Contents

CONTENTS

The Evolution
of Human Life History

Edited by Kristen Hawkes and Richard R. Paine

School of American Research Press
Santa Fe

James Currey
Oxford

School of American Research Press

Post Office Box 2188
Santa Fe, New Mexico 87504-2188

James Currey Ltd

73 Botley Road
Oxford OX2 0BS

Co-Director and Editor: Catherine Cocks
Manuscript Editor: Kate Talbot
Design and Production: Cynthia Dyer
Proofreader: Sarah Soliz
Indexer: Catherine Fox
Printer: Edwards Brothers Printing, Inc.

Library of Congress Cataloging-in-Publication Data:

The evolution of human life history / edited by Kristen Hawkes and Richard Paine.
    p. cm. — (School of American Research advanced seminar series)
Includes bibliographical references and index.
ISBN 1-930618-72-7 (pa : alk. paper)
1. Human evolution. 2. Human beings—Origin. 3. Fossil hominids. I. Hawkes, Kristen,
1944– II. Paine, Richard R. III. School of American Research (Santa Fe, N.M.) IV. Series.

GN281.E8926 2006
599.93'8—dc22

                    2006008207

British Library Cataloguing-in-Publication Data

The evolution of human life history.— (School of American Research advanced seminar
series)
   1.Human evolution 2.Human beings—Origin 3.Fossil hominids
   I. Hawkes, Kristen, 1944– II. Paine, Richard R. III. School of American Research
   (Santa Fe, N.M.)
   599.9'38

ISBN 10: 0-85255-170-3 (James Currey paper)
ISBN 13: 978-0-85255-170-7 (James Currey paper)

Cover illustration: *Baby boy (0–3 months) sleeping on mother's shoulder.*
AA052303 © 2004 Getty Images, Inc.

The Evolution
of Human Life History

**School of American Research
Advanced Seminar Series**

James F. Brooks
General Editor

The Evolution
of Human Life History

Contributors

Nancy Barrickman
Department of Biological Anthropology and Anatomy, Duke University

Meredith L. Bastian
Department of Biological Anthropology and Anatomy, Duke University

Nicholas Blurton Jones
Department of Anthropology, University of California, Los Angeles

Barry Bogin
Department of Behavioral Sciences, University of Michigan–Dearborn

Jesper L. Boldsen
Department of Anthropology, University of Southern Denmark

Kristen Hawkes
Department of Anthropology, University of Utah

Nicholas P. Herrmann
Department of Anthropology, University of Tennessee

Lyle W. Konigsberg
Department of Anthropology, University of Tennessee

Elissa B. Krakauer
Department of Biological Anthropology and Anatomy, Duke University

Richard R. Paine
Department of Anthropology, University of Utah

Shannen L. Robson
Department of Anthropology, University of Utah

Daniel W. Sellen
Department of Anthropology, University of Toronto

Matthew M. Skinner
Department of Anthropology, George Washington University

Maria A. van Noordwijk
Anthropologisches Institut und Museum, Universität Zürich

Carel P. van Schaik
Anthropologisches Institut und Museum, Universität Zürich

Bernard Wood
Center for the Advanced Study of Hominid Paleobiology,
George Washington University

Figures

Tables

The Evolution
of Human Life History

1

Introduction

Richard R. Paine and Kristen Hawkes

Human life history differs from that of other primates in several initially puzzling ways. Our children depend on others for subsistence much longer than do the offspring of any other mammal, yet we wean babies earlier than most other apes do. Our age at first reproduction is much older than that of other apes, but our fertility can be higher. We have the longest lifespan of any terrestrial mammal, yet women stop bearing children in the middle of it. Some of these apparent contradictions have been attributed to our big brains and to the nuclear families and sexual division of labor that ethnographers have found in all human societies. But over the past two or three decades, findings in hunter-gatherer ethnography, Paleolithic archaeology, human paleontology, and comparative primatology have raised questions about these long-standing ideas.

Recent applications of life history theory (Stearns 1992) to distinctive features of the human life course (for example, Smith and Tompkins 1995; Hill and Hurtado 1996; Hawkes et al. 1998; Kaplan et al. 2000) have helped fuel a more sophisticated debate over the evolution of human life history. This body of theory was developed in evolutionary biology to explain the diversity of life cycles among living things. To address that enormous variety, life history theoreticians make use of two fundamental principles: natural selection and the trade-offs required by the inevitable limits of time and energy (reviewed in Stearns 1992). Energy is allocated in three general ways: for growth, for maintenance and repair of somatic tissues, and for current reproduction. Because the energy available to an organism is limited and energy spent for one purpose cannot be used for another, more energy for one means less for another. Organisms face additional trade-offs within each of these categories; for example, investment in reproduction can go to parenting or mating, and investment in parenting is traded off between quantity and quality of offspring. Natural selection favors tendencies to allocate available energy in ways that maximize lifetime fitness. Because the final accounting of the fitness consequences of alternative allocations is over lifetimes, mortality risks affect the net gains and losses for each trade-off. Life history theoreticians therefore take a demographic perspective, looking at rates of survival and reproduction at each age class in a population.

THE ADVANCED SEMINAR

The School of American Research sponsored an advanced seminar titled "The Evolution of Human Life History," November 2 through 8, 2002. The seminar was organized with three clear goals: to identify the distinctive features of human life history, to debate current models of life history evolution, and to critically evaluate the data available for describing the evolution of human life history and testing current hypotheses. Current descriptions of variation in life history features among living species of mammals would provide a context for identifying the derived characteristics of human life histories—those that distinguish us from common ancestors with other primates—and would help focus questions about when and why those characteristics evolved in our lineage. These rate and timing variables not only shape individual lives but also are major determinants of the age structure of populations. Therefore, both our lives and the character of our societies depend on our life histories.

The defining feature of the advanced seminar was its interdisciplinary approach. The study of human life history evolution has been dominated by paleoanthropologists, primatologists, and evolutionary ecologists working with foragers. These specialists have brought the inquiry to a point of general agreement about some distinctive features of human life history. However, there is still strong disagreement about the key variables that promoted the evolution of these derived human traits.

This advanced seminar brought specialists in human paleontology, primatology, and hunter-gatherer behavioral ecology together with specialists in demography and paleodemography, human growth and development, nutrition, and the genomics of aging. The range of specializations was dictated by the central problems of identifying and explaining human life histories. Ethnographic observations of modern foragers capture activity differences by age and sex, patterns of growth and development, and age-specific fertility and mortality in conditions similar in many ways to those of people in the pre-agricultural past. Combined with the patterns of growth, development, and age-specific nutritional effects in humans who depend on other modes of subsistence, these ethnographic and demographic data indicate distinctive aspects of maturation and age-specific mortality in our species. Skeletal remains of past populations provide evidence about the antiquity of these patterns. Only the fossils and archaeology place the evolutionary changes in time and space, as well as in the ecological context in which they emerged and spread. Other lines of evidence illuminate phylogenetic changes. The human lineage is a part of the larger radiation of the primates, so any regularities in life history variation across living primate species set the general framework for the inquiry into what happened in human evolution. Even more broadly, the recent explosion of work in aging genomics provides a window into the enormous diversity of life cycles in the living world and hints at some of the possible mechanisms that pace life histories, including our own.

VOLUME ORGANIZATION

As we originally envisioned it, the advanced seminar would focus on two central issues: (1) the selective factors affecting the evolution of human life history and (2) our ability to reconstruct it, especially for hominids other than modern humans. Following the current wider debate, participants focused on several issues: offspring provisioning and child needs, learning and development, and survival of postreproductive women. Participants quickly (if provisionally) agreed that attention should be concentrated on a short list of derived features of human life histories that characterize our species: our relatively long potential lifespans, our relatively late maturity, our relatively early weaning at ages that precede feeding independence, and the relatively large divergence between curves of declining fertility and increasing mortality risk with greater age ("midlife menopause").

Participants also agreed that processes applicable to broad mammalian and specifically primate variation are likely to be implicated in our own evolution and that the derived human features are probably linked, especially in light of the cross-species regularities in mammalian life history variation. Two of the most promising explanatory models currently available, the Grandmother and Embodied Capital hypotheses, link all or most of the four derived features. The former builds on symmetry models for explaining mammalian life history variation, nominating the trade-offs in those models and a novel role for ancestral grandmothers to propel the evolution of the derived human features. The latter argues that the developmental requirements and behavioral advantages of expanding brains in the context of increased emphasis on hunting explain our delayed maturity and increased longevity. Hillard Kaplan (Kaplan et al. 2000; Kaplan and Robson 2002; Kaplan, Lancaster, and Robson 2003) has played the leading role in elaborating the Embodied Capital model and applying it to human evolution; we had hoped that he would participate in the seminar, but his other commitments intervened. Although we missed his active presence, his model is discussed, explained, and critiqued in several chapters.

Two of the original seminar participants, Leslie Aiello and Caleb Finch, do not have chapters in this volume. Their presentations and contributions to the discussions in Santa Fe enriched the advanced seminar. Those discussions had impacts not fully realized at the time, but the chapters here have been extensively revised in light of them.

In the second chapter, Shannen Robson, Carel van Schaik, and Kristen Hawkes assemble current evidence on the life histories of the living great apes to reconstruct the likely life history of our common ancestor. By comparing the most recent empirical data on orangutans, gorillas, chimpanzees, bonobos, and modern humans, the authors identify the longer adult lifespans, later age at first parturition, earlier weaning, and shorter interbirth intervals that distinguish human life history from those of our closest living relatives. Reconstructions of past taxa based on living descendents must always be provisional, but the comparisons strongly suggest that the human values on these traits are derived; that is, they evolved after our lineage separated from an ancestor in common with the living great apes. The living taxa do not, however, differ in the age at which female fertility declines, suggesting that this is a life history feature conserved from our common ancestor.

Robson and colleagues also report comparative data on brain growth and dental maturation. The brain growth data show that human and chimp infant brains approach adult size at about the same age, refuting the common assumption that humans require a much longer time to grow their big brains. The comparative data on dental development—a topic discussed by Hawkes in chapter 3 and in greater detail by Skinner and Wood in chapter 11—show that different aspects of dental development do not vary together as a correlated block within the great ape clade. Among these species, neither molar eruption ages nor crown formation times vary in tandem with variation in life histories. Skinner and Wood refer to these as "life history related variables" (LHRVs) and draw a clear distinction between LHRVs and life history variables (LHVs). The important lesson, often rediscovered, is that even though growth and development are not independent of life history, they themselves are not life history variables. Genera and species face different problems within life stages, and developmental patterns can be selected accordingly, with little or no alteration in the life history variables that determine population vital rates.

In chapter 3, Kristen Hawkes provides an historical overview of research on human life history evolution. First, she introduces the field of life history evolution, reviewing key assumptions and modeling tools, especially the Euler-Lotka equation and stable population theory. She discusses r and K selection (MacArthur and Wilson 1967), noting explanatory weaknesses of this widely cited model, and Charnov's (1993) alternative approach, which focuses on life history invariants. Steven Jay Gould (1977) linked developmental heterochrony with life history, and Hawkes uses his influential ideas about slow human maturation to lead off a review of work on each of the distinctive features of human life history. The chapter underlines the important difference between questions about mechanisms and about adaptive effects and considers some impacts of genomics on ideas about the evolution of life histories. It concludes with a discussion of the most influential adaptive hypothesis about human evolution, the Hunting hypothesis, and a brief summary of the empirical challenges that emerged at the end of the 1970s. This sets the stage for the next chapter's discussion of subsequent modifications and alternatives that are explicitly grounded in life history theory.

In chapter 4, Hawkes focuses on the slow-fast variation in mammalian life histories and Charnov's symmetry approach to explaining it. Hawkes summarizes data and theory indicating that adult mortality rates are likely determinants of other life history variables, including varying investment in individual offspring. She speculates that increased somatic maintenance, which slows aging in adults, also lowers mortality rates in juveniles, a possibility consistent with Kirkwood's (1977, 1981) Disposable Soma model. The novel suggestion she makes here is that higher levels of somatic repair might be a physiological reason for cross-species correlations between rates of aging and rates of offspring production. Slower-aging mammalian mothers may earn higher marginal gains for additional investment in offspring equipped to build more effective mechanisms for maintenance and repair. The slow-fast mammalian regularities and Charnov's mammal model are the foundation for the hypothesis that long human childhoods and more expensive youngsters are consequences of slowed aging and the novel productive role of aging females. She concludes by comparing and contrasting this Grandmother hypothesis with the influential Embodied Capital argument, which hypothesizes that our late maturity and expensive juveniles evolved because of ancestral reliance on investment from hunting fathers.

Carel van Schaik, Nancy Barrickman, Meredith Bastian, Elissa Krakauer, and Maria van Noordwijk (chapter 5) discuss some of the consequences of slow life histories for distinctive features of primate lives. They review life history variation across the order, giving particular attention to differences in brain size. Variability among primate species provides an opportunity to test hypotheses about causes and effects of slower life histories. The authors identify two main classes of models—those using demographic tools and those based in natural history—that have been proposed to explain the relatively long immaturity for a given body size that distinguishes primates in general, including humans, from nonprimate mammals. Charnov's demographic model assumes an allometric growth/production function and shows that age (and therefore size) at maturity is determined by the level of adult mortality. This model successfully explains major variation in mammalian life histories, including perhaps those of humans. The other class of models addresses lineage-specific details of natural history. The Juvenile Risks model associates large brain size to slow development and therefore late maturation, and the Skill Learning hypothesis suggests that a long period of immaturity is necessary to learn the numerous skills required for success as a reproducing adult. Both natural history models have broad support, though we currently lack empirical resolution to distinguish between them.

Van Schaik and colleagues argue that Charnov's (1991, 1993) demographic model is compatible with these developmental natural history models and propose that the latter may provide some of the mechanisms underlying the particular size allometries that play important roles in Charnov's model. The authors conclude that future work should concentrate on testing the critical predictions of the two natural history models and perhaps develop an overarching model that focuses on the role of adult brain size in the development of larger-brained organisms such as primates.

Like other primates, human newborns initially depend entirely on mother's milk. But weaning marks feeding independence for other primates, whereas human children continue to depend on supplements from others long after nursing ends. In chapter 6, Daniel Sellen reviews the distinctive and common features of human and nonhuman primate lactation. Though he laments the overall lack of data on the biology of lactation in nonhuman primates, especially apes, Sellen makes a number of basic biological comparisons. He pays special attention to transitional feeding in which infants begin to consume foods in addition to breast milk.

Early exclusive breastfeeding is enormously beneficial to human infants. After about six months of age, however, breast milk is no longer sufficient to meet typical infant nutritional needs. Sellen notes that our pattern of transitional feeding, which includes highly processed foods with breast milk, is a unique characteristic of humans. Infants continue to benefit from breastfeeding into their third year. From there, the marginal returns on continued breastfeeding diminish rapidly. These distinctively processed foods may enable infants to survive without breast milk at a much younger age, as well as smaller size, than infant apes.

Sellen argues that the use of highly processed, nutrient-rich, complementary foods was a derived feature that co-evolved with a reduction in the costs of lactation. Together, these made lactation shorter and reduced interbirth intervals without increasing maternal or infant mortality rates. Sellen goes on to suggest that behavioral and physiological shifts toward complementary feeding and early weaning may have promoted the evolution of distinctive patterns of human foraging, parenting, and social behavior.

Barry Bogin (chapter 7) discusses the physiological aspects of "childhood," which he argues provided crucial reproductive advantages to hominin mothers, and offers hypotheses from a human development perspective. Bogin defines childhood as the period from weaning to the onset of the juvenile growth period. During this time, human children must depend on older individuals for food and protection. In contrast, weaned chimpanzees and juveniles of other primate species must forage for their own food from the time they are weaned. In terms of physical growth, human childhood comprises seven to ten years of relatively slow growth after weaning. Following this period, humans experience a few years of rapid growth (the adolescent growth spurt) in virtually all skeletal dimensions of the body. Bogin argues that childhood made it possible for hominins to replace long lactation with cooperative provisioning, shortening a mother's interbirth intervals. The extensive learning and practice that take place during childhood constitute, he concludes, a secondary benefit of the stage.

Nicholas Blurton Jones uses his work among Hadza foragers in northern Tanzania to address four questions in chapter 8: (1) whether adult mortality rates observed among contemporary hunter-gatherers indicate species-specific adult mortality, (2) whether Charnov's (1993) growth function adequately captures Hadza children's growth, (3) whether improvements in foraging effectiveness with age among Hadza children support long-standing ideas that our late maturity results from the need for long periods of learning and practice to prepare for adulthood, and (4) whether Hadza women past childbearing age increase their fitness by helping descendants.

Blurton Jones summarizes results from his Hadza demography showing their low adult mortality and long average adult lifespans. The similar relationship between the length of the juvenile period and the average adult lifespan in humans and other primates challenges the long-standing assumption that our late maturity is due to a special human requirement for long periods of learning. He shows that Charnov's simple growth model can account for a large fraction of the variation in size with age among the Hadza. Using weanling size, age at first parturition, and maternal size, he shows that female chimpanzees, orangutans, and humans are on very similar growth curves. These demonstrations further underline the applicability of Charnov's (1991, 1993) model of mammalian life history variation to human evolution.

Blurton Jones also summarizes his series of experimental studies on variation with age in Hadza foraging efficiency. Sex differences in foraging activities and boarding school attendance provided a "natural experiment" for observing whether subjects of similar ages who differed in time spent learning and practicing various tests then differed in their foraging performance. Results gave no support to the proposition that long periods of learning are necessary to master these tasks. Differences in size and strength, not length of practice, account for differences in foraging efficiency.

The Grandmother hypothesis proposes that late maturity in humans results from the same trade-offs that Charnov (1991, 1993) has modeled to explain the relationship between age at first reproduction and average adult lifespans in other primates, namely, that our late maturity results from our unusual longevity. That unusual longevity evolved in our lineage when ecological circumstances allowed more vigorous peri- and postmenopausal females to increase their fitness by provisioning their grandchildren. Tests of this hypothesis include empirical measures of the effects of grandmothers' help. Blurton Jones discusses difficulties in measuring such effects and reports some results showing that older Hadza women are generally found where their help for descendants might be most valuable. The chapter concludes with a series of questions and points related especially to growth patterns, resource acquisition, and longevity.

Testing hypotheses of human life history evolution requires specific data for the key periods of human evolution. A central goal of the advanced seminar was to consider the direct evidence for the life histories of past populations. What was the lifespan of prehuman hominids? What was their age of reproductive maturity? What was the intensity of mortality, and how did it differ with age at each critical point? Did a significant number of individuals, particularly females, live past reproductive age (Trinkaus 1995)? Recent reevaluations of paleodemography have shown how difficult it is to reconstruct even age and sex for anatomically modern humans accurately and without bias (Bocquet-Appel and Masset 1982).

Lyle Konigsberg and Nicholas Herrmann (chapter 9) discuss the use of paleodemography to reconstruct ancient longevity, and they address the essential question of whether (anatomically modern) human aging patterns have changed during our past. They review three main sources of error that currently plague paleodemographic life tables: the assumption of demographic stationarity, which they dismiss as "fairly trivial"; misestimation of age at death from skeletal indicators; and nonrandom sampling with respect to age in death assemblages. Paleodemography is making important advances in improving age estimation methods, especially in dealing with reference sample bias (Hoppa and Vaupel 2002a). Konigsberg and Herrmann focus on this second problem, in particular, evaluating how reference sample bias (Bocquet-Appel and Masset 1982) can be eliminated from age-at-death distributions.

The authors illustrate how unbiased paleodemographic estimates of age distributions can be produced using a single age-at-death indicator, the sacroiliac joint. They use maximum likelihood methods to estimate the two Gompertz parameters in a Siler hazards model (Gage 1988), which give a mortality curve. They then apply their strategy to two southeastern skeletal series, Indian Knoll and Averbuch, and finally to Loisy-en-Brie, a French Neolithic site.

We may be able to assess whether rates of skeletal aging changed in the past with statistical approaches like those outlined in this chapter, combined with tooth cementum annulation studies as a proxy for known ages (Wittwer-Backofen and Buba 2002; Wittwer-Backofen, Gampe, and Vaupel 2004). The authors are encouraged that the life tables they generated for ancient populations, using unbiased statistics and uncertainty in age estimation, resemble the life tables of extant foragers and horticulturalists—unlike many paleodemographic life tables based on biased aging methods. However, they warn that we should approach current demographic reconstructions of any hominin besides anatomically modern *H. sapiens sapiens*, including recent studies of Neanderthal paleodemography (Trinkaus 1995; Bermúdez de Castro and Nicolás 1997; Bocquet-Appel and Arsuaga 1999), "with considerable caution."

The historical demographic record (Oeppen and Vaupel 2002) shows remarkable increases in life expectancy from the nineteenth century to the present. Until about 1950 these changes were due primarily to decreases in infant and juvenile mortality. The historical demographic record, though fragmentary, also suggests that there were improvements in adult life expectancy perhaps dating back to the fourteenth century (Russell 1948; Hollingsworth 1977). Richard Paine and Jesper Boldsen (chapter 10) look at paleodemographic evidence for changing selective pressures in the Holocene in an attempt to assess whether the historical observations represent a long-term trend or a more recent change. The period from the Mesolithic through the onset of historical demographic records (which become widespread in the seventeenth and eighteenth centuries) is characterized by increased population growth, urbanism, and expansion of trade networks. All of these facilitate the survival and transmission of epidemic diseases. Paine and Boldsen explore whether changes in patterns of epidemic disease during the Holocene could have raised levels of extrinsic mortality.

From the perspective of life history theory, differences in mortality rates with age are all important (Hawkes, chapter 3). Paine and Boldsen focus their attention on the mortality of subadults, between 2 years old and the onset of reproduction at about 18 years old, to estimate changes in extrinsic mortality that would have affected all ages. They chose the juvenile age span for two reasons: skeletons between these ages are well represented in excavated samples, and age estimation for these ages is relatively accurate. Paine and Boldsen model the effects of increasing epidemic frequency with a series of Leslie matrix projections and compare the age distribution of subadult death from the projections with historically reported subadult death patterns through the Holocene. Their modeling supports the contention that the frequency of epidemics increased throughout the period from the Mesolithic through the Middle Ages. Adult extrinsic mortality increased from the Mesolithic through about the Roman Iron Age and then began to decrease as shortened intervals transformed epidemic diseases into diseases of childhood. Elevated levels of extrinsic mortality lasted longer for children but eventually declined. A result of this pattern would be a temporary suppression of life expectancy. The model captures both widely observed paleodemographic patterns and historical trends, specifically, the historical pattern of adult life expectancy increases preceding improvements in life expectancy at birth. Paine and Boldsen suggest that historical demographic patterns may not be very good indicators of Pleistocene ones.

Matthew Skinner and Bernard Wood (chapter 11) address the deeper antiquity of human life history characteristics, this time from a paleoanthropological perspective. They discuss the hominid fossil record and what it might tell us about the sequence and timing of life history changes. They explain the methods paleoanthropologists use to organize fossil hominins into taxa, summarizing the hominin fossil record under two contrasting taxonomic schemes. The "long" taxonomy emphasizes discontinuities, a punctuated model of evolution, and a branching or cladogenetic interpretation of the fossil record and leads to a large number of species. The "short" taxonomy emphasizes morphological continuity and a more gradualistic view of evolution, leading to fewer species. They use the contrast in taxonomies to highlight the influence of taxonomic hypotheses on interpretations of the evolution of human life history.

Skinner and Wood then critically review inferences about life history characteristics from fossils and attempt to assess when and in what taxon various distinctive characteristics of human life history first appear. They distinguish between life history variables (LHVs)—such as age at weaning, age at sexual maturity, gestation length, and longevity—and life history related variables (LHRVs)—such as body mass, brain mass/endocranial volume, and patterns of dental development, which show correlations to LHVs among primates. No LHVs can be retrieved directly from the hard tissues studied by paleoanthropologists. Some morphological LHRVs, such as endocranial volume, can be estimated from hard tissues and have been used to estimate when the distinctive characteristics of human life history (LHVs) may have appeared. Because teeth preserve better than other skeletal tissues and their microstructure provides a precise record of the time course of their own development, these tissues are of special interest for reconstructing ontogeny. Skinner and Wood review features of dental development and compare modern humans with chimpanzees to show that aspects of dental development do not vary as a block across these taxa. Dental development provides LHRVs, not LHVs. The fact that these are distinct classes of variables (as Robson and colleagues discuss in chapter 2 and Hawkes chronicles in chapter 4) certainly complicates the process of reconstructing the life histories of past taxa, but coming to terms with the distinction is a necessary step to making that reconstruction possible.

As with living primate studies and the paleodemographic data, the picture Skinner and Wood present of the fossil record is necessarily far from complete and far from conclusive. Life history related variables—body mass, cranial volume, and dental development—present an inconsistent picture in which extinct taxa had life histories comparable to that of modern humans. The problem is most acute surrounding *H. ergaster* and *H. erectus*. Body mass estimates are similar to modern humans, but neither estimates of brain mass nor dental ontogeny conform to modern human patterns.

OUTCOMES OF THE ADVANCED SEMINAR

Participants found it surprisingly easy to agree on a short list of things that need explaining and on the contending explanations, but data necessary to more precisely characterize empirical patterns and test particular hypotheses proved surprising in another way. The limits of available data sets, as well as the precarious assumptions and extrapolations necessary for inferences about life history, emerged repeatedly in discussion. Those working on one line of evidence had assumed that experts on others had better data. Consequently, all saw that one outcome of the advanced seminar would be a relatively long wish list for comparative data on the nutrient needs and developmental patterns in nonhuman primates, as well as comparative physiological and behavioral measures of age-specific changes in performance to add to demographic measures of senescence.

The combination of data on living populations with archaeological and fossil evidence of past life histories resulted in bad and good news. On one hand, aspects of development do not directly index age at first parturition, an especially consequential life history variable. On the other hand, techniques for precisely aging dental events and calculating individual ages from teeth have great promise for extracting ontogenetic information from specimens dated to both the more recent and the deeper past, and the development of methods that deal probabilistically with the age estimates in skeletal samples makes possible a seriously informative paleodemography.

Other living primates are a potential source of information about life history evolution that has only begun to be tapped. Many features of growth, development, and aging are less well studied in our nearest living relatives, even though differences between humans and the other living apes are crucial for posing and testing hypotheses about human life history evolution. Overall, the advanced seminar increased the participants' appreciation of the difficulties of data collection and interpretation faced by their colleagues and the importance of the multiple lines of evidence needed for describing and explaining the evolution of human life histories.

The advanced seminar brought together scholars often separated by respective specialties in a remarkably collegial setting. This enabled us to discover that assumptions unexamined by one specialty were inconsistent with evidence well known in another and also that concepts, questions, and findings from one field could be of great use in another. Our respective research directions were clarified in unexpected ways, and our collective inquiry into the evolution of human life history much energized as a consequence. All the participants would like to thank the School of American Research once again for providing this unique opportunity.

Acknowledgments
We thank Ursula Hanly and especially Jennifer Graves for careful editing and tireless assistance in assembling the volume.

2

The Derived Features of Human Life History

**Shannen L. Robson, Carel P. van Schaik,
and Kristen Hawkes**

SUMMARY

*This chapter compares and contrasts the life histories of extant great apes
in order to construct a hypothetical life history of the last common ancestor of
all great apes and to identify features of human life history that have been
derived during the evolution of our lineage. Data compiled from the published
literature indicate some variation across the living taxa, but all great apes
have relatively long lifespans and late maturity. Therefore, we infer that a
slow life history is the ancestral state of all great apes.*

*We examine variation in the timing of brain growth and aspects of den-
tal development and find that they are not correlated in the life history variation across these species. We conclude that adjustment in growth and
development, though constrained by life history, are imperfect predictors of life
history variables.*

*Our comparisons show that humans have the slowest life history of the
great apes, with a notably longer adult lifespan and an older age at first birth.
We investigate the two important features of human life history that deviate
from the expected great ape pattern: shortened interbirth intervals and vigorous postmenopausal longevity. Human infants are weaned earlier than*

expected for their age at maturity and before they are capable of independent feeding. Because females conceive soon after weaning an infant, women typically have multiple dependent offspring simultaneously. The pattern of human age-related fertility decline appears to be conserved. Reproductive senescence occurs at essentially the same age among all great apes, suggesting that the marked postmenopausal survival of human females is a derived trait resulting from selection for slower rates of somatic aging. The human pattern of shortened interbirth intervals and "stacking" dependents could have evolved only if human mothers had reliable sources of help. Related post-menopausal and prereproductive females, without infants of their own, likely gained inclusive fitness benefits from supplying that help.

Despite variability in the statistics of deaths and births, every species shows strong central tendencies in demographic variables as a result of underlying, biologically anchored, individual predispositions for growth, development, reproduction, and aging (Harvey and Clutton-Brock 1985). Our species is no exception. Although there have been frequent allusions to dramatic changes in human life history as a result of changes in sources of mortality (Olshansky, Carnes, and Cassel 1998), our species shows all the hallmarks of one designed for slow development and long life, with female fertility declining to menopause well before aging advances in other physiological systems. Thus, like any other species, humans possess a clearly delimited life history. And, for other species, it is a productive working hypothesis to regard these features as adaptations that evolved through natural selection.

To set the agenda for the rest of this volume, it is essential that we obtain a clear picture of the changes that have taken place in hominin life history since the point of departure: the origin of the very first bipedal ape, five to seven million years ago. Ideally, we would also estimate when the major changes or novelties evolved during hominin evolution, associating the shifts with adaptations to the new habitats colonized and lifestyles adopted by new hominid species. This task is fraught with difficulties, however, because values for extinct species tend to be reconstructed through processes with many steps, each with a particular uncertainty, or through relationships of unknown validity for the species involved (Skinner and Wood, chapter 11, this volume).

We can map the similarities and differences between modern

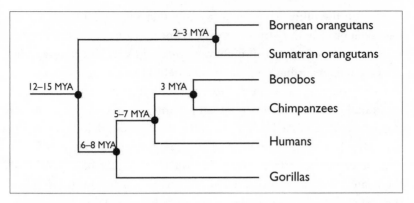

FIGURE 2.1

Phylogenetic relationships of the great ape species. Estimated time of divergence of the orangutan, gorilla, and chimpanzee/bonobo lineages from the hominid lineage (Glazko and Nei 2003). Estimated time of bonobo/chimpanzee divergence (Wildman et al. 2003). Estimated time of Bornean/Sumatran orangutan divergence (Zhang, Ryder, and Zhang 2001).

humans and our closest living relatives, the great apes, with much less uncertainty and use these comparisons to infer the likely changes in life history over the radiation of our own lineage.

DERIVED HUMAN LIFE HISTORY TRAITS

Humans are part of the wider radiation of great apes. As shown in figure 2.1, our closest relatives are the two species of chimpanzee (genus *Pan*): the common chimpanzee (*P. troglodytes*) and the bonobo (*P. paniscus*). There is one other extant African great ape, the gorilla (*Gorilla gorilla*), which comes in various distinct subspecies. In Asia, a separate lineage of great apes evolved, of which two species of orangutan (*Pongo pygmaeus* and *P. abelii*) are the only living representatives (Zhang, Ryder, and Zhang 2001).

Which Apes Resemble the First Hominin?

Using some composite estimates based on the living great apes to reconstruct the common ancestor at the root of the hominin lineage would be permissible only if these taxa have changed little since then. On one hand, there is some support for this assumption: the molecular and morphological similarities among the great apes suggest that they have been more conserved than the hominin radiation (Moore

1996). On the other hand, many assume that some parallel evolution has taken place in the African hominoid lineages, especially with respect to their locomotion. Because chimpanzees and gorillas are terrestrial knuckle walkers, it has long been considered parsimonious to assume that our common ancestor was too. However, Schmitt's (2003) recent examination of the locomotor biomechanics among extant primates suggests that human bipedalism most likely evolved independently from an arboreal ancestor. Because this change implies that the African great apes became more terrestrial over time, it may be argued that their late Miocene arboreal ancestors had slower life histories, given the general correlation between terrestriality and faster life history (van Schaik and Deaner 2003). If such parallel evolution is important to life history, then the still strictly arboreal orangutan may provide the best estimate for the earliest hominins. Therefore, if the African apes did not change independently, then the earliest hominins had a life history similar to our closest living relatives, the chimpanzee and bonobo, or if they did, one closer to the more arboreal orangutan. The utility of reconstructing a common ancestor from shared patterns and similarities between phylogenetically close extant relatives is obvious, but caution should be used in assuming that shifts in hominin life histories always favor one direction. The recently discovered *Homo floresiensis*, a "hobbit"-size hominid (Brown et al. 2004; Falk et al. 2005) may exemplify how selection can favor a faster life history from a slower ancestor within our genus.

Gorillas require special consideration because they are unusual among the great apes in that they achieve the largest body size in the shortest time. Adult body size is the result of both the duration and the rate of growth before maturity. Relative to other primates, all great apes grow for a longer time and achieve larger adult body sizes. Gorillas, however, grow much faster than the rest of us. On average, primates grow more slowly than other mammals and are therefore smaller at adulthood than nonprimate mammals of similar ages at first birth. Humans, chimpanzees, bonobos, and orangutans grow even more slowly than the primate average (Blurton Jones, chapter 8, this volume). But this is not true of gorillas. Variation in growth rate across the mammals is closely tied to variation in the rate of offspring production (Charnov 1991; Charnov and Berrigan 1993). Gorillas grow more quickly and also produce babies at shorter intervals than the other great apes (table 2.1). The reasons gorillas exhibit rapid growth are debated, but analyses by Leigh (1994) show that growth rates among primates co-vary with diet.

Leigh (1994) examined the diet ecology and growth rates of forty-two anthropoid primate species and found that those with more folivorous diets tend to grow faster than those with more frugivorous ones. All great ape species, including gorillas, favor fruit when it is abundant, but chimpanzees and orangutans specialize on fruit and extractive foods (such as insects) and sometimes vertebrate meat (chimpanzees more so). To some extent, bonobos (and gorillas, in particular) fall back on vegetative foods that tend to be abundant but of lower quality (Malenky et al. 1994; Conklin-Brittain, Knott, and Wrangham 2001). The first australopithecines were thought to have diets dominated by fruits and seeds (Schoeninger et al. 2001). If diet ecology influences growth trajectories, then we would expect the earliest hominins to have growth and reproductive rates closer to those of chimpanzees and orangutans than to gorillas. Also, fossil evidence suggests similarities between chimpanzees and australopithecines (versus gorillas) in body sizes (McHenry 1994). Average growth rates for living humans are close to the rates for chimpanzees, bonobos, and orangutans (Blurton Jones, chapter 8, this volume). For these reasons, we consider the values of chimpanzees and orangutans as the endpoints of the range of estimates for the first hominins and refer to gorillas only when relevant.

Data Sources

To develop proper comparisons between people and living great apes, we primarily rely on the life history parameters estimated from hunter-gatherers, because their diets, mobility, foraging styles, and population densities most likely resemble those of modern humans before the invention of agriculture. Although we note estimates for some of these variables from a broader range of human populations in the text, in table 2.1 we used composite estimates from different detailed studies of extant hunter-gatherers whenever possible. This reduces concern about possible effects of improved diets and medical care on rate of development and senescence. It can be argued that the estimates are conservative in that ethnographically known populations

TABLE 2.1

Primary Life History Parameters of Female Great Apes (Arranged by Phylogenetic Distance from Humans), Mainly for Wild Populations, Compared with Those of Humans, Mainly Foragers

Great Ape Species	Maximum Lifespan (Years)	Age at First Birth (Years)	Adult Female Weight (kg)	Gestation Length (Days)
Orangutan (*Pongo pygmaeus* and *P. abelii*)	58.7[a]	15.6[d]	36.0[i]	260[m]
Gorilla (*Gorilla gorilla*)	54.0[a]	10.0[e]	84.5 (71–98)[j]	255[m]
Bonobo (*Pan paniscus*)	50.0+[b]	14.2[f]	33.0 (27–39)[j]	244[n]
Chimpanzee (*Pan troglodytes*)	53.4[a]	13.3[g]	35.0 (25–45)[j]	225[m]
Human (*Homo sapiens*)	85.0[c]	19.5[h]	47.0 (38–56)[k]	270[m]

Sources: a. Judge and Carey (2000), b. Erwin et al. (2002), c. Hill and Hurtado (1996); Howell (1979); Blurton Jones, Hawkes, and O'Connell (2002), d. Wich et al. (2004), e. Alvarez (2000); for humans, only data from two foraging populations, the Ache and !Kung, f. Kuroda (1989), g. Average age at first birth for five *P. troglodytes* populations: Bossou, 10.9 years (Sugiyama 2004); Gombe, 13.3 years (Wallis 1997); Mahale, 14.56 years (Nishida et al. 2003); Tai, 13.7 years (Boesch and Boesch-Achermann 2000); and Kibale, 15.4 years (Wrangham in Knott 2001), h. Average age at first reproduction from four human foraging groups: Ache, 19.5 years (Hill and Hurtado 1996); !Kung, 19.2 years (Howell 1979); Hadza, 18.77 years (Blurton Jones, unpublished data); and Hiwi, 20.5 years (Kaplan et al. 2000), i. Smith and Jungers (1997); mean of subspecies, j. Average (range reported in parentheses) compiled from Smith and Jungers (1997); Zihlman (1997a); and Smith and Leigh (1998), k. Average of range (reported in parentheses) of ethnographic samples from Jenike (2001:table 5), m. Harvey, Martin, and Clutton-Brock (1987), n. Median gestation length for bonobos in captivity reported by de Waal and Lanting (1997:190) from Thompson-Handler (1990), o. Average of range (reported in parentheses) compiled from Smith and Jungers (1997); Zihlman

of hunter-gatherers occupied only a subset of habitats initially colonized by modern people, mostly environments that are marginal for agriculture.

The nonhuman great ape data primarily come from long-term field studies, and these data are improving over time (see table 2.1 for source references). In all the reports of wild studies, the ages of many adults were estimated; all maximum lifespans were based on estimates with unknown errors. Maximum lifespans in the table are therefore

Neonate Weight (kg)	Neonate as a % of Maternal Weight	Age at Weaning (Years)	Interbirth Interval (Years)	Age at Last Birth (Years)
1.56 (1.31–1.81)[o]	4.3%	7.0[e]	8.05[d]	>41[d]
1.95 (1.6–2.3)[o]	2.3%	2.8[e]	4.40[e]	–
1.38 (1.30–1.45)[o]	4.2%	–	6.25[r]	–
1.90 (1.4–2.4)[o]	5.4%	4.5[e]	5.46[s]	42[u]
3.00 (2.4–3.6)[p]	5.9% [q]	2.8[e]	3.69[t]	45[v]

(1997a); and Smith and Leigh (1998), p. Average neonatal weight of seventy-eight groups worldwide (range reported in parentheses) from Meredith (1970), q. Calculated from data reported by Poppitt and colleagues (1994) on linked maternal/neonatal weight for eight populations, r. Average of two *P. paniscus* populations: Wamba, 4.5 years (Takahata, Ihobe, and Idani 1996), and Lomako, 8.0 years (Fruth in Knott 2001), s. Average interbirth interval of six *P. troglodytes* populations: Bossou, 5.3 years (Sugiyama 2004); Gombe, 5.2 years (Wallis 1997); Mahale, 5.6 years (Nishida et al. 2003); Tai, 5.7 years (Boesch and Boesch-Achermann 2000); Kanywara, Kibale, 5.4 years (Brewer-Marsden, Marsden, and Emery-Thompson n.d.); and Budongo, 5.6 years (Brewer-Marsden, Marsden, and Emery-Thompson n.d.), t. Average human interbirth interval of three foraging groups: Ache, 3.2 years (Hill and Hurtado 1996); !Kung, 4.12 years (Howell 1979); and Hiwi, 3.76 years (Kaplan et al. 2000), u. Average of latest recorded age at last birth in four *P. troglodytes* populations: Gombe, 44 years (Goodall Institute); Mahale, 39 years (Nishida et al. 2003); Tai, 44 years (Boesch and Boesch-Achermann 2000); and Bossou, 41 years (Sugiyama 2004), v. Hill and Hurtado (1996); Howell (1979); and Martin and colleagues (2003).

taken from individuals of known ages in captivity. The mortality profiles constructed for wild populations do not indicate stable or growing populations for any of the species, which implies that observed mortalities are higher than they have generally been until quite recently.

LIFE HISTORY CONTRASTS

Comparisons of data in table 2.1 show that extant humans evolved the following changes in character states from the other great apes.

Maximum Potential Lifespan

The maximum potential lifespan of humans is clearly longer than that of the other great apes by several decades. Even among human foragers without access to any medical support, some people live into their 70s and 80s (R. B. Lee 1968; Howell 1979; Hill and Hurtado 1996; Blurton Jones, Hawkes, and O'Connell 1999, 2002). In contrast, chimpanzees in the wild usually die before they reach 45 (Hill et al. 2001), and orangutans before age 50 (Wich et al. 2004). This difference in lifespan remains even under captive and modern medical conditions; maximum recorded longevity for great apes is around 60 years (Erwin et al. 2002), whereas the oldest human on record died at 122 (Robine and Allard 1998). These data show that humans have gained an increase in maximum lifespan relative to the ancestral state of at least twenty to thirty years. Maximum lifespan and average adult lifespan are correlated variables (Sacher 1959; Hawkes, chapter 3, this volume). Chimpanzee (Hill et al. 2001) and orangutan (Wich et al. 2004) females in the wild who survive to age 15 can expect to live only an additional fifteen to twenty more years (probably more for orangutans), whereas hunter-gatherers at age 15 can expect to live about twice that long (Howell 1979; Hill and Hurtado 1996; Blurton Jones, Hawkes, and O'Connell 2002).

Longer adult lifespans reflect lower adult mortality. When extrinsic adult mortality is as low as it is among great apes, adults can live long enough to display signs of declining physiological performance and eventually die from age-specific frailty. Ricklefs (1998) showed that in species with adult lifespans similar to chimpanzees, about 69 percent of adult deaths result from age-related causes. Selection can favor slower rates of aging if the fitness benefits of extending vigorous physical performance exceed the costs of increased somatic maintenance and repair. Slower rates of aging may account for the difference between human and nonhuman great ape maximum lifespans (Hawkes 2003). There is little systematic evidence documenting age-specific declines in physical performance in nonhuman great apes, but qualitative descriptions suggest that, as expected from their relatively shorter lifespans, chimpanzees do age faster than humans. Goodall (1986) classified chimpanzees at Gombe as old aged beginning at age 33. Finch and Stanford (2004:4) report that individuals age 35 or more years "show frailty and weight loss" and the "external indications of senescence include sagging skin, slowed movements, and worn teeth." As chimpanzees in the wild reach their mid-30s, they appear to age rapidly and die within a decade. In contrast, studies of physical performance among people who hunt and gather for a living show that vigor declines more slowly with age. Measures such as muscle strength in hunter-gatherer women decrease slowly over many decades (Blurton Jones and Marlowe 2002; Walker and Hill 2003). Comparable systematic performance data on great apes are needed to test whether they do, in fact, age more quickly than people.

Age at First Birth

As expected from an extension in lifespan, age at first reproduction among humans is much later than among other great apes and has increased from the ancestral state by four to six years. The age at first birth of female chimpanzees and bonobos in the wild, while variable, shows a central tendency toward 13 and 14 years, respectively. For gorillas, the mean age at first birth is 10 years, and orangutans bear their first offspring around age 15.6 years. Mean age at first birth among human foraging populations is 19.5 years.

These central tendencies persist for all great ape species in spite of differences in environment and ecology among populations in the wild. The affluence of captivity seems to have only a modest effect on age at first birth. It is often assumed that superabundance enhances physical condition, accelerates the timing of first birth, and extends longevity. However, there is evidence that the husbandry practices and socioecological conditions of many captive colonies do not always maximize the welfare of great apes and often increase incidents of vascular disease, obesity, and stress (DeRousseau 1994; Finch and Stanford 2003). Captive chimpanzees and bonobos bear their first offspring when they are around 11 years old (Bentley 1999; Knott 2001; Sugiyama 2004). Even though this mean is earlier than the central tendency of age at first birth among their wild counterparts, it is within the age range of at least one wild population. Age at first birth for gorillas in captivity is virtually identical for those in the wild (9.3 versus 10 years). Captive orangutan females show the largest shift in age at first birth from their wild counterparts. Markham (1995) reports age at first birth for orangutans in captivity as 11.5 years, almost four years earlier than orangutans in the wild. Whether in the wild or captivity, though, orangutans have the latest age at first birth and remain the "slowest" of the nonhuman great ape species.

Similar to captive great apes, there is also surprisingly little variation in average age at first birth among humans. Even under current conditions of ample food supply and medical care, human females, on average and cross-culturally, bear their first offspring after they are 18 years old (Bogin 1999a; Martin et al. 2003). Data from historic human records indicate that average age at first birth occurred even later, in the early to mid-20s (Le Bourg et al. 1993; Westendorp and Kirkwood 1998; Korpelainen 2000, 2003; Low, Simon, and Anderson 2002; Smith, Mineau, and Bean 2003; Grundy and Tomassini 2005; Helle, Lummaa, and Jokela 2005; Pettay et al. 2005). These data emphasize the limited plasticity of life history traits even in light of resource abundance.

Maternal Body Size

Later age at first birth enables energy to be invested in growth over a longer juvenile period, so most mammals with slower life histories also have larger body sizes (Purvis and Harvey 1995). Of all the primates, great apes are the longest-lived and latest maturing, as well as the largest-bodied. As previously discussed, gorillas are unusual in that they grow faster than the other great apes, including humans, achieving a much larger adult size. The remaining great ape species share a similar growth rate and achieve body sizes that generally vary with the duration of growth before maturity (Blurton Jones, chapter 8, this volume).

Chimpanzees, bonobos, and orangutans bear their first offspring between the ages of 13 and 16 and have similar body weights, around 35 kg. Human females have a later average age at first birth, 19.5 years, increasing the duration of growth four to six years longer than *Pan* or *Pongo* species. As a result, human females in extant foraging societies are about 10–15 kg larger than chimpanzee, bonobo, or orangutan females. Modern foragers are generally smaller than the estimated body sizes for people before the Mesolithic (Ruff, Trinkhaus, and Holliday 1997; Jenike 2001). Ethnographic hunter-gatherer means may therefore underestimate the average maternal-size differences between humans and our common ancestor.

Gestation Length and Size at Birth

Larger mothers have greater resources for offspring production, and great ape mothers translate this energy into larger, more expensive babies (Stearns 1992; see Hawkes, chapter 4, this volume:figure 4.7). As noted above, the rate of offspring production co-varies with growth rate (Charnov and Berrigan 1993); gorillas grow faster and produce babies at shorter intervals than the other great apes. Chimpanzees, bonobos, orangutans, and humans grow more slowly, more slowly even than the average primate but for a longer period of time, resulting in large mothers who produce large babies. Human females, with the longest duration of growth, have the largest maternal body sizes and produce the largest offspring.

Larger human neonatal size is achieved through a comparably longer length of gestation, ten to thirty days longer than the other great apes (Haig 1999; Dufour and Sauther 2002). Although this difference seems slight, human newborns spend the last weeks before parturition accumulating remarkably large adipose fat stores (Southgate and Hey 1976), and these fat stores likely account for the comparatively larger size of human neonates. Across the mammals, neonatal fat stores scale allometrically with body size (Widdowson 1950). Human neonates, however, are more than three times fatter than expected for a mammal of their size (Kuzawa 1998). At birth, 12 to15 percent of human neonatal body weight is adipose tissue (Fomon et al. 1982). Although there are no data documenting the body fat of great ape infants, the qualitative difference in the amount of body fat between human and great apes is apparent. Schultz (1969:152) made the general observation that "most human babies are born well padded with a remarkable amount of subcutaneous fat, whereas monkeys and apes have very little, so that they look decidedly 'skinny' and horribly wrinkled."

Estimating neonatal size relative to maternal size is difficult because there is extreme variation in adult body size both inter- and intra-individually and within and among populations (see table 2.1 for ranges). Nevertheless, graphing data reported by Poppitt and colleagues (1994) show that neonatal weight scales allometrically with maternal weight (figure 2.2). Bigger mothers bear larger infants, but the increase in the ratio of neonatal mass to maternal mass declines allometrically (slope of 0.746) with maternal size—6.4 percent for the

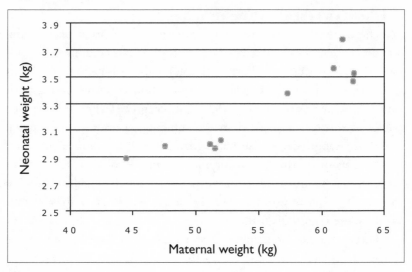

FIGURE 2.2

Neonatal weight relative to maternal weight (data from Poppitt et al. 1994). Neonatal weight scales allometrically with maternal weight at a slope of 0.746.

smallest mothers and 5.8 percent for the largest mothers in Poppit and colleagues' sample. Among extant human populations, neonatal size is somewhat larger relative to maternal body weight than other great ape species (Leuttenegger 1973). This difference is inflated when ethnographic hunter-gatherers are used to represent maternal size and may result from late Pleistocene decreases in adult size. Using two methods to estimate body mass, Ruff, Trinkhaus, and Holliday (1997) determined that adult individuals in our genus were about 10 percent larger during the Pleistocene.

Age at Weaning and Interbirth Intervals

Species with slow life histories generally have later ages at weaning and longer interbirth intervals. Great apes exemplify this pattern. They wean their dependent offspring relatively late, especially the frugivorous chimpanzees and orangutans (around ages 4.5 and 7 years, respectively), and have long interbirth intervals (5.5 and 8 years, respectively). Humans, however, have the slowest life history in many respects, but we wean our infants comparatively early. Human foragers typically wean their infants by age 3 and have mean interbirth intervals of around 3.7 years. Like age at first birth, human weaning ages are similar across a broad range of ecologies. Weaning age for humans is consistently "between 2 to 3 years and generally occurs about midway in that range" (Kennedy 2005:7).

Many ways have been proposed to estimate expected ("natural") weaning age from other human life history variables, and most predict later weaning age than practiced (Sellen 2001a). Harvey and Clutton-Brock (1985) predicted an average weaning age of 3.36 years based on a correlation between maternal and infant body size, but Charnov and Berrigan (1993) noted that mammalian infants are generally weaned when they achieve one-third of maternal body weight (Lee, Majluf, and Gordon 1991), which for humans occurs around 6.4 years. B. Smith (1992), following Schultz (1956), found that across a sample of primates, weaning age correlated with the eruption of the first permanent molar, around 6.5 years in humans. It is clear that the observed human weaning age of 2 to 3 years is earlier than these predictions. This is all the more remarkable because other aspects of our life history have slowed down relative to the ancestral state (Smith and Tompkins 1995).

Age at Last Birth and Menopause

Among mammals, oocytes are produced in the fetal ovaries until the third trimester of gestation, when the mitosis of germ cells ends. At this point, females have a fixed initial store of oocytes that is then subject to a process of continual depletion, or atresia, over their lifetime until the number of remaining follicles nears zero (vom Saal, Finch, and Nelson 1994; O'Connor, Holman, and Wood 2001; A. Cohen 2004). In humans, the cycle of ovulation and menstruation is generated by an endocrinological feedback loop that requires a sufficient oocyte store (J. Wood 1994). When there are too few oocytes remaining to stimulate ovulation, estimated at around one thousand follicles (Richardson, Senikas, and Nelson 1987), cycling ceases. All menstruating primates can potentially experience the senescent cessation of menses, or menopause, if they live long enough. In nonhuman species, however, reproductive senescence usually corresponds with somatic senescence, and few species live beyond the depletion of their oocyte store.

This is well documented in captive populations of macaques (for example, *M. fuscata*, Nozaki, Mitsunaga, and Shimizu [1995]; *M. mulatta*, M. Walker [1995]; *M. nemestrina*, Short et al. [1989]), where individuals live longer with senescent impairments than they can in the wild. Data on reproductive senescence in great apes is scant, but histological examination of captive chimpanzee females' ovaries suggests that the process of oocyte reduction is similar to that in humans (Gould, Flint, and Graham 1981). The few captive females that survived to menopause exhibited the same pattern of declining fecundity and variable cycling experienced by women (Tutin and McGinnis 1981) and around the same age (Gould, Flint, and Graham 1981).

Several years before menopause in women, the hormonal system that regulates menstrual cycles, the hypothalamic-pituitary-ovarian (HPO) axis, begins to break down because the number of oocytes necessary for ovarian steroid production is reduced below a necessary threshold. During this period of "perimenopause," cycle lengths become long and irregular, and many are anovulatory. Inconsistent functioning of the HPO axis and the increase in pregnancy failure during perimenopause result in a steep decline in the fertility of human females (Holman and Wood 2001). In noncontracepting human populations, average age at last birth precedes average age at menopause by about ten years (Gosden 1985). There are few data documenting the pattern of age-specific fertility decline in nonhuman great apes, but those available for chimpanzees suggest that fertility nears zero at 45 years of age (Nishida, Takasaki, and Takahata 1990; Boesch and Boesch Achermann 2000; Sugiyama 2004), as it does in humans (Howell 1979; Hill and Hurtado 1996; Muller et al. 2002; Martin et al. 2003). It appears that the age at which fertility declines in the other great apes is similar to that of humans (see Wich et al. 2004 on orangutans). This similarity suggests that we all share the ancestral pattern of ovarian ontogeny and what is derived in humans is not an unusual rate or timing of reproductive decline but a slowed rate of somatic aging and a vigorous, postmenopausal lifespan.

EFFECTS OF DERIVED HUMAN LIFE HISTORY

Many characteristics of growth and development depend on life history but are not, themselves, life history traits. The contrasts described above for females, excluding body size—maximum potential lifespan (or average adult lifespan), age at first birth, gestation length, interbirth intervals and age at weaning, and age at last birth—are directly linked to population vital rates. In this section, we discuss links between the derived features of human life history and aspects of human growth, development, and sociality.

Altriciality and Brain Growth

The postnatal growth requirements of human brains have long been seen as the source of our slow maturation. Compared with infants of the other great apes, human infants have been considered "helpless and undeveloped at birth" (Gould 1977:369), incapable of independent movement until at least 6 months of age; neonatal great apes are able to cling to their mothers from a very early age. This relative altriciality (Portmann 1941) has been attributed to the relatively small size of the human neonate's brain, under the assumption that a rapidly growing and developing brain is incapable of coordinating fully developed locomotor behavior (R. Martin 1990). There have been objections to both primary aspects of this widely accepted perspective. First, Schultz (1969:154) pointed out that the minimal locomotor development of humans at birth is not unusual, that, in fact, "the apes are born as helpless and immature as the exceptionally large human newborn." Because chimpanzee and gorilla infants are carried by their mothers for approximately twenty postnatal weeks, Schultz (1969:157) concluded that this "flatly contradicts the frequently heard vague claim that man is unique in his being born utterly helpless in such a very immature state as is very exceptional among primates." In addition, human babies are born with strong grasping reflexes equal to that of other primates (Konner 1972) and use sophisticated behavioral strategies to maximize their survival (Hrdy 1999). Together, these observations suggest that the motor skills of human neonates are no more altricial than those of other great apes and that infants are not behaviorally underdeveloped.

Second, human altriciality is said to be the result of a smaller relative brain size at birth due to an obstetrical constraint imposed by a pelvis shaped for bipedality. For most mammals, the rapid rate of fetal brain growth ends at, or just after, parturition. For humans, however, the fetal pattern of brain growth is comparably steeper and continues for almost a year after birth. The continuation of rapid fetal brain growth rates during the first twelve postnatal months led Portmann (1941) to suggest that humans really have a twenty-one-month gestation span: nine months in utero and twelve extra-uterine months that R. Martin (1990) termed "exterogestation." This suggests that human infants are born "early" because continued brain growth in utero would result in a head size too large for successful parturition (R. Martin 1983). Recent analyses comparing the patterns of brain growth in chim-pan-zees and humans (Leigh 2004) invite doubts about the uniqueness of rapid postnatal brain growth. We examine these data below.

There are few published data sets of brain sizes for individuals of known ages. Most authors present their original data in figures and report averages instead of original values, making intraspecies comparisons difficult (Jolicoeur, Baron, and Cabana 1988; Cabana, Jolicoeur, and Michaud 1993). Of the complete data sets published, most are derived from autopsy and necropsy records, a unique sample of individuals with various pathologies that possibly misrepresents the "normal" population. These are cross-sectional data, not longitudinal, repeated measurements on the same individual to assess individual variation in brain size and growth. However, these data currently provide the only opportunity for quantifying brain growth and development. Technological advances in brain imaging should make longitudinal data sets available for future comparison and analyses.

We calculated human brain measures from Marchand's (1902) data set, which reports brain weight (wet, including meninges, in grams), stature (in centimeters), sex, and known or estimated chronological age. Marchand assembled these data from German autopsy records documented between 1885 and 1900. The original data include a total of 716 human males and 452 females from birth to more than 80 years old. The variation in brain size with age and sex compares favorably with other reports (Dekaban and Sadowsky 1978; Kretschmann et al. 1979), indicating that Marchand's series can serve as a representative sample. Our calculations use his data on all individuals 3 years old and younger.

Brain weights for chimpanzees (*Pan troglodytes*) of known ages were drawn from necropsy data reported by Herndon and colleagues (1999). Brain weights were obtained fresh at Yerkes Regional Primate

Center from 76 captive individuals (33 females and 43 males) who died from natural causes or were euthanized when natural death was imminent. We used a subset of these data to calculate percent of adult brain weight at birth and to graph brain size from birth to 3 years.

These data, summarized in table 2.2 and plotted in figure 2.3, challenge three common assumptions about the uniqueness of human brain growth. First, chimpanzee and human infants are more similar in their percent of adult brain size at birth than usually assumed. It is conventionally reported that human neonatal brain weight is only 25 percent of adult size at birth whereas chimpanzee neonates have 50 percent of their adult brain weight at birth (Dienske 1986). But chimps are twice as close to adult size at birth as are humans; instead of a large interspecific difference in relative neonatal brain size, the difference is only about 10 percent. A larger sample of chimpanzee neonates may close this interval even more. This revision results from slightly lower percentage values for humans but primarily from the much smaller neonatal value for chimpanzees. Until now, relative chimpanzee neonatal brain size has been repeatedly based on the estimated cranial capacity of a single cranial specimen, known to be 74 days old at death (Schultz 1941). When plotted against Herndon and colleagues' (1999) values, this specimen is larger than neonatal size and falls where it should in the scatter, given its age of 2.5 months.

Second, we find that chimpanzees and humans share a very similar pattern of relative brain growth (see figure 2.2). Leigh (2004:152), using the same data to calculate brain growth trajectories for chimpanzees and humans, concluded that "after the first 18 months of life, *Pan* and *Homo* are not substantially different in terms of growth rates." Third, humans reach adult brain size much earlier than widely claimed, some individuals by 3 years of age. Kretschmann and colleagues (1979) used the Marchand (1902) data to show that, on average, males achieve 95 percent of total brain size by 3.82 years old and females reach 95 percent values by 3.44 years old. This is much earlier than assumed by most researchers.

Analyses indicate similarities in brain growth, relative neonatal brain size, and motor and behavioral skills at birth between humans and chimpanzees, challenging the characterization of humans as distinctively altricial. The similarities between chimps and humans do

TABLE 2.2

Human and Chimpanzee Brain Size at Birth and Adulthood by Sex

Species	Sex	Average Neonatal Brain Weight (g)[1]	Average Adult Brain Weight (g)[2]	Percent of Adult Total at Birth
Homo sapiens[3]				
	Males	371 (n = 16)	1404 (n = 150)	26.4
	Females	361 (n = 8)	1281 (n = 116)	28.2
Pan troglodytes[4]				
	Males	125 (n = 3)	406 (n = 17)	30.8
	Females	146 (n = 4)	368 (n = 17)	39.7

1. *Neonate* is defined as an individual between birth and 10 days old.
2. Average adult brain size was calculated as the mean of individuals between 20 and 40 years old by sex for humans and the mean of individuals between 7 and 30 years old for each sex in chimpanzees because this range safely precedes a known trend toward declining brain weight with age (Dekaban and Sadowsky 1978; Herndon et al. 1999).
3. References: Marchand (1902).
4. References: Herndon and colleagues (1999).

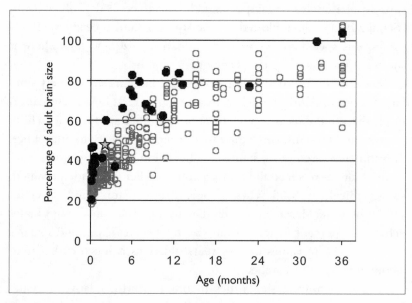

FIGURE 2.3

Percent of adult brain size achieved by age. Black dots are chimpanzees (Herndon et al. 1999; n = 26; males = 16, females = 10); open circles are humans (Marchand 1902; n = 160; males = 111, females = 49). The star represents Schultz's (1941) 74-day-old specimen.

not support the view that our juvenility is longer because of the growth requirements of our large brains.

Dental Development

Like brain growth and development, the pattern of dental growth and development is commonly used as a marker of life history events. Efforts have primarily focused on uncovering correlations between the timing and sequence of eruption of the permanent dentition and age at weaning and maturity. Relationships between dental markers and life history would provide a means to make direct interpretations of maturation schedules during hominin evolution based on fossil teeth. Given the systematic relationships among life history traits, establishing the timing of one would provide grounds for hypothesizing others. Teeth are less sensitive than other tissues to developmental insults and short-term ecological fluctuations (Nissen and Riessen 1964; Garn et al. 1973; Liversidge 2003), making them relatively reliable maturation markers. Schultz's often reprinted graph depicting variation in timing of life stages across the primates (for example, in Schultz 1969) used the emergence of the first permanent teeth to mark the end of infancy and the emergence of the last permanent teeth to mark the beginning of adulthood. Comparing primate species, Schultz (1949) also observed variation in the sequence of tooth eruption across the order. In species that are weaned relatively early, molars erupt before the deciduous teeth are lost and the emergence of the anterior permanent dentition. Schultz presumed that permanent molars erupted first so that infants would be prepared to masticate food when weaned, a generalization that B. Smith (2000) calls "Schultz's rule." Slower-developing humans show a distinctive eruption sequence: the permanent anterior dentition emerges before the molars. Schultz speculated that the human shift in eruption sequence is directly connected to slower human life history and, in particular, our much longer period of juvenility.

Building on Schultz's recognition of a connection between dental development and life history, B. Smith (1989a) showed that across the primates there is a strong correlation between the eruption of the first permanent molar (M1), weaning age and eruption of the third molar (M3), and age at first birth. In addition to eruption schedules, crown and root formation increments have been used to assess developmental age (Moorrees, Fanning, and Hunt 1963). The daily growth of

TABLE 2.3

Eruption and Crown Formation Schedules for Permanent Teeth

Species	Sex	M1 Eruption Mean (Years)	Age at Weaning (Years)[1]	M3 Eruption Mean (Years)[a]
Orang	Unknown	4.20 (~3.5–4.9)[a] ~3.5[a]	7.0	~10 ~10
Gorilla	Unknown	3.50 (3.0–4.0)[b] 3.50 (3.0–4.0)b	2.8	11.40 (9.70–13.10) 10.38 (8.70–12.10)
Chimp	Female	3.27 (2.75–3.75)[b] 3.19 (2.67–3.75)[b]	4.5	11.30 (9.75–13.08) 10.71 (9.00–13.08)
Chimp	Male	3.38 (3.00–3.75)[b] 3.33 (3.00–3.58)[b]	4.5	11.36 (10.00–13.58) 10.27 (9.00–11.08)
Chimp	Unknown	3.323 (2.2–4.1)[c] 3.218 (1.9–4.1)[c]	4.5	
Human	Female	6.35 sd 0.74[b] 6.15 sd 0.76[b]	2.8	20.50 20.40
Human	Male	6.40 sd 0.79[b] 6.33 sd 0.79[b]	2.8	20.50 19.80
Human	Unknown	5.84 (4.74–7.0)[d]	2.8	

Top values represent maxillary teeth, and lower line, mandibular teeth. Ranges are reported in parentheses.

a. Smith, Crummett, and Brandt (1994) and Kelley and Schwartz (2005)

b. Smith, Crummett, and Brandt (1994)

c. Conroy and Mahoney (1991) and Zihlman, Bolter, and Boesch (2004) report maxillary M1 at alveolar margin(estimating four months from gingival emergence) at 4.1 years in a wild chimpanzee; they report dental characteristics of seventeen immature wild chimps of known ages and conclude that "emergence of permanent teeth in wild chimpanzees is consistently later than 90 percent of captive individuals" (Zihlman, Bolter, and Boesch 2004:10541).

d. Liversidge (2003); mean (range) of fifty-six worldwide populations

e. Macho (2001); Kelley and Schwartz (2005)

f. Macho (2001)

g. Reid et al. (1998)

h. Liversidge (2000)

i. See table 2.1 for references.

Age at First Birth (Years)[i]	M1 Crown Formation (Years)	Average Molar Crown Formation (Years)[f]	I1 Crown Formation (Years)	I2 Crown Formation (Years)
15.6	3.01 (2.90–3.12)[e] 2.81[f]	3.13		
10.0	2.70[f] 2.90[f]	2.85		
13.3				
	2.85[f] 2.73[f]	3.39	4.00[g] 4.90 (4.45–5.35)[g]	4.50[g] 5.07 (5.00–5.15)[g]
19.5				
	3.03[f] 2.62[f]	3.07	4.29 (3.33–4.54)[h] 3.90 (3.12–4.50)[h]	4.42 (4.17–5.40)[h]

dental microstructures, primarily crown formation and enamel deposition, is an especially promising line of evidence that can link aspects of dental development to absolute calendar time (Bromage and Dean 1985; Benyon and Dean 1987). Like eruption schedules, crown formation is also broadly correlated with life history variation across the anthropoid primates (Macho 2001). This correlation fails, however, within the narrow phylogenetic range we consider here. Table 2.3 shows that the patterns of dental maturation and eruption in great apes do not always correspond with one another, nor with the order of fast-to-slow life histories among these species.

A comparison of age at weaning in table 2.1 with M1 eruption in table 2.3 illustrates this lack of correspondence. M1 eruption follows weaning age in gorillas and chimpanzees by nine months to one year, but by more than three years in humans, whereas it precedes weaning by a similar span in orangutans. Although the age of M3 eruption is much older in later breeding humans, M3s do not erupt at an older age in the later breeding chimps and orangutans, compared with gorillas. M3 eruption misestimates age at first birth in all the nonhuman great ape species by 1–5.5 years, erupting at around 11 years in gorillas and chimpanzees and 10 years in orangutans, whereas age at first birth occurs around 10, 13.3, and 15.6 years, respectively. These data show that the life history variation among the living great apes is not closely reflected in their molar eruption schedules.

Comparison of crown formation rates in table 2.3 shows that microstructure development and life history variables correspond even less well. Not only are crown formation times quite similar among the nonhuman apes, failing to track variation in either weaning ages or age at maturity, but also there is "considerable overlap among great apes and humans" in the formation rates of both incisors and molars (Macho and Wood 1995b:23). The data show that researchers must temper expectations that individual aspects of dental development (such as anterior crown formation times) are tightly tied to age at first birth (Ramírez Rozzi and Bermúdez de Castro 2004) and age at weaning (Macho 2001).

The timing of tooth eruption, crown maturation, and other aspects of dental development (Godfrey et al. 2003) varies among great ape species. Although the range of this variation is not independent of life history, the evidence reveals that the link is not a tight one. The robust associations among life history traits themselves reflect the necessary interdependence of population vital rates (Hawkes, chapter 3, this volume), but the demographic constraints on growth and development are quite indirect. Life histories may change without concomitant shifts in all aspects of development, and, conversely, selection might favor developmental adjustments within immature stages because of particular problems faced by infants and juveniles in each species (Godfrey et al. 2003).

Interbirth Intervals and Juvenile Foraging

A primary life history difference between human and nonhuman great apes is the faster rate of offspring production in human females. For large-bodied mammals that produce large-bodied babies, the span between two offspring (the interbirth interval) is typically long, resulting in slow female reproductive rates (Harvey and Clutton-Brock 1985). In primates, conception closely follows weaning of the preceding offspring (Pusey 1983; Graham and Nadler 1990; Watts 1991; Lee and Bowman 1995), suggesting that interbirth intervals end when an infant can successfully feed itself. Weaning is strictly defined as the cessation of infant suckling, but this definition conceals the fact that weaning is primarily a transitional process, a gradual reduction in the portion of milk ingested and a concomitant increase in solid food consumption, not an abrupt cessation of lactation (Sellen, chapter 6, this volume). From the start of transitional feeding, primate infants forage for the solid food they ingest, although they occasionally obtain non-milk resources through passive food sharing (Feistner and McGrew 1989). The period of transitional feeding and the interbirth interval generally end when mothers have less fitness to gain from continuing their investment in the growing offspring than from beginning another pregnancy (Trivers 1974), usually at a time when an infant can successfully obtain all its own daily calories.

Offspring dependence is generally defined as the period during which the offspring drinks milk from its mother, that is, the time from birth to weaning. Some suggest a broader definition of dependence, noting that the mother provides services in addition to lactation that contribute to offspring survival (for example, Pereira and Altmann

1985). Primate orphans provide a good measure of the timing of independence from the mother. The available data, although largely anecdotal, suggest that suckling infants generally do not survive the death of their mother. Great ape orphan survival approaches that of no orphans if the mother is not lost before weaning age (Pusey 1983; Goodall 1986; Nishida, Takasaki, and Takahata 1990; Watts and Pusey 1993). In contrast, human infants are weaned at an age when they are still largely incapable of independent foraging and therefore continue to depend on provisioning by older individuals (Lancaster and Lancaster 1983). Data for humans show that offspring suffer poor survivorship if the mother dies during the first years of a child's life (Hill and Hurtado 1991; Sear et al. 2002; Pavard et al. 2005). Thereafter, death of the mother has less effect, not because the child is independent but because others supply support (Mace and Sear 2005).

Weaning and nutritional independence are not synonymous in humans as they are among the other apes. Children are weaned earlier yet are nutritionally dependent much longer than expected for a primate with our age at maturity. It is generally assumed that children require provisioning because they lack the ecological knowledge and complex foraging skills to forage independently. Gaining these skills is thought to require a long period of learning and practice during juvenility, an "apprenticeship," in order for human children to forage competently for themselves (Kaplan et al. 2000; Kaplan, Lancaster, and Robson 2003).

Recent studies challenge two common assumptions about the limitations of children's foraging efforts and capabilities. First, many foraging skills do not require substantial time and practice for children to master (Bliege Bird and Bird 2002; Blurton Jones and Marlowe 2002). Rather, children's foraging strategies appear to be more strongly constrained by their diminutive size, strength, and speed than by age and experience (Bird and Bliege Bird 2005; Tucker and Young 2005). Because children cannot acquire resources that require adult size, they forage from a different diet breadth. Calculations of juvenile foraging returns in child-accessible patches reveal that children are optimal foragers, targeting resources that yield the maximum immediate return rate (Bird and Bliege Bird 2002, 2005). These studies show that when evaluated within the constraints of their small size and strength, children are strategic and skilled foragers.

Second, Hawkes, O'Connell, and Blurton Jones (1995) have shown that foraging children can contribute more to their own subsistence than is widely assumed. Hadza children actively participate in food acquisition soon after weaning and throughout childhood, and these efforts make important contributions to their own nutrition. A mother often incorporates the productivity of her offspring when selecting foraging locations or resources, by choosing the strategy "that maximizes the *team rate* she and her children earn collectively, *even if the rate she earns herself is less than the maximum possible*" (Hawkes, O'Connell, and Blurton Jones 1995:695, italics original). Nevertheless, even though human juveniles can forage on their own behalf, they reside in habitats selected by adults and rarely ideal for independent juvenile subsistence. Thus, human children, unlike other ape juveniles, remain dependent upon supplemental provisioning long after they are weaned.

Stacking and Cooperative Breeding

With an earlier age at weaning and shorter interbirth intervals, human mothers shoulder the simultaneous nutritional dependence of multiple sequential offspring, a phenomenon we may call "stacking": mothers move on to bear another baby before the preceding one is nutritionally independent. This characteristic of humans is absent among nonhuman great apes. Great ape mothers may be accompanied by weaned subadult offspring while carrying a dependent infant, but they do not provision their offspring once weaned. Sumatran orangutans (van Noordwijk and van Schaik 2005) tolerate the presence of weaned juveniles, but these juveniles feed themselves and tend to leave their mother before the next infant is 2 years old (although there may be a longer association in the eastern subspecies *P. pygmaeus morio* of the Bornean orangutans [Horr 1975; M. Ancrenaz, personal communication 2005]). Maternal association with multiple immature offspring is more apparent in chimpanzees when a just-weaned juvenile and an older juvenile approaching adolescence may travel with their mother but, again, feed themselves. Orangutan immatures develop foraging competence at about the same age chimpanzees do, and their later weaning ages may be a response to the low productivity of the Southeast Asian rainforest, in which mothers cannot afford to travel with both a new baby and a weaned juvenile (van Noordwijk and van

Schaik 2005). This finding highlights the benefits that juveniles gain from association with adults. In more gregarious species, mothers may have shorter interbirth intervals because their weaned offspring need not make independent ranging choices yet. Comparing weaning ages in orangutans, chimpanzees, and gorillas, interbirth intervals vary inversely with gregariousness, and intervals are shortest in our own, especially gregarious species.

Human juveniles not only remain in association with their mothers but also continue to depend on provisioning after the birth of a younger sibling. The caloric returns necessary for multiple dependents may exceed the abilities of a single individual forager and require contributions from helpers other than the mother (Kaplan et al. 2000).

Fathers have long been assumed to be the primary source of help. Men differ from the males in other great ape species by regularly acquiring food that is consumed by women and children, and it is assumed that paternal benefits to improved nutrition and survival of their own offspring account for the evolution of men's work (Kaplan et al. 2000). Forager men sometimes provide a substantial component of food for their own children (for example, Marlowe 2003); among hunter-gatherer societies, higher average subsistence contributions from men are associated with higher average female fertility (Marlowe 2001). But the motives for men's contributions and the benefits they earn are disputed. Social benefits may be more important than parenting benefits in shaping these male activities. The returns from men's hunting are unpredictable, making it an unreliable strategy for family provisioning among low-latitude foragers (Hawkes, O'Connell, and Blurton Jones 2001b). When a hunter is successful, the meat is widely shared, so his family gets little more than others (Hawkes, O'Connell, and Blurton Jones 2001a). As in primates generally, the association of adult males with youngsters can sometimes serve as mating effort, mate guarding, or social bridging (Flinn 1992; Smuts and Gubernick 1992; Kuester and Paul 2000). Nevertheless, even if competition for social standing is the main motivation for men's food acquisition, especially big game hunting, the result does provide benefits for mothers and their children (Hawkes and Bliege Bird 2002).

Features of our distinctive life history, long postmenopausal lifespans and late age at first birth, provide two more reliable sources of potential help to mothers with multiple dependents. Postmenopausal and adolescent females lack newborns of their own and are therefore inclined to provide allomaternal assistance to gain inclusive fitness benefits (Hrdy 1999). Ethnographic and historic data show that the presence of a grandmother (especially the maternal grandmother) increases the welfare of her grandchildren (Sear, Mace, and McGregor 2000, 2003; Jamison et al. 2002; Sear et al. 2002; Voland and Beise 2002; Lahdenpera et al. 2004; Ragsdale 2004; Tymicki 2004). When circumstances permit (Hames and Draper 2004), older adolescents provide important help to their mothers through the caretaking of younger siblings (Tronick, Morelli, and Ivey 1992). The fact that human mothers stack nutritionally dependent offspring points to the evolutionary importance of help from provisioners other than the mother in the evolution of our life histories (Hrdy 1999).

CONCLUSIONS

We have compared the life histories of humans and the living great apes to develop a hypothetical life history for a common ancestor and identify changes in our lineage. A general feature of living great apes is a slow life history, so we infer that this was also true of our common ancestor. Human life histories are even slower. Humans have a significantly longer lifespan, with adults living at least twenty-five years longer than the other great apes. Human age at first birth is four to six years older than for orangutans and chimpanzees, increasing the period of juvenility and opportunity for growth. Additional time to grow results in larger human mothers who produce absolutely and relatively larger babies.

Two striking deviations have shaped the pattern of slowing in human life histories: our short interbirth intervals and our vigorous postmenopausal longevity. First, slower life histories typically include longer interbirth intervals. Although humans have the longest subadult period, attain the largest body size, and produce the largest infants, we have the shortest interbirth intervals. Human infants are weaned several years earlier than might be expected of an ape with our age at maturity. Also, because women (like most primate females) conceive soon after a child is weaned, they bear another baby before the preceding one is capable of independent foraging. Second, women stop bearing offspring by their early 40s. The age at which fertility declines to menopause appears to be essentially the same in women as in the other apes, indicating that this trait may be conserved across the great ape radiation. The distinctively early weaning of human infants and stacking of dependent offspring could evolve only if human mothers had a reliable source of help. Postmenopausal grandmothers and adolescents, because they themselves did not have infants, likely supplied that help.

We have also highlighted the imperfect correspondence among various aspects of growth and development in brains and teeth and between those developmental variables and the life history traits that are tied to population vital rates. Our exploration of the cross-species variation among great apes and humans in these dimensions is only a beginning. More is clearly in order.

Acknowledgments

We thank Sarah Hrdy, Eric Rickart, Earl Keefe, Nick Blurton Jones, Dan Sellen, and the SAR participants for valuable input and discussion. We also thank Jennifer Graves for careful editing.

3

Life History Theory and Human Evolution

A Chronicle of Ideas and Findings

Kristen Hawkes

SUMMARY

Fertility ends at similar ages in women and female chimpanzees, but humans usually live longer and mature later. We also differ from our closest living relatives in weaning infants before they can feed themselves. The comparisons pose questions about when and why the distinctively human life history traits evolved in our lineage. Here I outline the basic framework of the field of life history evolution and, against that background, chronicle past inquiries into each of these distinctively human traits. The chronicle covers discovery and description, guided sometimes by hypotheses about underlying developmental mechanisms and sometimes by hypotheses about adaptive effects. Following the review, I discuss the continuing importance of distinguishing between questions about mechanisms and adaptive effects in light of accumulating fossil evidence and progress in genomics. I conclude with a brief reference to the most influential adaptive hypothesis to date, the Hunting hypothesis, and some of the accumulating empirical challenges to it, setting the stage for current debates addressed in subsequent chapters.

Human life histories differ from those of our nearest living relatives in several striking ways (Smith and Tompkins 1995; Bogin and Smith 1996; Robson, van Schaik, and Hawkes, chapter 2, this volume). We can live twice as long as chimpanzees can, having the greatest potential longevity of the terrestrial vertebrates (Carey and Judge 2000). Yet, fertility declines to essentially zero at about the age of 45 in both women and female chimpanzees (Gage 1998; Hawkes 2003; Nishida et al. 2003). Other aspects of human physiology age more slowly than our ovarian systems (Gosden 1985; Finch 1990; Hill and Hurtado 1991; Hughes et al. 2001; Blurton Jones and Marlowe 2002; Walker and Hill 2003), so, unlike other primates, we reach menopause before our geriatric years (Pavelka and Fedigan 1991). We mature very slowly. Average age at first birth is about six years later for humans than it is for chimpanzees (Robson, van Schaik, and Hawkes, chapter 2, this volume). But we wean infants earlier than chimpanzees do and have shorter birth spacing (Galdikas and Wood 1990; Robson, van Schaik, and Hawkes, chapter 2, this volume). Unlike other primate juveniles, our children continue to depend on feeding assistance after they are weaned and their mothers are nursing new babies (Lancaster and Lancaster 1983, 1987; Bogin 1999a).

These features of human life histories not only describe important aspects of our individual lives but also determine the age structure of human families, communities, and populations. Age composition of social groups determines many of the problems and possibilities of both conflict and cooperation. Accumulating evidence that our life history features are both distinctive and typical of human experience prompts questions about when and why they evolved. When and why did ancestral populations begin to have characteristically human age structures?

Modern humans are the only living representatives of a clade that has included many other species. Those previous members of our lineage and their distribution in time and space are known only through the fossil and archaeological record. Without that record, we would have no clues to the existence and distinctive character of either australopithecines or any species in the genus *Homo* except our own. The fragmentary evidence of hominin fossils and the archaeology associated with past populations are the key lines of evidence about how they differed from one another, when and how much they differed from living species, and when and why human life histories evolved.

A focus on life histories highlights questions about longevity and aging, age at maturity, rates of offspring production, and the population age structures that these imply. Life history evolution is a field that seeks to explain variation in probabilities of survival and reproduction across the lifespans of living things, highlighting interrelationships among these timing and rate variables. Questions about physiological (and now, increasingly, molecular) mechanisms that underlie the rate and timing of growth, development, reproduction, and aging occupy many researchers. Life history evolution focuses less on mechanisms and more on their fitness-related effects, that is, whether they are likely to result in relatively more descendants in future populations. These effects can explain why natural selection adjusts the timing and rate variables (and therefore the mechanisms underlying them) differently in different species. The goal of the field is to discover the fitness costs and benefits, the trade-offs that explain the diversity of life histories across the living world. Applied to our lineage, the theory, the models, and other conceptual tools help link multiple lines of evidence about our evolutionary heritage.

Following this introduction, I describe the field of life history evolution by characterizing a few of its key assumptions and models (for a review of the field, see Stearns 1992). In preparation for subsequent discussion, I then summarize r and K selection, some critiques, and Charnov's alternative scheme of dimensionless invariants.

Next, I turn to the history of ideas and findings about the appearance of four distinctive features of human life history: our late maturation, our potentially long lifespans, our slow aging, with fertility ending in women while other physiological systems maintain a substantial fraction of peak performance, and our children's continued dependence on feeding assistance after they are weaned.

After summarizing work on the evolution of each of those four features, I explicitly distinguish different kinds of explanations. The discussion follows the review of work because a different mix of explanatory frameworks has influenced inquiry into each of the four features of human life histories. Questions about causal mechanisms and about adaptive function have both been important. Distinguishing between them is too. Another distinction, between homologous features (those shared with immediate common ancestors) and homoplasies (similarities that newly appear in descendants), has also become especially important with the rise of cladistics and the explosive development of molecular techniques. The distinction between homologies and homoplasies is of primary import for investigators seeking to establish phylogenetic relationships among both modern and ancient taxa. Expansions of the hominin fossil record have exposed a great deal of independent variation in measurable traits, complicating phylogenetic assignments. More generally, developments in genomics reveal similar genetic pathways for phenotypic functions employed by species that are phylogenetically very distant from one another. These findings make mechanism questions seem potentially tractable and especially tantalizing. Only adaptive hypotheses, however, seek to explain why particular life history features evolve instead of others, why human life histories have taken their distinctive shape.

One adaptive hypothesis has provided especially influential guidance for research exploring changes in the human lineage. I turn to it in a brief concluding section. As Cartmill (1993:191) pointed out, "the hunting hypothesis was the first truly Darwinian explanation of human origins to be proposed." S. L. Washburn's (1960; Washburn and DeVore 1961; Washburn and Moore 1974) especially influential version of this hypothesis linked work in paleoecology, paleontology, Paleolithic archaeology, comparative primatology, and hunter-gatherer ethnography. Now the empirical record in each of the fields on which Washburn relied is much richer and more complex. The evidence no longer shows the temporal relationships among the appearances of human characteristics, which once seemed clear. Nevertheless, discovering what actually happened in the evolution of our lineage still involves pursuing Washburn's general research strategy. The same lines of inquiry he championed, as well as genomics, provide the evidence to build, correct, and revise hypotheses about what happened in the past. Explicit use of models that link life history features to one another is an additional tool to help us extract more from the hard evidence on the evolution of our lineage.

LIFE HISTORY EVOLUTION

Although the foundation goes back to Darwin (1859) and further to Euler (1760), the field-defining publications in life history evolution are mostly mid-twentieth century, including Fisher (1930), Cole

(1954), Williams (1957, 1966b), Hamilton (1966), MacArthur and Wilson (1967), Lack (1968), Tinkle (1969), and Gadgil and Bossert (1970). However, the pace of work accelerated so much in the late eighties and nineties that Stearns, in his 1992 textbook, could write that "analysis of the evolution of fitness components is a new field, life history evolution" (Stearns 1992:10).

The Demographic Foundation

Partridge and Harvey's (1988:1449) succinct definition of life histories as "the probabilities of survival and the rates of reproduction at each age in the life-span" highlights the demographic framework of the field and its ties with the conceptual tools of population genetics.

Stearns (1992:10) explained the framework this way:

> Life history evolution makes the simplifying claim that the phenotype consists of demographic traits—birth, age and size at maturity, number and size of offspring, growth and reproductive investment, length of life, death—connected by constraining relationships, tradeoffs...including those between current reproduction and survival, current reproduction and future reproduction, number, size, and sex of offspring.

The power of this simplification comes from models of population growth in age-structured populations (Cole 1954; Hamilton 1966; Gadgil and Bossert 1970; Charlesworth 1994).

The basic equation of both demography and life history evolution was discovered by Euler in the eighteenth century and rediscovered by Lotka in the twentieth (Euler 1760; Lotka 1922; Keyfitz 1977). Population growth rate (r) is determined by age-specific mortality and fertility rates. It depends on the probability of survival (l_x) and the average number of offspring produced (m_x) by those at each age (x). These variables are necessarily interdependent because the size of each newborn cohort depends on the number of females in the offspring-bearing ages and their fertility rates. Those females come from cohorts of past newborns. Thus, the number of females in the fertile ages depends on the number and fertility of females in the past, as well as the mortality rates of their offspring. When fertility and mortality rates are sustained for a few generations, they result in a population with a stable age distribution. This means that all the age classes then grow (or decline) at a constant exponential rate (r) and the fraction of the total population in each age class remains unchanged.

"Although most natural populations are rarely in stable age distribution, moderate deviations from stable age distributions do not often change qualitative predictions. The Euler-Lotka equation captures robust features of demography" (Stearns 1992:25). A mutation that alters the rate of fertility or mortality at any age can affect the population growth rate. Comparing the growth rate of the mutant with the growth rate of the background population therefore indicates the lifetime fitness effect of the mutation and whether it would spread or decline against the common type.

An additional simplifying assumption is sometimes used. Because stable populations grow (or decline) exponentially, growth rates must average near zero most of the time. Otherwise, populations either disappear or overrun the planet. In stationary (that is, nongrowing) populations ($r = 0$), each adult female, on average, exactly replaces herself. The number of surviving daughters produced by a female over her lifetime (R_0) is one. When $R_0 = 1$, the relationships among certain life history variables are necessarily fixed; therefore, assuming that populations are nongrowing can simplify modeling and analyses (Charnov 1991, 1993, 1997). Stationary populations also have standing age distributions that mirror the mortality schedule, a useful way to underline the fundamental link between life histories and the age structure of populations.

Life history analyses explore the costs and benefits of shifts in mortality and fertility by measuring the magnitude of their lifetime effects. Because time and energy are limited, more of one thing generally means less of something else (Maynard Smith 1978; Seger and Stubblefield 1996). Any increase in fertility or decrease in mortality at one age likely entails changes in those variables at other ages. Changes have different consequences for lifetime fitness, depending on which ages they affect (Cole 1954; Williams 1957; Hamilton 1966; Charlesworth 1994). These consequences and the life histories of ancestral populations determine the range of possible life histories in immediate descendants.

r and K Selection

Over the past several decades, r and K selection has been the most widely used theory of life history variation. The labels were introduced by MacArthur and Wilson (1967; Pianka 1970) to capture Dobzhansky's (1950) suggestion that in environments subject to extreme variation, populations will likely "crash." Mortality would then be independent of density and largely independent of individual competitive abilities. Under those conditions, selection would favor features that maximize the intrinsic rate of population growth (r). In relatively constant environments, populations would saturate carrying capacity, K (the conventional symbol for this variable in density-dependent models of population growth). Then mortality would be density-dependent and would differentially affect individuals, depending on their efficiency in acquiring resources. Under those conditions, selection would favor increased competitive ability. Pianka (1970) enumerated the contrasting characteristics expected for each kind of selection, with K-selected species investing more in fewer offspring that develop more slowly and delay reproduction to gain greater competitive ability and larger body size, living long lives and reproducing repeatedly.

The r and K scheme is intuitively appealing. As Stearns (1992:307) wrote, it "was suggestive and influential but incorrect." Problems with it include the following three (for example, see Promislow and Harvey 1990, 1991; Roff 1992; Stearns 1992; Charlesworth 1994). First, the associations postulated in the theory are often not found in the world. Stearns (1977:168) tested the dichotomy on published data on a wide array of taxa: "In about half the studies...the organisms fit the accepted scheme...; in the other half they did not." Promislow and Harvey (1991:124) noted that "K selection should, by definition, give rise to increased carrying capacity.... But larger individuals using a greater amount of resources might actually reduce carrying capacity." In fact, maximum densities of different species are negatively correlated with body mass, larger-bodied species living at lower maximum densities (Damuth 1981, 1987).

In addition to empirical failures, a second important problem is the coherence of the assumptions. As Stearns (1977:206) put it:

> Unlike r, K cannot be realistically expressed as a function of

life history traits....Thus r and K cannot be reduced to units of common currency. If they do trade off, so that higher r's imply lower K's, the mechanisms by which that tradeoff is accomplished are not demographic, but are bound up in physiology and social behavior, and as such could be expected to change from taxon to taxon.

It is especially important that the r and K distinction ignores differences in mortality rates with age, because changes in mortality rates have different consequences for life history evolution, depending on which ages are affected. A population in which growth is held in check by equal mortality increases on all age classes can be comparable to a population that is allowed to grow unchecked. Selection has the same effects on life history traits under both conditions (Charlesworth 1994). Equal mortality increases across all age classes are the same as no mortality changes at all.

A third problem is that the characteristics expected with either r or K selection can be generated and maintained in stationary (nongrowing) populations by models in which mortality varies with age (Kozlowski and Weiner 1997; Harvey and Purvis 1999). The circumstances postulated in the r and K scheme to explain each set of features are therefore not required for the evolution or maintenance of either one.

Nevertheless, "fast-slow" variation in life cycles and associations between timing variables and adult body size are empirical regularities in the living world (Bonner 1965; Western 1979; Clutton-Brock and Harvey 1983; McMahon and Bonner 1983; Peters 1983; Calder 1984). Scaling patterns are pervasive (Brown and West 2000). Roff (1992:45) criticized Pianka for using body lengths of vertebrates and insects to demonstrate r versus K selection, because "to compare vertebrates and insects is to compare apples and oranges." Still, within taxonomic groups, life history variation does generally fall along a fast-slow continuum that is associated with variation in body size. As Promislow and Harvey (1990:418) emphasized, however, "it is important to distinguish between the empirically observed fast-slow continuum in mammal life histories and the theoretically derived r-K continuum. There is no good evidence that increased competitive ability among mammals results in higher K."

Charnov's Symmetry Approach

An alternative scheme for broad regularities in life history variation has been developed by E. L. Charnov (1993, 2002), who has shown that mammals, birds, and fish can be distinguished by characteristic relationships among life history traits. The relationships among the traits reflect distinctive symmetries in each taxonomic group by remaining approximately constant—invariant—when the traits themselves change in value. For example, the ratio between species' average adult lifespan and average age at maturity is about 1.4 for mammals, 2.3 for birds, and 0.5 for fish (Charnov and Berrigan 1990a; Charnov 1993). To explain these taxonomically distinctive patterns, Charnov (2002:753) has constructed explanatory models in which "the optimal life history adjusts some life-history variables...in the face of tradeoffs with others.... [T]he dimensionless approach to life histories looks for *invariants* in the *outward life history*...and in the *tradeoffs* that generate the set of optimal life histories" (italics original).

Unlike r and K selection, Charnov's approach emphasizes both the differences among and the similarities within taxonomic groups. Three "dimensionless numbers, each a benefit-cost ratio summarizing reproductive timing, allocation and demography, are invariants and thus are useful to classify life histories"(Charnov 2002:749). He uses them to represent the distribution of life histories in three dimensions, a "life history cube." Mammals, birds, and fish occupy distinct positions in the cube, defined by their characteristic values on the life history ratios that delineate the edges: (1) the ratio of offspring size to maternal size, (2) the ratio of relative reproductive effort to adult mortality rate, and (3) the ratio of adult lifespan to age at maturity. The values for each variable are averages calculated over age-structured populations. Charnov (2002:757) wrote:

> This classification scheme for life histories differs from those such as "*r*- and *K*-selection"...in that these other schemes invariably use axes with dimensional magnitudes such as time or mass. Elephants and squirrels are at opposite poles in these schemes, and the suggestion is made that natural selection operates in fundamentally different ways when we contrast them (opportunistic versus equilibrium,

for example)....But when we remove absolute magnitude for time and mass, squirrels and elephants look a lot alike, and look different from fish or altricial birds. Selection may well operate similarly on squirrel and elephant life histories in the sense that...the trade-offs have the same dimensionless features. My working hypothesis...is that the trade-off features are the same *within* (say) altricial birds, mammals or indeterminate growers like fish, with major differences *between* these groups.

To the extent that this holds empirically, the distinctive characteristics of mammalian (or perhaps, more narrowly, primate) trade-offs should help students of human evolution hypothesize the ranges of possible life histories and population age structures of our ancestors and the extinct taxa in our lineage. A Grandmother hypothesis for the evolution of human life histories (Hawkes, O'Connell, and Blurton Jones 1997, 2003; Hawkes et al. 1998; Blurton Jones, Hawkes, and O'Connell 1999; O'Connell, Hawkes, and Blurton Jones 1999; Alvarez 2000; O'Connell et al. 2002; see Hawkes, chapter 4, this volume, for more detailed discussion) explicitly builds on Charnov's mammalian invariants.

THE EVOLUTION OF FOUR DISTINCTIVE FEATURES IN THE HUMAN LINEAGE

The empirical record of life history variation among living populations, the theory to explain that variation, and the fossil record of our own lineage have all expanded in the past few decades. For a much longer time, questions about the evolution of particular human life history features have preoccupied the curious. I largely restrict attention to work that addresses questions about the appearance of these features in the evolution of our lineage, and I discuss the four features in turn. Investigators often addressed these features two at a time, so the sections overlap. But each highlights different problems and different aspects of the record.

Models of life history evolution generally assume that mortality schedules determine optimal ages of first birth and rates of offspring production. On those grounds, I should discuss our low adult mortality (our long lifespans and slow aging) first, with postmenopausal longevity following, then slow maturation, and finally weaning age. I begin instead with slow maturation because S. J. Gould's (1977) *Ontogeny and Phylogeny* highlighted that feature especially, sketching a broad history of ideas about evolutionary change and raising issues that I touch on again in subsequent sections of this chapter. Gould's book continues to influence research on the evolution of human growth and development.

Slow Maturation

Gould is especially well known for his interest in the role of developmental mechanisms in shaping the diversity of life and for his critiques of "the adaptationist program" (for example, Gould and Lewontin 1979). *Ontogeny and Phylogeny* (1977), however, emphasized the fundamental adaptive importance of life history variation. Here are Gould's (1977:289–290) own words:

> I regard the rise of theoretical population ecology as one of the most significant events in evolutionary theory during the past twenty years. For…it has proved that the components of life history strategies—timing of reproduction, fecundity, and longevity, for example—are adaptations in themselves, not merely the consequences of evolving structure and function….In short, theoretical population ecology has given us a new set of parameters for assessing adaptation.

Gould (1977:2) wrote that he began his book about "the ancient subject of parallels between ontogeny and phylogeny" to rescue an important topic that was neglected at the time because of associations with erroneous ideas about evolution: "Properly restructured, it stands as a central theme in evolutionary biology because it illuminates two issues of great contemporary importance: the evolution of ecological strategies and the biology of regulation" (1977:2).

Gould (1977:2) characterized *Ontogeny and Phylogeny* as "primarily a long argument for the evolutionary importance of *heterochrony*—changes in the relative timing of appearance and rate of development for characters already present in ancestors." From the start of the book (here quoting Gould 1977:8), however, he emphasized that although "classical arguments [for the importance of heterochrony] are based upon the macroevolutionary significance of morphology," he had a different kind of evolutionary importance in mind: "I focus upon the immediate significance of acceleration and retardation in the evolution of life-history strategies for ecological adaptation. In this context, the timing of maturation assumes special importance" (1977:8).

Although morphological development is very much the subject of the book, the life history implications of morphology are repeatedly given priority of importance, for example, "the timing of maturation (rather than the morphology obtained by speeding up or slowing down)" (1977:289). In his treatment of human evolution, Gould (1977:399) reiterates that in discussing "the evolutionary significance of heterochrony, I have been trying to de-emphasize the traditional arguments of morphology while asserting the importance of life history strategies."

The r and K scheme was in wide use in the seventies and is a major theme of the book. Gould (1977:399–400) proposed that it had great promise for explaining macroevolutionary patterns:

> I have linked accelerated development to r-selective regimes and identified retarded development as a common trait of K strategists....I have also tried to link K selection to what we generally regard as "progressive" in evolution, while suggesting that r selection generally serves as a break upon such evolutionary change. I regard human evolution as a strong confirmation of these views.
>
> To begin with, we belong to a class of animals in which K selection dominates (Pianka 1970)....We belong to an order of mammals distinguished by their propensity for repeated single births, intense parental care, long life spans, late maturation, and a high degree of socialization—a point for point agreement with Pianka's listing of traits common to K strategists (1970).
>
> Human evolution has emphasized one feature of this common primate heritage—delayed development, particularly as expressed in late maturation and extended childhood. This retardation has reacted synergistically with other hall-

marks of hominization—with intelligence (by enlarging the brain through prolongation of fetal growth tendencies and by providing a longer period of childhood learning) and with socialization (by cementing family units through increased parental care of slowly developing offspring).

Gould (1977:9) argued that "neoteny has been a (probably the) major determinant of human evolution." In documenting both the history of the idea and the empirical evidence for it, he surmised:

> The notion of human neoteny has it roots in two obvious facts: the striking resemblances between juvenile pongids and adult humans and the obliteration of this similarity during pongid ontogeny by strong negative allometry of the brain and positive allometry of the jaws....[T]hese phenomena...had been recognized as soon as juvenile pongids had reached the zoos and museums of Europe. (Gould 1977:353)

In the 1920s, L. Bolk (for example, 1926) developed his fetalization theory of human evolution; the distinctive features of human body form are seen as fetal conditions in other primates but remain permanent in humans. Gould (1977:356) justified extended attention to the case Bolk made: "His insight has been ridiculed in the light of modern doctrine and dismissed in toto because he linked valid and important data to evolutionary views now rejected.... [But] the data that he presented can survive the collapse of his explanatory structure."

While the work of A. H. Schultz is under no such danger of dismissal, Gould's caveat about the value of the data, in spite of an unsustainable explanatory structure, applies to him as well. Schultz had a very orthogenetic view of primate evolution, but those errors in no way reduce the value of many of his insights, based as they are on his meticulous attention to measurements and patterns of variation both within and among populations. Gould uses Schultz's work to support his arguments about delayed maturation in humans.

Noting our common ancestry with the anthropoid apes, Schultz (1950:428) had this to say:

> Man became distinguished chiefly in connection with his

three outstanding specializations; the early and undoubtedly rapid acquisition of the erect posture, the later, gradual and ultimately great increase in relative brain-size, and the comparatively very recent prolongation of his main periods of life.

With the gradual accumulation of large series of monkeys and apes it has become possible to compare man with other primates on the basis of statistically adequate observations and at all stages of growth. Only in this way can it be decided whether a particular character is really distinctive in all cases within a representative, normal range of variations, or differs merely in regard to the frequency of occurrence, thus being of lesser significance. With the realization that any evolutionary change, apparent in the adult, is the result of some primary alteration in the processes of growth and development, it seems highly desirable to discover the condition in which human growth differs from the growth of non-human primates.

Schultz (1956:890) underlines the importance of variation in age at maturity across the primates:

In regard to all parts of post-natal life one can recognize a clear trend toward prolongation, beginning in monkeys, as compared to lemurs, more pronounced in gibbons, still more in all three great apes and by far the most marked in man. For instance, general growth, at least in length, is completed in only 3 years in prosimians, in 7 years in Old World monkeys such as macaques, in not over 9 years in gibbons, in 11 years in the large man-like apes, and in as much as 20 years in recent man. Of special biological significance is the fact that with the advance on the evolutionary scale of primates, puberty and the beginning of fertility become more and more chronologically retarded and thereby the interval between succeeding generations becomes steadily lengthened.

Schultz's view that these differences in the time to skeletal maturation represent a trend of progressive evolution is not consistent with modern evolutionary theory, but the differences he points to are real empirical phenomena. As the final sentence of the passage shows, he recognized that the demographic implications of age at maturity are especially important.

Schultz might have agreed with Gould's endorsement of Bolk's central point. Gould ends his chapter on human evolution by reasserting Bolk's (1926:470) question and answer: "What is the essential in man as an organism? The obvious answer is: the slow progress of his life's course." But Schultz's work also showed that slower life histories did not mean slower growth and development in all corresponding body parts. "With his fetalization theory, Bolk (1926) had called attention to ontogenetic retardation as a phylogenetic process. It can be shown today that accelerations in development have also played a role in human evolution" (Schultz 1956:888).

Well aware of this, Gould still claimed that neoteny has been the major determinant of human evolution, a claim that has been actively debated with many demonstrations of non-neotenous processes in human growth and development (for example, Shea 1989; McKinney and McNamara 1991; Godfrey and Sutherland 1996). Gould's 1977 book might have stimulated more attention to life history, but particular kinds of morphological heterochrony have been the focus of attention among students of growth and development (for example, Parker, Langer, and McKinney 2000; Minugh-Purvis and McNamara 2002; Thompson, Krovitz, and Nelson 2003).

Much of what has happened in studies of heterochrony is quite difficult for nonspecialists because of the emphasis on distinguishing different kinds of morphological heterochrony. Shea (2002:79), appraising the proliferation of recent work, commented:

> Certainly, one area where much attention has been focused involves the recognition and definition of the myriad types and categories of morphological heterochrony.... [While] debates over appropriate definitions and classifications are certainly a necessary and productive component of heterochronic research...they often seem, to insiders and outsiders alike, as exercises that dwell excessively on ever-growing mounds of tongue-twisting jargon of uncertain biological relevance.

Shea (1981, 1983a) demonstrated that no single heterochronic shift could account for the differences in either growth trajectories or adult form among the African apes (Leigh and Shea 1996). Subsequent work has underlined the generality of that finding. Leigh and Park (1998:348), investigating "the evolution of human growth prolongation," compared velocity curves of growth across many species of primates on an array of dimensions and found that

> relative size, velocity relative to size-for-age, and estimates of the pace of ontogeny (timing variables) show appreciable amounts of variation independent of adult size. Variation that is unrelated to adult size is typical during early periods of primate ontogeny, and may reflect a high degree of adaptive variation. Low phylogenetically adjusted correlations for some of these variables suggest that attributes of early growth periods and adult body size are often uncoupled, and evolve independently.

Such independence has repeatedly confronted analysts looking for correlated adjustments in morphological variation. Investigators exploring the mismatch between phenotypic and molecular similarities in papionin primates find substantial variation in growth patterns across the tribe (Collard and Wood 2001). Collard and O'Higgins (2001) and Leigh, Shah, and Buchanan (2003) measured crania from ontogenetic series of various genera to characterize the growth patterns that result in adult faces. Both studies not only improve understanding of the ontogeny and evolution of papionin faces but also reveal diversity in the patterns of growth and development. Leigh, Shah, and Buchanan (2003:307) concluded that "ontogenetic allometric data may not be informative regarding papionin taxonomy."

Schultz had pointed out that even though prolonged life periods distinguish people from other primates, this does not mean that all aspects of human growth and development are slower. In his 1960 review of "age changes in primates and their modification in man," Schultz (1960:19) referred to a large study of skeletal changes with age in young American males, which found maturation changes to share a common, orderly process. He remarked:

> Closely corresponding to this intraspecific constancy in gen-

eral sequence and variability in timing of the age changes of
man we find intergenerically among primates few major
deviations from one common pattern of development, but
many marked modifications in the relative timing during
the maturation of epiphyses, sutures, dentition, hair, etc.
(Schultz 1960:29)

Gould (1977) appreciated this variability. Recognizing that not only
neoteny but also multiple heterochronic processes are implicated in
human evolution, he wrote:

No Darwinian supporter of retardation as a major element
in human evolution can deny that many distinctive features
are not peadomorphic; the concept of mosaic evolution
practically requires such a belief....The evolutionary direction of each feature is controlled by natural selection; the
capacity for independent variation of characteristics is very
great. (Gould 1977:364–365)

Yet, at the same time, Gould pinned substantial hope on finding
that developmental mechanisms limit that independence. His claim
that "features of an organism are bound (often quite loosely) in covari-
ant sets, and these sets are often dissociable as blocks" (Gould 1982:341
–342) is cited by Shea (1983b:522), who explicitly hoped that "this
'shuffling' of the developmental trajectories of various body regions
may provide new adaptive morphological configurations with minimal
genetic changes."

Ontogeny and Phylogeny was published just after M.-C. King and A.
C. Wilson's (1975:107) summary showing that "the genetic distance
between humans and the chimpanzee is probably too small to account
for their substantial organismal differences." King and Wilson
(1975:107) hypothesized that "regulatory mutations account for the
major biological differences between humans and chimpanzees."
Citing their work, Gould (1977:9) wrote:

Humans and chimpanzees are almost identical in structural
genes, yet differ markedly in form and behavior. This paradox can be resolved by invoking a small genetic difference
with profound effects—alterations in the regulatory system
that slow down the general rate of development in humans.

> Heterochronic changes are regulatory changes; they require only an alteration in the timing of features already present.

The emphasis is on mechanisms. While Gould appreciated that demographic processes shape life histories and he recognized the capacity of selection to modify individual morphological features independently, he expected developmental mechanisms to explain human differences. The mechanisms that give rise to a variant and the net fitness benefits that spread and maintain it are equally important domains of inquiry. But they demand different kinds of research. Life history evolution generally seeks to explain species differences in age at maturity through the fitness effects of shifts in that trait under prevailing demographic constraints.

Long Lifespans and Slow Aging

Gould (1977) cited G. A. Sacher (1959; Sacher and Staffeldt 1974), who made especially important contributions to the evolution of longevity. A footnote in *Ontogeny and Phylogeny* (1977) mentioned the associations Sacher found between brain size and maturation time across the mammals as corroborating evidence for Gould's neoteny argument. Gould (1977:371n) concluded that "the neotenic hypothesis applies whether brain enlargement precedes more general retardation or vice versa." The associations between brain size and maturation time that Sacher discovered became a component of his inquiry into the evolution of longevity. Sacher (1975:417) argued that human longevity "is distinctive and important enough to merit being listed, along with symbolic and tool making behavior, as a distinguishing feature of the human species."

Finding a strong relationship between brain size and maximum lifespan across mammals, Sacher (1975:426) favored two mutually compatible hypotheses "about the causal processes responsible for the relation." One is that the brain "participates in the stabilization of the life processes of the organism....In other words, the brain is postulated to be an ORGAN OF LONGEVITY" (1975:426, emphasis original). The other is that "the evolution of a larger brain imposes on the species an added metabolic and developmental burden, and a consequent decreased reproductive rate that can only be compensated by means of an extension of the reproductive span, and hence of lifespan" (1975:426). He considered the second hypothesis to be confirmed by his finding that two brain size variables, neonatal brain weight and the ratio of neonatal to adult brain weight, are correlated with two life history variables, gestation time and litter size across ninety-one mammal species, including nineteen primates (Sacher 1975).

Sacher had earlier concluded (Sacher and Staffeldt 1974) that a common growth law for mammalian brains is the rate-limiting process for all other aspects of somatic growth. Therefore, brain size "provides an objective basis for the estimation of relative maturation times of related species that differ in brain size" (Sacher 1975:427). On those grounds, Sacher used cranial capacity to estimate both lifespan and maturation times in fossil hominin taxa. From the data available at the time, he estimated that australopithecines were later maturing and longer-lived than modern chimpanzees, that Neanderthals were similar to modern humans, and that *Homo erectus* was intermediate between australopiths and modern people.

Sacher's hypothesis that brains controlled both maturation and longevity was partly based on his (1959) finding that although brain weight is correlated with body weight across the mammals and body weight is correlated with lifespan, the correlation between lifespan and brain weight was significantly stronger. In response to Sacher, others showed that spleen, adrenal, and kidney mass are as well correlated with lifespan as is brain mass (Calder 1976; Economos 1980a; Prothero and Jürgens 1987). One recognized reason why organ weights show stronger correlations with life history variables than do body weights is that organ masses vary less among adults over time, making them more stable measures of animal size.

> The reason for the better prediction of life span from brain mass is that brain mass has less variability than body mass. The body mass of any individual or species can vary widely, depending upon its energy balance situation.... [W]ithin species, or when the mammals are treated together, the coefficient of variation for brain mass is less than half that for body mass. (Lindstedt and Calder 1981:12)

There is a substantial literature on brain-size/body-size measures and the relationships between them (for example, Prothero and Jürgens 1987; Pagel and Harvey 1989; Harvey and Krebs 1990; Barton 1999). Sacher (1959) devised an "index of cephalization" to measure brain size relative to body size, and much subsequent work has focused on the evolution of brains that are relatively large for body size, especially in primates (R. Martin 1990) and in the human lineage (for example, Jerison 1973; Aiello and Wheeler 1995; Allman 1999). Increases in this relative measure are correlated with increased lifespan in primates, but not in other mammalian orders (Austad and Fischer 1992; but see van Schaik et al., chapter 5, this volume).

Sacher's ideas about the role of brains in determining the pace of life histories do not include the usual assumption that the function of delayed maturity is to allow more time to learn. He cited Dobzhansky (1962) for the widespread claim "that the maturation times of hominids get longer because they have more to learn" (Sacher 1975: 429). "Hominids do indeed have more to learn," Sacher (1975:429) agreed, "but the essence of hominization is that they are able to learn more rapidly." Still, he favored the hypothesis that age at maturity depended on brain size: "A more reasonable assumption...is that the learning process speeds up to fit into the maturation period defined by an optimum pattern of mammalian brain growth" (1975:429).

Sacher's hypotheses about the causal mechanisms linking brains to life history variables have not fared well (see, for example, Allman 1999; Deaner, Barton, and van Schaik 2003; and Robson, van Schaik, and Hawkes, chapter 2, this volume, on brain growth patterns in humans and chimpanzees), but his discovery that lifespan is one of the life history features generally predictable from organism size remains extremely important. Calder (1984:4) summarized the importance of size this way:

> Suppose we encounter a new beast that we wish to understand....If we know only its "weight" we can predict (give or take 25% or so) a wide variety of its specifications and requirements: home range, heart and metabolic rates, life span—each from an empirical allometric equation based on body size.

Lifespan, usually (but not always) meaning observed maximum lifespan, has come to be a widely used measure of longevity (D. W. E. Smith 1993). But starting with Sacher's use of observed maximum lifespan in the 1959 Ciba symposium, it has drawn objections. G. C. Williams (1999:405) framed his long-standing complaint this way: "It is clearly true that different species have different demographies....This does not mean that any maximum observed age can be identified as a species characteristic." Williams (1999:405) worried that a specified maximum lifespan suggests erroneously that "death is a programmed event in life history," an idea inconsistent with evolutionary theories of aging. There are, nevertheless, ways that maximum lifespan is very useful in comparisons among populations and across species. The population average is the best single summary of lifetime survival, so life expectancy at birth or mean lifespan may seem a better single parameter than observed maximum lifespan to characterize a population's mortality experience. But mean lifespan does not distinguish differences in mortality with age. Consequently, it obscures both important cross-species differences and important intraspecies similarities.

Life expectancy is the probable number of additional years of life remaining for a cohort. Given a life table, which records the rates of death at each age, it can be calculated from any age. For example, life expectancy at the beginning of adulthood (at about 19 or 20 years of age for women [Robson, van Schaik, and Hawkes, chapter 2, this volume]) is the expectation of life for those who have reached adulthood, the average adult lifespan—a very useful parameter. When used without an age qualification, however, life expectancy refers to the expectation of life from birth. Because it is an average for an entire cohort, life expectancy at birth includes the lives of all who die as infants and juveniles. These short lives have large effects on the estimate.

Sacher (1959) focused attention on the important difference between life expectancy at birth and how long *adults* are likely to live. He said that he used "maximum documented longevity" in cross-species comparisons not only because complete life tables—necessary to calculate life expectancy—were available for so few species but also because life expectancy is not a stable parameter. "This is clearly seen in the life-tables of human populations in different countries or in the same country in different historical periods. Instances can be found in which life expectations vary by more than a factor of two, but even in these extreme cases the lifespans do not differ by as much as 20 percent" (Sacher 1959:115).

Williams also seconded the common concern that maximum observed age at death might be so highly sensitive to sample size that it could not be a stable index of adult mortality rates. Sacher (1959, 1975) showed that this concern was misplaced. The relevant probability estimates for the behavior of a variable like maximum recorded lifespan come from the statistics of extremes. When adult mortality follows a Gompertz function—increasing exponentially with age (as fish, bird, and mammal mortality schedules do)—the exponential term always dominates at advanced ages. Consequently, "the characteristic oldest age increases as a double logarithmic function of the cohort size" (Sacher 1959:115). "In consequence the maximum expected survival increases very slowly" with sample size (Sacher 1975:419). "What this means in practice, as I have now confirmed for a large number of species, is that as the number of maximum survival times from different zoos increases, the maximum of this set of values increases very slowly and becomes virtually stationary for practical purposes" (1975:419).

Sacher's attention to maximum lifespan as an especially useful variable played a significant role in developments in life history theory. R. J. H. Beverton and S. J. Holt participated in the 1959 Ciba conference where Sacher reported his methods and findings. Studying the effects of harvest rates on fish life histories, Beverton and Holt (1959; Beverton 1963) required an estimate of adult mortality rates. They found data available, even approximately, for very few populations of interest. Citing Sacher (1959) for pioneering the technique of using maximum lifespan as a stable measure of longevity, Beverton (1963) showed that the "characteristic maximum age," the oldest individual observed, provided a useful index of the adult mortality rate in a population. Beverton both evaluated and exploited Sacher's argument about the statistics of extremes, and Charnov subsequently used Beverton's work as a foundation for his symmetry approach. Following Beverton, Charnov (1993) found that maximum lifespan provided a useful index of average adult lifespan, the inverse of adult mortality rates.

Adult mortality is, in turn, linked with aging. It was G. C. Williams

(1957) who first used life history theory to lay out basic expectations about the evolution of senescence, defined as declines in fitness-related performance with age. Williams (1957) showed how the theory of natural selection can explain why organisms get old and why members of different species age at different rates. His model of "antagonistic pleiotropy" is an evolutionary explanation for aging that is built on the decline in force of selection with age. Because some mortality risk is inevitable—even without senescence—cohorts necessarily become smaller at each successive age. Consequently, selection acts more strongly on mutations that affect phenotypic performance at younger adult ages. When the same genes have effects at different adult ages, positive effects earlier in life are favored at the expense of consequent negative effects on performance at older ages. One expectation about rates of senescence that comes from evolutionary life history theory is that selection against senescence should be stronger—and therefore rates of aging slower—in species with low rates of adult mortality. Another is that selection against senescence should be stronger when fitness-increasing opportunities rise with adult age. W. D. Hamilton (1966) provided the classic formal demonstration of demographic constraints on senescence, using data on a human population to do so.

T. B. L. Kirkwood's (1977, 1981; Kirkwood and Rose 1991) "disposable soma" model has been an especially productive elaboration on these arguments because it focuses on the demographic effects of trade-offs between repair of somatic damage that slows senescence, on one hand, and investments in current reproduction, on the other. The processes of life result in inevitable damage to cells (for example, Beckman and Ames 1998). That damage can be lessened or repaired, but allocation to those processes leaves less for growth and reproduction. Given such a trade-off, selection can never favor perfect repair. Variants that invest too much in somatic maintenance have lower lifetime fitness and are outcompeted by alternatives that put less into somatic maintenance and more into producing descendants. Reviewing the history of ideas, R. Holliday (1995:102) noted that

> initially, the disposable soma theory took into account accuracy in macromolecular synthesis.... [Then] the metabolic

cost of repair of macromolecules was an obvious inclusion (Kirkwood 1981), and later on many other types of mechanism were discussed in terms of the maintenance of the adult organism.... Today the disposable soma theory includes the considerable metabolic expense of all such maintenance mechanisms and the tradeoff between this expense and the investment of resources into growth to adulthood and reproduction.

Kirkwood's model speaks to Williams' question, why do organisms age? and shows why disposable somas result from natural selection. It also speaks readily to the questions, why does aging ever slow? how can increased longevity evolve? If the lifetime fitness benefits for a marginally increased investment in somatic repair outweigh the benefits for the same investment in reproduction at younger ages, selection favors more somatic maintenance. If adult mortality rates go down, the chances of staying alive longer to benefit from a more durable soma increase, and selection favors increased somatic effort. As Williams (1957:404) noted, "*low adult death rates should be associated with low rates of senescence, and high adult death rates with high rates of senescence...*[so] we should be able to predict rates of senescence on the basis of adult mortality rates" (italics original). Subsequent work (for example, Ricklefs 1998) has confirmed that empirical correlations between adult mortality rates and aging rates across samples of mammals and birds are consistent with the theory (see Hawkes, chapter 4, this volume, for further discussion).

Long average adult lifespans characterize living human populations (Robson, van Schaik, and Hawkes, chapter 2, this volume). For past populations, the ages at death represented in skeletal assemblages would seem the obvious source of information about mortality rates. Researchers investigating aging have often relied on these data to estimate past mortality rates (Williams 1957; Austad 1997). Increasingly, though, paleodemographers have come to appreciate why the archaeological assemblages are not a straightforward reflection of population mortality rates (see Konigsberg and Herrmann, chapter 9, this volume). "[A] number of natural and cultural filters conspire to produce archaeological skeletal samples that cannot be considered as random samples of all members of a population who died within a certain period" (Konigsberg and Frankenberg 1994:92).

Among these filters, the following three are especially important for estimating rates of death at different ages from archaeological samples. First, taphonomic processes differentially affect bones by sex and age (P. L. Walker 1995). The surprising magnitude of possible preservation bias was demonstrated by Walker, Johnson, and Lambert (1988) on a cemetery in California where mission records showed that 53 percent of the adults interred in the cemetery were older than 45 years of age but only 7 percent of the adult skeletons recovered were older than 45. As the investigators cautioned, other things being equal, the magnitude of the age-related bias should be "roughly proportional to the length of time a group of burials has been in the ground" (Walker, Johnson, and Lambert 1988:188), a stark warning for Paleolithic samples.

The second problem of bias in the age-at-death distribution of skeletal assemblages is also serious. Remains of individuals of different ages and sexes may be deposited in different places. Among modern people, for example, juveniles and adults may be interred in cemeteries, but infants may not. Most Neanderthal remains have been discovered in cave deposits, and as E. Trinkaus (1995:138) noted, older individuals may be underrepresented if "the elderly were dying in or adjacent to shelters less frequently than younger members of the population."

Of remains that actually are recovered, age-at-death misestimation is a third substantial problem. J.-P. Bocquet-Appel and C. Masset's "Farewell to Paleodemography" (1982) was prompted by comparisons between the mortality schedules of Europeans constructed by historical demographers working with texts and those constructed by paleodemographers working with skeletal material often from related populations in similar time ranges. Bocquet-Appel and Masset showed the mismatch in estimated mortality schedules and found that the distinctive age structures produced by paleodemographers resulted from systematic biases due to the characteristics of the reference samples used in aging adult skeletons. They concluded that "early mortality of adults, overmortality of women, lack of old people in those populations, whether prehistoric or medieval: all these hackneyed notions were born from the misinterpretation of data. As they are in no way vindicated, we must get rid of them" (Bocquet-Appel and Masset 1982:329).

Assessing responses to these difficulties, L. W. Konigsberg and

S. R. Frankenberg (1994:93) concluded that "unfortunately there are no 'magic bullets' that can be uniformly applied to remove the biases caused by biological and cultural filters." Nevertheless, they pronounced paleoanthropology "not quite dead" because emerging methods promised much improved age-at-death estimates. Increasingly sophisticated mathematical tools extract more accurate, if less precise, information about the distribution of ages in modern human skeletal assemblages (Hoppa and Vaupel 2002a; Konigsberg and Herrmann, chapter 9, this volume). Analysts now recognize that they must *start* with a model of "how the chance of death varies with age" (Hoppa and Vaupel 2002b:3). This echoes a point N. Howell (1976a:25) made about the necessary reliance of paleodemography on the "uniformitarian assumption" that "the human animal has not basically changed in its direct biological response to the environment in processes of ovulation, spermatogenesis, length of pregnancy, degree of helplessness of the young and rates of maturation and senility over time."

If this holds across modern humans, what of other members of our evolutionary lineage? Konigsberg and Frankenberg (1994:92–93) assumed that "the evolutionary details that modified a basic pongid life history into a hominid one remain obscure, but aspects of recent demographic history are assailable. Study of the last 10,000 years or so is an important part of anthropological discourse." They went on to say that "with relatively new appreciation of the problems of age estimation, sample bias, and the complexity of relationships among fertility, mortality, population growth and life table analysis, we see paleodemography as just beginning to embark on what should be a truly productive phase of research" (Konigsberg and Frankenberg 1994:104).

Yet, some of the complexity they note, long recognized by demographers, still remains to be appreciated by students of human evolution. Of particular importance here, the erroneous inference that life expectancy (at birth) is an index of adult lifespans leads to mistaken assumptions about age structures in past human populations. The error was committed by S. L. Washburn (1981:11) decades ago: "In the last 100 years, the expectation of length of life for human beings has increased dramatically.... The result is a situation that is entirely new from the point of view of evolution—a very large number of human beings living to ages far beyond those that were normal for the species."

As Sacher had already observed, though, life expectancy is not a good index of longevity (and see D. W. E. Smith 1993). It is strongly affected by infant and juvenile mortality rates. Recently, J. Oeppen and R. W. Vaupel (2002) demonstrated the remarkably steady increase in the global record for national life expectancy, essentially linear since 1840. Emphasizing the importance of this persistent recent trend, they also noted that "before 1950, most of the gain in life expectancy was due to large reductions in death rates at younger ages" (Oeppen and Vaupel 2002:1029). In those populations with much lower life expectancies than the current record holders, people who did not die in childhood had long average adult lifespans, with good chances of living to a ripe old age (see Paine and Boldsen, chapter 10, this volume).

Demographers long ago demonstrated that variation in life expectancies in human populations have surprisingly small effects on adult age structure. Fertility levels have large effects (for example, Coale 1956; Coale and Demeny 1966 [second edition, 1983]). The Coale and Demeny model life tables for stable (human) populations show what initially seems counterintuitive. Holding fertility constant and tripling life expectancy from twenty to sixty years, the fraction of adults (those older than 15) who are older than 45 differs within only five percentage points. Also—perhaps initially paradoxically—the proportion of elders is largest when life expectancy is lowest (Hawkes 2004b; Hawkes and Blurton Jones 2005). Careful ethnographic demography of modern hunter-gatherers repeatedly finds life expectancies shorter than four decades and also finds the characteristic and distinctive feature of human age structures: about a third of the adults are older than 45 (Howell 1979; Hill and Hurtado 1996; Blurton Jones, Hawkes, and O'Connell 2002).

Both models and data show that it is incorrect to infer that people could not have had long lifespans in prehistory, because "life expectancies over forty years were never reported for any population prior to the late nineteenth and twentieth centuries" (Crews and Gerber 2003: 20). It is misleading to reason that "if typical life expectancy among our recent hominid predecessors was only three or four decades…less than half of the total lifespan of a typical individual would have been spent as an adult" (Krovitz, Nelson, and Thompson 2003:1).

The difficulties in estimating adult mortality rates from age-at-death estimates of past populations are increasingly well understood. Investigators continue to work at reducing biases in age estimation (for example, Aykroyd et al. 1999; Miles 2001; Hoppa and Vaupel 2002a; Konigsberg and Herrmann, chapter 9, this volume), and perhaps the taphonomic biases can be estimated. But neither of these correctives removes the "cultural filter" (Konigsberg and Frankenberg 1994) that makes skeletal assemblages a biased sample of deaths. As a consequence, body size continues to be a favored index, even by paleodemographers (Konigsberg and Frankenberg 1994), for estimating variation in lifespan across hominins. The cross-species associations between size and maximum lifespan recognized by Sacher have been confirmed in greater detail in expanded and improved data sets (Harvey and Clutton-Brock 1985; Finch 1990; Allman, McLaughlin, and Hakeem 1993; Hammer and Foley 1996; Barton 1999; Judge and Carey 2000; Deaner, Barton, and van Schaik 2003), and maximum lifespan is a useful index of average adult lifespans and adult mortality rates (Beverton 1963; Charnov 1993).

Size, however, is a variable with problems of its own, as noted above in regard to brains and bodies. Additional difficulties arise in estimating it from fossil specimens (for example, Kappelman 1996; R. Smith 1996), but there are some strong patterns. McHenry (1991, 1992) demonstrated that australopiths, even those with very robust crania, were substantially smaller in body size than early members of genus *Homo* (Wood and Collard 1999b). The change from a chimpanzee-size australopith ancestor to the first widely successful members of our genus, in which both brain size and maternal body size approximately doubled, signals a shift in life history (Smith and Tompkins 1995; O'Connell, Hawkes, and Blurton Jones 1999; Aiello and Key 2002; Aiello and Wells 2002; Hawkes, O'Connell, and Blurton Jones 2003).

Within genus *Homo*, brain size and body size do not always change together (Hawkes, O'Connell, and Blurton Jones 2003; Skinner and Wood, chapter 11, this volume). Ruff, Trinkaus, and Holliday (1997: 173–174) estimated body mass and cranial capacities for genus *Homo* across the Pleistocene and concluded that an apparent increase in body size from Early to Late Pleistocene "is largely an artifact of two confounding variables: sex and geography.... There is a bias toward males in our Late Pleistocene sample...[and] the apparent sudden increase in average body mass during the latter Middle Pleistocene is largely a result of the inclusion of higher-latitude specimens."

As to relative brain size, they found that

> early to early Middle Pleistocene (1,800–600 kyr BP) *Homo* was about one third less encephalized than recent humans, and there was no increase in encephalization quotient (EQ) throughout this time period. By the early Late Pleistocene (150–100 kyr BP), EQ had increased to values within about 10% of those of recent humans. (Ruff, Trinkaus, and Holliday 1997:175)

Finally, they show "that a decrease in average absolute brain size over the past 35,000 years within *H. sapiens* was paralleled by a corresponding decrease in average body size, supporting earlier suggestions of a general correlated size reduction in the human skeleton since the early Upper Paleolithic" (Ruff, Trinkaus, and Holliday 1997:175).

How big is a modern human? To the extent that body size can be estimated for a taxon and this can index longevity, the sample and estimates provided by Ruff and colleagues suggest no large differences between the early members of our genus (as defined by Wood and Collard 1999b), archaics, and Upper Paleolithic moderns. Brains, however, are larger and encephalization greater in Middle Paleolithic humans. If it is brain size that predicts longevity, then (as Sacher concluded) Neanderthals and moderns must have similar lifespans, longer than those of earlier members of the genus, with those, in turn, longer than those of australopiths.

Postmenopausal Longevity

When lifespans are longer—adult mortalities lower—selection against senescence is stronger, and aging is slower. However, the ovaries of living humans do not age any more slowly than those of living chimpanzees (Hawkes 2003; Robson, van Schaik, and Hawkes, chapter 2, this volume). We establish our maximum store of oocytes in fetal life, and the number of follicles remaining declines from birth onward (Block 1952; Richardson, Senikas, and Nelson 1987; O'Connor, Holman, and Wood 2001). Recent evidence in mice (Johnson, et al. 2004; Johnson, et al. 2005) challenges long-standing orthodoxy that, in mammals, no new follicles are produced during adulthood. Still, the net number of follicles declines with age across all mammalian clades (vom Saal, Finch, and Nelson 1994). The physiology of menopause, in particular, is known to be quite similar in humans, chimpanzees, and several species of macaques (Graham, Kling, and Steiner 1979; Gould, Flint, and Graham 1981; Nozaki, Mitsunaga, and Shimizu 1995; M. L. Walker 1995). Unlike other primates, however, humans reach terminal fertility and then menopause when aging is less advanced in other physiological systems (Gosden 1985; Hill and Hurtado 1991; Pavelka and Fedigan 1991; Caro et al. 1995).

Williams (1957) raised the topic of human mid-life menopause explicitly when he addressed the problem of aging from the perspective of evolutionary life history theory. Theory predicts that "there should be little or no post-reproductive period in the normal life of any species," but "at first sight it appears that this prediction is not realized. Long post-reproductive periods are known in many domesticated animals and in man himself. In man it may be even longer than the reproductive period" (1957:407). But Williams (1957:407) went on to say that "these observations lose much of their seeming importance when it is realized that they are largely artifacts of civilization. In very primitive conditions, such as prevailed throughout almost all of man's evolution post-reproductive individuals were extremely rare."

The evidence Williams (1957:407) cited for this rarity was a tabulation of estimated ages at death in a series of Paleolithic and Mesolithic skeletons in which only 3 of 173 specimens "were over fifty and none was much older than this." Twenty-two years later, Williams (1999:407) reiterated the same conclusion: "Young-adult mortality rates in the Stone Age were such that only a trivial minority would live beyond what we now call middle age." I reviewed biases inherent in estimating adult mortality rates and population age structures from such data above. Those known biases, combined with the data from careful hunter-gatherer demographies, are grounds for disputing the common claim, here coming from Williams, that old people are an artifact of civilization.

Williams' other hypothesis (1957:407–408) about the evolution of mid-life menopause in women was this:

> At some time during human evolution it may have become

advantageous for a woman of forty-five or fifty to stop dividing her declining faculties between the care of extant offspring and the production of new ones. A termination of increasingly hazardous pregnancies would enable her to devote her whole remaining energy to the care of her living children, and would remove childbirth mortality as a possible cause of failure to raise these children. Menopause, although apparently a cessation of reproduction, may have arisen as a reproductive adaptation to a life-cycle already characterized by senescence, unusual hazards in pregnancy and childbirth, and a long period of juvenile dependence.

This "stopping early" hypothesis has stimulated work on the optimal timing of menopause. Trade-offs like those hypothesized by Williams might explain why selection maintains the observed modal age of menopause in women (for example, Hill and Hurtado 1991, 1996; Rogers 1993; Packer, Tatar, and Collins 1998; Peccei 2001; Shanley and Kirkwood 2001). Noting that the age of fertility decline and menopause appears to be about the same in chimpanzees and people whereas human adult mortalities are much lower, Hawkes and colleagues (1998) pointed to the simplest phylogenetic inference: our longevity, not our age at menopause, is derived. Ovarian ontogeny may have remained more or less the same throughout both hominin and chimpanzee lineages from our common ancestor. If so, the age of menopause did not alter; it became a mid-life process when greater longevity evolved in the human lineage. That makes the evolutionary question, what could favor slower aging while not favoring later ages of childbearing at the same time?

E. Trinkaus and R. L. Tompkins (1987) proposed that our slower aging and longer lifespans may not have evolved until the appearance of moderns. They estimated the ages at death of individuals assumed to be among the oldest Neanderthal adults and, combining their findings with other reports, noted "the extreme rarity and possible absence of Neanderthals greater than 40 to 45 years in the fossil record" (Trinkaus and Tompkins 1987:128). Using these data and other lines of evidence, they proposed "the intriguing possibility" that "the significant postreproductive survival of recent humans had not yet emerged among these late archaic humans"; instead, "archaic members of the genus *Homo* [may have] had lifespans similar to those of wild chimpanzees" (Trinkaus and Tompkins 1990:174). They recognized that if this were so, age at maturity in Neanderthals must have been earlier as well. "Retarded developmental rates among Nean-derthals approaching that presumed for recent humans" could not have been favored if adult mortalities were so high (1990:159). Subsequently, concern about the age-at-death estimates on which they relied and about the viability of populations with chimpanzee adult mortality profiles and even slightly slower maturation than chimpanzees led Trinkaus to reconsider those earlier lifespan estimates. Revisiting the evidence, Trinkaus (1995:139) still surmised that young adult mortality must have been high compared with ethnographically known hunter-gatherers, but he concluded "that the Neanderthals had a demographic pattern similar to those of at least some modern human populations."

The under-representation of older adults in fossil remains of both Neanderthals and Neanderthal ancestors is a recurrent finding. Analyzing the assemblage of Middle Pleistocene Neanderthal ancestors from the Atapuerca Sima de los Huesos, J. M. Bermúdez de Castro and M. E. Nicolás (1997:333) reported that "longevity was probably no greater than 40 years." On the basis of more complete analysis of the assemblage and comparison with other Middle Pleistocene European assemblages, Bermúdez de Castro and colleagues (2004:22) concluded "from the fossil evidence that the effective life span of Middle Pleistocene populations in Europe probably did not exceed 40–45."

Employing the same toothwear seriation technique (Miles 1963) used by Bermúdez de Castro and colleagues to age adults, R. Caspari and S.-H. Lee (2004) produced an "OY ratio" of older to younger adults for skeletal dentitions from an array of hominin taxa: australopithecines, *Homo erectus*, Neanderthals, and Upper Paleolithic moderns. Their young adult category consisted of dentitions with the third molar erupted but limited tooth wear. "Older adults were defined as twice the age of reproductive maturation, the age at which one could theoretically first become a grandmother" (Caspari and Lee 2004:10896). The ratio of older to younger adults was taken to be an index of longevity. Caspari and Lee (2004:10898) wrote:

Two important conclusions emerge from this study: first, there is significant increased longevity between all groups, indicating a trend of increased survivorship of older adults through human evolution. Second, the increase is by far the greatest in the early modern humans of the Upper Paleolithic, when for the first time there are a larger number of older adults than younger adults in the death distribution. Whereas high levels of young adult mortality have been noted for Neanderthals (Trinkaus 1995), the magnitude of the increase in OY ratios in the Upper Paleolithic is nevertheless surprising.

Caspari and Lee's OY ratio was 0.39 for Neanderthals and 2.08 for Upper Paleolithic moderns, a fivefold difference.

Problems of taphonomic bias and age-at-death estimations, as well as the unknown relationship between the age distribution of skeletal assemblages and the mortality experience of populations, would apply to these dentitions. Another problem is specific to their definition of old and young adults. The scaling relationships in primate—and therefore probably in hominin—life histories mean that such an OY ratio would likely be insensitive to longevity.

Caspari and Lee chose this ratio because age at maturity is not known for the nonmodern taxa, but as Schultz (1956, 1960) and then B. H. Smith (1989a) had shown, eruption of the third molar is a useful marker of maturity across the primates. By choosing a trait that is "independent of actual ages," Caspari and Lee could avoid contention about the actual age estimates. However, the "invariant" relationship between age at maturity and adult mortality highlighted by Charnov's model of mammalian life history evolution implies that when old is defined as twice the age at maturity, the ratio of old to young adults might be similarly invariant. Because longevity and age at maturity are positively correlated across the mammals, including the primates—even modern humans (Charnov 1993; Charnov and Berrigan 1993; Hawkes et al. 1998; Alvarez 2000)— the same invariance likely held among past hominins. If the relationship between these two variables is approximately constant, then the fraction of adults that are more than double the age at maturity might be about the same, whether average adult lifespans are short or long.

Data on living populations illustrate exactly this (Hawkes and O'Connell 2005). The proportions of adults in the old categories defined as twice the age of M3 eruption can be calculated for standing populations of foraging people and chimpanzees, using data in Smith, Crummett, and Brandt's (1994) compendium of tooth eruption ages in primates, life tables for modern chimpanzees in the wild (Hill et al. 2001), and life tables for three modern hunter-gatherer populations (!Kung: Howell 1979; Ache: Hill and Hurtado 1996; Hadza: Blurton Jones, Hawkes, and O'Connell 2002). The central tendency of M3 eruption in Smith and colleagues' sample of female chimpanzees (n = 7) is 10.7 years; in their sample of women (n = 663), it is 20.4 years. Using Caspari and Lee's definitions, young adult chimpanzees are 10–19 and old chimpanzees, 20 and older. Young women are 20–39 and old women, 40 and older. Assuming that the life tables characterize stationary populations, the ratio of old adults to young adults is 1.09 for chimpanzees and 1.12 for people, very similar proportions of old adults in two species with different longevities.

Adding macaques underlines the point. For Smith, Crummett, and Brandt's (1994) sample of *Macaca fuscata* (n = 570), the central tendency of third molar eruption is 5.7 years. By Caspari and Lee's definition, young adults would be 5–9 and old adults, 10 and older. Using Pavelka and Fedigan's (1999) life table for *M. fuscata* at Arashiyama West and again assuming that the population is stationary, the ratio of old adults to young adults is 0.97. For people, chimpanzees, and Japanese macaques—species with widely differing longevities—the ratio of old to young adults is very similar because the definition of old is scaled to age at maturity.

Konigsberg and Herrmann (chapter 9, this volume) point out other reasons to be cautious about Caspari and Lee's analyses. Their chapter illustrates some of the increasingly sophisticated methods for dealing with the multiple and inevitable sources of error in estimating the age characteristics of death assemblages. Difficulties confronting paleodemographers are daunting but increasingly well recognized. Some, at least, can be corrected so that this line of hard evidence may begin to return solid findings.

More investigation of the similarities and differences among living species will improve understanding of the evolution of our postmenopausal longevity. For example, chimpanzees in the wild rarely live to menopausal ages. This mortality pattern, as well as numerous anecdotal descriptions of chimpanzees beginning to display geriatric symptoms in their mid-30s (Goodall 1986; Huffman 1990; Finch and Stanford 2004), supports the expectation that chimpanzees age faster than people do. In captivity, survival improves at all ages (Courtenay and Santow 1989; Dyke et al. 1995; Hill et al. 2001), so more will live to menopause. As increasing numbers of captives of known birth dates move into the ages of interest (Erwin et al. 2002), we have the opportunity to record variation in ages at menopause and to measure performance of other physiological systems across these ages. Systematic comparisons between humans and chimpanzees should show which functions decline with age at a slower rate in our own species.

Weaning before Independent Feeding

Humans wean infants earlier than they can feed themselves and at younger ages than chimpanzees or orangutans do (Robson, van Schaik, and Hawkes, chapter 2, and Sellen, chapter 6, this volume). This relatively early weaning runs counter to the broad pattern across primate species, in which longer adult lifespans and later ages at first birth are usually associated with later weaning ages (Smith and Tompkins 1995; Hawkes et al. 1998; Hawkes, O'Connell, and Blurton Jones 2003; Hawkes, chapter 4, this volume). Variation in rates of maturation to feeding independence has been a topic of special interest in primate life history evolution beginning with Schultz's use of dental markers to identify and compare aspects of primate ontogeny. Schultz (1960:11–13) wrote: "Of the many age changes in development, those regarding the dentition have been studied most intensively, not only because they can be readily observed but also because they serve generally for the estimation of the physiological age of living animals as well as skulls."

In particular, Gould (1977) mentioned Schultz's (1949) observation that in faster-maturing primates the molars appear before the deciduous teeth are shed, so when nursing ends, the molars are ready for mastication. By contrast, in humans the molars emerge after the anterior permanent teeth. Gould (1977:380) cited, in full, Schultz's interpretation that "this alteration is an adaptive requirement of delayed development." Schultz (1950:440) wrote:

It is tempting to speculate that this human distinction is the result of some natural selection, directly connected with the extreme prolongation of the period of growth in man. The deciduous teeth of man are not more durable than those of other primates, yet they have to serve in the former for much longer periods than in the latter. Hence this newly acquired precedence for the replacement of milk teeth over the addition of molars is undoubtedly beneficial, if not necessary, for man.

B. H. Smith (2000) has called this "Schultz's rule" and has used the differences that Schultz described in the dental emergence patterns of great apes and humans to assess the relative development of juvenile hominid fossils (B. H. Smith 1986). In Schultz's schematic depiction of variation in duration of life periods across the primates (for example, Schultz 1960, 1969), he used "the appearance of the first permanent teeth" to mark the termination of infancy (1969:147). Although we wean infants earlier, the eruption of the first permanent molars is much delayed in humans, compared with the living great apes (Robson, van Schaik, and Hawkes, chapter 2, this volume). Smith showed that juvenile *A. afarensis*, *A. africanus*, and *H. habilis* specimens fit pongid emergence standards better than human standards whereas a Neanderthal specimen fit the modern human pattern. Noting that "prolonged infant and child dependency appears consistently in theories of early cultural evolution," she concluded that her analysis did not support A. Mann's (1975) view that this was characteristic of hominids before the appearance of *Homo erectus* (B. H. Smith 1986:329).

Smith then investigated relationships between aspects of dental development and life history variables in a sample of twenty-one primate species (including prosimians and both New and Old World anthropoids) to build on Sacher's finding that brain size, longevity, and age at maturity are correlated across the mammals (B. H. Smith 1989a). She found that the ages of eruption of the first molar and of the last permanent teeth were especially well correlated with brain size, as well as with life history variables such as age at weaning, age at first birth, and lifespan. "The dentition has advantages over other markers of maturation in that it is robust to environmental perturbations and has relatively low variance. Thus the dentition provides a growth marker that is reliable...[and] can be extended to species in the fossil record" (B. H. Smith 1989a:686).

Smith used these associations, especially age of emergence of the first molar, to interpret hominin schedules of development, concluding that australopiths displayed maturation rates like modern apes whereas *Homo erectus* and Neanderthals had rates more similar to modern humans (B. H. Smith 1989b, 1991a, 1993, 1994; Smith and Tompkins 1995; Bogin and Smith 1996). Her findings then guided others seeking to explain the evolution of human life histories (Bogin 1999a; O'Connell, Hawkes, and Blurton Jones 1999; Kaplan et al. 2000; Hawkes, O'Connell, and Blurton Jones 2003).

Dental markers do not, however, escape the difficulties with other growth and development variables discussed under heterochrony above. Gould (1977) had used Mann's (1975) assessment that australopithecine juveniles had dental developmental patterns like modern humans and unlike modern apes as evidence of greater retardation in our lineage from its initial radiation. Smith's analyses challenged Mann's conclusions by showing that the relative timing of first molar eruption in australopiths was similar to modern apes and unlike modern humans. Only fossil specimens assigned to genus *Homo* displayed emergence sequences similar to modern humans (B. H. Smith 1994). Other aspects of dental development, however, do not show the same differences, so specialists have found the emphasis on first molar eruption difficult to justify (Macho and Wood 1995b). Macho (2001:189) wrote:

> The pattern and timing of tooth emergence is highly correlated with life-history variables and brain size. Conversely, a firm relationship between molar formation time and life-history variables has not yet been established. It seems counterintuitive that one aspect of dental development should be correlated with life history variables while the other should not.

Schultz had made the point that, compared with other modern primates, some aspects of skeletal development are slowed down in humans and others are not. The same holds for dental development. Crown formation is a variable of special interest because the process is punctuated by daily shifts that leave a record of the number of days it takes a tooth to form. Tooth microstructure thus provides an actual developmental clock for aging juvenile fossils (Beynon and Dean 1988) and perhaps for identifying absolute weaning ages (Katzenberg, Herring, and Saunders 1996; Wright and Schwarcz 1998; Rabb et al. 2004). Macho and Wood (1995b:23) report crown formation data for humans, chimpanzees, gorillas, orangutans, and two fossil hominins: "[A]vailable data on permanent incisor formation times indicate... considerable overlap among great apes and humans....Canine formation times vary substantially both within and between species....On the other hand crown formation times of molars are more similar between hominoid species."

With a phylogenetically wider sample of living and extinct primates covering a broader range of body sizes, Macho (2001) found correlations of crown formation times with life history variables and with brain size as well. But "the correlations are relatively high for only a few variables, notably age at weaning, brain size and body mass" (Macho 2001: 196). Considering only her subsample of humans, chimpanzees, gorillas, and orangutans, even these variables are not correlated with molar crown formation times (Robson, van Schaik, and Hawkes, chapter 2, this volume).

Examining a sample of modern humans and fossil relatives and African apes, Dean and others (2001) found enamel formation rates to be faster in anterior teeth of australopiths than in African apes. Although they confirm Smith's picture of eruption sequences in genus *Homo*, commenting that "radiographs, as well as direct observations of developing teeth, show that the sequence of key events during tooth growth in *H. erectus* was identical to that of modern humans" (Dean et al. 2001:629), they found enamel formation times for two *H. erectus* specimens to be faster than times for modern humans. Their analysis of crown formation rates found that only a Neanderthal specimen overlapped the modern human range (Dean et al. 2001). In a larger sample of Neanderthal anterior teeth and measuring a different feature of enamel formation, Ramírez Rozzi and Bermúdez de Castro (2004) found clearly faster formation in Neanderthals than in modern humans. From this, they infer a faster rate of maturation in Neanderthals "because dental growth is an excellent indicator of somatic development" (Ramírez Rozzi and Bermúdez de Castro 2004: 936). But this component of dental development, crown formation times, is not related to differences in age at maturity among living people and other great apes.

Other aspects of dental development and life history variation across primates have been explored by Godfrey and colleagues (2001). They measured dental development in two ways: (1) dental precocity, the fraction of postcanine teeth erupted at various ages, and (2) dental endowment at weaning, the fraction of adult postcanine occlusial area that was present at weaning. A strong association between these measures and adult brain size, but not a close correlation with life history traits, led them to "underscore just how variable dental development at weaning can be. One cannot assume...that dental maturation will be linked in a consistent manner to skeletal growth or reproductive maturation" (Godfrey et al. 2003:197). The details of particular measures, samples, and tests in these important challenges merit careful attention.

As shown by Robson, van Schaik, and Hawkes (chapter 2, this volume), commonly used markers of dental development are not correlated with weaning age across the living hominoids. Weaning does, however, leave an isotope signature in the microstructure of tooth enamel (Katzenberg, Herring, and Saunders 1996; Wright and Schwarcz 1998; Rabb et al. 2004). That could provide a way to identify this important life history variable (see Sellen, chapter 6, this volume) in fossil specimens.

DIFFERENT KINDS OF EXPLANATIONS BEFORE AND AFTER GENOMICS

Finding systematic relationships between life history features and variables that can be measured in bones and teeth is a necessary foundation for extracting life history information from the fossil record. Different frameworks of ideas have motivated that inquiry and will surely continue to do so in the future. Distinction between the proximate mechanisms that generate a morphological, physiological, or behavioral feature and the adaptive effects that explain why selection favored, spread, and maintained it goes back to Darwin. The apparent simplicity of this distinction seems increasingly deceptive, but that does not make it less important.

Causal Mechanisms, Adaptive Explanations, and Distinctions between Homology and Homoplasy

N. Tinbergen (1963) famously reminded evolutionary biologists that answers to proximate mechanism questions are not answers to questions about adaptive function, and vice versa. Different kinds of research programs, different data, different hypotheses address these different questions. Tinbergen distinguished four different questions researchers have in mind when they seek to explain a biological feature, four different "whys." One addresses the proximate mechanisms that cause the feature, how the underlying physiology works. This contrasts with functional questions that focus on adaptive effects, asking why selection maintains the feature of interest in the form observed. Perhaps paradoxically in this context, Tinbergen also distinguished both of those from questions about ontogeny or phylogeny. A different research agenda is necessary to discover how a feature develops over the life course of an individual organism, and another to determine when the feature arose in ancestral populations. Both mechanism and adaptive effect questions can also be asked about ontogenetic or phylogenetic patterns.

In the past few decades, the dominance of cladistics (Hennig 1966), the explosion of molecular techniques and data sets (Hillis 1994; Klein and Takahata 2002), and the addition to the comparative method of systematic procedures to correct phylogenetic sampling biases (Harvey and Pagel 1991) have highlighted new complications associated with the distinction between causal mechanisms and adaptive effects. On the one hand, cladistic methods assume that only similarities between taxa that are shared with their last common ancestor (homologies) are relevant to identifying phylogenetic relationships. Similarities between taxa that are not shared with their last common ancestor (homoplasies) are considered potentially misleading for phylogenetic questions.

On the other hand, current practice in testing adaptive hypotheses with cross-species comparisons requires the use of phylogenetically corrected data sets in which species that are homologous for the features of interest are not counted because they are not considered independent cases. Only homoplasies offer independent trials for testing adaptive hypotheses. Classic persuasive illustrations of the power of natural selection show different proximate mechanisms producing similar adaptive effects, for example, adaptations for flight in birds and bats, male and female individuals produced by diverse sex-determining mechanisms, and the convergent evolution of cephalopod and vertebrate eyes.

The distinction between homologous and homoplastic similarities can seem straightforward, but it has become increasingly vexed as phylogenetic relationships are explored in light of evidence of similarities and differences at many levels. Wake (1999:30–31) gives the following example:

> The condition of permanent larvae in salamanders has arisen many times independently...some bones never form in larvae, but even should a permanently larval species reproduce, the bones remain as latent elements. Imagine that [these bones] reappear in a derivative species. These would be identified as homoplasies...in phylogentic analysis, but a morphologist would insist that [each bone is the same] as in distantly related salamanders. It must be a homologue!

Lockwood and Fleagle (1999), reviewing treatments of homoplasy in primate and human evolution, noted that ideas about intrinsic progressive tendencies supported early twentieth-century expectations of widespread homoplasies in primate lineages because each lineage was expected to progress through time from lower to higher grades. After the modern synthesis, orthogenesis was abandoned, but not the idea of adaptive trends recognized as grade shifts progressively evolving more humanlike characteristics. As the primate fossil record expanded, however, "emphasis was placed on identifying unique features of modern taxa in fossils, without undue concern for the implications this may have for parallel evolution or reversals in other features" (Lockwood and Fleagle 1999:194).

With the expansion of cladistics into anthropology, "homoplasy was generally seen [at first] as the result of error due to bad choice of characters and misidentified homology. However, the 'reality' of homoplasy can be seen in the effect that fossil discoveries have had on phylogenies in recent years" (Lockwood and Fleagle 1999:194).

[It] has become common for fossil taxa to be found that belong to a particular clade based on selected data sets or traditional "key" characters, but at the same time reveal parallel evolution among various other traits....In other words, the combination of traits in the fossil taxon sets up a situation where one body of evidence (e.g., cranial, dental, or postcranial) is substantially homoplastic, and it is unclear which data set to prefer....Computer programs that are now available permit analyses of large data sets (numbers of taxa and characters) that often generate numerous equally parsimonious trees. (Lockwood and Fleagle 1999:196)

Unusual features of the primate fossil record, or of the features often chosen, might make anthropological cladistics especially thorny. But "statistics...are readily calculated to express the proportion of character change that reflects homology or homoplasy....Primates do not exhibit unusually high or low levels of homoplasy, and within primates, no single type of data appears to be less homoplastic than other types of data" (Lockwood and Fleagle 1999:196).

The problem is central for establishing phylogentic relationships, but it also plagues phenotypic reconstructions. Life history models show why, given stable population theory and assuming populations to be generally nongrowing, only certain combinations of life history traits can persist—but which, if any, features of the fossil specimens provide reliable signals of any of them?

After the Genomics Revolution

Problems of the homology/homoplasy opposition have emerged with special force from discoveries in evolutionary developmental genetics. The complexities apply not only to morphological and behavioral data sets but to molecular ones as well (Sanderson and Donoghue 1989; Patterson, Williams, and Humphries 1993). In light of "evo-devo" findings, Gould (2002:1062) appraised his treatment in *Ontogeny and Phylogeny* as reading

like a quaint conceptual fossil from an "ancient" time of cross bows and arquebuses....I can only express my joy and astonishment at a subsequent speed of resolution and discovery that has sustained my predictions, but also made my earlier book effectively obsolete...the field of evolutionary developmental biology...has invented the tools...for decoding the basic genetic structure of regulation.

Because "extensive genetic homology for fundamental features of development does hold across the most disparate animal phyla" (Gould 2002:1066), Gould (1123) concluded that evo-devo has finally laid "selectionist orthodoxy" to rest:

> This general shift in viewpoint—from a preference for atomistic adaptationism (favoring the explanation for each part as an independent and relatively unconstrained event of crafting by natural selection for current utility) to a recognition that homologous developmental pathways (retained from a deep and different past, whatever the original adaptive context) strongly shape current possibilities "from the inside"—has permeated phylogentic studies at all levels, from similarities among the most disparate phyla to diversity among species within small monophyletic segments of life's tree.

Gould (1123) summarizes "the homology of developmental pathways in homoplastic eyes of several phyla" to demonstrate that selection is subordinate to developmental mechanisms. However, the findings also highlight the power of natural selection. Reviewing the book, D. Futuyma (2002:661) wrote that "Gould's excitement (which I share) about contemporary 'evo-devo' is palpable.... (I, however, do not agree that the convergence of vertebrate and cephalopod eyes, in which some 'master' genes play common roles, has lost its role as testament to the power of natural selection)." Patterns of growth and development vary among closely related taxa with different elements of that variation uncoupled from one another, while the same genetic control mechanisms are found among taxa not only in different phyla but in different kingdoms.

> "The more we learn about the genome, the more it teaches us about our own place in the web of life," said Robert May , an evolutionary biologist and president of the Royal Society in Great Britain. "For example, we share half our genes with

the banana. (Actually, it would be more accurate to say bananas share half their genes with us, because their genome is smaller.) This is a fact more evident in some of my acquaintances than others." (*Discover* 2001:62)

The genomics revolution has provided a radically new view of the diversity of life (for example, Adoutte et al. 2000), to which phenotypic characteristics can be a poor guide. J. Klein and N. Takahata's (2002: 199) comments capture a "post genomics" view of human/chimpanzee comparisons:

> All the estimates obtained by both older and newer techniques have yielded very similar figures: the genomes of these two species differ at approximately 1–2 percent of their nucleotide sites....Science writers and even some scientists appear to be flabbergasted when confronted with the sequence divergence between the human and chimpanzee genomes, but they shouldn't be, because the observed value matches the expectation very well. It would be indeed astounding if the value had turned out to be much greater than 2 percent.

They suggest that "the impression of a gap between the small differences at the molecular level to the seemingly large differences at the phenotypic level may arise because the intervening steps between the genotype and the phenotype, between the DNA and the appearance of an organism, remain unidentified" (Klein and Takahata 2002:204).

The difference between people and chimpanzees also seems remarkable because of the tendency to misestimate the rate of change required to produce the phenotypic differences. As G. C. Williams (1992:132) pointed out:

> Data on Pleistocene human evolution are interpretable in various ways, but it is possible that the cerebrum doubled in size in as little as 100,000 years, or perhaps 3000 generations (Rightmire 1985). This according to Whiten and Byrne (1988) is a "unique and staggering acceleration in brain size." How rapid a rate is this really? Even with conservative assumptions on coefficient of variation (e.g., 10%) and her-

itability (30%) in this character, it would take only a rather weak selection (s = 0.03) to give a 1% change in a generation. This would mean a doubling in 70 generations. An early hominid brain could have increased to modern size, and back again, about 21 times while the actual evolution took place.

Thirty years ago, King and Wilson (1975) surmised that differences in regulatory mechanisms mostly account for the phenotypic differences between people and chimpanzees. This hypothesis continues to be a useful guide as new technology allows much more precise comparison of genomes. The two species differ in levels of gene expression, the location of recombination "hot spots," and the evident strength of selection on particular genes (Enard et al. 2002; Caceres et al. 2003; Olson and Varki 2004; Nielsen et al. 2005; Winckler et al. 2005). Insertions, deletions, and duplications account for more differences than single nucleotide substitutions (Cheng et al. 2005; The Chimpanzee Sequencing and Analysis Consortium 2005).

One genomic signal of the differences in life history is revealed by analyses of changes in gene expression with age in human and chimpanzee brains (Fraser et al. 2005). Now the power of molecular techniques to measure both similarities and differences far outstrips understanding of their phenotypic consequences. Positive selection can be detected in the absence of clues about the actual fitness costs and benefits conferred. The challenge is to link the evidence of selection to phenotypic consequences (Li and Saunders 2005). As S. B. Carroll (2005:1164) noted in an Allan Wilson Memorial Lecture, "the great and difficult challenge, with the genome sequences of humans, chimpanzees, and other mammals now available, is to map changes in genes to changes in traits."

Study of genetic correlations with intraspecific variation in aging rates among humans and among chimpanzees will also provide more evidence of how rates of aging shifted in our lineage. Genetic diversity in living human populations may even contain evidence of differences among nonmodern populations (Eswaran, Harpending, and Rogers 2005). For the most part, however, learning about the phenotypes of our ancestors and extinct cousins necessarily remains the "ancient" problem that Gould laid out in 1977: "The data of heterochrony represent the only confident estimate that classical macroevolutionary morphology can supply for the importance of changes in regulation" (Gould 1977:408). It is the fossil and archaeological record that can show where and when brains, bodies, and life histories changed in the hominin clade. Discovering what the lives of the ancestors and cousins of modern humans were like, how they differed from us and from other modern primates, how they differed from one another, what happened in our lineage before the appearance of modern humans, where, when, and why, requires placing the fossil and archaeological clues within frameworks for describing and explaining the variation we can examine in living species. To discover what phenotypes selection favored and when and why, we need well-warranted hypotheses about the variation in the present and also ways to take those hypotheses to the tangible remains of a different past.

ADAPTIVE HYPOTHESES ABOUT THE EVOLUTION OF HUMAN LIFE HISTORIES

Gould in 1977 had expected morphological variation to be mosaic because "the evolutionary direction of each feature is controlled by natural selection; the capacity for independent variation of characteristics is very great" (Gould 1977:364–365). He had also cited Cole's (1954) demonstration that life history features cannot vary independently. Subsequent work on evolution in age-structured populations has elaborated both the theory and the empirical record on relationships among age at maturity, annual fecundity, and adult and juvenile mortality. The life history models do not depend on particular mechanisms, applying as they do across species in which those mechanisms might (or might not) be different. That gives them a welcome generality for applications to a different past. At the same time, the estimates of life history variables in past populations must come from fossil evidence, so lineage-specific mechanisms that link morphological features to life history variables in primates—size and aspects of dental development, for example—become crucial tools. Genomics promises to add to this a much better understanding of what changed in the evolution of our own lineage and that of our sister species, chimpanzees. The fossil and archaeological records tie those changes to time and place, and a life history framework supplies the help of linking features to one another. When some life history traits can be confidently estimated, the result is a strong prediction about others. Explicit attempts to take advantage of those interrelationships in constructing and revising adaptive hypotheses are recent, but they build on a venerable foundation.

In the fifties and sixties, S. L. Washburn departed from most anthropologists in arguing that comparative morphology supported a quite recent common ancestor of modern humans and African apes, something the molecular evidence subsequently confirmed (Goodman 1962; Wilson and Sarich 1969; King and Wilson 1975). As Lockwood and Fleagle (1999:195) noted, Washburn and his students repeatedly pointed out that the "fossil phylogenies based on dental similarities [like tooth size] between particular 'Miocene apes' and living hominoid genera implied tremendous parallel evolution of postcranial similarities among modern hominoids." Contrary to many anthropologists, Washburn preferred a "more parsimonious phylogeny: a clade of Miocene apes preceding the radiation of living hominoids. This view in many ways laid the groundwork for current understanding of fossil hominoid relationships" (Lockwood and Fleagle 1999:195).

Washburn had the widest influence on thinking about human evolution through his elaboration of the Hunting hypothesis. Its satisfying, adaptive logic is one of the reasons it is so widely enlisted to explain human evolution. His emphasis was on links among hunting, tools, bipedalism, and brains, but he used these to explain what Gould called the "hallmarks of hominization." Building on Dart's (1949) savanna hypothesis about the likely importance of hunting and therefore tools and brains to explain the bipedalism of australopithecines, Washburn (1960) proposed that the combination of enlarging brains and a pelvis shaped for bipedalism created an "obstetrical dilemma" for mothers. Shifts in the timing and rate of fetal, infant, and juvenile development were necessary consequences. Most brain growth had to be postnatal, slowing other aspects of infant development. Undeveloped neonates required more maternal protection and support, and juveniles needed a longer developmental and learning period before reaching adulthood. The conflict between maternal care requirements and hunting led mothers to pair with hunting mates who supplied paternal provisioning to fund the greater dependence of human infants and juveniles for a longer time. A sexual division of labor with paternal provisioning made nuclear families into units of economic and reproductive cooperation. Gould (1977:400) mentioned Washburn as one who had recognized the significance of delayed maturation. But Washburn did more than that. He elaborated an adaptive hypothesis that linked slow development to the fitness benefits for an ape that could eat better by hunting in savanna environments (Washburn 1960; Washburn and Lancaster 1968; Washburn and Moore 1974).

Washburn drew comprehensively on hominid fossils, Paleolithic archaeology, comparative studies of nonhuman primates, and studies of modern hunter-gatherers. He used the consensus picture that had emerged in each of these fields through the sixties and early seventies to fill out the scenario. Ethnology gave a fundamental role to sexual divisions of labor, making nuclear families the basic elements of human social organization (for example, Murdock 1949; Sahlins 1972). Other primates generally, and other great apes in particular, lacked nuclear families and were not known to hunt (Lancaster and Lancaster 1983). The paleontological record suggested that bipedal locomotion and enlarged brains emerged contemporaneously, and this appeared to be more or less coincident in time with the earliest archaeology (Washburn 1960).

Challenges began to mount in the late seventies, with clear evidence that bipedalism preceded the appearance of stone tools and expanding brains by at least a million years (Johanson and White 1979; see Skinner and Wood, chapter 11, this volume). Chimpanzees were discovered to be regular hunters (Goodall 1968, 1986; Stanford 1999). The home base interpretation of concentrations of stone tools and the bones of large animals in Lower Paleolithic sites was critically questioned and largely rejected (Binford 1981; O'Connell, Hawkes, and Blurton Jones 1988; O'Connell et al. 2002). Archaeologists now recognize that clear evidence of hominin big-game hunting does not appear until the late Middle Pleistocene, more than 1.5 million years after the earliest stone tools and at least a million years after the appearance of genus *Homo* (O'Connell et al. 2002; Stiner 2002). Systematic study of foraging and food-sharing patterns among living hunter-gatherers showed that hunters provide little of the meat eaten by their own wives and offspring; most is eaten by consumers outside the hunter's own family (Kaplan and Hill 1985; Hawkes, O'Connell, and Blurton Jones 1991, 2001b; Hawkes 1993).

Some view the challenges as decisive grounds for rejecting the Hunting hypothesis (for example, Zihlmann and Tanner 1978; Dahlberg 1981; O'Connell, Hawkes, and Blurton Jones 1999; Hawkes, O'Connell, and Blurton Jones 2001a; O'Connell et al. 2002). Others argue that the Hunting hypothesis still captures major components of what happened in human evolution (Tooby and DeVore 1987; Deacon 1997; Kaplan et al. 2000). Adaptive hypotheses about the evolution of human life histories that are founded on these alternative assessments are discussed in chapter 4.

A lesson of this review is that what we know about the past is much more complicated than it used to be. Each line of inquiry develops conceptual and modeling tools and bodies of evidence that highlight different questions, driving what practitioners investigate, what they debate, and what they take for granted. That is supposed to be how knowledge increases. But the difficulty of conversation across lines of evidence grows as a consequence, and notions falsified in one field of inquiry remain common assumptions in others. Some things that seem contradictory may be what we should expect of a different past, as Gould anticipated in 1977 about heterochronic changes in human evolution. The problem of discovering which aspects of the fossil and archaeological record give the best indices of ancestral life history variables has no clear general solution, at least not yet. Alternative hypotheses applied to multiple lines of evidence expose many contradictions and pose new measurement and modeling challenges. The one certain thing is that recent developments give us all a lot to do.

Acknowledgments

I am grateful to all the participants in the advanced seminar for their contributions and collegiality and to the School of American Research for its grand hospitality. For especially useful advice on this chapter, I thank Nick Blurton Jones, Jim O'Connell, Shannen Robson, and Carel van Schaik.

4

Slow Life Histories and Human Evolution

Kristen Hawkes

SUMMARY

Compared with other mammals, including other primates, humans take a long time to reach adulthood. Our very late maturity is often attributed to developmental and learning requirements that evolved with ancestral reliance on hunting. But other determinants may explain it. Across the mammals, age at first birth is correlated with a set of life history variables along a fast-slow continuum. I review data and theory showing that adult mortality rates are likely determinants of both age at maturity and maternal investment in individual offspring. Noting the riddle posed by increasingly expensive babies as life histories slow, I speculate that mechanisms of aging might explain this mammalian pattern. Perhaps when selection favors greater allocation to somatic maintenance and repair to slow aging, this lowers juvenile mortality as well, raising the marginal survival gains for additional investment in individual offspring. Whatever the merits of this suggestion, the relationships among adult lifespan, age at maturity, and rate of offspring production documented for mammals form the foundation for a previously proposed hypothesis that our very slow life histories are due to a novel productive role for ancestral grandmothers. I conclude by comparing and contrasting that hypothesis with

a recent version of the more venerable alternative that attributes our late
maturity and expensive juveniles to ancestral reliance on hunting.

Slow human maturation has been a topic of interest in Western scholarship since before Darwin (Gould 1977). By mid-twentieth century, Adolph Schultz (1950, 1960) had shown variation in maturation rates across primates, noting that maturity seemed to be successively later in taxa more closely related to humans. A growing body of knowledge about primate social behavior led Sherwood Washburn and David Hamburg (1965:613) to surmise that "the adaptive function of prolonged biological youth is that it gives the animal time to learn." Washburn incorporated this idea about slow maturation in his influential elaboration of the Hunting hypothesis to explain the evolution of many distinctively human features. He proposed that human maturity was delayed by the learning required for successful hunting. Building on Raymond Dart's (1949) argument that the importance of hunting in savanna environments favored larger brains and bipedalism among human ancestors, Washburn argued that the shape of the pelvis in bipedal mothers, combined with the expanding brains of offspring, would create an obstetrical dilemma. Babies would have to be born at an "earlier stage of development" (Washburn 1960) and therefore need more care as infants, as well as a longer period of maternal dependence during which to grow and furnish those larger brains. This expanded offspring dependence would conflict with maternal hunting, leading mothers to pair with hunting mates. According to this hypothesis, nuclear families and sexual divisions of labor resulted from ancestral reliance on hunting because the larger brains favored in hunters necessitated the slow development and the extreme maternal dependence of human children.

Subsequent research showed the appearance of bipedalism, expanding brains, and archaeological evidence of big game hunting to be separated by millions of years (Johanson and White 1979; Klein 1999; Stiner 2000). Although the actual temporal record contradicted Washburn's version of the Hunting hypothesis, elements of the hypothesis still remain compelling to some (for example, Kaplan et al. 2000; Kaplan and Robson 2002; Robson and Kaplan 2003). The idea that we take so long to mature because of the time required to grow and outfit our big brains is especially persuasive to many. I will return to the Hunting hypothesis after a lengthier review of the background and content of an alternative to this persistent idea.

Instead of constraints of juvenile requirements shaping ontogeny, selection may adjust juvenile development as a consequence of changes in adult mortality rates. The assumption that selection adjusts maturation rates in the face of adult mortality constraints is commonly used in evolutionary life history theory, an approach that derives from a combination of demographic theory and theory about natural selection shaping phenotypic trade-offs (see chapter 3). In the evolutionary model that is most successful at explaining cross-species regularities in life history variation, adult mortality rates determine age at maturity. I review the background, evidence, and elements of this model, focusing on cross-species regularities in life history variation and the likely role of adult mortality rates as the pacemaker of life histories. I then draw special attention to implications for links between aging rates and benefits for investment in offspring. In conclusion, I discuss implications of these regularities for human evolution, reviewing the Grandmother hypothesis and contrasting it with recent versions of the Hunting hypothesis.

EVOLUTIONARY LIFE HISTORY THEORY

Evolutionary life history theory (Fisher 1930; Lack 1947; Williams 1957, 1966a, 1966b; Hamilton 1966; Stearns 1992; Charlesworth 1994) regularly employs both mathematical demography (Lotka 1922; Keyfitz 1977) and optimality models (Maynard Smith 1978; Seger and Stubblefield 1996) to explain the wide diversity of life cycles in living things. Stable population theory from demography explains the interdependence of population vital rates. Whenever age-specific birth and death rates remain constant for a few generations (and migration is negligible), populations reach stable age distributions. The proportion of individuals in each age class does not change, whether or not the population is growing. The relative lifetime fitness effect of any change in fertility or mortality at a particular age can be calculated by using stable population models. Modelers sometimes assume that populations are not only stable but also stationary (nongrowing), a simplification justified by the geometric effects of population growth rates. Even small departures from zero growth quickly lead to either extinction or unsustainably large populations, so growth rates must be near zero most of the time.

In addition to stable population models, evolutionary life history theorists use both standard and frequency-dependent optimality (or Evolutionarily Stable Strategy [ESS]) models to investigate the trade-offs imposed by a finite world. Because time and energy are limited, more allocated to one thing leaves less for something else. More into maintenance means less for current reproduction; more into individual offspring means fewer produced. The guiding premise is that natural selection favors tendencies and capacities to trade off these fitness components so as to enhance overall lifetime fitness. Because costs and benefits from various components depend both on an organism's own characteristics and on local circumstances, optimal allocations differ for individuals over time, among individuals within populations, and among populations of the same species. Capacities for adjustment to immediate circumstances might result in wide phenotypic variation. Yet, the strong regularities within taxonomic groups suggest that a limited number of fundamental trade-offs usually predominate (Charnov 1993; see Robson, van Schaik, and Hawkes, chapter 2, this volume).

Given general expectations about allocation trade-offs, some of the regular interrelationships among life history variables are initially puzzling. Paul Harvey and Timothy Clutton-Brock (1985) noted that in mammals generally and primates in particular, one might expect "compensation." Longer gestation length might mean shorter time to weaning, or later weaning might mean less time to maturity. Instead of negative correlations among these timing variables across primate species, though, they found just the reverse: "In particular, relative neonatal weight is positively correlated with relative gestational length, relative weaning age and relative age at maturity" (Harvey and Clutton- Brock 1985:578). These positive correlations multiply differences in potential reproductive rates, expanding the range of slow-fast variation.

Variation in adult body size is correlated with the slow-fast differences (Blueweiss et al. 1978; Western 1979; J. Eisenberg 1981; Western and Ssemakula 1982). Andrew Purvis and Paul Harvey (1995) compiled a mammalian life history data set that contains sixty-four species,

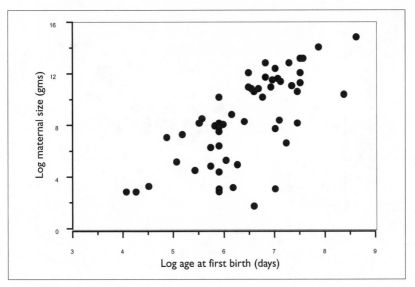

FIGURE 4.1

Natural log/log plot of adult body size by age at first birth across species of mammals. Data from Purvis and Harvey (1995) includes sixty-four species, ranging from rodents to elephants. This data set includes only two species of primates. Least squares regression r = 0.684.

ranging from rodents to elephants. Log/log plots of age at maturity and adult body size for these species (figure 4.1) confirm that larger-bodied species are slower to mature.

Because it takes longer to grow bigger, a correlation between age at maturity and body size is not surprising. But the magnitude of associated differences in reproductive rates can far outpace the differences of size: "For example, consider the smallest and the largest species of primate. A female mouse lemur (*Microcebus murinus*) born at the same time as a female gorilla (*Gorilla gorilla*) could leave 10 million descendants before the gorilla became sexually mature" (Harvey, Read, and Promislow 1989:14). After some feasible threshold, the time spent growing larger means reproduction foregone. There must be benefits that compensate this cost. Possible advantages for growing larger include predator defense, mobility over larger foraging ranges, and tolerance of lower diet quality or local resource fluctuations, all of which would reduce adult mortality risk (McNab 1963, 1980; Western 1979; Western and Ssemakula 1982; Clutton-Brock and Harvey 1983;

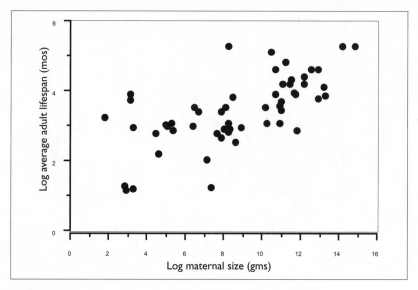

FIGURE 4.2

Natural log/log plot of average adult lifespan by adult body size. Data from Purvis and Harvey (1995); n = 63; r = 0.669 (missing data on one of the sixty-four species in this data set).

Pagel and Harvey 1993; Kozlowski and Weiner 1997). Growing larger might lower adult mortality.

Species with larger adult body sizes do have longer adult lifespans (figure 4.2), but the direction of causality could also run the other way. Larger body sizes could be a consequence of lower adult mortality risk. When this risk is lower, juveniles can afford a longer growth period and get larger before maturing (Kozlowski and Weigert 1987; Charnov 1990).

The positive correlation between adult lifespan and age at maturity is consistent with either direction of causality. Yet, the relationship between those timing variables remains when body size is removed (Harvey and Zammuto 1985; Sutherland, Grafen, and Harvey 1986; Read and Harvey 1989; Promislow and Harvey 1990). Average adult lifespan and age at maturity are more closely correlated with each other than either is with body size (figure 4.3; compare with figures 4.1 and 4.2).

Using order means as data points, Andrew Read, Paul Harvey, and Daniel Promislow (Read and Harvey 1989; Harvey, Read, and Promislow 1989) found that the relationship between adult lifespan and age at maturity remains but that orders change position relative to

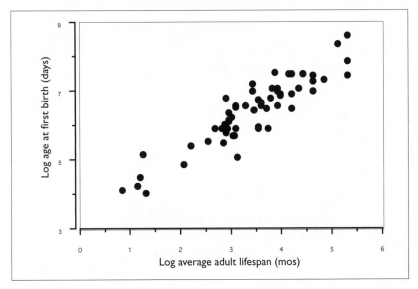

FIGURE 4.3

Natural log/log plot of age at first birth by average adult lifespan. Data from Purvis and Harvey (1995); n = 63; r = 0.913 (missing data on one of the sixty-four species in this data set).

each other on these fast-slow dimensions when body size is removed: "Species with high mortality rates for their body size had the suite of life history characteristics associated with the fast end of the fast-slow continuum: short gestation lengths, early ages at weaning and maturity, short periods from weaning to maturity, and large litters" (Harvey, Read, and Promislow 1989:23).

This could imply that adult mortality risk determines the other traits, with selection favoring delayed maturity when the mortality risk of waiting declines. Reproductive efficiency might, for example, improve with age (Harvey, Read, and Promislow 1989). Across the fast-slow continuum, the rate of offspring production is correlated with age at maturity, but the direction of the correlation is negative. Species that wait longer have babies at a slower rate (figure 4.4).

This is a central feature of slow mammalian life histories. Harvey, Read, and Promislow (1989:16–17) posed the puzzle this way: "[While] it is plausible that an upper limit on neonate size is sometimes set by the size of the birth canal or the ability of the placenta to sustain a large, growing fetus...it is by no means clear why elephants do not

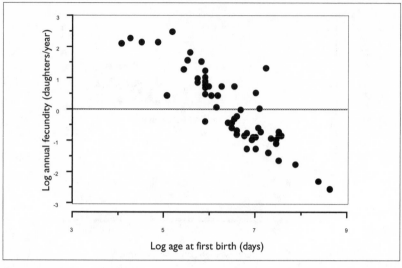

FIGURE 4.4

Natural log/log plot of annual fecundity (daughters/years) by age at first birth. Data from Purvis and Harvey (1995); n = 59; r = 0.880 (missing data on five of the sixty-four species in this data set).

produce two horse-sized or three hippopotamus-sized neonates, which together would weigh the same as an elephant at birth (and fit through the birth canal more easily)." In spite of the costs, baby size increases with the mother's size (figure 4.5). Greater postnatal investment in larger neonates then compounds the puzzle. Babies that are larger at birth are then larger at weaning (figure 4.6) (Millar 1977; Lee, Majluf, and Gordon 1991). Bigger mothers, instead of producing weanlings at a faster rate, produce bigger weanlings (figure 4.7).

This is part of the vast empirical evidence that selection does not simply maximize fertility. David Lack (1947, 1953) provided an explanation for the general pattern by pointing out the crucial trade-off between quantity and quality of offspring. Parents typically leave more *surviving* descendants when they divide their effort among fewer and allot more to each (Williams 1966b; Smith and Fretwell 1974). But why does greater investment in offspring quality regularly accompany delayed maturity, correlations that further reduce potential reproductive rates? Why do those who wait longer to mature then invest more in each baby, reducing their rates of offspring production even further?

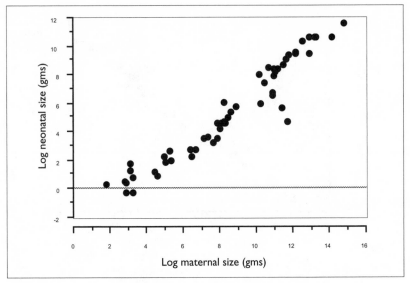

FIGURE 4.5

Natural log/log plot of neonatal size by maternal size. Data from Purvis and Harvey (1995); n = 60; r = 0.962 (missing data on four of the sixty-four species in this data set).

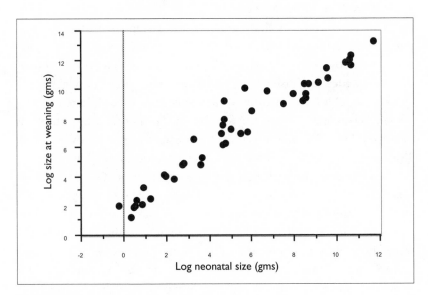

FIGURE 4.6

Natural log/log plot of weanling size by neonatal size. Data from Purvis and Harvey (1995); n = 43; r = 0.970 (missing data on twenty-one of the sixty-four species in this data set).

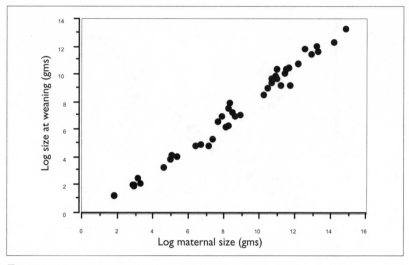

FIGURE 4.7

Natural log/log plot of weanling size by maternal size. Data from Purvis and Harvey (1995); n = 42; r = 0.991 (missing data on twenty-two of the sixty-four species in this data set).

CHARNOV'S 1991 MODEL

The description of these general regularities in mammals (and similar regularities in birds [Saether 1988]) and the evolutionary questions they pose were crucial developments in the late 1980s. Harvey and colleagues established the empirical associations among the life history variables and surmised that because the timing variables remain correlated when the effects of body size are statistically removed, body size might not be as important as previously assumed. Eric Charnov (1990) focused attention on indications that body size was nevertheless the scaffolding of the regularities. The timing variables all scale with body size in the same way. Consequently, the ratios of the variables (such as the ratio of age at maturity to average adult lifespan) remain the same across large changes in the individual variables themselves. Charnov underlined both the persistence of characteristic ratios across large changes of body size within taxa (for example, among mammals) and the differences in these ratios from one taxon to another (from fish to mammals to birds) (Charnov and Berrigan 1990b; Charnov 2002).

Charnov's (1991) model of mammalian life history evolution explained the invariance of these ratios across transformations of body

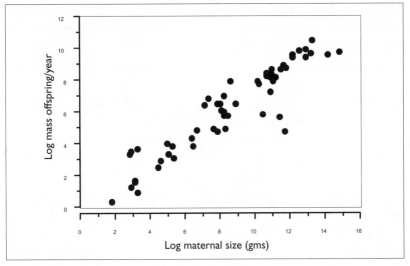

FIGURE 4.8

Natural log/log plot of offspring mass/year (neonatal weight times litter size times litters per year) by maternal size. Data from Purvis and Harvey (1995); n = 56; r = 0.929 (missing data on eight of the sixty-four species in this data set).

size. Building on his previous work and that of many others, he assumed a simple growth model in which a juvenile channels production into growing herself and at maturity redirects that production into offspring. Maternal body size is then the consequence of age at maturity. A simple exponential growth equation ($dW/dt = AW^{0.75}$) made growth an allometric function of body size (W) and a taxon-specific production function (A). As a juvenile grows bigger, she can mobilize more production for growing herself. The bigger she is at maturity, the more production she can put into growing offspring.

The simple growth model uses an average value (A) for the rate of production throughout juvenile life, ignoring the variation in growth trajectories at different ages. In exchange for subsuming those "evolutionarily labile" (Leigh and Park 1998) variables into rate averages, the model captures some broader patterns. Hill and Hurtado (1996) and Blurton Jones (chapter 8, this volume) show that it also accounts for general features of human growth. Charnov (1991) assumes that the benefit of growing larger is that larger mothers have more production available (mass/time) to put into babies (also a rate average). Figure 4.8 shows the broad mammalian relationship between maternal size and the annual mass of offspring produced; the slope of the best-fit linear regression of this log/log plot (equivalent to the exponent in the growth equation) is 0.728.

In addition to the simple growth model, Charnov used a simplified mortality assumption: a high burst of early mortality (during which any density-dependent mortality occurs) dropping to a constant adult rate before some feasible age at maturity. Optimal age at maturity (α) then depends on the trade-off between the gains for continuing to grow larger and the risk of dying before reproducing. Later maturity is favored when that risk of dying declines.

Charnov's model accounts for the tighter correlations between timing variables themselves than between any of them and body size by recognizing the importance of (average) growth rate differences (Case 1978) and the covariation of these with the rate of offspring production. Both are represented by one variable, the production coefficient (A). Species characterized by a low 'A' grow slowly and therefore are relatively small at a given age of maturity. They also have a low rate of offspring production at a given size (this variation contributes to the scatter in figures 4.1 and 4.2, compared with that in figure 4.3). Primates are smaller for a given age at maturity and produce babies at a slower rate than nonprimate mammals of a given size. Fitting data to the model, 'A' averages about 0.4 in primates, compared with about 1.0 in mammals generally (Charnov and Berrigan 1993).

The puzzle of why rates of offspring production (across species) go down as age at maturity goes up is treated in Charnov's mammal model as follows. Productive capacity scales up allometrically with size at about 0.75 power (see figure 4.8, slope 0.728), whereas offspring size increases almost isometrically with maternal size. Babies are nearly a constant fraction of their mother's mass (the slope of the line in figure 4.7 is 0.955). Because baby size goes up faster than maternal productive rate, bigger mothers take longer to grow their offspring to weaning size and must turn them out at a slower rate.

The model is clear, simple, and consistent with the data. It explains the empirical relationships by treating age at maturity as one optimization (assuming a fixed offspring size), followed by a subsequent and independent second optimization that establishes a new parental quantity/quality equilibrium (ESS) (Charnov 1993, 2001b). Maternal size and fecundity are assumed to be positively related within a species but negatively related across species because optimal investment per child changes among species. Across species, bigger mothers *do* make bigger babies (see figure 4.7), so they must make them at a slower rate. That is the empirical pattern. But the question raised by Harvey and colleagues above still has force: Why do bigger mothers make bigger, more expensive babies rather than use their greater productive capacity to make more babies?

Aspects of life histories not included in Charnov's initial mammal model might contribute to an explanation. Fast-slow life history variation entails not only differences in age at maturity and rates of offspring production but also varying rates of senescence. Both theory and data provide a basis for hypothesizing a link between aging and offspring investment.

AGING

Throughout an organism's life history, allocations to growth and reproduction compete with somatic maintenance (Williams 1957, 1966b; Gadgil and Bossert 1970). Kirkwood's (1977, 1981; Kirkwood and Rose 1991) disposable soma model focuses specifically on the question of varying allocation to maintenance. It is a version of Williams' (1957) antagonistic pleiotropy hypothesis about the evolution of aging, which explicitly focuses attention on the cost of maintenance and repair. If the processes of life result in inevitable damage to cells and tissues, accumulating impairment will increase vulnerability to mortality risks. The damage can be limited by buffering against it and can be reduced by repair, but allocation to somatic maintenance reduces allocation to growth and reproduction. From this perspective, accumulating damage is an intrinsic component of mortality risk that combines with extrinsic risks to determine the overall mortality rate (Cichon and Kozlowski 2000).

Trade-offs due to the cost of maintenance and repair imply a necessary qualitative relationship between extrinsic and intrinsic components of mortality risk. If extrinsic risk is high, then allocation to maintenance and repair is less beneficial because the chance of dying is high, no matter the repair. Conversely, if extrinsic risk is low, the chance of future benefit from repair is high. The present value of possible future payoffs may be considerable. Selection can favor trading off some growth and/or current reproduction for more maintenance

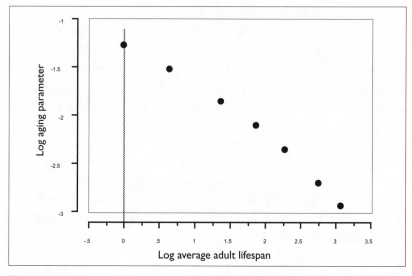

FIGURE 4.9

Natural log/log plot of rate of senescence (Ricklefs' aging parameter) by average adult lifespan. Estimates from Ricklefs (1998); modeling and data from eighteen bird species and twenty-seven mammal species.

and repair because an organism might live long enough to gain from persistent competence. As George Williams (1957:404) pointed out long ago, "*low adult death rates should be associated with low rates of senescence, and high adult death rates with high rates of senescence...*[so] we should be able to predict rates of senescence on the basis of adult mortality rates" (italics original).

Robert Ricklefs (1998) modeled and measured cross-species variation in intrinsic and extrinsic components of adult mortality in a sample of eighteen bird species and twenty-seven mammal species. He used the minimum mortality exhibited by an age class (the initial mortality rate) to estimate extrinsic mortality risks. Differences between the minimum rate and rates at older ages provided his estimate of intrinsic mortality, and a function fitted to changes in adult mortality with age indexed the rate of senescence.

Using these measures, Ricklefs showed two things. First, the rate of senescence increases with extrinsic mortality risk (figure 4.9). In species with high death rates, individuals age more quickly. Second, the fraction of adult mortality due to the intrinsic (senescent) component increases when adult lifespans lengthen (figure 4.10).

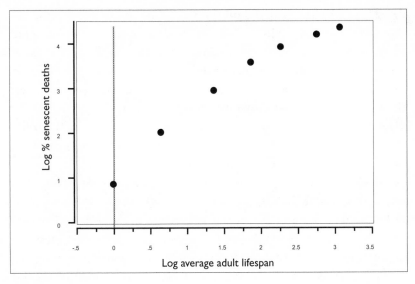

FIGURE 4.10

Natural log/log plot of the fraction of adult deaths due to senescence by average adult life-span. The proportion of age-specific mortality above the initial mortality rate is death that would not have occurred if mortality rates remained constant with adult age. This death is assumed to reflect declining fitness-related performance with age. Estimates from Ricklefs (1998); modeling and data from eighteen bird species and twenty-seven mammal species.

High extrinsic mortality favors less repair and senescence is faster, but most individuals die before they have a chance to grow old. Conversely, when extrinsic mortality is low and more repair slows aging, the proportion of deaths due to senescence becomes remarkably high. The older the age structure, the more aging-related adult deaths.

Ricklefs' empirical demonstration is consistent with the theoretical expectation that benefits for maintenance and repair increase with the chance of future survival. As adult lifespans lengthen, aging rates slow. As life histories slow and populations have older age structures, the proportion of senescent deaths increases. Imperfect repair allows damage to accumulate, or, perhaps, as modeled by Cichon and Kozlowski (2000), allocation to repair varies with age. Either way, intrinsic mortality plays an increasingly dominant role in survival schedules when extrinsic mortality is low and populations have an older age structure.

There is another variable that should affect optimal allocation to somatic maintenance and repair. Williams (1957:406) predicted that aging would be slower in organisms that continue to increase in fecundity after maturity: "[A]n increase in fecundity has the opposite effect from mortality." He was comparing the rapid senescence of determinant growers, such as mammals, with the slower senescence of indeterminant growers, such as many fish and invertebrates that continue to grow larger after maturity and produce more eggs as they get bigger. The point, however, is a general one. Charnov (1993) applied it to sex-changing fish. The same idea applies whenever individuals can have larger effects on their own fitness at older ages.

Greater allocation to somatic durability slows aging in adults. It might also shift life history allocations throughout development. More elaborate maintenance and repair might start early, perhaps from the initial stages of an individual's development, and affect the durability of juveniles similarly to that of adults. As more effective buffers against mortality are favored in adults, they will be reproduced in the offspring. Promislow and Harvey (1990) reported comparative results consistent with this reasoning. They found that "juvenile and adult mortality were significantly and positively correlated after removing the effects of body weight (which accounts for over 65% of the total variance in mortality). Species tend to have high or low mortality for their body weight throughout their lifetime" (Promislow and Harvey 1990:428).

The cross-species correlation between juvenile and adult mortality rates (figure 4.11) could result simply from adjustments in the timing of maturity as a consequence of adult mortality rates (Charnov 1991), as discussed above. If maturity is delayed when adult mortality is low, then the juvenile period includes more time at low mortality rates, reducing the average juvenile mortality rate. The correlation is also consistent with differences in somatic durability throughout life. Species with more durable adults may also have more durable juveniles.

Biodemographers use the minimum mortality rate exhibited by an age class (the initial mortality rate) to index extrinsic mortality (Finch 1990; and Ricklefs 1998, as discussed above). By the argument above, however, that rate is likely affected by intrinsic mortality buffers, not just extrinsic risk. Physiological processes of maintenance and repair should affect the vulnerability of juveniles just as they affect adults. Finch, Pike, and Whitten (1990) noted large differences in the initial mortality rates of various laboratory and captive populations.

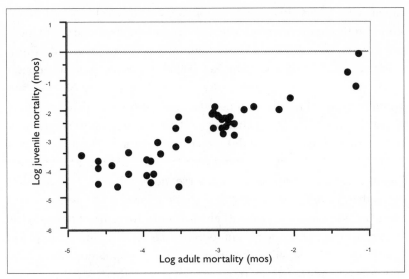

Figure 4.11

Natural log/log plot of juvenile mortality rate by adult mortality rate across mammals.
Data from Purvis and Harvey (1995); n = 49; r = 0.891 (missing data on twenty-five of
the sixty-four species in this data set).

Husbandry conditions are surely implicated, but other differences may also play a role. Because extrinsic sources of mortality are substantially reduced in captivity, initial mortality rates may also depend on intrinsic processes of maintenance and repair in juveniles. Finch and colleagues suggested that evolution might adjust not only rates of aging but also initial mortality rates.

If selection for more durable adults results in more durable infants and juveniles, then this might systematically shift the mother's gain curve for investment in each offspring. Greater marginal gains for additional investment could help explain why longer-lived mammalian mothers invest more in each offspring. This line of reasoning prompts the hypothesis that cell and molecular processes associated with differential aging may link adult mortality rates with juvenile mortality rates and also link mammalian aging rates with the optimal quality/quantity trade-off for offspring investment.

WHAT ABOUT HUMAN EVOLUTION?

These general mammalian fast-slow regularities provide a framework for investigating the evolution of human life histories. Modern humans are a very recent species, only one hundred thousand to two hundred thousand years old, whereas the ancestors we share with modern chimpanzees lived about six million years ago (King and Wilson 1975; Klein 1999; Glazko and Nei 2003). Over the past six million years, many different species evolved in our lineage (see Skinner and Wood, chapter 11, this volume). Genetic, morphological, and biochemical evidence from both living and ancient populations calibrates some of the similarities and differences among them. However, all past members of our lineage are known only from the fossil and archaeological record. It is impossible to observe their vital rates. This does not mean that the age structures of these populations could have been anything at all. Like the laws of physics and chemistry, demographic imperatives apply to persistent populations at any time and place, those in the past as well as the present. Ancient populations must have reproduced themselves at replacement rates; otherwise, they would have overrun the planet or disappeared. If we can infer some things about the life histories of individuals in past populations, this will dictate the probable range of other life history variables (Cole 1954; Keyfitz 1977; Charlesworth 1994; Charnov 1997).

The regularities of the fast-slow variation in mammalian life histories inspire even stronger presumptions. Life history variation reflects fundamental trade-offs for living primates, including the most unusual primate, modern humans. Therefore, those trade-offs likely applied to others in our hominin clade as well. Across the living primates, the fast-slow variation is broadly correlated with body size, for example, the mouse lemur/gorilla comparison. The data set compiled by Caroline Ross and Kate Jones (1999) shows that primates display the same relationships among life history variables and size found in the Purvis and Harvey (1995) data set for mammals as a whole. Primate species with longer adult lifespans mature later (figure 4.12). Species with later maturity are larger (figure 4.13). Larger species put more production into babies (figure 4.14). Bigger mothers have bigger newborns (figure 4.15), which they then nurse longer (figure 4.16). Having more expensive babies, mothers have them at a slower rate (figure 4.17). The later the age at maturity, the slower the rate of baby production (figure 4.18).

Body size and age at maturity are two variables that can be indexed in the fossil record (though not without difficulty; see, for example, Kappelman [1996]; R. Smith [1996]). The evolutionary life history

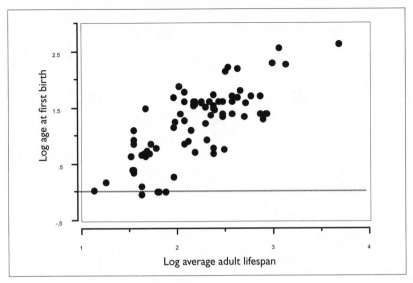

FIGURE 4.12

Natural log/log plot of age at first birth by average adult lifespan. Data in Ross and Jones (1999) includes one hundred primate species. Here n = 78; r = 0.754 (missing data on twenty-two of the one hundred species in this data set). Average adult lifespan is calculated from the maximum recorded longevity (Ross and Jones 1999:table 4.2) by Charnov's method (1993:104, fig. 5.6).

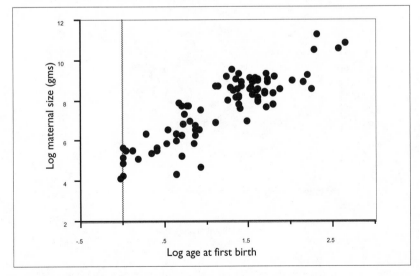

FIGURE 4.13

Natural log/log plot of adult body size by age at first birth. Data from Ross and Jones (1999); n = 88; r = 0.871 (missing data on twelve of the one hundred species in this data set).

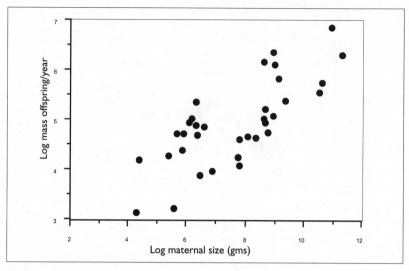

FIGURE 4.14

Natural log/log plot of offspring mass/year (neonatal size times litter size divided by inter-birth interval) by maternal size. Maternal size from Ross and Jones (1999); neonatal weights, litter size, and interbirth interval from Chapman, Walker, and Lefebvre (1990); n = 34; r = 0.755.

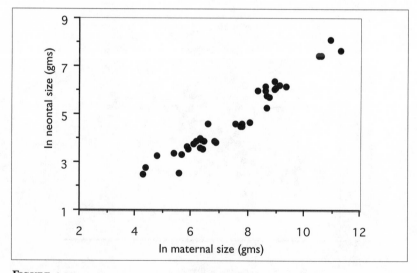

FIGURE 4.15

Natural log/log plot of neonatal size by maternal size. Data from Ross and Jones (1999) and Chapman, Walker, and Lefebvre (1990); n = 38; r = 0.970.

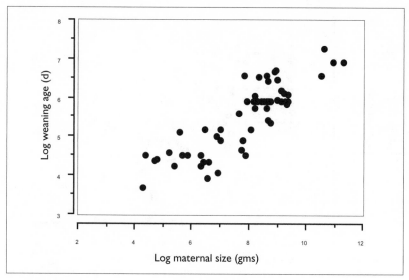

FIGURE 4.16

Natural log/log plot of weaning age by maternal size. Data from Ross and Jones (1999); n = 60; r = 0.852 (missing data on forty of the one hundred species in this data set).

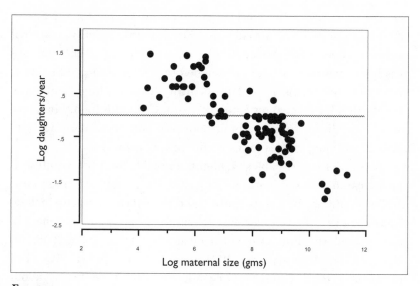

FIGURE 4.17

Natural log/log plot of annual fecundity (daughters per year) by maternal size. Data from Ross and Jones (1999); n = 88; r = 0.800 (missing data on twelve of the one hundred species in this data set).

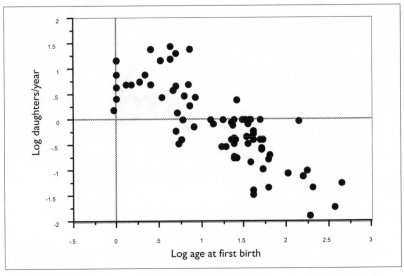

FIGURE 4.18

Natural log/log plot of annual fecundity (daughters/year) by age at first birth. Data from Ross and Jones (1999); n = 78; r = 0.83 (missing data on twenty-two of the one hundred species in this data set).

theory summarized above assigns the main causal role for the timing of maturation to adult mortality risk. From that perspective, maternal body size depends on the length of the juvenile period. When maturity is later, growth continues longer before it stops and production is redirected into offspring, so later maturity results in larger adult size (see Blurton Jones, chapter 8, this volume). Using this theory (and evidence from living species), adult body size and maturation age estimates imply likely ranges for other life history features.

Focus on these variables highlights a notable life history shift with the appearance of the first widely successful members of genus *Homo*. Earlier hominins, the australopiths (used in the broad sense to include *Australopithecus* and *Paranthropus*) are similar in body size and maturation to modern chimpanzees (Bromage and Dean 1985; B. Smith 1989a, 1991a; McHenry 1992, 1994; Smith and Tompkins 1995). The several taxa in this australopith radiation also have brains about the size of modern chimpanzees and have been characterized as "bipedal apes" (Klein 1999; see Skinner and Wood, chapter 11, this volume).

Brain size increases with the appearance of genus *Homo* around two million years ago. Because body size also increases substantially, though, the *relative* brain size change is less dramatic (McHenry 1992, 1994; Aiello and Wheeler 1995; Wood and Collard 1999b). Collard and Wood (1999:324) go so far as to suggest that "although there are twofold differences in the mean absolute brain size of early hominids, these differences are almost certainly not significant when body mass is taken into account. A notable effect of body-mass correction is that the absolutely larger brain of *H. ergaster* is 'cancelled out' by its substantial estimated body mass."

The larger body size of this taxon is associated with a later age at maturity than that which characterized the australopithecines (B. Smith 1991a, 1993). *H. ergaster/erectus* was similar to modern humans in body size and shape (Aiello and Key 2002), with maturation patterns perhaps in the range of modern humans (B. Smith 1994; Tardieu 1998; Clegg and Aiello 1999; Antón 2002a; S. Smith 2004; but see Dean et al. 2001; Skinner and Wood, chapter 11, this volume). The exceptionally large brains that distinguish modern humans, however, did not appear in our lineage until the radiation of "archaic" sapiens, which began at least a million years after the spread of the first widely successful members of our genus (see McHenry 1994; Ruff, Trinkaus, and Holliday 1997; Klein 1999; Skinner and Wood, chapter 11, this volume).

From the theoretical perspective outlined above, delay in maturity and growth to larger adult size are favored when lifespans lengthen. Otherwise, gains from growing larger are outweighed by the risk of dying before the benefits of larger size can be realized. Assuming that australopiths had life histories resembling those of modern chimpanzees (Smith and Tompkins 1995), they were at the slow end of the primate variation, with adult lifespans long enough to allow quite late maturity. Using Ricklefs' findings of the fraction of senescent deaths associated with chimpanzeelike lifespans, most adult deaths (about 70 percent) would have been due to senescent decline. What could have slowed rates of aging even further among the first widely successful members of our genus?

A GRANDMOTHER HYPOTHESIS

Observations among Hadza hunter-gatherers in northern Tanzania (Woodburn 1968; Blurton Jones et al. 1992) suggest an answer (Hawkes et al. 1998; Blurton Jones, Hawkes, and O'Connell 1999; O'Connell,

Hawkes, and Blurton Jones 1999). Among these modern people, children are productive and energetic foragers (Blurton Jones, Hawkes, and O'Connell 1989) but cannot effectively handle one essential dietary staple, the large root of a plant that is deeply buried and requires strength to excavate (Hawkes, O'Connell, and Blurton Jones 1995). Women past menopause are especially active tuber diggers (Hawkes, O'Connell, and Blurton Jones 1989). In this population, a mother's foraging effort has a measurable effect on her children's nutritional welfare, except when she bears another baby and turns her efforts to nursing her newborn. Then it is the work of postmenopausal grandmothers that differentially affects the nutritional welfare of weaned children (Hawkes, O'Connell, and Blurton Jones 1997).

The Hadza patterns underline an important consequence of the ecological changes that coincided with the appearance of our genus (O'Connell, Hawkes, and Blurton Jones 1999). Drying environments in the late Pliocene (Cerling 1992; deMenocal 1995) probably constricted the availability of foods that young juveniles can handle. Intensified aridity and seasonality would likely have favored plants that cope well with dry seasons, for example, by holding nutrients in hard-cased seeds, nuts, and underground storage organs. Such resources can give high return rates to human foragers with the strength and skill to extract and process them, which young juveniles lack. To depend on these resources and succeed in these environments, mothers have to provision offspring who are still too young to extract and process the foods for themselves. The mother-offspring provisioning allows the occupation of otherwise uninhabitable environments. The fossil and archaeological evidence shows that *Homo ergaster/erectus* is the first hominin found outside Africa, as far east as Indonesia, and as far north as latitude 45 degrees (Swisher et al. 1994; Gabunia et al. 2000; Larick et al. 2001; Zhu et al. 2001).

Such a difference in feeding ecology is proposed to have the following consequence for life history evolution: maternal provisioning of weaned offspring creates a novel fitness opportunity for older females whose own fertility is declining. If the older females help feed their weanling grandchildren, the mothers of those weanlings can have shorter interbirth intervals without reductions in offspring survivorship. Thus, the more vigorous elders without nursing infants of their own can raise their daughters' reproductive success, increasing the number of descendants who share their characteristics. By this pathway, selection would favor greater allocation to physiological processes that buffer against mortality risk, slowing the rate of senescence through enhanced somatic maintenance and repair.

More allocation to somatic maintenance means less to current reproduction. If the ancestors of our genus were close to evolutionary stability for that trade-off, more maintenance and repair (slower aging) could only be favored if there were a benefit that outweighed that cost in current reproduction during the childbearing years. In this Grandmother hypothesis, the cost is paid by the contribution the older females make to the fertility and survival of their younger kin.

TWO INVARIANTS, A FALSIFICATION, AND HUMAN AGE STRUCTURES

Hawkes and co-authors (1998) argued that differences between humans and other living apes on three life history variables—adult mortality (M), age at maturity (α), and annual fecundity (b)—are consistent with the Grandmother hypothesis and Charnov's (1991) mammal model. Alvarez (2000) compiled a sample of sixteen primate species to evaluate the similarities and differences statistically. If the entire adult lifespan in humans is spent contributing to the production of descendants, then age at maturity (α) should be adjusted to adult mortality (M). Alvarez used the foraging Aché (Hill and Hurtado 1996) to represent humans and confirmed that the late age of first birth in this population—similar to the age of first birth for the !Kung (Howell 1979) and the Hadza (Blurton Jones et al. 1992; Blurton Jones, Hawkes, and O'Connell 2002)—is the age of first birth (α) predicted by the mammalian invariant (αM). Ross and Jones' (1999) data set is larger and much noisier than the data used by Alvarez but shows the same thing. Humans are within the 95 percent confidence interval when age at maturity (α) is regressed on average adult lifespan (figure 4.12 shows the relationship between these variables).

Alvarez (2000) also found human annual fecundity to be higher than expected from the mammalian αb. The Aché birthrate (b, annual fecundity) is above the 95 percent confidence interval for the regression of (b) on age at maturity (α) in her sixteen-species sample. The Grandmother hypothesis predicts the human rate of baby production to be higher than that of a primate with our age at maturity and no grandmothering, because our childbearing rate is elevated by grand-mothers' help. Alvarez's (2000) statistical results are therefore consis-tent with the claim that Hawkes and colleagues (1998) made about high human fecundity based on comparisons among humans, chim-panzees, gorillas, and orangutans.

There is another implication of this argument to test from the same data, an implication highlighted by the previous discussion of connections between slowed aging and more expensive offspring. With humans' slow rates of aging, we should have very expensive babies. The Grandmother hypothesis predicts annual fecundity during the child-bearing years to be high for our age at maturity, not because human mothers favor more quantity and less quality than expected but because grandmothers' production subsidizes the production of the childbearers. If all the adult women are counted as contributors, the rate per contributor should be consistent with the mammalian invari-ant. Averaged over both childbearing and grandmothering years, human fecundity should be lower than the average in the other living apes and consistent with the rate predicted for a primate with our late age at maturity.

That test has now been superseded by Alvarez's subsequent work, investigating the possibility that we (Hawkes et al. 1998; Alvarez 2000) may have mistaken features resulting from high growth rates in human populations for real life history characteristics. Because human popu-lations are usually growing while many other primate populations, great apes in particular, are not, the life history differences we have inferred from using observed fecundities may be biased by the popu-lation growth differences. This is an important concern. Alvarez's (2004a) new analysis shows that we did indeed overestimate human fertility.

Charnov's mammal model assumes stationary populations. Adjusting observed values for both human and chimpanzee popula-tions to make them stationary, Alvarez (2004a) then used the station-ary models to estimate the variables just discussed. The stationary models retain the characteristic features of both species. Adult mortal-ities in humans are lower than in chimpanzees, so average adult life-spans are longer, with about a quarter of the adult women past childbearing age. The human fertilities are substantially lower than chimpanzee fertilities in the stationary populations. Whether calculated over the childbearing years only or over all the adult years, the human fertilities are within the confidence interval for fecundity regressed on age at maturity in Alvarez's sixteen-species sample.

Because average adult mortality rates are lower in the human than in the chimpanzee stationary models (as they are in observed populations), the rate at which juveniles become adults in human populations must also be slower than in chimpanzees. As in the observed populations, the fraction of adults past the childbearing age is large in the stationary human populations but negligible in the chimpanzees. Necessarily, then, the human rate of baby production is higher when calculated as fertility during the childbearing age than when averaged over all women. In contrast, for chimpanzee populations, whether baby production is distributed over all the adult females or only those of childbearing age makes little difference because so few females are alive after terminal fertility in that species. The results do not support our previous claims that human fertility is high for our late maturity, but they underline the distinctively long adult lifespans and old age structure of human populations. We put more into offspring and produce them at a slower rate, as expected for a primate with our old population age structure.

The old age structure of human populations is often mistakenly assumed to depend on long life expectancies. Life expectancies much over 40 may be a relatively recent novelty (Oeppen and Vaupel 2002), and many assume that long average adult lifespans are also recent (such as Washburn 1981; Crews and Gerber 2003; Kennedy 2003; Krovitz, Nelson, and Thompson 2003; Nelson, Thompson, and Krovitz 2003). But life expectancies are averages, strongly affected by the short lives of those who die as infants and juveniles. This is clearly illustrated by using the stable population models built by Coale and Demeny (1966) to examine the effects of varying mortality on population age structure. With fertility held constant, a tripling of life expectancy (from 20 to 60) makes little difference in the fraction of adults over 45 (Hawkes 2004a; Hawkes and Blurton Jones 2005). Moreover, the direction of the difference is opposite to usual intuition: the lower the life expectancy, the *larger* the fraction of women past the age of terminal fertility. In hunter-gatherer populations with life expectancies lower than 40, a quarter or more of the adult women are past the age of 45 (Hawkes 2003, 2004a; Hawkes, O'Connell, and Blurton Jones 2003; Hawkes and Blurton Jones 2005).

To explain this pattern, the Grandmother hypothesis proposes that aging slowed and adult lifespans lengthened in our lineage when females who were slightly more vigorous as their fertility declined could have a novel effect on their own fitness. Without infants of their own, the older females could help their daughters feed weanlings who were unable to handle increasingly important food resources. As more vigorous elders helped more, their vigor was represented in more descendants. Slower aging and longer average adult lifespans decreased the risk of waiting longer to mature, resulting in a larger pool of adolescents who might also help their mothers and younger siblings, while remaining immature longer. Middle-aged adults and teenagers are conventionally described as post- and prereproductive, but they contribute to the reproductive success of childbearers. Sarah Hrdy (1999, 2001) has characterized humans as cooperative breeders, underlining the importance of flows of help to mothers and young juveniles. Resource transfers, not only from mothers to offspring but also from grandmothers, older siblings, and others, are long appreciated features of the socioecology of our species (see Sahlins 1972; Davis and Daly 1997; Ivey 2000).

COMPARING GRANDMOTHERING WITH THE HUNTING HYPOTHESIS

This Grandmother hypothesis is similar in some meaningful respects to the Hunting hypothesis summarized at the beginning of this chapter. Both point to the same expanding savannas to trigger adaptive shifts in the human lineage. Both hypotheses involve resource transfers between generations—maternal and especially paternal provisioning, on one hand, and maternal and grandmaternal provisioning, on the other. Changes in aging rates, which are central to the Grandmother hypothesis, are also major elements of recent versions of the Hunting hypothesis (Kaplan et al. 2000).

A central difference is the grandmothering model's focus on female life history trade-offs. In contrast, the Hunting hypothesis makes the productivity of hunting *men* the source of payoffs for longer juvenile development (Hill and Kaplan 1999). Kaplan and colleagues have elaborated this in detail (Kaplan 1996, 1997; Kaplan et al. 2000; Kaplan and Robson 2002; Robson and Kaplan 2003), characterizing brains and learning as embodied capital that generates surplus production from hunting men. Using data on foraging return rates and time allocation among hunter-gatherers, they estimate average age- and sex-specific energy consumption and production rates and highlight the net energetic deficit imposed by juveniles, as well as the net energetic surplus provided by men's hunting. If the production profiles reflect age- and sex-specific capacities, then the surplus from men is necessary to pay the juvenile deficits. An economic and reproductive partnership between men and women is then required. Assuming that partnership, the number of new dependent juveniles that can be recruited depends on the size of the surplus. These assumptions justify the expectation that investments in growth and mortality reduction that maximize surplus production will be favored by selection. Modeling those investments, Kaplan and Robson (2002; Robson and Kaplan 2003) find that when greater investments in embodied capital raise the lifetime surplus produced, the surplus is further increased by investments in mortality reduction.

By contrast, the Grandmother hypothesis attends explicitly to female life history trade-offs, proposing that slowed aging is favored by the contribution that older females make to the survival and fertility of their junior kin. These fitness effects from grandmothering result in competitive advantages for lineages in which aging is slower than in ancestral populations. This results in lower adult mortality and consequent changes in other life history variables. Males and females are not assumed to have the same productive and reproductive interests.

Alternative models ignore different aspects of the empirical complexity. Choices among simplifications—as with everything else— involve trade-offs. The Grandmother hypothesis is built on a model of mammalian life history evolution, which, like much of life history theory, is about female trade-offs. For mammals, life history questions such as when to stop growing and have the first baby; whether to have singletons, twins, or more offspring per pregnancy; and when to wean and move on to the next baby are questions about female life histories. Males, of course, face life history trade-offs as well, but different ones.

Charnov's model of mammalian life history invariants provides "assembly rules" for female life histories. The variation in age at maturity and in annual fecundity across mammals generally, and within the order primates, is correlated with adult female lifespans—irrespective of male strategies.

In humans, as in most mammals, including other primates, childcare is women's work. Our species is unusual for the economic productivity of adult males. Men, unlike males in most primate species, expend substantial effort producing food that is consumed by females and juveniles. This surplus production, central to the Hunting or Embodied Capital hypothesis, plays no role in the Grandmother hypothesis. The omission is not because those investigating the evolutionary role of grandmothers dismiss the importance of hunting and men's activities. Our ethnographic experience confirms the high value placed on meat and hunting in modern hunting and gathering communities, prompting inquiry explicitly focused on hunting and men's foraging and reproductive strategies (Hawkes 1990, 1991, 1993, 2000, 2001, 2004a; Hawkes, O'Connell, and Blurton Jones 1991, 2001a, 2001b; Blurton Jones et al. 2000; Hawkes and Bliege Bird 2002; O'Connell et al. 2002). Main findings include the strategic adjustments that individuals of different ages and sexes make in their foraging behavior and the lesson that—in these ethnographic cases, at least—hunting is not satisfactorily explained as paternal provisioning. Hunting successes are unpredictable, meat is claimed by many, and the hunter does not control the distribution of shares. Differential nutritional benefits to the hunters (and their own wives and children) are all but absent. Yet, better hunters often spend more time hunting, inflating the contributions they make to others' consumption. Social benefits for the hunters seem more likely to explain the patterns than do nutritional benefits for their own families.

The ethnographic findings point to the importance of sexual selection (Darwin 1871) in human social behavior. Different reproductive interests of the sexes and the relevance of mating competition among males are central to the "ecological model" for explaining social arrangements in other primates (Wrangham 1979, 1980; van Schaik 1983, 1989, 1996; Kappeler and van Schaik 2002; Hawkes 2004b). Because the same things are important among modern humans, it is especially likely that they were also important in the lives of our ancestors. The earliest assemblages of stone tools and large animal bones are associated with ancestors who lacked the projectile weapons that make modern men such effective hunters. But social benefits to males for showing off their qualities as competitive scavengers can explain otherwise puzzling aspects of the early archaeology (O'Connell, Hawkes, and Blurton Jones 2002). Social competition and costly signaling models promise to be more effective than paternal provisioning in explaining the evolution and character of men's work (Hawkes and Bliege Bird 2002; Bliege Bird and Smith 2005).

The Grandmother hypothesis is silent on male life history trade-offs, except in one way. Arguments about slowed aging in our lineage do have implications for male longevity. As greater allocation to somatic maintenance and repair is favored through the increased fitness of more vigorous grandmothers, those characteristics would be represented in their descendants of both sexes. Longer-lived women not only have more expensive and longer-lived daughters (and granddaughters) but also longer-lived and more expensive sons (and grandsons). Male-male competition can lead to higher adult mortality rates in males than females, with higher aging rates expected as a consequence, but longevity in females is a good general predictor of longevity in males across primate species (Allman et al. 1998).

CONCLUDING COMMENT

The fast-slow life history continuum implies the predominance of a few basic trade-offs across the broad range of mammalian life histories. The evolutionary optimization model that best explains the cross-species patterns assumes that continued growth is current reproduction traded for greater reproductive capacity in the future. The present value of those future benefits depends on adult mortality risk. Theory, combined with the empirical patterns, also links mortality risk to variation in somatic durability, maintenance, and repair. More fitness opportunities at later ages increase the net benefits for somatic maintenance. Slower life histories favor more effective intrinsic buffers against somatic damage, so much so that the rate of aging can become the main determinant of adult mortality rates.

Varying investment in somatic maintenance and repair should also affect allocation to production of self (juvenile growth rate) and babies. In Charnov's 1991 model, he assumed growth and reproductive rates to be independent of mortality rates to explain the scaling regularities in adult lifespans, age at maturity, and annual fecundity. A recent (Charnov 2004) modification attends specifically to trade-offs between production (growth and reproduction) and maintenance, showing that longer-lived species may be more efficient at maintenance and repair. This model is of special interest because it also reproduces the scaling regularities in the life history variables that are real aspects of the empirical variation.

Ronald D. Lee (2003) has developed a formal theory of intergenerational transfers to explore the evolution of slower aging rates. Lee's model does not deal with scaling patterns among life history variables, but it does show that when intergenerational transfers of resources are important, it is the remaining economic productivity, not fertility, that determines the rate of senescence. Links between economic productivity and aging are also central to Kaplan and colleagues' Embodied Capital model. Their verbal arguments emphasize expanding brains and hunting, but their formal model (Kaplan et al. 2000; Kaplan and Robson 2002; Robson and Kaplan 2003) includes more general trade-offs among growth, mortality buffers, and production. Differences among these various approaches are not small ones. One of them, the role of the broader primate regularities in the Grandmother hypothesis, has been emphasized here. Also, there are important convergences. Kaplan and colleagues' models, the model built by Lee, and the Grandmother hypothesis recognize human longevity as an evolved trait—with help *from* elders, not *to* them—the source of the distinctive age structure of human populations. That agreement, in itself, indicates progress toward explaining our slow life histories as the evolutionary legacy of our ancestral past.

Acknowledgments

I am grateful to all the participants in the advanced seminar and also to the School of American Research. For especially useful advice on this chapter, I thank Helen Alvarez, Nick Blurton Jones, Jim O'Connell, Carel van Schaik, and Shannen Robson.

5

Primate Life Histories and the Role of Brains

Carel P. van Schaik, Nancy Barrickman,

Meredith L. Bastian, Elissa B. Krakauer,

and Maria A. van Noordwijk

SUMMARY

Primate life histories are among the slowest of all mammals, and those of great apes are the slowest among primates. Because humans show a further slowing down in some aspects of their life history, study of primate life histories is pertinent to the understanding of human life history. Slow life history influences behavior both directly and indirectly, by affecting the relative duration of components of the immature period. Among primates, slow life histories are characterized by a disproportional shortening of the relative duration of gestation, leading to greater vulnerability to infanticide by males. These direct and indirect effects on behavior may have selected for cognitively rich behavioral solutions.

We also draw attention to the increasingly well-documented correlation between slow life histories and large brain size. Demographic models have been fairly successful in explaining life history variation across taxa, but they ignore this correlation, which may explain the reduced growth and reproduction of some lineages. We explore several hypotheses developed to explain the correlation between brain size and life history, and we suggest that these ideas can be integrated into a single framework. On the one hand, the development of larger adult brains inevitably imposes a developmental cost on the organism, usually in terms of delayed maturity; this cost must be offset by fitness benefits, usually improved adult survival and therefore longer reproductive life. On the other hand, in species with slower life history, selection often favors larger brain size. We examine the relationship between this approach and the main competing models (such as the Grandmother and the Embodied Capital hypotheses) to explain the evolution of human life histories.

The huge variability of both mammalian and bird life histories can be arranged on a fast-slow continuum (Saether 1988; Promislow and Harvey 1990; Bennett and Owens 2002). Although position on the continuum is correlated with body size, the continuum itself is retained if the effect of body size is removed (see also Hawkes, chapter 4, this volume). Among mammals, primates have slow life histories (Read and Harvey 1989), which means that they mature late, have relatively low birthrates after long gestation, give birth to single young, and have long life expectancies as adults, especially when corrected for the possible confounding effects of body size. Among primates, great apes have particularly slow life histories. For instance, the orangutan (*Pongo abelii, P. pygmaeus*) has the latest age of first reproduction and the longest interbirth interval of any nonhuman primate (Robson, van Schaik, and Hawkes, chapter 2, this volume) and is among the slowest of all extant mammals. Human age of first reproduction and maximum lifespan are even later and longer, respectively, than those of great apes (Hawkes et al. 1998; Blurton Jones, Hawkes, and O'Connell 1999).

Insights into the determinants of life history variation among primates, and perhaps great apes in particular, should also enhance our understanding of humans. In this chapter, we place hypotheses for the derived features of human life history (Hawkes et al. 1998; Kaplan et al. 2000; Lancaster et al. 2000; see also Hawkes, chapter 4, this volume) into a broader primate context.

General life history explanations are based on demographic variables and focus on optimizing developmental and reproductive schedules in the face of externally imposed mortality rates (see Charnov 1993; Kozlowski and Weiner 1997; Hawkes, chapter 3, this volume). Charnov's demographic life history model combines the power of classic life history theory with the existence of lawlike allometric relationships between body size and relevant variables such as production. The production function has a 3/4 exponent and a constant (A), which varies between taxa. During immaturity, the production is channeled into growth; after maturity, it is channeled into reproduction. Despite its simplicity, the model elegantly explains much of the taxonomic variation in life history, and broad comparative tests have generally supported it (Purvis and Harvey 1995). The presence of the invariants proposed by the model has been questioned (Nee et al. 2005), but their values as predicted by Charnov's model are found to hold for humans (Hawkes et al. 1998) and a select set of primate species (Alvarez 2000). Hawkes (chapter 4, this volume) provides a concise overview of Charnov's model.

The present chapter has two goals. The first is to draw attention to important correlates of slow life histories with respect to behavior, cognitive abilities, and brain size, which apply to primates in general and should therefore be relevant to understanding humans. Our second goal is to explain the correlated evolution between life history and brain size and therefore cognitive abilities. Many ideas, in a research tradition separate from the one that spawned the demographic life history models, have been offered to explain this correlation. They were developed to explain the correlation between brain size and life-history pace, which is now well documented in primates (Allman, McLaughlin, and Hakeem 1993; Ross and Jones 1999; Deaner, Barton, and van Schaik 2003). We call them biological models because they focus on particular biological processes (explained in detail below) that link brain size to the duration of the developmental period or total lifespan.

Some reconciliation between these two independent approaches is required. One good reason to explore their compatibility is that the demographic model leaves some things unexplained. In particular, it predicts the relationships between production and body size but does not explain why these relationships vary so much, both between and within lineages. More specifically, the demographic model is consistent with the observation that primate growth rates are generally less than half of those in other mammals (for example, Case 1978) but does not explain this, nor does it explain why there is such variability in growth rates among primate species (for example, Leigh 2001). Aware of this incompleteness, Charnov and Berrigan (1993:193) suggested that primate biologists explore why this is, although they also suggested to look elsewhere than to the brain: "Primate biologists seem (to us) to be obsessed with the benefits of large brains."

The biological hypotheses examined here may therefore complement the demographic model (or models, if some modified version turns out to be more successful; for example, Kozlowski and Weiner [1997]), especially because they may explain a major input variable of the demographic model (parameter [A] in Charnov [1993]). We will present empirical evidence in favor of these hypotheses, which can be integrated into a single framework. We do not attempt here to compare this framework formally with the demographic model, but we do briefly examine the implications for our understanding of the origins of human life history.

BEHAVIORAL CORRELATES OF SLOW LIFE HISTORY

Stearns (1992:210) remarks that the constraints imposed by life history on behavioral evolution "are not surprising enough to catalyse interest." Up to a point, that is true: the consequences of life history differences—for instance, having large litters (of usually altricial young) instead of a single precocial offspring—are, in themselves, trivial and mapping them is straightforward. However, these consequences may add up to produce major differences between lineages in social organization. Exploring the behavioral correlates and consequences of slow life history is especially interesting because of the light it might shed on primate and human evolution.

Slow life history is expected to produce some systematic effects, which could modify behaviors found in animals across the life history spectrum and call forth behaviors peculiar to species with slow life histories (compare Kappeler, Pereira, and van Schaik 2003). The effects come in two main classes: the direct consequences of longer life expectancy, longer development periods, and lower demographic turnover and the indirect consequences of changes in the relative duration of developmental phases. We will discuss them in turn.

The direct consequences are varied. Slow life history should affect the costs of behavioral acts, lead to more time before maturity is reached, influence the local demographic situation, and increase the probability of encountering drastic environmental change. First, the costs of any behavioral act should be affected by life expectancy at the time. Animals with short life expectancies may be expected to accept higher mortality risks attached to fitness-enhancing behaviors (Janson 2003) as a result of high opportunity costs associated with postponing them, whereas those with slow life histories may be more conservative or risk-averse in their behaviors. Such risk aversion may be expressed in any behavior involving mortality risk, such as predation avoidance or escalated fighting. Consequently, species with slow life history should be more likely to follow behavioral tactics that reduce predation risk, such as grouping, vigilance behavior, and avoidance of high-risk micro-habitats. Janson (2003) suggests that the counterintuitive positive correlation between group size and body size in primates is due to the life history effect. Living in groups, especially if they are stable, is bound to produce greater social complexity, whereas a greater emphasis on predation avoidance inevitably affects food intake, thus reducing growth and reproduction.

Likewise, all other things being equal, an animal with a long life expectancy should avoid risky escalated fights if there is a chance that the benefits can be reaped at some future moment without such high risks. For instance, violent takeovers by outsider males have never been recorded for mountain gorillas (*Gorilla g. beringei* [Watts 2000]), whereas they are not uncommon in the faster-living Thomas langur (*Presbytis thomasi*), despite basically similar social organization (Steenbeek 2000). Compared with animals with shorter life expectancy, slow-living ones are generally more likely to go through much more elaborate assessment mechanisms before fighting erupts and to threaten rather than fight, thus finding nonviolent solutions to conflicts. This escalation avoidance may also impose greater cognitive demands.

Second, animals with slower life history have longer developmental periods and therefore more time available to explore their habitat and gain experience before breeding. They also have greater opportunity to form long-term relationships in which costly acts of the same modality are reciprocated or those of different modalities are interchanged (for example, agonistic support for the same support returned or for grooming or tolerance [de Waal 1992]). Slow life history, then, may favor investment in learning (see below) and increase the potential for more elaborate social interactions and long-term relationships. To the extent that socially biased learning of ecological and social skills enhances fitness, slow life history may also favor more tolerant social relationships in which such socially biased acquisition is more likely (van Schaik, van Noordwijk, and Nunn 1999).

A third direct impact of slow life histories is on the demographic situation, affecting turnover of breeding slots and operational sex ratios. Because slow life history is accompanied by lower mortality and, consequently, lower turnover of suitable social positions, we should expect greater competition or queuing for these positions. In pair-living territorial birds, the difficulty of finding a place to settle has favored staying in the natal territory and "helping at the nest" (Bennett and Owens 2002). In turn, this may have favored the evolution of decision-making mechanisms that are more conditional with respect to choices about staying, breeding, helping, allying with relatives, and so on. Similar patterns are expected in pair-living primates. In addition, all other things being equal, female breeding rates slow down more than male breeding potential among species with slow-paced life histories. As a result, the ratio of males ready to mate to females ready to mate (the operational sex ratio) tends to be more male-biased in species with slow life history. We should therefore expect more potential for male-male competition and harassment of females (Smuts and Smuts 1993), as well as, potentially, the presence of cognitively demanding solutions to these conflicts (for example, association and coalitions with protectors).

Finally, the longer an animal's life, the more likely it is to encounter some drastic change in its abiotic, biotic, or social environment. If flexible behavioral responses to these changes (general learning ability, allowing for rapid conditioning, capacious memory, or some form of more advanced reasoning) improve the chances of surviving them, one expects selection to favor increased cognitive abilities in longer-lived animals (Allman, McLaughlin, and Hakeem 1993).

The effects of life history reviewed above are direct, but there are also indirect effects, acting through changes in the duration of relevant stages. It appears that, at least among primates, the slowdown of life history phases is not proportional for all stages of development. Analyses based on species values indicated that as primate life history slows down, gestation becomes an increasingly small fraction of the total prereproductive span whereas the postnatal period of immaturity becomes an increasingly large fraction. When analyses were repeated, using independent contrasts to avoid the possible effects of phylogenetic nonindependence (Nunn and Barton 2001), the proportional duration of gestation decreased significantly with a slowdown in life history (figure 5.1a); as a result, its mirror image, postnatal immaturity, increased significantly, although the proportional duration of neither lactation nor juvenility plus adolescence shows a clear change (figure 5.1b, c).

That gestation becomes proportionately shorter with an overall slowdown in life history can perhaps be attributed to strong physical constraints on the size of infants at birth. Under Charnov's model, we would have expected that the relative duration of gestation plus lactation would increase, because slower life history generally means larger mothers and larger mothers take longer to produce young that are a constant proportion of their body size (Charnov 1993; see also Hawkes, chapter 4, this volume). However, we find no change among the primate data (independent contrasts) in the relative duration of dependence on the mother (gestation plus lactation). Because of limited statistical power, though, this negative result must be considered preliminary. Another interpretation of the whole pattern is that slow life history is accompanied by a greater need to learn vital skills before the offspring is mature. This is discussed in more detail below.

Regardless of the explanation, a striking consequence of the differential slowdown of gestation and postnatal phases with a general slowdown of life history is that lactation/gestation ratios become increasingly high, a result that also holds after controlling for phylogenetic nonindependence through independent contrasts (figure 5.2; compare van Schaik and Deaner 2003). This ratio is a good predictor of risk of infanticide, not only across orders of mammals but also among primates (van Schaik 2000). The risk of infanticide is likely to have produced year-round male-female association in primates (van Schaik and Kappeler 1997), as well as female sexual counterstrategies (van Schaik, van Noordwijk, and Nunn 1999; van Schaik, Pradhan, and van Noordwijk 2004), and may have contributed greatly to social and cognitive complexity in primates.

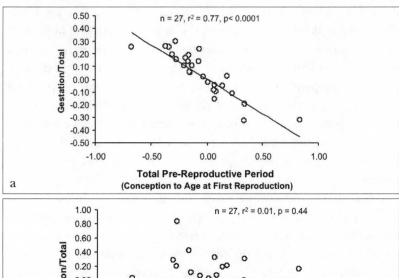

a

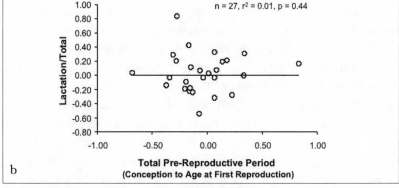

b

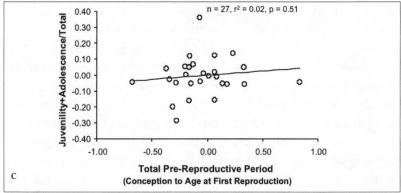

c

FIGURE 5.1

The relative duration of three stages of immaturity (5.1a, gestation; 5.1b, lactation; and 5.1c, juvenility plus adolescence) as a function of life history pace, indexed by age at first reproduction of the female (measured in months), across primate species. We included only information from long-term studies of wild primate populations. Shown are independent contrast values, calculated using Mesquite (Maddison and Maddison 2003). For the analysis, all branch lengths were set to 1 (raw species values show highly significant correlations, all P<0.01).

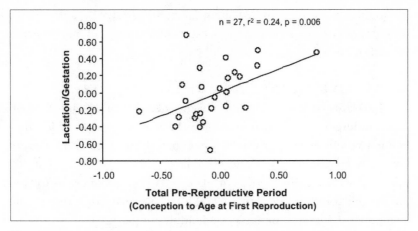

FIGURE 5.2

The lactation/gestation ratio as a function of life history pace, indexed by the age at first reproduction of the female, in the sample of primate species with reliable estimates of life history parameters. Shown are independent contrasts. Same conventions as in figure 5.1.

Overall, then, the effects of slower life history create conditions in which natural selection may favor greater cognitive abilities. The behavioral correlates of slow life history can be summarized as increased scope for gregariousness and long-term association among individuals and the resulting development of social relationships. The social interactions among these individuals may become more complex because of their tendency to avoid escalation of dangerous conflicts and because of increased mating conflict between the sexes, with resultant sexual coercion and possible female counterstrategies. Longer dependency enables longer periods of exploration and learning, which, in turn, may allow the evolution of cognitively more demanding ecologies (Deaner, Barton, and van Schaik 2003). The sum total of these effects and correlates is that animals with slow life histories have, on average, far greater opportunity to benefit from cognitively complex (conditional) behavioral strategies, including those that involve social manipulation.

It is, therefore, not entirely coincidental that many long-lived organisms show complex behavior and that these same organisms tend to be large-brained. Viewed in this light, humans are simply an extreme expression of a general pattern in nature, and some of our derived behavioral features, for instance, our general risk avoidance or complex social life, can be seen as a straightforward consequence of having the slowest life history among extant terrestrial mammals. We will now discuss the relationship between life history and one aspect of behavior, cognition.

COGNITIVE CORRELATES OF LIFE HISTORY

Biologists have long entertained the idea that brains and lifespan have undergone correlated evolution (Friedenthal 1910), which they tended to interpret as a direct physiological effect of brain size on longevity (Sacher 1959). Modern life history theory suggests that lifespan is just one of the various correlated components of life history, so the correlation could be with general life history pace or with separate components (developmental period, adult lifespan).

Theoreticians have generally been dismissive of a possible causal relationship (Harvey and Read 1988; Harvey and Purvis 1999) because it seemed like a special case alternative to the emerging broad demographic theory that emphasized the role of unavoidable mortality. They could do this more easily because the correlation between brain size and lifespan could potentially be a byproduct of the correlation between body size and lifespan (Economos 1980b; see also Prothero and Jürgens 1987).

Nonetheless, biologists and biological anthropologists have continued to argue in favor of correlated evolution between brain size and slow life history. In a study of primates, Allman, McLaughlin, and Hakeem (1993; Allman 1999) controlled for the possibility that the correlation between brain size and slow life history could be a byproduct of the errors in body size estimation, whereas Ross and Jones (1999) controlled for possible phylogenetic nonindependence. Both still found the correlation. Deaner, Barton, and van Schaik (2003) controlled for both these possible problems and also still found the correlation. They also controlled for possible effects of social (group size) and ecological (ranging, diet) variables and found that these were not responsible for the correlation between brains and life history. Barton (1999) and Allman (1999) also suggest that the influences of brains and socioecology on life history were independent.

More detailed analyses are needed to examine whether particular components of life history show a stronger relationship with brain size than others.

Direct developmental correlates of large brain size exist. Neonate mammals with larger brains are born after longer gestation, if the effects of body size are removed (Pagel and Harvey 1988). Therefore, growing an infant with a larger brain takes longer than growing a smaller-brained infant of similar body size. Barrickman and colleagues (2005) have recently confirmed this finding in primates, using independent contrasts. With respect to postnatal development, data on nonhuman primates show variable, interspecific correlations between brain size and age at first reproduction or other developmental landmarks, depending on the data set included, the taxa involved, the methods used, and the weighing of more recent or more ancient contrasts (Barton 1999; Ross and Jones 1999; Deaner, Barton, and van Schaik 2003; Ross 2003, 2004). In a large sample of primates, Ross and Jones (1999) found that juvenility is longer and age at first reproduction delayed in larger-brained organisms, after controlling for body size (see also Ross 2003, 2004; but see Deaner, Barton, and van Schaik 2003). Barrickman and colleagues (2005) found the same in a new sample containing only data gleaned from long-term field studies. Indeed, in a multiple regression analysis of twenty-seven independent contrasts, adult brain size predicted age at first reproduction far better than adult body size. The component of immaturity that was most responsive to brain size was juvenility plus adolescence, instead of lactation. Barrickman and colleagues (2005) showed that the duration of juvenility is correlated much more tightly (and significantly) with the amount of postnatal brain growth than with the amount of postnatal body growth. As a result, larger-brained primates mature later than smaller-brained ones, especially because they take longer after weaning (even though brain growth is largely complete by weaning in many species [R. Martin 1983, 1996; Leigh 2001]).

Regarding the correlation of increased brain size with adult performance, Deaner, Barton, and van Schaik (2003) found a significantly positive correlation between brain size and longevity, after controlling for body size and phylogenetic nonindependence (but see Ross and Jones 1999). In the small, wild-only sample, Barrickman and colleagues (2005) also found significantly positive correlations, using both maximum adult lifespan (maximum lifespan—age at first reproduction) and adult life expectancy (at age at first reproduction).

No study has found a positive effect of brain size on reproductive rates.

Deaner, Barton, and van Schaik (2003; van Schaik and Deaner 2003) extended this analysis to other mammalian orders as well but found significant correlations only in orders with relatively large brains, such as carnivores, cetaceans, and primates. However, moving to the highest level, that of eutherian orders, they still found a strong relationship between brain size and life history (from data compiled by Austad and Fischer 1992), provided that one extreme outlier was removed—bats, the only mammalian order with true flight (see Safi, Seid, and Dechmann [2005] for the flight-related selection on brain size in this group). The same relationship appears to hold across mammals as a whole. Moreover, recent and ongoing work even finds support in birds (Iwaniuk and Nelson 2003; Isler and van Schaik 2005).

Independent evidence for a link between brain size and life history comes from studies of domestication. Domestication generally produces increased growth rates and reproduction among adults (that is, a general increase in production function or a higher [A] [Charnov 1993]), in most cases because those are features directly targeted by the artificial selection. It is well known that domesticated animals have smaller brains than their wild ancestors, even though they have often ended up having larger adult body size (Kruska 1996; Zohary, Tchernov, and Horwitz 1998). This systematic effect of domestication is in keeping with the idea that faster life histories are inevitably accompanied by smaller brains.

Consistent with the proposed link, there are direct developmental correlates of large brain size. First, evidence from studies of aging indicates that the species with the most gradual aging-related increase in mortality (that is, those with the longest potential lifespans) are those with the largest brains (Promislow 1991; Ricklefs and Scheuerlein 2001): larger-brained animals are designed by selection to live longer. Second, developmental markers, such as patterns of dental eruption, show a tighter link with adult brain mass than with adult body mass in primates (Smith and Tompkins 1995; Godfrey et al. 2001), perhaps reflecting a mechanistic link between dental development (which is expected to be slower when the ability to feed and forage independently develops more slowly) and brain development (both develop from the neural plate [Lumsden 1988; Chai et al. 2000]).

In sum, the evidence for a link between life history pace and brain size and therefore cognitive abilities has now become too strong to ignore, and some reconciliation with the prevailing demographic theory of life history is needed. Either this theory can accommodate this correlation, or it needs to be amended.

EXISTING HYPOTHESES FOR CORRELATIONS BETWEEN BRAIN SIZE AND LIFE HISTORY

We will now briefly discuss the many ideas that have been proposed to explain correlated evolution between life history and brains and, as a consequence, cognitive abilities. These ideas have been organized and reviewed by Deaner, Barton, and van Schaik (2003; see also Ross and Jones 1999). We will ignore the hypotheses that posit direct physiological constraints of brains on lifespan, because they lack supporting evidence (Deaner, Barton, and van Schaik 2003). After reviewing these ideas, we will present our own synthesis, based on the allocation/trade-off perspective that combines many of these ideas into a single hypothesis.

We begin with one hypothesis that aims to explain longer lifespan in larger-brained organisms, and then we focus on three ideas proposed to explain the slowdown in development linked to larger brains. The latter differ from the predominantly demographic approach to life history in that they posit specific processes that link brain size to variation in development rather than to probabilities of survival.

Cognitive Buffer

Several authors have argued that increased (mature) brain size positively affects adult reproduction and survival (Allman 1999; Deaner, Barton, and van Schaik 2003) because it imparts better learning abilities and greater behavioral flexibility. Conversely, enhanced cognition can also be seen as buffering animals against unexpected ecological changes, which become more likely as animals are longer-lived.

Maturational Constraints

Large-brained organisms must develop slowly, according to this hypothesis, as a result of the time it takes for actively developing brains to reach functional maturity, even after mass growth has been completed (Deaner, Barton, and van Schaik 2003). The assumption is that immature nervous systems cannot function at the adult level, even in the face of adequate amounts of external stimulation.

Very small brains, such as those of the popular nematode *Caenorhabditis elegans*, are specified in detail by the genetic program. As brains increase in size, however, the developmental specifications must be increasingly open-ended (Deacon 1997), perhaps, in particular, for cortically mediated functions (Parker and McKinney 1999:320), forcing a lengthy period of adaptive modification in response to external inputs and interactions with other structures. Because more complex patterns of behavior and neural connectivity are built on simpler ones, complex behavior cannot emerge immediately (for example, Elman et al. 1996; Quartz and Sejnowski 1997; see Allman 1999), and larger brains take more time to mature than smaller ones.

This hypothesis explains why motor patterns, including many manipulative skills in humans (for instance, reaching, grasping, and tapping), develop progressively throughout juvenility (reviewed in Kuhtz-Buschbeck et al. 1998; Lemon 1999; and Schneiberg et al. 2002). For example, rapid hand movements increase in speed with age (Pisev 1985; Mueller and Loemberg 1992; Kuhtz-Buschbeck et al. 1998; Largo et al. 2001). Importantly, these motor patterns appear to emerge independently from learning or training (Mueller and Loemberg 1992), a conclusion also supported by the finding that many skills emerge at approximately the same age across individuals of a given species (reviewed by Parker and McKinney 1999), for instance, language in humans. Given the importance of motor skills to daily activities, from foraging to locomotion and social interactions, the observed delay in neurological maturation should result in a subsequent delay in overall development.

In the cerebral cortices of the primates examined thus far (macaques, marmosets, and humans), synaptic density peaks sometime after birth but is then pruned and reaches adult levels around puberty (Bourgeois 1997; Huttenlocher and Dabholkar 1997). The process of myelination continues long after the brain has reached adult size. It starts with subcortical structures and continues up through the highest cortical layers, also ending at approximately reproductive maturity in the primates studied thus far (humans [Giedd et al. 1996]; macaques [Gibson 1991]). Functional maturation of cortical areas in humans continues even past the age of first reproduction (Gogtay et al. 2004).

This hypothesis also explains both the timing and the amount of play in immature primates. Play in mammals reflects periods of brain differentiation. Byers and Walker (1995) suggested that one main function of play is "adaptive modification of the developing neuromuscular system" and that play is therefore timed to occur during the sensitive periods of synaptogenesis in the central nervous system (CNS) and of neuromuscular differentiation. Fairbanks (2000) evaluated this hypothesis for primates and found that the various kinds of play tended to peak during the sensitive periods of the relevant processes (for instance, activity play during peak cerebellar synaptogenesis, improving motor coordination), when primates are maximally responsive to external stimulation of the relevant neural pathways and selective synaptic pruning of unused pathways takes place (see also Lewis and Barton 2004).

Rates of play tend to peak when learning abilities are still immature (Fairbanks 2000), suggesting that play is not involved in the actual maturation of learning mechanisms or particular skills but rather prepares the brain for these capacities to emerge, inevitably leading to a delay in the emergence of skillful behaviors. Immature primates spend a remarkable amount of time in play (social, motor, or object-oriented): for instance, up to 25 percent of time among vervet infants (*Cercopithecus aethiops*) (Fairbanks 2000) and around 50 percent in 1- to 2-year-old wild orangutans (van Noordwijk and van Schaik 2005). Lewis (2003) recently compared play patterns across a number of primate species sampled using identical methods, and her data indicate a positive relationship between play activity and brain size (figure 5.3; compare Iwaniuk, Nelson, and Pellis 2001).

Skill Learning
Also known as the "Needing-to-Learn" hypothesis (Ross and Jones 1999), this idea argues that maturation is delayed in large-brained organisms because they need to learn vital skills for adult performance during development and that any attempt to reproduce earlier would be doomed to failure. The reasons for the delay in maturation are

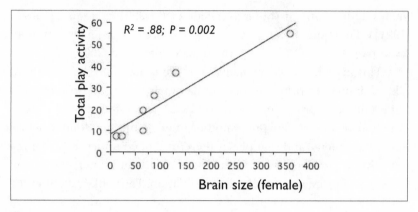

FIGURE 5.3

Time devoted to play in relation to brain size, from systematic observations using identical methods in a number of primate species. From data presented by Lewis (2000).

the attainment of specific skills, whereas under the Maturational Constraints hypothesis the delay is due to slow maturation of the nervous system, regardless of the details of the experience.

Following earlier allusions in the literature that higher juvenile mortality may be due to their inefficient foraging (Lack 1954; Ashmole 1963), MacLean (1986) and J. Brown (1987) specifically invoked lower foraging efficiency of juvenile birds as an explanation for delayed maturity. The basic argument is that improved survival and reproductive performance during adulthood compensate for delayed maturity caused by long periods of skill acquisition. These skills are usually thought to concern ecological performance, especially feeding (or also predation avoidance and nest building), although they may also refer to parenting or social skills.

Figure 5.4 (inspired by J. Brown 1987:figure 5.4) provides a graphic illustration of this idea, applied to mammals: weaning is possible after the immature's foraging efficiency exceeds a threshold value (W), and successful breeding is possible after threshold R is passed. Therefore, immatures can reach adulthood at different ages, depending on the age trajectory of foraging efficiency. The latter is a function of both an external (food types and abundance) component and an internal (skill learning) one, which, in turn, depend on the complexity of the diet (the extent of reliance on extractive foraging or capture after pursuit and the difficulty of locating and processing food items).

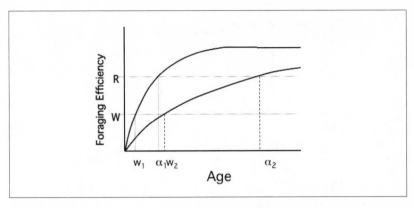

FIGURE 5.4

The Skill Learning hypothesis illustrated. Different age trajectories of foraging efficiency cross the threshold values for weaning (W) and breeding (R) at different ages (indicated by the dashed and dotted vertical lines: w = age at weaning, and a = age at first reproduction). Variation in the age trajectories can be caused by variation in food abundance or in dietary complexity (compare Brown 1987:figure 5.4).

Figure 5.4 shows two age trajectories; the upper curve reflects rapid learning of skills, high abundance of easy-to-acquire food, or a combination of the two (ignoring possible limitations due to narrow norms of reaction).

Numerous naturalistic observations of juvenile incompetence support the plausibility of this hypothesis, especially the ecological version. Lower foraging efficiency among immatures is commonly recorded among birds (Marchetti and Price 1989; Wunderle 1991), carnivores (Caro and Hauser 1992), cetaceans (Baird 2000), and primates (Boinski and Fragaszy 1989). Immature primates and several birds also tend to have so-called intermediate diets, differing from adult diets in excluding food items that are hard to obtain or to process (Pereira and Altmann 1985; Marchetti and Price 1989; Yoerg 1994).

Because of the widespread presence of these effects in birds, which generally reach adult body size around fledging (for example, Marchetti and Price 1989; Wunderle 1991), reduced juvenile foraging efficiency must reflect, at least in part, lack of experience instead of just smaller size and strength. The most convincing evidence that the acquisition of foraging skills may determine age at maturity comes from comparisons of closely related species (figure 5.5). MacLean

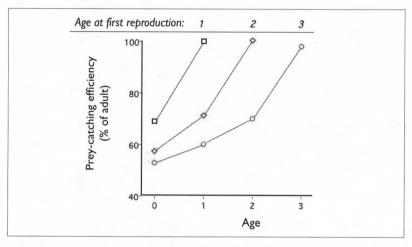

FIGURE 5.5

Age at first reproduction for three species of gull, in relation to the age trajectory of prey-catching efficiency of immatures (relative to adults; efficiency is measured as intervals between successful catches; after MacLean 1986). Note that reproduction starts at the age when adult-level efficiency is reached. The three species are Bonaparte's gull (Larus philadelphia), squares; ring-billed gull (L. delawarensis), diamonds; and herring gull (L. argentatus), circles.

(1986) showed that three species of gulls commence breeding when foraging efficiency reaches stable values, which happens at different ages.

Janson and van Schaik (1993) reviewed the literature on foraging in juvenile primates and concluded that lower efficiency among them was due more to smaller size than imperfect skills, throwing doubt on the explanatory value for primates of this hypothesis. It is most appropriate for species with complex foraging niches, such as those involving extraction and extensive food processing before ingestion of some of the diet, sometimes involving tool use. Therefore, it should apply especially to great apes, which have been characterized as occupying a cognitive foraging niche (Byrne 1997; see also van Schaik 2004). Indeed, the most complex techniques take long to mature in gorillas (Byrne and Byrne 1993), chimpanzees (Matsuzawa 1994; Boesch and Boesch-Achermann 2000), and orangutans (Fox, Sitompul, and van Schaik 1999). The slow attainment of competence may be due to the strong social component: learning often shows an alteration between periods of observational learning, as shown by the close attention juvenile apes pay to the processing techniques of older role models (for example, Myowa-Yamakoshi and Matsuzawa 2000), and periods of individual practice. Not surprisingly, skills practiced only after adolescence, such as group hunting by male chimpanzees, reach stable values even later in life (Boesch and Boesch-Achermann 2000).

This hypothesis is best tested in animals that are solitary during their active period, because in gregarious animals, ecologically incompetent immatures can parasitize on the knowledge of the spatiotemporal food distribution possessed by other group members. Krakauer (2005) conducted an experimental study of skill learning during development in captive aye-ayes (*Daubentonia madagascariensis*). Like great apes, aye-ayes are solitary and occupy a complex, extractive foraging niche. They engage in so-called "tap" foraging (Erickson 1991), locating larvae in wood through the acoustic feedback of rapidly tapping on the surface with their elongated finger. After locating the larvae, a small hole is gnawed and larvae extracted with that same finger. They also have an extremely slow developmental pace for a lemur, characterized by a long gestation period (167 days [Glander 1994]), a late age at weaning (well over one year [Feistner and Ashbourne 1994]), a late age at first reproduction, and a long interbirth interval (>4 years and ~2.7 years, respectively; captive values calculated from Feistner and Lind [2000]).

As predicted, immature aye-ayes forage less efficiently than experienced adults, and tap-foraging efficiency is constrained by lack of experience but not by size or strength limitations (Krakauer 2005). This study found that immatures require repeated exposure to extractive tasks in order to develop adult-level efficiency. Results also indicate that social learning mechanisms (including local enhancement and social facilitation, food sharing, and possibly observation) promote the development of tap-foraging skills (see Krakauer 2005).

In sum, the primate data indicate that immature primates must learn skills that are important for survival.

Brain Malnutrition Avoidance

Janson and van Schaik (1993) proposed that delaying maturity by reducing growth rates actually may, in some conditions, improve the probability of surviving to maturity, to the extent that it offsets the negative fitness effect of the time delay. Reducing juvenile growth rates reduces the risk of starvation and, consequently, mortality. The model assumes that other sources of mortality for immatures are sufficiently low to allow this lengthening to work. In particular, unavoidable predation is strongly reduced because of group living, generally arboreal habitat, and occupation by immatures of safe spatial positions and microhabitats (see also van Schaik and Deaner 2003; compare Janson 2003).

The main problem with this hypothesis is that somatic growth rates are not constant and starvation can be avoided by regulating them up or down in response to fluctuations in food abundance (for example, Bogin 1988), although this flexibility is not unlimited. This weakness is avoided by a more recently proposed variant, the Brain Malnutrition Avoidance hypothesis (Deaner, Barton, and van Schaik 2003), which is built on the well-documented vulnerability of the growing and differentiating brain to starvation as a result of inflexibility in brain growth rates among mammals (Tanner 1986; Schew and Ricklefs 1998; compare Nowicki, Searcy, and Peters 2002). Low rates of brain growth help to avert brain starvation, with its attendant cognitive deficits. Because body size must maintain some proportionality with brain size, somatic growth must lag behind as well. This hypothesis, then, assumes that conservative growth improves the probability of surviving to maturity while fully competent.

The Brain Malnutrition Avoidance hypothesis is consistent with the observation that rates of primate brain growth vary with the predictability of food supply. Growth rates are generally higher during gestation and lactation (R. Martin 1983, 1996) than during juvenility and generally drop following weaning, when inexperienced juveniles must support themselves. As expected, brain growth rates remain higher in species in which adults continue to provision immatures after weaning (Leigh 2004). The rate of brain growth is extremely high in young birds relative to mammals, perhaps because both bird parents usually provision and at exceedingly high rates compared with mammals (Drent and Daan 1980).

This hypothesis also explains intraspecific (individual or interpopulation) variation in development rate in relation to food abundance, if we are willing to assume that in periods or habitats with consistently greater food abundance, the probability of brain starvation is reduced and therefore brain growth rates can safely be set at higher levels. The faster growth and development found among zoo animals can be explained in the same way.

Relations among these Hypotheses

Because these ideas were proposed or applied to explain the same set of phenomena, their main predictions are, obviously, similar. Moreover, the selective benefits they are thought to provide are nonexclusive. Here, we must briefly examine the relations between the three ideas that purport to explain delayed maturity in ways other than through lower adult mortality and therefore longer adult lifespan. Brain Malnutrition Avoidance is not at odds with the other selective agents; it merely ascribes the slow pace of development to the low growth rate imposed by the avoidance of energy deficits to the growing brain, which is likely to lead to lack of physical maturation of the brain or a deficit in specific skills. It does, however, make one unique prediction—that larger-brained species should have at least equal probability of reaching adulthood relative to their smaller-brained relatives, despite the fact that it generally takes the larger-brained species longer. Unfortunately, there have been no studies yet to test this prediction, so no verdict is possible.

The two others, Maturational Constraints and Skill Learning, show great overlap, but the critical difference is that, according to Skill Learning, essential skills for successful reproduction do not reach adult levels until around the age at first reproduction, whereas according to Maturational Constraints, the delay is due to general immaturity, perhaps reflected in overall lack of integration and motivation or persistence. The critical prediction of the Skill Learning hypothesis is that ecological competence does not plateau until nearly the age at first reproduction.

When do learned skills mature in primates? In most primates, juveniles seem reasonably competent, with smaller size (instead of poorer skill) causing less foraging efficiency than found in adults (Boinski and Fragaszy 1989; Janson and van Schaik 1993), although some skills are known to mature much later (for instance, hunting skills in male chimpanzees [Boesch and Boesch-Achermann 2000]). Perhaps it is more interesting to examine this question in the most solitary primates, in which immatures less skilled in finding food cannot simply follow the

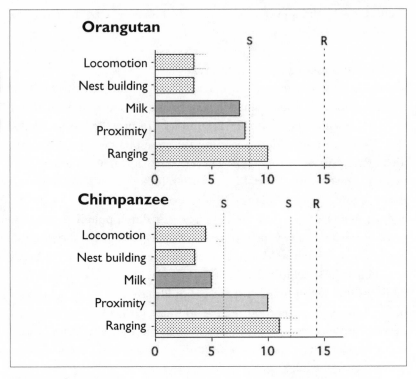

FIGURE 5.6

Comparison of developmental landmarks of wild orangutans (van Noordwijk and van Schaik 2005) and chimpanzees (Pusey 1983, 1990; Watts and Pusey 1993): s = birth of next sibling; r = age at first reproduction. Proximity refers to spending more than 50 percent of the time near the mother (<10 m in orangutans and <15 m in chimpanzees).

lead of others. Van Noordwijk and van Schaik (2005) report on a study of orangutan development at Suaq Balimbing, a Sumatran swamp forest with the most gregarious orangutan population on record (van Schaik 2004). Weaning age was estimated to be about 7 years, and the interbirth interval was estimated to be at least 8.2 years, several years longer than that of the chimpanzees (Pusey 1983, 1990; Watts and Pusey 1993). Figure 5.6 shows that orangutan immatures reached behavioral developmental markers at very similar ages to chimpanzees. Immatures of both species start to range independently only when they are around 10–11 years old. For both species, this is several years before either sex reaches adult body size and age of first reproduction.

The only real difference between the two species, then, is the age at weaning. We suggest that this is because chimpanzee mothers can afford ecologically to be accompanied by independent offspring while they have their next baby whereas orangutan mothers generally cannot (see van Noordwijk and van Schaik 2005 for details). It appears that the ability to select and process foods determines weaning age whereas skills at finding food or avoiding social risks (skills that can mature later in most gregarious species) determine complete independence. The data on aye-ayes, although collected in captivity, likewise suggest that their major food-processing skill (tap foraging) has reached adult skill levels around weaning age.

In summary, the results at hand suggest that food-processing skills have reached adult-level proficiency around weaning in most species, even though the juvenile period shows the strongest delay in species with larger brains. Even if other ecological skills mature later, they should delay maturity only in the most solitary species. If further detailed field studies confirm this preliminary conclusion, it appears that maturational constraints imposed by large brain size rather than by the time needed to learn essential skills are responsible for slow maturation among larger-brained primates.

HOW BRAINS AND LIFE HISTORY INTERACT: A SYNTHESIS

We have seen that a variety of biological hypotheses can potentially explain the observed correlation between brain size and life history pace but also that it is difficult to test them rigorously and decide between them. Here, we take an approach inspired by life history theory and the allocation trade-offs on which it is built, which can subsume most of the ideas presented above (compare Sacher 1975).

Brain tissue is metabolically among the most costly tissues in the body (Aiello and Wheeler 1995). In small-brained organisms, these costs may not reach quantitative values large enough to compete with the other targets for allocating limiting resources. As relative brain size increases, though, the brain inevitably usurps a greater proportion of the energy budget, gradually competing with other allocations, such as growth and reproduction, and eventually reaching a point where trade-offs between adult brain size and rates of growth and reproduction emerge. The brain's energy requirements are not a trivial proportion of the energy budget in larger-brained species: in chimpanzees, for instance, some 9 percent of resting metabolic rate goes to maintaining the brain (Leonard and Robertson 1992). Therefore, at least in taxa with relatively large brains, we cannot ignore the energy drain caused by the brain.

Now, suppose an organism increases its brain size relative to its ancestral state. All other things being equal, this organism must now bear some developmental cost imposed by the need to grow (and maintain) a larger brain, which, in organisms with single offspring, will generally be expressed in longer duration of immaturity. In general, then, we expect slower development in larger-brained organisms. This is, of course, what the data on primates confirm abundantly: controlling for body size, larger-brained species mature at a later age.

If this development cost applies, however, it must be offset by appreciable fitness benefits, or natural selection would not favor the brain increase (for example, Stearns 1992). The benefits can be of three kinds: improved probability of reaching adulthood, improved reproductive rates, or improved adult survival. The first prediction is that of the Brain Malnutrition Avoidance hypothesis, as yet untested. The second prediction is not met in primates, or mammals in general (Isler and van Schaik 2005), a finding that was not unexpected. However, the third benefit is both eminently plausible and, indeed, found to be universal, at least for primates, consistent with the Cognitive Buffer hypothesis.

This energetic perspective elegantly explains why mammals with larger brains mature more slowly but, once adult, live longer. If adult mortality is consistently reduced, we expect that selection would favor a design for increased longevity and that larger-brained organisms, over time, would also acquire increased maximum lifespan or longevity.

So far, we have only considered the effects of brain size on life history. However, all we have are correlations. We must also examine whether slower-paced life history can lead to larger brains. In interspecific correlations, the "causal" link can be direct or it can be indirect, in which changes in one variable favor evolutionary changes in the other variable. A direct effect of life history on brain size is not easily envisaged unless one posits a direct physiological link between them,

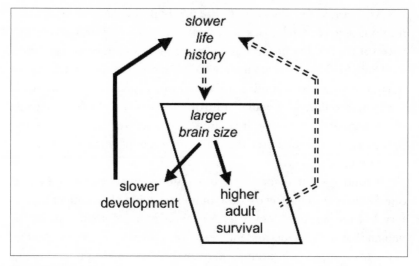

FIGURE 5.7

The feedback between life history pace and brain size, as argued in this chapter. A solid arrow indicates that a change in the source variable directly alters the variable at the end of the arrow. A dashed arrow indicates that a change in the source variable selectively favors a change in the target variable (provided that the benefit exceeds the development cost). The solid box indicates the subset of cases in which increased brain size actually enhances adult survival enough to compensate for the fitness imposed by slower development (in all other cases, selection will not favor the increase in brain size).

for which there is no evidence (see above). However, an indirect link is quite likely. Under slower life history, larger brain size may be selectively favored more strongly than under faster life history. First, as we argue above, slow life history per se may create various challenges that require cognitive solutions. Second, the benefit of increased brain size should be greater for long-lived organisms simply because they can benefit more from the same investment (the Delayed Benefits hypothesis of Deaner, Barton, and van Schaik [2003]). Finally, as adult lifespan increases, animals may have greater need to learn new skills because of changing environmental conditions or may draw benefits for longer from learning new skills (for example, Dukas 1998; Kaplan et al. 2000). The problem is that these benefits must be large enough to offset the direct costs of increased brain size, which may not always be the case.

As shown schematically in figure 5.7, both direct and indirect connections suggest a feedback loop between brain size and life history pace (of course, the positive feedback can go in both directions; compare Safi, Seid, and Dechmann [2005]). Among the species we can see today, the observed brain size and life history represent an equilibrium in which selection does not favor further increase in brain size, because the marginal benefits of increased adult survival or reproductive performance do not offset the marginal costs of increased development time.

A fundamental asymmetry is worth noting: a change in brain size, due to the brain's impact on development, should always affect life history, but the reverse is not true. Any change in the phenotype or the habitat that reduces unavoidable, extrinsic mortality will select for slower life history pace (Kirkwood and Austad 2000), and brain size change is only one of many such changes.

IMPLICATIONS FOR UNDERSTANDING HUMAN LIFE HISTORY

The presence of correlated evolution between brains and life histories has implications for our understanding of the evolution of human life histories. It seems that the demographic and biological approaches are compatible. The demographic approach explains the general pattern in life histories. The biological approach explains variation in the rate of development and reproduction (the production function in the demographic model), because energy allocation to the growing or mature brain necessitates a reduction in energy invested into these nonmaintenance functions.

This perspective may help us to place the main hypotheses for the evolution of human life history in context. The Grandmother hypothesis (Hawkes, chapter 4, and Blurton Jones, chapter 8, this volume) is built on Charnov's demographic model, arguing that reduced adult mortality led to later maturation and larger body size. The high birth rates of humans, relative to the other great apes, and our considerably increased maximum lifespan are ascribed to the switch in women around middle age from reproduction to allocare (midlife menopause). The only role for increased brain size is that it may have been instrumental in reducing adult mortality, resulting in later age at maturity and larger body size. If the model can ignore the effect of adult brain size on development time, this may be because the model makes comparisons with great apes, which are already large-brained, and because reliable provisioning of (prematurely) weaned juveniles by grandmothers may cancel any further slowdown due to the increase in brain size relative to the ancestral state of hominins.

The main competing model, the Embodied Capital hypothesis (Kaplan et al. 2000; Lancaster et al. 2000), is the Skill Learning hypothesis writ large. It suggests that extensive skill learning is required before reproduction is possible and that only massive adult-energy subsidies —in particular, by highly skilled, adult male hunters—make our long maturation demographically possible. As we note above, the data on nonhuman primates do not support this model, and we suggest that another, more general, model (Maturational Constraints) explains delayed maturation. Although a poor fit for nonhuman primates does not mean that the hypothesis cannot apply to humans, some studies on human skill development also find little support for it (Bliege Bird and Bird 2002; Blurton Jones and Marlowe 2002). Moreover, much of the general evidence in support of the Maturational Constraints hypothesis comes from humans.

A more quantitative approach is necessary to assess whether we need to insert the effects of larger brain size on development time and perhaps reproductive rate into the existing models to improve their predictive power. It is also possible, though, that the perspective based on the generally observed, correlated evolution between life history and brain size may, on its own, account for many of the changes observed during hominin evolution.

Species with larger brains show longer lifespan and longer periods of immaturity, and humans are no exception. Despite a threefold increase in our brain size, though, the developmental period in humans is slowed down relatively little compared with our great-ape relatives, and interbirth intervals have even decreased. The only way to make sense of these changes is to assume massive provisioning of immatures, which emerges as a critical human adaptation. The work reviewed here is silent on whether grandmothers, fathers, or still others did the provisioning.

Acknowledgments

We thank Rob Deaner, all the participants of the School of American Research advanced seminar, and especially Kristen Hawkes for valuable input, Tuck Finch for providing us with several relevant references, and Karin Isler for fruitful discussion.

6

Lactation, Complementary Feeding, and Human Life History

Daniel W. Sellen

SUMMARY

In this chapter, I review distinctive features of human lactation, highlight gaps in knowledge of nonhuman primate lactation, and draw conclusions about the adaptive significance of human complementary feeding. Breast milk nutrient composition does not indicate any special adaptations to adult diet or infant growth, and secretion rates conform to a pattern associated with reduced lactation stress and slow life history. Maternal daily costs of lactation are reduced in humans by mobilization of fat stores laid down in pregnancy, changes in physical activity level, and metabolic accommodation. Metabolic costs of maintenance, growth, and activity are also comparatively low in human infants. The scheduling of human weaning is unusually plastic, although the characteristics of young children suggest that the transition to adult foods evolved to occur over several years. Human infants outstrip the maternal supply of nutrients at about 6 months of age but are able to survive without breast milk at much younger ages and smaller body sizes than are other infant apes. Complementary feeding is probably a uniquely derived species characteristic that co-evolved with shifts in foraging, sharing, and food processing, underpinning an unusual capacity to reduce the length of exclusive lactation and transitional feeding without increasing juvenile mortality.

THE PROBLEM

The scheduling, duration, and physiology of lactation and the transition to weaning mediate several of the most important trade-offs in mammalian life history, such as those between current and future reproduction, number and quality of offspring, and body size and maturation. However, remarkably little work has been done to identify any phylogenetically distinctive features of human lactation and interpret them within an evolutionary framework linking shifts in foraging, care giving, and life history strategies. We do not fully understand the selection pressures that produced variation in the patterns of lactation and juvenile nutritional dependency seen across mammals, or the nature and extent of any differences between modern humans and other extant primates. The goals of this chapter are therefore to consider the complex trade-offs that likely shaped the evolution of lactation and weaning in mammals and to review comparative evidence that the scheduling and physiology of human lactation may be evolutionarily distinctive.

LACTATION IN MAMMALS: AN OVERVIEW

Before we can focus on a comparison of humans and other primates, it is helpful to consider the shared advantages of lactation to humans and other mammals and to identify the ancient, shared (that is, plesiomorphic) features of lactation biology.

Origin, Maintenance, Current Diversity

Lactation, the ability to secrete immunologically active and nutritious milk from ventral epidermal glands, is an ancient characteristic that evolved at the root of the adaptive radiation of mammals, probably between 210 and 190 MYA (Hartmann et al. 1984; Blackburn 1993; Luckett 1993; Cifelli et al. 1996). Its initial fitness advantages were likely three: early mammals could transfer the protective functions of a fully developed immune system across generations to benefit genetic relatives at a younger and more vulnerable age; they could reproduce successfully without access to an environment with special foods for their young; and they gained a new physiological tool for optimization of litter size, enabling titration of maternal investment across siblings in response to fluctuations in resource supply. Lactation physiology probably co-evolved with the efficient use of body fat and other stored nutrients in impoverished or disturbed Cenozoic habitats (Pond 1997).

Because all known mammals lactate, we cannot use the comparative method to test simple hypotheses about whether lactation per se is an adaptation. All extant species have retained both postnatal juvenile dependence on lactation and the ability of females to lactate (Hartmann, Morgan, and Arthur 1986), suggesting that it confers enormous adaptive advantages. Lactation facilitates integration of many functional characteristics of the adult and juvenile phases and increases physiological and behavioral flexibility of both mothers and offspring. Many features of lactogenesis (Hartmann 1973; Fleet, Goode, and Hamon 1975) and milk immunological activity (Goldman, Chheda, and Garofalo 1998) are remarkably conserved across species.

Despite such general functional similarities, the significant diversity in species-specific characteristics of lactation biology reflects a complex evolutionary history of adaptive shifts in disease ecology, foraging strategy, and patterns of growth and development. Milk composition varies with maternal diet, physiology, patterns of nutrient transfer, and care behavior (Gittleman and Thompson 1988). Relative milk energy yield varies with litter size, mass, and suckling pattern (R. Martin 1984). The energy density of milk varies more than fifteenfold among species (Oftedal 1986). Although poorly studied across species, the immune components in milk appear to vary with disease risk (Goldman, Chheda, and Garofalo 1998).

Humans represent another unique species within this universe of variation, but just how unique is human lactation biology and how has it co-evolved with shifts in diet and life history? Are human infants peculiarly vulnerable to the trade-offs involved in the transition from milk to other foods, and, if so, what species-specific parental and caregiver adaptations have evolved to protect them (Trevathan and McKenna 1994; McKenna and Bernshaw 1995)? Our challenge is to understand the selective mechanisms through which changes in the scheduling, duration, and physiology of lactation have intimately linked the evolution of patterns of parental investment and juvenile development in mammalian lineages, including hominids.

Lactation and Life History: Some Definitions

Before examining human lactation and life history in comparative perspective, it is helpful to dispel some confusion about the terms used in biomedicine, anthropology, and zoology. In the biomedical literature, *infant* refers to an age category instead of a nutritional phase.[1] By convention, the zoological literature tends to describe mammalian postnatal life history as infant (nutritionally dependent and nonreproductive), juvenile (nutritionally independent but nonreproductive), and adult (nutritionally independent and reproductive) phases (Pereira and Altmann 1985; Pagel and Harvey 1993). In this scheme, *infant* can refer to a young mammal feeding only on milk, only on provisioned food, or on some combination of the two. This makes sense for species in which juveniles and adults forage alone and fully independent foraging develops more abruptly. Among social foragers and communal breeders, however, the criterion of nutritional independence becomes unhelpful in distinguishing the infant and juvenile phases.

Mammalian feeding transitions scaffold a range of physiological, anatomical, behavioral, and developmental changes across the life course. The postnatal life of a mammal can be divided more specifically into at least three feeding phases (figure 6.1):[2] a primary phase of "exclusive suckling," in which all nutrition is derived from maternal milk; a secondary phase of "transitional feeding," when nutrition is derived from some combination of maternal milk and other foods foraged by the infant, its parents, or allocarers; and a final "weanling" phase, when the juvenile must forage for itself and subsist on foods similar or identical to those selected by adults.

Figure 6.1 summarizes the most common sequence of events and phases in the feeding development of a typical mammal. Juvenile daily intake of energy and specific nutrients increases from birth (a). This increase is entirely due to greater milk intake during an initial period of *exclusive suckling*. The ingestion of foraged foods (b) marks the beginning of a *transitional feeding* period during which milk continues to contribute to nutrition and immune protection and juveniles can increase intakes beyond peak maternal milk production. As juveniles begin to derive nutrients more efficiently from the environment than from the nipple (because of some combination of increased compe-

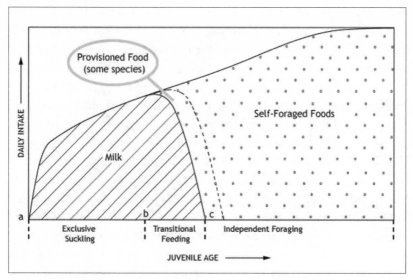

FIGURE 6.1

A simplified model of care and feeding in a generalized altricial mammal.

tency, decreased milk production, and increased maternal resistance to suckling), both the absolute and the proportional contributions of milk intake decrease until last suckling occurs (c). Note that the relative length of exclusive suckling (a–b) and transitional feeding (b–c) is generally reversed in precocious mammals such as primates or artiodactyls, which tend to have a long period of milk and a short period of mixed feeding. After weaning, further increase in total intake occurs by means of *independent foraging*. In a minority of species, juveniles may consume, both before and after weaning, provisioned foods for which mothers or allocarers have foraged.

For analysis of variation in the nature and duration of exclusive suckling and transitional feeding, we could construct several indicators, such as age at first ingestion of foods and age at last suckling. In theory, a suite of such indicators could be developed as biomarkers of the life history changes that occur during transitions between feeding phases. In practice, such indicators may have poor construct and/or measurement validity.[3] One key indicator, weaning, is a biologically significant event in a juvenile's life that marks the end of infancy.[4] For theoretical and comparative purposes, weaning is best defined as the cessation of maternal lactation investment in a specific offspring.[5] Last suckling would be the "gold standard" indicator of weaning, but observing this directly in the field for most species is very difficult.

Age at weaning has long been recognized both as a key intergenerational component of mammalian life history and as a maturational marker useful for comparative testing of evolutionary ecological hypotheses. In theory, the scheduling of weaning represents an evolutionary compromise between the point (from the mother's perspective) at which fitness costs of continued lactation (lost reproductive value) exceed fitness benefits (increased offspring survival and/or enhanced functional competence) and the point (from the infant's perspective) at which the increasing, relative fitness benefits of dietary independence exceed the decreasing, relative fitness benefits of taxing the mother's nutritional resources and time budget. Selection may result in age at weaning becoming more or less labile within species. On the one hand, age at weaning is an emergent feature of behavioral and physiological interactions between mothers and infants and should be exquisitely sensitive to local feeding and disease ecology. On the other hand, we can predict that reaction norms for age at weaning are under strong selection because fitness consequences of age at weaning are critical for both mother and offspring; also, the transition to weaning is tightly coordinated with other life history changes.

HUMAN LACTATION IN COMPARATIVE PERSPECTIVE

To develop predictions about what selective forces produce variation in lactation and transitional feeding patterns, we must consider separately the trade-offs involved for mothers and for infants. Mothers are born first and have evolved mechanisms for titration of reproductive effort in response to a rich suite of environmental factors (Hrdy 1999). Infants' interests largely overlap those of the mother but under some conditions may be selected to exploit her to their own fitness advantage (Trivers 1974; Haig 1993). In each case, the ideal approach is to examine the general nature of such trade-offs for all mammals and then to develop a comparative perspective on humans by identifying, wherever data are available, evolved differences between primates and other mammals, between apes and other nonhuman primates, and among humans and apes and hominins. As we will see, gaps in the comparative database severely hamper such an approach. Identifying such gaps is nevertheless useful for developing an agenda for further research on the evolution of human lactation and transitional feeding.

Constraints on Mothers

Lactation is an unambiguous form of maternal investment that entails a number of evolutionary trade-offs for the mother and creates special potential for conflicts of interest between mother and offspring and among siblings (Trivers 1972, 1974; Godfray 1995; Agrawal, Brodie, and Brown 2001). Any assessment of lactation's importance in structuring mammal, primate, and human life history must take into account the total costs and benefits of lactation for mothers, as well as the extent to which these are driven by infant requirements and accommodated by maternal adaptations. In this section, I consider several constraints on mothers that must have shaped the evolution of mammal, primate, and human lactation.

Maternal Costs of Lactation.

Several lines of evidence show that lactation biology is costly to evolve and maintain. It is monophyletic, rarely expressed in males (Francis 1994), and associated with high maternal-fitness costs (Altmann, Altmann, and Hausfater 1978; Clutton-Brock, Albon, and Guinness 1989). The maternal energetic cost of lactation depends on milk energy density and gross composition, rate of milk secretion, and efficiency of milk synthesis, but it accounts for more than three-quarters of the energetic costs of female reproduction in many species (Oftedal 1985). The energetic costs of lactation are often so high that they must be met by an increase in food intake or the depletion of stored fat and nutrients (Sadleir 1967; Vernon and Flint 1984; Loudon and Racey 1987; Dufour and Sauther 2002).

A variety of life history strategies have evolved to reduce the daily energetic cost of lactation and buffer against fluctuations in maternal food intake. Such strategies involve food stores, regulating use of body stores, seasonal changes in foraging activity and social provisioning, and the scheduling of lactation (Bronson 1989). A fundamental relationship between maternal dietary intake and milk yield varies in slope across taxa because of different patterns in use of body stores during lactation (Oftedal 1984b; Prentice and Prentice 1988). Marsupials commonly overlap lactation with gestation of younger offspring, which is unusual among placental mammals. Primates are characterized by a slow life history and a low production coefficient (Charnov and Berrigan 1993). Their long length of lactation exceeds that of gestation in all species (Hartmann et al. 1984).

Lactation performance is generally resilient to maternal undernutrition, suggesting that infant needs take precedence over those of the mother. Although all captive species studied show compromised lactation performance (measured in milk volume or composition or in litter growth) in response to severely restricted food intake (Rasmussen 1992), the extent of compromise depends on the type or combinations of nutrients restricted and the degree and duration of restriction. For example, rat pups reduce milk ingestion only when acute maternal dietary intake falls below 60 percent of ad libitum intake or chronic maternal dietary intake falls below 70 percent of ad libitum. A similar threshold of response is reported for baboons (Roberts, Cole, and Coward 1985). Such resilience is consistent with the hypothesis that a common selective advantage of lactation has been to provide a mechanism for buffering infants against ecological fluctuations in food supply.

Is milk synthesis more costly or less costly for female humans than for other primate species, and are human mothers more likely to be stressed to their physiological limits during lactation? In assessing the maternal costs of lactation, we must distinguish among (a) the comparative costs in milk production (volume, energy density, and gross composition), (b) the cumulative costs in infant intake during the period of lactation, and (c) the actual daily costs to lactating mothers (relative to a nonlactating baseline) after physiological and behavioral accommodation, including mobilization of fat stores. We can then consider the potential somatic costs to mothers under severe nutritional, social, or ecological constraints and the potential costs to mothers of *not* lactating. As we will see, the available data force us to focus mainly on total energy as the currency in which costs are measured.

Milk Production. Milk volume, gross composition, and peak yield are clearly linked to the behavioral ecology of infant care (Ben Shaul

1962; Oftedal and Iverson 1987). For example, marine mammals (such as phocids) produce concentrated fatty milks, terrestrial species that nurse episodically (such as felids and canids) produce milks high in fat and carbohydrates, and terrestrial species that nurse continuously (marsupials) or on demand (primates) produce dilute milks that are high in carbohydrates and low in fat and protein. Variation in milk energy density across mammals is largely a result of differences in lipid concentrations, which vary up to fiftyfold (Blaxter 1961). The concentration of lactose, the principal carbohydrate, varies by only 50 percent among distantly related species, and the gross protein and mineral content of milk is quite similar across mammals. Species with smaller bodies or faster life histories tend to secrete more nutrient-dense and fatty milk at higher rates. An allometric relationship also exists between maternal metabolic (that is, lean) body size and peak milk-energy yield, which decreases as one considers only species with many young, ungulates with single young, and primates with single young (Oftedal 1984a, 1984b; Lee and Bowman 1995).

After adjustment for body size, primates secrete low peak-milk volumes (Oftedal 1984b). Milk energy densities of primates studied fall in the lower portion of the range for all species studied (table 6.1) (Oftedal 1984b, 1986). Nonhuman primate milks show a low concentration of lipid, at less than one-third of milk dry matter. Among primates, in contrast to most other species, lipids provide only a little more than half of total milk energy. Protein levels are also comparatively low (approximately 10, 15, and 45 percent of the levels in sea lions, rabbits, and cows, respectively). Primate milks contain a high concentration of lactose (approximately 225, 270, and 1,750 percent of the levels of dogs, rats, and bears, respectively), which may be an adaptation for fueling rapid postnatal brain growth.

Available evidence suggests that the gross composition of milk does not vary widely across nonhuman primate species with differences in body size, reproductive rates, other life history characteristics, and patterns of maternal care (Fomon 1986; Kanazawa et al. 1991; Patino and Borda 1997; Dufour and Sauther 2002). One study suggests that prosimians that carry their young during lactation produce more dilute milks than do species that leave their young unattended for prolonged periods; however, current data are insufficient to characterize

TABLE 6.1

Estimates of Gross Milk Composition and Milk Production Reported for Selected Terrestrial Mammal Genera

Genus	Crude Protein (%)	Crude Fat (%)	Crude Sugar (%)	Gross Energy (kJ/g)	Milk Yield (g/kg$^{0.75}$/Day)	Milk Energy Output (kJ/kg$^{0.75}$/Day)
Primates:						
Homo	0.8	4.1	6.8	2.89	51	146.02
Papio	1.5	4.6	7.7	3.31	48	161.92
Macaca	1.8	–	–	3.35	–	–
Cercopithecus	2.1	3.0	7.2	2.80	–	–
Callithrix	2.7	3.6	7.4	3.22	–	–
Leontopithcus	2.6	5.2	7.2	3.77	–	–
Eulemur	1.3	–	–	3.26	–	–
Nonprimates:						
Carnivora						
Canis	7.5	9.5	3.8	6.11	158	966.50
Artiodactyla						
Sus	5.6	8.3	5.0	5.19	200	1,029.26
Cervus	7.1	8.5	4.5	5.73	56	320.49
Rangifer	9.5	10.9	3.4	6.95	94	332.21
Ovis	4.1	7.3	5.0	4.64	126	585.76
Rodentia						
Rattus	8.1	8.8	3.8	5.98	140	811.70
Lagomorpha						
Oryctolagus	10.3	15.2	1.8	8.54	89	765.67

Figures recalculated from Oftedal (1984b), Oftedal and Iverson (1987), and Power, Oftedal, and Tardif (2002).

these patterns properly (Tilden and Oftedal 1997). Gross energy density does not vary widely among anthropoids in comparison with variation within other orders (Power, Oftedal, and Tardif 2002).

Human milk production is similar to that of other anthropoids when measured on a volume yield and an energy output basis and scaled for body size (see table 6.1). A liter of mature human milk collected from healthy, well-nourished women at six months postpartum also contains approximately 72.0 ± 2.5 g lactose, 10.5 ± 2.0 g protein, and 39.0 ± 4.0 g fat (Institute of Medicine [US] Subcommittee on

Nutrition during Lactation 1991c). (Estimates from the literature vary; for slightly different estimates, see Picciano [2001].) Although this represents one of the lowest concentrations of protein (1.6 percent) and highest concentrations of carbohydrate (6.8 percent) of any mammal, it is not a remarkable outlier among primates (Macy, Kelly, and Sloan 1953; Ben Shaul 1962; Hambraeus 1982; Hartmann et al. 1984; Picciano 2001).[6] Moreover, there is no evidence for increased levels of long-chain, polyunsaturated fatty acids (LCPUFAs) in human milk relative to other primates (Robson 2004).

In sum, gross human-milk volume and composition do not differ widely from those of other primates, which appear to correlate with slow infant growth. There is little support for the hypothesis that protein and lipid composition of human milk may be designed for slower infant growth relative to other nonhuman primates (Bernhart 1961). No studies among wild or captive great apes have examined the volume and composition of milk in relation to maternal diet and activity, nor has anyone estimated the extent to which suckling increases metabolic demands for nutrients. Therefore, on current data, it is not possible to assess whether milk synthesis for humans is more costly or less costly than for other primates.

Milk Intake. Age-related change in infant demand for milk is barely studied for nonhuman primates. This limits our ability to evaluate the suckling dependency of primate infants and to draw conclusions about the degree to which human demand for milk is unusual.

Human infants born healthy at term are able to suckle very soon after birth, but initial intake may be constrained by the onset of copious milk production, which occurs up to three days postpartum in normal mothers (Lawrence 1994; Chapman and Pérez-Escamilla 1999a, 1999b; Neville and Morton 2001; Neville, Morton, and Umemura 2001; Grajeda and Pérez-Escamilla 2002). There is some evidence that human neonates are able to mobilize tissues laid down in gestation to meet metabolic needs while making the transition from umbilical to breast-feeding (Kuzawa 1998; Rodriguez et al. 2000). Few studies report the incidence of weight loss after birth, but most clinicians regard a perinatal loss of up to 10 percent of birth weight as normal (Manganaro 2001). Milk intake increases more gradually after five days

(Neville et al. 1988). At one to two weeks, when human milk becomes more dilute, energy intakes increase less steeply.

Infant demand is the main determinant of lactation performance in all populations studied (Lunn 1985; Dewey et al. 1991; Cohen et al. 1994; Daly and Hartmann 1995). Among exclusively breastfed infants, milk intake increases exponentially in the first five days after birth, to 500–600 ml/d (Howie and McNeilly 1982; Neville et al. 1988). Intakes average approximately 750–800 g/d in the first four to five months, with a considerable range of variation between 450 and 1,200 g/d (Institute of Medicine [US] Subcommittee on Nutrition during Lactation 1991b). Group mean volumes of milk produced at peak lactation are similar for mothers living in a wide variety of settings— approximately 820 g/day—again, with considerable individual variation (Prentice and Prentice 1988; Institute of Medicine [US] Subcommittee on Nutrition during Lactation 1991b; Prentice et al. 1996).

The crude energetic costs of human lactation have been estimated from measurements of daily milk intake among predominantly breastfed infants observed for two years postpartum (table 6.2, column 3). The cumulative maternal-energy cost of lactation can be estimated as ~1,686 MJ, more than half of which is borne in the first year of infant life. This corresponds to a mean daily additional cost of approximately 2.3 MJ/d (actually, 2.7 MJ/d in the first six months [Prentice et al. 1996]). Therefore, the daily cost of lactation is potentially high (~25–30 percent) in relation to average total energy expenditure for a moderately active (1.7 [TS] resting metabolic rate), nonpregnant, nonlactating woman weighing 50 kg (calculated from equations in Food and Nutrition Board 1989).

Maternal Accommodation. The energy costs of lactation are unknown for nonhuman primates, but several lines of evidence indicate that lactation places significant metabolic demands on mothers and that certain mechanisms accommodate these demands (Altmann, Altmann, and Hausfater 1978; Harcourt 1987; P. Lee 1987; Altmann and Samuels 1992; Dufour and Sauther 2002). Some field observations suggest that intake of high-energy foods (Boinski 1988), overall food energy (Stacey 1986; Sauther 1994), and time allocated to foraging (J. Altmann 1980; Dunbar and Dunbar 1988) increase among lactating

TABLE 6.2

Potential Energy Costs of Human Lactation[a]

	Milk Volume (g/d)	Potential Maternal Energy Requirement (MJ/d)[b]		
(A) Daily, by Month of Infant Life		*Total Energy Required for Milk Production (MJ/d)[c]*	*Balance Required If Milk Production Subsidized by Loss of Fat Stored in Pregnancy (MJ/d)[d]*	*Balance Required If Milk Production Subsidized by Fat Loss and Complementary Feeding (MJ/d)[e]*
0–1	680	2.380	1.730	1.730
1–2	780	2.730	2.080	2.080
2–3	820	2.870	2.220	2.220
3–6	820	2.870	2.220	0.780[f]
6–11	650	2.275	2.275	1.140
12–24	600	2.100	2.100	1.050
(B) Annual, by Month of Infant Life	*Cumulative Milk Volume (g)*	*Cumulative Energy Requirement (MJ)*		
0–11	262,742	919.598	800.999	279.164
12–24	218,952	766.332	766.332	383.166
0–24	481,694	1,685.930	1,567.331	662.330

a. Data are taken from a review of clinical studies by Prentice and colleagues (1996).

b. 1 MJ = 238.8 calories.

c. Assumes breast milk energy density of 2.80 kJ/g and 80 percent conversion efficiency of dietary to milk energy.

d. Assumes fat weight loss of 500 g/d, equivalent to energy saving of 650 kJ/d in the first six months.

e. Assumes that infant receives half of energy requirements from non–breast milk foods.

f. It must be noted that, although non–breast milk foods are commonly introduced between ages 3 and 6 months in contemporary populations, international advisory bodies now recommend exclusive breastfeeding for the first six months of life (Kramer and Kakuma 2002).

females, particularly when forage quality is poor (Dunbar, Hannah-Stewart, and Dunbar 2002). There is scant evidence, however, that wild, nonhuman primate mothers successfully accommodate the costs of protecting their infants against fluctuations in milk volume when conditions are adverse (Dufour and Sauther 2002). Captive studies suggest that, in some species, the energetic costs of lactation are met by a suite of energy-sparing adaptations that include, depending on the species and the individual, breakdown of tissue stores (Bercovitch 1987), greater efficiency of energy utilization (Roberts, Cole, and Coward 1985), reduced physical activity (Harrison 1983; Bercovitch 1987), and shared care of infants (Tardif, Harrison, and Simek 1993). Among humans, at least three types of accommodation occur.

First, depletion of the maternal fat reserves laid down before and during pregnancy has the potential to subsidize the additional energy costs of lactation by ~118.6 MJ (0.325 MJ/d) in the first year (table 6.3). (There is no evidence that human lactation performance is influenced by whether the energy to support it is derived from the diet or from fat stores.) A number of physiological mechanisms ensure that, in favorable conditions, the average woman begins lactation with approximately 125 MJ of additional fat accumulated during pregnancy (see table 6.3, column 3). This storage of fat demands the largest proportion (~71 percent) of additional energy needed to sustain a healthy pregnancy in nonchronically energy-deficient women (Durnin 1987; Lawrence et al. 1987; Prentice et al. 1996).[7] Yet, it is achieved with only modest alterations in maternal energy flux and metabolic partitioning. Studies among free-living women indicate that a proportion of the daily energy cost of pregnancy is often met by reductions in basal metabolic rates and physical activity (Durnin et al. 1985; Prentice et al. 1996) and that the average daily costs of pregnancy (~0.7 MJ/d) are low (~8 percent) in relation to the usual dietary-energy intakes and requirements of healthy nonpregnant, nonlactating women (~8.78 MJ/d).

Second, feeding nursing infants safe and nutritionally adequate complementary foods can result in maternal energy savings of almost 1.8 MJ/d in the first year (see table 6.2, column 4). The combined use of maternal body stores of energy and of complementary foods can reduce the net additional costs to mothers to as low as 0.9 MJ/d. For many women, this represents 10–20 percent of the usual total energy expenditure. Healthy people with unconstrained access to food or choice of activities can easily accommodate increases in daily energy requirements of up to 30 percent by increasing energy intake, decreasing physical activity, or both. Over two years, fat depletion and complementary feeding reduce the actual cost of lactation estimated to satisfy infant needs by 1,023.6 MJ, or almost 61 percent.

TABLE 6.3

Energy Cost of Human Pregnancy[a]

Component	Weight Gain (g)[b]	Total Energy Cost (MJ)	Proportion of Total Weight Gain	Proportion of Total Energy Cost (Protein)	Proportion of Total Energy (Fat)
Maternal fat stores	3,345	125.039	27%	1.1%	70.8%
Fetus	3,294	33.000	27%	7.3%	11.6%
Other maternal tissues[c]	5,744	15.905	46%	8.1%	1.1%
Total	12,383	173.944[d]	100%	16.5%	83.5%

a. Recalculated from Prentice and colleagues (1996).

b. Based on average pregnancy weight gain of 12.4 kg delivering a baby of 3.3 kg (Hytten and Chamberlain 1980).

c. Includes placenta, amniotic fluid, uterus, breast, blood, and extracellular, extravascular water.

d. Note that this figure may not represent the total cost of pregnancy because it does not include increases in energy expenditure during activity.

Third, although the daily energetic cost of lactation is potentially higher than that of pregnancy (~2.3 MJ/d versus ~0.7 MJ/d; see tables 6.2 and 6.3), additional metabolic compensatory mechanisms appear to exist. Most studies suggest that lactation performance is rarely compromised even when mothers are multiparous, marginally undernourished, engaged in high levels of physical activity, and losing weight and fat with age and by season (Prentice et al. 1981; Adair, Pollitt, and Mueller 1983; Lunn 1985; Brown et al. 1986; Prentice et al. 1986; Winkvist et al. 1994). To date, only a single intervention study has suggested that maternal food supplementation during lactation can improve milk production (Gonzalez-Cossio et al. 1998). Aerobic exercise and gradual weight loss have no adverse effect on milk volume or composition, infant milk intake, infant growth, or other metabolic parameters (Lovelady, Lönnerdal, and Dewey 1990; Dewey et al. 1994; McCrory 2000, 2001). (Studies of long-term, moderate exercise among groups of healthy, well-fed, lactating mothers indicate this.) Women in

poor communities may have smaller body size, eat less, and birth smaller babies than women in richer communities, but they do not produce
less milk (Prentice 1986; Institute of Medicine [US] Subcommittee on
Nutrition during Lactation 1991b; Rasmussen 1992). Breast milk composition is also resistant to reductions in maternal nutrient intake
(Institute of Medicine [US] Subcommittee on Nutrition during Lactation 1991a; L. H. Allen 1994).

In sum, clinical nutrition studies suggest that the net costs of lactation are low after mobilizing tissue stores and reducing basal metabolic rates and that humans do not need to substantially increase food
intakes or reduce activity during lactation (Prentice and Whitehead
1987; Prentice and Prentice 1988). During pregnancy, a combination
of energy-sparing and energy-storing adaptations function to protect
the growth of the fetus within a wide energetic margin and to reduce
the subsequent maternal energetic stress of lactation. Therefore, there
is indirect evidence that a tendency to gain fat during pregnancy
evolved as an adaptation to buffer milk production against acute
reductions in maternal food intake and that complementary feeding
evolved to reduce the maternal costs of milk production.[8]

Maternal Depletion.

Even when compensatory mechanisms are operating, mammalian
mothers face trade-offs between maintaining the quantity and quality
of milk and maintaining their own nutritional status and reproductive
potential. In wild ungulates, lactation has been observed to result in
irrecoverable weight loss and reduced survival, with subsequent reproduction among individual mothers subjected to particularly high seasonal, social, and physiological stress (Clutton-Brock, Albon, and Guinness
1989; Clutton-Brock 1991). At present, it is impossible to assess the
extent to which lactating nonhuman primate mothers are "buffered"
from nutritional depletion, because no field studies document such
costs of lactation.

Studies suggest that most well-nourished women can support the
extra energy costs of lactation without weight loss by increasing energy
intake or decreasing physical activity (Prentice and Prentice 1988).
(These studies were restricted to mothers of healthy body-mass index
who experienced normal weight gains during pregnancy and delivered
term babies within the normal birth-weight range.) The energetic data

described above suggest that women with adequate energy reserves can maintain milk energy output within the normal range even when losing weight (Brown and Dewey 1992). In fact, lactation does not result in maternal weight loss among sedentary women without caloric restriction (K. G. Dewey 1998), whereas well-fed but active women tend to lose about 0.5 kg/mo in the first six months (Butte et al. 1984). Therefore, maternal fat loss may not be a programmed component of human lactation (Prentice et al. 1996); rather, it may have evolved as a facultative strategy for scheduling reproduction across the lifespan.

Nevertheless, such buffering of lactation may have negative effects (P. T. Ellison 1995). If maternal nutrient needs are compromised before those of infants, the effects of maternal nutrition depletion and repletion over a reproductive cycle may have opposite effects on the well-being of mothers and children (Persson 2001). There is evidence that multiple gestation, frequent reproductive cycling, and overlap of pregnancy and lactation can lead to poor birth outcomes, poor infant weight gain, and mothers' poor micronutrient status and nutritional depletion (Merchant and Martorell 1988; Merchant, Martorell, and Haas 1990b; McDermott, Steketee, and Wirima 1995; Dijkhuizen et al. 2001). In subsistence populations, women typically gain less fat during pregnancy (Lawrence et al. 1987) and show parity-related decreases in weight and adiposity (Harrison, Boyce, and Platt 1975; Tracer 1991; Adair and Popkin 1992); during lactation, mothers lose body fat (Adair and Popkin 1992), particularly in lean seasons (Sellen 2000). In sum, when the nutritional supply is chronically restricted, maternal depletion may result (Winkvist, Rasmussen, and Habicht 1992).

Maternal Opportunity Costs.

The opportunity costs of lactation in terms of allocation of time and energy to other behaviors and physiological processes are very difficult to measure but are probably appreciable. Suckling interferes with maternal foraging and social activity among nonhuman primates and is accompanied by the energetic and practical burden of infant carrying (J. Altmann 1980; Nicolson 1987; Altmann and Samuels 1992). Among humans, material and psychosocial constraints clearly contribute to the widespread mismatch between recommended and actual young-child feeding practices (Morse, Jehle, and Gamble 1990; WHO 1996; Haggerty and Rutstein 1999; Esterik 2002; Sellen 2002).

In allocating time between work and other forms of care giving, mothers in subsistence societies experience acute conflicts (Panter-Brick 1995; Sellen 1998). Agriculture and pastoral production constrain maternal time allocation to infant feeding, resulting in reduced breastfeeding frequency, shorter duration of exclusive and continued breastfeeding, and complementary feeding by alternative caregivers (Panter-Brick 1991; Panter-Brick, Lotstein, and Ellison 1993; Marriott 1997; Sellen 2001c). Contrary to some predictions (Kolata 1974; Dumond 1975; R. B. Lee 1979a; Buikstra, Konigsberg, and Bullington 1986), comparative studies show that the availability of cereals and milk in agricultural and pastoral populations was not the major factor leading to shorter duration of exclusive and continued breastfeeding (Sellen 2001c). Rather, shortened duration occurs in populations in which women's activities entail physical separation from infants for extended periods of time (Nerlove 1974; McGuire and Popkin 1989). Indeed, changes in maternal work and childcare patterns may explain the increases in fertility that accompanied the adoption of agriculture (Ford 1945; Flannery 1973; M. Cohen 1977; R. B. Lee 1979b; Cohen and Armelagos 1984).

Whenever maternal work is arduous and food intake is low or unpredictable, mothers may perceive benefits of reduced breastfeeding in terms of balancing energy/nutrient flux and avoiding maternal depletion. Under extreme conditions, these perceptions may have some scientific validity (Merchant, Martorell, and Hass 1990a; Adair and Popkin 1992; P. T. Ellison 1995; Gray 1996; Prentice and Goldberg 2000). Also, the social opportunity costs of breastfeeding may be very high in some contexts (Cosminsky, Mhloyi, and Ewbank 1993; Mabilia 1996a, 1996b). Breastfeeding practices are extremely sensitive to cultural influences and have a history of variation through time (Wickes 1953a, 1953b, 1953c; Fildes 1982; Tonz 2000). Human mothers require significant social support, knowledge, and experience to initiate and maintain breastfeeding successfully (Righard and Alade 1992).

Maternal Benefits.

To assume that lactation entails only costs for mammal mothers is wrong. Lactation reduces the loss of young offspring to predation, disease, and starvation and may therefore reduce net maternal reproduction costs. In some species, the ability to convert encountered or captured food resources into milk enables the parking or caching of offspring. Then the mother is freed from the physical burden of carrying offspring and can avoid the risk of displacement by competitors while foraging. Such increases in maternal reproductive efficiency may possibly allow greater maternal allocation to somatic growth and maintenance, as well as longer lifespan. The potential role of lactation in improving age-specific fecundity and modifying female lifespan has not been investigated in nonhuman primates, but evidence from humans suggests that its importance during our evolution should not be underestimated.

Many mammals use lactation as a strategy for reducing the short-term costs of reproduction by spreading them over the long term. Lactation is the principal method of regulating fertility in primates (Hearn 1984) and has evolved as the focal mechanism for balancing current and future reproductive effort. Compared with most other mammals of similar size, primates live longer, produce few offspring, and have low intrinsic rates of natural increase (Charnov 1991; Charnov and Berrigan 1993; Ross 1998; Ross and Jones 1999). Primates also have smaller litters, long gestation, and slow fetal growth (Harvey, Martin, and Clutton-Brock 1987; Chapman, Walker, and Lefebvre 1990). These life history characteristics reduce the daily energetic costs of gestation despite faster and more energetically costly fetal brain growth (Martin and MacLarnon 1990; R. Martin 1996). In addition, slow postnatal growth and wide birth intervals result in lower requirements for nutrients and energy. This adaptation may allow infants to be sustained with small milk yields and dilute milk, reducing the selective pressures on lactating females to seek out foods of particularly high nutrient density (Oftedal 1991; Tilden and Oftedal 1997).

For contemporary human mothers, studies indicate possible health benefits of lactating (Labbok 2001): bone health (Cumming and Klineberg 1993; Melton et al. 1993), reduced risk of cancer (Rosenblatt and Thomas 1993; Newcomb et al. 1994), and earlier return to prepregnant weight (Dewey, Heinig, and Nommsen 1993). Initiation of breastfeeding increases oxytocin levels, resulting in reduced postpartum bleeding and more rapid uterine involution (Chua, Arulkumaran, and Lim 1994). Prolactin-mediated inhibition of ovulation (Short 1987; Gray et al. 1990; Kennedy and Visness 1992) protects against menstrual blood loss and nutrient deficiency (Labbok

1999). Because lactation places small demands on maternal iron stores (see below), increased spacing and survival of breastfed offspring may lower the cost of future reproduction by facilitating maternal iron repletion. Taken together, such observed health benefits to women who breastfeed can be understood as maternal adaptations to the evolutionary context in which breastfeeding patterns were shaped.

Constraints on Juveniles

A supply of milk obviates the need to forage, opens a developmental window of opportunity for play and learning, and enables young mammals to maintain high postnatal growth rates, though never as high as those in utero. At no other stage of life is a single food as adequate as the sole source of nutrition, nor as useful in protecting against infection. Young mammals can grow and be active while their ability to respond independently to unfamiliar pathogens and deficiencies in nutrient intake is limited by the immaturity of tissues and organs involved in immune response (the thymus, blood cells, lymphatic tissues) and nutrient metabolism (the gastrointestinal tract, liver, and kidneys).

However, lactation is a characteristic expressed in adults. Across mammals, age at weaning is associated with adult female body size, litter size, gestation length, aspects of maternal feeding ecology, and the ratio of adult-to-juvenile mortality (R. Martin 1984; Harvey and Clutton-Brock 1985; Harvey, Martin, and Clutton-Brock 1987; Promislow and Harvey 1990; Pagel and Harvey 1993). It is therefore a fallacy to assume that lactation evolved as a direct result of net fitness benefits for offspring. Rather, the availability of milk presents mammalian offspring with an evolutionary and developmental dilemma, the resolution of which must favor increased reproductive efficiency of the lactating parent.

The age at which a mammal can survive independently of milk is an evolved life history characteristic shaped by constraints on the developmental trajectory of offspring, the ecology of the adult feeding niche, and whether parents provision weanlings. On one hand, an early transition to complete nutritional and social independence may be risky because of developmental constraints, exposure to pathogens, seasonal absence of food resources, or lack of foraging experience.[9]

On the other hand, obligate dependency on an adequate milk supply becomes costly for infant fitness if the mother is in poor condition or at high risk of predation. In this section, I consider several constraints on juveniles that must have shaped the evolution of mammal, primate, and human lactation.

Nutrient Requirements.

Several lines of evidence indicate that primate milk components have evolved, in part, to satisfy infants' special nutrient needs. Compared with wild foods, human and nonhuman primate milk is a rich source of key nutrients such as vitamin A, vitamin D, iodine, and calcium and of essential long-chain, polyunsaturated fatty acids (LCPUFAs). In humans, lactose is readily absorbed from the infant gut and yields monosaccharides for immediate energy production. Protein provides essential amino acids for growth and protective factors (immunoglobulins, lysozyme, lactoferrin), carriers for vitamins (folate, vitamin D, vitamin B12), digestive enzymes (lipases, amylase), and hormones and growth factors (insulin, epidermal growth factor, prolactin). Lipids, at least 97 percent of which are triglycerides, compose the major energy-yielding fraction (45–55 percent of total energy). The water component (87 percent) is sterile and sufficient to keep exclusively breastfed infants cool by means of evaporative heat loss from the lungs (up to 25 percent of total [Bentley 1998]) and hydrated without ingestion of pathogens for up to 6 months of age (Almroth 1978). The highly complex biochemistry of human milk delivers a broad spectrum of nutritional benefits (Clifford 1985; R. Black 1998).

For either wild or captive nonhuman primates, few data are available on age-specific changes in energy requirements, the total energy costs of growth and maintenance during infancy, or the proportion met by milk consumed. S. Altmann's pioneering study of free-living yearling baboons (*Papio cynocephalus*) estimated their minimum total energy requirements for growth and maintenance at 0.871 MJ/d, or 0.383 MJ/kg/d (data recalculated from various tables in S. Altmann 1998). Careful interpretation of his results suggests that their mothers bore the cost of their minimal energy requirement (S. Altmann 1998). At this age, eight baboons in the sample were consuming a total 2.251 MJ of energy, of which approximately 40 percent (that is, 0.900 MJ/d) was estimated to come from milk. Observation of ad libitum intakes among several species of captive, large-bodied cercopithecine infants has produced appreciably higher estimates of average infant energy requirements, in the range of 0.837–1.255 MJ/kg/d (Nicolosi and Hunt 1979; National Academy of Sciences 1989). Such intakes, however, are likely to differ from either average requirements or usual intakes in the wild.

Reliable estimates of healthy human-infant energy requirements are available from clinical nutritional studies using a range of cross-validated methods (table 6.4). Human infants have three- to fourfold greater energy requirements per unit mass than adults because they are smaller and growing. Although a precipitous decrease in human infant growth rate occurs during the first year of life, daily energy requirement more than doubles because of increased body size and activity. Much more energy is expended in physical activity and metabolism than is laid down in infant tissue, and gender differences are small but biologically significant. Depending on age and sex, average energy requirements range widely between 1.3 and 3.5 MJ/d (370 to 870 kcal/d) (Butte, Henry, and Torun 1996). These estimates are regarded as universally valid because healthy infants from different geographic areas show relative uniformity of growth, behavior, and physical activity (Butte, Henry, and Torun 1996).

Although cumulative energy requirement between birth and 6 months of age may exceed 2,000 MJ (see table 6.4), human infants appear to have low energy requirements in comparison with other primates, likely because of slower growth. On a per kilo basis, average requirements fall far below those estimated for free-living yearling baboons and captive large-bodied cercopithecines and fall within the range of daily intakes observed in much smaller-size (average 2.27 kg) wild yearling baboons (S. Altmann 1998).

Attempts to assess the age-specific nutritional adequacy of human milk have focused on infant energy expenditure, infant growth, and sufficiency of vitamin A, iodine, iron, zinc, calcium, vitamin B6, and vitamin D, all of which are major determinants of survival and functional development in humans (L. Allen 1990). Human peak-milk volume corresponds to a mean infant-energy intake of 2.87 MJ/d, which is well in excess of healthy infant requirements in the first six

TABLE 6.4

Energy Cost of Human Infancy[a]

Sex and Age (Months)[b]	Weight (kg)	Weight Gain (g/d)	Energy Expenditure MJ/kg/d	MJ/d	Energy Deposition MJ/kg/d	MJ/d	Total Requirement MJ/kg/d	MJ/d
Boys								
0–1	3.80	29	0.255	0.954	0.109	0.473	0.364	1.427
1–2	4.75	35	0.268	1.255	0.109	0.473	0.377	1.728
2–3	5.60	30	0.280	1.540	0.100	0.569	0.381	2.109
3–4	6.35	21	0.289	1.816	0.059	0.377	0.347	2.192
4–5	7.00	17	0.301	2.071	0.038	0.259	0.339	2.330
5–6	7.55	15	0.310	2.314	0.025	0.205	0.335	2.519
6–9	8.50	13	0.335	2.778	0.013	0.117	0.347	2.895
9–12	9.70	11	0.364	3.439	0.008	0.079	0.372	3.519
Cumulative, 0–6				302.566		71.634		374.199
Cumulative, 0–12				869.781		89.574		959.355
Girls								
0–1	3.60	26	0.255	0.920	0.094	0.427	0.351	1.347
1–2	4.35	29	0.268	1.197	0.094	0.427	0.360	1.623
2–3	5.05	24	0.280	1.460	0.084	0.452	0.364	1.912
3–4	5.70	19	0.289	1.720	0.054	0.331	0.343	2.050
4–5	6.35	16	0.301	1.975	0.042	0.272	0.343	2.247
5–6	6.95	15	0.310	2.226	0.033	0.234	0.343	2.460
6–9	7.97	11	0.335	2.699	0.013	0.109	0.347	2.807
9–12	9.05	10	0.364	3.343	0.008	0.088	0.372	3.431
Cumulative, 0–6				227.813		58.722		286.535
Cumulative, 0–12				840.008		83.085		923.093

a. Data collated and recalculated from Butte (1996).
b. Estimated from pooled age-specific measurements of energy expenditure of healthy, breastfed human infants. Note that breastfed infants show a different pattern of growth than others and that boys differ from girls in size and growth rates.

months (see table 6.4). Although a difference between observed intakes and milk production may be partly attributable to increased intakes during or after infant illness, it also indicates that most breast-fed infants do not need additional sources of energy in the first six months. Despite lengthy debate among nutritionists and pediatricians over the optimal duration of exclusive breastfeeding among humans,[10] most experts now agree that when the mother and infant are not pre-viously undernourished, the nutrients in human milk are adequate to supply infant needs for at least the first six months of life.[11]

The distribution of mean intakes of human milk by healthy infants matches the distribution of energy, protein, and calcium requirements throughout the first six months of infancy, and the concentration of these nutrients in milk does not decrease with maternal intake (Butte, Lopez-Alarcon, and Garza 2002). Infants who are exclusively breastfed for their first six months experience less morbidity from gastrointestinal infection than those who receive other foods at 3 or 4 months of age but show no significant deficits in growth (Cohen et al. 1994; Dewey et al. 1999; Kramer and Kakuma 2002; Kramer et al. 2003). Even among low-birth-weight infants, exclusive breastfeeding to 6 months age does not compromise growth relative to infants given hygienically prepared, nutritious, complementary foods at age 4 months (Dewey et al. 1999). Breastfeeding is therefore recommended for the first six months of life (WHO Collaborative Study Team on the Role of Breastfeeding on the Prevention of Infant Mortality 2000; Kramer and Kakuma 2002). Although human milk is a poor source of iron and zinc relative to infant requirements (Domellöf et al. 2004), iron stores at birth are usually suf-ficient to meet the needs of healthy, term infants during the first six months of life. Similarly, the vitamin D content of human milk is insuf-ficient to meet infant requirements before 6 months of age, but prena-tal stores become depleted in normal infants only when exposure to sunlight is insufficient for them to synthesize vitamin D de novo.

Estimates of the subsequent contributions of breast milk to total energy intake during the transitional or complementary feeding phase vary widely with infant demand and with "complementary" feeding practices. Complementary foods[12] (sometimes referred to as "weaning food" or "breast milk supplement") are defined in the clinical litera-ture as any foods—whether manufactured or locally prepared, solid, liquid, or semi-solid—that are suitable as a complement to breast milk (or to infant formula) when it cannot satisfy an infant's nutritional requirements. Complementary feeding means that only a proportion of total energy required before the end of infancy (up to 3,000 MJ for some male infants) is obtained from milk consumed (approximately 45 percent when we compare cumulative totals 0–12 months in tables 6.2 and 6.3).

No study has demonstrated an age at which young children cease to benefit from consumption of some breast milk (Marquis and Habicht 2000), and there is no clinically defined upper limit to the duration of breastfeeding (Dettwyler 1995). Rather, the recommended twenty-four-month minimum duration of breastfeeding represents an age threshold below which breast milk consumption remains highly beneficial (WHO 1998; K. Dewey 2003). Contemporary clinical studies show that breast milk can provide a significant source of energy and other nutrients after complementary feeding begins and until at least the third year of human life. Breast milk helps young children meet their nutritional needs, which, it is important to emphasize, are very different from those of adults. Because of the immaturity of their digestive system, young children (that is, under 3 years of age) tolerate less sodium, sugar, and fiber (Akre 1990). They benefit more from dietary fat because it is energy-dense and used for neural myelinization. A higher metabolic rate and a greater chance of exposure to novel infections render them particularly vulnerable to micronutrient deficiencies.

Development of Feeding Capacity.

Researchers have barely explored the evolutionary significance of the timing, sequence, and degree of plasticity of human feeding capacity in its development. So few studies have examined the development of nonhuman primate feeding behaviors in detail that we can make no interspecific comparisons (Fairbanks and Pereira 1993; P. Lee 1997; S. Altmann 1998). We must await more study of postnatal feeding behavior among other primates before we can assess whether a fundamental shift in the dietary needs of young has taken place during the evolution of the human lineage. Nevertheless, the available data suggest that infant and young child development was likely shaped by the temporal availability of maternal milk and other foods among the immediate ancestors of early humans.

There is little contemporary geographic or ethnic variation in rates or sequencing of immunologic, alimentary, neurobehavioral, and psychomotor development (Pollitt 1984; Kaplan and Dove 1987; Tronick and Winn 1992). The relationship between infant development and feeding has likely remained similar in human populations since the species emerged in the Late Pleistocene.[13] Compared with great apes, human neonates are large (Leutenegger 1973; Zihlmann 1997b) and fat (Kuzawa 1998) but grow more slowly (Bogin, chapter 7, this volume). Throughout childhood, digestion of some foods and absorption of nutrients are constrained by small stomach size and short intestinal length (Hamosh 1995), and an immature immune system renders them susceptible to infections.

Normal breathing, feeding, and swallowing in humans develop through the integration of growth and neurological maturation, the influence of physiological, interpersonal, and cultural factors, and adaptation to minimize the chances of malnutrition and respiratory obstruction (McKenna 1990; Stevenson and Allaire 1991). Healthy, term, normal-birth-weight infants are clearly adapted to strip milk efficiently from the breast. Sucking and swallowing reflexes are established prenatally (Milla 1991), and most unimpeded newborns find a nipple and begin spontaneous sucking and rooting within an hour of birth, whether or not copious milk is yet available (Widström et al. 1996).

Modern humans seem to have prolonged dental maturation in comparison with apes, among whom there is wide heterochrony (Macho and Wood 1995). Components of the muscular coordination of chewing and related oral reflexes emerge sequentially after the first week, and fully functional stimulus-response patterns begin by 8 months of age (Sheppard and Mysak 1984; Stevenson and Allaire 1991). However, the eruption of primary teeth is not complete until the second year (B. Smith 1991a), so babies are limited in the range of foods they can chew. Relative to the permanent adult teeth, which do not begin to emerge until the fifth or six year, the deciduous primary teeth have thin enamel and short roots. In combination with small jaw size and the comparatively late appearance of molars in humans (Schultz 1950; also see Hawkes, chapter 4, and Skinner and Wood, chapter 11, this volume), this limits the ability of young children to process tough foods without the appreciable attrition observed in apes (Aiello, Montgomery, and Dean 1991). Such constraints could have been mitigated during human evolution only through continued lactation or feeding of softer foods to young.

The developmental rate of infant feeding skills (versus breastfeeding reflexes) varies with the texture and variety of complementary foods given and the method of feeding (Gisel 1991). Early flavor experiences influence food acceptance by infants and young children (Mennella and Beauchamp 1998; Gerrish and Mennella 2001; Wardle et al. 2003). Underlying these influences, however, is an unlearned shift from initial indifference to sweet, salty, and sour tastes between birth and ~4–6 months, to a heightened preference for them in middle childhood and adolescence (Bauchamp and Cowart 1987; Desor and Bauchamp 1987; Liem and Mennella 2003). The perception of bitter tastes, often signaling the presence of dietary inhibitors such as tannins, also declines with age (Drewnowski and Gomez-Carneros 2000; Drewnowski 2001). The development of phenotypic food preferences depends on interaction with multiple aspects of the eating environment (Birch 1999).

The timing of human adult-onset lactase decline may be an indicator of the age at which ancestral human infants weaned. We know that this characteristic is heritable (Flatz and Saengudom 1969; Sahi 1974; Montgomery et al. 1991), but also subject to positive selection in some populations that domesticated animals, within the past ten thousand years (McCracken 1971; Holden and Mace 1997). To some extent, lactase is an inducible enzyme. In most populations not subject to the recent adoption of dairying as a subsistence strategy, lactase decline occurs between the ages of 5 and 7 years, that is, in mid-childhood (Sahi et al. 1972; Lee and Krasinski 1998), suggesting ancestral age at weaning similar to that of great apes. However, we know of no data on the timing of adult-onset lactase decline in nonhuman primates, and we do not know how quickly lactase decline may track evolutionary decreases in lactation duration.

Development of Immune Competency.

The immune components and anti-inflammatory properties of milk vary widely across mammal species, presumably as a result of adaptation to varying disease ecology (Goldman, Chheda, and Garofalo 1998). Human infant survival and health heavily depend on the anti-infective effects of milk mediated through a combination of immunological and nutritional mechanisms (Hamosh 2001). Human milk shows strong and increasing similarities to the immune spectra of milks from Old World monkeys, great apes, and chimpanzees (Cole, Hale, and Sturzenegger 1992; Galili 1993; Goldman 2001), suggesting that humans and other apes show common adaptation to similar patho-gens. We have no direct data to show that immune protection is important for survival of wild nonhuman primates; we can only assume so. To evaluate this hypothesis properly, we need new data on the major pathogens infecting young wild apes and the mechanisms through which breast milk may provide immune protection.

Recent research on human milk has revealed a staggering range of bioactive cellular and molecular factors that function alone or in combination to reinforce and develop the infant immune system (Goldman 1993; Cummins and Thompson 1997; Goldman, Chheda, and Garafolo 1997; Hasselbalch et al. 1999; Hawkes, Neumann, and Gibson 1999). Some of these factors act directly to kill or inhibit pathogens or prevent adhesion at the intestinal mucosal surfaces; others regulate the immune response, prevent inflammation, or reduce the risk for allergic reaction. Human milk provides significant protection against diarrhea and acute respiratory and other infections (Jason, Neiburg, and Marks 1984; Cunningham 1988; Victora 1996; Lopez-Alarcon, Villalpando, and Fajardo 1997; WHO Collaborative Study Team on the Role of Breastfeeding on the Prevention of Infant Mortality 2000). Residual immune benefits of human milk are also observed in industrialized countries where many nutritional components of milk can be matched by processed formulas, and some data suggest that milk protects against chronic diseases for which infectious agents may yet be found.

It is important to emphasize that human milk is almost certainly more complex and finely evolved than current methods of description and analysis allow us to understand. Many constituents of human milk are "bioactive" instead of simply nutritive or immunological in function (Hamosh 2001; Lönnerdal and Lien 2003). A significant nonprotein nitrogen fraction (25 percent of total nitrogen) consists of more than two hundred compounds, including nucleotides that rapidly growing infant tissues may be unable to synthesize de novo. Enzymes, hormones, and growth factors secreted by the mother modulate gut function and promote tissue growth and cognitive development (Gordon 1997; Black and Bhatia 1998; Goldman 2000; Hamosh 2001). Denatured bioactive factors and nutrients are secreted as protein-bound components that offer protection from digestion and facilitate efficient absorption and utilization. Indeed, epidemiological studies suggest that immunological and nutritional milk factors function synergistically to protect contemporary infants and young children against undernutrition and infection (de Andraca, Peirano, and Uauy 1998; WHO Collaborative Study Team on the Role of Breastfeeding on the Prevention of Infant Mortality 2000; León-Cava et al. 2002).

Trade-offs and Conflicts of Interest in Human Lactation

Comparative biology shows us many ways in which mammals resolve the trade-offs and conflicts of interest between maternal and infant fitness that are imposed by the constraints described above. In this section, I review evidence suggesting that humans have been selected to resolve these trade-offs not through any major changes in the physiology of infant nutrient requirements or the composition of maternal milk, but through a reorganization of the general pattern of transitional feeding and scheduling of female reproduction across the lifespan. I argue that these changes were made possible by the preparation of complementary foods that mimicked some of the nutritional properties of ancestral human breast milk.

Resolution of Parent-Offspring Conflict.

There is a consensus that infant and weanling mortality is higher than at any other life stage and that weanlings are particularly susceptible to nutritional stress (S. Altmann 1998:23). In past human populations, weaning stress was often severe and affected health throughout the rest of the survivor's lifespan (Humphrey and Elford 1988; Goodman et al. 1992). However, evidence of weaning stress is not necessarily evidence of maternal-infant conflict over weaning; it may reflect ecological constraints operating on both infants and mothers. Dental evidence of severe physiological stress experienced around the age of weaning for extant apes (Lukacs 1999), extinct monkeys (Lukacs 2001), other nonhuman primates (Guatelli-Steinberg 2001), and humans may reflect the difficulty of the transition to independent feeding instead of resolution of parent-offspring conflict in favor of the mother.

Despite the influential predictions of theorists (Trivers 1972, 1974), there is little direct evidence for severe weaning conflict in mammals or humans (Bateson 1994). At least some mammals appear to have evolved physiological mechanisms to lower the maternal costs of lactation so that these do not exceed the inclusive fitness benefits accrued through increased survival of better-quality offspring. Little or no maternal-offspring conflict is observed in studies of weaning among some canids (Malm and Jensen 1997) and bovids (Cassinello 1997). Recent theoretical models suggest that evolution has produced mutually low-cost, evolutionarily stable strategies that favor efficient resolution of potential parent-offspring conflicts over weaning (Godfray 1995; Hardling et al. 2001). Moreover, a strong reciprocal association between the overall intensity and duration of lactation and the magnitude of delays in development of juvenile immune, digestive, and locomotor systems observed across species suggests that potential weaning conflicts are often resolved in the offspring's favor (Hartmann et al. 1984; Nicolson 1987; Cummins and Thompson 1997; Goldman, Chheda, and Garofalo 1998; Lambert 1998).

Transitional and Complementary Feeding.

Nonhuman primate infants begin to forage on foods similar to those selected by the mother, processing them largely for themselves. In this regard, they fit the general mammalian pattern depicted in figure 6.1. It is clear that provisioning never approaches the levels observed in human populations. It is not clear, however, to what extent transitional feeding occurs before weaning, that is, whether weaning is abrupt, gradual, or variable within or among species.

Because detailed studies of the diets and foraging behavior of nonhuman primate weanlings are too few, we cannot draw any firm conclusions. Recent detailed field studies suggest that the transition to weaning can be a gradual process in at least one other hominid, the orangutans (van Noordwijk and van Schaik 2005). Weaning age appears to be sensitive to ecological factors that constrain maternal ability to meet the increasing energy needs of growing offspring (Lee,

Majluf, and Gordon 1991). Variation in transitional feeding patterns is apparently wide both within and among species and has yet to be fully described and explained (P. Lee 1997, 1999). Whatever explanations emerge from future research, nonhuman primates have evolved a high degree of plasticity in weaning age.

Comparative analyses have generated several life history models to predict ages at which primates are adapted to terminate lactation: 1.5 times the length of gestation (Harvey and Clutton-Brock 1985), eruption of first molar teeth (B. Smith 1991a, 1992; see also Robson, van Schaik, and Hawkes, chapter 2, this volume), tripling (Lawrence 1989:245) or quadrupling (Lee, Majluf, and Gordon 1991) of birth weight, and attainment of one-third adult weight (Charnov 1993). However, no model reliably predicts age at weaning for all primate species. This again suggests that age at weaning is very labile relative to other life history traits.

Putting aside the question of whether weaning represents resolution of lactation conflicts in favor of the mother or the infant, human mothers are clearly adapted to exercise more behavioral flexibility in the patterns and duration of breastfeeding than are other primates. In all contemporary human populations, babies and toddlers receive specially prepared foods during the transitional feeding phase (figure 6.2). In most cases, this occurs long before weaning. Typically, these preparations are of a type not eaten by juveniles and adults and are actively prepared and fed by both the mother and other caregivers. These foods are often given in addition to milk from the breast of the mother or another woman, and, in many cases, can be referred to as "complementary foods" because they are nutritionally rich. This habit of preparing processed foods with high-energy and micronutrient density and feeding them to young children before they are weaned appears to have evolved uniquely in the human lineage.

Figure 6.2 summarizes the general sequence of events and phases recommended for the development of human feeding behavior, on the basis of both clinical observation and observation of children in many populations. The order of events and phases presented is known to promote optimal health and fitness outcomes for most healthy term babies and assumes no constraints on maternal and caregiver time allocation or access to food resources. Initiation of breastfeeding within one hour of birth (a) followed by a six-month period of *exclusive breast-feeding* promotes optimal growth and development of healthy newborns. Introduction of nutrient-rich and pathogen-poor complementary foods (b) is necessary until approximately 6 months of age to support increased daily dietary intake. The use of complementary foods (that is, nutritionally rich and sterile combinations of foods acquired and processed by caregivers and fed only to infants and toddlers) is unique to humans. During the period of *complementary feeding*, which continues through the second year of life, breast milk remains an important, sterile source of nutrients and immune protection. Family foods (that is, raw foods and combinations of foods collected, processed, and shared by older juveniles and adults), which are also unique to humans, begin to contribute to total dietary intakes during the second half of infancy (c) and increasingly so as chewing, swallowing, and tasting competencies develop in the second year of life. The frequency of suckling and volume of milk consumed diminish gradually in the second, third, and fourth year of life, but the age at weaning (d) is extremely variable and there is no upper age limit at which breastfeeding may cease to be of some benefit to children.

As a result of the invention of complementary feeding, the duration of transitional feeding is extremely labile across contemporary human populations. Among mammals, humans are unique in having evolved the capacity to rear a proportion of offspring to adulthood without suckling them. Humans also exhibit an unusually high degree of variation in weaning age (Hartmann et al. 1984). If initiated, the duration of human lactation ranges from a few hours to more than five years, spanning the entire range observed for all other species of mammal (Hartmann and Arthur 1986). Possibly in contrast to nonhuman primates, humans wean over a wide range of infant sizes and often after smaller postnatal weight gain (Hill and Hurtado 1996). Despite the potential costs to infants of early weaning, our infant feeding patterns are unusually plastic even in comparison with other primates.

Such flexibility almost certainly reflects an evolved maternal capacity to vary reproduction in relation to ecology (Caro and Sellen 1990; Blurton Jones 1993; P. T. Ellison 1994), the availability of alternative caregivers (Hrdy 1999), and the specific flux of environmental and

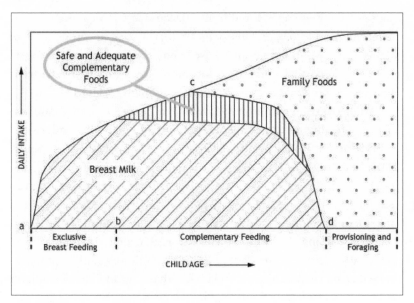

FIGURE 6.2

Evolved pattern of care and feeding in humans.

social factors influencing trade-offs affecting the timing of weaning (Sellen 2001c). Observation in contemporary human societies shows that lactation behavior is sensitive to maternal workload and the availability of cooperative childcare and feeding (see above). Human mothers show a strong tendency to reduce the frequency of suckling and the duration of lactation.[14] Indeed, increased behavioral control over the frequency and duration of suckling affords mothers a range of options that minimize the physiological and opportunity costs of lactation without compromising infant survival or functional development.

Given the potential flexibility and observed variation in transitional feeding patterns, it is difficult to draw a firm conclusion about whether humans have evolved a species-specific, global optimum pattern of infant feeding. Some indicators suggest that the age-related pattern for introduction of complementary foods and termination of breastfeeding concords closely with the current clinical recommendations for normal, healthy children (Sellen 2001c). For example, in a sample of 172 ethnographic reports published between 1873 and 1998, the central tendency for age of introduction of liquid and solid foods falls between ages 4 and 6 months, and age at weaning exceeds 24 months (table 6.5).[15] This suggests that a sizeable proportion of infants in these populations may have been exclusively breastfed for six months and partially breastfed for more than two years, patterns known to be optimal for growth and development (WHO 1979, 2001).

Other data show widespread mismatch between optimal and actual infant-feeding practices in contemporary populations (Underwood and Hofvander 1982; Quandt 1985; Huffman and Martin 1994; Sellen 2002). Common practices such as discarding of colostrum (Gunnlaugsson and Einarsdottir 1993; Rizvi 1993), use of prelacteal feeds (Pérez-Escamilla et al. 1996; Akuse and Obinya 2002), and reduced breast milk intake due to early introduction of formula and other substances and early weaning (Heinig et al. 1993) are associated with infant illness and death (Jones et al. 2003). Some evolutionary anthropologists argue that such associations are evidence that maternal needs trade off favorably against infant needs, but it is important to note that contemporary populations living in poverty in modern states are not in any kind of ecological equilibrium and that their conditions are far removed from those to which humans likely adapted. The existence of diversity in lactation and transitional feeding does, however, suggest that no single, global optimum pattern exists for all infants and mothers (McDade and Worthman 1998; Sellen 2001b).

Rescheduling of Reproductive Effort.

Among ancestral mothers, shortening the period of exclusive lactation or transitional feeding, or both, likely reduced birth intervals (by accelerating the return of menstrual cycling) and may have improved subsequent birth outcomes (by reducing maternal depletion). However, this would pay off evolutionarily only if the effect on older sibling mortality was marginal; reduced juvenile mortality may have been a salient evolutionary innovation among early humans (R. Foley 1995; Hammel 1996; Pennington 1996). This could be achieved if other kinds of foods were substituted for the nutritional and antibiotic components of breast milk or if infant development was accelerated so that the period of nutritional dependency was shortened.

Reduction of interbirth intervals relative to other hominoids has been proposed as an important factor in the evolution of the genus

TABLE 6.5

Comparison of Young Child Feeding Patterns among Nonindustrial Societies with Current Clinical Recommendations

Feeding Transition (Number of Cultures)	Average Age Reported as Typical for Transition (Months)[a]			Age Recommended (Months)[b]
	Mean ± Standard Deviation	*Median*	*Mode*	
Introduce non–breast milk liquids (18)	4.5 ±6.0	2.0	6.0	6.0
Introduce solids (42)	5.0 ±4.0	5.5	6.0	6.0
End breastfeeding (112)	29.0 ±10.0	29.5	30.0	>24.0

a. Sellen (2001a)
b. Kramer and Kakuma (2002)

Homo (O'Connell, Hawkes, and Blurton Jones 1999; Aiello and Key 2002). Comparative survival analysis of birth intervals in four hominoid species suggests that humans have the shortest closed birth intervals, rarely exceeding four years in natural fertility populations. In contrast, half of all randomly selected, closed birth intervals exceed four, five, and eight years in wild gorillas, chimpanzees, and orangutans, respectively (Galdikas and Wood 1990). Although more direct data are needed, this indicates that the human lactation span is short compared with other primates.

Shortened birth spacing would have increased maternal fitness only if it did not increase offspring mortality. In fact, humans are particularly good at keeping young alive despite shorter birth intervals (Robson, van Schaik, and Hawkes, chapter 2, this volume). Infant and weanling survival is much greater among foragers than among apes and is greater still in nonindustrial herding and farming economies (Hewlett 1991a; Hill and Hurtado 1996; Sellen and Mace 1999; Kaplan et al. 2001). Even after controlling for scaling effects and the wide variation in birth intervals among human foragers, humans have a high reproductive rate, which is almost entirely due to shorter inter-birth intervals rather than to increased twinning rates (Blurton Jones,

Hawkes, and O'Connell 1999). Recent simulations suggest that small improvements in young child survival could produce important changes in human demography (Bentley, Paine, and Boldsen 2001; Paine and Boldsen, chapter 10, this volume). We can surmise that even when improved young child survival may not have led to large increases in ancestral human population size, it had great potential to increase lineage fitness.

THE COMPLEMENTARY FEEDING HYPOTHESIS FOR HUMAN EVOLUTION

The various comparative observations outlined invite explanation in terms of a single, coherent evolutionary model for the appearance and persistence of certain distinctive features of human lactation and young child feeding. I hypothesize that complementary feeding was a key innovation that selected for increased flexibility in the duration of breastfeeding.

Evolution of Complementary Feeding

Some derived features of human life history (see Robson, van Schaik, and Hawkes, chapter 2, this volume) probably co-evolved with changes in patterns of transitional feeding, weaning, and subsequent juvenile provisioning and in the scheduling of the supply of maternal milk. Any changes in the timing of and progression to weaning would have depended on changes in diet and life history among human ancestors. When hominins began to target foraged foods yielding specific key nutrients and to render foraged foods more nutritious through complex processing, some of the constraints on mothers and infants would have been relaxed.

We can hypothesize that a key adaptive shift among human ancestors was the ability to select, process, and combine nutrient-dense, high-quality "juvenile" foods that increased weanling survival, growth, and functional development relative to abrupt weaning onto adult foods and reduced maternal costs of lactation. In other words, humans, or their ancestors, evolved complementary feeding as a derived and adaptive characteristic. Complementary feeding is an evolutionarily novel type of parental care-giving behavior that reduces both the maternal costs of lactation and the fitness costs to infants of the transition from mother's milk to foraged foods. The use of complementary foods made possible new shifts in life history, including shorter lactation, decreased infant mortality, closer birth spacing, long childhood, achievement of larger body size, and a postreproductive phase in females.

At some time since the split with the last common ancestor of hominins and African apes, selection likely began to favor dietary adaptations that accelerated the transition to weaning without decreasing survival or the development of functional competence. Safe complementary feeding could have evolved gradually through numerous subtle behavioral shifts. Group birthing, biparental care, food sharing, and alloparenting contributed to the evolution of more cooperative breeding. Selection of high-nutrient-density food sources through greater "ecological intelligence," cooperative foraging, and tool use improved diet quality. Food processing using various physical, chemical, and bacteriological means increased foraging returns and dietary quality.

Some combination of these changes would have created the conditions for three further shifts. The first of these was replacement of breast milk with nutrient-dense, high-quality complementary foods, which made possible the reduction of birth intervals without incurring a cost of increased mortality or compromised functional development of offspring (that is, dietary resolution of the quality/quantity trade-off). The second was an increased selective advantage for parents whose offspring were provisioned for many years after weaning, as well as for offspring who relied on this provisioning. The third was improvement in maternal diet and therefore birth outcomes and maternal survival, through consumption of these same foods across the lifespan as "family" foods. Therefore, I suggest that behavioral and physiological shifts toward complementary feeding with nutrient-rich foods and early weaning may also have triggered or facilitated the evolution of more general shifts in human foraging, parenting, and social behavior.

Implications

If true, this evolutionary scenario holds several implications. First, humans have evolved extreme plasticity in the duration of lactation and the timing of introduction of non–breast milk foods. This may explain our contemporary problems in defining optimal infant-feeding recommendations. Second, humans have not evolved accurate perceptual mechanisms for "quality control" of the nutritional composition of complementary foods per se. Rather, we have evolved the behavioral tendency to target and concentrate micronutrients and energy from the biotic environment and feed the results to our children. This may explain the use of nutritionally inappropriate complementary foods in agrarian populations, in which dietary diversity is greatly reduced. Third, the habit of experimenting with and eating highly processed, nutrient-dense, high-quality "baby" foods throughout the lifespan has ultimately led to the invention of industrially processed and "fast" foods, including infant formulas. The human species is the first mammal to eliminate lactation. As a consequence, modern populations are at increased risk of cancer, obesity, and cardiovascular disease, exemplifying how a behavioral trait becomes maladaptive in a novel social and technological environment.

To date, few anthropologists have called for a focus on hominid strategies to garner foods of special value to weanlings. A rare example is Binford and Binford's (1969) argument regarding scavenged bone marrow. Most attempts at characterizing ancestral diets fail to consider a number of important issues adequately. The Complementary Feeding hypothesis focuses attention on the fitness benefits of improved nutrition in terms of specific nutrients at a critically vulnerable phase in the life history. It utilizes knowledge of the evolved, specific nutrient needs and dietary propensities of humans and a life history perspective that, to date, have been only weakly integrated into theories of human dietary evolution.

CONCLUSION

This chapter reviews data to suggest that human lactation has a number of distinctive features and to develop a hypothesis for the adaptive significance of early complementary feeding among human ancestors. A major lesson learned is that we know vastly more about lactation biology in humans than in nonhumans, particularly the apes. Despite significant gaps in the data on nonhuman primate lactation biology, tentative conclusions about what is and is not distinctive about human lactation and transitional feeding are drawn as follows.

First, humans have retained an ancestral primate strategy of low daily investment in infants through lactation. Rates of milk secretion conform to a general primate pattern associated with reduced lactation stress and a slow life history. The gross composition of human milk does not differ notably from that of other primates. The nutrient composition of human milk does not indicate any special adaptations to dietary deficiencies or the needs of growing human infants, such as rapid brain growth. The costs of maintenance, growth, and activity of human infants are comparatively low in relation to body size and maternal capacity for milk production.

Second, human female reproductive scheduling is perhaps unusually geared to the energetic support of lactation, with significant fat storage during pregnancy. Natural selection appears to have produced efficient adaptations in human mothers whereby the daily costs of lactation are reduced by mobilization of fat stores laid down in pregnancy (which may be species-specific), changes in physical activity level, and metabolic accommodation.

Third, the feeding of highly processed foods in addition to breast milk has evolved as a unique characteristic of our species. Human infants outstrip the maternal supply of nutrients at about age 6 months and can survive without breast milk at much younger ages and smaller body sizes than can other infant apes. This was made possible by complementary feeding of specially collected and processed foods for the use of infants and young children. Complementary feeding is probably a derived feature that co-evolved with, and may have provided a selective advantage for, shifts in foraging.

Fourth, the scheduling of weaning is unusually plastic among humans, and transitional feeding appears to be fundamentally different. Humans have evolved an unusual capacity to reduce the length of exclusive and transitional feeding without increasing mortality. The characteristics of young children suggest that early childhood evolved in an environment in which the transition to adult foods occurred over several years.

Fifth and last, lactation remained a key life history component throughout hominid evolution. Infants have not evolved to make efficient use of other foods before 6 months of age. Breastfeeding remained a strongly selected component of ancestral maternal strategies because of its powerful anti-infective properties. Today, humans benefit enormously from early exclusive breastfeeding and from partial breastfeeding continued into the third year of life, after which the marginal returns on continued breastfeeding diminish.

In conclusion, the available data are sufficient to support a hypothesis that, at some point in the past seven million years, humans evolved an adaptive, species-typical pattern of facultative, shortened lactation without compromising offspring fitness. This was made possible by the concomitant evolution of complementary feeding behaviors, which are clearly species-specific. The advantages of complementary feeding may have selected for changes in many aspects of food acquisition, processing, and sharing. Changes in lactation may have also played a role in allowing other changes in life history.

Acknowledgments
Thanks to Kristen Hawkes and Rick Paine for the invitation to participate and to Richard Leventhal, Leslie Shipman, and all the staff at the School of American Research for their support of the advanced seminar. Discussions with Kay Dewey, John Kingston, and the seminar participants stimulated many of the ideas presented. Kristen Hawkes and Shannen Robson made helpful comments on the manuscript, and Kate Sellen assisted with the figures.

Notes
1. In clinical usage, the term *infant* is reserved for a child in the age range from birth to 12 months. This may be based on a questionable Western biomedical assumption analogous to that of weaned mammals of other species, that humans achieve a level of independence after age 12 months. Related and overlapping terms also used in both the social and health sciences include *baby* (0 to 2 years), *young child* (1 to 5 years), and *child* (the age range between 5 years and puberty).

2. Such a conceptual framework suggests a number of common events and processes that can be observed, measured, and compared in order to characterize variation within and among species. Transitional feeding in many species involves the infant's supplementing its diet of milk with self-collected wild foods. For example, in many predominantly herbivorous species, the transition to independent foraging is usually abrupt and does not involve provisioning (Clutton-Brock 1991). In other species, social group members (kin or nonkin) may provision the infant, either with unmodified raw foods or with partially processed foods such as butchered carcasses, peeled fruits, and premasticated substances. For example,

many predominantly carnivorous species have evolved a period of weanling provisioning before the offspring forage independently or cooperatively with other group members.

3. There has been debate over whether our conceptual models should characterize *weaning* as an event or a process (P. Martin 1984, 1985; Counsilman and Lim 1985; P. Lee 1997). In consequence, the term *weaning* has been used inconsistently to describe a developmental phase (the maturation of systems involved in independent feeding and foraging), a nutritional transition (the gradual reduction in the volume of milk consumed and its proportion in the diet), and a social process (decreasing frequency of interactions with mother and increasing frequency and complexity of interactions with others).

4. This usage should not be confused with a clinical one. In humans, weaning often does not coincide with the end of pediatric infancy at age 12 months (and strictly should not, because it is currently recommended to take place only after at least two years of life).

5. This definition is epistemologically precise, methodologically feasible, theoretically unambiguous, and thoroughly consistent with nomenclature currently used in clinical research on lactation in humans, the species in which it has been most intensively studied (WHO 1998).

6. The gross composition of human milk sampled after the first month of infant life approximates 87 percent water, 6.8 percent carbohydrate (mostly as lactose), 4.0 percent fat (mostly as triglycerides), 1.6 percent protein, and 0.2 percent mineral (WHO 1985).

7. In contrast, the fetus and its supporting tissues consume only 18.9 percent and 9.2 percent, respectively, of the energy costs of tissue deposition during pregnancy, even though, together, they constitute the largest proportion of weight gain during pregnancy (73 percent; see table 6.3).

8. Human nutritionists have hypothesized that pregnancy fat-storage adaptations are unique to humans (Prentice and Whitehead 1987; Prentice and Goldberg 2000). This appears to be in marked contrast to many other mammals, including nonhuman primates, and runs counter to suggestions by some primatologists that the energetics of human reproduction are similar to those of other anthropoids (P. Lee 1997, 1999; Ross 1998). Others argue that a current paucity of data on body composition changes in nonhuman primates makes it difficult to draw firm conclusions (Dufour and Sauther 2002). In fact, estimates of the total energy cost of human pregnancy differ enormously among individuals and among populations, suggesting that selection has favored considerable phenotypic

plasticity in these accommodations (one review reports a grouped mean range of ~78–~286 MJ [Durnin 1987]).

9. In humans, this trade-off has been characterized as the "weanling's dilemma," the challenge in weighing the known risks of introducing contaminated and nutrient-poor first foods against the theoretically diminishing adequacy of breast milk for satisfying infant energy and micronutrient requirements (Jelliffe and Jelliffe 1978; Rowland, Barrell, and Whitehead 1978; Waterlow 1981). In fact, there is no evidence for a weaning dilemma before 6 months of age. Based on observational studies, a recent WHO Expert Consultation concluded that the health benefits of waiting six months to introduce other foods outweigh the potential risks for most human babies (WHO 1998).

10. Exclusive breastfeeding (EBF) is defined as the practice of giving an infant no other food or drink apart from breast milk (not even water), either directly from the breast or after prior expression into a bottle, with the exception of drops or syrups consisting of vitamins, mineral supplements, or medicines.

11. Exclusive breastfeeding may not be adequate for preterm and low birth-weight babies with poor iron and zinc stores or when the amounts of vitamin A, vitamin B6, and folate in milk decrease in mothers who are marginally nourished (L. H. Allen 1994).

12. Not all non–breast milk substances fed to infants are "complementary" in this sense; in fact, some may be nutritionally inadequate and harmful. Clinical research has identified characteristics of complementary foods and methods of feeding them that maximize positive outcomes for children (K. Dewey 2003).

13. This is true even among African Pygmy populations that show growth suppression from birth due to decreased expression and function of type 1 IGF receptors (Bailey 1991; Shea and Bailey 1996; Geffner et al. 1998).

14. For many contemporary populations living in resource-poor conditions, short duration of breastfeeding and short birth intervals are clearly associated with higher infant mortality and poorer infant quality, but this is not evidence that maternal needs trade off favorably against infant needs.

15. Unfortunately, because the range of variation in reported ages at weaning among populations is considerable, it is not possible to ascertain the proportion of individual children fed according to the recommendations in these populations.

7

Modern Human Life History

The Evolution of Human Childhood and Fertility

Barry Bogin

SUMMARY

Life history theory needs to account for certain features of human social behavior and physical growth that are unusual compared with other primates. Human infants have a relatively early age for weaning (the cessation of breastfeeding)—on average, by age 36 months—but after weaning, human children are still dependent on older individuals for food and protection, until about age 7 years. Many members of the social group—older siblings, grand-mothers, fathers, other kin, even nonkin—take an active role in this provision-ing. Also, humans have seven to ten years of relatively slow growth following weaning and then a few years of rapid growth in virtually all skeletal dimen-sions of the body. No other primate species shares this pattern of skeletal growth.

A central question in life history evolution is, did these characteristics evolve as a package or as a mosaic? The evidence suggests a mosaic, with the evolution of a childhood life stage more than two million years ago as perhaps the earliest feature of modern human growth. The evolution of childhood occurred because it provided reproductive advantages to the mother—by weaning early, the mother was free to reproduce again, faster than any ape.

As a secondary benefit, the extra time for growth and development afforded by childhood enabled greater investments in physical and social capital of the youngster before maturation. These investments, especially in greater brain growth and behavioral complexity, may be inadvertent and chance consequences of the evolution of childhood. The primary driver of the evolution of human life history was the evolution of childhood and cooperative care of children. These allowed for more rapid reproduction, higher-quality offspring, and lower prereproductive mortality than ever before in mammalian history.

Consider the following two life histories. Fifi was born near the shores of Lake Tanganyika, Tanzania, probably in 1958. She gave birth for the first time at age 13 years. In the year 2003, at 44 years of age, she became a mother for the ninth time. Her first three births were spaced five years apart, but subsequent births occurred every four years. The exception to this pattern was her eighth birth, which occurred two years after the birth of her seventh infant. Fifi's seventh infant died shortly after its birth, and she became pregnant soon thereafter. Fifi has four living daughters, and the two oldest have blessed her with five grandchildren, of which four are alive. Fifi has four living sons. One of the older two, Frodo, is confirmed as father of three offspring, Fred, Titan, and Sherehe (Morin et al. 1994; Constable et al. 2001). Because of Fifi's involvement with her own offspring, she rarely invests time or resources in her grandchildren.

The second life history concerns Ethel, who was born in 1908 in the village of Gajsin, Ukraine. She gave birth to two daughters, the first at age 22 and the second at age 29. Both survived to adulthood and produced a total of five offspring. Because Ethel had no current children of her own to care for, she was able to invest time, energy, and resources in the care of her grandchildren. All the grandchildren survived to reproductive age and produced ten biological offspring, four of whom are of reproductive age (two males and two females). As of this writing, Ethel (age 97) and her daughters, grandchildren, and great grandchildren are all alive.

Fifi is a chimpanzee, one of the Gombe group studied by Jane Goodall since 1960 (Goodall 2003). Ethel is my maternal grandmother. Both are reproductively successful, though as of this writing, Ethel more so, because she has more confirmed living descendants. Ethel's family will increase further because her oldest grandchild (the present author) and his wife are in the process of adopting a 1-year-old infant. Chimpanzees living in the wild do not adopt the still-nursing infants of other females (Goodall 1983). Ethel's reproductive success is typical of *Homo sapiens* women, but Fifi is "a female that is off the charts in terms of reproductive success!" (Anne Pusey, personal communication 2004). More typically, a female chimpanzee reproduces only two off-spring that live to adulthood. Goodall (1983) reports that between the years 1965 and 1980, fifty-one births and forty-nine deaths occurred in one community of wild chimpanzees at the Gombe Stream National Park, Tanzania. During a ten-year period, Nishida, Takasaki, and Takahata (1990) observed "74 births, 74 deaths, 14 immigrations and 13 emigrations" in one community at the Mahale Mountains National Park, Tanzania. Chimpanzee population size in these two communities is, by these data, effectively in equilibrium.

The differences between Fifi's and Ethel's reproductive scheduling, longevity, and family social dynamics (including the behavior of grandmothers toward their grandchildren) illustrate many key features of human life history (see also Hawkes, chapters 3 and 4, Robson, van Schaik, and Hawkes, chapter 2, and Sellen, chapter 6, this volume). The human life cycle sharply contrasts with that of other mammal species, even other primates (van Schaik et al., chapter 5, this volume). Female chimpanzees at Gombe give birth to their first infant at an average age of 14 years; in traditional societies throughout the world today and in the historic past, human women do so at an average age of 19 years. Of course, some chimpanzees and women experience first births at younger and older ages. Chimpanzees usually continue to provide some breast milk to their infant for 4 years or longer and average 5.5 years between successful births. In traditional foraging and horticultural societies, human women can successfully reduce the interval to 3–4 years (Short 1976; Howell 1979; Blurton Jones et al. 1992; Hill and Hurtado 1996; Robson, van Schaik, and Hawkes, chapter 2, this volume), and even to 2.0 years in agricultural and industrial societies (Bogin 2001; Setty-Venugopal and Upadhyay 2002). Human birth intervals can be this short because of the early termination of breast-feeding in traditional societies—by a median age of 30 months (Dettwyler 1995) but as early as 9 months (Lee, Majluf, and Gordon

1991; Sellen, chapter 6, this volume). Another contrast is that chimpanzees continue to reproduce until death but human women stop well before death, usually by their mid-40s, and experience menopause by about age 50. It is possible that chimpanzee females experience menopause after age 50, as documented in one case (Finch and Stanford 2004), but chimpanzees rarely live beyond 50. Human women may live for decades beyond menopause and age 50 (Fedigan and Pavelka 1994).

THE HUMAN PARADOX

These contrasts between human women and our genetically closest primate cousin present a problem for students of the evolution of life history. Life history theory has to explain an apparent paradox, that humans successfully combine delayed reproduction, births to helpless newborns, and a relatively short duration of breastfeeding with an extended period of offspring dependency, menopause, and great longevity. Life history theory also has to explain the features of human social behavior and physical growth that are unique among primates. In terms of social behavior, after weaning (the cessation of breastfeeding), human children depend on older individuals for food and protection until about age 7 years. Other forms of physical, social, and economic dependency may continue into the third decade of life.

This dependency of human children is due to the immaturity of their dental, motor, cognitive, and linguistic abilities. Children cannot masticate adult-type foods until the first permanent molars and central incisors erupt, which takes place at an average age of 7 years (Smith, Crummett, and Brandt 1994). Children under 7 cannot walk as efficiently as older people; in traditional foraging and horticultural societies, this means that they cannot acquire sufficient amounts of their own food. Nakano and Kimura (1992) and Kramer (1998) find that by age 7 years, on average, humans can walk with almost adult-type efficiency and gait. Children under 7 use more energy per kilogram of body weight when walking than do adults. By 5 to 6 years of age, children are about 85 percent as efficient as adults. At 7 to 8 years of age, youngsters have more than 90 percent the efficiency of adults.

In what has come to be known as the "five to seven year shift" (Sameroff and Haith 1996), new learning and behavioral capabilities emerge, enabling greater social independence. Cognitive and emotional developments permit new levels of self-sufficiency (Tomasello and Call 1997). With little or no supervision, 7-year-olds can perform many basic tasks, including food preparation, infant care, and other domestic activities (Rogoff 1996; Weisner 1996). Finally, the 7-year-old human achieves new competencies in speech production and language usage. One quantitative change involves the relationship between pharynx height and oral cavity length, which changes from birth until 6–8 years of age, when it reaches and stabilizes at the (1:1) ratio that permits adult vowel production (Fitch and Giedd 1999; Lieberman et al. 2001). The 7-year-old also is more adultlike in production phonology, vocabulary, sentence length, and syntax (Locke and Bogin 2005).

Many members of the human social group, including older siblings, grandmothers, fathers, other kin, and nonkin, help provision and protect infants and children. In contrast, weaned chimpanzees and juveniles of other primate species must forage for most of their own food. The weaned young of some species (for instance, marmosets and tamarins) do receive assistance from their mothers and occasionally from the fathers, but much less often from other group members.

Another paradox for life history evolution is the human pattern of physical growth. Most primate species have rapid growth in length and body weight during infancy and then a declining rate of growth from weaning to adulthood (figures 7.1 and 7.2). In terms of physical growth, humans are unusual in having seven to ten years of relatively slow growth following weaning and then a few years of rapid growth in virtually all skeletal dimensions, called the "adolescent growth spurt." No other primate species, not even chimpanzees, exhibits this pattern of skeletal growth (Bogin 1999a; Hamada and Udono 2002; but see Leigh 2001 for evidence of growth spurts in body weight).

As mentioned before, a central question is whether these characteristics evolved as a package or as a mosaic. In other publications, I explain how the evidence suggests that human life history evolved as a mosaic and may have taken form over more than a million years (Bogin 1999a, 2001). In this chapter, I review the evolution of human childhood, a special life history stage. First, it is necessary to define some key terms, to review the stages of the human life cycle, and to show in more detail how human life history stands in contrast with

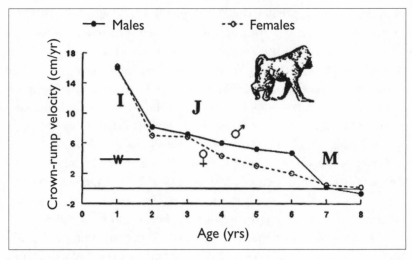

FIGURE 7.1

Baboon crown-rump-length velocity. Letters indicate the stages of growth: I, *infancy;* J, *juvenile; and* M, *mature adult. Weaning* (W) *may take place anytime between the ages of 6 and 18 months (from Bogin 1999a, after Coelho 1985).*

other mammals.

LIFE HISTORY AND LIFE CYCLES

Every species has its own pattern of ontogeny, that is, the process of growth, development, and maturation of the individual organism from conception to death. Every species also has distinct life history traits, that is, major events that occur between the conception and death of an organism. The events of life history "govern natality and mortality" (Cole 1954:103), as well as ontogeny (Charnov 1993, 2001a; Bogin 2001). Stearns (1992:vii) captures the essence of life history theory:

> Consider a zygote that is about to begin its life, and imagine that all opportunities are open to it. At what age and size should it start to reproduce? How many times in its life should it attempt reproduction—once, more than once, continuously, seasonally? When it does reproduce, how much energy and time should it allocate to reproduction as opposed to growth and maintenance? Given a certain allocation, how should it divide those resources up among off-

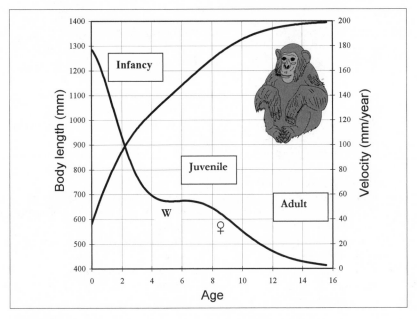

FIGURE 7.2

A model of distance and velocity curves for chimpanzee growth in body length: I, *infancy;* J, *juvenile; and* M, *mature adult. This is based on the longitudinal study of captive chimpanzee growth conducted by Hamada and Udono (2002). In the wild, weaning (W) usually takes place between 48 and 60 months of age (Pusey 1983).*

spring? Should they be few in number but high in quality and large in size, or should they be small and numerous and less likely to survive? Should it concentrate its reproduction early in life and have a short life as a consequence, or should it make less reproductive effort in any given attempt and live longer?

Perhaps it is best to conceptualize a species' pattern of life history as a series of trade-offs, or compromises, that an organism makes between principal biological or behavioral traits. Some mammalian life history traits and trade-offs are listed in table 7.1.

The following are principal traits for mammals, including human beings: the timing of birth versus continued fetal development, the length of the lactation stage versus weaning (the cessation of lactation), the size of the brain, the age at first reproduction, and the age

Table 7.1

Life History Principal Traits and Trade-offs for Mammals

Principal Traits	Tradeoffs

1. Size at birth
2. Growth patterns
  • Number of life cycle stages
  • Duration of each stage
3. Brain size at each life stage and
  at maturity
4. Age and body size at maturity
5. Sexuality: sexual reproduction,
  parthenogenesis, no reproduction?
  • Age at first reproduction
6. Age-, sex-, and size-specific
  reproductive investments
  • Age and size of offspring at
   weaning
7. Number, size, and sex ratio of
  offspring
8. Length of life
  • Reproductive lifespan
  • Age at last reproduction
  • Rate of aging/senescence
	1. Current reproduction versus future
	  reproduction
	2. Current reproduction versus
	  survival
	3. Number, size, and sex of offspring
	4. Parental reproduction versus
	  growth
	5. Number versus size of offspring
	6. Parental condition versus offspring
	  growth
	7. Offspring growth, condition, and
	  survival
	8. Parental versus offspring
	  reproduction

This is a partial list of the most important traits. The bulleted items under each principal trait are examples of specific characteristics of any species. The list is based on the discussion in Cole (1954) and Stearns (1992), who provide additional traits.

at death. The living mammals have greatly varying life history strategies, and examining what shapes these histories is one of the most active areas of research in whole-organism biology.

Bonner (1965) develops the idea that the stages of the life cycle of an individual organism, a colony, or a society are "the basic unit of natural selection." His focus on life cycle stages follows from the research of several nineteenth- and twentieth-century embryologists who proposed that speciation is often achieved by altering rates of growth of existing life stages and by adding or deleting stages. Bonner (1993:93) proposes that we should not think of organisms as *having* a life cycle but rather *as* life cycles: "The great lesson that comes from thinking of organisms as life cycles is that it is the life cycle, not just the adult, that evolves. In particular, it is the building period of the life cycle—the period of development—that is altered over time by natural selection. It is obvious that the only way to change the character of an adult is to change its development."

My goal in this chapter is to consider the following three topics: (1) the evolution of the childhood stage of modern human life history from the perspective of physical growth and development, (2) the basic trade-offs in growth and fertility that result from life history evolution, and (3) the genetic and hormonal basis of some life history traits.

HUMAN LIFE HISTORY

Stages in the human life cycle are listed and defined in table 7.2. The focus of this chapter is restricted to human life history from birth to adulthood. During this period, human beings have five life history stages: infant, child, juvenile, adolescent, and adult. These stage names are used here in ways that are biologically definable and meaningful, so their definition may differ considerably from common usage.

The term *childhood* commonly refers to any time before sexual maturation or before legal responsibility is socially recognized in an individual. This usage of *childhood* may cover the ages between birth and 12, 18, or 21 years. In contrast, the childhood stage of human life history in this chapter refers to a period between the ages of 3 and 7 years, on average. The restricted usage of *childhood* and the other life history stage names in this chapter is justified because each stage encompasses a set of biological and behavioral traits that define the stage. These traits have evolved and bestowed on the human species our special nature.

The stages of human life history from birth to adulthood are evident in graphs of body size growth (figure 7.3), showing the growth in height for normal boys and girls (growth in body weight is very similar). The amount of growth from year to year, the distance curve, is labeled on the y-axis on the right side of the graph in figure 7.3. The rate of growth in height during any year, the velocity curve, is labeled on the left side. Growth velocity is more pertinent to the discussion here because the velocity changes mark the division between human life history stages.

The most rapid growth velocity of any postnatal stage occurs in *infancy*, a stage that begins at birth and lasts until about age 3 years. The infant's growth rate is also characterized by a steep decline in velocity, a deceleration. The infant's curve of growth—rapid velocity

TABLE 7.2

Stages in the Human Life Cycle

Stage	Growth Events/Duration (Approximate or Average)
Prenatal Life	
Fertilization	
First trimester	Fertilization to twelfth week: Embryogenesis
Second trimester	Fourth through sixth lunar month: Rapid growth in length
Third trimester	Seventh lunar month to birth: Rapid growth in weight and organ maturation
Birth	
Postnatal Life	
Neonatal period	Birth to 28 days: Extrauterine adaptation, most rapid rate of postnatal growth and maturation
Infancy	Second month to end of lactation, usually by 36 months: Rapid growth velocity but with steep deceleration in growth rate, feeding by lactation, deciduous tooth eruption, many developmental milestones in physiology, behavior, and cognition
Childhood	Years 3–7: Moderate growth rate, dependency on older people for care and feeding, midgrowth spurt, eruption of first permanent molar and incisor, near completion of brain growth by end of stage
Juvenile	Years 7–10 for girls, 7–12 for boys: Slower growth rate, self-feeding capability, cognitive transition leading to learning of economic and social skills
Puberty	An event of short duration (days or a few weeks) at the end of the juvenile stage: Reactivation in central nervous system of sexual development, dramatic increase in secretion of sex hormones
Adolescence	The stage of development that lasts five to ten years after the onset of puberty: Growth spurt in height and weight, permanent tooth eruption almost complete, development of secondary sexual characteristics, sociosexual maturation, intensification of interest in and practice of adult social, economic, and sexual activities
Adulthood	
Prime and transition	From 20 years old to end of childbearing years: Homeostasis in physiology, behavior, and cognition; menopause for women by age 50
Old age and senescence	From end of childbearing years to death: Decline in the function of many body tissues or systems
Death	

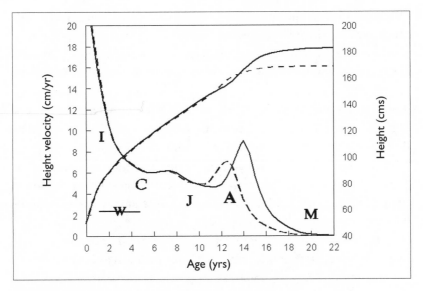

FIGURE 7.3

Average velocity and distance curves of growth in height for healthy girls (dashed lines) and boys (solid lines), showing the postnatal stages of human growth. In the velocity curves, note the spurts in growth rate at mid-childhood and adolescence for both girls and boys. The postnatal stages: I, infancy; C, childhood; J, juvenile; A, adolescence; and M, mature adult. In traditional human societies, weaning (W) of infants from any breastfeeding occurs at an average age of 30 months, with a range of 6–60 or more months (Dettwyler 1995; Sellen, chapter 6, this volume). The figure is based on original material from Bogin (1999a).

and deceleration—is a continuation of the fetal pattern, in which the rate of growth in length actually reaches a peak in the second trimester of gestation, and then begins a deceleration that lasts until childhood. The *childhood* stage follows infancy, encompassing the ages of about 3–7 years. The growth deceleration of infancy ends at the beginning of childhood, and the rate of growth levels off at about 6 cm per year. This leveling off in growth rate is unusual for mammals. Virtually all other species continue a pattern of deceleration after infancy that ends with sexual maturation (Bogin 1999a).

Another feature of the childhood growth phase is the modest acceleration in growth velocity that peaks at about 7 years of age (the midgrowth spurt). Some studies note the presence of the midgrowth spurt in the velocity curve of boys but not girls. Others find that up to two-thirds of boys and girls have midgrowth spurts. The midgrowth spurt is often linked with an endocrine event called "adrenarche," which results in a progressive increase in the secretion of adrenal androgen hormones. However, in a recent study measuring both growth and adrenal hormone production in a group of healthy children (Remer and Manz 2001), the increase in adrenal androgen production occurred one year after the midgrowth spurt. It seems that as-yet-unknown mechanisms are responsible for the midgrowth spurt. Whatever these mechanisms are, they cause the transient increase in growth rate and may also trigger changes in behavior and cognition (described in more detail below). With these changes, the childhood stage ends and the juvenile stage begins.

The human *juvenile* stage begins at about age 7 years and is characterized by the slowest rate of growth since birth. In girls, the juvenile period ends, on average, at about the age of 10, two years before it usually ends in boys; the difference reflects the earlier initiation of puberty and adolescence in girls. Puberty is an event of the neuroendocrine system (Grumbach and Styne 2003). The current understanding of the control of puberty is that one center (or perhaps a few centers) of the brain changes its pattern of neurological activity and its influence on the hypothalamus. The hypothalamus, which is basically inactive in terms of sexual development from about the age of 2 or 3 years, is again stimulated to produce gonadotrophic hormones, which, in turn, stimulate the maturation of the gonads.

Puberty is a relatively short-term event, but adolescence is a lengthy stage of development. During human *adolescence*, most boys and girls experience a rapid acceleration in the growth velocity of virtually all the bones of the body (the adolescent growth spurt). Adolescence is also the stage of life when much social, economic, and sexual maturation takes place. The duration of the adolescent growth spurt covers about eight or nine years, between (on average) ages 10 and 18 in girls and 12 and 20 or 21 in boys. Adolescence ends and early *adulthood* begins with the completion of the growth spurt. In any human population, there is individual variation in the exact ages of each life history stage. However, the modal ages given here do faithfully describe the typical human patterns of growth (see Bogin [1999a, 2001], for discussion of population variation in growth and other life history traits).

Adults achieve full reproductive maturity, meaning that they have the physical, economic, and psychosocial maturity and capacity to care for offspring successfully. Adolescents can bear offspring but usually cannot keep them alive without significant assistance from more competent adults. With the onset of adulthood, growth in height stops because the long bones of the skeleton (the femur, tibia, and humerus) lose their capability to lengthen. In adult humans, a trade-off is made between investing further time and energy in body growth versus reproduction.

LIFE HISTORY OF OTHER PRIMATES

The human pattern of growth velocity is distinct from that of other primates (Pereira and Fairbanks 1993). Leigh (1996) published an extensive review of primate growth in body weight. There are fewer studies of skeletal growth velocity. The results of two such studies appear in figures 7.1 and 7.2, for baboons and chimpanzees (see Robson, van Schaik, and Hawkes, chapter 2, and Sellen, chapter 6, in this volume for additional reviews of primate growth and development). Both species have three phases of postnatal growth: an infancy phase of rapid deceleration, a juvenile phase of less rapid or no deceleration, and a sexual maturation phase of steeper deceleration. In no phase are there growth spurts for body length. Both baboons and chimpanzees achieve reproductive maturation during the third phase of growth, and females may become pregnant while still in that third growth phase. The ♀ symbol indicates the average age at first sexual swelling for each species. In contrast with baboons and chimpanzees, human girls achieve menarche (first menstruation) about one year after the peak of the adolescent growth spurt. This is at about age 13 years in reasonably healthy populations (Bogin 2001). First pregnancy does not occur, on average, for about five years after menarche, when all skeletal growth is virtually complete.

TEETH, FEEDING, AND REPRODUCTION

In addition to changes in growth rate and the timing of first birth, each stage of the human life cycle may be defined by characteristics of dentition, changes in feeding methods, and physical and mental competencies (discussed briefly above and in more detail below). The postpubertal stages may also be characterized by maturation events of the reproductive system and by changes in sexual behavior.

For all mammals, infancy is the stage when the young are fed by maternal lactation. Human infancy requires the mother to provide nourishment to her offspring via lactation or some culturally derived imitation of lactation. During infancy, the deciduous dentition (the so-called "milk teeth") erupts through the gums. Human infancy ends when the child is weaned from the breast, which usually occurs between 24 and 36 months of age in traditional and pre-industrial societies (Dettwyler 1995). By this age, all the deciduous teeth have erupted, even for very late maturing infants (Demirjian 1986), and the young can move on to eating foods specially prepared for children.

One of the important physical developmental milestones of childhood is the replacement of the deciduous teeth with the first permanent teeth. First molar eruption takes place, on average, between the ages of 5.5 and 6.5 years for the majority of human children. Eruption of the central incisor quickly follows, or sometimes precedes, eruption of the first molar. By the end of childhood, usually at the age of 7 years, most children have in place the four first permanent molars and several permanent incisors. Along with growth in size and strength of the jaws and the muscles for chewing, these new teeth provide sufficient capabilities to eat a diet similar to that of adults.

Infancy and childhood are the times of the most rapid postnatal brain growth in human beings. The high rate of brain growth is energetically expensive. The human newborn uses 87 percent of its resting metabolic rate (RMR) for brain growth and function. By the age of 5 years, the percent of RMR usage is still high, at 44 percent, whereas in the adult human the figure is between 20 and 25 percent of RMR. At birth, chimpanzees have smaller brains than do humans, and the difference in size increases rapidly (Leigh 2004). Consequently, the RMR values for the chimpanzee are about 45 percent at birth, 20 percent at age 5 years, and 9 percent at adulthood (Leonard and Robertson 1994).

Table 7.3 lists the key features of human childhood. This suite of traits is not found in any other species of mammal. By the beginning of the juvenile stage (about age 7 years), the growth in weight of the brain is nearly complete (Cabana, Jolicoeur, and Michaud 1993; Robson, van Schaik, and Hawkes, chapter 2, this volume), but much

TABLE 7.3

The Traits Defining Human Childhood

- Period of age 3 to 7 years
- Slow and steady rate of growth and relatively small body size
- Large brain; from age 3 to 5 years, a fast-growing brain
- Higher resting metabolic rate than any other mammalian species
- Immature dentition
- Weaned from mother but dependent on older people for care and feeding for about four years
- Sensitive period for maturation of fundamental motor patterns
- Sensitive period for cognitive and language development
- Sensitive period for physical development, with plasticity to the environment

---

No other mammalian species has this entire suite of features.

physical and cognitive development must still take place. The nutrient requirements for brain growth diminish sharply. Moreover, cognitive and emotional capacities quickly mature to new levels of self-sufficiency during the "5-to-7-years-old transition" (see above). An important consequence of this cognitive transition is that juveniles can conceptualize themselves as independent of older people, something children cannot do. Even when suffering from abuse or neglect, children younger than 6 years old cannot seem to leave their homes. So-called "wolf children" and even "street children," who are sometimes alleged to live on their own, are either myths or not children at all. My search of the literature and personal communication with researchers of street children finds no case of a child (a youngster under the age of 6 years) living alone, either in the wild or on urban streets (see, for example, Panter-Brick, Todd, and Baker 1996). Street children are, in fact, street juveniles and adolescents.

The near completion of brain growth by the start of the juvenile stage enables more energy investment in body growth, but juveniles grow at the slowest rate since birth. A probable explanation for this paradox is that the slow growth of the juvenile body allows for a trade-off between growth, on the one hand, and learning and work, on the other. Studies of juvenile primates in the wild and human juveniles in many cultures indicate that the learning and practice of many food extraction and production skills and much social behavior take place during this stage (Birdsell 1979; J. Altmann 1980; Goodall 1986; Kaplan et al. 2000; van Schaik et al., chapter 5, this volume). Human and non-human primate juveniles learn much about important adult activities, including the preparation of food and methods of infant and childcare (Weisner 1987; Pereira and Fairbanks 1993). Because juveniles are pre-pubertal, they can attend to this kind of social learning without the distractions caused by sexual maturation. As an aside, the start of the human juvenile stage coincides with entry into traditional formal schooling in the industrialized nations. The connection is hardly a coincidence; the juvenile stage is suited for the kinds of learning and socialization found in school environments.

Human juveniles continue their dental maturation and usually have all permanent teeth, except the third molar, by the end of the stage. Indeed, the second permanent molar teeth erupt at a mean age of 10.5–12.0 years in both boys and girls. The eruption of the second molar coincides with the beginning of the adolescent stage, just as the eruption of the first molar marks the end of the childhood stage. No new teeth erupt during human adolescence. Rather, the adolescent stage of life is when social and sexual maturation takes place, largely driven by the hormonal changes of puberty. None of these endocrine changes can be detected directly without sophisticated technology, but the effects of puberty can be noted easily as visible and audible signs of sexual maturation. One such sign is a sudden increase in the density of pubic hair (indeed, the term *puberty* is derived from the Latin *pubescere*, "to grow hairy"). In boys, the deepening of the voice is another sign of puberty (Locke and Bogin 2005). In girls, a visible sign is the development of the breast bud, the first stage of breast development. The pubescent boy or girl, parents, relatives, friends, and sometimes everyone else in the social group can observe these signs of early adolescence.

The adolescent stage also includes development of the external genitalia, sexual dimorphism in body size and composition, and the onset of greater interest and practice of adult patterns of sociosexual and economic behavior. These physical and behavioral changes occur with puberty in many species of mammals, but two important differences distinguish human adolescence. The first is the length of time between the age at puberty and the age at first birth. Humans take, on average, at least ten years for this transition. The average ages for girls are 9 years at puberty (detected by hormonal changes) and 19 years at first birth; for boys, puberty takes place also at about age 9 and fatherhood, no earlier than 21–25, on average. The reasons for delay between puberty and first birth or fatherhood seem to be related to the added value of experience, learning, and physical development provided by the parents (Bogin 1999a, 1999b). The point here is that monkeys and apes take fewer than three years to make the transition from puberty to parenthood.

WHY DID THE HUMAN LIFE CYCLE EVOLVE? THE REPRODUCTIVE ADVANTAGES OF CHILDHOOD

The life stages of infant, juvenile, and adult are shared by most primates (see figures 7.1 and 7.2) and by many other social mammals (see reviews by Harvey, Martin, and Clutton-Brock 1987; Pereira and Fairbanks 1993; Leigh 1996; Bogin 1999a). The evolution of many details concerning the human stages of infancy, juvenile, adolescence, and adulthood are fascinating, but here I discuss only the evolution of human childhood.

Selection for increased reproductive success is the force that drives much of biological evolution. Reproductive success explains the evolution of childhood. Consider the data shown in figure 7.4, which depicts several hominoid developmental landmarks. Compared with living apes, human beings experience developmental delays in eruption of the first permanent molar, age at menarche, and age at first birth. However, humans have a shorter infancy and a shorter birth interval than apes (Robson, van Schaik, and Hawkes, chapter 2, and Sellen, chapter 6, this volume). Females of all other primate species cannot wean their current infant until two things happen: the first permanent molar (M1) must erupt so that the infant can eat an adult-type diet (B. Smith 1991b), and then the infant must learn to forage for itself.

For chimpanzees, this takes about five years. The chimpanzee infant's M1 erupts at a mean age of 3.1 years (Anemone, Mooney, and Siegel 1996; Smith, Crummett, and Brandt 1994), but the mother continues to nurse for about another two years as the infant learns how to acquire and process foods (Pusey 1983). Because of the infant's dependency on the mother, the average period between successful births in the wild is 5.2–5.6 years at the Gombe Stream and Mahale

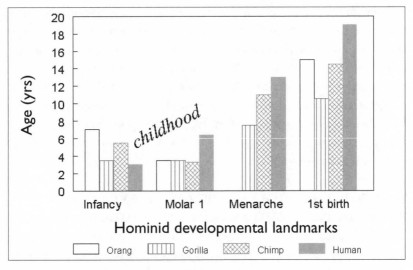

FIGURE 7.4

Hominoid developmental landmarks. Data based on observations of wild-living individuals or, for humans, healthy individuals from various cultures. Infancy/B.I. *is the period of dependency on the mother for survival, usually coincident with the mean age at weaning and/or a new birth* (B.I. *means "birth interval");* Molar 1 *is the mean age at eruption of the first permanent molar;* Menarche *is the mean age at first estrus or menstrual bleeding;* First Birth *is the mean age of females at first offspring delivery.* Orang, Pongo pygmaeus; *gorilla,* Gorilla gorilla; *chimp,* Pan troglodytes; *human,* Homo sapiens *(modified from Bogin 1999a).*

Mountain research sites in Tanzania (Teleki, Hunt, and Pfifferling 1976; Goodall 1983; Nishida, Takasaki, and Takahata 1990). At the Kibale Forest research site in Uganda, chimpanzees average 7.0 years between successful births (Pusey 2001). High-ranking females reproduce more rapidly (Fifi's birth interval averages 4.0 years) and have higher offspring survival (Pusey, Williams, and Goodall 1997).

Human women in traditional societies wait, on average, three to four years between births. The human M1 erupts at about 6 years of age, and human offspring have much to learn before they can survive on their own. The relatively early weaning of human infants is therefore quite unexpected when compared with other primates and mammals. However, the short birth interval gives women a distinct advantage over the apes: they can produce and rear two offspring through infancy in the time it takes chimpanzees or orangutans to produce and rear one offspring. The weaned infant, though, must survive to adulthood if the short human birth spacing is to result in a true reproductive advantage. How can human beings trade off early weaning for increased reproductive frequency and still ensure offspring survival?

Short birth intervals entail a life history compromise between maternal investments in a current infant and in a future infant. A mother who stops nursing her current infant leaves the infant in the predicament of how to eat. Human 3-year-olds cannot move on to the feeding semi-independence of the juvenile stage; they cannot forage for themselves. Even if children could get hold of food from others, they cannot process the diet of juveniles, adolescents, or adults because of immature dentition and the small size of the digestive tract (Behar 1977; Smith, Crummett, and Brandt 1994; Sellen, chapter 6, this volume). These children, then, need foods that are specially chosen and prepared, that is, "baby foods." Human mothers, however, do not have to provide 100 percent of nutrition and care directly to their children. Any older individuals in the social group can feed and protect weaned, dependent children. Indeed, traditional societies deal with the problem of childcare by spreading the responsibility among many individuals, including older juveniles, adolescents, grandmothers, and other adults (Blurton Jones, chapter 8, Hawkes, chapters 3 and 4, and Sellen, chapter 6, this volume).

For example, in Hadza society (African hunters and gatherers), grandmothers and great aunts supply a significant amount of food and care to children (Hawkes, O'Connell, and Blurton Jones 1997; Blurton Jones, chapter 8, this volume). In Agta society (Philippine hunter-gatherers), women hunt large game animals but still retain primary responsibility for childcare (Estioko-Griffin 1986). They accomplish this dual task by living in extended family groups—two or three brothers and sisters, their spouses, children, and parents—and sharing the childcare. Among the Maya of Guatemala (horticulturists and agriculturists), many people live together in extended family compounds. Women of all ages work together in food preparation, clothing manufacture, and childcare (Bogin field notes, 1988–1993). In some societies, including the Agta and the Aka pygmies, hunter-gatherers of central Africa (Hewlett 1991b), fathers provide significant childcare. Summarizing the data from many human societies, Lancaster and Lancaster (1983) call this kind of childcare and feeding "the hominid adaptation" because no other primate or mammal does all of this. The evolutionary reward is that by reducing the length of the infancy stage of life (that is, lactation) and by developing the special features of the human childhood stage, humans have the potential for greater lifetime fertility than any ape.

As shown in figure 7.4, the insertion of the human childhood stage "fills the gap" between the maternal dependence of infants and the relative independence of juveniles. The "bottom line," in a biological sense, is that the evolution of human childhood frees the mother from the demands of nursing and the inhibition of ovulation related to continuous nursing. This, in turn, decreases the interbirth interval and increases reproductive fitness. Investments from siblings, fathers, grandmothers, and others explain, in large part, why a greater percentage of human young survive to adulthood than the young of any other mammalian species. Such cooperative breeding behavior to enhance inclusive fitness has evolved in many independent taxonomic groups, such as insects, birds, and mammals (including primates), so finding it in our own species is no surprise (Clutton-Brock 2002).

BRAIN GROWTH AND LEARNING—A SECONDARY ADVANTAGE OF CHILDHOOD

Human life history—with nearly two decades of postnatal growth and development, including infant dependency and extended childhood, juvenile, and adolescent stages before social and sexual maturation—has long been considered to be advantageous for our species because it provides an extended period ("extra time") for brain development, for the acquisition of technical skills such as tool making and food processing, and for socialization, play, and the development of complex social roles and cultural behavior.

These are common rationalizations for the value of the human growth pattern. They emphasize the value of learning, an idea that Spencer (1886) popularized but which actually goes back to the dawn of written history (Boyd 1980). Learning as the reason for the evolution of several prolonged life stages preceding maturation was nicely summarized by Dobzhansky (1962:58): "Although a prolonged period of juvenile helplessness and dependency would, by itself, be disadvantageous to a species because it endangers the young and handicaps their parents, it is a help to man because the slow development provides time for learning and training, which are far more extensive in man than in any other animal." Allison Jolly (1985:44) also invoked the learning hypothesis for human ontogeny: "Human evolution is a paradox. We have become larger, with long life and immaturity, and few, much loved offspring, and yet we are more, not less adaptable." In an attempt to resolve the paradox of human evolution and our peculiar life history, Jolly (1985:44) concludes in the next sentence that "mental agility buffers environmental change and has replaced reproductive agility."

The reference to reproductive agility means that we are a reproductively frugal species compared with those that lavishly produce dozens, hundreds, or thousands of offspring in each brood or litter. It is fairly easy to argue that humans, with relatively low wastage of offspring, are somehow more "efficient" than other species. But a paradox still remains. The learning hypothesis does not explain how the pattern of human growth evolved. It does not provide a causal mechanism for the evolution of human growth. Rather, it is a tautological argument for the benefits of the simultaneous possession of brains that are large relative to body size, complex technology, and cultural behavior.

Research from hominin paleontology, animal ethology, and archaeology shows that these brain-behavior traits are not causally linked. Extinct hominin species and living primates of various species (and brain sizes) have complex technology and learned behavior (van Schaik et al., chapter 5, and Skinner and Wood, chapter 11, this volume). More to the point, the value of a larger brain, with all the clever learning that the brain can do, is of limited benefit during childhood. Only later in life do the "extra time" and "extra learning" pay off in terms of survival and reproductive success.

Empirical studies of mammalian development show that a childhood stage is not necessary for learning complex skills. Ethological observations of nonhuman primates, elephants, social carnivores, and other mammals show that, during their infant and juvenile stages of life, they can learn and practice all the feeding, social, and reproductive behavior they need. It may be argued that human beings have more to learn than nonhuman primates, such as symbolic language, kinship systems, and the use of technology. Perhaps extra developmental time is necessary to acquire it all. Kaplan and colleagues (2000) suggest that the more complex aspects of human food extraction (such as foraging for hidden foods), hunting animals, and sociosexual behavior may require twenty years or more to master. Maybe human childhood co-evolved with these behavioral complexes. Not so, according to several recent reports. A series of ethnographic studies in traditional societies around the world shows that learning the basics of food production does not take extra time (Bogin 1999a; Bock and Sellen 2002, and other papers in that same volume).

Curiously, Bock and Sellen (2002) cite me as the proponent of the learning hypothesis, despite my long-standing disagreement with both the brain growth and learning hypotheses as the primary reasons for the evolution of childhood (Bogin 1988). I contend that the reproductive advantage to adults is what explains the evolution of a prolonged childhood as a new life history stage for humans. The brain growth and learning hypotheses cannot account for the initial selective impetus for the evolution of childhood. Growing a larger (and more complex) brain may be a secondary benefit of childhood. The primary benefit still seems to be the reproductive advantages to the mother and her close genetic kin.

Maintaining Rapid Brain Growth

R. Martin (1983) and Leigh (2004) demonstrate that the chimpanzee pattern of brain and body growth, even when extended by several years, cannot result in a brain size much greater than 800 cc. This is well below the modern human average of 1,350 cc and below the average for many extinct hominins since the time of *Homo erectus*. Comparing human and chimpanzee brain growth reveals the telling difference (figure 7.5, from Leigh 2004). Before birth (not shown), both chimpanzees and humans have relatively fast *rates* of brain growth, which remain rapid for about eighteen months after birth. However, the total *amount* of growth in human brain mass increases much more rapidly than in chimpanzees. At birth, human brain weight averages 366 g and chimpanzees average 136 g (Robson, van Schaik, and Hawkes, chapter 2, this volume); at 18 months, human brains weigh more than 1,000 g and chimpanzee brains average about 300 g (see figure 7.5). After 18 months of age in both species, the rate of

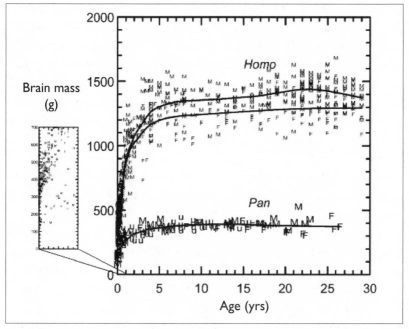

FIGURE 7.5

Brain-mass growth data for humans (Homo sapiens) *and chimpanzees* (Pan troglodytes). *Brain mass increases during the postnatal period in both species. Lines represent best-fit lowess regressions through the data points. M, males; F, females; and U, sex unidentified (Vrba 1998). The inset shows brain-mass growth for each species during the first postnatal year (reproduced from Leigh 2004, with kind permission of the author).*

brain growth declines, but more so in the chimpanzee. During the early phase of the human childhood stage (age 3–5 years), the rate and the amount of brain growth exceed those of the chimpanzee (see figure 7.5). Chimpanzee brain growth ends by 5 years of age, whereas human beings continue a slow but significant rate of brain growth for several more years (Vrba 1998; Leigh 2004; see figure 7.5). In sum, the greater amount of human brain growth before and after birth and the prolongation of "fetal-like" rates of brain growth during infancy and early childhood account for the large size of the human brain.

In the light of this, the "extra time" hypothesis for the evolution of childhood and brain growth is much too simplistic. We should no longer consider childhood an extension of the infancy developmental period but rather a distinct stage of life history between the infancy and juvenile stages. Childhood allows the young human being to continue a fast rate of brain growth because of, in large part, the deceleration of body growth during infancy and the slow rate of body growth of childhood. By the start of childhood at age 3 years, the body growth rate levels off at ~6 cm/year. This slow and steady rate of human growth maintains a relatively small-size body during the childhood years, but the child's brain continues a relatively fast rate of growth. In a classic life history trade-off, the child invests energy and material to build a bigger brain while delaying investment in a bigger body. The body will catch up to the brain, but not until the growth spurt during adolescence.

Other trade-offs also result from the insertion of childhood into human life history. The child's brain is relatively large, almost twice the size of an adult chimpanzee's brain. The child's brain is also quite active. As indicated above, at the age of 5 years the child uses, on average, 44 percent of its resting metabolic rate (RMR) for brain growth and function. The child's large, active, and still growing brain requires a diet that is dense in energy, lipids, and proteins. Moreover, the constraints of the child's immature dentition and small digestive system necessitate a diet that is easy to chew and swallow and is low in total volume. Children lack the motor and cognitive skills to prepare such a diet for themselves; they must depend on older individuals for care and feeding.

Fortunately, children are relatively inexpensive to feed. Their slower rate of body growth and smaller body size reduce competition with adults for food resources; slow-growing, small-bodied children require less food than bigger individuals. A 5-year-old child of average body size and activity, for example, requires 22.7 percent less dietary energy per day for maintenance and growth than does a 10-year-old juvenile of average body size (Ulijaszek and Strickland 1993; Guthrie and Picciano 1995). Therefore, provisioning children, though time-consuming, is not as onerous a task of investment as it would be, for instance, if both brain growth and body growth were progressing at the same rapid rate.

"BABYSITTING" FOR CHILDREN

Directly related to the care and feeding of children is the fact that many older persons can do the job. Because children do not require nursing, any competent member of a social group can provide food and care for them. Early neurological maturity and late sexual maturity enable juveniles and young adolescents to care for themselves and also for children (Bogin 1994). Grandmothers and other postreproductive women provide much childcare (Bogin and Smith 1996; Hawkes et al. 1998; Hawkes, chapter 4, and Blurton Jones, chapter 8, this volume). Again, this frees younger adults, especially the mother, for subsistence activity, adult social behaviors, and further childbearing. Caretaking of this type is rare in other primates, even for apes. Usually, the mother must care for her infant nonhuman primate, or it will die. Adoptions of orphaned infants by females do occur in chimpanzee social groups, but only infants older than 4 years and able to forage for themselves can survive more than a few weeks (Goodall 1983). Goodall noted deterioration in the health and behavior of infant chimpanzees whose mothers had died. The behavioral changes included depression, listlessness, whimpering, and less play. Health changes such as loss of weight were observed. Goodall reported that even those older infants who survived the death of their mothers were affected by delays in physical growth and maturation.

It is well known that human infants and children also show physical and behavioral pathology after the death of one or both parents (Bowlby 1969). However, it seems that the human infant can more easily make new attachments to other caretakers than can the chimpanzee infant (Chisholm 1999). The ability of a variety of human caretakers to attach to one or several human infants may also be an important factor. The psychological and social roots of this difference between human and nonhuman species in attachment behavior are not well understood. The flexibility in attachment behavior evolved by hominin ancestors contributed, in part, to the evolution of childhood and the reproductive efficiency of the human species.

One common pattern of childcare in many traditional cultures is to have juveniles assume caretaking responsibilities for children. This occurs among two well-studied, African hunting-gathering cultures, the !Kung and the Mbuti. Mothers carry their infants with them while foraging. Weaned children (nursing an infant to age 4 years is common in these cultures) must stay "home" at the base camp, for they have neither the strength nor stamina to follow their parents while gathering or hunting (Draper 1976; Konner 1976; Turnbull 1983a, 1983b).

At !Kung camps, children of various ages play together within the camp boundaries, and juveniles assume many caretaking functions for younger children. The children seem to transfer their attachment from parents and other adults to the juveniles, behaving toward them with appropriate deference and obedience. In the age-graded play-group, older generations transmit cultural behavior, as well as adult parental behavior (Konner 1976), to younger generations. Of course, the children and juveniles are never left entirely on their own. At least one adult is always in camp, though not directly involved in childcare. Rather, he or she is preparing food or tools or is otherwise engaged in adult activity.

The Mbuti (nomadic hunters and gatherers of central African rain forests) have a similar childcare arrangement. After weaning, toddlers enter the world of the *bopi*, the Mbuti term for a children's playground but also a place of age-graded childcare and cultural transmission. Between the ages of 2 or 3 to 8 or 9 years, children and juveniles spend almost all day in the bopi. There they learn physical skills, cultural values, and even sexual behavior. "Little that children [and juveniles] do in the bopi is not of full value in later adult life" (Turnbull 1983b: 43–44).

The age-graded playgroup accomplishes both caretaking and enculturation, freeing the adults to provide food, shelter, and other necessities for all the young at their various stages of development. A woman may be pregnant and simultaneously have a child weaned within the preceding year and one or more older offspring. Thus, adults can increase their net reproductive output in a relatively short time. This benefit, along with the selective advantage of numerous surviving offspring afforded by age-graded caretaking, may partially account for the initial evolution of the prolonged childhood life stage in modern humans. Later in human evolution, the role of the playgroup could have been co-opted to gain more time for brain development and learning. In the protective environment of the home base or camp, the playgroup gives children the freedom to explore and experiment, which has been shown to encourage learning, socialization, and even tool use (Beck 1980; Dolhinow 1999; Bogin 2002a).

PLASTICITY OF DEVELOPMENT

Another benefit of childhood is a better-adapted body and more behavioral flexibility with that body. The slow rate of body growth between ages 3 and 7 years provides a mechanism that allows more time for developmental plasticity (Lasker 1969). By this, I mean that a slow-growing child can more precisely "track" ecological conditions, with more growth under good conditions and less growth under bad circumstances. The fitness of a given phenotype (the physical features and behavior of an individual) varies across the range of variation in an environment. When phenotypes are fixed early in development, as in mammals that mature sexually soon after weaning (such as rodents), environmental change and high mortality are positively correlated. The human childhood stage adds four years of relatively slow physical growth and allows for physical and behavioral experience that further enhances developmental plasticity.

An example of the role of plasticity in human physical development comes from my research with the children of Guatemala Maya immigrants to the United States (Bogin and Loucky 1997; Bogin et al. 2002). This research began in 1992 with the measurement of body size in a sample of Maya children (n = 174), 6–12 years old, living in Florida and California. In 1999 and 2000 we measured another group of 6–12 year olds (n = 360) living in the same communities. We compared the older and newer samples with a sample of Maya schoolchildren living in rural Guatemala, measured in 1998–1999 (n = 1,297).

Mean values for height for each sample appear in figure 7.6. Reference data for height from the National Health and Nutrition Examination Surveys (*NHANES* in figure 7.6) I and II of the United States are used as a baseline for comparison in each graph. Maya children living in the United States, in both the 1992 (*Maya-USA1992* in figure 7.6) and the 1999 and 2000 (*Maya-USA2000*) samples, are significantly taller than Maya children living in Guatemala (*Maya-Guat*). The average difference in height between the Maya-USA 2000 and the Maya-Guat samples is 10.24 cm. This is possibly the largest difference in mean stature between migrants and *sedentes* (those who remain in the old country) ever recorded.

Further analysis of our data shows that about 70 percent (7 cm) of the increase in stature is due to the longer legs of the Maya living in the United States (Bogin et al. 2002). The children of the immigrants not only are significantly taller but also have significantly altered body proportions.

The greater stature and altered body proportions of the Maya living

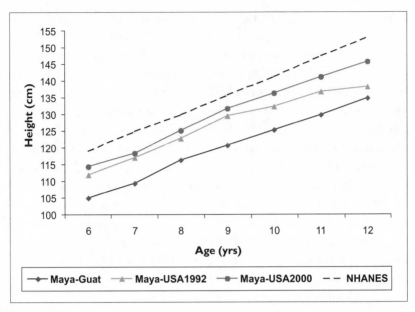

FIGURE 7.6

Mean height of Maya samples compared with the median height of the NHANES reference data (from Bogin and Varela Silva 2003).

in the United States are likely due to improvements in the environment for growth. All Maya in the United States have access to clean drinking water, health services, and education, which may not be so in Guatemala. In Florida, we know that almost all the Maya children participate in school breakfast and lunch programs. These health and nutritional changes are known to result in greater stature. Our findings show the extent and rapidity of plastic changes in human biology during the period of growth and development. Because the differences in height are established by age 6, the developmental plasticity must take place during the infant and childhood stages of development.

WHEN DID CHILDHOOD EVOLVE?

The evolution of new hominin species, such as *Homo habilis, H. ergaster, H. erectus,* and anatomically modern *H. sapiens,* is accompanied by novel patterns of growth in size and body proportion (Bogin and Rios 2003; Thompson, Krovitz, and Nelson 2003). It is not known to what extent the new fossil hominin species, their patterns of growth, and their life history stages are related. We can directly study the stages of the life cycle only for living species; however, we can postulate on the life cycle of extinct species. Such inferences for the hominins are, of course, hypotheses based on comparative anatomy, comparative physiology, comparative ethology, and archaeology.

I have written at some length about the timing of human life history evolution (Bogin 1999a, 2002b). Here I summarize those discussions by stating that the childhood stage of hominin life history may have appeared by two million years BP. Fossil species such as *Homo habilis, H. rudolfensis, H. ergaster,* or early *H. erectus* may have evolved childhood for the reproductive and adaptive plasticity advantages described above. In early *Homo,* childhood may have lasted only a year or so. Despite its short duration, childhood was inserted into early *Homo* life history at the end of the infancy stage. The reduction of infancy by even one year would offer a significant reproductive advantage to any hominin females whose offspring possessed this new life stage. The new life history adaptation of childhood would be favored by natural selection. Over time, further reduction of infancy and prolongation of childhood would be selected because hominin populations with this pattern of life history would out-reproduce those populations without a childhood stage. By the time of archaic *Homo sapiens,* the duration of childhood expanded to its current span of four years. Additional fossil evidence for the evolution of childhood is presented later in this chapter and in other chapters in this book (Skinner and Wood, chapter 11).

GENETIC AND HORMONAL REGULATION OF HUMAN LIFE HISTORY TRAITS

There must be a genetic basis for life history traits if such traits are to evolve over time. Indeed, a genetic basis for human life history markers such as the timing of tooth development, puberty, and menarche, as well as rates of growth for stature and body mass, is well established (see reviews by Bogin 1999a; Towne, Demerath, and Czerwinski 2002). The genetics for the timing of other human traits, such as weaning and age at first reproduction, is not established but likely exists, because there is a genetic basis for these types of traits in other species (Stearns 1992; Leips, Travis, and Rodd 2000; Lill 2001).

Genetics, however, is not the whole story. Hormones, as well as their complex interactions with genes and the environment, seem to play the central role in life history regulation and evolution. Finch and colleagues provide excellent reviews of these gene-hormone-environment interactions in life history schedules (Finch and Rose 1995; Finch and Kirkwood 2000; Finch and Ruvkun 2001; Finch 2002). The action of the thyroid hormones is particularly important in life history evolution because thyroid hormones regulate differentiation, development, and metabolism of tissues throughout the body. Gagneux and colleagues (2001) and Crockford (2003) have published original studies and reviews of thyroid research that relate directly to differences between humans and great apes.

The presence of an adolescent growth spurt in humans and its absence in the chimpanzee offer an example of gene-endocrine interaction in the regulation of life history traits. In both boys and girls, the rise of secretion of androgen hormones (such as testosterone), along with low doses of estrogens early in adolescence, seems to increase growth rates. Later in adolescence, the high doses of estrogens seem to decrease growth rates. During the growth acceleration phase, estrogens appear to stimulate the production of growth hormone (GH), and together these hormones result in the growth spurt (P. Ellison 2002; Hindmarsh 2002).

But more is involved. Roughly equivalent amounts of hormone production in both chimpanzees and humans result in strikingly different rates of growth. In the male chimpanzee, the concentration of testosterone in blood serum increases about thirty-one-fold from the pre-pubertal to pubertal state. In the human male, serum testosterone concentration increases about thirty-eight-fold, or 1.23 times the increase for the chimpanzee (reviewed in Bogin 1999a). Clearly, both chimpanzee males and human boys experience large increases in testosterone production after puberty, but the effects on skeletal growth are not as similar. Chimpanzees have a relatively small increase in the velocity of growth of individual long bones during puberty, "usually less than a centimeter" (Watts and Gavan 1982:58). Hamada and colleagues (1996) report little or no increase in the rate of skeletal growth at the time of puberty for their samples of male and female chimpanzees, despite marked increases in androgen and estrogen levels.

In sharp contrast to the chimpanzee research are the findings for human boys and girls, who show relatively large and easily detectable growth spurts for all the long bones and the vertebrae during adolescence. Cameron, Tanner, and Whitehouse (1982) performed a longitudinal analysis on the growth of individual limb segments in British boys. They found that the peak value in velocity during the adolescent growth spurt ranged between 1.34 cm/year for the forearm and 2.44 cm/year for the tibia. Satake, Kirutka, and Ozaki (1993) report that during human adolescence, peak velocity for sitting height (the length of head, neck, and trunk) equals 7.5 cm/year for Japanese boys and 6.2 cm/year for Japanese girls. These two studies show that growth response of the human skeleton to rising endocrine levels is significantly greater than that of the chimpanzee skeleton.

The skeleton's growth potential is likely to be regulated more by the sensitivity of neuroendocrine receptors and post-receptors (biological tissues) to growth stimuli (hormones) than by the rate or amount of production of the stimuli themselves. The differences in bone sensitivity to hormone levels between nonhuman and human primate growth are probably controlled at the genetic level. Given the overall similarity between humans and chimpanzees in structural genes (the DNA that codes for proteins), the variation in growth control likely lies in the regulatory genes (the noncoding DNA that controls the activity of structural genes). These regulatory genes seem to initiate and terminate each of the distinct periods of growth and control their duration (Davidson 2001). Research into the identification and function of regulatory gene domains, such as homeobox gene families (highly conserved sequences of DNA base pairs found in most eukaryotes), is very active at this time. Recent discoveries of homeobox domains for tooth development and skeletal development in mammals show the importance of interactions among regulatory genes, hormones, and growth (Cobourne and Sharpe 2003; Shibaguchi et al. 2003).

TEETH AND LIFE HISTORY

Long before the discovery of homeobox genes, it was known that the rate of formation of the crown and roots of teeth, as well as their size and shape, is under strong genetic control. The predictability of tooth formation and morphology, even under widely varying conditions for nutrition and health, attests to this strong genetic control (Demirjian 1986; Sullivan 1986; Hlusko, Weiss, and Mahaney 2002). Because of this, dental development schedules provide good correlates of many life history traits and events, as described for humans earlier in this chapter.

The idea of using dental eruption schedules as life history markers for primates originated with Schultz (1924; see Hawkes, chapter 3, this volume). Smith, Crummett, and Brandt (1994) updated Schultz's work with a review of dental eruption data for forty-six species of primates, representing all families. Primates are mammals, and all mammals have two sets of teeth, the deciduous or "milk" teeth and the permanent teeth. Moreover, all the anthropoid primates (Old World monkeys, the apes, and humans) have the same dental formula (the type and number of teeth). Teeth and their development provide a common basis for comparing all species of anthropoids. Smith, Crummett, and Brandt (1994) found that the first few permanent teeth to erupt provide the most information about life history. These authors reported a correlation coefficient of r = 0.72–0.92 for the mean age of first tooth eruption (usually M1) with mean adult body weight (an r = 1.0 would be a perfect relationship). The correlation between M1 eruption and mean adult brain weight is even stronger, r = 0.82–0.97. In another paper, B. Smith (1991b) reports that the correlation between M1 eruption and age at weaning is r = 0.96 (not statistically different from r = 1.0) in thirteen species of primates. Chimpanzees and humans are exceptions. Chimpanzees wean a year or more after eruption of M1, and humans wean several years before M1 eruption (see Robson, van Schaik, and Hawkes, chapter 2, this volume).

These dental comparisons reveal the slower rate of life history progression in apes and people. Smith, Crummett, and Brandt (1994) show that in many species of primates, the newborns have one or more deciduous teeth erupted at birth. The great apes and people, however, are usually toothless for at least a month after birth, and the slow rate of human dental development stands apart from that of the apes. Dean (2000:77) states, "All living great apes are dentally mature by about 11 [years of age], irrespective of their body mass." Humans are not dentally mature until 18–21 years of age. Dean points out that the difference is due mostly to a faster rate of root formation in the great apes than in humans. Formation of tooth crown enamel takes approximately the same time to form in apes and humans. Dean's point is that the dental evidence, as well as much other evidence from growth and development, shows that the evolution of human life history is derived from a general primate substrate.

Dean's conclusion, as well as my own, is that the regulation of tooth development is what separates living primates. And not just tooth development evolved by a change in gene-hormone regulation, but also most of the major features of primate life history. New fossil evidence and the careful analysis of existing fossil material are shedding much light on patterns of regulation in dental development and human evolution. Dean and colleagues (2001) analyzed tooth enamel growth patterns in thirteen fossil hominins. They found that fossils attributed to the australopithecines and early *Homo* (*H. habilis* and *H. erectus* types) are more similar to living African apes than to modern humans. These authors conclude that "truly modern dental development emerged relatively late in human evolution" (Dean et al. 2001:628). Several lines of evidence indicate that a truly modern human life history is no older than 800,000 BP and may be as young as 100,000 years old (Bermúdez de Castro et al. 1999; Thompson, Krovitz, and Nelson 2003).

CONCLUSION

The evolution of human childhood occurred because it provided reproductive advantages to the mother and other mature kin of the child. I have been emphasizing the importance of this reproductive advantage to the mother since the publication of the first edition of my book *Patterns of Human Growth* (Bogin 1988) and in subsequent publications (Bogin 1990, 1993, 1994, 1997, 1999a, 1999b, 2001, 2002b; Bogin and Smith 1996). Unfortunately, some of my readers believe that I favor learning and brain development as the prime movers in human evolution. For this reason, I emphasize here (in italic) the primary reason for childhood.

As a secondary benefit, the evolution of a childhood life history stage may have been co-opted to allow for greater plasticity in growth and for developing new types of investments in physical and social capital of the youngster before maturation. Investments in greater brain growth, symbolic language, and more complex social behavior may be secondary consequences of the evolution of childhood. When this "extra time" became available, human ancestors may have actively exploited childhood for the instruction, learning, and practice of many social and economic skills. But such learning was not the primary driver of human life history evolution. Rather, it was a new type of fertility that made us human—children no longer dependent on breastfeeding and mothers free to resume reproductive cycling more quickly than any other hominoid primate. In addition, cooperative care of children allowed for more rapid reproduction, higher-quality offspring, and lower prereproductive mortality. In sum, childhood and cooperative breeding helped evolve human life history.

Acknowledgments

Many thanks to Kristen Hawkes and Richard Paine for organizing the advanced seminar from which this chapter emerged. All the attendees contributed ideas and an esprit de corps that helped me to think and to write. I also thank the staff at the School of American Research.

8

Contemporary Hunter-Gatherers and Human Life History Evolution

Nicholas Blurton Jones

SUMMARY

In this chapter, I use data from contemporary hunter-gatherers to argue that human life history fits a general mammalian pattern and needs little "special pleading." Among hunter-gatherers, first birth occurs at the age we should predict for a great ape with a hunter-gatherer adult lifespan, so our long juvenile period needs no unique explanation. Archaeological demography, however, has suggested much higher adult mortality. I exclude modern influences on hunter-gatherer adult mortality and summarize problems in archaeological demography. Hunter-gatherer adult mortality resembles mortality in the rural third world and in historical pre-industrial populations.

Because of the many accounts of special features of human growth (such as the adolescent spurt), I was surprised to find that Charnov's growth function (an essential piece of his general mammalian life history theory) accounted for most of the variance in Hadza growth between weaning and maturity. Hunter-gatherers and great apes (except gorillas) grow at the same rate.

Young foragers have much to learn, but they seem able to learn it even when deprived of big stretches of their juvenile bush experience. Learning does not come to a halt when reproduction begins. We cannot argue that the human juvenile period is long because so much needs to be learned before reproduction.

Effects of grandmothers on younger kin (demonstrated in sedentary populations) could account for elongated adult life. Older Hadza women (but not men) live where their help to younger kin (if effective) would most enhance their own fitness. The opportunistic mobility of older Hadza women may make their demographic effects difficult to see.

Efforts to account for the evolution of human life history have traditionally emphasized its special features and the special theories needed to account for them. The importance of immaturity as a time for learning and brain development has been a constant theme, but many other issues have received close attention, such as special features of growth. Recently, some of us have tried to see how human life history fits with the very general mammalian patterns observed by authors such as Harvey and Clutton-Brock (1985) and Promislow and Harvey (1990), as well as with the theoretical effort to account for them set out by Charnov (1993), which Hawkes describes in chapters 3 and 4 of this volume. I review some of our recent work on the Hadza hunters and gatherers of northern Tanzania and use it to discuss the extent to which our species conforms to the general mammalian pattern.

Hunters and gatherers have attracted anthropologists' interest as one of our four key windows into the past. Paleoanthropology gives us direct data on what happened to anatomy. Archaeology gives us data from which we can test hypotheses about past behavior and ecology. Primatology gives us the comparative perspective on differences between modern humans and their closest relatives, as well as the patterns of variation particularly useful in studying life history. Although none are isolated from the modern world, contemporary hunters and gatherers let us see something of the ecological/economic circumstances that confront people living without agriculture. They may also enable us to see the growth and demographic patterns of people who live in that ecology. Some, like the Hadza, living in a relatively rich, wooded savanna in east Africa (Woodburn 1968), enable us to see people confronting the sub-Saharan savanna ecology, which is the closest we can get to the ecology that set the selection pressures that generated our species. Because life history is part of our adaptation to life in the savanna, hunter-gatherers should be informative. But if we believe that life history parameters may evolve more slowly than behavior, then we must temper our use of contemporary hunters and gatherers with questions about a longer time scale than we can observe. With patience and some difficulty, we can obtain data from contemporary hunter-gatherers in detail and volume, but we must consider the brief time period covered by these data and always use them alongside the data from paleoanthropology, archaeology, and primatology.

The length of the human juvenile period (weaning to first repro-duction) has also been a focus of anthropologists' interest. It is several years longer in humans than in our nearest relatives (see Robson, van Schaik, and Hawkes, chapter 2, this volume). Across a wide array of mammalian taxa, the length of the juvenile period bears a constant rela-tionship to the length of the adult lifespan. Charnov (1993) showed how the relationship arises from factors that influence the optimal age at first reproduction in females. This optimum reflects a trade-off between the reproductive advantages of greater size (a result of extended growth) and the average amount of time available to "cash in" these advantages during adult reproductive life. If adult mortality increases, then there is less time to cash in and a lower optimal age of first reproduction. If adult mortality declines, then optimal age at first reproduction is higher.

Thus, adult mortality is directly relevant to this long-discussed fea-ture of human life history—the length of the juvenile period. If adult mortality is similar to that observed among contemporary hunting and gathering societies, then the average age at first reproduction is much as predicted (Alvarez 2000). The length of the juvenile period requires no special explanation if we can explain adult longevity. Have modern populations such as Ache, !Kung, and Hadza led us to overestimate human longevity? Perhaps some of the much lower estimates from archaeological demography better represent our species. Then the shorter period of adult lifespan would imply that our longer juvenile period is exceptional and needs special explanation.

Charnov based his general mammal model (ELC) on a universal growth function: $dW/dt = AW^{0.75}$ (increase in weight per unit time = a taxonomic constant [A] times current weight to the .75 power). This is applied to the period from weaning to adulthood; before weaning, growth is a function of maternal size. We will take a preliminary look at Hadza growth data to see whether it conforms to Charnov's function or falls into the special pattern widely held to describe human growth. The latter places special emphasis on the adolescent growth spurt, which is universally reported in samples from industrial nations but is known to vary with nutrition and other factors.

Older literature accounts for the evolution of the juvenile period as the time needed to accomplish beneficial amounts of learning, especially of subsistence skills. Recently, Kaplan and colleagues (2000) have incorporated the idea in more sophisticated models. But some recent work suggests that subsistence skills depend on size and strength and can be learned quickly. I will summarize work on the Hadza and work by Bliege Bird and Bird on Merriam and Martu children.

The Grandmother hypothesis (GMH) is an application of Charnov's general mammal model. GMH tries to account for the reduction of adult mortality and elongation of adult life and allows other things to follow from ELC, particularly a longer juvenile period (to optimize age at first reproduction) and a greater body size (resulting from the prolonged period of growth). O'Connell, Hawkes, and Blurton Jones (1999) suggested that this set of features characterized *Homo erectus/ ergaster*. Hawkes, O'Connell, and Blurton Jones (2003) noted that these changes were accompanied by a very small change in relative brain size (see also Skinner and Wood, chapter 11, this volume, who describe the distribution of these features in the fossil record).

Is GMH correct in treating postreproductive life in the same way that Charnov's model treats average adult lifespan—a shorter or longer period of reproduction during which the reproductive gains of longer growth time and larger size are cashed in? If an increase in adult female lifespan was selected for the fitness gains to the older female from helping her younger kin, then this aspect of GMH is correct. Data are accumulating that support the view that older females also increase the reproductive success of their younger kin (Sear, Mace, and McGregor 2000; Lahdenpera et al. 2004). So far, though, we lack such evidence for mobile hunter-gatherers. I will discuss what I see as some difficulties in our current attempts to test for demographic effects of grandmothers. The way in which grandmothers distribute their help, while conforming to expectations for a fitness maximizer, may obscure these effects.

Most of the data reported here have been published elsewhere —modern influences on mortality (Blurton Jones, Hawkes, and O'Connell 2002; Hawkes and Blurton Jones 2005); learning and the length of the juvenile period (Blurton Jones and Marlowe 2002); and residence patterns of grandmothers and grandfathers (Blurton Jones, Hawkes, and O'Connell 2005). New data reported here for the Hadza come from an exploratory "first cut" at anthropometric data gathered alongside a series of censuses started in 1985 and ending in 2000. Age estimates may need some revision, and all charts contain embarrassing outliers (sometimes arising from mistaken identity!). All resulting parameters may eventually be adjusted, but such adjustments are likely to be quite small.

ADULT MORTALITY

Estimates of human longevity, or adult mortality rates from contemporary hunter-gatherers, suggest much lower adult mortality than among great apes (Robson, van Schaik, and Hawkes, chapter 2, this volume) and a lengthier postreproductive life. Ache, !Kung, and Hadza hunter-gatherer women aged 45 can expect, on average, another twenty-one years of life (Blurton Jones, Hawkes, and O'Connell 2002). Among the Hadza, 71 percent of individuals who reach adulthood (say, at age 20) survive to the end of their childbearing years (Hawkes, O'Connell, and Blurton Jones 2003:table 9.2). Early and Headland (1998) report a higher mortality level for the Agta during a period of extreme hardship at the hands of expanding populations of neighbors. Even among the Agta, though, 59 percent of those who reach 20 appear to survive past the age of 40, which is close to last childbirth among the Agta (calculated from q_x figures in Early and Headland 1998:table 8.1, forager phase).

The observations support the values for adult mortality used in Alvarez (2000) and her conclusion that the length of the human juvenile period is close to that expected from adult mortality. Note that we are concerned with survivorship, from the age of 20 or 45 to 70 or so. The issue is whether humans live longer than other great apes. None in these forager societies have been encountered who we can be convinced lived into their 90s or beyond, barely any in their 80s. Some demographers are nowadays concerned with survival beyond the 80s and 90s in industrial societies, and many physicians are concerned with diseases such as Alzheimer's, which most often strikes people only at the very end of the observable lifespan of any hunter-gatherer.

In striking contrast, many archaeological demographic reports suggest barely any survivors past age 45, which puts human lifespan quite close to chimpanzee lifespan. A widely cited and very thoroughly conducted example is the paleodemographic study by Lovejoy and colleagues (1977) and Mensforth and Lovejoy (1985) of a very large sample of skeletons from the Libben site in Ohio, dated around AD 800–1100. This population is reported to have an age structure strikingly younger than that of either living hunter-gatherers or the highest-mortality model populations in Coale and Demeny (1983). A plot of its l_x curve (l_x is the proportion of those born who live to age x) falls intermediate between the !Kung (Howell 1979) and the chimpanzee for the first thirty years, followed by a precipitate drop from about age 35 until the last few individuals die at about the same age as the oldest wild chimpanzees, between 45 and 50. This strongly contrasts with modern hunter-gatherers—not only in apparent mortality of middle-aged adults but also, as Howell (1982) pointed out, in a most unusual ratio of caregivers to dependents—and must have included many orphans and almost no grandparents.

Why do estimates of lifespan for contemporary hunter-gatherers differ so much from the results of archaeological demography studies? What kind of data should we take as representing the evolved human life history? Hawkes and Blurton Jones (2005) reviewed this issue at some length. First, the use of a single measure, life expectancy at birth, can be misleading. Life expectancy at birth is a poor indicator of adult mortality. It is heavily influenced by infant and juvenile mortality and therefore by fertility (more babies arrive in the population to live their too brief lives, thus lowering the average lifetime lived by a newborn). In ELC, adult mortality is expressed as the instantaneous adult mortality rate, treated as though it remained unchanged throughout adult life. For humans, who show a clear increase in mortality rate at high ages, other measures may be more convenient. Life expectancy at early adulthood (say, age 20) is one useful measurement. This is the average number of years of life remaining to an individual who reaches the age of 20. For Hadza, it is 41.4 years, for !Kung, 34.0, and for Ache in the forest period, 39.8 (sources in Blurton Jones, Hawkes, and O'Connell [2002]; my latest estimate for Hadza, which uses all the data from 1985–2000, is 39.1 years). Life expectancy at age 45 is a useful indicator of postmenopausal life (see figures above). The maximum age ever recorded is also a surprisingly good indicator of adult mortality rate in many animals (Charnov 1993:104; see Hawkes, chapter 3, this volume). The percentage of the population aged more than, say, 20 or 45 indicates that some number of individuals survive to adulthood or beyond the childbearing years, but infant and child mortality and population increase or decrease also influence this percentage. Population increase lowers the proportion of older individuals; population decrease raises it.

Second, the contemporary hunter-gatherer data differ only a little from contemporary data on rural populations in developing countries. The data on contemporary hunter-gatherers also closely resemble the data presented by historical demographers such as Laslett (1995) on European and other populations from a time before modern medicine. Furthermore, some of the historical populations—for example, Roman Egypt (Bagnall and Frier 1994; Parkin 2003) and China from about AD 100 (Zhao 1997)—date from before some of the archaeological populations studied in North America. The key difference is not time but whether the data were contemporary written records or excavated bones.

The methods of archaeological demography have been subject to much scrutiny. Important studies compare written and archaeological records of the same population. The Spitalfields study (Molleson et al. 1993) showed that among individuals older than about 40, ages estimated from bones were significantly younger than those indicated from recorded birth dates for the same individuals. Walker, Johnson, and Lambert (1988) demonstrated the poor preservation of the very young and the old in a California mission cemetery. The bones gave a demographic picture quite similar to other archaeological studies in North America. The mission records of the same cemetery at the same time showed an age-at-death distribution much more typical of contemporary hunter-gatherers. It is interesting that the novel methods set out in this volume by Konigsberg and Herrmann (chapter 9) result in an age structure that falls within the range of the Coale and Demeny

(1983) models derived from living populations. This arrival of some "bone populations" inside the range of the very large number of known "written populations" is quite comforting.

As a field worker on contemporary foragers, my approach has been to look for effects of the modern world on the hunter-gatherer populations that are studied. The belief that modern hunting and gathering societies can be extrapolated backward to the pre-agricultural past has been strongly challenged by Schrire (1980) and Wilmsen (1989), along with many others. How much has the modern world increased adult survivorship among the people we have most closely studied? In a recent paper, I examined this issue in detail for the Hadza and discussed observations from !Kung and Ache (Blurton Jones, Hawkes, and O'Connell 2002). We discussed the extent to which the finding could be explained away by errors in age estimation and by population decrease (which would lead to an older population—but Hadza and Ache have been increasing). Estimating individual ages was a very large and important part of each demographic study. Each research group used different combinations of known birth dates, historical markers, and relative ages to estimate the ages of nearly all individuals in their study populations. Each group used several methods for checking the accuracy of the estimates. No one relied on asking the research subjects their age. At the time of the studies, almost no one in these societies knew his or her age or even the calendar year.

It is easy to think of possible modern influences, and with the Hadza data, I examined the following.

- *Medical Help Given by Researchers.* We decided that it was unethical to withhold from Hadza any help that we felt able to give to ourselves or one another while at our remote field sites. Sometimes we drove very ill people to clinic or hospital, if requested by their families. Reviewing notebooks, we found that these were mainly men and that most died, so our help was ineffective. We may have saved the lives of two children; others were treated for very mild complaints that probably would not have killed them. We probably saved one woman, aged about 30, who had acute pneumonia.

- *Access to Medical Services in the Surrounding Area.* All the Hadza camps were within a day and a half walk of government rural health clinics. Hadza tended to avoid the clinics, claiming that there would be no medicine (sometimes true). The walk would be nearly impossible for a very sick person.

- *Epidemics.* Surrounding populations of farmers and townspeople are much denser today than in a world of foragers among foragers, creating a larger reservoir of disease. Contemporary foragers may try to keep themselves apart from neighbors, but the effectiveness of self-isolation and the net result are hard to assess. Higher mortality in the less populous distant past seems unlikely, though.

- *Sanitary Engineering.* During the 1985–2000 study period, only one Hadza had access to piped water, and none to sewage systems.

- *Law and Order.* Was homicide reduced? German colonization may have saved the Hadza from extinction at the hands of expanding Maasai in the late 1800s. During the twentieth century, a low rate of killings between Hadza and their Datoga herder neighbors continued. Access to forces of law and order is limited; few police have the facilities for making arduous trips into the bush. Until the late 1990s, Hadza displayed no understanding that external authorities could or should be called upon in cases of murder. They now widely recognize this right and duty.

- *Refuge for the Elderly and Infirm.* Do elderly and infirm take refuge in villages and live "unnaturally long"? Quantitative data show that as people age, they stay away from villages.

- *Farmer and Herder Neighbors.* Do more settled neighbors protect Hadza from effects of food shortages? We can see no differences in mortality related to distance from farmers. Sometimes neighbors do give food to Hadza, as well as trade maize for meat at a seemingly derisive exchange rate, but they have also greatly degraded the environment. Their net effect may well be to make the forager life more difficult.

- *Reduction in Death by Predation.* Predators may have become scarce or intimidated. Death from large predators is very rare in each population. Predators were abundant in Hadza country (and !Kung and Ache country) during the study periods. The practices of East African herders may intimidate lions, which Blurton Jones and Konner (1976) suggested might account for the difference between Hadza and !Kung methods of scavenging from lions. We suspect that deaths from predators have been rare throughout the time that people have used bows.

- *Change in Attitudes toward Abandonment.* Outsiders may have changed forager attitudes about leaving elderly people behind. Striking examples from bushmen or Eskimos can be contrasted with striking tales of survival by Ache and Hadza. Polar and desert habitats demand much more extreme decisions than do more moderate tropical habitats, in which camp movements are shorter (in our series of censuses, the average person of any age was 16 km from where we had last seen him or her) and many people can choose to stay with an invalid.

We concluded that the influence of these possible factors was minimal, and we drew up an estimate of the "Hadza worst case," which gave an adult survivorship close to that of !Kung (as described by Howell 1979) before the 1960s. The Ache in the forest period before "contact" provide the strongest case, but even here modern influences can be proposed. Hill and Hurtado (1996) note the number of Ache shot by Paraguayan farmers, sometimes while raiding the farmers' fields. Certainly, had the Paraguayan farmers no guns, those Ache would have lived longer, but the positive effects of being able to steal food from fields are much more difficult to assess. Balee (1992) has suggested that the forest inhabited by Ache shows signs of previous felling and agriculture. This may best explain the distribution of orange trees, which are used by Ache to some extent, but some of Balee's more extensive claims seem to arise from misunderstanding the relationships among geology, climate, and forest profiles.

The adult survivorship of these modern foragers, which varies so little among the three populations, is also close to that observed in the much larger sample of populations without access to modern medicine—pre-1800 Europe and recent, rural, third-world populations. Putting these together, we can argue for a species-specific pattern, an adult lifespan much longer than that of our closest relatives, the great apes. When people everywhere, even under the poorest of conditions, have such low adult mortality and such long lives, how do we account for the difference from the much shorter lifespans implied by the archaeological population studies mentioned above?

Few traditional explanations survive scrutiny. This universally high level of longevity is not due to agriculture; it is found in hunter-gatherers. It is not firmly associated with recent times; some of the historical demography populations date from before the "bone populations." Some say that the observed longevity is due to "culture," sometimes specifying care of the sick or infirm. Are we to suppose that the members of the "bone populations," foragers and farmers, cared less for their sick and infirm than the Hadza, !Kung, or Ache? Lovejoy and colleagues (1977) offered an explanation based on increases in immunological competence among those heavily exposed to infection early in life. The "bone populations" are implied to represent more isolated, less exposed populations, whereas the "anthropological populations" are "virtually all contact societies" with exposure to a wider array of pathogens (Lovejoy et al. 1977:293). This could conceivably apply to the New World samples, but we might wonder, on the one hand, how it would apply in the Old World and to the likely lack of isolation among prehistoric populations and, on the other hand, we might find it seriously impaired by the Ache data from Paraguay. The values we have reported for Ache come from Hill and Hurtado's (1996) findings on the period before recent contact, and adult lifespans were similar to other modern hunter-gatherers. Hill and Hurtado, however, also report Ache mortality during the time of contact and during the later "reservation period." There were changes, as expected, but far too weak to account for the difference between the apparently short-lived "bone populations" and the evidently long-lived historical and anthropological populations. The contradiction remains. We believe that the lifespans implied by the bone data are very questionable and that a definitive resolution is yet to be reached.

The modern world has changed adult mortality for some, the members of modern industrial and fast-developing nations. Where do they belong in an account of the evolution of human life history? We should separate two processes. First, improvements in infant and child survival have occurred, usually credited to science-based medicine, progress in sanitary engineering, and better diet. More recently, survival of the very old, the over 80, has increased in industrial nations. Eighty is close to the age of the oldest individual Hadza, !Kung, or Ache. If this modern extension of adult longevity simply reflects the removal of some important pathogens and the technical fixes for the degenerative diseases of senescence, it is of relatively little evolutionary interest. But if it reflects some underlying reaction norm concerning lifetime scheduling of investment in immune systems or other maintenance systems, it may be profoundly relevant to life history theory. A lively recent literature deals with some aspects of extreme old age (for example, Vaupel 1997; Partridge and Mangel 1999).

CHARNOV'S GROWTH FUNCTION AND PATTERNS OF GROWTH IN CONTEMPORARY HUNTER-GATHERERS

Three recently studied hunter-gatherer populations (Ache, !Kung, and Hadza) each show an average age of 19 years at first birth for mothers. The ratio of juvenile period (weaning to first birth) to adult lifespan is therefore close to the higher primate value, as Alvarez (2000) and Hawkes (chapter 4, this volume) have reported. If we take these populations as representing *Homo sapiens*, the length of our juvenile period would not appear to be anything special and would require no explanation. But a large literature has suggested otherwise. For example, the existence of an adolescent growth spurt is widely reported as a well-established difference between humans and other animals (although an adolescent spurt has been claimed for some other primates). On one hand, Bogin (1999a; chapter 7, this volume) has made the interesting suggestion that the pre-adult period of humans be divided into a slow-growing childhood, when tasks other than growth (such as learning) may be better recipients of time and energy, and adolescence, when growth becomes a premier adaptive task. On the other hand, Charnov's 1993 model employs a simple growth model to represent a general mammalian pattern. Is it a good enough model of hunter-gatherer growth? Does Charnov's growth equation provide a universal mammal "baseline," upon which special human features are added as small deviations?

Charnov (1993) proposes that growth before weaning is at a high rate, determined by the mother's productivity, and that after weaning, growth falls to a rate determined by the juvenile's own productivity. Growth then proceeds according to $dW/dt = AW^{0.75}$, where W is weight and (A) is a constant for each major taxon. This "productivity function" plays an important role in Charnov's theory, quantitatively predicting constant relationships between various other life history parameters. The function gives a weight curve that accelerates imperceptibly at first but eventually climbs quite strikingly. Finally, approaching adulthood in a determinate grower, growth must slow and cease. Is the adolescent growth spurt merely what we see when a very long-lived species follows Charnov's equation? Note that the animal literature attends primarily to growth in weight (except in studies of fish, in which length is often used) whereas researchers on human growth have been much more interested in height. In humans, weight is extremely variable across populations, among individuals, between sickness and health, and even from week to week. Understandably, weight can be thought to indicate less about attained size. Height may also be behaviorally salient to people in ways we have not identified in quadrupedal species. As Bogin (1999a; chapter 7, this volume) points out, many have tried to describe human growth by a simple equation, and such models have failed to represent all the interesting features of the pattern. Researchers on human growth (with a few exceptions) have also differed from theoreticians such as Charnov in seeking functions that describe the entire growth curve from birth to maturity, without initial regard for the biological significance of different parts of the curve.

Hill and Hurtado (1996) fitted Charnov's growth function to Ache data and reported a good fit to growth of children older than 6 but with an (A) much lower than among most other primates (0.29 for girls from age 6 to 15, 0.23 for boys from age 6 to 18). They do not report results for fits from weaning, nor do they comment on why they chose age 6 (weight 18 kg).

I examined the fit of Hadza growth data to the productivity equation as follows. Our measurements of Hadza include many people measured more than once. I calculated gains in height and weight between measurements fewer than four years apart (the mean length of these intervals was 1.85 years), and we can plot growth rate (cm/yr and kg/yr) against age. The raw data were differences in weight between one occasion and the next for the same individual, stored as changes in kg/year. There were 580 records of weight changes for females, 530 for males under age 25. Each measurement of rate of weight gain began at a starting weight. The starting weight (W) was converted to $W^{0.75}$ for every record, giving a measure called "wtpowr." A linear curve was fitted to weight gain in kg/year predicted by wtpowr, with the curve going through the origin. The fit was very close: r = 0.91 for females and 0.89 for males, and the coefficient (A) was 0.23 for males (aged 2–18) and 0.26 for females (aged 2–16). These figures are remarkably close to those obtained by Hill and Hurtado (1996) for Ache. Our results imply that Charnov's equation accounts for a very large proportion of the variance in Hadza juvenile growth velocity (83 percent for females, 79 percent for males).

Figures 8.1 and 8.2 plot the average, observed, annual weight gain (the average of all the individual longitudinal changes beginning in that year of age) and the values predicted by the productivity equation. The predictions were calculated beginning at age 3, which is just after weaning (30 months appears to be the age at which 50 percent of children are still seen, or reported to be, suckling and 50 percent are reported as having ceased suckling), with a weight of 10 kg and using the values for (A) derived above. The girls' observed average annual weight gain follows the predicted line quite well until age 17 years. The boys also follow up to about 17, but then, like the girls, their weight gain declines far below the predicted rates, even though, unlike the girls, they continue to gain weight at a significant rate into their mid-20s and beyond. Because triceps skinfolds stay at a minimal 4–6 mm in adult Hadza men, this weight gain probably comprises increased muscle. The observed weight growth rate for females aged 2–17 correlates with the predicted rate, with r = 0.93.

The productivity equation used by Charnov (1993), summarizing growth in weight of many species, aptly describes growth of Hadza children from weaning until shortly before first reproduction. The values for (A) that we have obtained from hunter-gatherer growth are much lower than the 0.42 obtained for primates as a group by Charnov (1993) and the 0.47 estimated from a larger sample by Ross and Jones (1999). In general, though, (A) for chimpanzees, bonobos, and orangs may also be lower than for the primates (see Robson, van Schaik, and Hawkes, chapter 2, this volume, who remark on the striking difference in the growth rates of gorillas and other apes). The adult female sizes, age at maturity, and lengths of the juvenile periods imply that (A) for *Pongo pygmaeus*, *Pan troglodytes*, and *Pan paniscus* would be very similar to those found for human foragers. Data summarized in Ross (2003) and Robson, van Schaik, and Hawkes (chapter 2, this volume), shown in table 8.1, allow us to plot the size at first reproduction for chimpanzee, bonobo, orangutan, and Hadza and the weight at weaning

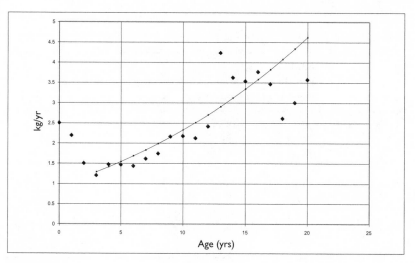

FIGURE 8.1

Hadza male weight changes plotted by age at start of interval (to the nearest year). The value at each age is the mean of all the pairs of measurements that begin at that age. Intervals vary between 1 year and 4 years (mean 1.85 years), and weight changes are pro-rated to a single year. The solid line is change predicted by the dW/dt = AW$^{0.75}$ equation, beginning with a weight of 10 kg at age 3 years, and the fitted male, A = .23.

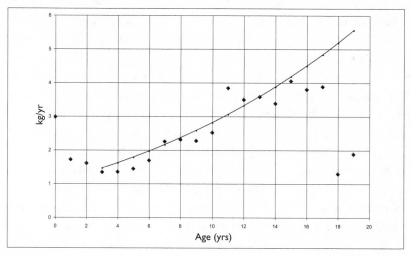

FIGURE 8.2

Hadza female weight changes plotted by start of interval. The solid line is change predicted by the dW/dt = AW$^{0.75}$ equation, beginning with a weight of 10 kg at age 3 years, and the fitted male, A = .26.

TABLE 8.1

Great Ape Life History Variables Used for Figure 8.3

	Adult Female Weight	Age at First Birth	Weaning Weight	Weaning Age	Alpha
P. troglodytes	40.3,[1] 35,[2] 33.7[3]	13,[1] 13.3[2]	8.5[1]	4.5[2]	8.36,[1] 8[3]
P. paniscus	33.2,[1] 33[2]	14.2[2]	8.5[1]		
Pongo pygmaeus	37.1,[1] 36[2]	9.68,[1] 15.6[2]		7[2]	7.88[1]

1. Ross (2003)
2. Robson, van Schaik, and Hawkes (chapter 2, this volume)
3. Ross and Jones (1999)

for chimpanzee and Hadza on a chart (figure 8.3) that shows weights predicted by $dW/dt = AW^{0.75}$ with the Hadza female (A) (0.26) and a narrow range of assumptions about weaning weight and weaning age. This plot shows that contemporary hunter-gatherers and great apes (excluding *Gorilla*) must have very similar (A); that is, they must grow at similar rates.

One of the most widely observed special features of human growth is the adolescent growth spurt. Despite its apparent link to the endocrine processes developing primary and secondary sexual characteristics, we have asked whether the adolescent spurt could be explained away when Charnov's equation is applied to a very late-maturing species in which the gradually increasing weight gains would become noticeable. Do Hadza have an adolescent growth spurt, if we define it as an increase in growth rate greater than predicted by the Charnov growth equation? In figure 8.1, we can see a couple points where male weight increase falls clearly above the value predicted by Charnov's function. Some studies already show variation in the visibility of the adolescent growth spurt (for example, Frisancho and Baker 1970), perhaps with variation in nutrition, and some show a pattern of growth somewhat different from that usually observed in industrial societies.

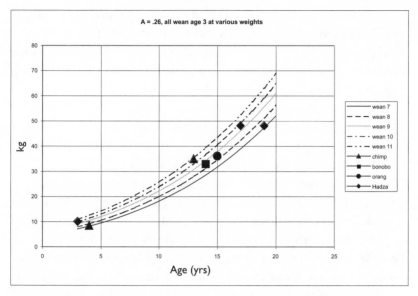

FIGURE 8.3

Comparing great ape and hunter-gatherer juvenile female growth rates. The continuous lines represent the body weight predicted by dW/dt = AW$^{0.75}$, beginning with a variety of notional weaning weights from 7 to 11 kg at age 3. Solid marks are the observed values of weaning weight and the weight at first reproduction for chimpanzee, bonobo, orangutan, and Hadza. A second mark for Hadza is placed at the age at which female growth stops.

For example, when Datoga or Turkana pastoralist heights are plotted on North American standards, the pastoralists fall ever more below the third percentile during the teen years. The data, however, give some indication that 20-year-olds eventually reach the third percentile (Little, Galvin, and Mugambi 1983; Sellen 1999). Herder boys and men are growing slower than Americans, but for longer periods and more steadily, with less of a spurt. Draper and Howell (2005) show similar plots of height data for !Kung in the 1960s. !Kung males and females fell increasingly behind during their teens but approached the third percentile in their 20s. Preliminary plots of the means of height from a much larger sample of Hadza (828 measurements of males aged up to 20, 821 females) appear in figures 8.4 and 8.5 with CDC standards. (Incidentally, the final heights and weights of our Hadza sample in 1985–2000 are very similar to the mean adult heights and weights of Hadza in 1966–1967 reported by Hiernaux and Hartono

[1980].) Figures 8.4 and 8.5 suggest a similar phenomenon to Draper and Howell's and Sellen's results. Does this mean that the adolescent growth spurt is much dampened or absent among hunter-gatherers? We saw above that weight followed a pattern close to Charnov's equation, with only a weak indication of any acceleration above that line to indicate an adolescent spurt.

The anthropometry tradition regards height as more meaningful than weight, so let us look at our data on Hadza height changes, from repeated measurements of the same individuals (425 height changes for males, 479 for females, under age 25), extracted from our very "mixed longitudinal" sample. Among the girls (figure 8.6), except for a small spike for intervals starting at age 11, rate of increase in height declines from early childhood and is almost finished by about 18. There is an unconvincing indication of an adolescent spurt in height, and it is surprisingly early. Among the boys (figure 8.7), there is a more convincing indication of a spurt in height. Growth rates increase and stay high from age 12 to 14. They then decline until the early 20s.

In any population, the adolescent growth spurt occurs at different ages in different individuals, so it is difficult to demonstrate without a closely spaced series of measures on the same individuals. If we add error under harsh field conditions and the errors in age estimation for people such as the Hadza, it may be no surprise that we see only poor indications of a height spurt from our sample of pairs of measurements, often more than a year apart. Consequently, I extracted data for only those forty-three young people who had been measured in five or more different years. For thirty-five of these, the measurements well spanned the teen years. Among them, we can see a teenage year with much faster growth in height for fifteen out of the sixteen boys, though for only four out of the nineteen girls. Something of the adolescent growth spurt exists in Hadza boys, but not in the girls. It is obvious in the field, though, that skinny little Hadza children quickly become muscular young men and shapely young women sometime in their teens. As in any other population, secondary sexual characteristics appear, and "young adults" differ distinctly from children.

We have very limited data from the Hadza on other changes at puberty. Some information on breast stage and menarche was gathered in 1990, and we may be able to test whether the sequence of

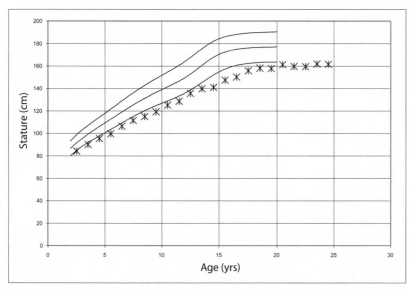

FIGURE 8.4

The height of Hadza boys plotted alongside the CDC (2000) height standards. Continuous lines represent the ninety-seventh, fiftieth, and third percentiles in the CDC standards.

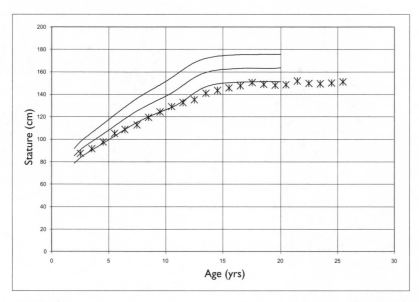

FIGURE 8.5

The height of Hadza girls plotted alongside the CDC (2000) height standards.

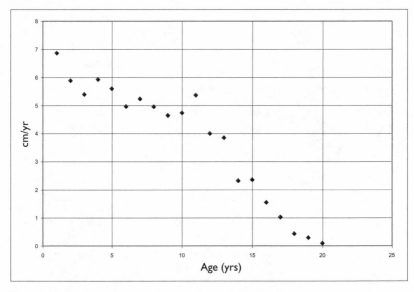

FIGURE 8.6

Hadza female height changes plotted by age at start of interval. (The details are the same as in figure 8.1.)

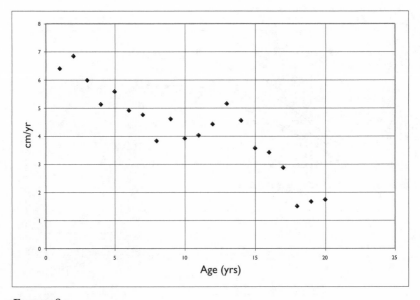

FIGURE 8.7

Hadza male height changes plotted by age at start of interval. (The details are the same as in figure 8.1.)

development during puberty resembles that in other populations. We have also repeatedly measured upper arm circumference (UAC) and triceps skinfolds. In boys, UAC increases appear to peak at an older age than do increases in height. If UAC growth represents mostly muscle growth (fatness, as measured by triceps skinfolds, decreases in males during this period), then muscle growth follows peak height velocity, just as in industrial and agricultural populations. We have yet to separate the individuals who attended boarding school. Already, we have shown that they tend to grow heavier (Blurton Jones and Marlowe 2002), but we should examine the growth patterns separately for the school attenders and the nonattenders.

The best summary of these very preliminary analyses seems to be that the Charnov equation accounts for most of the general pattern of Hadza growth during the juvenile period but that a very limited adolescent spurt is superimposed on this pattern. Hadza males show some indication of a growth spurt but continue to grow for a longer time than Western adolescents. Hadza females show only weak indications of a growth spurt, almost none for height. Their growth continues later than Western children's, but even their weight gain ceases by the end of the teen years. Frisancho and Baker (1970) describe children in high-altitude Peru as having a slow rate of growth, a prolonged growth period lasting to age 22, and a late and poorly defined growth spurt. The description could fit the Hadza data presented here. Is the growth spurt so expendable that it disappears when resources are scarce? Do contemporary forager levels of resources and growth represent our species before agriculture? Why would we have this facultative response? Does it reflect a hierarchy of uses for resources—grow at all costs, grow tall if you have spare resources, especially if you are male?

Most contemporary hunter-gatherers are very small (see Robson, van Schaik, and Hawkes, chapter 2, this volume), and most scholars who research growth are quick to label them as "undernourished." This implies that their growth is therefore "abnormal" and less representative of our species than is the growth of industrial populations, who are increasingly described as undergoing an "obesity crisis." The ecology of contemporary tropical hunters and gatherers certainly resembles, in many ways, the ecology containing the selection pressures that brought about our life history; however, we do not know how the nutritional intake of prehistoric tropical foragers compares with the nutrition of modern foragers. We do have archaeological evidence that some prehistoric samples were heavier than modern foragers, in low latitudes and high (Ruff, Trinkaus, and Holliday 1997).

Scholars often argue that a reduction in robusticity accompanied improvement in tools and weapons, assuming that strength was no longer as valuable. Do contemporary hunter-gatherers merely continue trends toward smaller size in recent times and in lower latitudes? We also have plenty of reason to believe that more food is advantageous, up to a certain quantity (for example, see Bairagi et al. 1985). Sociologists have demonstrated advantages in greater height in industrial societies, but there are indications that large size can be disadvantageous in other circumstances. Larger individuals perform less effectively or safely in severe heat conditions (for example, see Kerslake 1972; Baker 1988; Wright et al. 2002 and references therein). Medium-height !Kung men have tended to be more successful hunters than taller men (R. B. Lee 1979b:figure 10.1).

R. A. Foley (1982) pointed out another peculiarity of African hunter-gatherers. They occupy the extremes of rainfall, with Pygmies in high-rainfall forest, Hadza and San in very low-rainfall savanna and desert. Pastoralists occupy the 500–1,500 mm/yr rainfall savanna where large mammal biomass is highest. Foley is arguing about the likely proportions of plant and animal food in forager diets. But we may wonder whether the overall resources available to foragers in the 500–1,500 mm/yr areas might have been greater. If more resources were available to each individual (instead of the population being more dense), and in view of the larger stature of hunters and gatherers in the Upper Paleolithic (see Ruff, Trinkaus, and Holliday 1997; Skinner and Wood, chapter 11, this volume), we might decide that the growth patterns of Hadza and !Kung—and even Ache, whose calorie intake and adult weight are much higher—tell us little about a species-specific human growth pattern.

If larger, better-fed foragers typified our species, they may also have matured earlier. In modern populations, individual age at maturity varies with growth rate. Having matured earlier, the ancient foragers may have also had their first births earlier. These better-fed foragers might also have survived better than our contemporary examples.

Then the ratio of juvenile span to adult span would be a little lower than Alvarez (2000) and Hawkes and colleagues (1998) have reported. Our juvenile span would be shorter than expected. We should not overlook the possibility that an increase in resources can be allocated either to greater numbers, greater weight, or greater height. Aboriginal women (Eveleth and Tanner 1976) weighed about the same as Hadza women but were much taller. Ache men and women are about the same height as Hadza men and women but are much heavier.

Charnov's life history theory accounts for the general patterns of variation of life history among great numbers of species. At its core, the general growth equation applies well to hunter-gatherer growth. But the general pattern may vary in any species, as one can see from any of the graphs in Charnov's book or Hawkes' chapter 4, this volume. Humans need be no exception. Although Charnov's equation accounts for much of hunter-gatherer juvenile growth and clearly puts human growth in the same range as that of the other great apes, certain details of human growth and its variation require explanation. These might be better understood by trying to replace the traditional "balloon" model (the more food you pump in, the bigger they get) with a model that includes regulation (as in catch-up growth) and allocation of resources. Individuals must allocate resources among growth, maintenance, and reproduction (at any one time, as well as throughout the life history) and perhaps among muscle, fat, and bone, between strength and height, between economic and social functions.

We need more adaptationist thinking about hunter-gatherer growth before we conclude that the human juvenile period is so radically different in its pattern of growth that we need to invoke special reasons for the evolution of its length. Almost all the literature on human growth is presented in a causal perspective: more or less of this or that nutrient "produces" more or less height, muscle, fat (much of the evidence is correlational). We have made very little effort to think through ways in which natural selection might "design" the details of a growth system, setting tasks for proximate mechanisms of regulation of growth, despite early indications of powerful regulation as discussed in literature on "catch-up growth." Bogin's (chapter 7, this volume) suggestions about the differing tasks of childhood and adolescence are a promising beginning.

LEARNING AND THE LENGTH OF THE JUVENILE PERIOD

Hunter-gatherers have great knowledge and mastery of essential skills. Each generation has much to learn—the habitats and seasons of numerous plant foods, habits and movements of numerous animals, behavior of prey and predators. They must acquire skills for making and using tools. In addition to all this, they must acquire knowledge common to any society: kin and kinship terminology, proscriptions and prescriptions. All this must be learned. But is this why the juvenile period is so long? Most of us have assumed that it is. We have taken observations of children foraging, or playing at foraging skills, as indications of the length of time needed to learn these skills. Quantitative data showing increases in skill with age have also been interpreted as indicating the role of learning. Bock (2002) has shown how parents appear to trade off the immediate returns from children's work against the implied value of their play through its effect on acquisition and development of skills. But the Charnov model implies that we do not need a special explanation for the length of the juvenile period, and, recently, other kinds of evidence against the traditional skill acquisition assumptions have been presented.

In a series of simple experiments conducted with Hadza in 1997, Blurton Jones and Marlowe (2002) tested young and adult Hadza at digging tubers, climbing baobab trees, and shooting arrows, each a component of major subsistence activities. Hadza could not survive without these skills. Boys and girls dig shallow tubers for themselves from about age 5 to about 12. After this, boys dig much less than girls, spending more time wandering the bush with a bow and arrows. The girls accompany women to dig deep tubers, often in rocky ground. By the time they are adult, girls have spent their entire juvenile period digging almost daily and have had twice as much practice time as boys (Blurton Jones, Hawkes, and O'Connell 1997). When paid to dig tubers, in separate groups of males or females, boys and men were just as efficient as girls and women (forty-one males, thirty-eight females). Learning to locate and dig tubers does not take the entire juvenile period.

We tested boys and men for climbing. Men climb baobab trees, cutting pegs from small bushes to hammer into the trunk to form a kind of ladder. Baobab trees are climbed to get *Apis mellifera* honey. The work is very dangerous. Serious accidents and a few deaths have resulted from falls from baobab trees. We found that several willing young subjects were forbidden by adults because, even though we limited the climb to a very few feet off the ground, the task was considered too dangerous, or we were told that the boy could not do this yet. Those who did attempt the task performed as fast as the adult men. There was no increase with age, no sign of a deficit (in this very small climbing sample) in those who had lost bush time in boarding school.

We tested one hundred men and boys at archery, a key component of hunting. Here we found a clear increase in accuracy with age, but accuracy is as well predicted by strength and by strength of bow as by age. Since 1990, many Hadza children have been taken away to boarding school, and some stay several years. We looked for an effect on shooting accuracy from losing years of bush life in boarding school. There was no indication of an effect. A series of efforts to massage the data into giving an effect failed. It does not take the whole juvenile period for a boy to become an expert marksman. Men's accuracy seemed to increase well into the adult years, paralleling the improvement of hunting success reported for Ache hunters (Walker et al. 2002) and the age course of Hadza men's reputations as successful hunters. We also looked for effects of boarding school on efficiency at finding and digging tubers and, again, could see no indication of any effect.

These experiments suggested to us that we have been wrong to interpret increases in foraging efficiency with age as indications of increased skill or of the time needed to acquire and fine-tune these skills. Increases in size, weight, and strength seem to be important factors.

Studies of children's foraging by Bird and Bliege Bird (2000, 2002; Bliege Bird and Bird 2002) on Mer in the Torres Straits also suggest that we have been too quick to interpret the differences between children's foraging and adults' as signs of low skill or lack of knowledge. Merriam children are efficient foragers for shellfish, targeting an optimal set of prey for people of their height and walking speed. As spear fishers, children excel over all but the oldest adults. Recent studies of foraging among the Martu of western Australia by Bird and Bliege Bird (2005) support a similar conclusion. It appears that children target prey and patches that are optimal for people of their height and walking speed. If they get less than adults, it is not because they are more ignorant, but just smaller.

Tucker and Young (2005) found that Mikea children dig deep tubers in sandy soil quite efficiently but achieve low yields because of their distractibility and playfulness. We do not know what their return rates would be if they were experimentally given some added incentive to dig. This illustrates another "forgotten factor," motivation and its effect on concentration and persistence. This may account for some part of the increase in men's hunting success, which is reported to continue well after marriage and birth of the first children (Kaplan et al. 2000; Walker et al. 2002).

These recent studies should make us rethink our long-held belief that the juvenile period exists for learning. Much depends on the form in which we state our belief. Traditionally, it has been stated in terms of the juvenile period being stretched to allow enough time to learn subsistence skills. This formulation implies that less skill is achieved if less time is available—which is evidently not true for Hadza and quite implausible for Merriam spear fishers. Human-specific arguments for the length of the juvenile period may be not only unnecessary but also based on erroneous interpretations of juvenile behavior and the age changes in their subsistence.

It makes sense to think of the juvenile period as a useful time to do some learning but as primarily "waiting time," waiting to grow to the optimal size to begin reproducing. If any learned task is useful, learning it sooner rather than later would be helpful, unless the task is dangerous to learn when a youngster is too small (such as scavenging from lions and hyenas) or unnecessary until adulthood (such as politics). The recent findings are also quite compatible with the suggestion (Bogin 1999a; chapter 7, this volume) that the juvenile period be divided into an early phase of little growth and much learning and a later phase of rapid growth. In this connection, it is important to point out that those Hadza children in school attend during their teens, not in early or middle childhood. There may be additional tasks for adolescence or childhood, such as gaining status or a reputation, particularly in a population (like all hunter-gatherer societies) in which most of the people you interact with as an adult are people you have interacted with on and off throughout your childhood.

The recent findings must also be considered in relation to Kaplan and colleagues (2000). In their written account, Kaplan and colleagues appear to interpret all age increases in foraging success as a result of learning and to favor the traditional "we need all those years to get skilled" view; however, their formal model and conclusions are different. They model two roles for learning. First, learning skills or acquiring knowledge in the juvenile period that will lower adult mortality will, by the effect of mortality on optimal age at maturity, lengthen the juvenile period. Second, in Kaplan's model, increases in the reproductive benefit that accrues from time as a juvenile also lead to a later optimal age at maturity. Learning could play this role, just as growth does. Here, they seem to be implying that faster-growing individuals mature later. The opposite is generally observed among humans and other mammals.

The traditional literature on learning as a reason for the juvenile period includes a splendid array of strange ideas about brain development. Many of these ideas overlook two simple observations: (1) being born a few months "early" (but are we?—see Robson, van Schaik, and Hawkes, chapter 2, this volume) does not account for a juvenile period several years longer than that of our closest relatives, nor is it clear how early birth makes for a more efficient brain; and (2) most brain development is completed by about age 5 (see Robson, van Schaik, and Hawkes, chapter 2, this volume), not surprising if we have to put this excellent learning machine to great use and in only a limited time. If the length of the juvenile period was set by the growth and adult mortality trade-off, yet there was much to learn, selection may have favored not a lengthening of the juvenile period, but an improvement in learning mechanisms, the evolution of very rapid forms of learning.

All the recent studies concern modern humans with modern human brains. We learn many things very, very rapidly by observation and by hearsay. When did we acquire this ability? Did earlier ancestors have as much to learn? Did our small-brained, not-so-smart ancestors take eighteen years to learn how to do whatever it was they did for a living? Studies of actual learning curves for subsistence skills would be valuable. Eighteen years is an awfully slow learning curve. Members of The Society for Primitive Technology might be the ideal research subjects. Because they are eager but naive about the particular skills of

Ache, !Kung, Hadza, or Martu, one could measure the speed with which they reach the ability of local experts.

RESIDENCE PATTERNS AND THE GRANDMOTHER HYPOTHESIS

The view that the human juvenile period is of the length expected for an animal of our lifespan rests on the view that "postreproductive" individuals are nonetheless "reproducing," continuing to "cash in" their investment in body size, enhancing their own fitness during these postreproductive years. Therefore, it is very important to show whether older individuals, particularly grandmothers, actually do help their descendants. Evidence has begun to accumulate (Sear, Mace, and McGregor 2000; Lahdenpera et al. 2004), but more is needed. No direct evidence of elders' demographic effect on their younger kin's reproductive success is available from mobile hunter-gatherer societies.

In preparing to test for demographic effects of Hadza grandmothers, we have been cautioned by remarks of Hill and Hurtado (1996) concerning helpers. Helpers tend to obscure the effects of various risk factors, including costs and benefits involved in life history trade-offs. At the same time, they tend to obscure their own effects. For example, if grandmother goes to help her inept daughter, neglecting her accomplished daughter, and her help is effective, we see little difference when comparing the success of these daughters with and without grandmother. First, we need to look at the way older women distribute their help. Assuming that helping those with whom one resides is easier than helping those camped far away, we (Blurton Jones, Hawkes, and O'Connell 2005) looked at those with whom Hadza women (and men) aged 45 or more lived (in the same camp, during our ten censuses). This leads us into a wider issue about residence patterns.

The Grandmother hypothesis has been criticized on the grounds that the predominant human and great ape residence pattern is patrilocal. In a powerfully argued and supported paper, Alvarez (2004b) reviews the anthropological theory and ethnographic evidence behind the view that patrilocality was predominant among recent hunters and gatherers. Most of the widely used classifications are based on totally inadequate data and ignore insightful discussions that took place in early anthropology. The few ethnographies in which camp census data are available reveal an unclassifiable complex, supporting the view that individuals use a variety of kin and other links to decide where to live and with whom. The only discernable statistical bias was in favor of mother-daughter links. Marlowe (2004) also concludes that we have overestimated the prevalence of patrilocality. Alvarez points out that recent work on great ape society reveals a similar complexity and opportunism.

Our recent analysis (Blurton Jones, Hawkes, and O'Connell 2005) of 213 Hadza camp compositions tested seven predictions about where older women would reside if their presence was helpful and they were distributing their help in a way that increased their own fitness. If a woman over 45 has grown children, she is

1. *More* likely to be in camp with her daughter than with her son

2. *More* likely to be with her daughter if the daughter has children under age 7 years

3. *More* likely to be with her daughter if the daughter is suckling a baby

4. *Less* likely to be with her daughter if the daughter has a teenage daughter of her own (significant food producer)

5. *Not less* likely to be with the daughter if that daughter has a teenage son (*not* reliable deliverer of food)

6. *More* likely to be in camp with her son if his wife has no mother than if the son's wife's mother is alive

7. *Less* likely to be with a chronically infertile daughter than with another daughter

The data supported all seven predictions. If confirming predictions verifies the assumptions from which the predictions were derived, then these observations uphold the view that grandmothers' help does increase grandmothers' fitness. Alvarez's (2000) proposal of opportunistically strategizing individuals is also strongly supported by these data. Idle curiosity (as opposed to reasoned, if unsurprising, prediction) led us to two more results. The older woman is

1. *More* likely to be in camp with a daughter who is over 18 and is single than with one who is married

2. *More* likely to be in camp with an unmarried daughter who has children under 7 than with a married daughter who has children the same age

These two results may mean that a conflict of interest may exist between wives and husbands about where to live or (as most have believed) that husbands are helpers whose missing help is important to replace (Marlowe 2003). Even if this is so, it seems to have little influence over men's residence patterns. We tested these predictions for men, and only one was significant. We also found that when a mother of young children dies, the children are *less* likely to be with their father than they were when their mother was living.

The strategic location of grandmothers illustrates the suggestion made by Hill and Hurtado (1996) that helpers tend to complicate measuring costs and benefits of behavior. If grandmothers go where they are most needed and their help is effective, this obscures the effects of the "need," as well as the effects of their help (because they more often give to those in danger of doing badly). We must be very careful when trying to test for grandmothers' demographic effects. All these findings were statistically significant but fairly weak, suggesting that there is plenty of variance to play with but rather many factors to control for.

Although life history theory in biology deals almost entirely with females, human males have caused enough trouble to draw attention (Wrangham and Peterson 1996). Proponents of the view that patrilocality characterized great apes and hunter-gatherers have suggested an important role in evolution for groups of cooperating male kin. If matrilocality was common among our ancestors, human evolution was proceeding just as much around groups of cooperating and competing unrelated males. Then we might be provoked into investigating the nature of the cooperation and competition in a way we would not if we thought only of groups of close male kin. Papers by Bird, Smith, and Bird (2001), Hawkes (1991), and Hawkes and Bliege Bird (2002) seem to me to offer promise for an approach to the evolution of politics and of seemingly wasteful but highly noted, and sometimes archaeologically visible, products of culture.

DISCUSSION

In this chapter, I have attempted to apply data from hunters and gatherers to the question, is human life history an example of a general mammal pattern as described by Charnov (1993) and others, or is it, as many in anthropology and human biology have proposed, a very peculiar life history that requires special explanation? For example, many have treated the human juvenile period as being particularly long, exhibiting special characteristics and unique meaning. Charnov's (1993) general mammalian model emphasizes the constant relationship between adult mortality and length of the juvenile period, which is held to arise from selection for an optimal age at first reproduction. Reproductive capacity increases with size; size results from growth, according to a simple model (which is nonetheless instrumental in generating quantitative predictions about several constant relationships observed between life history variables). Delaying reproduction pays if predictable average adult lifespan is sufficient to "cash in" the advantages of prolonged growth. Selection will favor some compromise between continued growth and a longer time spent reproducing. Alvarez (2000) showed that humans fit on the same line relating length of juvenile period to adult mortality as other higher primates, which implies that we need no special arguments to account for the length of the human juvenile period. Referring to data on contemporary hunter-gatherers, I examined some potential counter-arguments:

1. If the adult mortality data for contemporary hunter-gatherers poorly represent the evolved human life history, the general mammalian model and GMH provide a less suitable account than we thought. Modern hunter-gatherer adult mortality is much lower than that estimated by archaeological demographers. However, modern hunter-gatherers resemble all human populations for which we have written records of birth and death dates (the poorest in the contemporary third world and the premedicine populations studied by historical demographers) in their low adult mortality and long lifespan, much longer than any other primate's. Some key studies (Walker, Johnson, and Lambert 1988; Molleson et al. 1993) imply serious problems with the conclusions from archaeological demography. Konigsberg and Herrmann (chapter 9, this volume) summarize new methods that bring at least one archaeological population into the

range of variation known from the hundreds of populations for whom written records of birth and death exist. But there could be another potential problem. Contemporary hunter-gatherer mortality may be reduced by influences from the modern world that surrounds them. I summarized evidence that these effects were small in the case of the Hadza, the !Kung, and especially the Ache. The mortality schedules observed in these populations are probably a very good representation of our evolved mortality.

2. Human growth has been described in detail and with much emphasis on its differences from growth of other animals. Does a general mammalian model, Charnov's growth function ($dW/dt = AW^{0.75}$), adequately describe growth between weaning and adulthood in contemporary hunter-gatherers? If not, then the usefulness of the general mammalian model for understanding evolution of human life history comes into doubt because this function is so important in predicting other very generally observed relationships. Fitting this function to Hadza data produced an extremely close fit for each sex, with results very similar to those obtained by Hill and Hurtado (1996) on Ache. Chimpanzees, bonobos, and orangutans seem to grow at much the same rate (similar [A]) as hunter-gatherers. Charnov's function could appear to mimic an adolescent growth spurt in a long-lived species, but the growth spurt has often been proposed as something unique to human growth and therefore a life history character requiring special explanation. Charnov's life history theory accounts for major variation across large numbers of species. Each may have its own deviations from the major trends and its own evolutionarily intriguing characteristics. Like other peoples living under hard conditions, Hadza show only weak indications of an adolescent growth spurt, and it is more evident in boys than in girls.

Do these contemporary hunter-gatherers represent the species-specific growth pattern we should be trying to explain? In that case, the very small adolescent spurt can be regarded as a marginally significant wrinkle added to the general mammalian pattern. The spurt, however, is universally found among industrial populations, who presumably have more to eat, and in those populations it is more striking among individuals who are growing the fastest. Perhaps the adolescent growth spurt is a facultative response to high nutrition: when resources are plentiful, more are allocated to the growth spurt. It might be useful to generate an adaptationist perspective on growth, which would replace the current "balloon theory" (the more you put in, the bigger they get) and emphasize the allocation of resources among survival, reproduction, and growth and between weight and height, growth and maintenance, and growth and number of offspring. Hunter-gatherers in pre-agricultural times were larger than contemporary hunter-gatherers, so we can probably assume that they had more visible adolescent growth spurts. What are the adaptive advantages of increased height? Why would males show a more obvious spurt than females? We should bear in mind Richard Lee's (1979b) observation that the tallest !Kung were not the best hunters and that large size has its drawbacks.

3. A widely favored alternative and special explanation for the length of the human juvenile period has been that foragers must delay reproduction while they learn because they have so much to master. Foragers do have much to learn, but they continue to do so after reproduction begins, which weakens the view that they must delay reproduction for this purpose. Observations widely interpreted as evidence that juveniles need eighteen years to learn how to be foragers have been shown to be better interpreted in other ways. Merriam and Martu children pursue different targets from adults, not because of ignorance but because they are efficient foragers and small (Bird and Bliege Bird 2005). Large chunks of the juvenile period spent away from the bush did not impair development of important Hadza foraging skills (Blurton Jones and Marlowe 2002). Some skills are not practiced until late in development, and individuals become more skilled during adulthood, when they are married with children (Blurton Jones and Marlowe 2002; Walker et al. 2002).

4. The Grandmother hypothesis (GMH) attends to one special feature of human ecology that it adds to the general mammalian pattern. Hunter-gatherer habitats are rich in resources that are difficult for juveniles to acquire. These resources can be exploited only if adults give food to juveniles, opening an opportunity for helpers to be more effective. If an aging, recently postreproductive female (or a still reproductive, aging male) can acquire food and pass it to younger kin, it may significantly affect the elder's fitness. Selection could then act to prolong the survival and vigor of the elder. GMH holds this to be the selection pressure for decreased adult mortality and elongated adult

lifespan, which then gives a selective advantage to a longer juvenile period. It makes sense only if the "postreproductive" period is actually part of the time when the reproductive advantages of delayed maturity are cashed in.

Direct observation of women's work patterns and children's growth suggests that, among Hadza, postreproductive life does enhance the fitness of the older person by enhancing the fitness of younger kin (Hawkes, O'Connell, and Blurton Jones 1997). Before looking for actual demographic effects of elders upon numbers and survival of children as recorded among more sedentary populations (Sear, Mace, and McGregor 2000; Lahdenpera et al. 2004), we had to attend to an important problem in studying effectiveness of helpers. If helpers go where they will be most effective—for example, to live with a daughter who has three small children, ignoring a daughter who has just one— then we might observe similar child mortality in the family with a resident grandmother as in the family with no grandmother present.

We have presented data showing that older Hadza women (but not older Hadza men) live where we would expect if they are behaving in ways that maximize their fitness through help to younger kin. This is consistent with the idea that they are effective, but it falls short of showing a demographic effect and indicates that demonstrating such an effect in very mobile populations might be difficult. The opportunistic mobility of older Hadza women makes us question evolutionary accounts based on the belief that patrilocality characterizes humans and our closest relatives. We suggest that thinking about the behavior of collaborating and competing *un*related males may give rewarding insights into human evolution.

I have reported data that bear on the question of whether we can adequately account for human life history as part of a general mammalian pattern or we can only describe and explain it by a collection of special arguments. The general pattern does very well, but, as in any species, there are local deviations. These are interesting, perhaps deserving explanation, but do not constitute a central account of evolution of human life history.

Kaplan and colleagues (2000) present an alternative general model that is designed to accommodate the nature of human life histories. Like GMH, it emphasizes the economic importance of older people, arguing that in subsistence societies only elders produce surplus food. Young parents are unable to produce as much as their offspring consume. These authors emphasize the economic role of men over that of women. Although in several ways the Kaplan model resembles Charnov's, Kaplan centers his model on a concept of "embodied capital," which extends beyond growth and "productivity" in Charnov's sense to include skills, knowledge, and immune competence. Thus, juvenile learning is seen as contributing to embodied capital. Kaplan points out that if skills that lower adult mortality can be learned during pre-adult life, selection will favor later first reproduction and thereby a longer juvenile period. Thus, a skill-based subsistence might be expected to lead to a long juvenile period.

Kaplan and his co-authors do not appear to dissent from either the adult mortality observed among contemporary foragers as the best estimate of our species' adult mortality or the idea that postchildbearing adults continue to reproduce in the sense that they enhance their fitness by helping their children and grandchildren. Kaplan and colleagues suggest that their model predicts that brain size, later maturity, larger size, slower growth, and lower mortality are linked and evolve together. Paleoanthropological literature appears to imply something different (see Skinner and Wood, chapter 11, this volume; Ruff, Trinkaus, and Holliday 1997), especially an early increase in body size and little relative increase in brain size with the origin of *Homo erectus/ergaster* and a much later increase in relative brain size with no increase in body size (Hawkes, O'Connell, and Blurton Jones 2003).

We should note that (as discussed more fully in Hawkes, chapter 4, this volume) Charnov recently extended his model to include a term to cover investment in maintenance, separated from the growth function. Ultimately, a theory of life history evolution that can explain adult mortality rates and taxonomic variation in growth rates must be superior to a theory that cannot. Charnov (2001a) begins to deal with variation in these rates by the addition of maintenance to a model that continues to predict the constants relating various life history parameters to one another. Kaplan and colleagues (2000) also deal explicitly with changes in these rates, but with a more complicated model, and they make no reference to the constant relationships among life history parameters.

Acknowledgments

I wish to thank the Tanzania Commission on Science and Technology for permission to conduct research in Tanzania, several hundred individual Hadza for their patience and good spirits, and our field assistants, Gudo Mahiya and the late Sokolo Mpanda, for their expertise and collegiality. Lars C. Smith introduced us to the Hadza and allowed us to use data from his 1977 census of the eastern Hadza. David Bygott and Jeannette Hanby provided a home away from home and vital logistic facilities. I am grateful to Professors C. L. Kamuzora and Audax Mabulla of the University of Dar es Salaam and to numerous officials and citizens of Mbulu and Karatu districts for help and friendship. The research was funded by the National Science Foundation, the Swan Fund, the University of Utah, and the University of California, Los Angeles. I thank the organizers of the School of American Research advanced seminar and the setting and participants for encouraging some heretical thinking.

9

The Osteological Evidence for Human Longevity in the Recent Past

Lyle W. Konigsberg and Nicholas P. Herrmann

SUMMARY

Paleodemography is the study of age and sex composition of populations before recorded history, and more specifically, the study of groups for which information on the age and sex of the (once) living or the dead is not available from documents. Because written records lack these essential descriptors of populations, we must determine age and sex from osteological or dental remains. This is rarely, if ever, a simple task, and a number of interpretive difficulties can lead to substantial biases on estimated population parameters. To discuss these problems, we use two recent prehistoric samples, the Late Archaic Indian Knoll Site and the Mississippian Averbuch Site, as examples and show that it is difficult to justify one of the primary assumptions in paleodemography, that people senesced in the past at the same rates as they do today. We discuss how this assumption can be examined within what has come to be known as the "Rostock Manifesto" (Hoppa and Vaupel 2002a) for paleodemographic analysis. In closing, we briefly discuss the problems awaiting paleodemographic analyses that probe further back into the evolution of human life history.

One central tenet of paleodemography is that humans age now in the same way they aged in the past. This is not to say that demographic history itself has remained static, but rather that ontogenetic "clocks" in the musculoskeletal system are assumed to be constant across the globe and across the span of prehistoric time. As happens when we make assumptions, we cling to the notion that human skeletal ontogeny is fixed, because this makes our analyses easier. To quote from Love and Müller (2002:185), "Any assumption that is weaker would make the analysis virtually impossible." Although this "uniformitarian" assumption (Howell 1976b) has become a comfortable crutch in the past quarter century, we have found occasional unsettling indications that it is untrue. In this chapter, we sketch some ways to test the assumption. From one of these approaches, we also present evidence indicating that a particular developmental system is proceeding at a faster pace now than it did in our prehistoric past.

The primary task of this chapter is to examine the osteological evidence for human longevity. Clearly, we can make little progress in this direction unless we first grapple with the issue of uniformity of skeletal aging. To this end, we first examine the pattern of senescence in the auricular surface of the ilium, using a large sample of "known" age skeletons (*known* is in quotes because, as noted below, the ages are not well documented). Following this analysis, we estimate Gompertz mortality models for a Late Archaic skeletal collection from Indian Knoll (Herrmann 2002; Herrmann and Konigsberg 2002; Morey et al. 2002) and for a Mississippian skeletal collection from Averbuch (L. Eisenberg 1989, 1991; Konigsberg and Frankenberg 1994). In the ensuing discussion, we compare estimated mortality among these two collections and a French Neolithic sample and then return to the question of the tempo of skeletal aging in the past.

AN INTRODUCTION TO THE "DEVILISHLY DIFFICULT" FIELD OF PALEODEMOGRAPHY

Nancy Howell (1976b:25) opened a chapter on paleodemography with the statement that "paleodemography is a subject which is simultaneously intensely interesting and devilishly difficult." Five years after writing this, she turned to an analysis of the Libben Site, a late prehistoric cemetery from Ohio for which Lovejoy and colleagues (1977) had previously published a life table. Using computer simulation,

Howell (1982:268) was able to show "that about 5% of the children age 0 to 9 have one or more living grandparent, and no one over age 10 has any." As a consequence of the harsh mortality regime suggested in the Libben life table, Howell indicated that the people at Libben would have been beset by "difficult childcare requirements."

Ultimately, Howell (1982:269) raised the question of whether prehistoric lifespan and mortality differed substantially from what is documented in recent history or whether the Libben analysis was "a 'reductio ad absurdum' shedding doubt on the literal accuracy of the life table itself." The simplest interpretation is probably the latter, that the Libben life table is fraught with estimation errors and biases. Unfortunately, the implausible Libben life table is not unique among published paleodemographic analyses or analyses of extant foraging societies. Gage and colleagues (1989:48–50) have written that "the high rate of aging in the paleodemographic tables and in the Yanomama is particularly intriguing. It may be a result of the error intrinsic in estimating ages in ethnographic populations and ages at death in paleopopulations, or it might represent some real differences in the dynamics of aging in these populations."

Hill and Hurtado (1996:193) write in their study of the Ache that the "study provides no support for the mortality profiles commonly reported in paleodemographic studies. Interpretations of remains from past populations have often suggested that virtually no adults survived beyond age 45–50 among our distant human ancestors....No living human population has ever been observed with such high adult mortality rates, and...recent mortality studies of isolated primitive peoples...should make us increasingly skeptical of such interpretations."

These quotes represent but smatterings of the assessments of paleodemography indicating that previous reconstructions of prehistoric human life history are highly questionable. It is now widely acknowledged that there are three main sources of error in previous estimates of paleodemographic life tables. The first, and probably the least damaging, is the assumption of a non-zero growth rate when, indeed, the prehistoric population was not demographically stationary. Sattenspiel and Harpending (1983) give a detailed account of this problem, which has also been recounted in a number of other sources (Johansson and Horowitz 1986; Konigsberg and Frankenberg 1994; Wood et al. 2002). Recently, Wood and colleagues (2002) suggested that it may be possible to estimate the growth rate simultaneously while estimating mortality parameters. In any event, the impact of generally assuming a stationary population when, in fact, there was a non-zero growth rate is trivial compared with the second form of estimation error.

The second source of error is misestimation of ages at death, the basic source data for all further paleodemographic calculations. This is such a salient problem in past paleodemographic analyses that we describe it in detail here, even though an extensive literature on the subject already exists (Bocquet-Appel and Masset 1982, 1985; Bocquet-Appel 1986; Konigsberg and Frankenberg 1992, 1994; Konigsberg, Frankenberg, and Walker 1997; Aykroyd et al. 1999; Hoppa and Vaupel 2002a). The third source of error is the non-random sampling with respect to age that often occurs in the production of death assemblages. Hoppa (1996) has extensively discussed this problem, and Moore, Swedlund, and Armelagos (1975) have examined the most common form of biased sampling, the under-enumeration of subadult deaths. The remainder of this chapter follows Moore, Swedlund, and Armelagos's (1975:60) lead in considering life expectancies at older ages only, because these are "mathematically unaffected" by "changes in infant representation." Consequently, we examine life expectancy at age 15 and older because, for one of the samples, there is strong evidence for the under-enumeration of subadults.

Bayesian versus Maximum Likelihood Estimation of Age-at-Death Structure

Konigsberg and Frankenberg (1992) have noted that previous analyses of age-at-death structure from human skeletal material have tended to take an implicit Bayesian approach. This point was made earlier in paleodemography (Bocquet-Appel and Masset 1982) and even earlier in a much different context—the fisheries literature (Kimura 1977; Westrheim and Ricker 1978). Because past analyses have been Bayesian in flavor, the age structure of the reference (known age) sample has tended to influence the reconstruction of the target (paleodemographic) sample. Simply stated, the age distribution in the reference sample conditioned on some "indicator of age" is influenced by the overall age distribution of the reference sample (Konigsberg and Frankenberg 2002). In contrast, maximum likelihood estimation of

TABLE 9.1

An Example of Bayesian and Maximum Likelihood Estimation of Age-at-Death Structure

	Stage		
Korean War	I–III	IV–VI	Total
15–24 years	224	16	240
25+ years	26	92	118
Total	*250*	*108*	*358*
Bayes	I–III	IV–VI	Total
15–24 years	262.53	103.26	365.79
25+ years	30.47	593.74	624.21
Total	*293*	*697*	*990*
MLE	I–III	IV–VI	Total
15–24 years	98	7	105
25+ years	195	690	885
Total	*293*	*697*	*990*

The first contingency table gives the distribution of pubic symphyseal stages against age in the reference sample. The target sample has 293 individuals in stages I–III and 697 in stages IV–VI, for a total of 990 individuals (italic). The actual number of individuals in the target sample younger than age 25 years is 105; the actual number at age 25 years or older is 885.

the age-at-death distribution for a target sample is not directly influenced by the age distribution from the reference sample. The contrast between Bayesian and maximum likelihood estimation in paleodemography is not immediately obvious, so in this section we present a few brief examples.

In table 9.1, we give a two-by-two cross-tabulation of two pubic symphyseal stages against two age classes from a sample of 358 individuals from the Korean War (McKern and Stewart 1957). The pubic symphysis is a portion of the innominate bone that undergoes age-related changes. In our table, we count the number of symphyses in Suchey-Brooks phases I–III and IV–VI (Katz and Suchey 1986). These two categories essentially contrast symphyses with incomplete dorsal margins and/or ventral ramparts with ones in which the margin and rampart are complete. The age classes we give are for ages 15–24 and 25 years or older. These data are taken from a study of the pubic symphyseal casts stored at the US National Museum.

Now we will assume that we have a second skeletal sample consisting of 990 individuals; 105 died between ages 15 and 25, and 885 died at age 25 or older. If the individuals from this second (fictitious) sample aged in the same way as did the individuals from the Korean War dead sample, then there should be

$$105 \left(\frac{224}{240}\right) + 885 \left(\frac{26}{118}\right),$$

or 293 skeletons in stages I–III. The remaining 697 skeletons would then be in stages IV–VI. From these counts of skeletons in the two stages, we want to estimate the (unknown) age-at-death distribution—that is, the proportion of deaths at age 25 years or older.

From table 9.1, we could find the expected number of skeletons under the age of 25 in stages I–III as

$$293 \left(\frac{224}{250}\right),$$

or 262.53, so the remaining 30.47 skeletons in stages I–III must be age 25 years or older. Similarly, the expected number of skeletons in stages IV–VI age 25 or older is

$$697 \left(\frac{92}{108}\right),$$

or 593.74, with the remaining 103.26 individuals in stages IV–VI having died before age 25. Summing the second row, we get 30.47 + 593.74, or 624.21 individuals who died at age 25 or older, instead of the actual 885. The analysis we have just attempted is a Bayesian one because it uses the proportion of individuals age 25 or older in the reference sample as an informative prior for the proportion age 25 or older in the target sample. We can see this more clearly by rewriting the problem as a linear regression. Using a result in Konigsberg, Frankenberg, and Walker (1997), we can write the estimated number of individuals in the target sample who are age 25 or older as

$$990 \left(\frac{118}{358} (1-r^2) + r^2 \left(\frac{885}{990}\right)\right) = 624.21. \tag{1}$$

Here r^2 is the squared Pearson correlation between age class and phase from the reference sample, in which phases I–III are scored as 0, phases IV–VI as 1, the age class 15–24 as 0, and the age class 25 or older as 1. The squared correlation in the Korean War sample is 0.533214, which from equation 1 gives a count of 624.21, identical with our preceding calculation. This Bayesian estimator uses the age proportion from the reference sample (118/358) as an informative prior. For example, if there is no correlation between the indicator and age, then we would predict the number of individuals in the target sample who are age 25 or older to be

$$990 \left(\frac{118}{358}\right) = 326.31,$$

which simply substitutes the reference sample age structure for the target sample.

In contrast to the Bayesian estimator, we can consider the maximum likelihood estimator. In this setting, we seek the age distribution for the target sample that best explains the observed distribution of indicator counts in the target, subject to the indicator aging in the same fashion as implied in the reference sample. From table 9.1, we let D_{25} equal the (unknown) number of individuals in the target sample who died at the age of 25 years or older. Now we can write

$$D_{25} \left(\frac{26}{118}\right) + \left(990 - D_{25}\right) \left(\frac{224}{240}\right) = 293, \qquad (2)$$

and solve for D_{25}, which is 885, equal to the true number. By subtraction, the number of individuals under age 25 is 105, and we can find the remainder of cell counts by using the appropriate conditional probabilities from the reference sample. Also, we can find the number of individuals age 25 years or older by using the regression approach we mentioned for Bayesian estimation. If we regress phase on age class (again using zeros and ones for scores) and then solve the regression equation for age class, we get the following estimator for the number of individuals age 25 or older:

$$990 \left(1.402536 \left(\frac{697}{990}\right) - 0.093502\right) = 885. \qquad (3)$$

This is known as a classical calibration estimate, and its properties are well characterized. Specifically, the method is the maximum likelihood estimator. Equation 1 is known as an inverse calibration estimate and also a Bayesian estimator that, as already noted, uses the reference sample age distribution as an informative prior. Konigsberg, Frankenberg, and Walker (1997) provide a discussion of classical and

TABLE 9.2

A Second Example for Bayesian and Maximum Likelihood Estimation of Age-at-Death Structure

	Stage			
Korean War	I–II	III–IV	V–VI	Total
15–24 years	165	73	2	240
25+ years	2	82	34	118
Total	*167*	*155*	*36*	*358*
Suchey Sample	I–II	III–IV	V–VI	Total
15–24 years	167	17	1	185
25+ years	33	179	340	552
Total	*200*	*196*	*341*	*737*
Expected	163.61	424.09	149.30	

The first contingency table gives the distribution of pubic symphyseal stages against age in the reference sample, and the second gives a similar table for the target sample. The bottom line for the target sample also gives the expected counts in stages, given the estimated age structure.

inverse calibration within the context of age estimation, and Konigsberg and colleagues (1998) extend the discussion to stature estimation.

Our example is decidedly artificial, so we will consider a more complicated example, using actual data for both the reference and target samples. Table 9.2 gives a contingency table, again for the Korean War dead but this time showing classification into phases I–II, III–IV, and V–VI. Also shown in table 9.2 is a similar contingency table for 737 males in Judy Suchey's forensic sample (Katz and Suchey 1986), which we will treat as a target sample. From the information in table 9.2, we can write the probability of getting the observed counts in phases from Suchey's sample conditional on the proportion of individuals age 25 or older in the sample. Ultimately, from this we can draw the full posterior density for this proportion, as in figure 9.1 (the maximum likelihood estimate is at the top of the peak, shown with a dashed line). This can be compared with the actual proportion, the Bayesian estimate, and the proportion from the reference (Korean War) sample (figure 9.1).

It is clear from the figure that the Bayesian estimate greatly underestimates the actual proportion, specifically because the Korean War dead sample has such a low frequency of deaths at age 25 or older. However, the maximum likelihood estimator (mle) is also too low. The

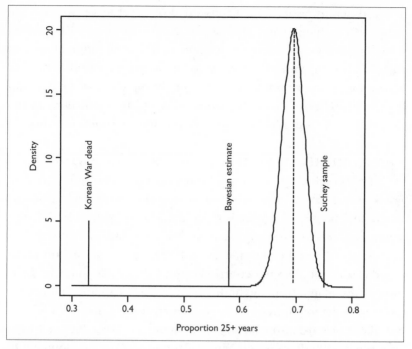

FIGURE 9.1

The maximum likelihood estimation (mle) of the proportion of individuals age 25 years or older in the Suchey sample, based on the contingency table from the Korean War dead. The vertical lines show actual proportions and the Bayesian estimate. The dashed vertical line shows the mle. Note that both the Bayesian and mle methods underestimate the true proportion in the Suchey sample.

actual proportion occurs at the upper 0.002 tail of the posterior density for the mle. It is disturbing that neither method produces an unbiased estimate of the actual proportion. Even more disturbing is that, had this been an actual paleodemographic analysis, we would have no way to check estimates against actual values.

With the maximum likelihood estimator, however, we can calculate the expected counts within phases for the target sample and compare these with the observed counts. These expected counts appear at the bottom of table 9.2 and form the basis for a chi-square test with one degree of freedom. The chi-square value from these counts of 377 is enormous, showing that the model does not do a good job of recovering the actual counts in stages. Typically, the model will fail if the samples age in different fashions or if substantial observer error prevents the samples from being scored comparably. In the current case, the model failed because we used a reference sample with a very limited age distribution, which does not allow us to characterize the full pattern of aging. A more important lesson from this example is that the Bayesian approach would not have enabled us to catch this error because the method exactly reproduces the observed counts in indicator states.

THE AURICULAR SURFACE AND HUMAN AGING

The preceding section discusses what Konigsberg and Frankenberg (2002) have referred to as "contingency table paleodemography" because it proceeds from simple cross-tabulations of stage against age class. This approach makes poor use of existent data because it reduces the known ages of the reference sample to (often) broad classes and does not effectively model the development of skeletal features related to aging. In the following, we abandon contingency table paleodemography in favor of newer, more effective methods. Specifically, we use ordinal categorical methods (Long 1997; Johnson and Albert 1999; Powers and Xie 2000) to model the development of skeletal features against age, and we use hazard models (Gage 1988; Wood, Holman et al. 1992, Wood et al. 2002) to produce a fuller description of the estimated age-at-death structure.

For the remainder of this chapter, we use the auricular surface of the ilium as the age "indicator" in our analyses. The auricular surface is the ear-shaped sacroiliac joint, where the sacral alae meet the posterior portion of the ilia (figure 9.2). Lovejoy, Meindl, Pryzbeck, and Mensforth (1985) introduced the auricular surface of the ilium as an age indicator for human skeletal material, defining eight ordered stages in the development of this surface. Others have examined the utility of this and other methods when applied to known age material (Murray and Murray 1991; Santos 1995; Buckberry and Chamberlain 2002; Schmitt et al. 2002; Igarashi et al. 2005).

For the study reported here, the second author scored auricular surfaces on 779 individuals from the Terry Anatomical Collection (Hunt and Albanese 2005), using Lovejoy and colleagues' eight-phase system. Although this collection is often referred to as being of "known age," very few skeletons in the collection have documented dates of

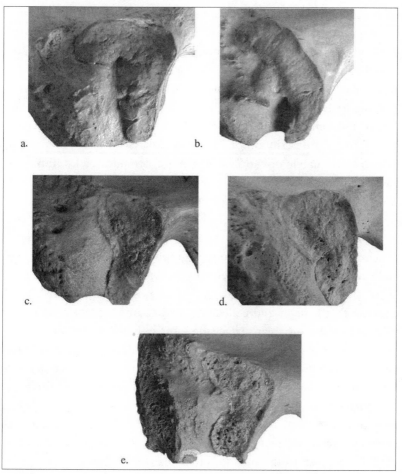

FIGURE 9.2

Representative auricular surfaces from the ilium, with the age at death and scoring on Lovejoy, Meindl, Pryzbeck, and Mensforth's (1985) system: (a) stage 1, Terry 1591, age 19; (b) stage 3, Terry 1215, age 25; (c) stage 5, Terry 717, age 29; (d) stage 7, Terry 1368, age 37; and (e) stage 8, Terry 639, age 82.

birth, and the age distribution for the collection shows very obvious digit preferences (for ages such as 40, 50, 60, 65, 70, 75, and 80 years). Although we do not believe that this age heaping necessarily has an adverse effect on our modeling of auricular surface development against age, we must acknowledge this deficit in the data.

To model the development of the auricular surface, we need a statistical method that is general enough to capture the progression through ordered categories but simple enough that we can apply the method to other skeletal collections. For this chapter, we use proportional-odds probit regression. This is a commonly applied model for ordered categorical data (Agresti and Finlay 1997; Long 1997; Johnson and Albert 1999; Venables and Ripley 1999; Powers and Xie 2000; Fox 2002). Boldsen and colleagues (2002) discuss the proportional odds model in their description of "transition analysis" for age estimation, but they ultimately opt for using a more complicated continuation ratio method. In the following, we describe the proportional odds model and apply it in analyses of the Terry Collection data.

A Binary Age-Dependent Trait

It is customary in the paleodemography literature to refer to "age indicators." In point of fact, referring to various traits as "age-dependent" is much more correct. To simplify our presentation, we will first pretend that Lovejoy and colleagues made a much coarser definition of stages for the auricular surface, defining only two stages. "Stage one" comprises Lovejoy and colleagues' stages 1–4, and "stage two" comprises stages 5–8 (in figure 9.2, this would group a and b together and contrast them with $c–e$). We can fit a probit regression so that the binary variable "stage" is regressed on age, which we do using the "glm" function in the statistical package "R." This function returns parameters in the form of a generalized linear model, but it is a simple matter to convert these to the mean and standard deviation for the age at which individuals move out of stage one and into stage two. In probit regression, the underlying model is a normal distribution, so in our context, we are estimating the mean age and standard deviation for the transition from stage one to stage two, assuming a normal distribution for the age at transition.

Boldsen and colleagues (2002) give an extensive presentation of applying such models (which they refer to as "transition analysis"). They use logistic regression, which produces a logistic distribution instead of a normal for the age at transition. In our analysis, with the two stages in the Terry sample we found a mean age at transition of 36.64 years, with a standard deviation of 18.85 years. In figure 9.3, we plot the probability conditional on age that an individual is in stage two

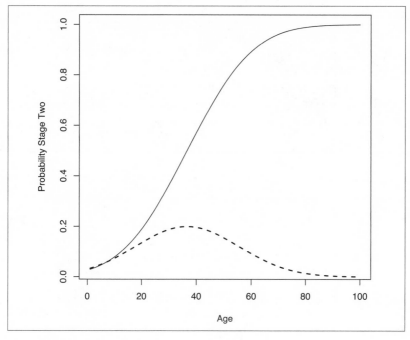

FIGURE 9.3

The solid line is the probability conditional on age from the Terry Collection that the auric-ular surface is in stage two (Lovejoy and colleagues' stages 5–8). The heavy dashed line is the distribution of transition ages.

and the distribution of transition ages for moving from stage one to stage two (see Boldsen et al. [2002] for a much more detailed presentation of the transition analysis paradigm).

A Three-Stage, Age-Dependent Trait

Now we will assume that Lovejoy and colleagues made a less coarse classification than our two-stage system, specifically, that they scored a stage one (Lovejoy and colleagues' stages 1 and 2), a stage two (their stages 3–5), and a stage three (their stages 6–8). We can view this as a cumulative problem, so we fit probit regressions in two analyses: stage one versus the combined stages two and three and the combined stages one and two versus stage three. The first analysis gives us the transition distribution for moving from stage one into stage two; the second gives us the distribution for moving from stage two into stage three.

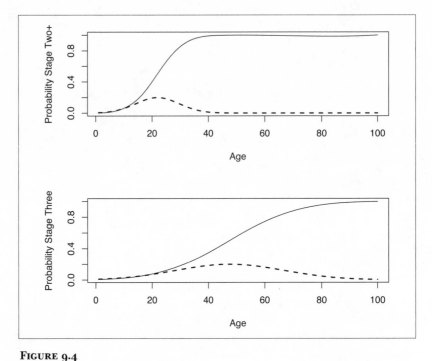

FIGURE 9.4

Top: *the probability of being in stage two or three (Lovejoy and colleagues' stages 3–8) and distribution of transition ages for moving out of stage one into stage two.* Bottom: *the probability of being in stage three (Lovejoy and colleagues' stages 6–8) and distribution of transition ages for moving out of stage two into stage three.*

The mean age and standard deviations for the 1→2 transition are estimated at 21.96 and 7.69 years, respectively, and for the 2→3 transition, 47.48 and 19.16 years, respectively. Figure 9.4 graphs the transition distributions (and cumulative distributions) in the same manner as figure 9.3. One important point to be gleaned from figure 9.4 is that the distribution of transition ages is more dispersed for the transition from stage two to stage three than from stage one to stage two. Consequently, the aging process becomes more variable with advancing age. This is an extremely common finding in studies of growth and aging. As we point out in introductory classes, we often speak about people in their 60s looking "good for their age," but such comments are not made about children. This is a simple result of the fact that we all start at approximately the same developmental point at birth and

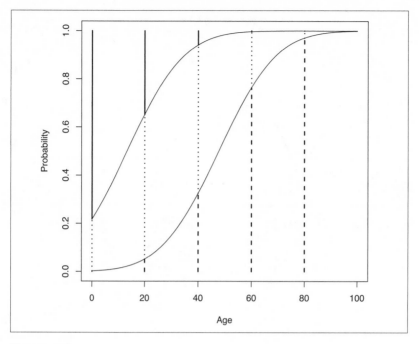

FIGURE 9.5

A proportional odds probit regression model for three stages (Lovejoy and colleagues' stages 1 and 2, 3–5, and 6–8). The two probit regression lines contrast the three stages, with the middle stage grouped with the first and then the last stage. The vertical lines give the probabilities of being in each stage at twenty-year intervals (the solid line gives the probability of being in stage one; the dotted line, stage two; and the dashed line, stage three).

then diverge on our own growth and senescence trajectories. While this is hardly a novel concept, we must be careful to ensure that our models maintain this important detail of the senescence process.

The statistical model we have used is the basis for both the proportional odds method and the continuation ratios used in Boldsen and colleagues (2002). The proportional odds method fits cumulative probabilities, comparing stage one with stages two and three combined and then stages one and two combined with stage three. In the proportional odds method, we require that all transitions have a common standard deviation. Then, by subtraction, we can find the probability of being in an internal stage (that is, not the first or last stage). Consequently, the probability of being in stage two at a particular age is the

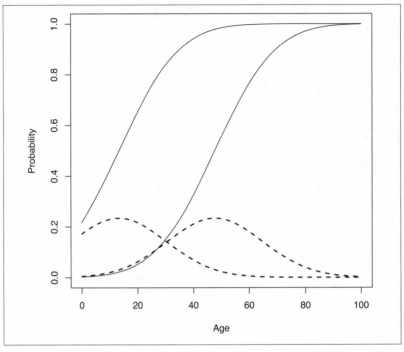

FIGURE 9.6

A continuation of the example from figure 9.5, showing the distribution of transition ages as dashed lines.

probability of being in stage two or three minus the probability of being in stage three. This is shown in figure 9.5, where we have plotted the two probit lines (cumulative probabilities). These lines yield mean ages to transition of 13.29 and 47.71 for the transitions from stage one to two and stage two to three, with a common standard deviation of 17.05 years.

Figure 9.6 shows the same example but with the addition of the distribution of transition ages. Note that the two transition distributions have an identical dispersion, which is an undesirable aspect of the proportional odds model. To circumvent this problem, we do the probit regression with age measured in a natural log scale. Figure 9.7 shows how this scale produces the desired effect of an increasing dispersion for transitions between higher (later) stages. In figure 9.7, the mean ages to transition are 20.47 and 45.45; the standard deviation of transition is 0.3579 on the natural log scale.

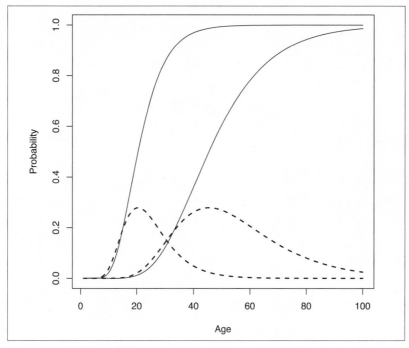

FIGURE 9.7

A proportional odds model from figures 9.5 and 9.6, but with the probit regressions done on the natural log of age.

Lovejoy and Colleagues' Eight Auricular Stages and a Reduced Five-Stage System

Lovejoy and colleagues' eight-stage system has never been systematically examined to determine whether the eight categories are distinguishable. In particular, we would like to know whether some of the stages should be collapsed together because they do not represent distinct phases. To answer this question, we have fit the proportional odds probit regression model to the eight stages, with age measured on a natural log scale. At any age, we can find the probability that an individual is in each of the eight stages, as we did in figure 9.5 for three stages. Love and Müller (2002) have referred to these probabilities as "invariant weight functions," with the hope that the probability functions are indeed invariant across samples. As we will see in a later section, there is empirical evidence that the functions may not be invariant for the auricular surface.

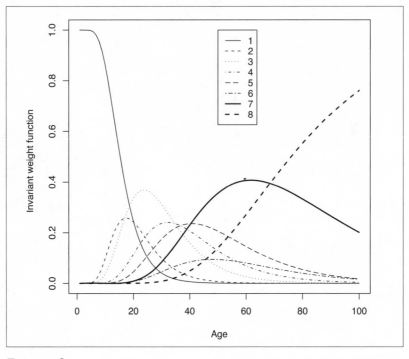

FIGURE 9.8

The probability of being in each of Lovejoy and colleagues' eight auricular stages conditional on age (from a proportional odds probit regression of stage on the natural logarithm of age in 779 individuals from the Terry Anatomical Collection).

Figure 9.8 displays the resulting invariant weight functions for the Terry Anatomical Collection scored in eight stages. The graph shows that a number of the stages should be subsumed under adjacent stages, and we have consequently fit a five-stage model. This re-scoring collapses Lovejoy and colleagues' stages 1 and 2 into one phase, maintains their stage 3 as a separate phase, combines their stages 4 and 5 into one phase, combines their stages 6 and 7 into one phase, and maintains their stage 8 as a single phase. Figure 9.9 shows the invariant weight functions for the five stages.

Just as we used a chi-square test to determine whether our model in "contingency table paleodemography" correctly recovered counts in indicator states, we can use a similar test for the auricular surface. If we write a hazard model to represent the age-at-death structure for the

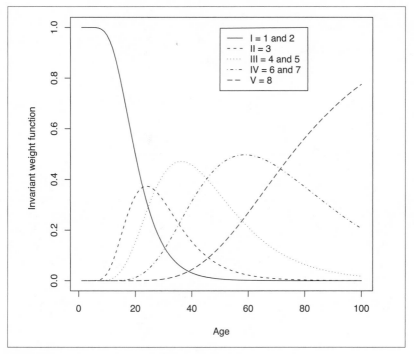

FIGURE 9.9

The probabilities of being in each of five stages (Roman numerals) formed from Lovejoy and colleagues' auricular stages (Arabic numerals).

779 individuals we selected from the Terry sample, then the integral across age for the probability of death multiplied by the weight functions gives the expected proportion of individuals in each stage of the auricular surface. This is the basis for what has come to be known as the "Rostock Manifesto" for paleodemography and, indeed, is the first equation listed in the Rostock volume (Hoppa and Vaupel 2002a) detailing the manifesto. Hoppa and Vaupel (2002a:3) wrote, "The basic strategy is to choose the parameters of the model of the lifespan distribution…to maximize the 'fit' between the observed frequencies of the morphological characteristics and the underlying probabilities of these characteristics." We do this with the Terry data using a Gompertz model of mortality, setting survivorship at age 15 to 1.0 because throughout this chapter we are ignoring subadult mortality.

Figure 9.10 shows the empirical survivorship from the recorded

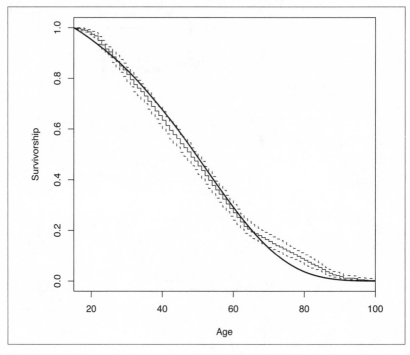

FIGURE 9.10

The empirical survivorship for 779 individuals sampled from the Terry Collection, based on recorded age (step function with 95 percent confidence intervals) and estimated from the auricular surface data using a five-phase proportional odds model (the heavy line).

ages and estimated from the counts in auricular stages, which are modeled using the proportional odds method with age on a log scale and Gompertz mortality. Not surprisingly, the Gompertz model survivorship estimated from the auricular stages is quite similar to the empirical survivorship from recorded ages. In paleodemographic settings, though, we do not have the luxury of comparing lifespan estimates from the bones with the known lifespan data from ages at death. We can, however, examine the fit between estimated and observed counts in auricular stages, as Hoppa and Vaupel suggested in the Rostock Manifesto and as we have done in our contingency table examples. This can be accomplished with a Pearson chi-square, with two degrees of freedom in our particular example. With five stages, four parameters (the frequency in each of four stages, with the fifth constrained to sum to 1.0 with the other four) fully specify the observed data, whereas the Gompertz is a two-parameter model. The difference in number of parameters yields two degrees of freedom in this case. The observed counts in the five stages are 60, 94, 219, 264, and 142; the estimated counts are 60.44, 93.64, 218.14, 265.22, and 141.56. This yields a Pearson chi-square value of 0.0150, which, with two degrees of freedom, gives a probability value of about 0.9925. Consequently, we suggest that the proportional odds probit model and the Gompertz model of mortality, together, do a quite reasonable job of reproducing the observed counts in stages for the Terry sample.

ESTIMATION OF LONGEVITY FOR INDIAN KNOLL

It should be a relatively straightforward process to apply the information on auricular surface aging from the Terry Collection to Indian Knoll and thus estimate the two Gompertz parameters for this site. The observed counts in stages for Indian Knoll are 117, 78, 162, 61, and 21, which leads to estimates of a and b in the Gompertz model of 0.0409 and 0.0249, respectively, translating into a life expectancy at age 15 of 16.8 years. Unfortunately, these Gompertz parameters do not do a good job of recovering the observed counts in stages, yielding expected counts of 106.83, 106.38, 132.70, 74.68, and 18.41. The Pearson chi-squared statistic comparing these expected counts with the observed counts is 19.90, which, with two degrees of freedom, yields a probability value of less than 0.0001.

Two possible reasons account for the discrepancy between predicted and observed counts. The first explanation is that observer error has reared its ugly head, and, consequently, the Indian Knoll sample does not appear to age in the same way as the Terry Collection (because the samples were not scored in the same way). Indeed, we have made the argument elsewhere (Konigsberg and Frankenberg 2003) that inter-observer error was the source of such a discrepancy in another analysis using a modern reference sample and a different modern target sample. For the Indian Knoll case, the second author scored both Indian Knoll and the Terry Collection, so any scoring error is due to the observer. The second, and we think more reasonable, explanation for the discrepancy is that the Indian Knoll sample senesced on a different schedule than the Terry Collection.

To examine the possibility that the people from the Indian Knoll site were on a different senescent path, we consider proportional odds

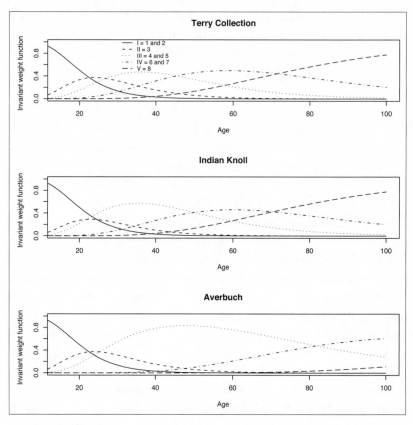

FIGURE 9.11

A comparison of invariant weight functions for the Terry Collection, Indian Knoll, and Averbuch.

probit regression models that have the same standard deviation for transitions (on the log age scale) as for the Terry Collection but differ in their mean ages to transition. This has the effect of maintaining the same overall strength of association between age and stage for the two samples but altering the specific timing of transitions between stages. Ideally, we would use some formal type of model fitting to estimate the new intercepts for Indian Knoll, but, with only two degrees of freedom available, there simply is not enough information. Instead, we have had to resort to trial-and-error selection of new mean ages to transition.

Table 9.3 lists the new values for Indian Knoll that give a reasonable fit between the observed counts in stages and the predicted

TABLE 9.3

Mean Transition Ages in Years

Sample	I/II	II/III	III/IV	IV/V
Terry Collection	19.98	28.68	45.83	75.45
Indian Knoll	19.98	*26.38*	*49.63*	75.45
Averbuch	19.98	28.68	*80.48*	*157.18*

Mean transition ages estimated from the Terry Collection and applied to Indian Knoll and Averbuch. The standard deviation for transitions is 0.3719 on the log age scale. Supplied transition ages that differ from the Terry Collection are italicized.

counts. Figure 9.11 compares the "invariant" weight functions for the Terry Collection, Indian Knoll, and Averbuch. Using the adjusted mean ages to transition for Indian Knoll, the predicted counts in stages are 111.73, 80.56, 166.91, 63.31, and 15.85, which are close to the observed counts of 117, 78, 162, 61, and 21. This gives a relatively small chi-square value of 2.23, but how to interpret this statistic is unclear. Even though we started with two available degrees of freedom, much of this information was lost when we adjusted two of the mean ages at transition. In any event, the adjustments to the transition ages do not have a substantial effect on the estimated Gompertz model. The estimated Gompertz a and b parameters are 0.0494 and 0.0126, respectively. If we integrate the survivorship, this yields an Indian Knoll life expectancy at age 15 of about 17.1 years, not much different from our previous calculation of 16.8.

ESTIMATION OF LONGEVITY FOR AVERBUCH

Armed with the knowledge that the invariant weight functions from the Terry Collection did not do a reasonable job of reproducing observed counts for Indian Knoll, we need to examine their performance similarly for Averbuch. In the case of the Averbuch site, there is an additional complication: the observer who scored this material was not the same observer who scored the Terry Collection. Averbuch was scored primarily by Dr. Samantha Hens, who was a graduate student at the University of Tennessee at the time. The observed counts in stages for Averbuch are 38, 47, 162, 46, and 5. The predicted counts using the Terry invariant weight functions and estimating the Gompertz parameters ($a = 0.0015$ and $b = 0.2416$) for Averbuch are 30.93, 73.10, 129.09,

58.85, and 6.03. As with Indian Knoll, this gives an unacceptably large chi-square of 22.31, which, with two degrees of freedom, yields a probability of less than 0.0001.

The life expectancy at age 15 from this Gompertz model is 18.79 years. If we re-estimate the Gompertz model using the adjusted mean transition ages shown for Averbuch in table 9.3, then the expected counts are 39.52, 44.94, 162.19, 46.75, and 4.60. This yields a Pearson chi-square statistic of 0.1999. The re-estimated Gompertz values of $a = 0.0201$ and $b = 0.0109$ yield an Averbuch life expectancy at age 15 of 34.95 years, substantially higher than our initial calculation of 18.79 years.

THE HISTORY OF RECENT HUMAN LONGEVITY

In addition to our results from Indian Knoll and Averbuch, we can include results from a French Neolithic site, Loisy-en-Brie. Bocquet-Appel and Bacro (1997) reported the raw data on femoral head involution from this site, as well as information on a reference collection of known age. Konigsberg and Frankenberg (2002) reanalyzed the data using hazard models and fit a Siler model. To date, Loisy-en-Brie, Indian Knoll, and Averbuch are the only sites we are aware of that have been analyzed using maximum likelihood estimation to model the progression through skeletal stages. It would be useful to compare the demographic reconstructions for these three sites to a general paleodemographic model (O'Connor 1995), as well as to demographic data from extant foraging and horticultural societies.

Drawing comparative data from extant foragers is not as easy a task as one might initially think. Early and Headland (1998), in their careful comparative study of forager demography, quote from Kelly (1995:205–209), who wrote that "any attempt to understand hunter-gatherer demography must confront the scanty data at our disposal. Given the importance often ascribed to population as a prime mover of cultural evolution, it is surprising that we have few accurate data on hunter-gatherer demography. Although we can compile a fairly impressive list...the accuracy of many of these data is unknown for a variety of reasons....All of these factors mean that we should regard hunter-gatherer [demographic] data with a healthy amount of skepticism."

In the end, Early and Headland found only six hunter-gatherer groups for which they thought the demographic data might be reliable. Of these, only half—the San Ildefonso Agta, the Ache, and the !Kung—have mortality data. For these three groups, we have estimated four-parameter Siler models that fit juvenile mortality as a negative Gompertz equation and adult mortality as a positive Gompertz. This is the Siler model (Gage and Dyke 1986; Gage 1988; Wood et al. 2002) with the baseline hazard (the a_2 parameter) set equal to zero. To fit this model, we started from the age-specific probabilities of death for foragers listed in Early and Headland's table 12.1 (with the substitution of the correct probability of death between zero and one, from their table 8.1, to replace a typographical error in table 12.1).

For horticulturalists, we have used data from the Yanomami because they have figured heavily in previous anthropological demography analyses. We used mortality data from two sources. Hill and Hurtado (1996:134) comment on Neel and Weiss's (1975) study of the Yanomami that "the difference between the Ache and the Yanomamo may be due to underestimation of the age of Yanomamo older adults (age estimates for the Yanomamo were assigned based on the ethnographer's visual assessment and genealogical clues)." We have already quoted Gage and colleagues' (1989:48–50) comment that the Yanomami analysis as represented in Neel and Weiss's study may "be a result of the error intrinsic in estimating ages in ethnographic populations." Such appears to be the case from Gage's 1988 study. As a consequence, in place of Neel and Weiss's now classic study, we use more reliable mortality data from Early and Peters' (1990) study of the Mucajai Yanomami and Early and Peters' (2000) study of the Xilixana Yanomami.

In figure 9.12a, we have plotted life expectancy at each age for the five extant samples described above (the !Kung, Xilixana Yanomami, Mucajai Yanomami, Ache, and Agta). As Hill and Hurtado (1996) have previously noted, the Ache, !Kung, and Yanomami have very similar mortality patterns, as reflected in their similar life expectancies. The Agta have lower life expectancies at all ages. For example, compared with the Xilixana Yanomami, the Agta have a life expectancy that is 16.5 years shorter at birth, 12.4 years shorter at age 20, 8.5 years shorter at age 40, and 4.3 years shorter at age 60. Still, the Agta life expectancies are within the range of those reported from model life tables.

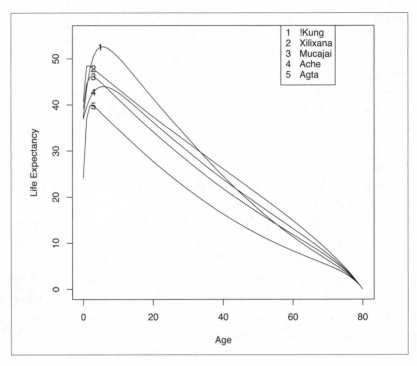

FIGURE 9.12A

A comparison of life expectancies for extant hunter-gatherer groups with reliable data.

In figure 9.12b, we compare the results from paleodemographic analyses of Averbuch, Loisy-en-Brie, and Indian Knoll with life expectancies from the extant hunter-gatherers. For Loisy-en-Brie, there are interval-censored observations on ages at death for those who died before age 23. Consequently, we show the entire life-expectancy curve for this Neolithic site, using the parameters estimated in Konigsberg and Frankenberg (2002) (a_1 = 0.0220, b_1 = 0.1144, a_2 = 0.0054, a_3 = 0.0026, and b_3 = 0.0507). Compared with extant hunter-gatherer life expectancies (shown hatched in figure 9.12b), nothing in our reanalysis of Loisy-en-Brie suggests a departure from the pattern of mortality among extant "anthropological" populations (save for under-enumeration of infant deaths). This is also the case for Averbuch, where we have plotted life expectancy starting at age 15, using the adjusted transition ages from table 9.3.

For the Averbuch cemetery, we cannot plot life expectancies under

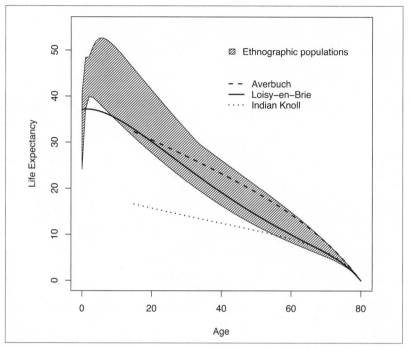

FIGURE 9.12B

A comparison of life expectancies for Averbuch, Loisy-en-Brie, and Indian Knoll with those of extant hunter-gatherers.

age 15 because the site has substantial under-enumeration of subadults. This under-enumeration is documented by the biased representation of subadults buried in house floors at the site. Because the cemeteries were completely excavated but the village house floors were not, we do not know in what proportion to combine the two samples. Figure 9.12b also contains a plot of life expectancy for Indian Knoll, again using the transition ages adjusted as in table 9.3. Indian Knoll life expectancies fall well below those for extant hunter-gatherers. Because we have used maximum likelihood estimation instead of the (informal) Bayesian methods previously common in paleodemography, it would be difficult to argue that we have systematically misestimated ages for this site. Rather, the more likely explanation is that many older individuals were not returned for burial in this seasonally migratory population.

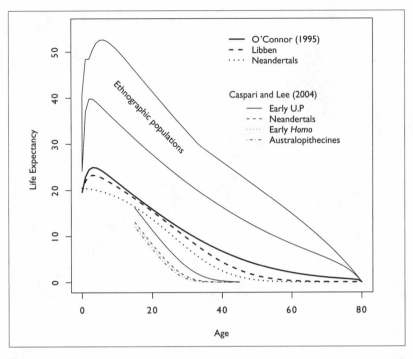

FIGURE 9.12C

A comparison of life expectancies for samples, with ages at death estimated using non-mle methods, with those of extant hunter-gatherers.

To complete figure 9.12, we show results in figure 9.12c from a number of paleodemographic studies that have used more traditional methods for age estimation. In order of overall decreasing life expectancies, the highest paleodemographic example is from O'Connor's (1995) model based on twelve paleodemographic life tables analyzed with Siler models. Next is the Libben analysis done by Gage (1988) with a Siler model. Below this is a Siler model from 206 Neandertals reported in Trinkaus (1995). We do not make a distinction here between "attritional" and "catastrophic" Neandertal samples (Bocquet-Appel and Arsuaga 1999). Beneath the Neandertals are Gompertz model life expectancies, starting at age 15 for four groups (early Upper Paleolithic, Neandertals, early *Homo*, and Australopithecines, in that order) reported in Caspari and Lee (2004). In the conclusion section, we discuss at length how these life expectancies for the Caspari and Lee study were calculated here. It is clear from this final part of figure 9.12 that the paleodemographic estimates from traditional methods give results that are not consonant with what we know from extant hunter-gatherer and horticultural groups.

In summary, we have shown that published paleodemographic life tables produce life expectancies that are considerably lower than those for extant "anthropological" populations. In contrast, our maximum likelihood estimates of life expectancy for Loisy-en-Brie and Averbuch are in line with life expectancies for the Ache, !Kung, Yanomami (from Early and Peters 1990, 2000), and Agta. In contrast, Indian Knoll appears to demonstrate under-representation of older adults, instead of under-estimation of ages. These results indicate that mortality experience in human prehistory did not differ from what has been documented for small-scale extant populations, but we need to return to our original question of whether rates of senescence have changed over time.

THE CHANGING TEMPO OF SENESCENCE?

Figure 9.11 suggests that, for the auricular surface of the ilium, there are not "invariant weight functions" but rather functions that differ across prehistory. Regardless of this variation or the presumed differences in age structure among the Terry Collection, Indian Knoll, and Averbuch, in figure 9.13 we show that the posterior density for age in the last auricular stage extends well beyond sixty years. This finding is reassuring because it indicates that when we find auricular surfaces in the last stage, we have no reason to infer that "everyone is dead by 50."

Lovejoy and colleagues' (1997) recent review of the "biology of the hominoid pelvis" provides much of the detail for evaluating the senescence of the auricular surface. Because the sacroiliac joint (the union of the sacral auricular surface with the auricular surface of the ilium) has been consistently implicated as a source of low back pain in the past few years (Daum 1995), the literature on the joint has been burgeoning. Further, the development of new imaging and clinical assessment methods (Braun, Sieper, and Bollow 2000) has contributed substantially to our understanding of this complex joint, as have recent studies of the histology (Kampen and Tillmann 1998), gross morphology of aging (Shibata, Shirai, and Miyamoto 2002), and kinematics of the joint (Sturesson, Udén, and Vleeming 2000).

Functionally, the joint is often classified as a diarthrosis (a mobile

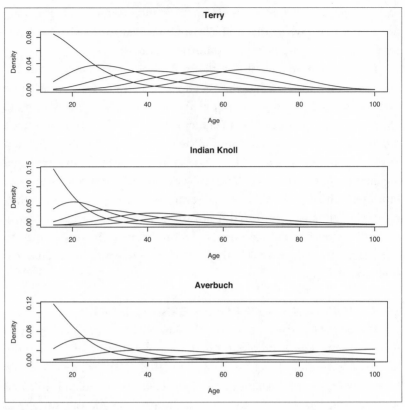

FIGURE 9.13

Posterior densities of age conditional on auricular surface stage. Note that these densities depend on both the pattern of auricular surface development against age and the age structure of the sample.

joint) because it contains a synovial capsule and the sacral surface is lined with articular hyaline cartilage, both of which are characteristics of diarthroses. Until recently, it was thought that the iliac surface was lined throughout life by fibrocartilage, which would be very atypical for a diarthrosis. Recent work by Kampen and Tillmann (1998:511) has shown that "large parts of the iliac cartilage are clearly hyaline in the adult." The sacroiliac bears many similarities to other mobile joints, except that its motion is severely restricted by the joint's geometry and the surrounding soft tissues. Consequently, some refer to the sacroiliac joint as an amphiarthrosis, and, indeed, motion in the joint is quite minimal (Sturesson, Udén, and Vleeming 2000). The joint is substantially weight-bearing. As Mooney (1997) notes, the sacroiliac joint has greater shear strength than the compressive strength of the third lumbar vertebra (both measured in vitro).

Taken together, in the sacroiliac joint we have a weight-bearing diarthrodial joint that shows patterns of aging. These patterns include both normal "physiological aging" and degeneration at later ages. Shibata, Shirai, and Miyamoto (2002) have commented that by ages 50 and above, all the individuals in their sample showed some form of joint degeneration, though this includes joint space narrowing that would not be visible osteologically. Regarding the sacroiliac cartilages, Kampen and Tillmann (1998:511) write that "genuine degeneration, comparable to osteoarthrosis in other diarthrodial joints, is set against 'physiological changes' appearing during aging." This information suggests that for transitions between earlier stages of joint surface development, we might expect uniform patterns across populations. For populations subject to different levels of physical activity, however, it may not be reasonable to assume that the later transitions are nearly as uniform. Indeed, this is what we appear to have found for Averbuch, where the pace of later transitions is much slower than we find in the Terry Collection.

Interestingly, Konigsberg and Frankenberg (2002) found no evidence that the pattern of femoral head involution had changed over the four-thousand-some years separating Loisy-en-Brie from Bocquet-Appel and Bacro's (1997) reference sample. Currently, we have no way of predicting a priori whether various anatomical systems followed the same pattern of senescence in the past as they do today. Certainly, when the osteological "age indicators" focus on degenerative changes, we are on much shakier ground in assuming universal patterns of aging. This problem makes paleodemographic reconstruction much more complicated, but it also introduces a new area of study. Specifically, we are beginning to approach a phase in research when it may be possible to look not only at human longevity in the past but also at changing tempos of senescence. In the remainder of this section, we discuss additional avenues for studying rates of senescence in the past.

Do Skeletons Wear Wristwatches?

"Skeletons do not have a wrist watch" was a section heading for one of Boquet-Appel's (1986) articles. This referred to the fact that none of the age "indicators" in use at that time had a correlation with age above 0.8, so we could never *know* the age at death for adult skeletal remains. Recently, Wittwer-Backofen and Buba (2002) have described refinements to age determination from the counting of dental cementum annulations. In their pilot validation study on a modern sample, they found a correlation of 0.94 between estimated and known age; in a more recent study (Wittwer-Backofen, Gampe, and Vaupel 2004), the correlation was in the vicinity of 0.98. Although skeletons do not wear wristwatches, the cementum annulation ages appear to be accurate enough to be used in place of known ages, provided that the method can be applied to archaeologically recovered teeth.

This opens the avenue to two kinds of studies. First, it may soon be possible to obtain "known" ages from archaeological skeletons by using cementum annuli counts, to treat these as a reference sample to derive the pattern of osteological aging, and then to apply these results back to skeletons that cannot be aged by annuli. In this way, the reference sample is entirely appropriate for the target sample, and we need not worry that aging patterns may have differed in the past (or across different populations). The second type of study, and the more interesting for the purpose of looking at human life history, is to treat skeletons with annuli counts as being of known age and then compare the patterns of osteological aging across archaeological time.

The High Dimensional Nature of Human Skeletal Aging

We have argued elsewhere (Herrmann and Konigsberg 2002) that correlations in the senescence of skeletal systems are substantial. Traditionally, these correlations have been assumed to equal zero after the effect of age is removed (Kolakowski and Bock 1981; Roche, Chumlea, and Thissen 1988; Lucy et al. 1996; Boldsen et al. 2002). This assumption of a zero correlation is called the "conditional independence assumption," and the logic is that skeletal age "indicators" are correlated with one another only because of their common correlations with age. Remove the effect of age, and the partial correlations between the indicators should be zero. Such an assumption does not make much sense because it argues that, for example, the partial correlation between suture closures at two distant sites across the vault should be zero and that the partial correlation between suture closures at two adjacent sites should also be zero. The conditional indepen-

dence assumption consequently ignores the topology and spatial organization of the skeleton. Still, osteologists have tended to cling to this
assumption because it vastly simplifies statistical calculations. If,
instead, we do not assume these partial correlations away, then there is
another possible venue for assessing change in the patterns of skeletal
aging. We describe this possible future research below.

In multivariate calibration problems, a number of dependent variables are used to estimate the predictor (or independent) variable. For
example, in allometric analysis we may use the size of two or more
organs to try to estimate overall body size. In allometric analysis, organs
are clearly dependent on body size, though it is often body size that we
want to estimate when only organs (such as bones) are available for
study. Similarly, in age estimation studies we can view various skeletal
attributes as being dependent on age. The causal direction is quite
clear because, for example, it is advancing age that causes one to gain
cementum annulations, not vice versa.

Whenever there are two or more dependent variables and one predictor, it is possible to test cases with unknown predictor values against
the reference (calibration) set, to see whether the test cases are outliers
(Brown and Sundberg 1987; P. Brown 1993). Outliers can come in two
forms. Specifically, in the age estimation context the test cases might be
much younger or older than is typical for the known-age reference
data set. This is not a particularly interesting result because usually the
reference data have been selected in some way to provide general cov-
erage across the age span. A more interesting result is when statistical
testing demonstrates that the age indicators senesce in a discordant
fashion from that seen in the reference data. Konigsberg and colleagues (1998) have made such an analysis for stature estimation,
examining humerus and femur length for fossils against a large reference set that includes measured statures. In addition to testing
whether fossil hominids were taller or shorter than modern humans,
they were able to test for differing proportionality. Konigsberg and
Frankenberg (2002) note that a similar analysis could be made in the
context of skeletal aging. To date, this has not been done.

The Constancy of Skeletal Senescence in Extant Populations

If we are to argue that there are universal weight functions
for skeletal aging that apply across time and space, then we must be

able to demonstrate that these functions apply for a variety of extant populations. So far, the record for these comparisons has not been encouraging. Hoppa (2000:190) examined pubic symphyseal development for three known-age skeletal collections and noted that "differences in the timing of age-related changes for osteological criteria may be significant." Most recently, Jackes (2003) has applied information from Judy Suchey's known-age pubic symphyseal data from Los Angeles to an analysis of known-age material from Coimbra, Portugal (Santos 1995). Jackes (2003:386) found substantive differences between the two collections and suggested that "population differences, derived from genetic or life factors, or some incalculable mixture of the two, could be the root cause." Konigsberg and Frankenberg (2003) suggested instead that the differences between the two samples could be traced to inter-observer error in the scoring of the pubic symphyses. In a broader study, Schmitt and colleagues (2002) compared aging in the "sacro-pelvic surface" and the pubic symphysis across a number of skeletal collections from recent populations. After observing interpopulation variation in skeletal aging, they noted "the necessity to use population-specific standards" (Schmitt et al. 2002:1207).

Unfortunately, the previous analyses of interpopulation variation in skeletal aging have not always been well designed. We are currently working on an analysis of between-sample variation in pubic symphyseal aging, so our comments here must be quite preliminary. One of the first considerations in any such study must be the role of inter-observer error. Some observations (such as the closure of cranial sutures) are relatively simple and easy to make, but others (such as observations on the auricular surface) are much harder. Ideally, in comparisons between samples the observations should have been made by the same observer, or at least by individuals from the same lab.

In addition to data-quality issues, a number of complicated statistical issues surround the analysis of interpopulation variation in skeletal aging. To date, the usual design has been to treat one sample as a reference sample and the other as a target and then to demonstrate that age estimation in the target fails. This is a wasteful data analysis strategy because with two (or more) known-age samples we should be able to make a direct comparison of patterns of skeletal aging. Such comparisons are, however, further complicated by the possibility of different age structures for samples.

This problem is easiest to demonstrate by thinking of a continuous age "indicator" (y) that depends, in part, on age (x). Now, we have two or more samples, and we want to determine whether the pattern of senescence for y varies across samples. This is an analysis of a covariance type of setting, in which the samples represent "treatments," the y variable is the variable of interest, and x (age) is the covariate. In a series of articles and comments (Evans and Anastasio 1968; Sprott 1970; Harris, Bisbee, and Evans 1971; Overall and Woodward 1977), researchers have pointed out that when the treatment and covariate are confounded, the statistical interpretation can be spurious. This problem could be circumvented by using samples that are age-matched, but we are unaware of any such analyses from known-age skeletal material.

CONCLUSION

As should be clear from this chapter, much work remains to be done in paleodemography. We have maximum likelihood estimates of hazard models that incorporate uncertainty in age estimation for only a very small handful of sites. What is encouraging about these few analyses is that they appear to generate life tables that are virtually indistinguishable from those of extant foragers and horticulturalists. The next step, aside from extending analyses to other places, is to extend analyses back in time. This will be critical in dating the emergence of our current life history. Although analyses of Neandertal paleodemography have begun to appear within the past decade (Trinkaus 1995; Bermúdez de Castro and Nicolás 1997; Bocquet-Appel and Arsuaga 1999), our track record with the demography of the recent past suggests that we must approach such studies with considerable caution. As a consequence, in this final section we make an in-depth examination of a recent publication (Caspari and Lee 2004) that claims "older age becomes common late in human evolution."

The Caspari and Lee analysis (also referred to in Hawkes, chapter 3, this volume) makes use of dental wear data to attempt to reconstruct demographic aspects of Australopithecines, early *Homo*, Neandertals, and early Upper Paleolithic peoples. Following Miles' (1963) method of "internal calibration," Caspari and Lee use dental wear to distinguish individuals who died between ages 15 and 30 years from those who died beyond 30 years of age. They make a number of unsubstantiated claims about the nature of their data, and we are forced to make a number of assumptions about these data in order to glean anything from them. First and foremost, we must assume that the ages of 15 and 30 years are correctly defined. All that is important, Caspari and Lee attempt to argue, is that the second age be twice that of the first age. If this is the only requirement, then it leads to too many alternative ways of explaining the data.

Caspari and Lee work with ratios of counts of "old" individuals (ages at death older than 30 years) to "young" individuals (ages at death between 15 and 30 years). Our preference is to work with deaths at ages older than 30 years in proportion to deaths at ages older than 15 years. If we define survivorship at age 15 as 1.0 (that is, we treat the cohort as only those individuals who reach the age of 15), then the proportion of deaths over age 30 from this cohort is just the survivorship to age 30. If we further assume that mortality follows a Gompertz model with an initial mortality rate (IMR) of 0.0002 at age 15 (this IMR value is given in Finch, Pike, and Witten [1990] for modern humans), then we can numerically solve for the mortality rate doubling (MRD) time. In this model, the IMR is what we have previously referred to in the Gompertz model as the a parameter and the MRD is $\ln(2)/b$ (see Finch, Pike, and Witten 1990).

Under these conditions, the MRD for Australopithecines from Caspari and Lee (2004) is 1.18. It is 1.24 for early *Homo*, 1.27 for Neandertals, and 1.53 for early Upper Paleolithic peoples. These values are remarkable because they indicate that (rounding to the nearest year) the mortality rate doubles for every year of life past age 15 in Australopithecines, early *Homo*, and Neandertals and doubles every two years in Upper Paleolithic peoples. In modern humans, doubling of the mortality rate takes about eight years (Finch, Pike, and Witten 1990). The Gompertz model is sensitive to the value selected for the IMR, so we tried a fivefold greater value of 0.001. At this IMR, the MRD times are 1.50 years for Australopithecines, 1.59 for early *Homo*, 1.65 for Neandertals, and 2.14 for early Upper Paleolithic peoples. Again, these doubling times seem incredibly fast. More to the point, we should ask whether they differ significantly between taxonomic groups.

Caspari and Lee (2004) argue that all the death ratios in their study are significantly different, but they base this argument on a misapplication of the bootstrap. Specifically, they treat one of their samples as if the death ratio was known without sampling error and then bootstrap another sample (at the wrong sample size) to approximate the sampling error in the second sample. A likelihood ratio or Pearson chi-square test for the two-by-two contingency table would be a perfectly reasonable approach here (where one classification is taxonomic and the other is 15–30 years versus 30+ years of age).

Before briefly reanalyzing Caspari and Lee's data here, we should point out at least one interpretive problem. Statistical significance of the differences in proportions of deaths over age 30 does not necessarily translate into statistical, or at least biological, significance of the differences in the living age distribution. This is demonstrated graphically in figure 9.14, which shows the proportion of those in the living population over age 15 who are also over age 30 years. For Australopithecines, 0.6 percent of the living group over age 15 would also be over age 30. For early *Homo*, this rises slightly to 1.56 percent; for Neandertals, to 2.49 percent; and for early Upper Paleolithic peoples, it rises substantially to 13.65 percent. In terms of "dependency ratios," it would be hard to argue that, with the exception of the Upper Paleolithic, any of the groups differ from one another in any meaningful way. Therefore, if we want to discuss "life history" instead of "death history," it would seem that the only meaningful contrast is between the Upper Paleolithic and all antecedent groups.

In reanalyzing Caspari and Lee's data, we should also point out that they make a very critical assumption that we believe is untenable. Specifically, they assume that there is little to no misclassification on their assignment of individuals to two age classes (15–30 years and 30+ years). If classification rates from a known-age sample were available, then we could solve for the death proportion much as we did in our example from table 9.1. Further, we could test for the significance of differences in death proportions that accounts for the uncertainty in age assignment. In the absence of such information, we have examined possible correct classification values between 60 and 100 percent and have assumed that misclassification is symmetric. In other words, if we assume that 80 percent of individuals over age 30 are correctly classified as being "old" (and that 20 percent are misclassified as "young"), then we also assume that 80 percent of those individuals under age 30

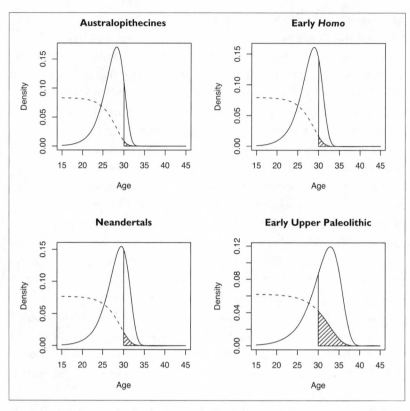

FIGURE 9.14

Implied living age distributions (dashed lines) and age-at-death distributions (solid lines) under the assumption of an IMR of 0.001. The vertical lines at age 30 years divide the age-at-death distributions into the observed proportions from Caspari and Lee (2004). The hatched regions are the implied proportions of living individuals age 30 years or older out of all individuals age 15 years or older.

are correctly classified as "young" (and 20 percent are misclassified as "old"). Under this assumption, we can find the 95 percent confidence intervals for the proportion of actual deaths over age 30 (out of those over age 15) by using standard likelihood methods.

Figure 9.15 shows a graph of these results. The first point to glean from the graph is that—if we assume 100 percent correct classification when, in fact, the correct classification is lower—we will obtain biased estimates. Specifically, if the death proportion is less than 0.5, then we will overestimate it; if it is greater than 0.5, we will underestimate it.

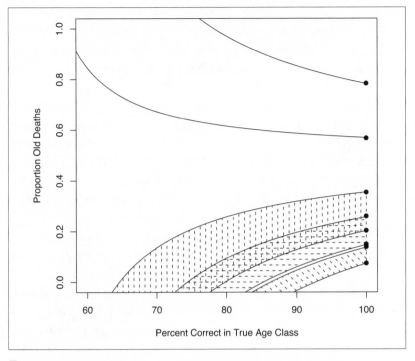

FIGURE 9.15

Ninety-five percent confidence intervals on the proportions of old age deaths for
Australopithecines *(hatched at – 45 degrees),* early Homo *(horizontal hatching),*
Neandertals *(vertical hatching), and the early Upper Paleolithic (no hatching). These*
intervals are plotted against the assumed-percent correct classifications into the "young"
and "old" age categories. The marked points at 100 percent correct classification show the
bootstrap 95 percent confidence intervals for one million draws with each taxon.

This is a well-known effect that follows from the "algebra of misclassification" (see Fleiss, Levin, and Paik 2003:565–569). We can also see
from figure 9.15 that the confidence interval widths for death proportions increase with decreasing correct classification, though this point
is somewhat masked by the fact that the death proportion must be
between zero and one.

Another salient point is that, despite Caspari and Lee's claim that
the early *Homo* and Neandertal death ratios are significantly different
(Caspari and Lee's bootstrap estimate of the p-value is 0.0133), when
both taxa are allowed to have their own confidence intervals, these

overlap substantially. Caspari and Lee treated the Neandertal data as if the death ratio was known instead of estimated. Finally, figure 9.15 also shows parametric bootstrap estimates of the 95 percent confidence intervals around the death proportions assuming 100 percent correct classification. These intervals were found using the empirical 0.025 and 0.975 quantiles from one million samples for each taxon, where the binomial is used for the parametric model. These Monte Carlo confidence intervals are indistinguishable from the likelihood-derived intervals, showing that Caspari and Lee's Monte Carlo approach was unnecessary (save for the fact that confidence intervals on ratios are computationally more difficult to find than confidence intervals on proportions).

We have been harsh in our closing criticism of the Caspari and Lee (2004) study, but it is our firm belief that we cannot make progress in paleodemographic interpretations through the blind statistical treatment of data. We must realistically re-examine the quality of our data, evaluate the strength of any necessary assumptions we make, and check our results against other data sources (such as modern primate data) to avoid the continual pitfalls that have beset paleodemographic analyses and interpretations in the past decades. Only in this way can we continue to discuss what paleodemography tells us about life history in the past and to argue whether our paleoanthropological "facts" about life history are any better than ill-supported hunches.

Acknowledgments

The collection of data from the Averbuch site was supported by NSF 9307693. Collection of reference sample data was supported by NSF 9727386. We thank the co-organizers of the advanced seminar and the participants for their invaluable input and the School.

10

Paleodemographic Data and Why Understanding Holocene Demography Is Essential to Understanding Human Life History Evolution in the Pleistocene

Richard R. Paine and Jesper L. Boldsen

SUMMARY

Most studies of human life history focus on either our Pleistocene fossil relatives or contemporary foragers, assuming that these populations best represent our "environment of evolutionary adaptedness" (Hill and Hurtado 1996). In this chapter, we use a large database of skeletal series from northern and central Europe dating from the Mesolithic through the late Middle Ages to explore selective pressures, specifically, cycles of epidemic disease among (demographically) prehistoric Holocene agricultural populations. Employing a series of mathematical population projections, we test the hypothesis that patterns of child death observed in the database reflect epidemic cycles, which escalate as populations grow and become more interconnected. The projections capture the trends in child death from the skeletal populations, suggesting that epidemic waves increased in frequency between the Mesolithic and the Medieval periods. If true, this would have led to marked increases in extrinsic mortality. The projections also suggest that these increases in extrinsic mortality would have been transitional.

We then explore some of the implications of the epidemic model for Holocene life histories. Although life expectancy at birth decreases throughout most of the simulation, increases in age-specific life expectancy reach younger and younger age groups as epidemic cycles become shorter. Adult life expectancy increases as life expectancy at birth declines, an apparent paradox we found in some sixteenth-to-eighteenth-century historical demographic records. The projections also demonstrate that, mirroring nineteenth-to-early-twentieth-century historical demographic records, life expectancy at birth does not lengthen dramatically until epidemic intervals become very short and increases in infant and child survival take hold. Infant and juvenile mortality has a disproportionately large effect on life expectancy at birth; it represents a large percentage of deaths, and each early death has a disproportionate mathematical impact. The projections call into question the widespread assumption based on historical demography that before the nineteenth century, few individuals lived past age 50.

Our Pleistocene fossil relatives (see Clegg and Aiello 1999; O'Connell, Hawkes, and Blurton Jones 1999) and contemporary foragers (see Hill and Hurtado 1996; Hawkes et al. 1998; Blurton Jones, Hawkes, and O'Connell 1999) tend to be emphasized in studies of human life history. We have assumed that the selective pressures these populations encounter(ed) are the most important for the development of the life history characteristics we find most interesting (Robson, van Schaik, and Hawkes, chapter 2, this volume). This may be true. However, we cannot view the life history of Pleistocene foragers without looking through the lens of Holocene farmers. Farming in the Holocene transformed human life, bringing with it a new suite of selective pressures. Virtually all living populations, including contemporary foraging populations, have been affected by the dramatic growth of Holocene farming populations.

This chapter has two purposes. We want to convey how important the understanding of Holocene agriculturalists is to our overall understanding of human life history evolution. Specifically, we examine possible effects of Holocene epidemic disease cycles on life expectancy at different ages. Using the results, we address the question of whether historically observed demographic trends of recent Holocene agricultural societies extend into our Pleistocene foraging past. Historical demographic data show remarkable increases in life expectancy since the eighteenth century. We would like to know whether this is a long-term trend. Another purpose is to provide an example of how pale-odemography, for all its limitations (for example, see Bocquet-Appel and Masset 1982, 1996; Walker, Johnson, and Lambert 1988; Wood, Milner et al. 1992; Paine 1997; Hoppa and Vaupel 2002b; Hawkes, chapter 3, and Konigsberg and Herrmann, chapter 9, this volume), might be used to examine life history change.

Two models currently dominate the literature on the evolution of human life history: the Embodied Capital hypothesis (Kaplan et al. 2000; Kaplan and Robson 2002; Kaplan, Lancaster, and Robson 2003) and the Grandmother hypothesis (Hawkes et al. 1998). Each is treated in greater detail elsewhere in this volume, especially by Hawkes (chapter 4). Both models are rooted in changes in Pleistocene foraging strategies. Embodied Capital posits that increased brain size and longevity co-evolved as responses to new, learning-intensive foraging strategies and a dietary shift toward resources that were high-quality and nutrient-dense but difficult to acquire (Kaplan, Lancaster, and Robson 2003). The Grandmother hypothesis emphasizes the role of postreproductive women in provisioning the weaned young children of their daughters. This enabled the younger women to maintain short-er interbirth intervals and improved the nutritional welfare of their liv-ing children. Proponents (such as Hawkes, O'Connell, and Blurton Jones 1989, 1995, and 1997; Blurton Jones, Hawkes, and O'Connell 1999; Hawkes, chapter 4, and Blurton Jones, chapter 8, this volume) cite impacts of grandmother provisioning on child welfare among con-temporary Hadza foragers as evidence of the potential benefit of long postreproductive lifespans. O'Connell, Hawkes, and Blurton Jones (1999) further argue that the changing foraging environment of the Pleistocene, particularly a heightened use of tubers, which small chil-dren are unable to harvest, would have increased reproductive advan-tages associated with grandmothers' provisioning. Robson and Kaplan (2003:150) extol the primacy of Pleistocene foraging when they state that "the economics of hunting and gathering *must have driven* the biological evolution of human characteristics, since hunter-gatherer societies prevailed for the two million years of human history" (italics ours).

Both hypotheses assume low levels of juvenile and adult mortality. The Embodied Capital theory (Robson and Kaplan 2003) treats our long childhood dependence and large brains as investments in stocks of somatic or embodied capital. Extended human lifespan and large brain size "are the results of a long learning process that is necessary for successful foraging" (Kaplan et al. 2000).[1] This investment involves three important costs: low juvenile productivity, delayed reproduction, and a "very expensive brain to grow and maintain" (Kaplan et al. 2000:161). The return on this investment comes at later ages, with lower mortality and increased (especially male) adult productivity, which translate into an intergenerational flow of food and higher reproductive success. Longer lifespans magnify this return. Increases in juvenile and adult mortality depreciate the value of investments in somatic and learned capital (Robson and Kaplan 2003). The Grandmother hypothesis is based on Charnov's identification of invariant relationships among life history characteristics (Charnov 1993). It attributes a driving role to adult mortality in determining other life history characteristics, including body (and brain) size and age at maturity (see Hawkes, chapter 4, this volume, for a detailed discussion of Charnov's models).

Several investigators (for example, Walker and Leakey 1993; B. Smith 1994; Clegg and Aiello 1999—see Skinner and Wood, chapter 11, this volume, for a summary of the paleontological evidence) have argued that the central life history features of modern humans might extend back to *Homo ergaster*. Proponents of both the Grandmother (O'Connell, Hawkes, and Blurton Jones 1999) and Embodied Capital (Kaplan et al. 2000) hypotheses seem to favor this timing. When Gage (1998:218; Gage cites Bogin and Smith 1996 as supporting this contention) argues that delayed maturation evolved "rather late," he means (most likely) only after *Homo erectus*. However, as Skinner and Wood (chapter 11, this volume) point out, the situation for *H. ergaster* is far from "tidy."

What does this have to do with the Holocene? Widespread acceptance of one model over the other may hinge upon whether we can credibly estimate adult life expectancy, or some proxy for it, for Pleistocene foragers. In particular, the Grandmother hypothesis depends on the assumption of significant (from an evolutionary perspective) numbers of long-lived, postreproductive females among Pleistocene hominins. Many authors (such as Washburn 1981; Weiss 1981; Kennedy 2003) have argued that regular survival past the end of the female reproductive period was a rarity before the very recent past. Kennedy (2003:561) summarizes this perspective forcefully: "[T]hese data strongly suggest that the debate over the significance of a woman's long postreproductive life (and the GMH) is moot prior to the industrial revolution and, even then, such long survival applied only to women living in the more industrialized societies."

Echoing Weiss and others, Kennedy acknowledges that older individuals have "always" been present, but not in sufficient numbers to perform the provisioning role asserted in the Grandmother hypothesis. Based on Holocene demographic trends, this argument is critical to hypotheses of life history evolution and cannot be tested without data from historical demography and especially paleodemography.

HISTORICAL DEMOGRAPHY

Historical demography can give us some picture of trends in the survivorship of postreproductive women in several European populations at least back into the eighteenth century, offering hints back several more centuries. Nation-level demographic statistics become commonplace in the mid-nineteenth century (Human Mortality Database 2005). During the nineteenth century, European nations show consistent increases in life expectancy at birth ($\mathring{e}_0$), life expectancy at 25 years ($\mathring{e}_{25}$), and the proportion of women surviving to ages 40 and 65 (table 10.1; figure 10.1 shows life expectancy trends in more detail for Sweden). The proportion of adults (those who have already survived to 18 years) who reach these ages changes very little until the last quarter of the century (see table 10.1). Oeppen and Vaupel (2002) show that, in nations where demographic records are available, female life expectancy at birth has risen by an amazing three months per year since 1860. However, they note that before the twentieth century, this was primarily the result of increased infant and child survival.

In Europe, the eighteenth century was also characterized by increases in life expectancy, especially adult life expectancy. Johansen and Oeppen (2001) report that Denmark and Sweden experienced a long upward trend in life expectancy at birth, after a nadir around 1710. Life expectancy for young adults ($\mathring{e}_{25}$) has been generally increasing since the mid-seventeenth century in England and Wales (Wrigley et al. 1997:281). However, life expectancy at birth, which will increase

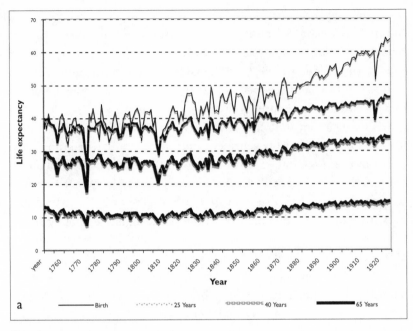

FIGURE 10.1

*Changing life expectancy, by age, for Swedish women in 1751–1925, based on period life
tables (data drawn from the Human Mortality Database 2005). A single-year-period life
table represents all deaths during the given year, as distinguished from a cohort life table,
which is based on the births of a single cohort. Figure 10.1a represents the raw data. In*

so dramatically in later centuries, shows no clear change before 1750 in
England and Wales (table 10.2) or among eighteenth-century French
women (table 10.3; Blayo 1970).

In England and Wales, life expectancy at birth ($\mathring{e}_0$) generally
declines in the seventeenth century, though the trend is jagged
(Wrigley and Schofield 1989; see table 10.2). At the same time, British
peerage records indicate that life expectancy among postreproductive
females ($\mathring{e}_{50}$) increased consistently from the mid-sixteenth century
through the mid-eighteenth century (table 10.4). The disparity probably reflects the impact of several episodes of crisis/epidemic mortality,
which differentially affected adults and children who had not been
previously exposed to these diseases. A shortening of intervals between
epidemic events transformed rapidly spreading infectious diseases into
diseases of childhood (McNeil 1977). Adult risk declined because of

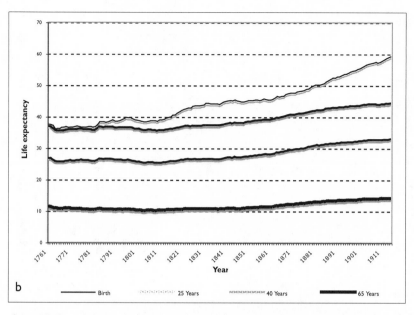

b ———— Birth ⋯⋯⋯⋯ 25 Years ▩▩▩▩▩ 40 Years ▬▬▬ 65 Years

figure 10.1b, we have smoothed the data by taking a twenty-year running average. Note the dampening of yearly variation in life expectancy at greater ages, the result of acquired immunities among older individuals. This is particularly clear for the 1918 flu epidemic (the final downward spike in life expectancy visible in figure 10.1a). There, life expectancy at birth drops nearly ten years (from 60.1 years in 1917 to 51.46 years in 1918), whereas life expectancy at 65 is virtually unchanged (13.85 years in 1917 and 13.66 years in 1918).

selective mortality (Vaupel, Manton, and Stallard 1979) and immunities acquired through surviving the same diseases in childhood.

Attempts to extend historical demography back past the seventeenth century tend to be limited to specialized populations. These include monks (Harvey 1993), British peers (Hollingsworth 1977), medieval vassals and tenants (Russell 1948), and the children of kings (Russell 1948). Hollingsworth's (1977) study of the British peerage (see table 10.4) suggests that life expectancy at birth changed very little before 1700. Like the general population, the British peerage shows declines in overall life expectancy through much of the seventeenth century (Hollingsworth 1977), probably related to increased child mortality. However, peer life expectancy at 50 ($\mathring{e}_{50}$) shows consistent increases from the latter sixteenth century onward, as does the proportion of 25 year olds who survived to reach 55 years ($_{30}P_{25}$). The

TABLE 10.1
Female Life Expectancy and Survivorship Figures for Selected European Countries in the Nineteenth and Early Twentieth Centuries

Country	Date	$\overset{\circ}{e}_0$	$\overset{\circ}{e}_{25}$	$\overset{\circ}{e}_{40}$	$_{40}P_0$	$_{65}P_0$	Adult Survival to 40 Years $_{22}P_{18}$	Adult Survival to 65 Years $_{47}P_{18}$
Denmark	1835	40.28	37.98	27.97	0.523	0.316	0.814	0.492
	1850	45.19	39.44	28.85	0.593	0.382	0.836	0.539
	1875	45.48	38.76	28.57	0.595	0.384	0.823	0.532
	1900	53.59	42.11	30.44	0.712	0.499	0.881	0.618
	1925	62.70	45.37	32.56	0.833	0.626	0.926	0.696
England and Wales	1841	42.33	37.49	27.76	0.549	0.336	0.799	0.490
	1850	43.63	37.97	28.10	0.568	0.352	0.808	0.502
	1875	43.13	36.72	26.43	0.579	0.331	0.799	0.456
	1900	48.15	39.25	27.48	0.664	0.398	0.881	0.528
	1925	60.85	44.95	27.86	0.812	0.601	0.926	0.685
Sweden	1751	39.94	36.89	26.98	0.527	0.310	0.813	0.478
	1775	39.29	36.60	26.59	0.520	0.298	0.812	0.466
	1800	33.22	34.71	24.26	0.451	0.230	0.812	0.415
	1825	47.64	39.99	28.80	0.637	0.406	0.860	0.548
	1850	47.32	39.13	28.13	0.634	0.400	0.853	0.538
	1875	46.49	39.81	29.06	0.613	0.402	0.847	0.555
	1900	53.65	42.90	31.61	0.695	0.506	0.867	0.631
	1925	63.73	46.05	33.66	0.828	0.639	0.910	0.702
France	1899	47.00	39.86	29.03	0.622	0.411	0.845	0.558
	1925	56.72	42.62	30.77	0.754	0.533	0.883	0.624

Data are drawn from period life tables in which the date indicated is the year of death (data drawn from the Human Mortality Database 2005). Percent adult survival to 40 or 65 years is the percentage of 18 year olds who survive to 40 or 65 years.

TABLE 10.2

The Cambridge Group Reconstruction of Life Expectancy at Birth ($\overset{\circ}{e}_0$), England and Wales, 1541 to 1841

Sexes Combined

Year	$\overset{\circ}{e}_0$	Year	$\overset{\circ}{e}_0$
1541	33.8	1701	37.1
1561	27.8	1721	32.5
1581	41.7	1741	31.7
1601	38.1	1761	34.2
1621	40.0	1781	34.7
1641	33.7	1801	35.9
1661	35.7	1821	39.2
1681	28.5	1841	40.3

After Wrigley and Schofield (1989). Data for five-year intervals, centered on the years indicated, are based on back-projection estimates. Note the instability of life expectancy before 1741, here and in table 10.3; then contrast it to life expectancy at age 50 years in table 10.3. For a discussion of back-projection estimates, see Wrigley and Schofield, chapter 7.

TABLE 10.3

Female Life Expectancy at Birth and at Age 25 Years, Eighteenth-Century France

Period	$\overset{\circ}{e}_0$	$\overset{\circ}{e}_{25}$
1740–1749	25.7	31.2
1750–1759	28.7	34.1
1760–1769	29.0	33.6
1770–1779	29.6	34.4
1780–1789	28.1	33.3

After Dupaquier (1995).

main feature of Russell's (1948) mortuary inquisitions is the impact of the Black Death on life expectancy for all ages ($\overset{\circ}{e}_0$, $\overset{\circ}{e}_{25}$, $\overset{\circ}{e}_{45}$). Life expectancy decreases for every cohort born between 1276 and 1348, then rebounds through the mid-fifteenth century (table 10.5).

To summarize, the historical demographic record shows dramatic increases in life expectancy at birth since at least the eighteenth century, when such records became widespread. Much of this increase

TABLE 10.4

Hollingsworth's (1977) Estimates of Life Expectancy, by Age and Proportion Surviving to Given Ages, from the British Peerage Registers

Birth Cohort	$\overset{\circ}{e}_0$	$\overset{\circ}{e}_{25}$	$\overset{\circ}{e}_{40}$	$\overset{\circ}{e}_{65}$	$_{25}P_0$ (Sexes Combined)	$_{40}P_0$ (Sexes Combined)	$_{30}P_{25}$ (Sexes Combined)
1550–1574	38.19	28.15	18.75	7.50	0.688	0.549	0.417
1575–1599	38.34	27.89	18.38	9.26	0.667	0.509	0.452
1600–1624	35.89	27.04	19.09	8.64	0.625	0.456	0.433
1625–1649	34.19	26.66	19.01	10.40	0.589	0.429	0.434
1650–1674	33.69	29.99	23.02	10.97	0.547	0.394	0.480
1675–1699	35.28	29.42	22.23	10.72	0.585	0.432	0.508
1700–1724	37.53	32.29	24.51	10.82	0.599	0.462	0.551
1725–1749	37.42	34.56	26.26	11.92	0.601	0.494	0.620
1750–1774	45.85	36.82	27.34	12.30	0.704	0.590	0.653
1775–1799	49.20	38.76	29.19	12.76	0.727	0.621	0.699

Life expectancy figures are female. Proportions surviving are for sexes combined. Estimates are based on twenty-five-year birth cohorts. Gavrilova and colleagues (2004) have argued that long-lived people have a better chance of being mentioned in incomplete genealogies. This is because their longer life leads to a greater paper trail in various archives. If true, this could lead to overrepresentation of long-lived people. Gavrilova and colleagues made this argument specifically in reference to the British peerage data, but it potentially applies to all early records.

TABLE 10.5

Life Expectancy for Medieval English Men, Based on Russell's (1948) Reconstruction

25-Year Cohort	$\overset{\circ}{e}_0$	$\overset{\circ}{e}_{25}$	$\overset{\circ}{e}_{45}$
Before 1276	35.28	25.56	15.51
1276–1300	31.30	23.47	14.78
1301–1325	29.84	21.36	13.93
1323–1348	30.22	20.98	16.14
1348–1375	17.33	22.89	16.79
1376–1400	20.53	22.54	16.10
1401–1425	23.78	27.50	16.58
1426–1450	32.75	25.54	18.09

Russell used records of mortuary inquisitions originally performed for tax purposes.

resulted from improvements in child survival, which began in the mid-eighteenth century and became more pronounced in the nineteenth and early twentieth centuries. Before approximately 1750, periodic epidemic episodes caused life expectancy at birth to fluctuate, with no clear trend. However, adult life expectancy, especially beyond the female reproductive years, displays an overall upward trend from at least the time of the Black Death in the fourteenth century. The plague itself depressed life expectancy to a significant, if unknown, degree. It is currently impossible to determine whether upward trends that characterize the historical demographic record represent long-term trends or recovery from a temporary low. If these adult trends do extend back beyond the plague years into demographic prehistory, they might imply low numbers of postreproductive women in prehistory more generally. If true, this would support contentions that few postreproductive women would be found among Pleistocene foragers.

PALEODEMOGRAPHIC EVIDENCE

Paleodemography is notoriously poor at estimating life expectancy (Sattenspiel and Harpending 1983; Johannson and Horowitz 1986; Paine 1989; Wood, Milner et al. 1992) and at estimating the ages/proportions of older individuals in a sample (Walker, Johnson, and Lambert

1988). The paleodemographic record does appear, *at first glance*, to suggest that prehistoric individuals who lived past 50 years of age were relative rarities. Several highly influential studies (such as Acsadi and Nemeskeri 1970; Lovejoy et al. 1977) have highlighted low mean age at death and small numbers of older individuals in prehistoric skeletal series. These studies have been cited (for example, Weiss 1973, 1981; Kennedy 2003) as evidence of low life expectancy in prehistory. Paleodemographers, however, have been arguing as long as the field has existed whether this is an accurate depiction of past conditions (see Howell 1976b, 1982; Lovejoy et al. 1977) or an artifact of archaeological recovery and age estimation bias (see Lovejoy, Meindl, Mensforth, and Barton 1985; Walker, Johnson, and Lambert 1988; P. Walker 1995; Gage 1998). Konigsberg and Herrmann (chapter 9, this volume) address this issue in detail from a statistical and methodological perspective.

Our analysis focuses on skeletal evidence of child (here defined as from age 2 years to physical maturity, at around 18 years, encompassing Bogin's childhood and adolescence; see Bogin, chapter 7, this volume) death patterns between the Mesolithic and the early advent of historical records in the late Medieval period. We focused on childhood death for several practical reasons. Age estimates for subadults, which are based on developmental stages (such as dental development and epiphyseal union) are generally considered more accurate, as well as less affected by reference sample bias, than measures used for adults. We believe that the age categories used in our analyses (2–5 years, 5–18 years, and 18+ years) are sufficiently conservative as to minimize the problem of inter-observer differences in age estimation (see Konigsberg and Herrmann, chapter 9, this volume). Children under 2 years of age were omitted from the analysis because of preservation and recovery problems.

The Historical Perspectives on Human Demography Database

The Historical Perspectives on Human Demography Database (HPHD) was compiled from existing site reports and more widely published data. It includes 14,089 anatomically aged individuals, age 2 years and older at death, from more than seventy-five sites in central Europe, primarily Germany, Austria, and Hungary, and in the Czech

Republic and Denmark. The database is large, but because of difficulties in data control and compatibility, it serves better as a source of hypotheses than as definitive data. Skeletal age-at-death estimates in the database were produced by a large number of osteologists using a variety of techniques. Despite recent and ongoing attempts to better quantify estimation techniques (Boldsen 1988, 1997; Konigsberg and Frankenberg 1992; Skytthe and Boldsen 1993; Konigsberg, Frankenberg, and Walker 1997; Milner, Boldsen, and Usher 1997), traditional methods rely on unquantifiable and often investigator-specific weightings of categorical observations (Maples 1989). Inter-observer differences present an obvious problem in aggregated samples such as this one. The sample also includes skeletons from a wide range of preservation conditions.

Preliminary examinations of the HPHD database (Boldsen and Paine 1995, n.d.; Paine and Boldsen 1997, 2002) yielded a series of age-at-death patterns that diverge from modern or historic patterns but resemble paleodemographic patterns found elsewhere. These include a low proportion of infants, which probably results from factors of preservation and recovery; a correspondingly high proportion of young adults; apparent sex differences in adult mortality (Boldsen and Paine 1995); and two very persistent trends in childhood death, summarized below. The lattermost are the focus of this analysis.

Child Death Patterns

In contemporary human populations, child death is heavily weighted toward the very young. Studies of child death in the HPHD database show something else. Between the Mesolithic period and the Iron Age, the weight of child mortality—as measured by the death rate ratio, or **drr** (Boldsen and Paine n.d.)—shifts toward older childhood (figure 10.2).[2] After the Iron Age, the trend reverses and child death becomes concentrated in earlier ages. By the late Medieval period, the pattern more closely resembles both the Mesolithic and contemporary patterns. The **drr** is a good statistic for paleodemographic cross-period comparisons. It is limited to broad age categories and is relatively insensitive to changes in population growth (Boldsen and Paine n.d.).

The consistency of the pattern, before and after the reversal point sometime during the European Iron Age, led us to believe that the

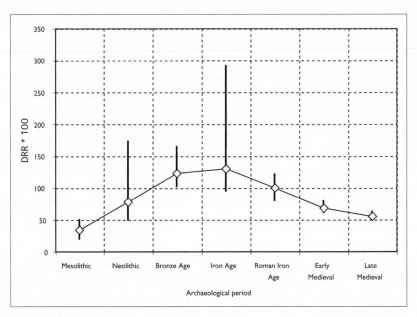

FIGURE 10.2

*The death rate ratio (**drr**)[1] tracks the ratio of late childhood (5–18 years) to early childhood (2–5 years) death, by archaeological period. A higher **drr** indicates relatively higher death rates among older children. The error bars represent bootstrapped 95 percent confidence intervals.*

pattern implied more than changing archaeological recovery conditions or biases in skeletal aging techniques. We sought an explanation that would be biologically meaningful, would fit with archaeologically and historically derived records of population change, and would be testable (Paine and Boldsen 2002). Relationships between the growth of large settled populations and increases in disease have long been a focus of paleodemographic interest (see M. Cohen 1977; Cohen and Armelagos 1984; Wood, Milner et al. 1992). We decided to test the hypothesis that increases in frequency of epidemic events, as the European population grew and became increasingly connected to the larger Old World population system, could have caused the two trends in child death. We drew heavily on McNeil's (1977) studies of the relationships among population growth, movement, and the frequency of epidemic events in the historical record.

The hypothesis made biological sense. The micro-organisms that cause epidemic diseases (for example, measles) require a constant supply of new hosts to survive (F. Black 1975; Top and Wehrle 1976). Both population size and density increased in Europe during the time period covered by the HPHD. Although this growth of the European population was not necessarily even over time or space, the overall pattern is clear (McKeown 1976). Connections between the northern and central European populations represented by the HPHD and the larger Old World population system, particularly Asia and the Mediterranean, also increased. Specific historical instances, including the intrusions of such groups as the Romans and the Avars, dramatically illustrate this process, which culminated in the highly integrated trade economy of the later Middle Ages.

Computer models offer paleodemographers an excellent tool for testing hypotheses. Computer models enable us to link demographic processes in living populations to the skeletal record (see Keckler 1997; Paine 1997, 2000; Paine and Boldsen 2002). The purpose of the analysis presented here was to test whether increasing the frequency of epidemic events and obeying some very basic assumptions could have created the general pattern of child death we observed in the HPHD.

Through a series of Leslie matrix projections, we (Paine 2000; Paine and Boldsen 2002) simulated the effects of epidemic events occurring at decreased intervals. Contemporary demographers use Leslie matrices (Leslie 1945; Caswell 1989) to project population size and age structure forward in time. Data produced by a Leslie matrix projection can be used to compute vital rates, as well as full life tables, for projected populations at any stage of the projection. This is particularly interesting when, as part of the projection, a model population is perturbed and becomes unstable. The short- and long-term effects of the perturbation can then be tracked through the projection (for a paleodemographic example, see Paine 2000).

We used the Brass (1971) LOGIT life table models to define the parameters of the basic population matrix. The Brass standard model fertility schedule was set to yield a total fertility rate (TFR) of 6.1, corresponding to the average TFR for natural fertility populations surveyed by Campbell and Wood (1988). Survivorship probabilities were generated from a Brass standard model (α = .65, and β = .95). This yields mortality characteristics close to anthropologists' stereotypes of

TABLE 10.6
Demographic Characteristics of the Model Stable Population Used in the Six Projections

α	β	$\mathring{e}_0$	TFR	CBR	CDR	r
.65	.95	22.05	6.1	45.23	44.49	.00074

The first two columns are parameter values for the Brass (1971) relational model life tables. The other demographic values—life expectancy at birth ($\mathring{e}_0$), the total fertility rate (TFR), the crude birth rate (CBR), the crude death rate (CDR), and the intrinsic rate of growth (r)—were derived from the model life table generated after projecting the model population one hundred years to achieve a stable age distribution.

preindustrial agrarian populations (table 10.6; Paine 2000). We projected the Leslie matrix described above for one hundred cycles (equivalent to one hundred years) to generate an initial population vector for subsequent projections. This population vector was stable but growing slowly (crude rates in table 10.6 are those of the stable population), as usually assumed for early Holocene populations.

Acquired disease resistance is a central assumption of our hypothesis. Exposure to an acute, epidemic disease typically results in one of two outcomes: either the host dies, or the host successfully defends itself against the disease and develops long-term resistance (Top and Wehrle 1976). It is also reasonable to assume that individuals who survive repeated insults are less frail than those who succumb to them (Vaupel, Manton, and Stallard 1979; Wood, Milner et al. 1992). We kept the rules for the projections simple. The first time a cohort is subjected to an epidemic year, each member's probability of surviving that year (P) is reduced by 30 percent; for example, in the twelve-year interval projection, the P of 9 year olds decreases from .993 to .693. During sub-sequent epidemic years, survivors of those cohorts that have been subjected to a single epidemic year have their probability of survival reduced by 10 percent, so in the six-year interval, the P of 9 year olds decreases from .993 to .893. If a cohort is subjected to more than two epidemic years, the probability of survival is not affected after the second.

In each projection, plague years (represented by their own matrices) are interspersed at regular intervals from three years to ninety-six years. Nonepidemic years are represented by the original matrix, which was used to create the initial stable population. Each projection is ter-

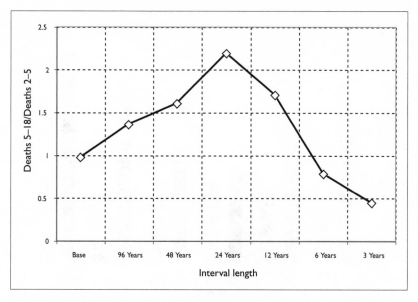

FIGURE 10.3

The ratio of older child deaths (5–18 years) to younger child deaths (2–5 years) for seven population projections. Deaths are cumulative over the course of seventy-five-year projections. The x axis indicates the interval length between epidemic years in each projection.

minated after ninety-five cycles (ninety-five model years). Arbitrarily, the first epidemic year is always year two of the projection. Epidemic cycles then repeat according to the interval being simulated. New population structures, which reflect the impact of the "epidemic," are no longer stable; even a single perturbation reverberates through the age structure for nearly one hundred years (Paine 2000). Each new population vector was recorded in a spreadsheet in which crude birth rates, death rates, and population growth, as well as the age structure of death, were tracked.

Results

The projections clearly show that decreasing the interval between epidemic years mimics the changes in child age at death seen in the HPHD (figure 10.3). The projections capture the shift toward later childhood death and the subsequent recompression of death into early childhood. As long as the interval between epidemic years is longer than eighteen years, shortening it increases the proportion of older

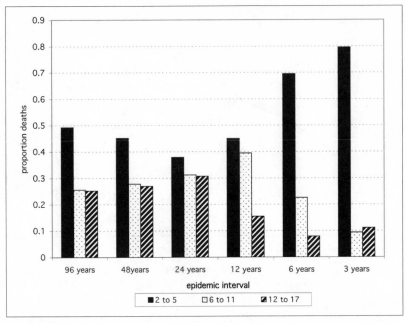

FIGURE 10.4

The proportion of child deaths, by age interval, in six population projections. The figures are based on cumulative deaths at the end of each projection. Note that these distributions do not reflect stable populations. They reflect both the crisis mortality years and unstable population structures during most noncrisis years.

child death by increasing the number of intervals in which subadult (for present purposes, age 2–18 years) mortality is dominated by age-independent death (figure 10.4). When the interval is shortened below 18 years, childhood mortality is slowly compressed until a pattern reminiscent of modern child mortality is reached. The fact that the epidemic cycle projections capture Holocene trends in child death (from the HPHD) so well lends strong support to the contention that accelerating epidemic cycles characterized the period (McNeil 1977). The historical demographic record (see Wrigley et al. 1997) also demonstrates that intermittent years of crisis mortality were a feature of life through the eighteenth century.

Extending Model Results

Among the issues paleodemographers have to deal with is apparent bias in skeletal recovery and in aging methods. We tend to be very unsure of our ability to represent the very young (birth to 2 years) and postreproductive (older than 45 years or so) adults (for an illustrative case, see Walker, Johnson, and Lambert 1988). The infant problem is most likely related to archaeological recovery. Infant bones are small and light, leading to poor preservation and under-recovery. Current aging methods usually underestimate the age of individuals more than 40 years old at death (Lovejoy, Meindl, Mensforth, and Barton 1985; Meindl et al. 1985). Walker and colleagues (Walker, Johnson, and Lambert 1988; P. Walker 1995) have also demonstrated under-representation of older individuals in cemeteries with known age distributions. The following example uses survival and death rates generated from the death distributions of the Leslie matrix projections, instead of the HPHD data, to look at some of the wider implications of epidemic frequency for life history.

Changes in Life Expectancy over Time.

The model results also capture patterns observed in the historical demographic record. Overall life expectancy (life expectancy at birth) decreases throughout most of the simulation. However, different levels of epidemic frequency have different life expectancy implications for different ages. As the interval between epidemics is decreased, the first age groups to recover are the oldest ones, because they have already survived insults and are no longer affected by subsequent epidemics. A pattern emerges in which increases in age-specific life expectancy reach younger and younger age groups as epidemic cycles become shorter. The projections capture, and provide some explanation of, a seemingly paradoxical observation from historical demography: in the sixteenth-to-eighteenth century, adult life expectancy increased as life expectancy at birth declined (table 10.7). In the projections, life expectancy at birth improves only after infant and child survival increases at the very end of the simulation, when epidemic intervals become very short. As Oeppen and Vaupel (2002) demonstrate, improvements in infant and child survival also drive the substantial increases in female life expectancy at birth in the nineteenth century. Infant and juvenile mortality has a large effect on life expectancy at birth across populations, for two reasons. It has a disproportionate mathematical

TABLE 10.7

The Life Expectancy and Proportion Surviving, by Age, for Model Populations in the Epidemic Frequency Projections

Epidemic Interval	$\mathring{e}_0$	$\mathring{e}_{15}$	$\mathring{e}_{25}$	$\mathring{e}_{45}$	$_{18}P_0$	Adult Survival to 40 Years $_{22}P_{18}$	Adult Survival to 65 Years $_{47}P_{18}$
96 years	22.7	34.5	30.0	20.6	0.413	0.644	0.280
48 years	22.4	33.9	31.2	20.7	0.401	0.642	0.298
24 years	24.8	33.0	30.4	20.4	0.452	0.627	0.281
12 years	23.8	38.5	34.2	22.0	0.394	0.726	0.364
6 years	22.9	40.1	33.7	21.6	0.379	0.749	0.365
3 years	22.4	40.1	33.7	21.7	0.376	0.750	0.368

Readers should note several aspects of these figures. First, the life tables used to estimate life expectancy are based on d_x values, not living population structure. This makes them comparable to both the period life-table figures above and paleodemographic life tables. Second, they do not represent stable populations. Life expectancy estimates are affected by the unstable age-at-death distribution of the projected population. Third, the age-at-death distributions used to generate the statistics are one-hundred-year cumulative death distributions for the projections. Each represents periods of crisis mortality and normal attritional mortality.

impact on life expectancy statistics, and infant and child deaths represent a large percentage of overall deaths (upwards of 30 percent in most nonindustrialized populations) across populations.

It is critical to remember that these changes in apparent life expectancy, as well as the patterns of change in life expectancy for different ages, all occur without any change to the underlying (stable) characteristics of the model population. All the changes are brought about by extrinsic mortality. They imply no change in the basic organism but suggest that changes in life expectancy observed in the seventeenth-to-nineteenth-century historical demographic record represent a recovery from a short-term perturbation instead of a long-term trend.

DISCUSSION

Life history investigators tend to view, explicitly or implicitly, the life history of anatomically modern *Homo sapiens* as more or less constant and primarily the product of our foraging past. This is what Nancy Howell (1976b, 1982) referred to as the "uniformitarian view." Paleo-demographers (such as Lovejoy et al. 1977; Paine 1997; Gage 1998; see Konigsberg and Herrmann, chapter 9, this volume, for further discussion) have been much more divided on this issue. Gage (1998:198–199) argued that the uniformitarian assumption would be reasonable only if "all human groups shared the same genes and environments....While there is currently little evidence that human groups differ with respect to genetics influencing demographic characteristics, it is clear that all human populations do not share similar environments."

Therefore, Gage argues, the uniformitarian view is "overly simplistic" and "clearly incorrect" at some level of specificity. Gage is correct, *at some level of specificity*. For example, one reason the Brass (1971) LOGIT models used in this analysis were developed is that child mortality in developing African nations took a different shape than child mortality in the Coale and Demeny (1966, 1983) "West" models, because of the differences in the risk of death from infectious disease. Unfortunately, these differences would be difficult, or impossible, to identify in a paleodemographic sample, given the imprecision of age estimates (even for young children) and problems of preservation.

The central question, beyond what causes paleodemographic samples to differ from modern populations, is whether the "level of specificity"—where ancient populations may differ from uniformitarian patterns in contemporary ones—is relevant from an evolutionary perspective. From a broad perspective (such as comparing human life history characteristics with overall primate life history), the uniformitarian view is certainly reasonable. On the more detailed level, using modern or historical patterns to evaluate life history predictions, for example, it is less certain whether there were sufficient numbers of postreproductive women in Pleistocene populations to be selectively relevant.

Our view is that observed differences between modern patterns and those observed in archaeological skeletal series are points of departure. We should not assume that they represent real biological differences among past populations or that they are purely artifacts of paleodemographic bias. We repeat our own call (Paine 1997) for explicit, testable models to identify how cultural and biological processes manifest themselves in the paleodemographic record and whether reasonable processes in living systems could produce the patterns we observe. We need to base our models in known human biology, meaning that they should account for observed uniformitarian patterns of human biology and demography. The study discussed here is an example of this approach.

The historical demographic record displays a consistent trend toward increased life expectancy among adults from the eighteenth century onward. Fragmentary records, such as the British peerage registers, suggest that this trend could be pushed back into the sixteenth century or earlier. On the surface, this could be seen as evidence for the conclusion (Washburn 1981; Weiss 1981; Kennedy 2003, among others) that few ancient humans lived far beyond their 45th birthday. Paleodemographers have often reached a similar, but far from reliable, conclusion. This conclusion would be damaging to either the Embodied Capital or the Grandmother hypothesis. It would be fatal to the latter. The paleodemographic record from Holocene Europe offers both an alternative trajectory and a possible explanation for the rapid increase in adult life expectancy observed in the historical record.

The model presented here, based on long-term trends in child death patterns between the Mesolithic and the early Medieval period, suggests that the frequency of epidemic waves increased over that time span. If true, this would have led to marked increases in extrinsic mortality. Child death patterns also support McNeil's (1977:116) contention that these pressures would have been short-lived: "As encounters with such epidemics increased, however, death tolls decreased.... An infectious disease, which immunizes those who survive, and which returns at intervals of five to ten years, automatically becomes a childhood disease.... This process of epidemiological adjustment was energetically underway in Europe as a whole during the so-called Dark Ages. As a result, the crippling demographic consequences of exposure to unfamiliar diseases disappeared within a few centuries."

While supporting the overall conclusion, our data would suggest that this process was drawn out over several millennia, instead of centuries. The trend we observe in the **drr** is fully consistent with this conclusion, as our projections demonstrate. Based on this reconstruction, we would expect to find that adult life expectancy began to rebound from a temporary nadir reached sometime around the European Iron Age. This increase would be expected to have continued across the boundary from demographic prehistory to demographic history. The model predicts that adult life expectancy increases would precede increases in life expectancy at birth, a pattern borne out by the historical demographic record.

For studies of human life history evolution, the most important implication of this study is that the upward trends in life expectancy characterizing the historical record may not represent a long-term trend. Instead, they may be a recovery from a short-term (from an evolutionary perspective) perturbation. This perturbation, the effect of epidemic disease associated with greater sedentism and population growth, brought new selective pressures. It raised the level of extrinsic mortality and lowered life expectancy. This has important implications for theories of life history evolution that focus on the Pleistocene—especially the Grandmother hypothesis, because it suggests, however tentatively, that historical demographic records are not a good indicator of Pleistocene mortality levels.

Paleodemography is currently in the throes of a long, often demoralizing, period of self-critique (Bocquet-Appel and Masset 1982, 1996; Wood, Milner et al. 1992; Konigsberg and Frankenberg 1994). We believe that this study demonstrates how paleodemography, despite its clear deficiencies, can contribute to the reconstruction of Holocene selective pressures, at least on a general level, and to the dialogue on life history evolution. By judiciously combining Holocene paleodemographic data with basic predictions from life history theory, we should be able to recognize, if not estimate, changes in selective pressure associated with extrinsic mortality over time.

Acknowledgments

We would like to thank the Danish Center for Demographic Research, the A. P. Sloan Foundation, the Carlsberg Foundation, and the University Research Committee of the University of Utah for financial support. For facilities and logistical support, we thank the Danish Center for Demographic Research and the Max Planck Institute for Demographic Research. We also thank Jennifer Graves for her terrific work in helping to prepare the manuscript.

Notes

1. Several chapters of this volume delve more into the relationship between learning and extended dependency. Bogin (chapter 7) discusses childhood patterns. Blurton Jones (chapter 8) examines the learning time and skills needed for Hadza foraging. Van Schaik and colleagues (chapter 5) provide a comparative perspective on skill acquisition, based on studies of orangutans.

2. The death rate ratio, $\mathbf{drr} = d_{5-18}/d_{2-5}$, where $\mathbf{d_{2-5}}$ is the mean death rate of ages 2–5 years. $d_{2-5} = 1 - (S_5/S_2)^{1/3}$, and $\mathbf{d_{5-18}}$ is the mean death rate from ages 5–18 years. $d_{5-18} = 1 - (S_{18}/S_5)^{1/13}$.

11

The Evolution of Modern Human Life History

A Paleontological Perspective

Matthew M. Skinner and Bernard Wood

SUMMARY

This contribution addresses the evolution of modern human life history from a paleontological perspective. First, we present two taxonomic hypotheses summarizing the hominin fossil record and then discuss the reliability of collecting data on life history variables for fossil taxa. We then examine age at weaning, body mass, brain size, and the growth, timing, and pattern of tooth formation, presenting a comparative analysis of these variables among hominin taxa. In many respects, the earliest hominin taxa demonstrate life history patterns that resemble those of extant apes, but some taxa (particularly the megadont australopiths) likely possessed unique life history patterns that were neither apelike nor modern humanlike, nor directly transitional between the two. Based on the few life history variables for which data are available from the hominin fossil record, a modern human pattern of life history does not appear to have been present in any hominin taxon before the appearance of our own species.

We can define and distinguish living taxa by using one or more of five categories of evidence: genotype, ontogeny, adult phenotype, behavior, and life history (the last is the focus of this volume). With the possible exception of the genotype, these categories are neither discrete nor independent (Müller and Newman 2003) but provide a heuristically useful way of subdividing an integrated whole. The order of the first three categories reflects the way we perceive them to operate. The genotype is the blueprint for an organism's ontogeny, which determines its adult phenotype and behavioral repertoire. Life history—that is, the way an organism times important events in its life cycle and, in particular, configures its reproductive effort—is almost certainly under the control, directly or indirectly, of the genotype. It is related, causally or otherwise, to an animal's ontogeny, adult phenotype, and behavior, especially its behaviors related to reproduction.

The taxon to which anatomically modern humans belong, *Homo sapiens*, can be distinguished from its close living relatives, the other great apes, in all the categories set out above (for example, Shoshani et al. 1996; Whiten et al. 1999; Bogin and Smith 2000; Gagneux and Varki 2001; Gibbs, Collard, and Wood 2002). With respect to life history, modern humans develop more slowly than the other great apes and, as a result, are the only living higher primate to have childhood and adolescent growth phases (Bogin 2003; but see Leigh 2001 for a contrasting view of human childhood/adolescent growth uniqueness). Compared with the other great apes, modern humans have a higher survival rate, live longer lives, start their reproductive effort later, and have shorter interbirth intervals so that parental investment per individual is high (reviewed in Leigh 2001; Robson, van Schaik, and Hawkes, chapter 2, this volume). But what factors have determined the distinctive life history of modern humans? What is its comparative context, and to what extent can we reconstruct its recent and deeper evolutionary history?

Researchers address these questions in several ways. In the first, they document details of the life history of contemporary or subrecent populations of modern humans. In many modern societies, life history has been significantly affected by advances in technology and concomitant changes in modern human behavior (such as diet and barrier and pharmaceutical means of birth control). Researchers need to know what modern human life history was like *before* these factors took effect. To do this, they can observe the life history and ecology of peoples whose lifestyles are judged to be aboriginal or close to aboriginal, and they can examine the historical records and skeletal remains of subrecent, anatomically modern humans.

The second research strategy is to study the life history and ecology of living primates closely related to modern humans. These comparative life history data enable researchers to generate hypotheses about the derived features of modern human life history. Information about the comparative ecology of the closely related higher primates also helps to inform hypotheses about the adaptive nature of higher primate life history. Data about the life history related variables (such as dental development) of living higher primates can be obtained from live animals or from museum collections of higher primate skeletons. By meticulous observation of living higher primates in the field and in captivity, researchers have discovered direct evidence about life history (see Kappeler and Pereira 2003; van Schaik et al., chapter 5, this volume).

This contribution concerns a third approach: the use of fossil evidence to investigate the evolutionary context of modern human life history. To do this, researchers must learn what they can about the life history of extinct hominin taxa (that is, fossil taxa more closely related to modern humans than to any other living taxon). Even though they are restricted to making inferences from the fossilized remains of hard tissues, even indirect information about the life history of fossil hominins is useful. A taxon that is directly ancestral to modern humans (but see below for the reasons, in most cases, this hypothesis is difficult to test and verify) can shed light on an earlier stage in the evolution of modern human life history. A taxon that belongs to an extinct hominin subclade might help throw light on the factors that determine and constrain how life history is configured more widely within the hominin clade.

Molecular biology has revolutionized our knowledge of the relationships within the great ape branch, or clade, of the Tree of Life. For information about relatedness, we can now pursue relationships among organisms at the level of the genome (that is, DNA) rather than rely on morphology (traditional hard- and/or soft-tissue anatomy or the morphology of proteins). Comparisons among the DNA of organisms have involved two methods. In DNA hybridization, the

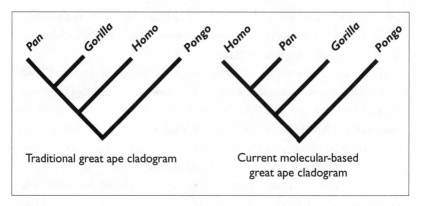

FIGURE 11.1

Traditional and current great ape cladistic relationships.

entire DNA is compared, but at a relatively crude level. In DNA sequencing, the base sequences of similar sections of DNA are determined and then compared. The results of hybridization (for example, Caccone and Powell 1989) and sequencing studies of both nuclear DNA and mtDNA (for example, Bailey et al. 1992; Horai et al. 1992; see reviews by Gagneux and Varki 2001; Wildman, Grossman, and Goodman 2002; Wildman et al. 2003) suggest that modern humans and modern chimpanzees are more closely related to each other than either is to the gorilla or to the orang (figure 11.1). Most attempts to calibrate the date of the *Pan/Homo* dichotomy (such as Shi et al. 2003) suggest that the hypothetical ancestor of modern humans and chimpanzees lived between about five and eight million years ago (Ma), but some researchers favor a substantially earlier date, 10–14 Ma (Arnason and Janke 2002).

If we make the untested assumption that the common ancestor of the *Pan/Homo* clade had a life history more like that of modern chimpanzees than of modern humans, we must then look at the fossil evidence of creatures more closely related to modern humans than to *Pan* (that is, the hominin part of the clade) in order to investigate the recent evolution of modern human life history. This chapter addresses three questions: First, did the unique features of modern human life history appear suddenly as one integrated package or evolve independently and incrementally? Second, did the onset of modern human life history coincide with the appearance of larger-bodied hominins with a modern human's skeletal proportions, or did it appear later in human evolution? Third, are modern human and modern chimp life histories the only ways that life history has been configured within the *Pan/Homo* clade, or does the fossil hominin record contain evidence of creatures that developed a different life history pattern?

The first section of this chapter explains how paleoanthropologists organize the hominin fossil record into taxa. To examine the influence of differing taxonomic hypotheses on an analysis of hominin life history patterns, we provide a speciose (splitting) taxonomy and a less speciose (lumping) taxonomy (table 11.1). The characteristics of each taxon, along with some indication of the quality and quantity of evidence available for that taxon under a splitting and then a lumping taxonomy, are summarized in appendixes I and II, respectively.

The second section of this chapter explains how we can infer life history from fossil evidence. First, we outline the difficulty involved in collecting standard life history data for fossil taxa. Second, we consider variables that influence life history, such as body mass and brain size, or can serve as proxies for life history, such as dental development. When the data are available, supporting tables provide the parameters of life history related variables for each of the fossil hominin taxa summarized in appendixes I and II. We then review the implications of these data when hominin taxa are organized according to their presumed phylogenetic relationships, and we summarize what can be deduced about the evolution of the major elements of life history within the hominin clade. This includes an assessment of when and in which taxa the distinctive aspects of modern human life history make their appearance. Finally, we consider the implications of these data for hypotheses about the first appearance of a modern humanlike life history.

ORGANIZING THE HOMININ FOSSIL RECORD

The classification of the hominin fossil evidence is controversial. However, a sound taxonomy is a prerequisite for any paleontological investigation, including one that addresses the evolution of modern human life history, for the allocation of individual fossils to each hominin taxon determines the inferences drawn about the life history

TABLE 11.1

*(A) Splitting and (B) Lumping Hominin Taxonomies and Skeletal Representation[1]
within a Splitting Hominin Taxa*

Informal Group	(A) Splitting Taxonomy	Age (Ma)
Basal australopiths	S. tchadensis	7.0–6.0
	O. tugenensis	6.0
	Ar. ramidus s.s.[2]	5.7–4.5
Australopiths	Au. anamensis	4.2–3.9
	Au. afarensis s. s.	4.0–3.0
	K. platyops	3.5–3.3
	Au. bahrelghazali	3.5–3.0
	Au. africanus	3.0–2.4
Megadont australopiths	Au. garhi	2.5
	P. aethiopicus	2.5–2.3
	P. boisei s. s.	2.3–1.3
	P. robustus	2.0–1.5
Primitive *Homo*	H. habilis s. s.	2.4–1.6
	H. rudolfensis	2.4–1.6
Archaic *Homo*	H. ergaster	1.9–1.5
	H. erectus s. s.	1.8–0.2
	H. floresiensis[3]	0.074–0.012
Homo of modern aspect	H. antecessor	0.7–0.5
	H. heidelbergensis	0.6–0.1
	H. neanderthalensis	0.2–0.03
	H. sapiens s. s.	0.19–present

Informal Group	(B) Lumping Taxonomy	Age (Ma)
Basal australopiths	Ar. ramidus s. l.	7.0–4.5
Australopiths	Au. afarensis s. l.	4.2–3.0
	Au. africanus	3.0–2.4
Megadont australopiths	P. boisei s. l.	2.5–1.3
	P. robustus	2.0–1.5
Primitive *Homo*	H. habilis s. l.	2.4–1.6
Archaic *Homo*	H. erectus s. l.	1.9–0.018
Homo of modern aspect	H. sapiens s. l.	0.7–present

1. Skeletal representation key: X, present; ff, fragmentary specimens; ?, taxonomic affiliation of fossil specimen(s) uncertain.

2. Recently, some specimens included in *Ar. ramidus s. s.* have been raised to a separate species, *Ar. kadabba* (Haile-Selassie, Suwa, and White 2004); however, this taxonomic distinction has not been incorporated into our analyses.

3. Given the recent and limited publication of this taxon and its current interpretation as an isolated endemic dwarf descendent of *H. erectus s. s.*, *H. floresiensis* is not included in our comparisons or analyses of life history patterns in fossil hominins.

Type Specimen	Crania	Dentition	Axial	Upper Limb	Lower Limb
TM 266-01-060-1	X	X			
BAR 1000'00		X		X	X
ARA-VP-6/1	X	X		X	ff
KNM-KP 29281	ff	X		X	X
LH 4	X	X	X	X	X
KNM-WT 40000	X	X			
KT 12/H1		X			
Taung 1	X	X	ff	X	X
BOU-VP-12/130	X	X		?	?
Omo 18.18	X	X			
OH 5	X	X		?	?
TM 1517	X	X		X	X
OH 7	X	X	X	X	X
KNM-ER 1470	X	X			?
KNM-ER 992	X	X	X	X	X
Trinil 2	X	X		X	X
LB1	X	X	ff	X	X
ATD6-5	X	X			
Mauer 1	X	X		ff	X
Neanderthal 1	X	X	X	X	X
None designated	X	X	X	X	X

Taxa Included from Splitting Taxonomy

Ar. ramidus s. s., S. tchadensis, O. tugenensis
Au. afarensis s. s., Au. anamensis, Au. bahrelghazali, K. platyops
Au. africanus
P. boisei s. s., P. aethiopicus, Au. garhi
P. robustus
H. habilis s. s., H. rudolfensis
H. erectus s. s., H. ergaster, H. floresiensis
H. sapiens s. s., H. antecessor, H. heidelbergensis, H. neanderthalensis

of that taxon. The debate about how to define living species is a lively one, so it should be no surprise that there is a spectrum of opinion about how the species category should be applied to fossil evidence. We are attracted by Eldredge's (1993) suggestion that all species should be regarded as "individuals" with their own "history." Therefore, each species has a "beginning" (the result of a speciation event), a "middle" (the duration of the species' existence), and an "end" (either extinction or participation in another speciation event).

We observe living species during what is just a "snapshot" in their history. In the hominin fossil record, the same species may be sampled several times during its history. Paleoanthropologists must decide whether they are looking at several samples of the same taxon or of different taxa. When making these judgments, they should strive not to underestimate or overestimate the actual number of species represented in the hominin fossil record.

One of the many factors paleoanthropologists must take into account is that the fossil record with which they work is confined to remains of the hard tissues (bones and teeth). From living animals, we know that many uncontested species (for example, *Cercopithecus* species) are difficult to distinguish by using bones and teeth. There are sound, logical reasons to suspect that a hard tissue–bound fossil record is always likely to underestimate the number of species, recently referred to as "Tattersall's Rule" (Antón 2003). When researchers stress discontinuities (as in so-called "taxic" interpretations) and adopt a punctuated equilibrium model of evolution, along with a branching (cladogenetic) interpretation of the fossil record, they tend to split the hominin fossil record into a larger rather than smaller number of species. This should be the preferred approach for life history studies; the results are less prone to producing "chimeric" life histories (Smith, Crummet, and Brandt 1994).

Conversely, other researchers emphasize morphological continuity instead of discontinuity, seeing species as longer-lived and more prone to substantial changes in morphology through time. Combining this philosophy with a more gradualistic (anagenetic) interpretation of evolution, these researchers tend to resolve the hominin fossil record into fewer, more inclusive species. This is also the case when researchers think in terms of allotaxa (for example, C. Jolly 2001; Antón 2003) and allow

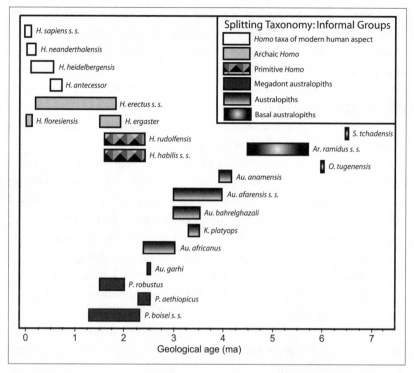

FIGURE 11.2

The more speciose (splitting) taxonomy favored by the authors. Informal groupings are based on brain size, body mass, postcanine tooth-size estimates, and locomotor mode. No ancestor-descendant relationships are implied between taxa.

a single species to manifest substantial regional and temporal variation.

For these reasons, the taxonomic hypothesis we favor is a relatively speciose taxonomy (referred to here as the "splitting" taxonomy; see table 11.1(A), figure 11.2, and appendix I), but we also provide an example of a less speciose taxonomy (the "lumping" taxonomy; see table 11.1(B) and appendix II). While some researchers might contest the specific details of each, we consider that these two taxonomies are a pragmatic way to present the hominin fossil record to the reader and to address the influence of taxonomic hypotheses on how we interpret the evolution of modern human life history. We have deliberately not sorted morphological features discussed in appendixes I and II into "primitive" (plesiomorphic), "derived" (synapomorphic), and "unique" (autapomorphic) because this suggests that hominin cladograms are more reliable than we believe them to be. Further details about most of the taxa and a more extensive bibliography can be found in Wood and Richmond (2000); this chapter cites only selected recent references. The reader can find recent relevant reviews of many taxa in Hartwig (2002) and Wood and Constantino (2004).

Two "technical" taxonomic conventions require explanation. First, when a taxon has been moved from its initial genus, the original reference appears in parentheses, followed by the revised reference. Second, some taxon names are used in different senses in the splitting and lumping taxonomies. When we refer in the text to the *hypodigm* (the fossil evidence referred to that taxon) of a taxon in the splitting taxonomy (appendix I), we follow the taxon name with *sensu stricto* (such as *Au. afarensis sensu stricto* or its abbreviation, *Au. afarensis s. s.*). We are using the taxon name in the strict sense. When we refer to the hypodigm that reflects a more inclusive interpretation of that taxon (that is, the hypodigm is larger; appendix II), the Linnean binomial is followed by *sensu lato* (for example, *Au. afarensis sensu lato* or *Au. afarensis s. l.*). We are using the taxon name in a looser sense. To save endless repetition, readers should assume that when we use a species name without a postfix, we are using it in the strict sense. The postfix *s. l.* here implies a more inclusive interpretation of that taxon.

We have created six informal groupings of hominin taxa under both the lumping and splitting taxonomies as a means of summarizing, for those less familiar with the hominin fossil record, the general similarities among various taxa. Table 11.1 and figure 11.2 list these informal groupings. The first three groups include taxa in the subtribe Australopithecina; the latter three groups include taxa in the subtribe Hominina. The first group, basal australopiths, refers to Late Miocene/Early Pliocene taxa that are temporally close to the split between hominins and panins (taxa more closely related to modern chimpanzees than to modern humans). At the early stages in hominin evolution, the lack of panin synapomorphies or subtle derived differences in the size and shape of the canines, the detailed morphology of the limbs, or some unique combination of such traits likely mark out creatures more closely related to modern humans than to modern chimpanzees. The hominin status of some of these taxa is debated.

The second group, australopiths, includes Pliocene taxa from East and southern Africa that exhibit morphology consistent with facultative bipedalism, but these taxa are broadly similar to chimpanzees in brain and body size. The third group, megadont australopiths, includes Plio-Pleistocene taxa from southern and East Africa whose morphology also suggests facultative bipedalism but which are differentiated by large jaws and extremely large postcanine teeth. This group includes taxa many researchers categorize in the genus *Paranthropus*. The fourth group, primitive *Homo*, includes Late Pliocene/Early Pleistocene taxa from East and southern Africa that exhibit morphology consistent with facultative bipedalism, a slightly larger brain, and postcanine teeth that, when related to body size, are larger than those seen in archaic *Homo* (see below). We placed these taxa in their own group to recognize the ongoing debate about their inclusion in the genus *Homo* (see Wood and Collard 1999b).

The fifth group, archaic *Homo*, includes Pleistocene taxa present in Africa and Asia that possess morphology consistent with obligate bipedalism, a medium-size brain, and absolutely and relatively small postcanine teeth. We include in this group the recently reported taxon *Homo floresiensis* from the island of Flores, Indonesia (Brown et al. 2004; Morwood et al. 2004). This species appears to represent a late surviving *Homo erectus* descendant; however, given suggestions that its morphology represents a case of endemic dwarfing (unique within the hominin clade), it is not included in comparisons of life history among hominin taxa. The final group, referred to as *Homo* of modern aspect, includes taxa located throughout the globe that exhibit morphology similar, if not identical, to modern *Homo sapiens* (the only extant hominin taxon).

Readers should be aware of two caveats with respect to the splitting taxonomy illustrated in figure 11.2. First, the age of the first and last appearances of any taxon in the fossil record—called the "first appearance datum" (FAD) and "last appearance datum" (LAD), respectively—almost certainly underestimates the temporal range of each taxon. It is very unlikely that we have a complete record of hominin taxonomic diversity, particularly in the pre–4 Mya phase of hominin evolution. This is because intensive explorations of sediments of this age not only have been conducted for less than a decade but also have been restricted in

TABLE 11.2

Life History Variables and Their Present Availability for Extant and Extinct Taxa

Life History Variables (LHVs)	Category[1]	Sex	Available for Extant Taxa	Presently Available for Extinct Taxa[2]
Gestation period	A	m/f	Yes	No
Age at weaning	A	m/f	Yes	Yes?
Age at sexual maturity	A	m/f	Yes	No
Length of estrous cycle	A	f	Yes	No
Age at first reproduction	A	f	Yes	No
Interbirth interval	A	f	Yes	No
Mean lifespan	A	m/f	Yes	Yes?
Maximum lifespan	A	m/f	Yes	No
Litter size	A	f	Yes	No

Life History Related Variables (LHRVs)

Non-dental				
Body mass, adult	C	m/f	Yes	Yes
Body mass, neonatal	C	m/f	Yes	Yes???
Brain mass, adult[3]	C	m/f	Yes	Yes
Brain mass, neonatal[3]	C	m/f	Yes	Yes???
Dental				
Tooth crown and root formation times	B	m/f	Yes	Yes?
Timing of tooth formation and eruption	B/C	m/f	Yes	Yes?

1. Categories of life history variables: A, directly measurable variables that contribute to the life history pattern; B, variables that elucidate ontogeny; and C, variables that are correlated with LHVs.
2. Availability designated as Yes means that reasonable sample sizes (but not necessarily reliable estimates) are available for most taxa; Yes? means that it is possible to collect data for this variable from the fossil record but sample sizes are currently too small to be meaningful for many taxa; and Yes??? means that it is theoretically possible to get data for this variable in the fossil record but sample sizes may never be large enough to make meaningful inferences.
3. Estimated from endocranial volume in extinct taxa.

their geographical scope. Therefore, the data set we are working with in the early phase of hominin evolution is almost certainly incomplete. We should bear this in mind when formulating and testing hypotheses about any aspect of hominin evolution, including the evolution of modern human life history. Nonetheless, FADs and LADs provide an approximate temporal sequence for the hominin taxa.

Second, we made a deliberate decision not to use lines to connect the taxa in figure 11.2. This reflects our view that within the constraints of existing knowledge are only two well-supported subclades within the hominin clade, one for *Paranthropus* taxa and the other for post–*H. ergaster* taxa assigned to the *Homo* clade. Without well-supported subclades, attempts to identify specific taxa as ancestors or descendants of other taxa are probably unwise.

INFERRING THE LIFE HISTORY OF EXTINCT HOMININ TAXA

Many lists of "life history variables" are potentially confusing conflations of three categories of information. The first category (A) consists of variables such as gestation length, age at weaning, and longevity that directly record the timing of life history related events. We refer to these as "life history variables" (LHVs). With the exception of the age at weaning (Aiello, Montgomery, and Dean 1991; Skinner 1997), we cannot yet make direct observations about life history variables (table 11.2) on an extinct taxon, but this may change as new methods are devised and applied to the fossil record. Unless researchers discover sites that have very different taphonomic biases, however, infant specimens of early hominins are always likely to be scarce.

The second category (B) subsumes qualitative or quantitative information that can be gleaned from the hominin fossil record about ontogeny. The third category (C) consists of information from the hominin fossil record about variables (such as body mass and brain size) that have been shown empirically within primates to influence life history or to be correlated with LHVs (for example, Sacher 1975; R. Martin 1981, 1983; Hofman 1984; B. Smith 1989a, 1992; Smith, Gannon, and Smith 1995; Smith and Tompkins 1995; Godfrey et al. 2003). To distinguish them from life history variables, we refer to the variables in categories B and C as "life history related variables" (LHRVs) (see table 11.2). In the next part of this section, we consider in more detail how (and, more importantly, how reliably) one LHV, age at weaning, and the LHRVs listed in table 11.2 can be inferred from the hominin fossil record.

Age at Weaning

Age at weaning is an indicator of relative offspring dependence, maternal investment, and interbirth interval (because lactation suppresses ovulation in great apes and humans) (Galdikas and Wood 1990; Robson, van Schaik, and Hawkes, chapter 2, this volume). Among living primates, weaning appears to coincide with eruption of the permanent mandibular first molar (B. Smith 1991b), but within the hominin clade, some evidence suggests that weaning may predate first molar emergence (Aiello, Montgomery, and Dean 1991; Dean 2000). This is certainly the case for modern human groups who wean infants by about age 2.5 years (Robson, van Schaik, and Hawkes, chapter 2, and Sellen, chapter 6, this volume), although the first permanent mandibular molar does not erupt until approximately age 6 years. Kennedy (2005) has recently suggested that the derived condition of early weaning in modern humans is the result of selection for early brain growth, which cannot be sustained by mother's milk alone (see Robson, van Schaik, and Hawkes, chapter 2, this volume, for brain growth data). Determining *when* during human ancestry this derived condition of early weaning appeared has proven difficult. Researchers have determined age at weaning in fossil hominins based on an assessment of the degree and timing of deciduous dental attrition associated with dietary supplementation. Comparative assessments of age at weaning among fossil hominin species, however, are limited by the relative dearth of infant and juvenile hominin specimens.

Aiello, Montgomery, and Dean (1991) showed that specimens of *P. boisei* and *P. robustus*, judged to be 2.5–3.5 years of age, exhibit high levels of deciduous dental attrition compared with specimens of *Au. afarensis*, judged to be 3–4 years of age and exhibiting minimal dental wear. *Au. africanus* also appeared to exhibit greater deciduous tooth wear than *Au. afarensis*. These authors concluded that this could relate to dietary differences and/or earlier age at weaning.

In comparing the age of onset of deciduous dental attrition in European Middle Paleolithic *H. neanderthalensis* and Upper Paleolithic *H. sapiens* dentitions, Mark Skinner (1997) concluded that *H. sapiens* children were weaned one year earlier than Neanderthal children (that is, at approximately 2 years of age in the former and 3 years of age in the latter). He also ventured that the subsequently reduced interbirth interval of *H. sapiens* might be linked with their demographic increase during

344

the Upper Paleolithic. Confirmation of these differences in the timing of weaning would have important implications for life history studies, demonstrating that small but perhaps significant differences in life history can occur among fossil hominin species that, on the basis of body mass and brain size, would be inferred to have similar life histories.

Using dental attrition as a proxy for weaning is problematic because the inclusion of dietary supplementation, which increases dental attrition, does not always coincide with the cessation of breastfeeding and, in great apes, can predate it by a number of years (Aiello, Montgomery, and Dean 1991; Sellen, chapter 6, this volume). Therefore, even a precise determination of the timing of particular levels of deciduous tooth wear in fossil hominins may not be an accurate proxy for weaning age (if one is interested in the actual completion of weaning). A potential solution to this problem may be to detect the cessation of breastfeeding via changes in the stable isotope composition of enamel formed around the time of complete weaning (Humphrey, Dean, and Jeffries 2005).

Body Mass

Body mass plays an important role in Charnov's dimensionless assembly rules for mammalian life histories (Charnov 1993; see Hawkes, chapter 4, this volume, for a discussion of Charnov's model) and is positively correlated with many life history variables across a range of mammalian taxa (Harvey and Read 1988; Hawkes, chapter 4, this volume). Specifically, strong correlations are found between body mass and LHVs such as gestation length, weaning age, age at first reproduction, interbirth interval, and maximum lifespan across subfamilies of primates (Harvey and Clutton-Brock 1985). How reliably can we estimate body mass by using skeletal fragments sampled from extinct taxa? Did increases in hominin body mass occur gradually within the history of species or quickly with the appearance of new species? When in hominin evolution did body mass reach the levels we see in contemporary and subrecent modern humans?

The most reliable estimates of body mass are made when the skeletal fragment is known to belong to a group for which regressions can be determined using actual body masses and skeletal measurements. This is clearly not the case for fossil hominins, for the regressions have to be generated using data from extant, more or less closely related groups such as the hominoids, anthropoids, or simians (for example, Aiello and Wood 1994). In addition, Richard Smith (1996) has cautioned that paleontologists' reliance on proxies for body mass in fossil-only taxa inevitably introduces error into attempts to estimate the body mass of fossil hominin taxa.

Traditionally, the most reliable body-mass estimates for living taxa have come from the postcranial skeleton. In the hominin fossil record, however, reliably associated postcranial remains are rare, and some early hominin taxon hypodigms include little or no postcranial evidence. This has led to attempts to use cranial variables as proxies for body mass (for example, Aiello and Wood 1994; Kappelman 1996). In the splitting and lumping hominin taxonomies (table 11.3), we have compiled body-mass estimates for taxa from the literature using both postcranial and cranial methods. The published body-mass estimates for *H. rudolfensis* in table 11.3 are more speculative than most because they are based on postcranial fossils whose assignment to *H. rudolfensis* are tentative and questionable. However, when Aiello and Wood (1994) used orbit dimensions to predict body mass directly from the KNM-ER 1470 cranium (the lectotype of *H. rudolfensis*), the 95 percent CIs (confidence intervals) they derived for its body mass (approximately 43–67 kg) (Aiello and Wood 1994:421, table 8) are very similar to the species 95 percent CIs given in table 11.3.

The 95 percent CIs around the means show that the estimates vary greatly in their reliability. As one would expect, there are differences in the parameters of those taxa (such as *H. habilis s. l.* and *H. habilis s. s.*) that have more inclusive and less inclusive interpretations. Whether one uses the lumping or the splitting taxonomy, there is apparently a substantial increase in the mean body mass of some hominin taxa with FADs around 2 Ma (figures 11.3 and 11.4). Before 2 Ma, the estimated body mass of each hominin taxon did not appear to differ markedly from any other or from the average body mass of modern chimpanzees (approximately 30–40 kg). An exception to this pattern is the estimated body mass of *Homo rudolfensis* and *Homo habilis s. l.* (taxon F in figure 11.3 and D in figure 11.4); at 2.4 Ma, these have an estimated mean body mass of 55 kg and 46 kg, respectively. It is important to note that, in both cases, the specimens from which body mass is actually being estimated and which give a reasonably large body-mass estimate for

TABLE 11.3

Body-Mass Estimates: Splitting and Lumping Hominin Taxonomies[1]

Taxonomy	Species		Male	Female	Body Mass	Method[4]
(A) SPLITTING	MEAN (KG)	95% CI[2]	MEAN (KG)	MEAN (KG)	SD[3]	
S. tchadensis	?	?	?	?	–	–
O. tugenensis	?	?	?	?	–	–
Ar. ramidus s. s.	40	?	?	?	–	D
Au. anamensis	42	- 72–156	51	33	1.54	A
Au. afarensis s. s.	38	31–45	45	29	1.55	A
K. platyops	?	?	?	?	–	–
Au. bahrelghazali	?	?	?	?	–	–
Au. africanus	34	30–38	41	30	1.36	A
Au. garhi	?	?	?	?	–	–
P. aethiopicus	38	?	38	?	–	B
P. boisei s. s.	41	- 52–134	49	34	1.44	A
P. robustus	36	27–45	40	32	1.25	A
H. habilis s. s.	33	25–41	37	32	1.16	A
H. rudolfensis	55	46–64	60	51	1.18	A
H. ergaster	64	53–76	68	54	1.26	E
H. erectus s. s.	58	50–65	59	57	1.04	C, B, E
H. antecessor	?	?	?	?	–	–
H. heidelbergensis	71	62–80	84	78	1.08	E
H. neanderthalensis	72	69–76	76	65	1.17	E
H. sapiens s. s.	64	63–66	68	57	1.19	E
(B) LUMPING						
Ar. ramidus s. l.	40	?	?	?	–	F
Au. afarensis s. l.	39	32–45	46	30	1.53	F
Au. africanus	34	30–38	41	30	1.36	F
P. boisei s. l.	40	21–59	43	34	1.26	F
P. robustus	36	27–45	40	32	1.25	F
H. habilis s. l.	46	34–57	52	41	1.27	F
H. erectus s. l.	61	55–66	65	57	1.14	F
H. sapiens s. l.	66	6– 67	70	59	1.19	F

1. See appendix III for fossil specimens included in the estimation of body mass for each taxon.
2. The 95 percent confidence intervals are calculated using a quantile from Student's t distribution, instead of a quantile of 1.96 from the normal distribution. This gives a more realistic estimate of the confidence interval for a mean derived from very small sample sizes (for example, *P. boisei s. s.*).
3. Body-mass sexual dimorphism (SD) calculated as the ratio of the estimated male mean and the estimated female mean body mass.
4. Method key: A, based on a modern human regression of hindlimb joint size; B, based on a hominoid-derived regression of orbital area; C, based on a hominoid-derived regression of orbital height; D, a comparative estimate of upper limb joint size of *Ar. ramidus* and AL 288-1 (*Au. afarensis*); E, based on regressions of femoral head diameter and/or stature and bi-iliac breadth (see Ruff, Trinkaus, and Holliday 1997); and F, body mass estimates for the more inclusive taxa, calculated as the mean value of all specimens from appropriate individual taxa listed in the splitting hominin taxonomy.

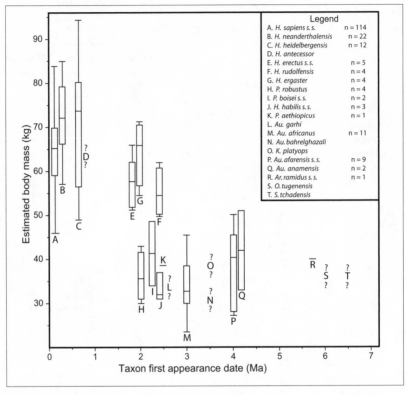

FIGURE 11.3

Estimated body mass plotted against first appearance date for the fossil hominin taxa recognized in the splitting taxonomy. Box and whisker plots show the median, upper, and lower quartiles (box) and the maximum and minimum values (whiskers). The number of individual estimates (n) used for each variable in this comparison is listed in the legend. Taxa represented by a single horizontal line have only a single estimate for this variable. Taxa with no data for this variable appear between question marks; their position along the vertical axis is determined by their informal group membership (see figure 11.2).

H. rudolfensis and *H. habilis s. l.*, respectively, date to ~1.8 Ma. This apparent difference in the pattern and timing of body size evolution within hominins demonstrates the influence of differing taxonomic hypotheses on the interpretation of life history evolution.

Body mass can increase during hominin evolution because both males and females within a taxon are larger or because there is a selective increase in female body mass and therefore a reduction in body-mass sexual dimorphism. Female body mass has long been considered

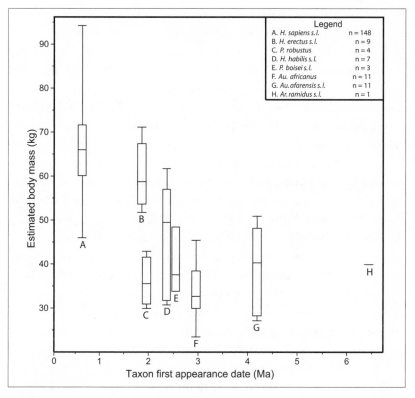

FIGURE 11.4

Estimated body mass plotted against first appearance date for the fossil hominin taxa recognized in the lumping taxonomy. Box and whisker plots show the median, upper, and lower quartiles (box) and the maximum and minimum values (whiskers). The number of individual estimates (n) used for each variable in this comparison is listed in the legend. Taxa represented by a single horizontal line have only a single estimate for this variable. Taxa with no data for this variable appear between question marks; their position along the vertical axis is determined by their informal group membership (see figure 11.2).

a critical life history related variable (for example, Harvey and Clutton-Brock 1985), so it is of particular interest in hominin evolution when there is evidence of any significant reduction in the high levels of overall body-size sexual dimorphism seen in Miocene higher primates and in at least some australopith taxa, such as *Au. afarensis* and *P. boisei* (Lockwood et al. 1996; Silverman, Richmond, and Wood 2001; but see Reno et al. 2003 for a different interpretation of the extent of sexual dimorphism in the former).

We calculated sexual dimorphism as the ratio of male-to-female estimated body mass. In the splitting hominin taxonomy (see table 11.3),
body mass sexual dimorphism appears to be greater than or equal to
that of chimpanzees (~1.25) until the appearance of early *Homo* and
becomes only slightly less so from 2 Ma to present. The lumping
hominin taxonomy (see table 11.3) presents a similar pattern, with
early australopith taxa (for example, *Au. afarensis s. l.* and *Au. africanus*)
exhibiting higher levels of body-mass sexual dimorphism than chimpanzees. *Paranthropus* taxa and *Homo habilis s. l.* exhibit levels similar to
those of chimpanzees, and sexual dimorphism decreases to modern
levels with the appearance of *Homo erectus s. l.* Working back from
extant *H. sapiens*, the pattern of moderate levels of body-mass sexual
dimorphism therefore seems to be consistent back to and including *H.
ergaster*, with greater body-mass differences between presumed males
and presumed females in the australopiths. The larger mean body
mass of *H. ergaster*, which is temporally the earliest taxon included in
H. erectus s. l., seems to result from two factors: an increase in absolute
body mass in both sexes and a larger increase in female body mass.

Brain Mass/Endocranial Volume

Researchers have shown that brain size is also highly correlated
with many life history variables (Sacher 1975; Harvey and Clutton-
Brock 1985). Although it is impossible to make direct measurements of
brain size by using fossil evidence, it is possible, with varying degrees of
precision, to measure the volume of the cranial cavity, otherwise
known as "endocranial volume." Brain mass can be derived from brain
volume, and brain volume can be derived from endocranial volume if
allowance is made for the space occupied by endocranial vasculature
and the intracranial, extracerebral cerebrospinal fluid. Few fossil
hominin crania are preserved well enough for endocranial volume to
be measured with the precision and accuracy one can achieve using
museum specimens of extant taxa. Holloway (1983a) attempted to classify endocranial volumes recorded from fossil hominin crania according to what he considered was the likelihood that measured volumes
accurately reflected the actual volume. Most published endocranial
volumes of fossil hominins lack any assessment of the precision or
accuracy of the estimated volumes.

TABLE 11.4

Cranial Capacity Estimates: Splitting and Lumping Hominin Taxonomies[1]

Taxonomy	Mean Cranial Capacity (cm³)	95% CI[2]	N
(A) SPLITTING			
S. tchadensis	365	?	1
O. tugenensis	?	?	–
Ar. ramidus s. s.	?	?	–
Au. anamensis	?	?	–
Au. afarensis s. s.	458	335–580	4
K. platyops	?	?	–
Au. bahrelghazali	?	?	–
Au. africanus	464	426–502	8
Au. garhi	450	?	1
P. aethiopicus	410	?	1
P. boisei s. s.	481	454–507	10
P. robustus	563	- 542–1668	2
H. habilis s. s.	609	544–674	6
H. rudolfensis	726	501–950	3
H. ergaster	764	640–888	6
H. erectus s. s.	1003	956–1051	36
H. antecessor	1000	?	1
H. heidelbergensis	1204	1130–1278	17
H. neanderthalensis	1426	1351–1501	23
H. sapiens s. s.	1478	1444–1512	66
(B) LUMPING[3]			
Ar. ramidus s. l.	365	–	1
Au. afarensis s. l.	458	335–580	6
Au. africanus	464	426–502	8
P. boisei s. l.	472	447–498	12
P. robustus	563	- 542–1668	2
H. habilis s. l.	648	579–716	9
H. erectus s. l.	969	919–1019	42
H. sapiens s. l.	1418	1384–1452	108

1. See appendix III for fossil specimens included in the estimation of cranial capacity for each taxon.
2. The 95 percent confidence intervals are calculated using a quantile from Student's t distribution, instead of a quantile of 1.96 from the normal distribution. This gives a more realistic estimate of the confidence interval for a mean derived from very small sample sizes (for example, *P. robustus*).
3. Cranial capacity estimates for these more inclusive taxa are calculated as the mean value of all specimens from appropriate individual taxa listed in the splitting hominin taxonomy above.

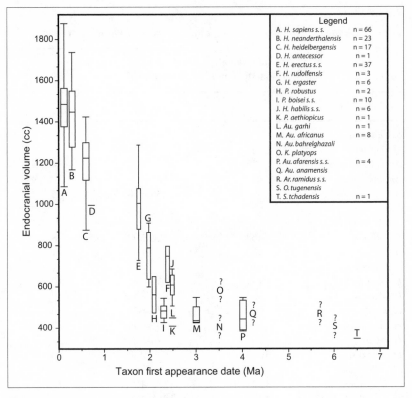

FIGURE 11.5

Estimated endocranial volume plotted against first appearance date for the fossil hominin taxa recognized in the splitting taxonomy. Box and whisker plots show the median, upper, and lower quartiles (box) and the maximum and minimum values (whiskers). The number of individual estimates (n) used for each variable in this comparison is listed in the legend. Taxa represented by a single horizontal line have only a single estimate for this variable. Taxa with no data for this variable appear between question marks; their position along the vertical axis is determined by their informal group membership (see figure 11.2).

Parameters for the cranial capacity (that is, endocranial volume) of hominin taxa in the splitting and lumping taxonomies are listed in table 11.4 and illustrated in figures 11.5 and 11.6. The confidence intervals (CIs) in table 11.4 reflect inter-individual variation within each taxon but take no account of the precision and accuracy of each individual endocranial-volume measurement. All australopith taxa have brain sizes that do not differ significantly from *P. troglodytes* (~400 cc). The brain sizes of *H. habilis s. s.*, *H. rudolfensis*, *H. habilis s. l.*, *H. ergaster,*

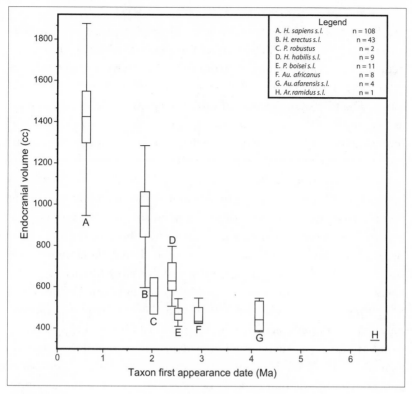

FIGURE 11.6

Estimated endocranial volume plotted against first appearance date for the fossil hominin taxa recognized in the lumping taxonomy. Box and whisker plots show the median, upper, and lower quartiles (box) and the maximum and minimum values (whiskers). The number of individual estimates (n) used for each variable in this comparison is listed in the legend. Taxa represented by a single horizontal line have only a single estimate for this variable. Taxa with no data for this variable appear between question marks; their position along the vertical axis is determined by their informal group membership (see figure 11.2).

and *H. erectus s. s.* are intermediate between the values for *P. troglodytes* and *H. sapiens* (see table 11.4). The value for *H. erectus s. s.* is the only one in this group closer to the value for *H. sapiens* than to that of *P. troglodytes*. Only *H. neanderthalensis* and *H. heidelbergensis* have brain sizes that are indistinguishable from those of *H. sapiens* (see table 11.4). In summary, the modern human expression of two important LHRVs, body mass and brain size, first appear at different times and in different taxa during human evolution.

Dental Life History Related Variables (LHRVs)

Teeth make up the majority of the fossil record, and researchers who try to reconstruct life history in fossil taxa rely heavily on ontogenetic data that can be collected from teeth (see Hawkes, chapter 3, this volume). For the purpose of this discussion, these data come in two forms. The first is an assessment of the microstructure of dental hard tissues to determine and compare the rate and pattern of crown and root formation, which have been shown to be positively correlated with age at weaning (an LHV) and with LHRVs such as female body mass and brain size (Macho 2001:table II). The second source of data is information about the relative timing of tooth formation and eruption into the jaws, using measures of dental microstructure and of the relative growth of tooth crowns and roots within the forming dentition. Because the timing and pattern of overall dental development are considered proxies for somatic growth and therefore life history, inferences about shared or distinct life history patterns can be generated using these data (Robson, van Schaik, and Hawkes, chapter 2, this volume). When dental microstructural analysis can be used in specimens to determine the age at death of individuals whose dentition is not fully formed, we can examine modern human and extant ape samples of known age and/or other fossil specimens to compare the absolute, instead of relative, timing of dental development.

Crown and Root Formation Times.

Because the rhythm of the incremental growth of the dental hard tissues is regular, those cycles of cellular activity can serve as a clock to time the onset, duration, and offset of the cellular activity responsible for depositing dental hard tissues in fossils (Dean 1987; Macho and Wood 1995b; Schwartz and Dean 2000; and B. Wood 2000 provide reviews of the cellular basis of dental ontogeny). Specifically, the crystalline matrix secreted by enamel-forming cells (ameloblasts) and dentine-forming cells (odontoblasts) shows two sets of discrete periodicities: a "short period" (approximately twenty four hours) and a "long period" (approximately six to nine days). In enamel, these are called "cross-striations" and the "brown striae of Retzius," respectively (Schwartz and Dean 2000). Their equivalents in dentine are "von Ebner's" and "Andresen's lines," respectively (Dean 1995b, 1998, 2000; Fitzgerald 1998). Also, therapeutic injections of antibiotics have shown these markers to be synchronic between enamel and dentine (Dean and Scandrett 1996). For fossil teeth that are not naturally fractured or from which thin sections cannot be made, determining crown formation time involves summing the estimated duration of appositional enamel growth (that is, enamel covering the cusp of a tooth whose long-period lines do not reach the surface of the crown) and the duration of imbricational enamel growth (that is, the product of the number of perikymata—defined as striae of Retzius that reach the surface of the enamel in the form of steps that resemble those of a tiled roof— and an estimated long-period duration of six to nine days).

In a recent analysis of enamel formation times in the incisors and canines of early hominins, Dean and colleagues (2001) counted long-period cross-striations and then used an empirically derived modal periodicity of nine days to calculate enamel formation times, plotting these against enamel thickness. The analyses show that archaic hominins take, on average, one hundred days fewer than modern humans to reach an enamel thickness of 1,000 mm. The authors conclude that "none of the trajectories of enamel growth in apes, australopiths or fossils attributed to *Homo habilis*, *Homo rudolfensis*, or *Homo erectus* falls within that of the sample from modern humans" (Dean et al. 2001:629). Similarly, in Dean's (1995b) analysis of root formation time in OH 16 (a specimen assigned to *H. habilis*), he identified it as unlike the modern human pattern.

Generally, crown formation times of anterior teeth are related to crown height (the taller the tooth, the longer it takes to form); those of postcanine teeth are related to overall crown size (Macho and Wood 1995b). Within fossil hominin taxa, the major exception to these generalizations is that the premolar and molar crowns of *P. boisei* take the same time, or less, to form than do those of modern humans and chimps, despite their having crowns approximately twice the overall size of modern humans. This is due to a combination of more enamel secretion per day by ameloblasts and a faster rate of ameloblast activation (Beynon and Wood 1987). We need more information to determine whether these differences are due to selection operating on life history or diet, or on a combination of the two. In Macho's (2001) analysis of crown formation times and life history evolution, she suggests that the rapid crown formation times of *P. boisei* are due to a disjunction between body mass and brain mass. However, the estimated body mass she uses for *P. boisei* differs little from that of modern humans. In fact, the available evidence suggests that neither *P. boisei s. s.* nor *P. boisei s. l.* is likely to have been significantly heavier than other australopith taxa (see table 11.3). In this respect at least, there is no evidence for a unique life history pattern for this hominin taxon.

Ramírez Rozzi and Bermúdez de Castro (2004) used perikymata packing patterns on the anterior dentition as a proxy for crown formation times; that is, closely spaced perikymata reflect decreased rates of maturation of enamel-forming ameloblasts and therefore longer crown formation times. They concluded that *H. antecessor* and *H. heidelbergensis* had shorter periods of dental growth than *H. sapiens* (both modern and Upper Paleolithic–Mesolithic) and that *H. neanderthalensis* had decreased crown formation times that were derived with respect to *H. antecessor* and *H. heidelbergensis*, suggesting a shorter period of somatic growth in this taxon (contra Dean and colleagues [2001], who concluded, albeit from analysis of a single specimen, that *H. neanderthalensis* shared similar enamel growth rates with modern humans). Ramírez Rozzi and Bermúdez de Castro (2004) attribute the apparent disconnect between the large brain and body size of *H. neanderthalensis* and this taxon's apparently rapid dental growth to high adult mortality rates. Therefore, as a proxy for somatic growth rate, crown and root formation times of fossil taxa do not resemble a modern human pattern before Upper Paleolithic *H. sapiens*.

Timing of Tooth Formation and Eruption.
    One of the many features that distinguish modern humans from the other great apes is the relative difference in the timing of tooth formation within the dental arcade and the sequence of tooth eruption into the jaw. In the nonhuman great apes, the first molar is the first permanent tooth to erupt, followed by the incisors and premolars, the second molar, and then the canine. In modern humans, the first molar and first incisor erupt close together, followed by the second incisor, with the canine, premolars, and second molar subsequently erupting close together (Mann, Lampl, and Monge 1990; Conroy and Vannier 1991a). Dean and Wood (1981) published a provisional chart comparing modern human, panin, and gorillin tooth crown and root development, with subsequent modifications (the important contributions of Anemone, Conroy, and Kuykendall are summarized in Kuykendall

2002); the chart is still used today. However, the proximate cause of these differences in eruption sequence has much more to do with the roots than with the crowns. For example, one main difference between the dental development of modern humans and extant panins and gorillins is the late eruption of the first molar in the former. This is caused by a temporal retardation in the final stages of root formation so that first molar eruption in modern humans occurs well after the crown and most of the root are formed (Dean 1995a; Macho and Wood 1995b).

The extent of root development in the teeth of living taxa can be assessed crudely by radiography and more precisely if the teeth are available for sectioning and histological analysis (Anemone 2002). Unfortunately, all these methods are more difficult to apply to fossil hominin jaws. The mineralized bone of most fossils is resistant to conventional radiographic techniques, but images can be obtained by using computerized tomography (for example, Conroy and Vannier 1987). Developments in both hardware and software are leading to expanded data sets for those fossil hominin taxa with large hypodigms, but the data for most extinct hominin taxa are still not sufficient to justify detailed interpretation. As noted more than a decade ago by Conroy and Vannier (1991b), just because the eruption sequence differs between modern humans and living chimpanzees, it does not follow that fossil hominin taxa, whose eruption sequence is the same as that of modern humans, had modern human rates of dental development.

Figure 11.7 emphasizes the complex interactions among several aspects of the development of lower incisors and molars in modern humans, living chimpanzees, and *Paranthropus* taxa. Despite similarities in gross dental ontogeny between *Pan* and *Paranthropus* (that is, eruption of M1 at ~3 years of age), their different incisor crown-formation times result in different eruption sequences. Modern humans and *Paranthropus* have similar eruption sequences, but their rates of crown and root formation show marked differences. Similar eruption sequences can mask differences in other aspects of dental development, but it is nonetheless a truism that eruption sequences are bound to differ among hominin taxa unless all aspects of dental ontogeny change their rates proportionally (Macho and Wood 1995a). Shared eruption sequences do not mean a shared ontogeny, but different eruption sequences do mean different ontogenies.

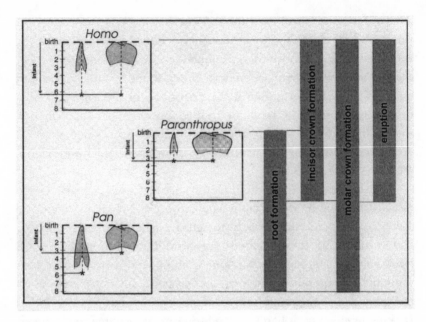

FIGURE 11.7

The relationship between crown formation and eruption sequence in modern humans, Pan, *and* P. boisei. *The vertical dashed line represents the time from the onset of crown formation to eruption. The height of the crown represents the approximate time taken for crown formation; the balance of the period to eruption represents the time taken for the root to form. The tooth crowns are approximately to scale. Infancy is taken to cease at the time of M1 eruption (*). The vertical gray bars indicate rates and patterns in common among the taxa. All three genera share similar molar crown formation times, but* Pan *differs from the other two in eruption schedules and* Homo *in root formation times. Adapted from Macho and Wood (1995b).*

In comparing the timing of relative tooth formation in a variety of hominin taxa (represented by particular fossil specimens), modern humans, and great apes, Bermúdez de Castro and colleagues (2003) found similarity between great apes and australopiths, on the one hand, and *H. antecessor*, *H. erectus s. s.*, *H. heidelbergensis*, and modern humans, on the other. *H. ergaster* (or early *H. erectus s. l.*, depending on your taxonomic hypothesis) specimens appeared intermediate between these two groups.

In appropriate juvenile fossil-hominin specimens, it is possible to use aspects of dental microstructure, assessments of dental attrition, and sequence of tooth eruption to determine age at death and thus to compare dental development among apes, modern humans, or other fossil hominin specimens of the same age. Bromage and Dean (1985) pioneered this approach by using counts of perikymata on the central incisor crown, assuming the time it takes to begin calicifying the tooth and forming the root. They were able to age fossil specimens more accurately, thus enabling comparisons with modern human dental specimens at a similar stage of development. Doing this for several fossil hominin mandibles—LH 2 (*Au. afarensis*), Sts 24 (*Au. africanus*), SK 63 (*P. robustus*), and KNM-ER 820 (*H. ergaster*)—Bromage and Dean concluded that the timing and duration of dental development resembled that of chimpanzees more than modern humans. Although perikymata counts made up about 90 percent of the age estimates for LH 2 and Sts 24, the majority of the elapsed time for KNM-ER 820 was based on assumptions, not observations, about ontogeny.

Subsequent studies (such as Dean et al. 1993; Moggi-Cecchi, Tobias, and Beynon 1998) have achieved greater accuracy and precision by sectioning whole teeth to recover information about the cellular events involved in tooth development. Age-at-death estimates for other early *Homo* specimens (such as KNM-ER 1590 and KNM-WT 15000 [B. Smith 1991a]) assigned to *H. rudolfensis* and *H. ergaster* (or *H. erectus s. l.*), respectively, also suggest that the timing of these taxa's dental development was not modern humanlike. However, any inferences drawn from these results must be tentative until we repair our ignorance of the extent, if any, of variation in dental development within in regional samples of *H. sapiens* (Liversidge 2003) and in wild-versus-captive samples of nonhuman, extant, higher primate taxa (Zihlman, Bolter, and Boesch 2004).

Within the context of dental LHRVs, such as crown and root formation time and the relative timing of tooth formation and eruption, no hominin taxa other than Upper Paleolithic *H. sapiens* exhibit teeth that suggest a modern humanlike pattern in all developmental aspects. Available evidence suggests that australopith hominins were chimpanzeelike, as were primitive *Homo* taxa. Later *H. erectus s. s.*, *H. antecessor*, and *H. heidelbergensis* exhibit patterns of dental development that, although derived in the direction of modern humans, are not identical to *H. sapiens* when compared with australopiths and primitive *Homo*. Apparently, *H. neanderthalensis* is derived with respect to its Middle

Pleistocene ancestors, but in the direction of more rapid dental growth. In this taxon, this contradicts predictions about life history patterns based on brain and body size.

PHYLOGENETIC TRENDS IN FOSSIL HOMININ LIFE HISTORY RELATED DATA

If the application of cladistic methods to the hominin fossil record generates robust hypotheses about the structure of the hominin clade, then we should be able, in theory, to predict the primitive condition of LHRVs for each of the hominin subclades, look for any evidence of homoplasy in life history, and determine at what stage in human evolution the distinctive aspects of modern human life history made their appearance. However, researchers disagree about the reliability of results from cladistic analyses of the hominin fossil record based on traditional metrical or nonmetrical data. Some are willing to accept these as reliable even when based on very small samples of early hominin taxa (Strait and Grine 2001, 2004). Other researchers (for example, Corruccini 1994)—including those who have tried to test the validity of these methods by applying them to living higher taxa for which we have independent molecular evidence about taxonomic relationships (Collard and Wood 2000)—are more skeptical. We tend towards the skeptical end of this spectrum.

Just as we need a well-supported hypothesis about evolutionary relationships among the living higher primates (see above) to predict the primitive condition for life history in the hominin clade, we need a robust hypothesis about evolutionary relationships among extinct hominin taxa to explore the evolution of life history within the hominin clade. There have been many attempts to determine phylogenetic relationships within the hominin clade. Most differ in their detailed conclusions, but nearly all (for example, Chamberlain and Wood 1987; Skelton and McHenry 1992; Strait, Grine, and Moniz 1997) share the conclusion that, around 2.5 Ma, the hominin clade split into two major subclades: one clade containing megadont archaic hominins referred to the genus *Paranthropus* and the other containing the clade that includes the only living hominin, *H. sapiens.*

If we were to accept that a genus should be both a clade and a grade (see Wood and Collard 1999a, 2001, for a discussion), then we would naturally want to know whether all the taxa included in

Paranthropus, on the one hand, and in *Homo*, on the other, have the same life history. There is widespread acknowledgment that a substantial body of phenotypic evidence supports a separate subclade (or monophyletic group) for *Paranthropus* species. Despite this consensus (Strait and Grine 2001), some evidence is still more consistent with robust australopith paraphyly (B. Wood 1988). The data gathered for this review suggest that there is no evidence in the *Paranthropus* clade for any significant increase in body mass and, compared with modern chimpanzees, there is only a slight increase in endocranial volume. However, enamel and dentine formation are faster in *Paranthropus* taxa (see above) than for any other member of the *Pan/Homo* clade for which data are available. This suggests that the pattern of *Paranthropus* life history was most likely distinct from the life histories of modern humans and chimpanzees (Kuykendall 2003).

Researchers also disagree about the criteria used to determine whether a taxon should be included within *Homo* and therefore where we should place the boundary between *Homo* and non-*Homo* hominin taxa (Wood and Collard 1999a, 1999b). As seen below in a summary of LHRVs present in fossil hominid taxa (just one of several categories of evidence that could be used to determine the boundaries of a genus), there is little evidence to support a grade distinction that applies to all the taxa presently included in the genus *Homo*.

IMPLICATIONS OF FOSSIL HOMININ LIFE HISTORY RELATED DATA FOR HYPOTHESES ABOUT THE EVOLUTION OF MODERN HUMAN LIFE HISTORY

The life history of modern humans differs substantially from the life history of our closest living relatives, the extant taxa within the genus *Pan* (Robson, van Schaik, and Hawkes, chapter 2, this volume). A summary table outlining the presence of modern humanlike LHRVs within a splitting hominin taxonomy is presented in table 11.5. Before primitive *Homo*, there is no evidence of any hominin taxon possessing a body size, a brain size, or aspects of dental development that diverge significantly from what we assume (but remember, this is an untested assumption) to be the primitive life history pattern for the *Pan/Homo* clade.

Within primitive *Homo*—that is, *H. habilis s. s.* and *H. rudolfensis* (or *H. habilis s. l.*, for those unconvinced that this hypodigm subsumes

TABLE 11.5

The Presence of Modern Humanlike LHRVs within the Taxa Recognized in a Splitting Hominin Taxonomy

Informal Group	Splitting Taxonomy	Body Size	Brain Mass	Crown & Root Formation	Timing of Tooth Formation & Eruption
Basal australopiths	S. tchadensis	?	N	?	?
	O. tugenensis	?	?	?	?
	Ar. ramidus s. s.	N	?	?	?
	Au. anamensis	N	?	?	?
	Au. afarensis s. s.	N	N	N	?
Australopiths	K. platyops	?	?	?	?
	Au. bahrelghazali	?	?	?	?
	Au. africanus	N	N	N	N
	Au. garhi	?	N	?	?
Megadont australopiths	P. aethiopicus	N	N	?	?
	P. boisei s. s.	N	N	N	N[1]
	P. robustus	N	N	N	N[1]
Primitive *Homo*	H. habilis s. s.	N	N	N	N
	H. rudolfensis	Y	N	?	?
Archaic *Homo*	H. ergaster	Y	N	N	N
	H. erectus s. s.	Y	N	N	N
Homo of modern aspect	H. antecessor	?	N	N	Y
	H. heidelbergensis	Y	Y	N	Y
	H. neanderthalensis	Y	Y	N	Y
	H. sapiens s. s.	Y	Y	Y	Y

1. Sequence but not timing.

more than one taxon)—what we can infer about LHRVs is consistent. With the possible exception of *H. rudolfensis* body mass, no LHRVs suggest the type of prolonged ontogeny seen in modern humans. The situation is only slightly different for *H. ergaster* and *H. erectus s. s.* Despite body-mass estimates similar (if not necessarily identical) to those of modern humans, the brain size, the crown and root formation times, and the timing and sequence of dental eruption are inconsistent with a modern human pattern. Middle Pleistocene *H. erectus s. s.* may be more modern humanlike in its dental development, but the evidence is often conflicting (for example, Sangiran 4 being more modern humanlike [Dean et al. 2001] and Sangiran 7 less so [Antón 2003]). Noncraniodental evidence for fossil hominin growth and development in *H. ergaster/H. erectus s. s.* is sparse and conflicting. Some workers interpret the pattern of growth and development of the postcranial skeleton in these taxa as compatible with that of modern humans (Clegg and Aiello 1999; S. Smith 2004); others point to subtle but significant differences (Tardieu 1998) from the ontogeny of modern humans.

The fossil material attributed to *H. antecessor* does not provide a good estimate of body mass, and it indicates a brain size similar to that of *Homo erectus s. s.* The crown formation times of *H. antecessor* are not yet modern, but there is some evidence for modern humanlike timing of tooth formation and eruption. The body and brain sizes of *H. heidelbergensis* and *H. neanderthalensis* are consistent with a modern human life history; however, while both appear to possess a modern humanlike pattern of dental development, the crown formation times of the former are similar to *H. antecessor*, and those of the latter appear to be autapomorphically rapid. Depending on the weight one wants to give to these LHRVs, a modern human pattern of life history may have been present in *H. heidelbergensis* and *H. neanderthalensis*, but it is also possible that the combination of features that distinguish the life history of modern humans may have evolved as recently as the Upper Paleolithic, that is, within the past forty thousand years.

CONCLUSIONS

Using the hominin fossil record, we investigated (a) whether the unique features of modern human life history appeared suddenly as an integrated package; (b) whether the presence in the fossil record of large-bodied hominins with modern human skeletal proportions signaled its appearance; and (c) whether modern human and modern chimpanzee life histories are the only ways that life history has been configured within the *Pan/Homo* clade. The clear contrasts between the life history of modern humans and the life history of our closest living relatives, the chimpanzees, have perhaps lulled researchers into the expectation that, at a point in evolutionary history, all these variables switched simultaneously from their primitive, nonhuman condition to the modern human condition. The reality seems to be more complicated. Some LHVs and LHRVs (for example, body mass) shifted to the modern human condition earlier; others, such as dental development, appear to have shifted much later.

Initial attempts to describe the dental ontogeny of fossil hominins were confined mostly to statements about whether it was "modern humanlike" or "apelike." Additional data and more sophisticated ways of displaying those data brought the realization that the dental ontogeny of many early hominins was distinctive, not an amalgam of some modern humanlike characteristics and some apelike ones (Bromage 1987; Kuykendall 2003). As we come to know more about the life histories of hominin taxa, we are also discovering that they can have distinctive life histories that do not conform to any living model (see Kelley [1997, 2002], for insightful reviews of life history evolution within living and extinct higher primates). At least one extinct clade, *Paranthropus*, has a pattern of dental LHRVs that most likely sets it apart from the life histories of both modern humans and chimpanzees.

Life history is an important component of the shared adaptive mix that justifies grouping taxa into genera. The tantalizing glimpses revealed by existing data and methods into the life history of taxa included in *Homo* suggest that this genus, as traditionally defined, subsumes at least two patterns of life history. If LHRVs are used to reconstruct life history, then primitive *Homo* and archaic *Homo* taxa appear to differ from each other, as well as from *Homo* taxa of modern aspect that appear in the Middle Pleistocene. How these differences relate to hominin ecology and patterns of social and cultural evolution within the hominin clade poses pressing research problems.

Clearly, the evolution of modern human life history is complex. The task of using the hominin fossil record to document and help understand that complexity has only just begun.

Acknowledgments

Bernard Wood is grateful to the organizers for their invitation to contribute to this volume, as well as to the other participants in the SAR advanced seminar (especially to Leslie Aiello) for their suggestions and advice. We thank the many researchers who generously responded to our requests for information about individual hominin specimens. We thank Daniel Temple for his considerable help in compiling the cranial capacity, dental, and mandibular data, as well as Justin Bedard for his help with the preparation of the chapter. Matthew M. Skinner is supported by a George Washington University Selective Excellence Graduate Fellowship; Bernard Wood is supported by The Henry Luce Foundation and the National Science Foundation.

APPENDIX 1

Splitting (Speciose) Hominin Taxonomy

Basal Australopiths.

This group includes one taxon, *Ardipithecus ramidus s. s.*, which is probably a member of the hominin clade, and two taxa, *Orrorin tugenensis* and *Sahelanthropus tchadensis*, which may be hominins.

Taxon name: *Sahelanthropus tchadensis* **Brunet et al. 2002**

Temporal range: About 7–6 Ma.

How dated: Relative dating by matching fossil evidence found in the same layers as the hominins with absolutely dated fossil sites in East Africa (Vignaud et al. 2002).

Initial discovery: TM 266-01-060-1—an adult cranium, Anthrocotheriid Unit, Toros-Menalla, Chad, 2001 (Brunet et al. 2002).

Type specimen: (See above.)

Source(s) of the evidence: Known only from localities in Toros-Menalla, Chad, and Central Africa.

Nature of the evidence: A plastically deformed cranium, a mandible, and some teeth; no postcranial evidence.

Characteristics and inferred behavior: A chimp-size animal displaying a

novel combination of primitive and derived features. Much about
the base and vault of the cranium is chimplike, but the anterior
placement of the foramen magnum is homininlike. The supraor-
bital torus, lack of a muzzle, small apically worn canines, low
rounded molar cusps, thick tooth enamel, and thick mandibular
corpus (Brunet et al. 2002) suggest that *S. tchadensis* does not
belong in the *Pan* clade. Either it is a primitive hominin, or it
belongs to a separate clade of homininlike apes.

Life history related data: Dental development, no; body mass, no;
endocranial volume, yes.

Taxon name: *Orrorin tugenensis* **Senut et al. 2001**

Temporal range: About 6.0 Ma.

How dated: Fossils found in sediments that lie between a 6.2 Ma volcanic trachyte below and an absolutely dated 5.6 Ma volcanic sill
above.

Initial discovery: KNM LU 335—left mandibular molar-tooth crown,
"thick, pink sandy and gritty horizon," middle Member A,
Lukeino Formation, Tugen Hills, Baringo, Kenya, 1974 (Pickford
1975).

Type specimen: BAR 1000'00—fragmentary mandible, Kapsomin,
Lukeino Formation, Tugen Hills, Baringo, Kenya, 2000 (Senut et
al. 2001).

Source(s) of the evidence: The relevant remains come from four localities
in the Lukeino Formation, Tugen Hills, Kenya.

Nature of the evidence: The thirteen specimens include three femoral
fragments.

Characteristics and inferred behavior: The femoral morphology has been
recently interpreted (Pickford et al. 2002; Galik et al. 2004) as
suggesting that *O. tugenensis* is an obligate biped, but other
researchers interpret the radiographs and CT scans of the
femoral neck as indicating a mix of bipedal and nonbipedal
locomotion. Otherwise, the discoverers admit that much of the
critical dental morphology is "ape-like" (Senut et al. 2001:6).
O. tugenensis may prove to be a hominin, but, equally and perhaps
more likely, it may belong to another part of the adaptive radiation that included the common ancestor of panins and hominins.

Life history related data: Dental development, no; body mass, no; endocranial volume, no.

Taxon name: *Ardipithecus ramidus sensu stricto* **(White, Suwa, and Asfaw 1994); White, Suwa, Asfaw and Asfaw 1995**

Temporal range: About 5.7–4.5 Ma.

How dated: Absolutely dated layers of volcanic ash above and below the fossil-bearing sediments.

Initial discovery: ARA-VP-1/1—right M3, Aramis, Middle Awash, Ethiopia, 1993 (White, Suwa, and Asfaw 1994). (n.b. If a mandible, KNM-LT 329, from Lothagam, Kenya, proves to belong to the hypodigm, then it would be the initial discovery.)

Type specimen: ARA-VP-6/1—associated upper and lower dentition, Aramis, Middle Awash, Ethiopia, 1993 (White, Suwa, and Asfaw 1994).

Source(s) of the evidence: The initial evidence for this taxon came as approximately 4.5 Ma fossils recovered from a site called "Aramis" in the Middle Awash region of Ethiopia. A second suite of fossils, including a mandible, teeth, and postcranial bones, was recovered in 1997 from five localities in the Middle Awash that range in age from 5.2 to >5.7 Ma (Haile-Selassie 2001).

Nature of the evidence: The published evidence consists of isolated teeth, a piece of the base of the cranium, and fragments of mandibles and long bones.

Characteristics and inferred behavior: The remains attributed to *Ar. ramidus* share some features with living species of *Pan*, others with the African apes in general, and, crucially, several dental and cranial features only with later hominins such as *Au. afarensis.* Therefore, the discoverers suggested that the material belongs to a hominin species. They initially allocated the new species to *Australopithecus* (White, Suwa, and Asfaw 1994) but subsequently assigned it to a new genus, *Ardipithecus* (White, Suwa, and Asfaw 1995), which the authors suggest is significantly more primitive than *Australopithecus.* Judging from the size of the shoulder joint, *Ar. ramidus* weighed about 40 kg. Its chewing teeth were relatively small, and the position of the foramen magnum suggests that the posture and gait of *Ar. ramidus* were, respectively, more upright and bipedal than is the case in the living apes. The thin enamel covering on the teeth suggests that the diet of *Ar. ramidus* may have resembled that of the chimpanzee more than modern humans'. Haile-Selassie, Suwa, and White (2004) have suggested that the hypodigm of the subspecies *Ar. ramidus kadabba* should be distinguished at the species level as *Ar. kadabba*. Even if this taxonomic change is accepted, the inferences about the life history of these taxa remain virtually unchanged.

Life history related data: Dental development, no; body mass, yes; endocranial volume, no.

Australopiths.

This group includes all the remaining hominin taxa not conventionally included in *Homo* and *Paranthropus*. It subsumes two genera, *Australopithecus* and *Kenyanthropus*. *Australopithecus* as used in this taxonomy and many others is almost certainly not a single clade. Until researchers can generate a reliable hominin phylogeny, however, there is little point in revising its generic terminology.

Taxon name: *Australopithecus anamensis* **Leakey et al. 1995**

Temporal range: About 4.2–3.9 Ma.

How dated: Mainly from absolutely dated layers of ash above and below the sediments bearing the hominin fossils.

Initial discovery: KNM-KP 271—left distal humerus, Naringangoro Hill, Kanapoi, Kenya, 1965 (Patterson and Howells 1967).

Type specimen: KNM-KP 29281—an adult mandible with complete dentition and a temporal fragment that probably belongs to the same individual, Kanapoi, Kenya, 1994.

Source(s) of the evidence: Allia Bay and Kanapoi, Kenya; Middle Awash, Ethiopia.

Nature of the evidence: The evidence consists of jaws, teeth, and postcranial elements from the upper and lower limbs.

Characteristics and inferred behavior: The main differences between *Au. anamensis* and *Au. afarensis* relate to details of the dentition. In some respects, the teeth of *Au. anamensis* are more primitive than those of *Au. afarensis* (such as the asymmetry of the premolar crowns and the simple crowns of the deciduous first mandibular molars). In others (for example, the low cross-sectional profiles and bulging sides of the molar crowns), they show similarities to *Paranthropus* (see below). The upper limb remains are australopithlike, but a tibia attributed to *Au. anamensis* has features associated with bipedality.

Life history related data: Dental development, no; body mass, yes; endocranial volume, no.

Taxon name: *Australopithecus afarensis sensu stricto* Johanson, White, and Coppens 1978

Temporal range: About 4–3 Ma.

How dated: Mainly from absolutely dated layers of ash above and below the sediments bearing the hominin fossils.

Initial discovery: AL 128-1—left proximal femur fragment, Sidi Hakoma Member, Hadar Formation, Afar, Ethiopia, 1973 (Johanson and Taieb 1976).

Type specimen: LH 4—adult mandible, Laetolil Beds, Laetoli, Tanzania, 1974.

Source(s) of the evidence: Laetoli, Tanzania; White Sands, Hadar, Maka, Belohdelie, and Fejej, Ethiopia; and Allia Bay, West Turkana, and Tabarin, Kenya.

Nature of the evidence: Au. afarensis s. s. is the earliest hominin to have a comprehensive fossil record, including a skull, fragmented skulls, many lower jaws, and sufficient limb bones to be able to estimate stature and body mass. The collection includes a specimen, AL-288, that preserves just less than half the skeleton of an adult female.

Characteristics and inferred behavior: The range of body-mass estimates is 31–45 kg, and the endocranial volume of *Au. afarensis s. s.* is estimated to be 400–500 cm^3. This is larger than the average endocranial volume of a chimpanzee, but if the estimates of the body size of *Au. afarensis s. s.* are approximately correct, then the brain of *Au. afarensis s. s.*, relative to estimated body mass, is not substantially larger than that of *Pan.* It has incisors that are much smaller than those of extant chimpanzees, but its premolars and molars are relatively larger than those of chimpanzees. The hind limbs of AL-288 are substantially shorter than those of a modern human of similar stature. The appearance of the pelvis and the relatively short lower limb suggests that although *Au. afarensis s. s.* was capable of bipedal walking, it was not adapted for long-range bipedalism. This indirect evidence for the locomotion of *Au. afarensis s. s.* is complemented by the discovery at Laetoli of several trails of fossil footprints. These provide very graphic, direct evidence that a contemporary hominin, presumably *Au. afarensis s. s.*, was capable of bipedal locomotion. The upper limb, especially the hand, retains morphology that most likely reflects a significant element of arboreal locomotion. The size of the footprints, the length of the stride, and stature estimates based on the length of the limb bones suggest that the standing height of adult individuals in this early hominin species was 1.0–1.5 m. Most researchers interpret the fossil evidence for *Au. afarensis s. s.* as consistent with a substantial level of sexual dimorphism, but a recent study argues that sexual dimorphism in this taxon is poorly developed (Reno et al. 2003).

Life history related data: Dental development, yes; body mass, yes; endocranial volume, yes.

Taxon name: *Kenyanthropus platyops* **Leakey et al. 2001**

Temporal range: About 3.5–3.3 Ma.

How dated: Mainly from absolutely dated layers of ash above and below the sediments bearing the hominin fossils.

Initial discovery: KNM-WT 38350—left maxilla fragment, Lomekwi Member, 17 m above the Tulu Bor Tuff, Lomekwi, West Turkana, Kenya, 1998 (Leakey et al. 2001).

Type specimen: KNM-WT 40000—a relatively complete cranium that is crisscrossed by matrix-filled cracks, Kataboi Member, 8 m below the Tulu Bor Tuff and 12 m above the Lokochot Tuff, Lomekwi, West Turkana, Kenya, 1999 (Leakey et al. 2001).

Source(s) of the evidence: West Turkana and perhaps Allia Bay, Kenya.

Nature of the evidence: The initial report lists the type cranium and the paratype maxilla plus 34 specimens—three mandible fragments, a maxilla fragment, and isolated teeth. Some may also belong to the hypodigm, but at this stage the researchers are reserving their judgment about the taxonomy of many of these remains (Leakey et al. 2001). Some of them have only recently been referred to *Au. afarensis s. s.* (Brown, Brown, and Walker 2001).

Characteristics and inferred behavior: The main reasons Leakey and colleagues (2001) did not assign this material to *Au. afarensis s. s.* are its reduced subnasal prognathism, anteriorly situated zygomatic root, flat and vertically orientated malar region, small but thick-enameled molars, and the unusually small M1 compared with the size of the P4 and M3. Some of the morphology of the new genus, including the shape of the face, is *Paranthropus*-like yet lacks the postcanine megadontia that characterizes *Paranthropus*. The authors note that the face of the new material resembles that of *Homo rudolfensis* (see below), but they rightly point out that the postcanine teeth of the latter are substantially larger than those of KNM-WT 40000. *K. platyops* apparently displays a hitherto unique combination of facial and dental morphology.

Life history related data: Dental development, no; body mass, no; endocranial volume, no.

Taxon name: *Australopithecus bahrelghazali* **Brunet et al. 1996**
Temporal range: About 3.5–3.0 Ma.
How dated: Relative dating based on matching mammalian fossils found in the caves with fossils from absolutely dated sites in East Africa.
Initial discovery: KT 12/H1—anterior portion of an adult mandible, Koro Toro, Chad, 1995 (Brunet et al. 1996).
Type specimen: (See above.)
Source(s) of the evidence: Koro Toro, Chad.
Nature of the evidence: Published evidence is restricted to a fragment of the mandible and an isolated tooth.
Characteristics and inferred behavior: Its discoverers claim that its thicker enamel distinguishes the Chad remains from *Ar. ramidus* and that its smaller mandibular symphysis and more complex mandibular premolar roots distinguish it from *Au. afarensis*. Otherwise, there is too little evidence to infer any behavior.
Life history related data: Dental development, no; body mass, no; endocranial volume, no.

Taxon name: *Australopithecus africanus* **Dart 1925**
Temporal range: About 3*–2.4 Ma. (*n.b. It remains to be seen whether the associated skeleton StW 573 from Mb2 [Clarke and Tobias

1995; Clarke 1998, 1999, 2002] and twelve hominin fossils recovered from the Jacovec Cavern since 1995 [Partridge et al. 2003] belong to the *Au. africanus* hypodigm.)

How dated: Mostly relative dating based on matching mammalian fossils found in the caves with fossils from absolutely dated sites in East Africa. Samples of quartz grains from Mb2 and the Jacovec Cavern have recently been dated to about 4.0–4.2 Ma using ratios of the radionuclides [29]Ae and [10]Be (Partridge et al. 2003),but other faunal and uranium series dates suggest a much younger (ca. 2.5 Ma) age for StW 573.

Initial discovery: Taung 1—a juvenile skull with partial endocast, Taung (formerly Taungs), now in South Africa, 1924.

Type specimen: (See above.)

Source(s) of the evidence: Most of the evidence comes from two caves, Sterkfontein and Makapansgat, with other evidence coming from Taung and Gladysvale.

Nature of the evidence: This is one of the better fossil records of an early hominin taxon. The cranium, mandible, and dentition are well sampled. The postcranium, particularly the axial skeleton, is less well represented in the sample, but there is at least one specimen of each of the long bones. Many of the fossils, however, were crushed and deformed by falling rocks before fully fossilized.

Characteristics and inferred behavior: The picture emerging from morphological and functional analyses suggests that although *Au. africanus* was capable of walking bipedally, it was probably not an obligate biped. It had large chewing teeth, and apart from the reduced canines, the skull is apelike. This means that endocranial volume, a reasonable proxy for brain size, is 464 cm^3. The Sterkfontein evidence suggests that males and females of *Au. africanus* differed substantially in body size, but probably not to the degree they did in *Au. afarensis* (see above).

Life history related data: Dental development, yes; body mass, yes; endocranial volume, yes.

Megadont Australopiths.

This group includes hominin taxa conventionally included in the genus *Paranthropus* and one *Australopithecus* species, *Au. garhi*. The genus *Paranthropus* was reintroduced when cladistic analyses suggested that the three species listed in this section formed a clade. Two genera, *Zinjanthropus* and *Paraustralopithecus*, are subsumed within the genus *Paranthropus*.

Taxon name: *Paranthropus aethiopicus* **(Arambourg and Coppens 1968); Chamberlain and Wood 1985**

Temporal range: About 2.5–2.3 Ma.

How dated: Mainly from absolutely dated layers of ash above and below the sediments bearing the hominin fossils.

Initial discovery: Omo 18.18 (or 18.1967.18)—an edentulous adult mandible, Locality 18, Section 7, Member C, Shungura Formation, Omo region, Ethiopia, 1967.

Type specimen: (See above.)

Source(s) of the evidence: Shungura Formation, Omo region, Ethiopia; and West Turkana, Kenya.

Nature of the evidence: The hypodigm includes a well-preserved cranium from West Turkana (KNM-WT 17000) together with mandibles (for example, KNM-WT 16005) and isolated teeth from the Shungura Formation. No postcranial fossils have been assigned to this taxon.

Characteristics and inferred behavior: Similar to *P. boisei* except that the face is more prognathic, the cranial base is less flexed, the incisors are larger, and the postcanine teeth are not as large or as morphologically specialized. The only source of endocranial volume data is KNM-ER WT 17000. When *P. aethiopicus* taxon was introduced in 1968, it was the only megadont hominin in this time range. With the discovery of *Au. garhi* (see below), robust mandibles with long premolar and molar tooth rows apparently are being associated with what are claimed to be two distinct forms of cranial morphology.

Life history related data: Dental development, yes; body mass, yes; endocranial volume, yes.

Taxon name: *Australopithecus garhi* **Asfaw et al. 1999**

Temporal range: About 2.5 Ma.

How dated: From absolutely dated layers of ash above and below the sediments bearing the hominin fossils.

Initial discovery: GAM-VP-1/1—left side of mandibular corpus, Gamedah, Middle Awash, Ethiopia, 1990.

Type specimen: BOU*-VP-12/130—a cranium from the Hata Member, Bouri, Middle Awash, Ethiopia, 1997. (*The prefix *ARA* was erroneously used in the text of Asfaw et al. 1999.)

Source(s) of the evidence: Bouri, Middle Awash, Ethiopia.

Nature of the evidence: A cranium and two partial mandibles.

Characteristics and inferred behavior: *Australopithecus garhi* combines a primitive cranium with large-crowned postcanine teeth. Unlike *Paranthropus* (see above), the incisors and canines are large, and the enamel lacks the extreme thickness seen in the latter taxon. A partial skeleton combining a long femur with a long forearm was found nearby but is not associated with the type cranium (Asfaw et al. 1999), and these fossils have not been formally assigned to *Au. garhi*.

Taxonomic note: The mandibular morphology of *Au. garhi* is, in some respects, like that of *P. aethiopicus*. If it is demonstrated that the type specimen of *P. aethiopicus* belongs to the same hypodigm as the mandibles that match the *Au. garhi* cranium, then *P. aethiopicus* would have priority as the name for the hypodigm presently attributed to *Au. garhi*.

Life history related data: Dental development, no; body mass, no; endocranial volume, yes.

Taxon name: *Paranthropus boisei sensu stricto* (Leakey 1959); Robinson 1960

Temporal range: About 2.3–1.3 Ma.

How dated: Mainly from absolutely dated layers of ash above and below the sediments bearing the hominin fossils.

Initial discovery: OH 3—deciduous mandibular canine and molar, BK, Lower Bed II, Olduvai Gorge, Tanzania, 1955 (L. Leakey 1958).

Type specimen: OH 5—adolescent cranium, FLK, Bed I, Olduvai Gorge, Tanzania, 1959 (L. Leakey 1959).

Source(s) of the evidence: Olduvai and Peninj, Tanzania; Omo Shungura Formation and Konso, Ethiopia; Koobi Fora, Chesowanja, and West Turkana, Kenya; and Malema, Malawi.

Nature of the evidence: P. boisei s. s. has a comprehensive craniodental
fossil record. There are several skulls (the one from Konso being
remarkably complete and well preserved), several well-preserved
crania, and many mandibles and isolated teeth. There is evidence
of both large- and small-bodied individuals, and the range of the
size difference suggests a substantial degree of sexual dimorphism. There are no postcranial remains that can, with certainty,
be assigned to *P. boisei s. s.*

Characteristics and inferred behavior: Paranthropus boisei s. s. is the only
hominin to combine a massive, wide, flat face, massive premolars
and molars, small anterior teeth, and a modest endocranial volume (approximately 480 cm³). The face of *P. boisei s. s.* is larger
and wider than that of *P. robustus,* yet their brain volumes are
similar. The mandible of *P. boisei s. s.* has a larger and wider body
or corpus than any other hominin (see *P. aethiopicus* above).
The tooth crowns apparently grow at a faster rate than has been
recorded for any other early hominin. Unfortunately, there is no
postcranial evidence that can, with certainty, be attributed to *P.
boisei s. s.* The fossil record of *P. boisei sensu stricto* extends across
about one million years of time, during which there is little evidence of any substantial change in the size or shape of the components of the cranium, mandible, and dentition (Wood, Wood,
and Konigsberg 1994).

Life history related data: Dental development, yes; body mass, yes;
endocranial volume, yes.

Taxon name: *Paranthropus robustus* **Broom 1938**

Temporal range: About 2.0–1.5 Ma.

How dated: Relative dating based on matching mammalian fossils
found in the caves with fossils from absolutely dated sites in East
Africa.

Initial discovery: TM 1517—an adult, presumably male, cranium and
associated skeleton, "Phase II Breccia," now Mb3, Kromdraai B,
South Africa, 1938.

Type specimen: (See above.)

Source(s) of the evidence: Kromdraai, Swartkrans, Gondolin, Drimolen,
and Cooper's caves, all situated in the Blauuwbank Valley, near

Johannesburg, South Africa.

Nature of the evidence: The fossil record is similar to, but less than, that of *Au. africanus.* The dentition is very well represented, some of the cranial remains are well preserved, but most of the mandibles are crushed or distorted. The postcranial skeleton is not well represented. Research at Drimolen was initiated in 1992, yet more than eighty hominin specimens have already been recovered, and it promises to be a rich source of evidence about *P. robustus.*

Characteristics and inferred behavior: The brain, face, and chewing teeth of *P. robustus* are larger than those of *Au. africanus,* yet the incisor teeth are smaller. What little is known about the postcranial skeleton of *P. robustus* suggests that the morphology of the pelvis and the hip joint is much like that of *Au. africanus.* It was most likely capable of bipedal walking but was not an obligate biped. The thumb of *P. robustus,* it has been suggested, would have been capable of the type of grip necessary for stone tool manufacture, but not all researchers accept this claim.

Life history related data: Dental development, yes; body mass, yes; endocranial volume, yes.

Primitive Homo.

This group contains the earliest members of the genus *Homo.* Some researchers (such as Wood and Collard 1999a) have suggested that these taxa (*H. habilis sensu stricto* and *H. rudolfensis*) may not belong in the *Homo* clade. Until we can generate sound phylogenetic hypotheses about these taxa and the australopiths, it is not clear what their new generic attribution should be. For the purposes of this review, these two taxa are retained within *Homo.* It is also noteworthy that this group subsumes a wide range of absolute and relative brain size (see below).

Taxon name: *Homo habilis sensu stricto* **Leakey, Tobias, and Napier 1964**

Temporal range: About 2.4–1.6 Ma.

How dated: Absolute dates from layers of volcanic ash and basalt above and below the fossil horizons.

Initial discovery: OH 4—fragmented mandible, MK, Bed I, Olduvai Gorge, Tanzania, 1959.

Type specimen: OH 7—partial skull cap and hand bones, FLKNN, Bed I, Olduvai Gorge, Tanzania, 1960.

Source(s) of the evidence: Olduvai Gorge, Tanzania; Koobi Fora and perhaps Chemeron, Kenya; Omo (Shungura) and Hadar, Ethiopia, East Africa; and perhaps also Sterkfontein, Swartkrans, Kromdraai, and Drimolen, South Africa.

Nature of the evidence: Mostly cranial and dental evidence, with only a few postcranial bones that can, with some confidence, be assigned to *H. habilis s. s.*

Characteristics and inferred behavior: The endocranial volume of *H. habilis s. s.* ranges from just less than 500 cm^3 to about 600 cm^3. All the crania are wider at the base than across the vault, but the face is broadest in its upper part. The only postcranial fossils that can be assigned with confidence to *H. habilis s. s.* are the postcranial bones associated with the type specimen, OH 7, and the associated skeleton, OH 62. Isolated postcranial bones from Olduvai Gorge (for example, OH 10) could belong to *P. boisei s. s.* (B. Wood 1974). If OH 62 is representative of *H. habilis s. s.*, the skeletal evidence suggests that its limb proportions and locomotion were australopithlike. The curved proximal phalanges and well-developed muscle markings on the phalanges of OH 7 indicate that the hand of *H. habilis s. s.* was capable of the type of powerful grasping needed for arboreal activities. The inference that *H. habilis s. s.* was capable of spoken language was based on links between endocranial morphology, on the one hand, and language comprehension and production, on the other; these links are no longer valid.

Life history related data: Dental development, yes; body mass, yes; endocranial volume, yes.

Taxon name: *Homo rudolfensis* Alexeev 1986 (Groves 1989); Wood 1992

Temporal range: About 2.4–1.6 Ma.

How dated: Mainly, absolute dates for volcanic ash layers above and below the fossil horizons.

Initial discovery: KNM-ER 819—Area 1, Okote Member, Koobi Fora
  Formation, Koobi Fora, Kenya, 1971.

Type specimen: Lectotype—KNM-ER 1470, Area 131, Upper Burgi
  Member, Koobi Fora Formation, Koobi Fora, Kenya, 1972
  (R. Leakey 1973).

Source(s) of the evidence: Koobi Fora and perhaps Chemeron, Kenya;
  and Uraha, Malawi.

Nature of the evidence: Several incomplete crania, two well-preserved
  mandibles, and several isolated teeth.

Characteristics and inferred behavior: Homo rudolfensis and *H. habilis s. s.*
  show different mixtures of primitive and derived, or specialized,
  features. For example, the absolute size of the brain case is
  greater in *H. rudolfensis*, and its face is widest in its midpart,
  whereas the face of *H. habilis s. s.* is widest superiorly. Despite the
  absolute size of its brain (approximately 726 cc) when related to
  estimates of body mass, the brain of *H. rudolfensis* is not substantially larger than those of the australopiths. The more primitive
  face of *H. rudolfensis* is combined with a robust mandible and
  mandibular postcanine teeth with larger, broader crowns and
  more complex premolar root systems than those of *H. habilis s. s.*
  At present, no postcranial remains can be reliably linked with
  H. rudolfensis. The mandible and postcanine teeth are larger than
  one would predict for a generalized hominoid of the same estimated body mass, suggesting that its dietary niche made mechan-
  ical demands similar to those of the megadont australopiths.

Life history related data: Dental development, yes; body mass, yes;
  endocranial volume, yes.

Archaic Homo.

This group includes two Pleistocene *Homo* taxa that exhibit modern humanlike body proportions, are thought to be the first *Homo*
taxa for which obligate bipedalism is strongly supported, but possess
only medium-size brains. It also includes the recently discovered
Homo floresiensis, which is characterized as a *Homo erectus* descendent
that has undergone endemic dwarfing on the island of Flores,
Indonesia.

Taxon name: *Homo ergaster* **Groves and Mazák 1975**

Temporal range: About 1.9–1.5 Ma.

How dated: Mainly, absolute dates for volcanic ash layers above and below the fossil horizons.

Initial discovery: KNM-ER 730—corpus of an adult mandible with worn teeth, Area 103, KBS Member, Koobi Fora, Kenya, 1970.

Type specimen: KNM-ER 992—well-preserved adult mandible, Area 3, Okote Member, Koobi Fora Formation, Koobi Fora, Kenya, 1971.

Source(s) of the evidence: Koobi Fora and West Turkana, Kenya; and possibly Dmanisi, Georgia.

Nature of the evidence: Cranial, mandibular, and dental evidence and an associated skeleton of a juvenile male individual from Nariokotome, West Turkana.

Characteristics and inferred behavior: Two sets of features are claimed to distinguish *H. ergaster* from *H. erectus s. s.* The first comprises features for which *H. ergaster* is more primitive than *H. erectus s. s.*, with the most compelling evidence coming from details of the mandibular premolars. The second set comprises features of the vault and base of the cranium for which *H. ergaster* is less specialized, or derived, than *H. erectus s. s.* Overall, *H. ergaster* is the first hominin to combine modern human-size chewing teeth with a postcranial skeleton (such as long legs and a large femoral head) apparently committed to long-range bipedalism. It lacks morphological features associated with arboreal locomotion. The small chewing teeth of *H. ergaster* imply that it was either eating different food than the australopiths or was consuming the same food but preparing it extra-orally. This preparation could have involved the use of stone tools, cooking, or a combination of the two. Although its dentition and postcranial skeleton are much more like those of later *Homo* than the australopiths', the absolute endocranial capacity of *H. ergaster* (mean = about 760 cc) does not reach the levels seen in later *Homo*. When scaled to body mass, it shows little advance over the levels seen in the australopiths (Wood and Collard 1999b).

Life history related data: Dental development, yes; body mass, yes; endocranial volume, yes.

Taxon name: *Homo erectus sensu stricto* **(Dubois 1892); Weidenreich 1940**

Temporal range: About 1.8 Ma to 200,000 years ago (Ka).

How dated: A mixture of biochronology and a few absolute dates that are tenuously linked with the fossiliferous horizons.

Initial discovery: Kedung Brubus 1—mandible fragment, Kedung Brubus, Java (now Indonesia), 1890.

Type specimen: Trinil 2—adult calotte, Trinil, Ngawi, Java (now Indonesia), 1891.

Source(s) of the evidence: Sites in Indonesia (such as Trinil, Sangiran, and Sambungmachan), China (such as Zhoukoudian and Lantian), and Africa (such as Olduvai Gorge and Melka Kunture).

Nature of the evidence: Mainly cranial, with some postcranial evidence but little or no evidence of the hand or foot.

Characteristics and inferred behavior: The crania belonging to *H. erectus s. s.* have a low vault, a substantial more-or-less continuous torus above the orbits, and a sharply angulated occipital region. The inner and outer tables of the cranial vault are thick. The body of the mandible is less robust than that of the australopiths. In this respect, it resembles *Homo sapiens*, except that the symphyseal region lacks the well-marked chin that is a feature of later *Homo* and modern humans. The tooth crowns are generally larger and the premolar roots more complicated than those of modern humans. The cortical bone of the postcranial skeleton is thicker than is the case in modern humans. The limb bones are modern humanlike in their proportions and have robust shafts, but the shafts of the long bones of the lower limb are flattened from front to back (femur) and side to side (tibia) relative to those of modern humans. All the dental and cranial evidence points to a modern humanlike diet for *H. erectus s. s.*, and the postcranial elements are consistent with a habitually upright posture and obligate, long-range bipedalism. There is no fossil evidence relevant to assessing the dexterity of *H. erectus s. s.*, but if *H. erectus s. s.* manufactured Acheulean artifacts, then dexterity would be implicit.

Life history related data: Dental development, yes; body mass, yes; endocranial volume, yes.

Taxon name: *Homo floresiensis* **Brown et al. 2004**

Temporal range: About 95–18 Ka.

How dated: Radiocarbon, luminescence, uranium-series, and electron spin resonance dates on associated sediments and faunal specimens and dated horizons above and below skeletal material (Morwood et al. 2004).

Initial fossil discovery: LB1—associated partial adult skeleton.

Type specimen: LB1—associated partial adult skeleton.

Source(s) of the evidence: Known only from Liang Bua, a cave 500 m above sea level and 25 km from the north coast of Flores. The cave is in a limestone hill on the southern edge of the Wae Racang Valley.

Nature of the evidence: A partial adult skeleton (LB1) with some components still articulated, as well as cranial and postcranial remains of other individuals (Morwood et al. 2005).

Characteristics and inferred behavior: This hominin displays a unique combination of *H. ergaster*-like cranial and dental morphology, a hitherto unknown suite of pelvic and femoral features, a small brain (approximately 380 cm^3), small body mass (25–30 kg), and small stature (1 m).

Taxonomic note: The researchers responsible for the find decided to recognize its morphological affinities with *Homo*, despite the small brain size, and to refer LB1 to a new species within the genus *Homo*.

Life history related data: Dental development, no; body mass, no; endocranial volume, yes (but not included in this analysis).

Homo *Taxa of Modern Human Aspect.*
This group includes hominin taxa that are similar, if not identical, to modern humans in body size, body proportions, brain size, and dental morphology.

Taxon name: *Homo antecessor* **Bermúdez de Castro et al. 1997**

Temporal range: About 700–500 Ka.

How dated: Biochronology.

Initial discovery: ATD6-1—left mandibular canine, Level 6, Gran Dolina, Spain, 1994.

Type specimen: ATD6-5—mandible and associated teeth, Level 6, Gran Dolina, Spain, 1994.

Source(s) of the evidence: Gran Dolina, Atapuerca, Spain.

Nature of the evidence: The partial cranium of a juvenile, parts of mandibles and maxillae, and isolated teeth.

Characteristics and inferred behavior: Researchers who found the remains claim that the combination of a modern humanlike facial morphology with the large and primitive crowns and roots of the teeth is not seen in *H. heidelbergensis* (see below). The Gran Dolina remains also show no sign of any derived *H. neanderthalensis* traits. Its discoverers suggest that *H. antecessor* is the last common ancestor of *Neanderthals* and *H. sapiens*.

Life history related data: Dental development, no; body mass, no; endocranial volume, yes.

Taxon name: *Homo heidelbergensis* **Schoetensack 1908**

Temporal range: About 600–100 Ka.

How dated: Mostly biochronological, with some uranium series and ESR absolute dates.

Initial discovery: Mauer 1—adult mandible, Mauer, Heidelberg, Germany, 1907.

Type specimen: (See above.)

Source(s) of the evidence: Sites in Europe (such as Mauer, Petralona); Near East (such as Zuttiyeh); Africa (such as Kabwe, Bodo); China (such as Dali, Jinniushan, Xujiayao, and Yunxian); and possibly India (such as Hathnora).

Nature of the evidence: Many crania but little mandibular and postcranial evidence.

Characteristics and inferred behavior: What set this material apart from *H. sapiens* and *Homo neanderthalensis* (see below) are the morphology of the cranium and the robusticity of the postcranial skeleton. Some brain cases are as large as those of modern humans but are always more robustly built, with a thickened occipital region, a projecting face, and large separate ridges above the orbits, unlike the more continuous brow ridge of *H. erectus s. s.* Compared with *H. erectus s. s.* (see above), the parietals are expanded, the occipital is more rounded, and the frontal bone is broader. The crania of *H. heidelbergensis* lack the specialized features of *H. neanderthalensis,* such as the anteriorly projecting midface and the distinctive swelling of the occipital region.

H. heidelbergensis is the earliest hominin to have a brain as large as anatomically modern *H. sapiens,* and its postcranial skeleton suggests that its robust long bones and large lower-limb joints were well suited to long-distance bipedal walking.

Taxonomic note: Researchers who see distinctions between the African part and the rest of this hypodigm refer the former component to *Homo rhodesiensis.*

Life history related data: Dental development, no; body mass, yes; endocranial volume, yes.

Taxon name: *Homo neanderthalensis* King 1864

Temporal range: About 200–30 Ka.

How dated: A mix of techniques, including radiocarbon, uranium series, and ESR.

Initial discovery: Engis 1—a child's cranium, Engis, Belgium, 1829.

Type specimen: Neanderthal 1—adult calotte and partial skeleton, Feldhofer Cave, Elberfield, Germany, 1856.

Source(s) of the evidence: Fossil evidence for *H. neanderthalensis* has been found throughout Europe (with the exception of Scandinavia), as well as in the Near East, the Levant, and western Asia.

Nature of the evidence: Many are burials, so all anatomical regions are represented in the fossil record.

Characteristics and inferred behavior: The distinctive features of the cranium of *H. neanderthalensis* include thick, double-arched brow ridges; a face that projects anteriorly in the midline; a large nose; laterally projecting and rounded parietal bones; and a rounded, posteriorly projecting occipital bone (that is, an occipital "bun"). The endocranial volume of *H. neanderthalensis* is, on average, larger than that of modern humans. Mandibular and dental features include a retromolar space and distinctively high incidences of nonmetrical dental traits. Postcranially, Neanderthals were stout, with a broad rib cage, a long clavicle, a wide pelvis, and generally robust limb bones with well-developed muscle insertions. The distal extremities tend to be short compared with most modern *H. sapiens*, but Neanderthals were evidently obligate bipeds. The generally well-marked muscle attachments and the relative thickness of long bone shafts point to a strenuous lifestyle. The size and wear on the incisors suggest that the Neanderthals regularly used their anterior teeth as "tools" for food preparation or for gripping hide or similar material.

Taxonomic note: The scope of the hypodigm of *H. neanderthalensis* depends on how inclusively the taxon is defined. For some researchers, the taxon is restricted to fossils from Europe and the Near East that used to be referred to as "Classic" Neanderthals. Others interpret the taxon more inclusively and recognize, within the hypodigm, fossil evidence that is generally older and less derived (for example, Steinheim, Swanscombe, and Atapuerca [Sima de los Huesos]).

Recent developments: Researchers have recovered short fragments of mitochondrial DNA from the humerus of the Neanderthal type specimen (Krings et al. 1997; Krings et al. 1999). The fossil sequence falls well outside the range of variation in a diverse sample of modern humans. Researchers suggest that Neanderthals would unlikely have made any contribution to the modern human gene pool, estimating that this amount of difference points to 550–690 Kyr of separation. Subsequently, mtDNA has been recovered at other Neanderthal sites, from rib fragments of a child's skeleton at Mezmaiskaya (Ovchinnikov et al. 2000), Vindija (Krings et al. 2000), Les Rochers-de-Villeneuve (Beauval et al. 2005), and El Sidrón (Lalueza-Fox et al. 2005). The differences among the fossil mtDNA fragments studied are similar to the differences among the same number of randomly selected African modern humans, but the differences between the fossil mtDNA and that of modern humans are substantial and significant (Knight 2003). The fragments of mtDNA that have been studied are short, but repeating the findings of the three studies summarized by Krings and colleagues (2000) for other parts of the genome would greatly strengthen the case for placing Neanderthals in a separate species from modern humans on the basis of their skeletal peculiarities.

Life history related data: Dental development, yes; body mass, yes; endocranial volume, yes.

Taxon name: *Homo sapiens sensu stricto* **Linnaeus 1758**

Temporal range: About 190–200 Ka to the present day.

How dated: A mix of techniques, including radiocarbon, uranium series, ESR, and some $^{40}\text{Ar}/^{39}\text{Ar}$ dates.

Initial fossil discovery: With hindsight, the first recorded evidence to be recovered was the "Red Lady of Paviland," Wales, 1824.

Type specimen: Linnaeus did not designate a type specimen.

Source(s) of the evidence: Fossil evidence of *H. sapiens* has been recovered from sites on all continents except Antarctica. The earliest absolutely dated remains are from Kibish (Omo) and Herto in Ethiopia (McDougall et al. 2005; White et al. 2003).

Nature of the evidence: Many are burials, so the fossil evidence is good. In some regions of the world (such as West Africa), however, remains are few and far between.

Characteristics and inferred behavior: The earliest evidence of anatomically modern human morphology in the fossil record comes from sites in Africa and the Near East. Also in Africa is evidence for a likely morphological precursor of anatomically modern human morphology. This takes the form of crania that are generally more robust and archaic-looking than those of anatomically modern humans yet not archaic enough to justify their allocation to *H. heidelbergensis* or derived enough to be *H. neanderthalensis* (see above). Specimens in this category include Jebel Irhoud from North Africa, Omo 2 and Laetoli 18 from East Africa, and Florisbad and Cave of Hearths in southern Africa. Undoubtedly, an existing gradation in morphology makes it difficult to set the boundary between anatomically modern humans and *H. heidelbergensis*. Unless at least one other taxon is recognized, however, the variation in the later *Homo* fossil record is too great to be accommodated in a single taxon.

Taxonomic note: Researchers who want to make a taxonomic distinction between fossils such as Florisbad, Omo 2, and Laetoli 18 and subrecent and living modern humans refer the earlier African subset to *Homo* (*Africanthropus*) *helmei* (Dreyer 1935).

Life history related data: Dental development, yes; body mass, yes; endocranial volume, yes.

APPENDIX 2

Lumping (Less Speciose) Hominin Taxonomy

Basal Australopiths.

Only one genus and species, *Ardipithecus ramidus sensu lato*, is recognized in the more inclusive taxonomy. This taxon incorporates remains attributed to *S. tchadensis* and *O. tugenensis*.

Taxon name: *Ardipithecus ramidus sensu lato* **(White, Suwa, and Asfaw 1994); White, Suwa, and Asfaw 1995**

Temporal range: About 7.0–4.5 Ma.

How dated: Biochronological dating for the older part of the hypodigm and absolutely dated layers of volcanic ash above and below the fossil-bearing sediments for the approximately 5 Ma evidence.

Initial discovery: ARA-VP-1/1—right M3, Aramis, Middle Awash, Ethiopia, 1993 (White, Suwa, and Asfaw 1994). (n.b. If a mandible, KNM-LT 329, from Lothagam, Kenya, proves to belong to the hypodigm, this would be the initial discovery.)

Type specimen: ARA-VP-6/1—associated upper and lower dentition, Aramis, Middle Awash, Ethiopia, 1993 (White, Suwa, and Asfaw 1994).

Source(s) of the evidence: Aramis and other localities, Middle Awash,
Ethiopia; Lukeino, Kenya; and Toros-Menalla, Chad.

Nature of the evidence: The published evidence consists of a partial
cranium, a piece of the base of the cranium, fragments of
mandibles, isolated teeth, and long bones.

Characteristics and inferred behavior: The remains attributed to *A.
ramidus s. l.* have some features in common with living species of
Pan, others with the African apes in general. Crucially, several
dental and cranial features are shared only with later hominins.

Life history related data: Dental development, no; body mass, yes;
endocranial volume, yes

Australopiths.

In the more lumping taxonomy, one monospecific genus,
Kenyanthropus, and two *Australopithecus* species, *Au. bahrelghazali* and
Au. anamensis, are sunk into *Au. afarensis sensu lato*. Otherwise, the
taxa remain the same as in the splitting taxonomy.

**Taxon name: *Australopithecus afarensis sensu lato* Johanson, White, and
Coppens 1978**

Temporal range: About 4.5–3.0 Ma.

How dated: Absolutely dated layers of ash above and below the sediments bearing the hominin fossils.

Initial discovery: AL 128-1—left proximal femur fragment, Sidi
Hakoma Member, Hadar Formation, Afar, Ethiopia, 1973
(Johanson and Taieb 1976).

Type specimen: LH 4—adult mandible, Laetolil Beds, Laetoli, Tanzania,
1974.

Source(s) of the evidence: Laetoli, Tanzania; White Sands, Hadar, Maka,
Belohdelie, and Fejej, Ethiopia; Allia Bay, Lothagam, West
Turkana, and Tabarin, Kenya; and Koro Toro, Chad.

Nature of the evidence: Au. afarensis s. l. is the earliest hominin to have a
comprehensive fossil record that includes a skull, fragmented
skulls, many lower jaws, and sufficient limb bones to be able to
estimate stature and body mass. The best-preserved postcranial
specimen in the enlarged hypodigm is still the partial skeleton of

an adult female, AL-288.

Characteristics and inferred behavior: The parameters of the more inclusive interpretation of *Au. afarensis s. l.* are much the same as those for *Au. afarensis s. s.*, except that the body mass of some individuals of the more inclusive taxon may be larger and there may be a greater range of postcranial morphology.

Life history related data: Dental development, yes; body mass, yes; endocranial volume, yes.

Megadont Australopiths.

In the more inclusive taxonomy, two species, *P. aethiopicus* and *Au. garhi*, are sunk into *P. boisei sensu lato.* Otherwise, the taxa remain the same as in the splitting taxonomy.

Taxon name: *Paranthropus boisei sensu lato* **(Leakey 1959); Robinson 1960**

Temporal range: About 2.5–1.3 Ma.

How dated: Mainly from absolutely dated layers of ash above and below the sediments bearing the hominin fossils.

Initial discovery: OH 3—deciduous mandibular canine and molar, BK, Lower Bed II, Olduvai Gorge, Tanzania, 1955 (L. Leakey 1958).

Type specimen: OH 5—adolescent cranium, FLK, Bed I, Olduvai Gorge, Tanzania, 1959 (L. Leakey 1959).

Source(s) of the evidence: Olduvai and Peninj, Tanzania; Omo Shungura Formation and Konso, Ethiopia; Koobi Fora, Chesowanja, and West Turkana, Kenya; and Malema, Malawi.

Characteristics and inferred behavior: Paranthropus boisei sensu lato is the only hominin to combine a massive, wide, flat face; massive premolars and molars; and a modest-size neurocranium (approximately 470 cm^3). The face of *P. boisei s. l.* is larger and wider than that of *P. robustus*, yet their brain volumes are similar. The mandible of *P. boisei s. l.* has a larger and wider body or corpus than any other hominin. The tooth crowns apparently grow at a faster rate than has been recorded for any other early hominin. Unfortunately, there is no postcranial evidence that can, with certainty, be attributed to *P. boisei s. l.* The fossil record of *P. boisei s. l.*

extends across more than one million years of time, during which there is evidence of only one significant episode (approximately 2.3 Ma) of any significant change in the size and shape of the mandible and dentition (Suwa 1988; Wood, Wood, and Konigsberg 1994).

Life history related data: Dental development, yes; body mass, yes; endocranial volume, yes.

Primitive Homo.

In the lumping taxonomy, *H. habilis sensu lato* subsumes *H. rudolfensis* and *H. habilis s. s.*

Taxon name: *Homo habilis sensu lato* **Leakey, Tobias, and Napier 1964**
Temporal range: About 2.4–1.6 Ma.
How dated: Absolute dates from layers of volcanic ash and basalt above and below the fossil horizons.
Initial discovery: OH 4—fragmented mandible, MK, Bed I, Olduvai Gorge, Tanzania, 1959.
Type specimen: OH 7—partial skull cap and hand bones, FLKNN, Bed 1, Olduvai Gorge, Tanzania, 1960.
Source(s) of the evidence: Olduvai Gorge, Tanzania; Koobi Fora and perhaps Chemeron, Kenya; Omo (Shungura) and Hadar, Ethiopia; and perhaps Sterkfontein, Swartkrans, and Drimolen, South Africa.
Nature of the evidence: Mostly cranial and dental evidence, with only a few postcranial bones that can, with some confidence, be assigned to *H. habilis s. l.*
Characteristics and inferred behavior: The mean endocranial volume of *H. habilis sensu lato* is 648 cm³. All the crania are wider at the base than across the vault, but the location of the maximum breadth of the face varies. In some individuals, it is the upper face, and in others, the midface. The only postcranial evidence that can, with confidence, be assigned to *H. habilis s. l.* is the following: the postcranial bones associated with the type specimen, OH 7, and the associated skeleton, OH 62. If OH 62 is representative of *H. habilis s. l.*, then the skeletal evidence suggests that its limb pro-

portions and locomotion were australopithlike. The curved proximal phalanges and well-developed muscle markings on the phalanges of OH 7 also indicate that the hand was used for more powerful grasping (such as would be needed for arboreal activities) than is the case in any other species of *Homo*. The inference that *H. habilis s. l.* was capable of spoken language was based on links between endocranial morphology, on the one hand, and language comprehension and production, on the other; these links are no longer valid.

Life history related data: Dental development, yes; body mass, yes; endocranial volume, yes.

Archaic Homo.

In the more inclusive taxonomy, *H. erectus sensu lato* subsumes *H. erectus s. s.*, *H. ergaster*, and *H. floresiensis* (although the reader is reminded that the LHRVs associated with this taxon were not included in the analyses).

Taxon name: *Homo erectus sensu lato* (Dubois 1892); Weidenreich 1940

Temporal range: About 1.8 Ma–18 Ka.

How dated: A mixture of biochronology and a few poorly correlated absolute dates.

Initial discovery: Mandible fragment at a site called "Kedung Brubus," Java (now Indonesia), 1890.

Type specimen: Trinil 2—adult calotte, Trinil, Ngawi, Java (now Indonesia), 1891.

Source(s) of the evidence: Sites in Indonesia (such as Trinil, Sangiran, and Sambungmachan), China (such as Zhoukoudian and Lantian), and Africa (such as Olduvai Gorge and Melka Kunture).

Nature of the evidence: Mainly cranial, with some postcranial evidence, but little or no evidence of the hand or foot.

Characteristics and inferred behavior: The crania of *H. erectus s. l.* have a low vault and a substantial, more-or-less continuous torus above the orbits; the occipital region varies from weakly to sharply angulated. The inner and outer tables of the cranial vault vary in thickness. The body of the mandible is less robust than that of the australopiths, but no more robust than that of modern humans when body size is taken into account. The mandibles lack the well-marked chin that is a feature of modern humans. The tooth crowns are generally larger and the premolar roots more complicated than those of modern humans, but relative to body size, there is no evidence of any postcanine megadontia. The cortical bone of some postcranial remains is generally thicker than is the case in modern humans. The limb bones are modern humanlike in their proportions and have robust shafts, but the shafts of some of the long bones of the lower limb are flattened from front to back (femur) and side to side (tibia) relative to those of modern humans. All the dental and cranial evidence points to a modern humanlike diet for *H. erectus s. l.*, and the postcranial elements are consistent with a habitually upright posture and obligate, long-range bipedalism. There is no fossil evidence relevant to assessing the dexterity of *H. erectus s. l.*, but if *H. erectus s. l.* manufactured Acheulean artifacts, then dexterity would be implicit.

Life history related data: Dental development, yes; body mass, yes; endocranial volume, yes.

Homo *of Modern Aspect.*

In the lumping taxonomy, *H. sapiens s. l.* subsumes *H. antecessor*, *H. heidelbergensis*, *H. neanderthalensis*, and *H. sapiens s. s.* An even more conservative taxonomy (for example, Wolpoff et al. 1994; Tobias 1995) suggests that all taxa within *Homo*, including *H. erectus s. l.*, should be sunk into *H. sapiens sensu lato*.

Taxon name: *Homo sapiens sensu lato* Linnaeus 1758

Temporal range: About 600 Ka to the present day.

How dated: A mix of techniques, including radiocarbon, uranium series, and ESR.

Initial fossil discovery: With hindsight, the first evidence to be recovered was the "Red Lady of Paviland," Wales, 1824.

Type specimen: Linnaeus did not designate a type specimen.

Source(s) of the evidence: Fossil evidence, if *H. sapiens s. l.* has been recovered from sites on all continents except Antarctica.

Nature of the evidence: Many are burials, so the fossil evidence is good. In some regions of the world (such as West Africa), however, remains are few and far between.

Characteristics and inferred behavior: The earliest evidence for this taxon comes from sites such as Kabwe and Bodo in Africa. This takes the form of crania that are generally more robust and archaic-looking than those of anatomically modern humans yet lack the derived features of *H. erectus s. l.*

Life history related data: Dental development, yes; body mass, yes; endocranial volume, yes.

APPENDIX 3

Notes for Body Mass and Brain Size Data Used in Tables 11.3 and 11.4

TABLE 11.3 BODY MASS ESTIMATES

Splitting Taxonomy

Ar. ramidus s. s. Wood and Richmond (2000). Estimate based on the observation that the shoulder joint size of *Ar. ramidus* is 30 percent larger than that of AL 288-1 (30 kg).

Au. anamensis. Male estimate from Leakey and colleagues (1995). The female estimate is from McHenry and Coffing (2000) and is derived from the male estimate using their ratio of male to female body mass from *Au. afarensis.*

Au. afarensis s. s. Adapted from McHenry (1992). Based on AL 333-3, 333-4, 333-7, 333w-56, 333x-26 for male and on 129-1a, 129-1b, 288-1, 333-6 for female.

Au. africanus. Adapted from McHenry (1992). Based on Sts 34, Stw 99, 311, 389 for male and on Sts 14, Stw 25, 102, 347, 358, 392, TM 1512 for female.

P. aethiopicus. Taken from Kappelman (1996). Based on KNM-WT 17000 for male.

P. boisei s. s. Adapted from McHenry (1992). Based on KNM-ER 1464 for male and on KNM-ER 1500 for female.

P. robustus. Adapted from McHenry (1992). Based on SK 82, 97 for male and on SK 3155, TM 1517 for female.

H. habilis s. s. Adapted from McHenry (1992). Based on KNM-ER 3735 (1503) for male and on OH 8, 35 for female.

H. rudolfensis. Adapted from McHenry (1992). Based on KNM-ER 1481, 3228 for male and on KNM-ER 813, 1472 for female. Some or all of these specimens possibly belong to *H. ergaster* and not *H. rudolfensis.*

H. ergaster. Adapted from Ruff, Trinkaus, and Holliday (1997). Based on KNM-ER 736, 1808, KNM-WT 15000 for male and on KNM-ER 737 for female.

H. erectus s. s. Taken from Aiello and Wood (1994; Sangiran 17 = male) and Kappelman (1996; Zhoukoudian XI = female) and adapted from Ruff, Trinkaus, and Holliday (1997; OH 28 and OH 34 = female; Zhoukoudian FeIV = no sex determination).

H. heidelbergensis. Adapted from Ruff, Trinkaus, and Holliday (1997); Rosenberg, Lu, and Ruff (1999; Jinniushan); and Arsuaga and colleagues (1999; Atapuerca-SH-1). Species estimate is based on Atapuerca (SH) Pelvis 1 (m), Broken Hill 689, Broken Hill 690, Broken Hill 691, Broken Hill 719 (m), Broken Hill 907, Boxgrove 1 (m), Jinniushan (f), Arago 44 (m), Gesher-Benot-Ya'acov, KNM-BK 66, and Ain Maarouf 1. Male (n = 4) and female (n =1) estimates are based on sex determinations taken from references and are denoted by (m) and (f), respectively.

H. neanderthalensis. Adapted from Ruff, Trinkaus, and Holliday (1997). Species estimate is based on Amud 1 (m), La Chapelle-aux-Saints (m), La Ferrassie 1 (m), La Ferrassie 2 (f), Kebara 2 (m), Neanderthal 1 (m), La Quina 5, Regourdou 1, Saint-Cesaire 1 (m), Spy 1 (f), Spy 2 (m), Shanidar 1 (m), Shanidar 3 (m), Shanidar 5 (m), Krapina 207 (m), Krapina 208 (f), Krapina 209 (f), Krapina 213 (m), Krapina 214 (f), Shanidar 2 (m), Shanidar 4 (m), Shanidar 6 (f), and Tabun C1 (f). Male (n = 14) and female (n = 7) estimates are based on sex determinations taken from Ruff, Trinkaus, and Holliday (1997) and are denoted by (m) and (f), respectively.

H. sapiens s. s. Adapted from Ruff, Trinkaus, and Holliday (1997). Species estimate is based on Qafzeh 3 (f), Qafzeh 7 (m), Qafzeh 8 (m), Qafzeh 9 (f), Skhul 4 (m), Skhul 5 (m), Skhul 6 (m), Skhul 7 (m), Skhul 7a (f), Skhul 9 (m), and 104 specimens (49 male, 31 female, and 24 unsexed) dated to 10–35ky BP. Male (n = 56) and female (n = 36) estimates are based on sex determinations from Ruff, Trinkaus, and Holliday (1997) and are denoted by (m) and (f), respectively.

Lumping Taxonomy

Au. afarensis s. l. Includes specimens attributed to *Au. afarensis s. s.* and *Au. anamensis.* Sample sizes: species estimate (n = 11); male (n = 6), female (n = 5).

P. boisei s. l. Includes specimens attributed to *P. boisei s. s.* and *P. aethiopicus.* Sample sizes: species estimate (n = 3); male (n = 2), female (n = 1).

H. habilis s. l. Includes specimens attributed to *H. habilis s. s.* and *H. rudolfensis.* Sample sizes: species estimate (n = 7); male (n = 3), female (n = 4). Some or all of the specimens attributed to *H. rudolfensis* in this calculation might actually belong to *H. ergaster. H. erectus s. l.* includes specimens attributed to *H. erectus s. s.* and *H. ergaster.* Sample sizes: species estimate (n = 9); male (n = 4), female (n = 4).

H. sapiens s. l. Includes specimens attributed to *H. sapiens s. s., H. neanderthalensis,* and *H. heidelbergensis.* Sample sizes: species estimate (n = 148); male (n = 74), female (n = 42).

TABLE 11.4 CRANIAL CAPACITY ESTIMATES

Splitting Taxonomy

S. tchadensis. Based on TM 266-01-060-1 (Zollikofer et al. 2005).

Au. afarensis s. s. Based on AL 162-28, 333-45 (Delson et al. 2000), 333-105 (adult estimate; Holloway 1983b), 444-2 (Kimbel, Rak, and

Johanson 2004).

Au. africanus. Based on MLD 1, 37/38; Sts 19/58, 5, 60, 71; Taung (adult estimate; Delson et al. 2000); Stw 505 (550 cc; Holloway, personal communication 2003).

Au. garhi. Based on BOU-VP-12/130 (Asfaw et al. 1999).

P. aethiopicus. Based on KNM-WT 17000 (Walker et al. 1986).

P. boisei s. s. Based on KGA 10-125 (Suwa et al. 1997), KNM-ER 406, 13750; Omo L338y-6 (Delson et al. 2000), KNM-ER 407, 732; OH 5 (Falk et al. 2000), KNM-ER 23000; Omo 323-1976-896, KNM-WT 17400 (Brown et al. 1993); and KNM-ER 13750 (Holloway 1988).

P. robustus. Based on SK 1585 (Falk et al. 2000), TM 1517 (Broom and Robinson 1948).

H. habilis s. s. Based on KNM-ER 1805, 1813; OH 7, 13, 24 (Delson et al. 2000), OH 16 (adult estimate; Tobias 1971).

H. rudolfensis. Based on KNM-ER 1470, 1590, 3732 (Delson et al. 2000).

H. ergaster. Based on D2280, 2282 (Gabunia et al. 2000), 2700 (Vekua et al. 2002); KNM-ER 3733, 3883 (Delson et al. 2000); KNM-WT 15000 (Begun and Walker 1993). Note that the inclusion of the recently discovered KNM-ER 42700 does not change the average cranial capacity of *H. ergaster* by more than 10 cm^3 if the actual capacity is close to 720, as tentatively reported (Leakey et al. 2003).

H. erectus s. s. Based on BOU-VP-2/66 (Asfaw et al. 2002); Ceprano (Ascenzi et al. 2000); Gongwangling 1/Lantian (Woo 1966); Hexian/PA 830 (Wu and Dong 1982); Narmada/Hathnora (mean of 1155 and 1421 cc in Wolpoff 1999); Ngandong 1, 5, 6, 10, 11; Sambungmacan 1; Sangiran 4/Pith IV (Delson et al. 2000); Ngandong 7, 12; Sangiran 2/Pith II, 10/Pith VI, 17/Pith VIII; Trinil 2/Pith I; Zhoukoudian II/D, X/L1, XI/L2, XII/L3 (Grimaud-Herve 1997); Ngandong 9; Zhoukoudian III/E1, Zhoukoudian VI (Weidenreich 1943); Ngawi (Wolpoff cited in Antón 2002b); OH 9, 12 (Holloway 1983b); Perning 1/Mojokerto (adult estimate; Antón 1997); PL-1/Poyolo (Mowbray et al. 2000); Sambungmacan 3

(Márquez et al. 2001), 4 (Baba et al. 2003); Nanjing 1 (Liu, Zhang, and Wu n.d.); Sangiran 12/Pith VII (Holloway 1981a), Sangiran IX (Anton and Swisher III, personal communication 2003); and Zhoukoudian V/H3 (Chiu et al. 1973).

H. antecessor. Based on ATD-15 (Bermúdez de Castro et al. 1997).

H. heidelbergensis. Based on Arago 21; Broken Hill-1/Kabwe; Petralona 1; Reilingen; Swanscombe 1; Vertesszollos II (Delson et al. 2000); Atapuerca 4, 5 (Arsuaga et al. 1997), 6 (Ruff, Trinkaus, and Holliday 1997); Bodo (Conroy et al. 2000); Dali 1 (Wu 1981); Florisbad (Beaumont and colleagues cited in Aiello and Dean 1990); Jinniushan (Wolpoff 1999); Ndutu (Brauer 1984); Saldanha/Hopefield /Elandsfontein (Drennan cited in Brauer 1984); Sale (Holloway 1981b); and Steinheim (Ruff, Trinkaus, and Holliday 1997).

H. neanderthalensis. Based on Amud 1; Biache-Saint Vaast; Ganovce 1; Krapina 2/B, 3/C, 4/D; La Quina 5; Monte Circeo I/Guattari 1; Neanderthal; Saccopastore I, II; Tabun C1 (Delson et al. 2000); Ehringsdorf 9; Gibraltar 1; La Chapelle-aux-Saints; La Ferrassie 1; Le Moustier 1; Teshik-Tash 1 (Grimaud-Herve 1997); La Quina 18 (adult estimate); Shanidar 5 (Ruff, Trinkaus, and Holliday 1997), 1 (Stewart cited in Day 1986); and Spy 1, 2 (Holloway 1983b).

H. sapiens s. s. Arene Candide 1, 1-IP, 2, 4, 5; Barma Grande 2; Bruniquel 2; Cap Blanc 1; Dolni Vestonice III; Grotte des Enfants 4, 5, 6; Minatogawa 1, 2, 4; Mladec 1; Nazlet Khater 1; Oberkassel 2; Paderbourne; Pataud 1; Qafzeh 11; San Teodoro 1, 2, 3, 5; St. Germain-la-Riviere 1; Veryier 1; Zhoukoudian Upper Cave 1, 2, 3 (Ruff, Trinkaus, and Holliday 1997); Asselar (Tobias 1971); Border Cave 1 (de Villiers 1973); BOU-VP-16/1 (White et al. 2003); Brno II and III; Dolni Vestonice XIII, XIV, XV, XVI; Pavlov 1 (Vlcek cited in Schwartz and Tattersall 2002); Combe-Cappelle; Predmosti 3, 9 (Grimaud-Herve 1997); Cro-Magnon 3; Mladec 2, 5 (Wolpoff 1999); Eyasi 1 (Protsch cited in Brauer 1984); Jebel Irhoud 1 (Holloway 1981b), 2 (Ennouchi cited in Brauer 1984); Kanjera 1 (Coon cited in Brauer 1984); LH 18/Ngaloba (Brauer 1984); Omo-Kibish 1, 2 (Day cited in Brauer 1984); Qafzeh 6 (Vallois and Vandermeersch 1972), 9

(Genet-Varcin cited in Brauer 1984); Singa 1 (Wells cited in Stringer 1979); Skhul 4 (McCown and Keith cited in Brauer 1984); Brno I; Chancelade 1;
Cro-Magnon 1; Oberkassel 1; Predmosti 4, 10; Skhul 5, 9; and Yinkou (Delson et al. 2000).

Lumping Taxonomy

P. boisei s. l. Includes specimens attributed to *P. boisei s. s.* and *P. aethiopicus.*

H. habilis s. l. Includes specimens attributed to *H. habilis s. s.* and *H. rudolfensis.*

H. erectus s. l. Includes specimens attributed to *H. erectus s. s.* and *H. ergaster.*

H. sapiens s. l. Includes specimens attributed to *H. sapiens s. s., H. neanderthalensis, H. heidelbergensis, H. antecessor,* and Fontechevade (Delson et al. 2000).

References

Acsadi, G., and J. Nemeskeri
1970 History of Human Lifespan and Mortality. Budapest: Akademai Kiado.

Adair, L. S., E. Pollitt, and W. H. Mueller
1983 Maternal Anthropometric Changes during Pregnancy and Lactation in a Rural Taiwanese Population. Human Biology 55:771–787.

Adair, L. S., and B. M. Popkin
1992 Prolonged Lactation Contributes to Depletion of Maternal Energy Reserves in Filipino Women. Journal of Nutrition 122:1643–1655.

Adoutte A., G. Balavoine, N. Lartillot, O. Lespinet, B. Prud'homme, and R. de Rosa
2000 The New Animal Phylogeny: Reliability and Implications. Proceedings of the National Academy of Sciences USA 97:4453–4456.

Agrawal, A. F., E. D. Brodie, and J. Brown
2001 Parent-Offspring Coadaptation and the Dual Genetic Control of Maternal Care. Science 292:1710–1712.

Agresti, A., and B. Finlay
1997 Statistical Methods for the Social Sciences. 2d ed. Upper Saddle River, NJ: Prentice-Hall.

Aiello, L. C., and C. Dean
1990 An Introduction to Human Evolutionary Anatomy. London: Academic Press.

Aiello, L. C., and C. Key
2002 Energetic Consequences of Being a *Homo erectus* Female. American Journal of Human Biology 14:551–565.

Aiello, L. C., C. Montgomery, and C. Dean
1991 The Natural History of Deciduous Tooth Attrition in Hominoids. Journal of Human Evolution 21:397–412.

Aiello, L. C., and J. C. K. Wells

2002   Energetics and the Evolution of the Genus *Homo*. Annual Review of Anthropology 31:323–338.

Aiello, L. C., and P. Wheeler

1995   The Expensive-Tissue Hypothesis: The Brain and the Digestive System in Human and Primate Evolution. Current Anthropology 36:199–221.

Aiello, L. C., and B. Wood

1994   Cranial Variables as Predictors of Hominine Body Mass. American Journal of Physical Anthropology 95:409–426.

Akre, J.

1990   Infant Feeding: The Physiological Basis. Geneva: World Health Organization.

Akuse, R. M., and E. A. Obinya

2002   Why Healthcare Workers Give Prelacteal Feeds. European Journal of Clinical Nutrition 56:729–734.

Alexeev, V.

1986   The Origin of the Human Race. Moscow: Progress Publishers.

Allen, L.

1990   Functional Indicators and Outcomes of Undernutrition. Journal of Nutrition 120:924–932.

Allen, L. H.

1994   Maternal Micronutrient Malnutrition: Effects on Breast Milk and Infant Nutrition, and Priorities for Intervention. SCN News 11:21–24.

Allman J., A. Rosin, R. Kuman, and A. Hasenstaub

1998   Parenting and Survival in Anthropoid Primates: Caretakers Live Longer. Proceedings of the National Academy of Sciences USA 95:6866–6869.

Allman, J. M.

1999   Evolving Brains. New York: Scientific American Library.

Allman, J. M., T. McLaughlin, and A. Hakeem

1993   Brain Weight and Life-Span in Primate Species. Proceedings of the National Academy of Sciences USA 90:118–122.

Almroth, S. G.

1978   Water Requirements of Breastfed Infants in Hot Climates. American Journal of Clinical Nutrition 31:1154.

Altmann, J.

1980   Baboon Mothers and Infants. Cambridge, MA: Harvard University Press.

Altmann, J., S. A. Altmann, and G. Hausfater

1978   Primate Infant's Effects on Mother's Future Reproduction. Science 201:1028–1030.

Altmann, J., and A. Samuels

1992   Costs of Maternal Care: Infant Carrying in Baboons. Behavioral Ecology and Sociobiology 29:391–398.

Altmann, S. A.

1998   Foraging for Survival: Yearling Baboons in Africa. Chicago: Chicago University Press.

Alvarez, H. P.

2000   Grandmother Hypothesis and Primate Life Histories. American Journal of Physical Anthropology 133:435–450.

2004a   Primate Life Histories, Grandmothering and the Evolution of Human Longevity. Ph.D. diss., University of Utah, Salt Lake City.

2004b   Residence Groups among Hunter-Gatherers: A View of the Claims and Evidence for Patrilocal Bands. *In* Kinship and Behavior in Primates, edited by B. Chapais and C. M. Berman, pp. 420–442. New York: Oxford University Press.

Anemone, R. L.

2002   Dental Development and Life History in Hominid Evolution. *In* Human Evolution through Developmental Change, edited by N. Minugh-Purvis and K. J. McNamara, pp. 249–280. Baltimore, MD: Johns Hopkins University Press.

Anemone, R. L., M. P. Mooney, and M. I. Siegel

1996   Longitudinal Study of Dental Development in Chimpanzees of Known Chronological Age: Implications for Understanding the Age at Death of Plio-Pleistocene Hominids. American Journal of Physical Anthropology 99:119–133.

Antón, S. C.

1997   Developmental Age and Taxonomic Affinity of the Mojokerto Child, Java, Indonesia. American Journal of Physical Anthropology 102:497–514.

2002a   Cranial Growth in *Homo erectus*. *In* Human Evolution through Developmental Change, edited by N. Minugh-Purvis and K. J. McNamara, pp. 349–380. Baltimore, MD: Johns Hopkins University Press.

2002b   Evolutionary Significance of Cranial Variation in Asian *Homo erectus*. American Journal of Physical Anthropology 118:301–323.

2003   Natural History of *Homo erectus*. Yearbook of Physical Anthropology 46:126–169.

Arambourg, C., and Y. Coppens

1968   Decouverte d'un Australopithecine Nouveau dans les Gisements de L'Omo (Ethiopie). South African Journal of Science 64:58–59.

Arnason, U., and A. Janke

2002   Mitogenomic Analyses of Eutherian Relationships. Cytogenetic and Genome Research 96:20–32.

Arsuaga, J. L., C. Lorenzo, J. M. Carretero, A. Gracia, I. Martínez, N. García, J. M. Bermúdez de Castro, and E. Carbonell
1999   A Complete Human Pelvis from the Middle Pleistocene of Spain. Nature 399:255–258.

Arsuaga, J. L., I. Martínez, A. Garcia, and C. Lorenzo
1997   The Sima de los Huesos Crania (Sierra de Atapuerca, Spain). A Comparative Study. Journal of Human Evolution 33:219–281.

Ascenzi, A., F. Mallegni, G. Manzi, A. G. Segre, and E. S. Naldini
2000   A Re-appraisal of Ceprano Calvaria Affinities with *Homo erectus*, after the New Reconstruction. Journal of Human Evolution 39:443–450.

Asfaw, B., B. M. Gilbert, Y. Beyene, W. K. Hart, P. R. Renne, G. Woldegabriel, E. S. Vrba, and T. D. White
2002   Remains of *Homo erectus* from Bouri, Middle Awash, Ethiopia. Nature 416:317–320.

Asfaw, B., T. White, O. Lovejoy, B. Latimer, S. Simpson, and G. Suwa
1999   *Australopithecus garhi*: A New Species of Early Hominid from Ethiopia. Science 284:629–635.

Ashmole, N. P.
1963   The Regulation of Numbers of Tropical Oceanic Birds. Ibis 103:458–473.

Austad, S. N.
1997   Postreproductive Survival. *In* Between Zeus and the Salmon: The Biodemography of Longevity, edited by K. Wachter and C. Finch, pp. 161–174. Washington, DC: National Academy Press.

Austad, S. N., and K. E. Fischer
1992   Primate Longevity: Its Place in the Mammalian Scheme. American Journal of Primatology 28:251–261.

Aykroyd, R. G., D. Lucy, A. M. Pollard, and C. A. Roberts
1999   Nasty, Brutish, But Not Necessarily Short: A Reconsideration of the Statistical Methods Used to Calculate Age at Death from Adult Human Skeletal and Dental Age Indicators. American Antiquity 64:55–70.

Baba, H., F. Aziz, Y. Kaifu, G. Suwa, R. T. Kono, and T. Jacob
2003   *Homo erectus* Calvarium from the Pleistocene of Java. Science 299:1384–1388.

Bagnall, R., and B. Frier
1994   The Demography of Roman Egypt. Cambridge: Cambridge University Press.

Bailey, R. C.
1991   The Comparative Growth of Efe Pygmies and African Farmers from Birth to Age 5 Years. Annals of Human Biology 18:113–120.

Bailey, W. J., K. Hayasak, C. G. Skinner, S. Kehoe, L. U. Sieu, J. L. Slighthom, and M. Goodman
1992   Reexamination of the African Hominoid Trichotomy with Additional

Sequences from the Primate Beta-Globin Gene. Molecular Phylogenetics and Evolution 1:97–135.

Bairagi, R., M. K. Chowdury, Y. J. Kim, and G. T. Curlin
1985   Alternative Anthropometric Indicators of Mortality. American Journal of Clinical Nutrition 42:296–306.

Baird, R.
2000   The Killer Whale: Foraging Specializations and Group Hunting. *In* Cetacean Societies: Field Studies of Dolphins and Whales, edited by J. Mann, R. C. Connor, P. L. Tyack, and H. Whitehead, pp. 127–153. Chicago: University of Chicago Press.

Baker, P. T.
1988   Human Adaptability. *In* Human Biology: An Introduction to Human Evolution, Variation, Growth, and Adaptability, edited by G. A. Harrison, J. M. Tanner, D. R. Pilbeam, and P. T. Baker, pp. 439–543. Oxford: Oxford University Press.

Balee, W.
1992   People of the Fallow: A Historical Ecology of Foraging in Lowland South America. *In* Conservation of Neotropical Forests: Working from Traditional Resource Use, edited by K. H. Redford and C. Padoch, pp. 35–57. New York: Columbia University Press.

Barrickman, N., M. Bastian, K. Isler, and C. P. van Schaik
2005   Life History Correlates of Brain Size: A New Test Using Primates. Unpublished manuscript.

Barton, R.
1999   The Evolutionary Ecology of the Primate Brain. *In* Comparative Primate Socioecology, edited by P. C. Lee, pp. 167–203. Cambridge Studies in Biological and Evolutionary Anthropology, vol. 22. Cambridge: Cambridge University Press.

Bateson, P.
1994   The Dynamics of Parent-Offspring Relationships in Mammals. Trends in Ecology and Evolution 9:399–403.

Bauchamp, G. K., and B. L. Cowart
1987   Development of Sweet Taste. *In* Sweetness, edited by J. Dobbing, pp. 127–138. Berlin: Springer-Verlag.

Beauval, C., B. Maureille, F. Lacrampe-Cuyaubere, D. Serre, D. Peressinotto, J. G. Bordes, D. Cochard, I. Couchoud, D. Dubrasque, V. Laroulandie, A. Lenoble, J. B. Mallye, S. Pasty, J. Primault, N. Rohland, S. Pääbo, E. Trinkaus
2005   A late Neandertal femur from Les Rochers-de-Villeneuve, France. Proceedings of the National Academy of Sciences 102:7085-7090.

Beck, B. B.
1980   Animal Tool Behavior. New York: Garland.

Beckman, K. B., and B. N. Ames

1998 The Free Radical Theory of Aging Matures. Physical Review 78:547–581.

Begun, D., and A. Walker

1993 The Endocast. *In* The Nariokotome *Homo Erectus* Skeleton, edited by A. Walker and R. Leakey, pp. 326–358. Cambridge, MA: Harvard University Press.

Behar, M.

1977 Protein-Calorie Deficits in Developing Countries. Annals of the New York Academy of Sciences 300:176–187.

Ben Shaul, D. M.

1962 The Composition of the Milk of Wild Animals. International Zoological Yearbook 4:333–342.

Bennett, P., and I. Owens

2002 Evolutionary Ecology of Birds: Life Histories, Mating Systems and Extinction. Oxford: Oxford University Press.

Bentley, G. R.

1998 Hydration as a Limiting Factor in Lactation. American Journal of Human Biology 10:151–161.

1999 Aping Our Ancestors: Comparative Aspects of Reproductive Ecology. Evolutionary Anthropology 7:175–185.

Bentley, G. R., R. R. Paine, and J. L. Boldsen

2001 Fertility Changes with the Prehistoric Transition to Agriculture. *In* Reproductive Ecology and Human Evolution, edited by P. T. Ellison, pp. 203–321. New York: Aldine de Gruyter.

Bercovitch, F. B.

1987 Female Weight and Reproductive Condition in a Population of Olive Baboons (*Papio anubis*). American Journal of Primatology 12:189–195.

Bermúdez de Castro, J. M., J. L. Arsuaga, E. Carbonell, A. Rosas, I. Martínez, and M. Mosquera

1997 A Hominid from the Lower Pleistocene of Atapuerca, Spain: Possible Ancestor to Neandertals and Modern Humans. Science 276:1392–1395.

Bermúdez de Castro, J. M., M. Martinón-Torres, M. Lozano, S. Sarmiento, and A. Muela

2004 Paleodemography of the Atapuerca–Sima de los Huesos Hominin Sample: A Revision and New Approaches to the Paleodemography of the European Middle Pleistocene Population. Journal of Anthropological Research 60:5–26.

Bermúdez de Castro, J. M., and M. E. Nicolás

1997 Paleodemography of the Atapuerca-SH Middle Pleistocene Hominid Sample. Journal of Human Evolution 33:333–355.

Bermúdez de Castro, J. M., F. Ramírez Rozzi, M. Martinón-Torres, S. Sarmiento Pérez, and A. Rosas

2003   Patterns of Dental Development in Lower and Middle Pleistocene Hominins from Atapuerca (Spain). *In* Patterns of Growth and Development in the Genus *Homo*, edited by J. L. Thompson, G. E. Krovitz, and A. J. Nelson, pp. 246–270. Cambridge: Cambridge University Press.

Bermúdez de Castro, J. M., A. Rosas, E. Carbonell, M. E. Nicolás, J. Rodriguez, and J. L. Arsuaga

1999   A Modern Human Pattern of Dental Development in Lower Pleistocene Hominids from Atapuerca-TD6 (Spain). Proceedings of the National Academy of Sciences 96:4210–4213.

Bernhart, F. W.

1961   Correlation between Growth Rate of the Suckling of Various Species and the Percentage of Total Calories from Protein in the Milk. Nature 191:358–360.

Beverton, R. J. H.

1963   Maturation, Growth, and Mortality of Clupeid and Eugraulid Stocks in Relation to Fishing. Rapp. P.-V. Reun. Cons. Int. Explor. Mer 154:44–67.

Beverton, R. J. H., and S. J. Holt

1959   A Review of the Lifespans and Mortality Rates of Fish in Nature and the Relation to Growth and Other Physiological Characteristics. *In* Ciba Foundation Colloquia on Ageing, vol. 5, The Lifespan of Animals, edited by G. E. W. Wolstenholme and M. O'Connor, pp. 142–177. London: Churchill.

Beynon, A., and B. Wood

1987   Patterns and Rates of Enamel Growth in the Molar Teeth of Early Hominids. Nature 326:493–496.

Beynon, A. D., and M. C. Dean

1987   Crown-Formation Time of a Fossil Hominid Premolar Tooth. Archives of Oral Biology 32:773–780.

1988   Distinct Dental Development Patterns in Early Fossil Hominids. Nature 335:509–514.

Binford, L. R.

1981   Bones: Ancient Men and Modern Myths. New York: Academic Press.

Binford, S. R., and L. R. Binford

1969   Stone Tools and Human Behavior. Scientific American 220:555–565.

Birch, L. L.

1999   Development of Food Preferences. Annual Review of Nutrition 19:41–62.

Bird, D. W., and R. Bliege Bird

2000   The Ethnoarchaeology of Juvenile Foragers: Shellfishing Strategies among Merriam Children. Journal of Anthropological Archaeology 19:461–476.

2002   Children on the Reef: Slow Learning or Strategic Foraging. Human Nature 13:269–298.

2005   Martu Children's Hunting Strategies in the Western Desert, Australia: Foraging and the Evolution of Human Life Histories. *In* Hunter-Gatherer Childhoods, edited by B. S. Hewlett and M. E. Lamb, pp. 129–146. New Brunswick, NJ, and London: Aldine Transaction.

Bird, R. B., E. A. Smith, and D. W. Bird
2001   The Hunting Handicap: Costly Signaling in Human Foraging Strategies. Behavioral Ecology and Sociobiology 50:9–19.

Birdsell, J. B.
1979   Ecological Influences on Australian Aboriginal Social Organization. *In* Primate Ecology and Human Origins, edited by I. S. Bernstein and E. O. Smith, pp. 117–151. New York: Garland.

Black, F. L.
1975   Infectious Diseases in Primitive Populations. Science 187:515–518.

Black, R. F.
1998   The Immunology of Breastfeeding. *In* The Science of Breastfeeding, edited by R. F. Black, L. Jarman, and J. B. Simpson, pp. 155–178. Lactation Specialist Self-Study Series, vol. 3. Boston: Jones and Bartlett.

Black, R. F., and J. Bhatia
1998   The Biochemistry of Human Milk. *In* The Science of Breastfeeding, edited by R. F. Black, L. Jarman, and J. B. Simpson, pp. 103–152. Lactation Specialist Self-Study Series, vol. 3. Boston: Jones and Bartlett.

Blackburn, D. G.
1993   Lactation: Historical Patterns and Potential for Manipulation. Journal of Dairy Science 46:3195–3212.

Blaxter, K. L.
1961   Lactation and Growth of the Young. *In* Milk: The Mammary Gland and Its Secretion, vol. 2, edited by S. K. Kon and A. T. Cowie, pp. 305–361. London: Academic Press.

Blayo, Y.
1970   La Mortalite en France de 1740 a 1829. Population 30:123–142.

Bliege Bird, R., and D. Bird
2002   Constraints of Knowing or Constraints of Growing? Fishing and Collecting by the Children of Mer. Human Nature 13:239–267.

Bliege Bird, R., and E. A. Smith
2005   Signaling Theory, Strategic Interaction, and Symbolic Capital. Current Anthropology 46:221–248.

Block, E.
1952   Quantitative Morphological Investigation of the Follicular System in Women. Acta Anatomica 14:108–123.

Blueweiss, L., H. Fox, V. Kudzma, D. Nakashima, R. Peters, and S. Sams

1978　Relationships between Body Size and Some Life History Parameters. Oecologia 37:257–272.

Blurton Jones, N.

1993　The Lives of Hunter-Gatherer Children: Effects of Parental Behavior and Parental Reproductive Strategy. *In* Juvenile Primates: Life History, Development, and Behavior, edited by M. E. Pereira and L. A. Fairbanks, pp. 309–326. New York: Oxford University Press.

Blurton Jones, N. G., K. Hawkes, and J. F. O'Connell

1989　Studying Costs of Children in Two Foraging Societies: Implications for Schedules of Reproduction. *In* Comparative Socioecology of Mammals and Man, edited by V. Standon and R. Foley, pp. 365–390. London: Blackwell.

1997　Why Do Hadza Children Forage? *In* Genetic, Ethological and Evolutionary Perspectives on Human Development. Essays in Honor of Dr. Daniel G. Freedman, edited by N. L. Segal, G. E. Weisfeld, and C. C. Weisfeld, pp. 279–313. Washington, DC: American Psychological Association.

1999　Some Current Ideas about the Evolution of the Human Life History. *In* Comparative Primate Socioecology, edited by P. C. Lee, pp. 140–166. Cambridge Studies in Biological and Evolutionary Anthropology, vol. 22. Cambridge: Cambridge University Press.

2002　The Antiquity of Post-reproductive Life: Are There Modern Impacts on Hunter-Gatherer Post-reproductive Life Spans? American Journal of Human Biology 14:184–205.

2005　Older Hadza Men and Women as Helpers: Residence Data. *In* Hunter-Gatherer Childhoods, edited by B. S. Hewlett and M. E. Lamb, pp. 214–236. New Brunswick, NJ, and London: Aldine Transaction.

Blurton Jones, N. G., and M. J. Konner

1976　!Kung Knowledge of Animal Behavior. *In* Kalahari Hunter-Gatherers, edited by R. B. Lee and I. DeVore, pp. 325–348. Cambridge, MA: Harvard University Press.

Blurton Jones, N. G., and F. W. Marlowe

2002　Selection for Delayed Maturity: Does It Take 20 Years to Learn to Hunt and Gather? Human Nature 13:199–238.

Blurton Jones, N. G., F. Marlowe, K. Hawkes, and J. F. O'Connell

2000　Paternal Investment and Hunter-Gatherer Divorce. *In* Adaptation and Human Behavior: An Anthropological Perspective, edited by L. Cronk, N. Chagnon, and W. Irons, pp. 61–90. New York: Aldine de Gruyter.

Blurton Jones, N. G., L. C. Smith, J. F. O'Connell, K. Hawkes, and C. Kamazura

1992　Demography of the Hadza, an Increasing and High Density Population of Savanna Foragers. American Journal of Physical Anthropology 89:159–181.

Bock, J.

2002   Learning, Life History, and Productivity: Children's Lives in the Okavango Delta, Botswana. Human Nature 13:161–197.

Bock, J., and D. W. Sellen

2002   Childhood and the Evolution of the Human Life Course. Human Nature B13:153–159.

Bocquet-Appel, J.-P.

1986   Once upon a Time: Palaeodemography. Mitteilungen der Berliner Gesellschaft für Anthropolgie, Ethnologie und Urgeschichte 7:127–133.

Bocquet-Appel, J.-P., and J.-L. Arsuaga

1999   Age Distributions of Hominid Samples at Atapuerca (SH) and Krapina Could Indicate Accumulation by Catastrophe. Journal of Archaeological Science 26:327–338.

Bocquet-Appel, J.-P., and J. N. Bacro

1997   Brief Communication: Estimates of Some Demographic Parameters in a Neolithic Rock-Cut Chamber (Approximately 2000 BC) Using Iterative Techniques for Aging and Demographic Estimators. American Journal of Physical Anthropology 102:569–575.

Bocquet-Appel, J.-P., and C. Masset

1982   Farewell to Paleodemography. Journal of Human Evolution 11:321–333.

1985   Paleodemography: Resurrection or Ghost? Journal of Human Evolution 14:107–111.

1996   Paleodemography: Expectancy and False Hope. American Journal of Physical Anthropology 99:571–583.

Boesch, C., and H. Boesch-Achermann

2000   The Chimpanzees of the Tai Forest: Behavioural Ecology and Evolution. Oxford: Oxford University Press.

Bogin, B.

1988   Patterns of Human Growth. Cambridge: Cambridge University Press.

1990   The Evolution of Human Childhood. Bioscience 40:16–25.

1993   Why Must I Be a Teenager at All? New Scientist 137:34–38.

1994   Adolescence in Evolutionary Perspective. Acta Paediatrica Scandinavia. Suppl. no. 406:29–35.

1997   Evolutionary Hypotheses for Human Childhood. Yearbook of Physical Anthropology 40:63–89.

1999a   Patterns of Human Growth. 2d ed. Cambridge: Cambridge University Press.

1999b   Evolutionary Perspectives on Human Growth. Annual Review of Anthropology 28:109–153.

2001   The Growth of Humanity. New York: Wiley-Liss.

2002a   Childhood, Play and Growth. In Human Growth from Conception to Maturity, edited by G. Gilli, L. Schell, and L. Benzo, pp. 35–50. London: Smith-Gordon.

2002b   The Evolution of Human Growth. *In* Human Growth and Development, edited by N. Cameron, pp. 295–320. Amsterdam: Academic Press.

2003   The Human Pattern of Growth and Development in Paleontological Perspective. *In* Patterns of Growth and Development in the Genus *Homo*, edited by J. L. Thompson, G. E. Krovitz, and A. J. Nelson, pp. 15–44. Cambridge: Cambridge University Press.

Bogin, B., and J. Loucky
1997   Plasticity, Political Economy, and Physical Growth Status of Guatemala Maya Children Living in the United States. American Journal of Physical Anthropology 102:17–32.

Bogin, B., and L. Rios
2003   Rapid Morphological Change in Living Humans: Implications for Modern Human Origins. Comp Biochem Physiol A Mol Integr Physiol 136:71–84.

Bogin, B., and B. H. Smith
1996   Evolution of the Human Life Cycle. American Journal of Human Biology 8:703–716.

2000   Evolution of the Human Life Cycle. *In* Human Biology: An Evolutionary and Biocultural Perspective, edited by S. Stinson, B. Bogin, R. Huss-Ashmore, and D. O'Rourke, pp. 377–424. New York: Wiley-Liss.

Bogin, B., P. K. Smith, A. B. Orden, M. I. Varela Silva, and J. Loucky
2002   Rapid Change in Height and Body Proportions of Maya American Children. American Journal of Human Biology 14:753–761.

Bogin, B., and M. I. O. Varela Silva
2003   Anthropometric Variation and Health: A Biocultural Model of Human Growth. Journal of Children's Health 1:149–172.

Boinski, S.
1988   Sex Differences in the Foraging Behavior of Squirrel Monkeys in a Seasonal Habitat. Behavioral Ecology and Sociobiology 32:177–186.

Boinski, S., and D. Fragaszy
1989   The Ontogeny of Foraging in Squirrel Monkeys, *Saimiri oerstedi*. Animal Behaviour 37:415–428.

Boldsen, J. L.
1988   Two Methods for the Reconstruction of the Empirical Mortality Profile. Human Evolution 3:335–342.

1997   Transitional Analysis: A Method for Unbiased Age Estimation from Skeletal Traits. Abstract. American Journal of Physical Anthropology. Suppl. no. 24:79.

Boldsen, J. L., G. R. Milner, L. W. Konigsberg, and J. M. Wood
2002   Transition Analysis: A New Method for Estimating Age from Skeletons. *In* Paleodemography: Age Distributions from Skeletal Samples, edited by R. D. Hoppa and J. W. Vaupel, pp. 73–106. New York: Oxford University Press.

Boldsen, J. L., and R. R. Paine

1995   Defining Extreme Longevity from the Mesolithic to the Middle Ages: Estimates Based on Skeletal Data. *In* Exceptional Longevity: From Prehistory to Present, edited by B. Jeune and J. W. Vaupel, pp. 25–36. Odense: Odense University Press.

n.d.   Paleodemographic Evidence of the Evolution of Childhood Disease Patterns in Holocene Europe. Unpublished manuscript, in prep.

Bolk, L.

1926   On the Problem of Anthropogenisis. Proc. Section Sciences Kon. Akad. Wetens. Amsterdam 29:465–475.

Bonner, J. T.

1965   Size and Cycle. Princeton, NJ: Princeton University Press.

1993   Life Cycles: Reflections of an Evolutionary Biologist. Princeton, NJ: Princeton University Press.

Bourgeois, J.

1997   Synaptogenesis, Heterochrony and Epigenesis of Mammalian Neocortex. Acta Paediatrica. Suppl. no. 422:27–33.

Bowlby, R.

1969   Attachment and Loss. New York: Basic Books.

Boyd, E.

1980   Origins of the Study of Human Growth, edited by B. S. Savara and J. F. Schilke. Eugene: University of Oregon Press.

Brass, W.

1971   On the Scale of Mortality. *In* Biological Aspects of Demography, edited by W. Brass, pp. 69–110. London: Taylor and Francis.

Brauer, G.

1984   A Craniological Approach to the Origin of Anatomically Modern *Homo sapiens* in Africa and Implications for the Appearance of Modern Europeans. *In* The Origin of Modern Humans: A World Survey of the Fossil Evidence, edited by F. H. Smith and F. Spencer, pp. 327–410. New York: Alan R. Liss.

Braun, J., J. Sieper, and M. Bollow

2000   Imaging of Sacroilititis. Clinical Rheumatology 19:51–57.

Brewer-Marsden, S., D. Marsden, and M. Emery-Thompson

n.d.   Demographic and Female Life History Parameters of Free-Ranging Chimpanzees at the Chimpanzee Rehabilitation Project, River Gambia National Park. International Journal of Primatology, in press.

Bromage, T. G.

1987   The Biological and Chronological Maturation of Early Hominids. Journal of Human Evolution 16:257–272.

Bromage, T. G., and M. C. Dean
1985   Re-evaluation of the Age at Death of Immature Fossil Hominids. Nature 317:525–527.

Bronson, F. H.
1989   Mammalian Reproductive Biology. Chicago: University of Chicago Press.

Broom, R.
1938   The Pleistocene Anthropoid Apes of South Africa. Nature 142:377–379.

Broom, R., and J. T. Robinson
1948   Size of the Brain in the Ape-Man, Plesianthropus. Nature 161:438.

Brown, B., F. H. Brown, and A. Walker
2001   New Hominids from the Lake Turkana Basin, Kenya. Journal of Human Evolution 41:29–44.

Brown, B., A. Walker, C. V. Ward, and R. E. Leakey
1993   New *Australopithecus boisei* Calvaria from East Lake Turkana, Kenya. American Journal of Physical Anthropology 91:137–159.

Brown, J.
1987   Helping and Communal Breeding in Birds. Princeton, NJ: Princeton University Press.

Brown, J. H., and G. B. West, eds.
2000   Scaling in Biology. Oxford: Oxford University Press.

Brown, K. H., N. A. Akhtar, A. D. Robertson, and M. G. Ahmed
1986   Lactational Capacity of Marginally Nourished Mothers: Relationships between Maternal Nutritional Status and Quantity and Proximate Composition of Milk. Pediatrics 78:909–919.

Brown, K. H., and K. G. Dewey
1992   Relationships between Maternal Nutritional Status and Milk Energy Output of Women in Less Developed Countries. *In* Mechanisms Regulating Lactation and Infant Nutrient Utilization, edited by M. F. Picciano and B. Lönnerdal, pp. 77–95. New York: Wiley-Liss, Inc.

**Brown, P., T. Sutikna, M. J. Morwood, R. P. Soejono, Jatmiko,
E. Wayhu Saptomo, and Rokus Awe Due**
2004   A New Small-Bodied Hominin from the Late Pleistocene of Flores, Indonesia. Nature 431:1055–1061.

Brown, P. J.
1993   Measurement, Regression, and Calibration. New York: Oxford University Press.

Brown, P. J., and R. Sundberg
1987   Confidence and Conflict in Multivariate Calibration. Journal of the Royal Statistical Society B 49:46–57.

Brunet, M., A. Beauvilain, Y. Coppens, E. Heintz, A. H. E. Moutaye, and D. Pilbeam

1996   *Australopithecus bahrelghazali,* une Nouvelle Espece d'Hominide Ancien de la Region de Koro Toro (Tchad). Comptes Rendus de l'Academie des Sciences 322:907–913.

Brunet, M., F. Guy, D. Pilbeam, H. T. Mackaye, A. Likius, D. Ahounta, A. Beauvilain, C. Blondel, H. Bocherens, J.-R. Boisserie, L. de Bonis, Y. Coppens, J. Dejax, C. Denys, P. Duringer, V. Eisenmann, F. Gongdibe, P. Fronty, D. Geraads, T. Lehmann, F. Lihoreau, A. Louchart, A. Mahamat, G. Merceron, G. Mouchelin, O. Otero, P. P. Campomanes, M. P. De Leon, J.-C. Rage, M. Sapanet, M. Schuster, J. Sudre, P. Tassy, X. Valentin, P. Vignaud, L. Viriot, A. Zazzo, and C. Zollikofer

2002   A New Hominid from the Upper Miocene of Chad, Central Africa. Nature 145:145–151.

Buckberry, J. L., and A. T. Chamberlain

2002   Age Estimation from the Auricular Surface of the Ilium: A Revised Method. American Journal of Physical Anthropology 119:231–239.

Buikstra, J. E., L. W. Konigsberg, and J. Bullington

1986   Fertility and the Development of Agriculture in the Prehistoric Midwest. American Antiquity 51:528–546.

Butte, N. F.

1996   Energy Requirements of Infants. European Journal of Clinical Nutrition 50:S24–S36.

Butte, N. F., C. Garza, J. E. Stuff, E. O. B. Smith, and B. L. Nichols

1984   Effect of Maternal Diet and Body Composition on Lactational Performance. American Journal of Clinical Nutrition 39:296–306.

Butte, N. F., C. J. K. Henry, and B. Torun

1996   Report of the Working Group on Energy Requirements of Infants, Children and Adolescents. European Journal of Clinical Nutrition 50:S188–S189.

Butte, N. F., M. Lopez-Alarcon, and C. Garza

2002   Nutrient Adequacy of Exclusive Breastfeeding for the Term Infant during the First Six Months of Life. Geneva: World Health Organization.

Byers, J., and C. Walker

1995   Refining the Motor Training Hypothesis for the Evolution of Play. American Naturalist 146:25–40.

Byrne, R., and J. Byrne

1993   Complex Leaf-Gathering Skills of Mountain Gorillas (*Gorilla g. beringei*): Variability and Standardization. American Journal of Primatology 31:241–261.

Byrne, R. W.

1997   The Technical Intelligence Hypothesis: An Additional Evolutionary
Stimulus to Intelligence? *In* Machiavellian Intelligence II: Extension and
Evaluations, edited by A. Whiten and R. W. Byrne, pp. 289–311.
Cambridge: Cambridge University Press.

Cabana, T., P. Jolicoeur, and J. Michaud

1993   Prenatal and Postnatal Growth and Allometry of Stature, Head
Circumference, and Brain Weight in Québec Children. American Journal
of Human Biology 5:93–99.

Caccone, A., and J. R. Powell

1989   DNA Divergence among Hominoids. Evolution 43:925–942.

**Caceres, M., J. Lachuer, M. A. Zapala, J. C. Redmond, L. Kudo,
D. H. Geschwind, D. J. Lockhart, T. M. Preuss, and C. Barlow**

2003   Elevated Gene Expression Levels Distinguish Human from Non-human
Primate Brains. Proceedings of the National Academy of Sciences USA
100:13030–13035.

Calder, W. A.

1976   Ageing in Vertebrates: Allometric Considerations of Spleen Size and
Lifespan. Federal Proceedings 35:96–97.

1984   Size, Function, and Life History. Cambridge, MA: Harvard University
Press.

Cameron, N., J. M. Tanner, and R. H. Whitehouse

1982   A Longitudinal Analysis of the Growth of Limb Segments in Adolescence.
Annals of Human Biology 9:211–220.

Campbell, K. L., and J. W. Wood

1988   Fertility in Traditional Societies. *In* Natural Human Fertility: Social and
Biological Determinants, edited by P. Diggory, M. Potts, and S. Teper,
pp. 39–69. London: Macmillan.

Carey, J. R., and D. S. Judge

2000   Longevity Records: Life Spans of Mammals, Birds, Amphibians, Reptiles,
and Fish. Monographs on Population Aging, 8. Odense: University Press.

Caro, T., and M. Hauser

1992   Is There Teaching in Nonhuman Animals? Quarterly Review of Biology
67:151–174.

Caro, T. M., and D. W. Sellen

1990   On the Reproductive Advantages of Fat in Women. Ethology and
Sociobiology 11:51–66.

**Caro, T. M., D. W. Sellen, A. Parish, R. Frank, D. M. Brown, E. Voland,
and M. Borgerhoff Mulder**

1995   Termination of Reproduction in Nonhuman and Human Female
Primates. International Journal of Primatology 16:205–220.

Carroll, S. B.

2005   Evolution at Two Levels: On Genes and Form. PLOS Biology 3:1159–1166.

Cartmill, M.

1993   A View to a Death in the Morning: Hunting and Nature through History. Cambridge, MA: Harvard University Press.

Case, T. J.

1978   On the Evolution and Adaptive Significance of Postnatal Growth Rates in Terrestrial Vertebrates. Quarterly Review of Biology 53:243–282.

Caspari, R., and S.-H. Lee

2004   Older Age Becomes Common Late in Human Evolution. Proceedings of the National Academy of Sciences USA 101:10895–10900.

Cassinello, J.

1997   Mother-Offspring Conflict in the Saharan Arrui, *Ammotragus lervia sahariensis*: Relation Weaning and Mother's Sexual Activity. Ethology 103:127–137.

Caswell, H.

1989   Matrix Population Models. Sunderland, MA: Sinauer Associates.

Centers for Disease Control, National Center for Health Statistics

2000   CDC Growth Charts. United States.

Cerling, T. E.

1992   Development of Grasslands and Savannas in East Africa during the Neocene. Palaeogeography, Palaeoclimatology, Palaeoecology 97:241–247.

Chai, Y., X. Jiang, Y. Ito, P. Bringas Jr., J. Han, D. H. Rowitch, P. Soriano, A. P. McMahon, and H. M. Sucov

2000   Fate of the Mammalian Cranial Neural Crest during Tooth and Mandibular Morphogenesis. Development 127:1671–1679.

Chamberlain, A. T., and B. A. Wood

1985   A Reappraisal of the Variation in Hominid Mandibular Corpus Dimensions. American Journal of Physical Anthropology 66:399–403.

1987   Early Hominid Phylogeny. Journal of Human Evolution 16:119–133.

Chapman, C. A., S. Walker, and L. Lefebvre

1990   Reproductive Strategies of Primates: The Influence of Body Size and Diet on Litter Size. Primates 31:1–13.

Chapman, D. J., and R. Pérez-Escamilla

1999a   Does Delayed Perception of the Onset of Lactation Shorten Breastfeeding Duration? Journal of Human Lactation 15:107–111.

1999b   Identification of Risk Factors for Delayed Onset of Lactation. Journal of the American Dietetic Association 99:450–454; quiz 455–456.

Charlesworth, B.

1994   Evolution in Age Structured Populations. 2d ed. Cambridge: Cambridge University Press.

Charnov, E. L.

1990 On the Evolution of Age of Maturity and the Adult Lifespan. Journal of Evolutionary Biology 3:139–144.

1991 Evolution of Life History Variation in Female Mammals. Proceedings of the National Academy of Sciences USA 88:1134–1137.

1993 Life History Invariants: Some Explorations of Symmetry in Evolutionary Ecology. Oxford, New York, Toronto: Oxford University Press.

1997 Trade-Off-Invariant Rules for Evolutionarily Stable Life Histories. Nature 387:393–394.

2001a Evolution of Mammal Life Histories. Evolutionary Ecology Research 3:521–535.

2001b Reproductive Efficiencies in the Evolution of Life Histories. Evolutionary Ecology Research 3:873–876.

2002 Reproductive Effort, Offspring Size and Benefit-Cost Ratios in the Classification of Life Histories. Evolutionary Ecology Research 4:749–758.

2004 The Optimal Balance between Growth Rate and Survival in Mammals. Evolutionary Ecology Research 6:307–313.

Charnov, E. L., and D. Berrigan

1990a Dimensionless Numbers and the Assembly Rules for Life Histories. Philosophical Transactions of the Royal Society London, Series B 332:241–248.

1990b Dimensionless Numbers and Life History Evolution: Age of Maturity versus the Adult Lifespan. Evolutionary Ecology 4:273–275.

1993 Why Do Female Primates Have Such Long Lifespans and So Few Babies? Or, Life in the Slow Lane. Evolutionary Anthropology 1:191–194.

Cheng, Z., M. Ventura, X. She, P. Khaitovich, T. Graves, K. Osoegawa, D. Church, P. DeJong, R. K. Wilson, S. Pääbo, M. Rocchi, and E. E. Eichler

2005 A Genome-wide Comparison of Recent Chimpanzee and Human Segmental Duplications. Nature 437:88–93.

The Chimpanzee Sequencing and Analysis Consortium

2005 Initial Sequence of the Chimpanzee Genome and Comparison with the Human Genome. Nature 437:69–87.

Chisholm, J. S.

1999 Sex, Hope, and Death. Cambridge: Cambridge University Press.

Chiu, C. L., Y. M. Ku, Y. Y. Chang, and S. S. Chang

1973 Peking Man Fossils and Cultural Remains Newly Discovered at Choukoutien. Vertebrata Palasiatica 11:109–131.

Chua, S., S. Arulkumaran, and I. Lim

1994 Influence of Breast Feeding and Nipple Stimulation on Postpartum Uterine Activity. British Journal of Obstetrics and Gynaecology 101:804–805.

Cichon, M., and J. Kozlowski

2000   Ageing and Typical Survivorship Curves Result from Optimal Resource Allocation. Evolutionary Ecology Research 2:857–870.

Cifelli, R. L., T. B. Rowe, W. P. Luckett, J. Banta, R. Reyes, and R. I. Howes

1996   Fossil Evidence for the Origin of the Marsupial Pattern of Tooth Replacement. Nature 379:715–718.

Clarke, R. J.

1998   First Ever Discovery of a Well-Preserved Skull and Associated Skeleton of *Australopithecus*. South African Journal of Science 94:460–463.

1999   Discovery of Complete Arm and Hand of the 3.3 Million-Year-Old *Australopithecus* Skeleton from Sterkfontein. South African Journal of Science 95:477–480.

2002   Newly Revealed Information on the Sterkfontein Member 2 *Australopithecus* Skeleton. South African Journal of Science 98:523–526.

Clarke, R. J., and P. V. Tobias

1995   Sterkfontein Member 2 Foot Bones of the Oldest South African Hominid. Science 269:521–524.

Clegg, M., and L. C. Aiello

1999   A Comparison of the Nariokotome *Homo erectus* with Juveniles from a Modern Human Population. American Journal of Physical Anthropology 110:81–93.

Clifford, W. L.

1985   Human Milk: Nutritional Properties. *In* Nutrition in Pediatrics, edited by W. A. Walker and J. B. Watkins, pp. 797–813. Boston: Little, Brown.

Clutton-Brock, T.

2002   Breeding Together: Kin Selection and Mutualism in Cooperative Vertebrates. Science 296:69–72.

Clutton-Brock, T. H.

1991   The Evolution of Parental Care. Princeton, NJ: Princeton University Press.

Clutton-Brock, T. H., S. D. Albon, and F. E. Guinness

1989   Fitness Costs of Gestation and Lactation in Wild Mammals. Nature 337:260–262.

Clutton-Brock, T. H., and P. H. Harvey

1983   The Functional Significance of Variation in Body Size among Mammals. *In* Recent Advances in the Study of Mammalian Behavior, edited by J. F. Eisenberg and D. G. Kleiman, pp. 662–663. Special Publication of the American Society of Mammalogists, no. 7.

Coale, A. J.

1956   The Effects of Changes in Mortality and Fertility on Age Composition. The Milbank Memorial Fund Quarterly 34:79–114.

Coale, A. J., and P. Demeny

1966   Regional Model Life Tables and Stable Populations. Princeton, NJ:

Princeton University Press.

1983   Regional Model Life Tables and Stable Populations. 2d ed. New York: Academic Press.

Cobourne, M. T., and P. T. Sharpe

2003   Tooth and Jaw: Molecular Mechanisms of Patterning in the First Branchial Arch. Archives of Oral Biology 48:1–14.

Coelho, A. M., Jr.

1985   Baboon Dimorphism: Growth in Weight, Length and Adiposity from Birth to 8 Years of Age. *In* Nonhuman Primate Models for Human Growth, edited by E. S. Watts, pp. 125–159. New York: Alan R. Liss.

Cohen, A. A.

2004   Female Post-reproductive Lifespan: A General Mammalian Trait. Biological Reviews of the Cambridge Philosophical Society 79:733–750.

Cohen, M. N.

1977   The Food Crisis in Prehistory. New Haven, CT: Yale University Press.

Cohen, M. N., and G. J. Armelagos

1984   Paleopathology at the Origins of Agriculture. New York: Academic Press.

Cohen, R., K. H. Brown, J. Canahuati, L. L. Rivera, and K. G. Dewey

1994   Effects of Age of Introduction of Complementary Foods on Infant Breast Milk Intake, Total Energy Intake, and Growth: A Randomised Intervention Study in Honduras. The Lancet 344:288–293.

Cole, L. C.

1954   The Population Consequences of Life History Phenomena. Quarterly Review of Biology 29:103–137.

Cole, M. F., C. A. Hale, and S. Sturzenegger

1992   Identification of Two Subclasses of IgA in the Chimpanzee (*Pan troglodytes*). Journal of Medical Primatology 21:275–278.

Collard, M., and P. O'Higgins

2001   Ontogeny and Homoplasy in the Papionin Monkey Face. Evolution and Development 2:322–331.

Collard, M. C., and B. A. Wood

1999   Grades among the African Early Hominids. *In* African Biogeography, Climate Change, and Human Evolution, edited by T. G. Bromage and S. Friedemann, pp. 316–327. Oxford: Oxford University Press.

2000   How Reliable Are Human Phylogenetic Hypotheses? Proceedings of the National Academy of Sciences 97:5003–5006.

2001   Homoplasy and the Early Hominid Masticatory System: Inferences from Analyses of Extant Hominoids and Papionins. Journal of Human Evolution 41:167–194.

Conklin-Brittain, N. L., C. D. Knott, and R. W. Wrangham

2001   The Feeding Ecology of Apes. Conference Proceedings. *In* The Apes: Challenges for the Twenty-First Century, pp. 167–174. Brookfield, NY: Brookfield Zoo.

Conroy, G. C., and C. J. Mahoney

1991   Mixed Longitudinal Study of Dental Emergence in the Chimpanzee, *Pan troglodytes* (Primates, Pongidae). American Journal of Physical Anthropology 86:243–254.

Conroy, G. C., and M. Vannier

1987   Dental Development of the Taung Skull from Computerized Tomography. Nature 329:625–627.

1991a   Dental Development in South African Australopithecines, Part I, Problems of Pattern and Chronology. American Journal of Physical Anthropology 86:121–136.

1991b   Dental Development in South African Australopithecines, Part II, Dental Stage Assessment. American Journal of Physical Anthropology 86:137–156.

Conroy, G. C., G. W. Weber, H. Seidler, W. Recheis, D. Z. Nedden, and J. H. Mariam

2000   Endocranial Capacity of the Bodo Cranium Determined from Three-Dimensional Computed Tomography. American Journal of Physical Anthropology 113:111–118.

Constable, J., M. Ashley, J. Goodall, and A. Pusey

2001   Noninvasive Paternity Assignment in Gombe Chimpanzees. Molecular Ecology 10:1279–1300.

Corruccini, R. S.

1994   How Certain Are Hominoid Phylogenies? The Role of Confidence Intervals in Cladistics. *In* Integrative Paths to the Past, Paleoanthropological Advances in Honor of F. Clark Howell, edited by R. S. Corruccini and R. L. Ciochon, pp. 167–183. Englewood Cliffs, NJ: Prentice Hall.

Cosminsky, S., M. Mhloyi, and D. Ewbank

1993   Child Feeding Practices in a Rural Area of Zimbabwe. Social Science and Medicine 36:937–947.

Counsilman, J. J., and L. M. Lim

1985   The Meaning of Weaning: Response to P. Martin. Animal Behavior 33:1023–1024.

Courtenay, J., and G. Santow

1989   Mortality of Wild and Captive Chimpanzees. Folia Primatologica 52:157–177.

Crews, D. E., and L. M. Gerber

2003   Reconstructing Life History of Hominids and Humans. Collegium Antropologicum 27:7–22.

Crockford, S. J.

2003   Thyroid Hormone Rhythms and Hominid Evolution: A New Paradigm Implicates Pulsitile Thyroid Hormone Secretion in Speciation and Adaptation Changes. International Journal of Comparative Biochemistry and Physiology, Part A 135:105–129.

Cumming, R. G., and R. J. Klineberg

1993   Breastfeeding and Other Reproductive Factors and the Risk of Hip Fractures in Elderly Women. International Journal of Epidemiology 22:684–691.

Cummins, A., and F. Thompson

1997   Postnatal Changes in Mucosal Immune Response: A Physiological Perspective on Breastfeeding and Weaning. Immunology and Cell Biology 75:419–429.

Cunningham, A. S.

1988   Studies of Breastfeeding and Infections. How Good Is the Evidence? A Critique of the Answer from Yale. Journal of Human Lactation 4:54–56.

Dahlberg, F., ed.

1981   Woman the Gatherer. New Haven, CT: Yale University Press.

Daly, S. E. J., and P. E. Hartmann

1995   Infant Demand and Milk Supply. Part 1: Infant Demand and Milk Production in Lactating Women. Part 2: The Short-Term Control of Milk Synthesis in Lactating Women. Journal of Human Lactation 11:21–37.

Damuth, J.

1981   Population Density and Body Size in Mammals. Nature 290:699–700.

1987   Interspecific Allometry of Population Density in Mammals and Other Animals: The Independence of Body Mass and Population Energy-Use. Biological Journal of the Linnean Society 31:193–246.

Dart, R. A.

1925   *Australopithecus africanus*: The Man-Ape of South Africa. Nature 115:195–199.

1949   The Predatory Implemental Technique of *Australopithecus*. American Journal of Physical Anthropology 7:1–38.

Darwin, C.

1859   The Origin of Species. London: J. Murray.

Daum, W. J.

1995   The Sacroiliac Joint: An Underappreciated Pain Generator. American Journal of Orthopedics 24:475–478.

Davidson, E.

2001   Genomic Regulatory Systems: Development and Evolution. San Diego: Academic Press.

Davis, J., and M. Daly

1997   Evolutionary Theory and the Human Family. Quarterly Review of Biology 72:407–435.

Day, M. H.

1986   Guide to Fossil Man. London: Cassell.

de Andraca, I., P. Peirano, and R. M. D. P. D. Uauy

1998   Nutrition and Care in the Preterm and Neonatal Periods and Later Development: Human Milk Is Best for Optimal Mental Development. Washington, DC: Pan American Health Organization.

de Villiers, H.

1973   Human Skeletal Remains from Border Cave, Ingwavuma District, Kwazulu, South Africa. Annals of the Transvaal Museum 28:229–256.

de Waal, F.

1992   Coalitions as Part of Reciprocal Relations in the Arnhem Chimpanzee Colony. *In* Coalitions and Alliances in Humans and Other Animals, edited by A. H. Harcourt and F. B. M. de Waal, pp. 233–258. Oxford: Oxford University Press.

de Waal, F., and F. Lanting

1997   Bonobo: The Forgotten Ape. Berkeley: University of California Press.

Deacon, T. W.

1997   The Symbolic Species: The Co-evolution of Language and the Brain. New York: W.W. Norton.

Dean, M. C.

1987   The Dental Development Status of Six East African Juvenile Fossil Hominids. Journal of Human Evolution 16:197–213.

1995a   Developmental Sequences and Rates of Growth in Tooth Length in Hominoids. *In* Proceedings of the 10th International Symposium on Dental Morphology, edited by R. J. Radlanski and H. Renz, pp. 308–313. Berlin: C & M Brünne.

1995b   The Nature and Periodicity of Incremental Lines in Primate Dentine and Their Relationship to Periradicular Bands in OH 16 (*Homo habilis*). *In* Aspects of Dental Biology: Palaeontology, Anthropology and Evolution, edited by J. Moggi-Cecchi, pp. 239–265. Florence: International Institute for the Study of Man.

1998   Comparative Observation on the Spacing of Short-Period (von Ebner's) Lines in Dentine. Archives of Oral Biology 43:1009–1021.

2000   Progress in Understanding Hominoid Dental Development. Journal of Anatomy 197:77–101.

Dean, M. C., A. D. Beynon, J. F. Thackeray, and G. A. Macho

1993   Histological Reconstruction of Dental Development and Age at Death of a Juvenile *Paranthropus robustus* Specimen, SK 63, from Swartkrans, South Africa. American Journal of Physical Anthropology 91:401–419.

Dean, M. C., M. G. Leakey, D. Reid, F. Schrenk, G. T. Schwartz, C. Stringer, and A. Walker

2001   Growth Processes in Teeth Distinguish Modern Humans from *Homo erectus* and Earlier Hominins. Nature 414:628–631.

Dean, M. C., and A. E. Scandrett

1996   The Relation between Long-Period Incremental Markings in Dentine and Daily Cross-Striations in Enamel in Human Teeth. Archives of Oral Biology 41:233–241.

Dean, M. C., and B. A. Wood

1981   Developing Pongid Dentition and Its Use for Ageing Individual Crania in Comparative Cross-sectional Growth Studies. Folia Primatologica 36:111–127.

Deaner, R. O., R. A. Barton, and C. P. van Schaik

2003   Primate Brains and Life Histories: Renewing the Connection. *In* Primate Life Histories and Socioecology, edited by P. Kappeler and M. Pereira, pp. 233–265. Chicago: University of Chicago Press.

Dekaban, A. S., and D. Sadowsky

1978   Changes in Brain Weights during the Span of Human Life: Relation of Brain Weights to Body Heights and Body Weights. Annals of Neurology 4:345–356.

Delson, E., I. Tattersall, J. A. Van Couvering, and A. S. Brooks, eds.

2000   Encyclopedia of Human Evolution and Prehistory. New York: Garland Publishing.

deMenocal, P. B.

1995   Plio-Pleistocene African Climate. Science 270:53–59.

Demirjian, A.

1986   Dentition. *In* Human Growth, vol. 2, Postnatal Growth, edited by F. Falkner and J. M. Tanner, pp. 269–298. New York: Plenum.

DeRousseau, C. J.

1994   Primate Gerontology: An Emerging Discipline. *In* Biological Anthropology and Aging: Perspectives on Human Variation over the Lifespan, edited by D. E. Crews and R. M. Garruto, pp. 127–153. Oxford: Oxford University Press.

Desor, J. A., and G. K. Bauchamp

1987   Longitudinal Changes in Sweet Preference in Humans. Physiology and Behavior 39:639–641.

Dettwyler, K. A.

1995   A Time to Wean: The Hominid Blueprint for the Natural Age of Weaning in Modern Human Populations. *In* Breastfeeding: Biocultural Perspectives, edited by P. Stuart-Macadam and K. A. Detwyller, pp. 39–73. New York: Aldine de Gruyter.

Dewey, K.

2003   Guiding Principles for Complementary Feeding of the Breastfed Child. Geneva: World Health Organization.

Dewey, K. G.
1998   Effects of Maternal Caloric Restriction and Exercise during Lactation. Journal of Nutrition 128. Suppl. no. 2:386.

Dewey, K. G., R. J. Cohen, K. H. Brown, and L. L. Rivera
1999   Age of Introduction of Complementary Foods and Growth of Term, Low-Birth-Weight, Breast-Fed Infants: A Randomized Intervention Study in Honduras. American Journal of Clinical Nutrition 69:679–686.

Dewey, K. G., M. J. Heinig, and L. A. Nommsen
1993   Maternal Weight-Loss Patterns during Prolonged Lactation. American Journal of Clinical Nutrition 58:162–166.

Dewey, K. G., M. J. Heinig, L. A. Nommsen, and B. Lönnerdal
1991   Maternal versus Infant Factors Related to Breast Milk Intake and Residual Milk Volume: The DARLING Study. Pediatrics 87:829–837.

Dewey, K. G., C. A. Lovelady, L. A. Nommsen, M. A. McCrory, and B. Lönnerdal
1994   A Randomized Study of the Effects of Aerobic Exercise by Lactating Women on Breastmilk Volume and Composition. New England Journal of Medicine 330:449–453.

Dienske, H.
1986   A Comparative Approach to the Question of Why Human Infants Develop So Slowly. In Primate Ontogeny, Cognition and Social Behaviour, edited by J. G. Else and P. C. Lee, pp. 147–154. New York: Cambridge University Press.

Dijkhuizen, M. A., F. T. Wieringa, C. E. West, Muherdiyantiningsih, and Muhilal
2001   Concurrent Micronutrient Deficiencies in Lactating Mothers and Their Infants in Indonesia. American Journal of Clinical Nutrition 73:786–791.

Discover
2001   Your Cousin, the Banana. Discover (January):62.

Dobzhansky, T.
1950   Evolution in the Tropics. American Scientist 38:209–221.
1962   Mankind Evolving. New Haven, CT: Yale University Press.

Dolhinow, P.
1999   Play: A Critical Process in the Developmental System. In The Non-Human Primates, edited by P. Dolhinow and A. Fuentes, pp. 231–236. Mt. View, CA: Mayfield.

Domellöf, M., B. Lönnerdal, K. G. Dewey, R. J. Cohen, and O. Hernell
2004   Iron, Zinc, and Copper Concentrations in Breast Milk Are Independent of Maternal Mineral Status. American Journal of Clinical Nutrition 79:111–115.

Draper, P.
1976   Social and Economic Constraints on Child Life among the !Kung. In Kalahari Hunter-Gatherers, edited by R. B. Lee and I. DeVore, pp. 199–217. Cambridge, MA: Harvard University Press.

Draper, P., and N. Howell

2005   The Growth and Kinship Resources of Ju/'hoansi Children. *In* Hunter-Gatherer Childhoods, edited by B. S. Hewlett and M. E. Lamb, pp. 262–281. New Brunswick, NJ, and London: Aldine Transaction.

Drent, R., and S. Daan

1980   The Prudent Parent: Energetic Adjustments in Avian Breeding. The Integrated Study of Bird Populations, edited by H. Klomp and J. Woldendorp, pp. 225–252. Amsterdam: North-Holland Publishing Company.

Drewnowski, A.

2001   The Science and Complexity of Bitter Taste. Nutrition Reviews 59: 163–169.

Drewnowski, A., and C. Gomez-Carneros

2000   Bitter Taste, Phytonutrients, and the Consumer: A Review. American Journal of Clinical Nutrition 72:1424–1435.

Dreyer, T. F.

1935   A Human Skull from Florisbad, Orange Free State, with a Note on the Endocranial Cast by C. V. Ariens Kappers. Proceedings of the Academy of Science Amsterdam 38:119–128.

Dubois, E.

1892   Palaeontologische Andrezoekingen op Java. Versl. Mijnw. Batavia 3:10–14.

Dufour, D. L., and M. L. Sauther

2002   Comparative and Evolutionary Dimensions of the Energetics of Human Pregnancy and Lactation. American Journal of Human Biology 14:584–602.

Dukas, R.

1998   Evolutionary Ecology of Learning. *In* Cognitive Ecology: The Evolutionary Ecology of Information Processing and Decision Making, edited by R. Dukas, pp. 129–174. Chicago: University of Chicago Press.

Dumond, D. E.

1975   The Limitation of Human Population: A Natural History. Science 187:713–721.

Dunbar, R. I. M., and P. Dunbar

1988   Maternal Time Budgets of Gelada Baboons. Animal Behaviour 36:970–980.

Dunbar, R. I. M., L. Hannah-Stewart, and P. Dunbar

2002   Forage Quality and the Costs of Lactation for Female Gelada Baboons. Animal Behaviour 64:801–805.

Dupaquier, J.

1995   Histoire de la Population Francaise 2 / de la Renaissance a 1789. Paris: Presses Universitaires de France.

Durnin, J. V., F. M. McKillop, S. Grant, and G. Fitzgerald
1985   Is Nutritional Status Endangered by Virtually No Extra Intake during
        Pregnancy? The Lancet 2:823–825.

Durnin, J. V. G. A.
1987   Energy Requirements of Pregnancy: An Integration of the Longitudinal
        Data from the Five-Country Study. The Lancet 2:1131.

Dyke, B., T. Gage, P. Alford, B. Swenson, and S. Williams-Blangero
1995   Model Life Table for Captive Chimpanzees. American Journal of
        Primatology 37:25–37.

Early, J. D., and T. N. Headland
1998   Population Dynamics of a Philippine Rain Forest People: The San
        Ildefonso Agta. Gainesville: University Press of Florida.

Early, J. D., and J. F. Peters
1990   The Population Dynamics of the Mucajai Yanomama. New York: Academic
        Press.
2000   The Xilixana Yanomami of the Amazon: History, Social Structure, and
        Population Dynamics. Gainesville: University of Florida Press.

Economos, A. C.
1980a   Brain-Lifespan Conjecture: A Reevaluation of the Evidence. Gerontology
        26:82–89.
1980b   Taxonomic Differences in the Mammalian Life Span–Body Weight
        Relationship and the Problem of Body Weight. Gerontology 26:90–98.

Eisenberg, J. F.
1981   The Mammalian Radiations. Chicago: University of Chicago Press.

Eisenberg, L. E.
1989   On Gaming Pieces and Culture Contact. Current Anthropology 30:345.
1991   Mississippian Cultural Terminations in Middle Tennessee: What the
        Bioarchaeological Evidence Can Tell Us. In What Mean These Bones?
        Studies in Southeastern Bioarchaeology, edited by M. L. Powell, P. S.
        Bridges, and A. M. W. Mires, pp. 70–88. Tuscaloosa: University of Alabama.

Eldredge, N.
1993   What, If Anything, Is a Species? In Species, Species Concepts, and Primate
        Evolution, edited by W. H. Kimbel and L. B. Martin, pp. 3–20. New York:
        Plenum Press.

Ellison, P.
2002   Puberty. In Human Growth and Development, edited by N. Cameron,
        pp. 65–84. Amsterdam: Academic Press.

Ellison, P. T.
1994   Advances in Human Reproductive Ecology. Annual Review of
        Anthropology 23:255–275.
1995   Breastfeeding, Fertility, and Maternal Condition. In Breastfeeding:

Biocultural Perspectives, edited by P. Stuart-Macadam and K. A. Dettwyler, pp. 305–345. Foundations of Human Behavior. New York: Aldine de Gruyter.

Elman, J. L., E. A. Bates, M. H. Johnson, A. Karmiloff-Smith, D. Parisi, and K. Plunkett

1996   Rethinking Innateness: A Connectionist Perspective on Development. Cambridge, MA: The MIT Press.

Enard, W., P. Khaitovich, J. Klose, S. Zöllner, F. Heissig, P. Giavalisco, K. Nieselt-Struwe, E. Muchmore, A. Varki, R. Ravid, G. M. Doxiadis, R. E. Bontrop, and S. Pääbo

2002   Intra- and Interspecific Variation in Primate Gene Expression Patterns. Science 296:340–343.

Erickson, C.

1991   Percussive Foraging in the Aye-Aye (*Daubentonia madagascariensis*). Animal Behaviour 41:793–801.

Erwin, J. M., P. R. Hof, J. J. Ely, and D. P. Perl

2002   One Gerontology: Advancing Understanding of Aging through Studies of Great Apes and Other Primates. *In* Aging in Nonhuman Primates, edited by J. M. Erwin and P. R. Hof, pp. 1–21. Interdisciplinary Topics in Gerontology, vol. 31. Basel, Switzerland: Karger.

Esterik, P. V.

2002   Contemporary Trends in Infant Feeding Research. Annual Review of Anthropology 31:257–278.

Estioko-Griffin, A.

1986   Daughters of the Forest. Natural History 95:36–43.

Eswaran, E., H. C. Harpending, and A. R. Rogers

2005   Genomics Refutes an Exclusively Out-of-African Origin for Humans. Journal of Human Evolution 49:1–18.

Euler, L.

1760   Recherchés Generales sur la Mortalite: La Multiplication du Genre Humain. Memoirs of the Academy of Sciences, Berlin 16:144–164.

Evans, S. H., and E. J. Anastasio

1968   Misuse of Analysis of Covariance When Treatment Effect and Covariate Are Confounded. Psychological Bulletin 69:225–234.

Eveleth, P. B., and J. M. Tanner

1976   Worldwide Variation in Human Growth. Cambridge and London: Cambridge University Press.

Fairbanks, L.

2000   The Developmental Timing of Primate Play: A Neural Selection Model. *In* Biology, Brains, and Behavior: The Evolution of Human Development, edited by S. Parker, J. Langer, and M. McKinney, pp. 131–158. School of American Research. Santa Fe, NM: SAR Press.

REFERENCES

Fairbanks, L. A., and M. E. Pereira
1993   Juvenile Primates: Dimensions for Future Research. *In* Juvenile Primates:
         Life History, Development, and Behavior, edited by M. E. Pereira and L. A.
         Fairbanks, pp. 359–366. New York: Oxford University Press.

**Falk, D., C. Hildebolt, K. Smith, M. J. Morwood, T. Sutikna, P. Brown, Jatmiko,
E. Wayhu Saptomo, B. Brunsden, and F. Prior**
2005   The Brain of LB1, *Homo floresiensis*. Science 308:242–245.

**Falk, D., J. C. Redmond Jr., J. Guyer, G. C. Conroy, W. Recheis, G. W. Weber,
and H. Seidler**
2000   Early Hominid Brain Evolution: A New Look at Old Endocasts. Journal of
         Human Evolution 38:695–717.

Fedigan, L. M., and M. S. M. Pavelka
1994   The Physical Anthropology of Menopause. *In* Strength in Diversity, edited
         by A. Herring and M. S. M. Pavelka, pp. 103–126. Toronto: Canadian
         Scholars Press.

Feistner, A., and C. Ashbourne
1994   Infant Development in a Captive Bred Aye-Aye (*Daubentonia madagascarien-
         sis*) over the First Year of Life. Folia Primatologica 62:74–92.

Feistner, A., and J. Lind
2000   International Studbook for the Aye-Aye (*Daubentonia madagascariensis*).
         Jersey: Durrell Wildlife Conservation Trust.

Feistner, A. T. C., and M. C. McGrew
1989   Food-Sharing in Primates: A Critical Review. *In* Perspectives in Primate
         Biology, edited by P. K. Seth and S. Seth, pp. 21–36. New Delhi: Today &
         Tomorrow's Printers and Publishers.

Fildes, V.
1982   The Age of Weaning in Britain 1500–1800. Journal of Biosocial Science
         14:223–240.

Finch, C. E.
1990   Longevity, Senescence, and the Genome. Chicago: University of Chicago
         Press.
2002   Evolution and the Plasticity of Aging in the Reproductive Schedules in
         Long-Lived Animals: The Importance of Genetic Variation in
         Neuroendocrine Mechanisms. Hormones, Brain and Behavior 4:799–820.

Finch, C. E., and T. B. L. Kirkwood
2000   Chance, Development, and Aging. New York: Oxford University Press.

Finch, C. E., M. C. Pike, and M. Whitten
1990   Slow Mortality Rate Accelerations during Aging in Some Animals
         Approximate That of Humans. Science 249:902–905.

Finch, C. E., and M. R. Rose
1995   Hormones and the Physiological Architecture of Life History Evolution.
         The Quarterly Review of Biology 70:1–52.

Finch, C. E., and G. Ruvkun

2001   Genetics of Aging. Annual Review of Genomics and Human Genetics 20:435–462.

Finch, C. E., and C. B. Stanford

2003   Lipoprotein Genes and Diet in the Evolution of Human Intelligence and Longevity. *In* Brain and Longevity, edited by C. E. Finch, J.-M. Robine, and Y. Christen, pp. 36–68. Heidelberg: Springer-Verlag.

2004   Meat-Adaptive Genes and the Evolution of Slower Aging in Humans. Quarterly Review of Biology 79:3–50.

Fisher, R. A.

1930   The Genetical Theory of Natural Selection. Oxford: Oxford University Press.

Fitch, W. T., and J. Giedd

1999   Morphology and Development of the Human Vocal Tract: A Study Using Magnetic Resonance Imaging. Journal of the Acoustical Society of America 106:1511–1522.

Fitzgerald, C. M.

1998   Do Enamel Microstructures Have Regular Time Dependency? Conclusions from the Literature and a Large-Scale Study. Journal of Human Evolution 35:371–386.

Flannery, K. V.

1973   The Origins of Agriculture. Annual Review of Anthropology 2:271–310.

Flatz, G., and C. Saengudom

1969   Lactose Tolerance in Asians: A Family Study. Nature 224:915–916.

Fleet, I. R., J. A. Goode, and M. H. Hamon

1975   Secretory Activity of Goat Mammary Glands during Pregnancy and the Onset of Lactation. Journal of Physiology 251:763–773.

Fleiss, J. L., B. Levin, and M. C. Paik

2003   Statistical Methods for Rates and Proportions. 3d ed. Hoboken, NJ: John Wiley and Sons.

Flinn, M. V.

1992   Paternal Care in a Caribbean Village. *In* Father-Child Relations: Cultural and Biosocial Contexts, edited by B. S. Hewlett, pp. 57–84. New York: Aldine de Gruyter.

Foley, R.

1995   Evolution and Adaptive Significance of Hominid Behaviour. *In* Motherhood in Human and Nonhuman Primates, edited by C. R. Pryce, R. D. Martin, and D. Skuse, pp. 27–36. Basel, Switzerland: Karger.

Foley, R. A.

1982   A Reconsideration of the Role of Predation on Large Mammals in Tropical Hunter-Gatherer Adaptation. Man (n.s.) 17:383–402.

Fomon, S. J.

1986   Breast-Feeding and Evolution. Journal of the American Dietary Association 86:317–318.

Fomon, S. L., F. Haschke, E. E. Ziegler, and S. E. Nelson

1982   Body Composition of Reference Children from Birth to Age 10 Years. American Journal of Clinical Nutrition 35:1169–1175.

Food and Nutrition Board

1989   Energy. *In* National Research Council: Recommended Dietary Allowances, pp. 24–38. Washington, DC: National Academy Press.

Ford, C. S.

1945   A Comparative Study of Human Reproduction. Yale University Publications in Anthropology, vol. 32. New Haven, CT: Yale University Press.

Fox, E. A., A. F. Sitompul, and C. P. van Schaik

1999   Intelligent Tool Use in Wild Sumatran Orangutans. *In* The Mentality of Gorillas and Orangutans, edited by S. T. Parker, L. Miles, and R. Mitchell, pp. 99–116. Cambridge: Cambridge University Press.

Fox, J.

2002   An R and S-PLUS Companion to Applied Regression. Thousand Oaks, CA: Sage Publications.

Francis, C.

1994   Lactation in Male Fruit Bats. Nature 367:691–692.

Fraser, H. B., P. Khaitovich, J. B. Plotkin, S. Pääbo, and M. B. Eisen

2005   Aging and Gene Expression in the Primate Brain. PLOS Biology 3:e274. www.plosbiology.org (last accessed September 2005).

Friedenthal, H.

1910   Uber die Gültigkeit der Massenwirkung für den Energieumsatz der lebendigen Substanz. Zentralblatt für Physiologie 24:321–327.

Frisancho, A. R., and P. T. Baker

1970   Altitude and Growth: A Study of the Patterns of Physical Growth of a High-Altitude Peruvian Quechua Population. American Journal of Physical Anthropology 32:279–292.

Futuyma, D. J.

2002   Stephen Jay Gould à la Recherché du Temps Perdu. Science 296:661–663.

Gabunia, L., A. Vekua, D. Lordkipanidze, C. C. Swisher III, R. Ferring, A. Justus, M. Nioradze, M. Tvalchrelidze, S. C. Antón, G. Bosinski, O. Jöris, M.-A. de Lumley, G. Majsuradze, and A. Mouskhelishvili

2000   Earliest Pleistocene Hominid Cranial Remains from Dmanisi, Republic of Georgia: Taxonomy, Geological Setting, and Age. Science 288:1019–1025.

Gadgil, M., and W. Bossert

1970   Life History Consequences of Natural Selection. American Naturalist 104:1–24.

Gage, T. B.

1988   Mathematical Hazard Models of Mortality: An Alternative to Modal Life Tables. American Journal of Physical Anthropology 76:429–441.

1998   The Comparative Demography of Primates, with Some Comments on the Evolution of Life Histories. Annual Review of Anthropology 27:197–221.

Gage, T. B., and B. Dyke

1986   Parameterizing Abridged Mortality Tables: The Siler Three-Component Hazard Model. Human Biology 58:275–291.

Gage, T. B., J. M. McCullough, C. A. Weitz, J. S. Dutt, and A. Abelson

1989   Demographic Studies and Human Population Biology. *In* Human Population Biology: A Transdisciplinary Science, edited by M. A. Little and J. D. Haas, pp. 45–65. New York: Oxford University Press.

Gagneux, P., B. Amess, S. Diaz, S. Moore, T. Patel, W. Dillman, R. Paekh, and A. Varki

2001   Protemoic Comparison of Human and Great Ape Blood Plasma Reveals Conserved Glycosylation and Differences in Thyroid Hormone Metabolism. American Journal of Physical Anthropology 115:99–109.

Gagneux, P., and A. Varki

2001   Genetic Differences between Humans and Great Apes. Molecular Phylogenetics and Evolution 18:2–13.

Galdikas, B. M. F., and J. W. Wood

1990   Birth Spacing Patterns in Humans and Apes. American Journal of Physical Anthropology 83:185–191.

Galik, K., B. Senut, M. Pickford, D. Gommery, J. Treil, A. J. Kuperavage, and R. B. Eckhardt

2004   External and Internal Morphology of the BAR 1002'00 *Orrorin tugenensis* Femur. Science 305:1450–1453.

Galili, U.

1993   Evolution and Pathophysiology of the Human Natural Anti-alpha-galactosyl gG (Anti-Gal) Antibody. Springer Seminars in Immunopathology 15:155–171.

Garn, S. M., S. T. Sandusky, J. M. Nagy, and F. L. Trowbridge

1973   Negro-Caucasoid Differences in Permanent Tooth Emergence at a Constant Income Level. Archives of Oral Biology 18:609–615.

Gavrilova, N. S., L. A. Gavrilov, V. G. Semyonova, and G. N. Evdokushkina

2004   Does Exceptional Human Longevity Come with High Cost of Infertility? Testing the Evolutionary Theories of Aging. Annals of the New York Academy of Sciences 1019:513–517.

Geffner, M. E., Y. Hattori, J. Vera, R. C. Bailey, and D. W. Golde

1998   IGF-II Mediates Mitogenic Signaling in IGF-I-Resistant Efe Pygmy T-Cell Lines* 424. Pediatric Research Program Issue APS-SPR. Suppl. no. 2:75.

Gerrish, C. J., and J. A. Mennella
2001   Flavor Variety Enhances Food Acceptance in Formula-Fed Infants. American Journal of Clinical Nutrition 73:1080–1085.

Gibbs, S., M. Collard, and B. A. Wood
2002   Soft-Tissue Anatomy of the Extant Hominoids: A Review and Phylogenetic Analysis. Journal of Anatomy 200:3–49.

Gibson, K.
1991   Myelination and Behavioral Development: A Comparative Perspective on Questions of Neotony, Altriciality and Intelligence. *In* Brain Maturation and Cognitive Development: Comparative and Cross-Cultural Perspectives, edited by K. Gibson and A. Petersen, pp. 29–63. Hawthorne, NY: Aldine de Gruyter.

Giedd, J., L. Snell, N. Lange, J. Rajapakse, B. Casey, P. Kozuch, A. Viatuzis, Y. Vauss, S. Hamburger, D. Kaysen, and J. Rapoport
1996   Quantitative Magnetic Resonance Imaging of Human Brain Development: Ages 4–18. Cerebral Cortex 6:551–560.

Gisel, E. G.
1991   Effect of Food Texture on the Development of Chewing of Children between Six Months and Two Years of Age. Developmental Medicine and Child Neurology 33:69–79.

Gittleman, J. L., and S. D. Thompson
1988   Energy Allocation in Mammalian Reproduction. American Zoologist 28:863–875.

Glander, K.
1994   Morphometrics and Growth in Captive Aye-Ayes (*Daubentonia madagascariensis*). Folia Primatologica 62:108–114.

Glazko, G. V., and M. Nei
2003   Estimation of Divergence Times for Major Lineages of Primate Species. Molecular Biology and Evolution 20:424–434.

Godfray, H. C. J.
1995   Evolutionary Theory of Parent-Offspring Conflict. Nature 376:133–138.

Godfrey, L. R., K. E. Samonds, W. L. Jungers, and M. R. Sutherland
2001   Teeth, Brains, and Primate Life Histories. American Journal of Physical Anthropology 114:192–214.

2003   Dental Development and Primate Life Histories. *In* Primate Life Histories and Socioecology, edited by P. Kappeler and M. Pereira, pp. 177–203. Chicago: University of Chicago Press.

Godfrey, L. R., and M. R. Sutherland
1996   Paradox of Peramorphic Paedomorphosis: Heterochrony and Human Evolution. American Journal of Physical Anthropology 99:17–42.

Gogtay, N., J. N. Giedd, L. Lusk, K. M. Hayashi, D. Greenstein, A. C. Vaituzis, T. F. Nugent III, D. H. Herman, L. S. Clasen, A. W. Toga, J. L. Rapoport, and P. M. Thompson
2004   Dynamic Mapping of Human Cortical Development during Childhood through Early Childhood. Proceedings of the National Academy of Sciences 101:8147–8179.

Goldman, A. S.
1993   The Immune System of Human Milk: Antimicrobial, Anti-inflammatory and Immunomodulating Properties. Pediatric Infectious Disease Journal 12:664–671.

2000   Modulation of the Gastrointestinal Tract of Infants by Human Milk. Interfaces and Interactions. An Evolutionary Perspective. The Journal of Nutrition. Suppl. no. 130:426S–431S.

2001   The Immunological System in Human Milk: The Past—A Pathway to the Future. Advances in Nutritional Research 10:15–37.

Goldman, A. S., S. Chheda, and R. Garofalo
1997   Spectrum of Immunomodulating Agents in Human Milk. International Journal of Pediatric Hematology and Oncology 4:491–497.

1998   Evolution of Immunologic Functions of the Mammary Gland and the Postnatal Development of Immunity. Pediatric Research 43:155–162.

Gonzalez-Cossio, T., J. Habicht, K. M. Rasmussen, and H. L. Delgado
1998   Impact of Food Supplementation during Lactation on Infant Breast-Milk Intake and on the Proportion of Infants Exclusively Breast-Fed. Journal of Nutrition 128:1692–1702.

Goodall, J.
1968   Behaviour of Free-Living Chimpanzees in the Gombe Stream Area. In Animal Behavior Monograph, vol. 1, pt. 3, edited by J. M. Cullen and C. G. Beer, pp. 165–311. London: Balliere, Tindall, and Casell.

1983   Population Dynamics during a 15-Year Period in One Community of Free-Living Chimpanzees in the Gombe National Park, Tanzania. Zietschrift für Tierpsychologie 61:1–60.

1986   The Chimpanzees of Gombe: Patterns of Behavior. Cambridge, MA: Harvard University Press.

2003   What's New at Gombe. National Geographic Magazine (April):76–89.

Goodman, A. H., G. H. Pelto, L. H. Allen, and A. Chavez
1992   Socioeconomic and Anthropometric Correlates of Linear Enamel Hypoplasia in Children from Solis, Mexico. Journal of Paleopathology 2:373–380.

Goodman, M.
1962   Immunochemistry of the Primates and Primate Evolution. Annals of the New York Academy of Science 102:219–234.

Gordon, N.
1997   Nutrition and Cognitive Function. Brain and Development 19:165–170.

Gosden, R. G.
1985   Biology of Menopause: The Causes and Consequences of Ovarian Ageing. London: Academic Press, Inc.

Gould, K. G., M. Flint, and C. E. Graham
1981   Chimpanzee Reproductive Senescence: A Possible Model for Evolution of the Menopause. Maturitas 3:157–166.

Gould, S. J.
1977   Ontogeny and Phylogeny. Cambridge, MA: Belknap Press.
1982   Change in Developmental Timing as a Mechanism of Macroevolution. *In* Evolution and Development, edited by J. T. Bonner, pp. 333–346. Berlin: Springer-Verlag.
2002   The Structure of Evolutionary Theory. Cambridge, MA: Belknap Press.

Gould, S. J., and R. C. Lewontin
1979   The Spandrels of San Marco and the Panglossian Paradigm: A Critique of the Adaptationist Program. Proceedings of the Royal Society of London, Series B 205:581–598.

Graham, C. E., O. R. Kling, and R. A. Steiner
1979   Reproductive Senescence in Female Non-human Primates. *In* Aging in Nonhuman Primates, edited by D. M. Bowden, pp. 183–202. New York: Van Nostrand Reinhold Co.

Graham, C. E., and R. D. Nadler
1990   Socioendocrine Interactions in Great Ape Reproduction. *In* Socioendocrinology of Primate Reproduction, edited by T. E. Ziegler and F. B. Bercovitch, pp. 33–58. New York: Wiley-Liss.

Grajeda, R., and R. Pérez-Escamilla
2002   Stress during Labor and Delivery Is Associated with Delayed Onset of Lactation among Urban Guatemalan Women. Journal of Nutrition 132:3055–3060.

Gray, R. H., O. M. Campbell, R. Apelo, S. S. Eslami, H. Zacur, R. M. Ramos, J. C. Gehret, and M. H. Labbock
1990   Risk of Ovulation during Lactation. The Lancet 335:25–29.

Gray, S. J.
1996   Ecology of Weaning among Nomadic Turkana Pastoralists of Kenya: Maternal Thinking, Maternal Behavior and Human Adaptive Strategies. Human Biology 68:437–465.

Grimaud-Herve, D.
1997   L'Evolution de l'Encephale chez *Homo erectus* et *Homo sapiens*. Paris: CNRS.

Groves, C. P.
1989   A Theory of Human and Primate Evolution. Oxford: Oxford University Press.

434

Groves, C. P., and V. Mazák

1975   An Approach to the Taxonomy of the Hominidae: Gracile Villafranchian Hominids of Africa. Casopis Pro Mineralogii a Geologii 20:225–247.

Grumbach, M. M., and D. M. Styne

2003   Puberty: Ontogeny, Neuroendocrinology, Physiology, and Disorders. *In* Williams Textbook of Endocrinology, 10th ed., edited by P. R. Larsen, H. M. Kronenberg, S. Melmed, and K. S. Polonsky, pp. 1115–1286. Philadelphia: W. B. Saunders.

Grundy, E., and C. Tomassini

2005   Fertility History and Health in Later Life: A Record Linkage Study in England and Wales. Social Science and Medicine 61:217–228.

Guatelli-Steinberg, D.

2001   What Can Developmental Defects of Enamel Reveal about Physiological Stress in Nonhuman Primates? Evolutionary Anthropology 10:138–151.

Gunnlaugsson, G., and J. Einarsdottir

1993   Colostrum and Ideas about Bad Milk—A Case-Study from Guinea-Bissau. Social Science and Medicine 36:283–288.

Guthrie, H., and M. F. Picciano

1995   Human Nutrition. St. Louis, MO: Mosby.

Haggerty, P. A., and S. O. Rutstein

1999   Breastfeeding and Complementary Infant Feeding, and the Postpartum Effects of Breastfeeding. Demographic and Health Surveys Comparative Studies, vol. 30. Calverton, MD: Macro International, Inc.

Haig, D.

1993   Genetic Conflicts in Human Pregnancy. Quarterly Review of Biology 68:495–532.

1999   Genetic Conflicts of Pregnancy and Childhood. *In* Evolution of Health and Disease, edited by S. Sterns, pp. 77–90. New York: Oxford University Press.

Haile-Selassie, Y.

2001   Late Miocene Hominids from the Middle Awash, Ethiopia. Nature 412:178–181.

Haile-Selassie, Y., G. Suwa, and T. D. White

2004   Late Miocene Teeth from Middle Awash, Ethiopia, and Early Hominid Dental Evolution. Science 303:1503–1505

Hamada, Y., and T. Udono

2002   Longitudinal Analysis of Length Growth in the Chimpanzee (*Pan troglodytes*). American Journal of Physical Anthropology 118:268–284.

Hamada, Y., T. Udono, M. Teramoto, and T. Sugawara

1996   The Growth Pattern of Chimpanzees: Somatic Growth and Reproductive Maturation in *Pan troglodytes*. Primates 37:279–295.

Hambraeus, L.

1982   Food and Growth in Children with Special Reference to Breast Feeding versus Formula Feeding. Journal of Food and Nutrition 39:1–13.

Hames, R., and P. Draper

2004   Women's Work, Child Care, and Helpers-at-the-Nest in a Hunter-Gatherer Society. Human Nature 15:319–341.

Hamilton, W. D.

1966   The Molding of Senescence by Natural Selection. Journal of Theoretical Biology 12:12–45.

Hammel, E. A.

1996   Demographic Constraints on Population Growth of Early Humans. Human Nature 7:217–255.

Hammer, M. L. A., and R. A. Foley

1996   Longevity and Life History Evolution in Hominid Evolution. Human Evolution 11:61–66.

Hamosh, M.

1995   Lipid Metabolism in Pediatric Nutrition. Pediatric Clinics of North America 42:839.

2001   Bioactive Factors in Human Milk. Pediatric Clinics of North America 48:69–86.

Harcourt, A. H.

1987   Dominance and Fertility among Female Primates. Journal of Zoology London 213:471–487.

Hardling, R., H. G. Smith, V. Jormalainen, and J. Tuomi

2001   Resolution of Evolutionary Conflict: Costly Behaviors. Evolutionary Ecology Research 3:829–844.

Harris, D. R., C. T. Bisbee, and S. H. Evans

1971   Further Comments: Misuse of Analysis of Covariance. Psychological Bulletin 75:220–222.

Harrison, G. A., A. J. Boyce, and C. M. Platt

1975   Body Composition Changes during Lactation in a New Guinea Population. Annals of Human Biology 2:395–398.

Harrison, M. J. S.

1983   Age and Sex Differences in the Diet and Feeding Strategies of the Green Monkey, *Cercopithecus sabaeus*. Animal Behavior 31:969–977.

Hartmann, P. E.

1973   Changes in the Composition and Yield of the Mammary Secretion of Cows during the Initiation of Lactation. Endocrinology 59:231–247.

Hartmann, P. E., and P. G. Arthur

1986   Assessment of Lactation Performance in Women. *In* Human Lactation 2:

Maternal and Environmental Factors, edited by M. Hamosh and
A. S. Goldman, pp. 215–230. New York: Plenum Press.

Hartmann, P. E., S. Morgan, and P. Arthur
1986   Milk Letdown and the Concentration of Fat in Breast Milk. *In* Human
Lactation 2: Maternal and Environmental Factors, edited by M. Hamosh
and A. Goldman, pp. 275–281. New York: Plenum Press.

Hartmann P. E., S. Rattigan, C. G. Prosser, L. Saint, and P. G. Arthur
1984   Human Lactation: Back to Nature. *In* Physiological Strategies in Lacation,
edited by M. Peaker, R. G. Vernon, and C. H. Knight, pp. 337–368.
London: Academic Press.

Hartwig, W. C., ed.
2002   The Primate Fossil Record. Cambridge: Cambridge University Press.

Harvey, B.
1993   Living and Dying in England 1100–1540: The Monastic Experience.
Oxford: Oxford University Press

Harvey, P. H., and T. H. Clutton-Brock
1985   Life History Variation in Primates. Evolution 39:559–581.

Harvey, P. H., and J. R. Krebs
1990   Comparing Brains. Science 249:140–146.

Harvey, P. H., R. D. Martin, and T. H. Clutton-Brock
1987   Life Histories in Comparative Perspective. *In* Primate Societies, edited
by B. B. Smuts, D. L. Cheney, R. M. Seyfarth, R. W. Wrangham, and
T. T. Struhsaker, pp. 181–196. Chicago: University of Chicago Press.

Harvey, P. H., and M. D. Pagel
1991   The Comparative Method in Evolutionary Biology. Oxford: Oxford
University Press.

Harvey, P. H., and A. Purvis
1999   Understanding the Ecological and Evolutionary Reasons for Life History
Variation: Mammals as a Case Study. *In* Advanced Ecological Theory:
Principles and Applications, edited by J. McGlade, pp. 232–248. Oxford:
Blackwell Science.

Harvey, P. H., and A. F. Read
1988   How and Why Do Mammalian Life Histories Vary? *In* Evolution of Life
Histories of Mammals, edited by M. S. Boyce, pp. 213–232. New Haven,
CT: Yale University Press.

Harvey, P. H., A. F. Read, and D. E. L. Promislow
1989   Life History Variation in Placental Mammals: Unifying Data with Theory.
Oxford Surveys in Evolutionary Biology 6:13–31.

Harvey, P. H., and R. M. Zammuto
1985   Patterns of Mortality and Age at First Reproduction in Natural Populations
of Mammals. Nature 315:319–320.

Hasselbalch, H., M. D. Engelmann, A. K. Ersboll, D. L. Jeppesen, and K. Fleischer-Michaelsen

1999   Breast-Feeding Influences Thymic Size in Late Infancy. Journal of Pediatrics 158:964–967.

Hawkes, J. S., M. A. Neumann, and R. A. Gibson

1999   The Effect of Breast Feeding on Lymphocyte Subpopulations in Healthy Term Infants at 6 Months of Age. Paediatric Research 45:648–651.

Hawkes, K.

1990   Why Do Men Hunt? Some Benefits for Risky Strategies. In Risk and Uncertainty in Tribal and Peasant Economies, edited by E. Cashdan, pp. 145–166. Boulder, CO: Westview Press.

1991   Showing Off: Tests of an Hypothesis about Men's Foraging Goals. Ethology and Sociobiology 12:29–54.

1993   Why Hunter-Gatherers Work: An Ancient Version of the Problem of Public Goods. Current Anthropology 34:341–361.

2000   Big Game Hunting and the Evolution of Egalitarian Societies: Lessons from the Hadza. In Hierarchies in Action: Cui Bono?, edited by M. Diehl, pp. 59–83. Center for Archaeological Investigations, Occasional Papers no. 27. Carbondale: Southern Illinois University Press.

2001   Is Meat the Hunter's Property? Ownership and Explanations of Hunting and Sharing. In Meat-Eating and Human Evolution, edited by C. Stanford and H. Bunn, pp. 219–236. Oxford: Oxford University Press.

2003   Grandmothers and the Evolution of Human Longevity. American Journal of Human Biology 15:380–400.

2004a   Mating, Parenting and the Evolution of Human Pair Bonds. In Kinship and Behavior in Primates, edited by B. Chapais and C. Berman, pp. 443–473. Oxford: Oxford University Press.

2004b   The Grandmother Effect. Nature 428:128–129.

Hawkes, K., and R. Bliege Bird

2002   Showing Off, Handicap Signaling, and the Evolution of Men's Work. Evolutionary Anthropology 11:58–67.

Hawkes, K., and N. G. Blurton Jones

2005   Human Age Structures, Paleodemography, and the Grandmother Hypothesis. In Grandmotherhood: The Evolutionary Significance of the Second Half of Life, edited by E. Voland, A. Chasiotis, and W. Schiefenhovel, pp. 118–140. New Brunswick, NJ: Rutgers University Press.

Hawkes, K., and J. F. O'Connell

2005   How Old Is Human Longevity? Journal of Human Evolution 49:650–653.

Hawkes, K., J. F. O'Connell, and N. G. Blurton Jones

1989   Hardworking Hadza Grandmothers. In Comparative Socioecology of Mammals and Man, edited by V. Standon and R. Foley, pp. 341–366. London: Blackwell.

1991 Hunting Income Patterns among the Hadza: Big Game, Common Goods, Foraging Goals, and the Evolution of the Human Diet. Philosophical Transactions of the Royal Society London, Series B 334:243–251.

1995 Hadza Children's Foraging: Juvenile Dependency, Social Arrangements, and Mobility among Hunter-Gatherers. Current Anthropology 36:688–700.

1997 Hadza Women's Time Allocation, Offspring Provisioning, and the Evolution of Post-menopausal Lifespans. Current Anthropology 38:551–578.

2001a Hunting and Nuclear Families: Some Lessons from the Hadza about Men's Work. Current Anthropology 42:681–709.

2001b Hadza Meat Sharing. Evolution and Human Behavior 22:113–142.

2003 Human Life Histories: Primate Tradeoffs, Grandmothering Socioecology, and the Fossil Record. In Primate Life Histories and Socioecology, edited by P. Kappeler and M. Pereira, pp. 204–227. Chicago: University of Chicago Press.

Hawkes, K., J. F. O'Connell, N. G. Blurton Jones, H. Alvarez, and E. L. Charnov
1998 Grandmothering, Menopause, and the Evolution of Human Life Histories. Proceedings of the National Academy of Sciences USA 95:1336–1339.

Hearn, J. P.
1984 Lactation and Reproduction in Non-human Primates. Symposium of the Zoological Society of London 51:327–335.

Heinig, M. J., L. A. Nommsen, J. M. Peerson, B. Lönnerdal, and K. G. Dewey
1993 Intake and Growth of Breast-Fed and Formula-Fed Infants in Relation to the Timing of Introduction of Complementary Foods: The DARLING Study. Acta Paediatrica 82:999–1006.

Helle, S., V. Lummaa, and J. Jokela
2005 Are Reproductive and Somatic Senescence Coupled in Humans? Late, But Not Early, Reproduction Correlated with Longevity in Historical Sami Women. Proceedings of the Royal Society London, Series B 272:29–37.

Hennig, W.
1966 Phylogenetic Systematics. Urbana: University of Illinois Press.

Herndon, J. G., J. Tigges, D. C. Anderson, S. A. Klumpp, and H. M. McClure
1999 Brain Weight throughout the Lifespan of the Chimpanzee. Journal of Comparative Neurology 409:567–572.

Herrmann, N. P.
2002 Biological Affinities of Archaic Period Populations from West-Central Kentucky and Tennessee. Ph.D. diss., University of Tennessee, Knoxville.

Herrmann, N. P., and L. W. Konigsberg
2002 A Re-examination of the Age-at-Death Distribution of Indian Knoll. In Paleodemography: Age Distributions from Skeletal Samples, edited by R. D. Hoppa and J. W. Vaupel, pp. 243–257. New York: Cambridge University Press.

Hewlett, B. S.

1991a Demography and Childcare in Preindustrial Societies. Journal of Anthropological Research 47:1–37.

1991b Intimate Fathers: The Nature and Context of Aka Pygmy Paternal Infant Care. Ann Arbor: University of Michigan Press.

Hiernaux, J., and D. B. Hartono

1980 Physical Measurements of the Adult Hadza of Tanzania. Annals of Human Biology 7: 339–346.

Hill, K., C. Boesche, J. Goodall, A. Pusey, J. Williams, and R. Wrangham

2001 Mortality Rates among Wild Chimpanzees. Journal of Human Evolution 39:1–14.

Hill, K., and H. Kaplan

1999 Life History Traits in Humans: Theory and Empirical Studies. Annual Reviews in Anthropology 28:397–430.

Hill, K. R., and A. M. Hurtado

1991 The Evolution of Premature Reproductive Senescence and Menopause in Human Females: An Evaluation of the "Grandmother" Hypothesis. Human Nature 2:313–350.

1996 Ache Life History: The Ecology and Demography of a Foraging People. Hawthorne, NY: Aldine de Gruyter.

Hillis, D. M.

1994 Homology in Molecular Biology. In Homology: The Hierarchical Basis of Comparative Biology, edited by B. K. Hall, pp. 339–368. New York: Academic Press.

Hindmarsh, P. C.

2002 Endocrinology of Growth. In Human Growth and Development, edited by N. Cameron, pp. 85–101. Amsterdam: Academic Press.

Hlusko, L. J., K. M. Weiss, and M. C. Mahaney

2002 Statistical Genetic Comparison of Two Techniques for Assessing Molar Crown Size in Pedigreed Baboons. American Journal of Physical Anthropology 117:182–189.

Hofman, M. A.

1984 On the Presumed Coevolution of Brain Size and Longevity in Hominids. Journal of Human Evolution 13:371–376.

Holden, C., and R. Mace

1997 Phylogenetic Analysis of the Evolution of Lactose Digestion in Adults. Human Biology 69:605–628.

Holliday, R.

1995 Understanding Ageing. Cambridge: Cambridge University Press.

Hollingsworth, T. H.

1977 Mortality in the British Peerage Families since 1600. Population. Suppl. no. 32:323–352.

Holloway, R. L.

1981a   The Indonesian *Homo erectus* Brain Endocast Revisited. American Journal
         of Physical Anthropology 55:503–521.

1981b   Volumetric and Asymmetry Determination on Recent Hominid Endocasts:
         Spy I and II, Djebel Irhoud I and the Sale *Homo erectus* Specimens, with
         Some Notes on Neandertal Brain Size. American Journal of Physical
         Anthropology 55:385–393.

1983a   Human Brain Evolution: A Search for Units, Models and Synthesis.
         Canadian Journal of Anthropology 3:215–230.

1983b   Human Paleontological Evidence Relevant to Language Behavior. Human
         Neurobiology 2:105–114.

1988   "Robust" Australopithecine Brain Endocasts: Some Preliminary
         Observations. *In* Evolutionary History of the "Robust" Australopithecines,
         edited by F. Grine, pp. 97–105. New York: Aldine de Gruyter.

Holman, D. J., and J. W. Wood

2001   Pregnancy Loss and Fecundability in Women. *In* Reproductive Ecology
         and Human Evolution, edited by P. T. Ellison, pp. 15–38. New York: Aldine
         de Gruyter.

Hoppa, R. D.

1996   Representativeness and Bias in Cemetery Samples: Implications for
         Paleodemographic Reconstruction of Past Populations. Ph.D. diss.,
         McMaster University, Hamilton, Ontario.

2000   Population Variation in Osteological Aging Criteria: An Example from the
         Pubic Symphysis. American Journal of Physical Anthropology 111:185–191.

Hoppa, R. D., and J. W. Vaupel

2002a   The Rostock Manifesto for Paleodemography: The Way from Stage to Age.
         In Paleodemography: Age Distributions from Skeletal Samples, edited by
         R. D. Hoppa and J. W. Vaupel, pp. 1–8. New York: Cambridge University
         Press.

Hoppa, R. D., and J. W. Vaupel, eds.

2002b   Paleodemography: Age Distributions from Skeletal Samples. Cambridge:
         Cambridge University Press.

**Horai, S., Y. Satta, K. Hayasaka, R. Kondo, T. Inoue, T. Ishida, S. Hayash,
and N. Takahata**

1992   Man's Place in Hominoidea Revealed by Mitochondrial DNA Genealogy.
         Journal of Molecular Evolution 35:32–43.

Horr, D. A.

1975   The Borneo Orangutan: Population Structure and Dynamics in
         Relationship to Ecology and Reproductive Strategy. *In* Primate Behavior:
         Development in Field and Laboratory Research, edited by L. A.
         Rosenblum, pp. 307–323. New York: Academic Press.

Howell, N.

1976a   Toward a Uniformitarian Theory of Human Paleo-demography. Journal of Human Evolution 5:25–40.

1976b   Toward a Uniformitarian Theory of Human Paleodemography. *In* The Demographic Evolution of Human Populations, edited by R. H. Ward and K. M. Weiss, pp. 25–40. New York: Academic Press.

1979   Demography of the Dobe !Kung. New York: Academic Press.

1982   Village Composition Implied by a Paleodemographic Life Table: The Libben Site. American Journal of Physical Anthropology 59:263–269.

Howie, P. W., and A. S. McNeilly

1982   Effect of Breastfeeding Patterns on Human Birth Intervals. Journal of Reproduction and Fertility 65:545–557.

Hrdy, S. B.

1999   Mother Nature: A History of Mothers, Infants, and Natural Selection. New York: Pantheon, Random House.

2001   Mothers and Others. Natural History 110:50–62.

Huffman, M. A.

1990   Some Socio-behavioral Manifestations of Old Age. *In* The Chimpanzees of the Mahale Mountains: Sexual and Life History Strategies, edited by T. Nishida, pp. 237–245. Tokyo: University of Tokyo Press.

Huffman, S. L., and L. H. Martin

1994   First Feedings: Optimal Feeding of Infants and Toddlers. Nutrition Research 14:127–159.

Hughes, V. A., W. R. Frontera, M. Wood, W. J. Evans, G. E. Dallal, R. Roubenoff, and M. A. F. Singh

2001   Longitudinal Muscle Strength Changes in Older Adults: Influence of Muscle Mass, Physical Activity, and Health. Journal of Gerontology: Biological Sciences 56A:B209–B217.

Human Mortality Database

2005   University of California, Berkeley, and Max Planck Institute for Demographic Research (Germany). www.mortality.org or www.humanmortality.de (last accessed September 2005).

Humphrey, C., and J. Elford

1988   Social Class Differences in Infant Mortality: The Problem of Competing Hypotheses. Journal of Biosocial Science 20:497–504.

Humphrey, L. T., M. C. Dean, and T. E. Jeffries

2005   Identification of the Neonatal Line Using LA-ICP-MS. American Journal of Physical Anthropology. Suppl. no. 40:119–120.

Hunt, D. R., and J. Albanese

2005   History and Demographic Composition of the Robert J. Terry Anatomical Collection. American Journal of Physical Anthropology 127:406–417.

Huttenlocher, P., and A. Dabholkar

1997   Regional Differences in Synaptogenesis in Human Cerebral Cortex.
        Journal of Comparative Neurology 387:167–178.

Hytten, F., and G. Chamberlain, eds.

1980   Clinical Physiology in Obstetrics. Oxford: Blackwell Scientific Publications.

Igarashi, Y., K. Ueso, T. Wakebe, and E. Kanazawa

2005   New Method for Estimation of Adult Skeletal Age at Death from the
        Morphology of the Auricular Surface of the Ilium. American Journal of
        Physical Anthropology 128:324–339.

Institute of Medicine (US) Subcommittee on Nutrition during Lactation

1991a   Milk Composition. In Nutrition during Lactation, pp. 113–152.
        Washington, DC: National Academy of Sciences.

1991b   Milk Volume. In Nutrition during Lactation, pp. 80–112. Washington, DC:
        National Academy of Sciences.

1991c   Nutrition during Lactation. Washington, DC: National Academy of Sciences.

Isler, K., and C. P. van Schaik

2005   Untitled, unpublished manuscript.

Ivey, P. K.

2000   Cooperative Reproduction in Ituri Forest Hunter-Gatherers: Who Cares
        for Efe Infants? Current Anthropology 41:856–866.

Iwaniuk, A. N., and J. E. Nelson

2003   Developmental Differences Are Correlated with Relative Brain Size in Birds:
        A Comparative Analysis. Canadian Journal of Zoology 81:1913–1928.

Iwaniuk, A. N., J. E. Nelson, and S. M. Pellis

2001   Do Big-Brained Animals Play More? Comparative Analyses of Play and
        Brain Size in Mammals. Journal of Comparative Psychology 115:29–41.

Jackes, M.

2003   Testing a Method: Paleodemography and Proportional Fitting. American
        Journal of Physical Anthropology 121:385–386.

Jamison, C. S., L. L. Cornell, P. L. Jamison, and H. Nakazato

2002   Are All Grandmothers Equal? A Review and a Preliminary Test of the
        "Grandmother Hypothesis" in Tokugawa Japan. American Journal of
        Physical Anthropology 119:67–76.

Janson, C. H.

2003   Puzzles, Predation, and Primates: Using Life History to Understand
        Selection Pressures. In Primate Life Histories and Socioecology, edited by
        P. M. Kappeler and M. E. Pereira, pp. 103–131. Chicago: University of
        Chicago Press.

Janson, C. H., and C. P. van Schaik

1993   Ecological Risk Aversion in Juvenile Primates: Slow and Steady Wins the
        Race. In Juvenile Primates: Life History, Development, and Behavior, edit-
        ed by M. E. Pereira and L. A. Fairbanks, pp. 57–74. New York: Oxford
        University Press.

Jason, J. M., P. Neiburg, and J. S. Marks
1984   Mortality and Infectious Diseases Associated with Infant Feeding Practices in Developing Countries. Pediatrics 74:702–727.

Jelliffe, D. B., and E. F. Jelliffe
1978   The Weanling's Dilemma. The Lancet 1:611.

Jenike, M. R.
2001   Nutritional Ecology: Diet, Physical Activity, and Body Size. *In* Hunter-Gatherers: An Interdisciplinary Perspective, edited by C. Panter-Brick, R. H. Layton, and P. Rowley-Conway, pp. 205–238. Cambridge: Cambridge University Press.

Jerison, H. J.
1973   Evolution of the Brain and Intelligence. New York: Academic Press.

Johansen, H. C., and J. Oeppen
2001   Danish Population Estimates 1665–1840. Research Report no. 21. Odense: Danish Center for Demographic Research.

Johanson, D. C., and M. Taieb
1976   Plio-Pleistocene Hominid Discoveries in Hadar, Ethiopia. Nature 260:293–297.

Johanson, D. C., and T. D. White
1979   A Systematic Reassessment of Early African Hominids. Science 202:321–330.

Johanson, D. C., T. D. White, and Y. Coppens
1978   A New Species of the Genus *Australopithecus* (Primates: Hominidae) from the Pliocene of East Africa. Kirtlandia 28:1–14.

Johansson, S. R., and S. Horowitz
1986   Estimating Mortality in Skeletal Populations: Influence of the Growth Rate on the Interpretation of Levels and Trends during the Transition to Agriculture. American Journal of Physical Anthropology 71:233–250.

Johnson J., J. Bagley, M. Skaznik-Wikiel, H.-J. Lee, G. B. Adams, Y. Niikura, K. S. Tschudy, J. Canning Tilly, M. L. Cortes, R. Forkert, T. Spitzer, J. Lacomini, D. T. Scadden, and J. L. Tilly
2005   Oocyte Generation in Adult Mammalian Ovaries by Putative Germ Cells in Bone Marrow and Peripheral Blood. Cell 122:303–315.

Johnson, J., J. Canning, T. Kaneko, J. K. Pru, and J. L. Tilly
2004   Germline Stem Cells and Follicular Renewal in the Postnatal Mammalian Ovary. Nature 428:145–150.

Johnson, V. E., and J. H. Albert
1999   Ordinal Data Modeling. New York: Springer-Verlag.

Jolicoeur, P., G. Baron, and T. Cabana
1988   Cross-sectional Growth and Decline of Human Stature and Brain Weight in Nineteenth-Century Germany. Growth, Development, and Aging 52:201–206.

Jolly, A.
1985 The Evolution of Primate Behavior. 2d ed. New York: Macmillan.

Jolly, C. J.
2001 A Proper Study for Mankind: Analogies from the Papionin Monkeys and Their Implications for Human Evolution. Yearbook of Physical Anthropology 44:177–204.

Jones, G., R. W. Steketee, R. E. Black, Z. A. Bhutta, S. S. Morris, and The BCSS Group
2003 How Many Child Deaths Can We Prevent This Year? The Lancet 362:65–71.

Judge, D. S., and J. R. Carey
2000 Postreproductive Life Predicted by Primate Patterns. Journal of Gerontology: Biological Sciences 55A:B201–B209.

Kampen, W. U., and B. Tillmann
1998 Age-Related Changes in the Articular Cartilage of Human Sacroiliac Joint. Anatomical Embryology 198:505–513.

Kanazawa, A. T., T. Miyazawa, H. Hirono, M. Hayashi, and K. Fujimoto
1991 Possible Essentiality of Docosahexaenoic Acid in Japanese Monkey Neonates: Occurrence in Colostrum and Low Biosynthetic Capacity in Neonate Brains. Lipids 26:53–57.

Kaplan, H., and H. Dove
1987 Infant Development among the Ache of Eastern Paraguay. Developmental Psychology 23:190–198.

Kaplan, H. S.
1996 A Theory of Fertility and Parental Investment in Traditional and Modern Societies. Yearbook of Physical Anthropology 39:91–135.

1997 The Evolution of the Human Life Course. In Between Zeus and the Salmon: The Biodemography of Longevity, edited by K. Wachter and C. Finch, pp. 175–211. Washington, DC: National Academy of Sciences.

Kaplan, H. S., and K. R. Hill
1985 Food Sharing among Ache Foragers: Tests of Explanatory Hypotheses. Current Anthropology 26:223–246.

Kaplan, H. S., K. R. Hill, A. M. Hurtado, and J. B. Lancaster
2001 The Embodied Capital Theory of Human Evolution. In Reproductive Ecology and Human Evolution, edited by P. T. Ellison, pp. 293–317. New York: Aldine de Gruyter.

Kaplan, H. S., K. R. Hill, J. B. Lancaster, and A. M. Hurtado
2000 A Theory of Human Life History Evolution: Diet, Intelligence, and Longevity. Evolutionary Anthropology 9:156–185.

Kaplan, H. S., J. B. Lancaster, and A. J. Robson
2003 Embodied Capital and the Evolutionary Economics of the Human Lifespan. Population and Development Review. Suppl. no. 29:152–182.

Kaplan, H. S., and A. J. Robson
2002   The Co-evolution of Intelligence and Longevity and the Emergence of Humans. Proceedings of the National Academy of Sciences USA 99:10221–10226.

Kappeler, P. M., and M. Pereira, eds.
2003   Primate Life Histories and Socioecology. Chicago: University of Chicago Press.

Kappeler, P. M., M. E. Pereira, and C. P. van Schaik
2003   Primate Life Histories and Socioecology. *In* Primate Life Histories and Socioecology, edited by P. M. Kappeler and M. E. Pereira, pp. 1–20. Chicago: University of Chicago Press.

Kappeler, P. M., and C. P. van Schaik
2002   Evolution of Primate Social Systems. International Journal of Primatology 23:707–740.

Kappelman, J.
1996   The Evolution of Body Mass and Relative Brain Size in Fossil Hominids. Journal of Human Evolution 30:243–276.

Katz, D., and J. M. Suchey
1986   Age Determination of the Male os pubis. American Journal of Physical Anthropology 69:427–435.

Katzenberg, A. M., D. A. Herring, and S. R. Saunders
1996   Weaning and Infant Mortality: Evaluating the Skeletal Evidence. Yearbook of Physical Anthropology 39:177–199.

Keckler, C. N. W.
1997   Catastrophic Mortality in Simulations of Forager Age-at-Death: Where Did All the Humans Go? *In* Integrating Archaeological Demography: Multidisciplinary Approaches to Prehistoric Population, edited by R. R. Paine, pp. 205–228. Center for Archaeological Investigations, Occasional Papers no. 24. Carbondale, IL: Southern Illinois University Press.

Kelley, J.
1997   Paleobiological and Phylogenetic Significance of Life History in Miocene Hominoids. *In* Function, Phylogeny, and Fossils: Miocene Hominoid Evolution and Adaptations, edited by D. R. Begun, C. V. Ward, and M. D. Rose, pp. 173–208. New York: Plenum Press.
2002   Life History Evolution in Miocene and Extant Apes. *In* Human Evolution through Developmental Change, edited by N. Minugh-Purvis and J. A. McNamara, pp. 223–248. Baltimore, MD: Johns Hopkins University Press.

Kelley, J., and G. T. Schwartz
2005   Histologically Determined Age at First Molar Emergence in *Pongo pygmaeus*. American Journal of Physical Anthropology. Suppl. no. 40:128.

Kelly, R. L.

1995   The Foraging Spectrum. Washington, DC: Smithsonian Institution Press.

Kennedy, G. E.

2003   Palaeolithic Grandmothers? Life History Theory and Early Homo. The Journal of the Royal Anthropological Institute (n.s.) 9:549–572.

2005   From the Ape's Dilemma to the Weanling's Dilemma: Early Weaning and Its Evolutionary Context. Journal of Human Evolution 48:109–217.

Kennedy, K. I., and C. M. Visness

1992   Contraceptive Efficacy of Lactational Amenorrhoea. The Lancet 339:227–230.

Kerslake, D.

1972   The Stress of Hot Environments. Cambridge: Cambridge University Press.

Keyfitz, N.

1977   Applied Mathematical Demography. New York: Wiley.

Kimbel, W., Y. Rak, and D. Johanson

2004   The Skull of *Australopithecus afarensis*. New York: Oxford University Press.

Kimura, D. K.

1977   Statistical Assessment of the Age-Length Key. Journal of the Fisheries Research Board of Canada 34:317–324.

King, M.-C., and A. Wilson

1975   Evolution at Two Levels in Humans and Chimpanzees. Science 188:107–116.

King, W.

1864   The Reputed Fossil Man of the Neanderthal. Quarterly Journal of Science 1:88–97.

Kirkwood, T. B. L.

1977   The Evolution of Aging. Nature 270:301–302.

1981   Repair and Its Evolution: Survival versus Reproduction. *In* Physiological Ecology: An Evolutionary Approach to Resource Use, edited by C. R. Townsend and P. Calow, pp. 165–189. Oxford: Blackwell Scientific.

Kirkwood, T. B. L., and S. N. Austad

2000   Why Do We Age? Nature 408:233–238.

Kirkwood, T. B. L., and M. R. Rose

1991   Evolution of Senescence: Late Survival Sacrificed for Reproduction. Philosophical Transactions of the Royal Society London, Series B 332:15–24.

Klein, J., and N. Takahata

2002   Where Do We Come From? The Molecular Evidence for Human Descent. Berlin: Springer Verlag.

Klein, R. G.

1999   The Human Career: Human Biological and Cultural Origins. 2d ed. Chicago: University of Chicago Press.

447

Knight, A.

2003   The Phylogenetic Relationship of Neandertal and Modern Human Mitochondrial DNAs Based on Informative Nucleotide Sites. Journal of Human Evolution 44:627–632.

Knott, C.

2001   Female Reproductive Ecology of the Apes: Implications for Human Evolution. *In* Reproductive Ecology and Human Evolution, edited by P. Ellison, pp. 429–463. New York: Aldine de Gruyter.

Kolakowski, D., and R. D. Bock

1981   A Multivariate Generalization of Probit Analysis. Biometrics 37:541–551.

Kolata, G. B.

1974   !Kung Hunter-Gatherers: Feminism, Diet and Birth Control. Science 185:932–934.

Konigsberg, L. W., and S. R. Frankenberg

1992   Estimation of Age Structure in Anthropological Demography. American Journal of Physical Anthropology 89:235–256.

1994   Paleodemography: "Not Quite Dead." Evolutionary Anthropology 3:92–105.

2002   Deconstructing Death in Paleodemography. American Journal of Physical Anthropology 117:297–309.

2003   Reply to Comments by Jackes: Inter-observer Error and Goodness of Fit Tests in Paleodemography. American Journal of Physical Anthropology 121:387–388.

Konigsberg, L. W., S. R. Frankenberg, and R. B. Walker

1997   Regress What on What? Paleodemographic Age Estimation as a Calibration Problem. *In* Integrating Archaeological Demography: Multidisciplinary Approaches to Prehistoric Population, edited by R. R. Paine, pp. 64–88. Center for Archaeological Investigations, Occasional Papers no. 24. Carbondale, IL: Southern Illinois University Press.

Konigsberg, L. W., S. M. Hens, L. M. Jantz, and W. L. Jungers

1998   Stature Estimation and Calibration: Bayesian and Maximum Likelihood Perspectives in Physical Anthropology. Yearbook of Physical Anthropology 41:65–92.

Konner, M. J.

1972   Aspects of the Developmental Ethology of a Foraging People. *In* Ethological Studies of Child Behavior, edited by N. Blurton Jones, pp. 285–304. Cambridge: Cambridge University Press.

1976   Maternal Care, Infant Behavior and Development among the !Kung. *In* Kalahari Hunter-Gatherers, edited by R. B. Lee and I. DeVore, pp. 218–245. Cambridge, MA: Harvard University Press.

Korpelainen, H.

2000   Fitness, Reproduction, and Longevity among European Aristocratic and Rural Finnish Families in the 1700s and 1800s. Proceedings of the Royal Society London, Series B 267:1765–1770.

2003   Human Life Histories and the Demographic Transition: A Case Study from Finland, 1870–1949. American Journal of Physical Anthropology 120:384–390.

Kozlowski, J., and R. G. Weigert

1987   Optimal Allocation of Energy to Growth and Reproduction. Theoretical Population Biology 29:16–37.

Kozlowski, J., and J. Weiner

1997   Interspecific Allometries Are Byproducts of Body Size Optimization. American Naturalist 149:352–380.

Krakauer, E. B.

2005   Development of Aye-Aye (*Daubentonia madagascariensis*) Foraging Skills: Independent Exploration and Social Learning. Ph.D. diss., Duke University, Durham, NC.

Kramer, M. S., T. Guo, R. W. Platt, Z. Sevkovskaya, I. Dzikovich, J.-P. Collet, S. Shapiro, B. Chalmers, E. Hodnett, I. Vanilovich, I. Mezen, T. Ducruet, G. Shishko, and N. Bogdanovich

2003   Infant Growth and Health Outcomes Associated with 3 Compared with 6 Mo of Exclusive Breastfeeding. American Journal of Clinical Nutrition 78:291–295.

Kramer, M. S., and R. Kakuma

2002   The Optimal Duration of Exclusive Breastfeeding: A Systematic Review. Geneva: World Health Organization.

Kramer, P.

1998   The Costs of Human Locomotion: Maternal Investment in Infant Transport. American Journal of Physical Anthropology 107:71–85.

Kretschmann, H. J., A. Schleicher, F. Wingert, K. Zilles, and H. J. Loblich

1979   Human Brain Growth in the 19th and 20th Century. Journal of the Neurological Sciences 40:169–188.

Krings, M., C. Capelli, F. Tschentscher, H. Geisert, S. Meyer, A. von Haeseler, K. Grossschmidt, G. Possnert, M. Paunovic, and S. Pääbo

2000   A View of Neandertal Genetic Diversity. Nature Genetics 26:144–146.

Krings, M., H. Geisert, R. W. Schmitz, H. Krainitzki, and S. Pääbo

1999   DNA Sequence of the Mitochondrial Hypervariable Region II from the Neandertal Type Specimen. Proceedings of the National Academy of Sciences 96:5581–5585.

Krings, M., A. Stone, R. W. Schmitz, H. Krainitzki, M. Stoneking, and S. Pääbo

1997   Neandertal DNA Sequences and the Origin of Modern Humans. Cell 90:19–30.

REFERENCES

Krovitz, G. E., A. J. Nelson, and J. L. Thompson
2003   Introduction. *In* Patterns of Growth and Development in the Genus *Homo*,
        edited by J. L. Thompson, G. E. Krovitz, and A. J. Nelson, pp. 1–11.
        Cambridge Studies in Biological and Evolutionary Anthropology, vol. 37.
        Cambridge: Cambridge University Press.

Kruska, D.
1996   The Effect of Domestication on Brain Size and Composition in the Mink
        (*Mustela vison*). Journal of Zoology London 239:645–661.

Kuester, J., and A. Paul
2000   The Use of Infants to Buffer Male Aggression. *In* Natural Conflict
        Resolution, edited by F. Aureli and F. B. M. de Waal, pp. 91–93. Berkeley
        and Los Angeles: University of California Press.

Kuhtz-Buschbeck, J. P., H. Stolze, K. Johnk, A. Boczek-Funcke, and M. Illert
1998   Development of Prehension Movements in Children: A Kinematic Study.
        Experimental Brain Research 122:424–432.

Kuroda, S.
1989   Developmental Retardation and Behavioral Characteristics in the Pygmy
        Chimpanzee. *In* Understanding Chimpanzees, edited by P. G. Heltne and
        L. Marquardt, pp. 184–193. Cambridge, MA: Harvard University Press.

Kuykendall, K. L.
2002   An Assessment of Radiographic and Histological Standards of Dental
        Development in Chimpanzees. *In* Human Evolution through
        Developmental Change, edited by N. Minugh-Purvis and J. A. McNamara,
        pp. 281–304. Baltimore, MD: Johns Hopkins University Press.
2003   Reconstructing Australopithecine Growth and Development: What Do We
        Think We Know? *In* Patterns of Growth and Development in the Genus
        Homo, edited by J. L. Thompson, G. E. Krovitz, and A. J. Nelson,
        pp. 191–218. Cambridge: Cambridge University Press.

Kuzawa, C. W.
1998   Adipose Tissue in Human Infancy and Childhood: An Evolutionary
        Perspective. Yearbook of Physical Anthropology 41:177–209.

Labbok, M. H.
1999   Health Sequelae of Breastfeeding for the Mother. Clinics in Perinatology
        26:491–503.
2001   Effects of Breastfeeding on the Mother. Pediatric Clinics of North America
        48:143–158.

Lack, D.
1947   The Significance of Clutch Size. Ibis 89:302–352.
1953   The Evolution of Reproductive Rates. *In* Evolution as a Process, edited by
        J. S. Huxley, E. B. Ford, and A. C. Hardy, pp. 143–156. London: Allen and
        Unwin.

1954   The Natural Regulation of Animal Numbers. Oxford: Clarendon Press.

1968   Ecological Adaptations for Breeding in Birds. London: Metheun.

Lahdenpera, M., V. Lummaa, S. Helle, M. Tremblay, and A. F. Russell
2004   Fitness Benefits of Prolonged Post-reproductive Lifespan in Women.
        Nature 428:178–181.

Lalueza-Fox, C., M. L. Sampietro, D. Caramelli, Y. Puder, M. Lari, F. Calafell,
C. Martinez-Maza, M. Bastir, J. Fortea, M. de la Rasilla, J. Bertranpetit, A. Rosas
2005   Neandertal evolutionary genetics: mitochondrial DNA data from the
        Iberian Peninsula. Molecular Biology and Evolution 22:1077-81.

Lambert, J. E.
1998   Primate Digestion: Interactions among Anatomy, Physiology, and Feeding
        Ecology. Evolutionary Anthropology 7:8–20.

Lancaster, J. B., H. Kaplan, K. Hill, and A. M. Hurtado
2000   The Evolution of Life History, Intelligence and Diet among Chimpanzees
        and Human Foragers. Perspectives in Ethology: Evolution, Culture, and
        Behavior 13:47–72.

Lancaster, J. B., and C. S. Lancaster
1983   Parental Investment: The Hominid Adaptation. *In* How Humans Adapt:
        Biocultural Odyssey, edited by D. J. Ortner, pp. 33–65. Washington, DC:
        Smithsonian Institution Press.

1987   The Watershed: Change in Parental-Investment and Family Formation
        Strategies in the Course of Human Evolution. *In* Parenting across the Life
        Span: Biosocial Dimensions, edited by J. B. Lancaster, J. Altmann, A. S.
        Rossi, and L. R. Sherrod, pp. 187–205. Hawthorne, NY: Aldine de Gruyter.

Largo, R. H., J. A. Caflisch, F. Hug, K. Muggli, A. A. Molnar, and L. Molinari
2001   Neuromotor Development from 5 to 18 Years. Part 2: Associated
        Movements. Developmental Medicine and Child Neurology 43:444–453.

Larick, R., R. Ciochon, Y. Zaim, Sudijono, Suminto, Y. Rizal, F. Aziz, M. Reagan,
and M. Heizler
2001   Early Pleistocene 40Ar/39Ar Ages for Bapang Formation Hominins,
        Central Java, Indonesia. Proceedings of the National Academy of Sciences
        USA 98:4866–4871.

Lasker, G. W.
1969   Human Biological Adaptability. Science 166:1480–1486.

Laslett, P.
1995   Necessary Knowledge: Age and Aging in the Societies of the Past. *In* Aging
        in the Past: Demography, Society, and Old Age, edited by D. I. Kertzer and
        P. Laslett, pp. 3–77. Berkeley: University of California Press.

Lawrence, M., F. Lawrence, W. A. Coward, T. J. Cole, and R. G. Whitehead
1987   Energy Requirements of Pregnancy in the Gambia. The Lancet
        2:1072–1076.

Lawrence, R. A.
1994   Physiology of Human Lactation. *In* Breastfeeding: A Guide for the Medical Profession, edited by R. A. Lawrence, pp. 59–89. St. Louis, MO: Mosby.

Lawrence, R. A., ed.
1989   Breastfeeding: A Guide for the Medical Profession. St. Louis, MO: Mosby.

Le Bourg, E., B. Thon, J. LeGare, B. Desjardins, and H. Charbonneau
1993   Reproductive Life of French-Canadians in the 17th–18th Centuries: A Search for a Trade-off between Early Fecundity and Longevity. Experimental Gerontology 28:217–232.

Leakey, L. S. B.
1958   Recent Discoveries at Olduvai Gorge, Tanganyika. Nature 181:1099–1103.
1959   A New Fossil Skull from Olduvai. Nature 184:491–493.

Leakey, L. S. B., P. V. Tobias, and J. R. Napier
1964   A New Species of the Genus *Homo* from Olduvai Gorge. Nature 202:7–9.

Leakey, M. G., C. S. Feibel, I. McDougall, and A. Walker
1995   New Four-Million-Year-Old Hominid Species from Kanapoi and Allia Bay, Kenya. Nature 376:565–571.

Leakey, M. G., F. Spoor, F. H. Brown, P. N. Gathogo, C. Kiarie, L. N. Leakey, and I. McDougall
2001   New Hominin Genus from Eastern Africa Shows Diverse Middle Pliocene Lineages. Nature 410:433–440.

Leakey, M. G., F. Spoor, F. H. Brown, P. N. Gathogo, and L. N. Leakey
2003   A New Hominin Calvaria from Ileret (Kenya). American Journal of Physical Anthropology. Suppl. no. 36:136.

Leakey, R. E. F.
1973   Evidence for an Advanced Plio-Pleistocene Hominid from East Rudolf, Kenya. Nature 242:447–450.

Lee, M.-F., and S. D. Krasinski
1998   Human Adult-Onset Lactase Decline: An Update. Nutrition News 56:1–8.

Lee, P. C.
1987   Nutrition, Fertility and Maternal Investment in Primates. Journal of Zoology, London 213:409–422.
1997   The Meaning of Weaning: Growth, Lactation, and Life History. Evolutionary Anthropology 5:87–96.
1999   Comparative Ecology of Postnatal Growth and Weaning among Haplorhine Primates. *In* Comparative Primate Socioecology, edited by P. C. Lee, pp. 111–139. Cambridge Studies in Biological and Evolutionary Anthropology, vol. 22. Cambridge: Cambridge University Press.

Lee, P. C., and J. E. Bowman
1995   Influence of Ecology and Energetics on Primate Mothers and Infants. *In* Motherhood in Human and Nonhuman Primates, edited by C. R. Pryce,

R. D. Martin, and D. Skuse, pp. 47–58. Basel, Switzerland: Karger.

Lee, P. C., P. Majluf, and I. J. Gordon

1991   Growth, Weaning, and Maternal Investment from a Comparative Perspective. Journal of Zoology London 225:99–114.

Lee, R. B.

1968   What Hunters Do for a Living, or, How to Make Out on Scarce Resources. *In* Man the Hunter, edited by R. B. Lee and I. DeVore, pp. 30–48. Chicago: Aldine Publishing Company.

1979a   Production and Reproduction. *In* The !Kung San: Men, Women and Work in a Foraging Society, edited by R. B. Lee, pp. 329–330. Cambridge: Cambridge University Press.

Lee, R. B., ed.

1979b   The !Kung San: Men, Women and Work in a Foraging Society. Cambridge: Cambridge University Press.

Lee, R. D.

2003   Rethinking the Evolutionary Theory of Aging: Transfers, Not Births, Shape Senescence in Social Species. Proceedings of the National Academy of Sciences USA 100:9637–9642.

Leigh, S. R.

1994   Ontogenetic Correlates of Diet in Anthropoid Primates. American Journal of Physical Anthropology 94:499–522.

1996   Evolution of Human Growth Spurts. American Journal of Physical Anthropology 101:455–474.

2001   The Evolution of Human Growth. Evolutionary Anthropology 10:223–236.

2004   Brain Growth, Life History, and Cognition in Primate and Human Evolution. American Journal of Primatology 62:139–164.

Leigh, S. R., and P. B. Park

1998   Evolution of Human Growth Prolongation. American Journal of Physical Anthropology 107:331–350.

Leigh, S. R., N. F. Shah, and L. S. Buchanan

2003   Ontogeny and Phylogeny in Papionin Primates. Journal of Human Evolution 45:285–316.

Leigh, S. R., and B. T. Shea

1996   Ontogeny of Body Size Variation in African Apes. American Journal of Physical Anthropology 99:43–65.

Leips, J., J. Travis, and F. H. Rodd

2000   Genetic Influences on Experimental Population Dynamics of the Least Killifish. Ecological Monographs 70:289–309.

Lemon, R. N.

1999   Neural Control of Dexterity: What Has Been Achieved? Experimental Brain Research 128:6–12.

453

León-Cava, N., C. Lutter, J. Ross, and L. Martin

2002   Quantifying the Benefits of Breastfeeding: A Summary of the Evidence. Washington, DC: Pan American Health Organization (PAHO) and Academy for Educational Development (AED).

Leonard, W. R., and M. L. Robertson

1992   Nutritional Requirements and Human Evolution: A Bioenergetics Model. American Journal of Human Biology 4:179–195.

1994   Evolutionary Perspectives on Human Nutrition: The Influence of Brain and Body Size on Diet and Metabolism. American Journal of Human Biology 6:77–88.

Leslie, P. H.

1945   On the Uses of Matrices in Certain Population Mathematics. Biometrika 33:183–212.

Leuttenegger, W.

1973   Maternal-Fetal Weight Relationships in Primates. Folia Primatologica 20:280–293.

Lewis, K.

2000   A Comparative Study of Primate Play Behaviour: Implications for the Study of Cognition. Folia Primatologica 71:417–421.

2003   A Comparative Analysis of Play Behaviour in Primates and Carnivores. Ph.D. diss., University of Durham, UK.

Lewis, K., and R. Barton

2004   Playing for Keeps: Evolutionary Relationships between Social Play and the Cerebellum in Nonhuman Primates. Human Nature 15:5–21.

Li, W.-H., and M. A. Saunders

2005   The Chimpanzees and Us. Nature 447:50–51.

Lieberman, D. E., R. C. McCarthy, K. M. Hiiemae, and J. B. Palmer

2001   Ontogeny of Postnatal Hyoid and Larynx Descent in Humans. Archives of Oral Biology 46:117–128.

Liem, D. G., and J. A. Mennella

2003   Heightened Sour Preferences during Childhood. Chemical Senses 28:173–180.

Lill, J. T.

2001   Selection on Herbivore Life-History Traits by the First and Third Trophic Levels: The Devil and the Deep Blue Sea Revisited. Evolution 55:2236–2247.

Lindstedt, S. T., and W. A. Calder

1981   Body Size, Physiological Time, and Longevity of Homeothermic Animals. Quarterly Review of Biology 56:1–16.

Linnaeus, C.

1758   Systema Naturae. Stockholm: Laurentii Salvii.

Little, M. A., K. Galvin, and M. Mugambi
1983   Cross-sectional Growth of Nomadic Turkana Pastoralists. Human Biology 55:811–830.

Liu, W., Y. Zhang, and X. Wu
n.d.   A Middle Pleistocene Human Cranium from Tangshan, Nanjing of Southeast China: A Comparison with *Homo erectus* from Eurasia and Africa Based on New Reconstruction, in prep. American Journal of Physical Anthropology.

Liversidge, H. M.
2000   Crown Formation Times of Human Permanent Anterior Teeth. Archives of Oral Biology 45:713–721.

2003   Variation in Modern Human Dental Development. *In* Patterns of Growth and Development in the Genus *Homo*, edited by J. L. Thompson, G. E. Krovitz, and A. J. Nelson, pp. 73–113. Cambridge: Cambridge University Press.

Locke, J. L., and B. Bogin
2005   Language and Life History: A New Perspective on the Development and Evolution of Human Language. Behavioral and Brain Sciences. Available online at http://www.bbsonline.org/preprints/Locke-06252004/references/

Lockwood, C. A., and J. G. Fleagle
1999   The Recognition and Evaluation of Homoplasy in Primate and Human Evolution. Yearbook of Physical Anthropology 42:189–232.

Lockwood, C. A., B. G. Richmond, W. L. Jungers, and W. H. Kimbel
1996   Randomization Procedures and Sexual Dimorphism in *Australopithecus afarensis*. Journal of Human Evolution 31:537–548.

Long, J. S.
1997   Regression Models for Categorical and Limited Dependent Variables. Thousand Oaks, CA: Sage Publications.

Lönnerdal, B., and E. L. Lien
2003   Nutritional and Physiologic Significance of a-lactalbumin in Infants. Nutrition Reviews 61:295–305.

Lopez-Alarcon, M., S. Villalpando, and A. Fajardo
1997   Breast-Feeding Lowers the Frequency and Duration of Acute Respiratory Infection and Diarrhea in Infants under Six Months of Age. Journal of Nutrition 127:436–443.

Lotka, A.
1922   The Stability of the Normal Age Distribution. Proceedings of the National Academy of Sciences USA 8:339–345.

Loudon, A. S. I., and P. A. Racey
1987   Reproductive Energetics in Mammals. Oxford: Clarendon Press.

Love, B., and H. G. Müller
2002   A Solution to the Problem of Obtaining a Mortality Schedule for
        Paleodemographic Data. *In* Paleodemography: Age Distributions from
        Skeletal Samples, edited by R. D. Hoppa and J. W. Vaupel, pp. 181–192.
        New York: Cambridge University Press.

Lovejoy, C. O., R. S. Meindl, R. P. Mensforth, and T. J. Barton
1985   Multifactorial Determination of Skeletal Age at Death: A Method and
        Blind Tests of Its Accuracy. American Journal of Physical Anthropology
        68:1–14.

**Lovejoy, C. O., R. S. Meindl, T. R. Pryzbeck, T. S. Barton, K. G. Heiple,
and D. Kotting**
1977   Paleodemography of the Libben Site, Ottawa County, Ohio. Science
        198:291–293.

Lovejoy, C. O., R. S. Meindl, T. R. Pryzbeck, and R. P. Mensforth
1985   Chronological Metamorphosis of the Auricular Surface of the Ilium: A
        New Method for the Determination of Adult Skeletal Age at Death.
        American Journal of Physical Anthropology 68:15–28.

Lovejoy, C. O., R. S. Meindl, R. G. Tague, and B. Latimer
1997   The Comparative Senescent Biology of the Hominoid Pelvis and Its
        Implications for the Use of Age-at-Death Indicators in the Human
        Skeleton. *In* Integrating Archaeological Demography: Multidisciplinary
        Approaches to Prehistoric Population, edited by R. R. Paine, pp. 43–63.
        Carbondale: Southern Illinois University Press.

Lovelady, C. A., B. Lönnerdal, and K. G. Dewey
1990   Lactation Performance of Exercising Women. American Journal of
        Clinical Nutrition 52:103–109.

Low, B. S., C. P. Simon, and K. G. Anderson
2002   An Evolutionary Ecological Perspective on Demographic Transitions:
        Modeling Multiple Currencies. American Journal of Human Biology
        14:149–167.

Luckett, W. P.
1993   An Ontogenetic Assessment of Dental Homologies in Therian Mammals.
        In Mammal Phylogeny, edited by F. S. Szalay, M. J. Novacek, and
        M. C. McKenna, pp. 182–204. New York: Springer.

Lucy, D., R. G. Aykroyd, A. M. Pollard, and T. Solheim
1996   A Bayesian Approach to Adult Human Age Estimation from Dental
        Observations by Johanson's Age Changes. Journal of Forensic Sciences
        41:189–194.

Lukacs, J. R.
1999   Enamel Hypoplasia in Deciduous Teeth of Great Apes: Do Differences in
        Defect Prevalence Imply Differential Levels of Physiological Stress?
        American Journal of Physical Anthropology 110:351–363.

2001   Enamel Hypoplasia in the Deciduous Teeth of Great Apes: Variation in
            Prevalence of Defects. American Journal of Physical Anthropology
            116:199–208.

Lumsden, A.
1988   Spatial Organization of the Epithelium and the Role of Neural Creset
            Cells in the Initiation of the Mammalian Tooth Germ. Development.
            Suppl. no. 1:155–169.

Lunn, P. G.
1985   Maternal Nutrition and Lactational Infertility: The Baby in the Driving
            Seat. *In* Maternal Nutrition and Lactational Infertility, edited by J.
            Dobbing, pp. 41–64. Vevey, Switzerland: Nestle Nutrition; New York: Raven
            Press.

Mabilia, M.
1996a   Beliefs and Practices in Infant Feeding among the Wagogo of Chigongwe
            (Dodoma Rural District), Tanzania. 1. Breastfeeding. Ecology of Food and
            Nutrition 35:195–207.

1996b   Beliefs and Practices in Infant Feeding among the Wagogo of Chigongwe
            (Dodoma Rural District), Tanzania. 2. Weaning. Ecology of Food and
            Nutrition 35:209–217.

MacArthur, R. H., and E. O. Wilson
1967   Theory of Island Biogeography. Princeton, NJ: Princeton University Press.

Mace, R., and R. Sear
2005   Are Humans Communal Breeders? *In* Grandmotherhood: The
            Evolutionary Significance of the Second Half of Human Life, edited by
            E. Voland, A. Chasiotis, and W. Schiefenhoevel, pp. 143–159. New
            Brunswick, NJ: Rutgers University Press.

Macho, G. A.
2001   Primate Molar Crown Formation Times and Life History Evolution
            Revisited. American Journal of Primatology 55:189–201.

Macho, G. A., and B. A. Wood
1995a   Evolution of Modern Dental Ontogeny Revisited. Anthropologie 33:57–62.
1995b   The Role of Time and Timing in Hominid Dental Evolution. Evolutionary
            Anthropology 4:17–31.

MacLean, A.
1986   Age-Specific Foraging Ability and the Evolution of Deferred Breeding in
            Three Species of Gulls. Wilson Bulletin 98:267–279.

Macy, I. C., H. J. Kelly, and R. E. Sloan
1953   The Composition of Milks. Washington, DC: National Research Council.

Maddison, W. P., and D. R. Maddison
2003   Mesquite: A Modular System for Evolutionary Analysis. Version 1.0.
            http://www.mesquiteproject.org, (last accessed September 2005).

Malenky, R. K., S. Kuroda, E. O. Vineberg, and R. W. Wrangham
1994   The Significance of Terrestrial Herbaceous Foods for Bonobos, Chimpanzees, and Gorillas. *In* Chimpanzee Cultures, edited by R. W. Wrangham, M. C. McGrew, F. B. M. de Waal, P. G. Heltne, and L. A. Marquardt, pp. 59–76. Cambridge, MA: Harvard University Press.

Malm, K., and P. Jensen
1997   Weaning and Parent-Offspring Conflict in the Domestic Dog. Ethology 103:653–664.

Manganaro, R.
2001   Incidence of Dehydration and Hypernatremia in Exclusively Breast-Fed Infants. Journal of Pediatrics 139:673–675.

Mann, A., M. Lampl, and J. Monge
1990   Patterns of Ontogeny in Human Evolution: Evidence from Dental Development. Yearbook of Physical Anthropology 33:111–150.

Mann, A. E.
1975   Paleodemographic Aspects of South African Australopithecines. University of Pennsylvania Publications in Anthropology 1:171.

Maples, W. R.
1989   An Improved Technique Using Dental Histology for Estimating Adult Ages. Journal of Forensic Science 24:168–174.

Marchand, F.
1902   Ueber das Hirngewicht des Menschen. Leipzig: B.G. Teubner.

Marchetti, K., and T. Price
1989   Differences in the Foraging of Juvenile and Adult Birds: The Importance of Developmental Constraints. Biological Reviews 64:51–70.

Markham, R.
1995   Doing It Naturally: Reproduction in Captive Orangutans (*Pongo pygmaeus*). *In* The Neglected Ape, edited by R. D. Nadler, B. M. F. Galdikas, L. K. Sheeran, and N. Rosen, pp. 273–278. New York: Plenum Press.

Marlowe, F.
2001   Male Contribution to Diet and Female Reproductive Success among Foragers. Current Anthropology 42:755–760.
2003   A Critical Period for Provisioning by Hadza Men: Implications for Pair Bonding. Evolution and Human Behavior 24:217–229.
2004   Marital Residence among Foragers. Current Anthropology 45:277–283.

Márquez, S., K. Mowbray, G. J. Sawyer, T. Jacob, and A. Silvers
2001   New Fossil Hominid Calvaria from Indonesia—Sambungmacan 3. The Anatomical Record 262:344–368.

Marquis, G. S., and J. Habicht
2000   Breastfeeding and Stunting among Toddlers in Peru. *In* Short and Long Term Effects of Breast Feeding on Child Health, edited by B. Koletzko,

K. F. Michaelsen, and O. Hernell, pp. 163–172. New York: Kluwer
Academic Plenum Publishers.

Marriott, H.
1997   Juggling Time and Dropping the Baby? Constraints Faced by Malian
Women. *In* Population Dynamics: Some Past and Emerging Issues, edited
by R. A. Powell, E. A. Mwafeni, and A. Ankomah, pp. 74–83. Exeter:
University of Exeter.

**Martin, J. A., B. E. Hamilton, P. D. Sutton, S. J. Ventura, F. Menacker,
and M. L. Munson**
2003   Births: Final Data for 2002. National Vital Statistics Reports, vol. 52, no.
10. Hyattsville, MD: National Center for Health Statistics.

Martin, P.
1984   The Meaning of Weaning. Animal Behaviour 32:1257–1259.
1985   Weaning: A Reply to Counsilman and Lim. Animal Behaviour
33:1024–1026.

Martin, R. D.
1981   Relative Brain Size and Basal Metabolic Rate in Terrestrial Vertebrates.
Nature 293:57–60.
1983   Human Brain Evolution in an Ecological Context. Fifty-Second James
Arthur Lecture on the Evolution of the Human Brain. New York:
American Museum of Natural History.
1984   Scaling Effects and Adaptive Strategies in Mammalian Lactation. Symposia
of the Zoological Society of London 51:87–117.
1990   Primate Origins and Evolution: A Phylogenetic Reconstruction. London:
Chapman and Hall.
1996   Scaling of the Mammalian Brain: The Maternal Energy Hypothesis. News
in Physiological Science 11:149–156.

Martin, R. D., and A. M. MacLarnon
1990   Reproductive Patterns in Primates and Other Mammals: The Dichotomy
between Altricial and Precocial Offspring. *In* Primate Life History and
Evolution, edited by C. J. De Rosseau, pp. 47–79. New York: Wiley-Liss.

Matsuzawa, T.
1994   Field Experiments on Use of Stone Tools by Chimpanzees in the Wild.
In Chimpanzee Cultures, edited by R. W. Wrangham, W. C. McGrew,
F. B. M. de Waal, P. G. Heltne, and L. A. Marqandt, pp. 351–370.
Cambridge, MA: Harvard University Press.

Maynard Smith, J.
1978   Optimization Theory in Evolution. Annual Review of Ecology and
Systematics 9:31–56.

McCracken, R. D.
1971   Lactase Deficiency: An Example of Dietary Evolution. Current
Anthropology 12:479–517.

McCrory, M. A.

2000 Aerobic Exercise during Lactation: Safe, Healthful, and Compatible. Journal of Human Lactation 16:95–98.

2001 Does Dieting during Lactation Put Infant Growth at Risk? Nutrition Reviews 59:18–27.

McDade, T. W., and C. M. Worthman

1998 The Weanling's Dilemma Reconsidered: A Biocultural Analysis of Breastfeeding Ecology. Journal of Developmental and Behavioral Pediatrics 19:286–299.

McDermott, J. M., R. Steketee, and J. Wirima

1995 Mortality Associated with Multiple Gestation in Malawi. International Journal of Epidemiology 24:413–419.

McDougall, I., F. H. Brown, and J. G. Fleagle

2005 Stratigraphic placement and age of modern humans from Kibish, Ethiopia. Nature 433:733-6.

McGuire, J., and B. Popkin

1989 Beating the Zero-Sum: Women and Nutrition in the Third World, Part 1. Food and Nutrition Bulletin 11:38–63.

McHenry, H. M.

1991 Petite Bodies of the "Robust" Australopithecines. American Journal of Physical Anthropology 86:445–454.

1992 Body Size and Proportions in Early Hominids. American Journal of Physical Anthropology 87:407–431.

1994 Behavioral Ecological Implications of Early Hominid Body Size. Journal of Human Evolution 27:77–87.

McHenry, H. M., and K. Coffing

2000 *Australopithecus* to *Homo*: Transformations in Body and Mind. Annual Review of Anthropology 29:125–46.

McKenna, J. J.

1990 Evolution and Sudden Infant Death Syndrome (SIDS). Part II: Why Human Infants? Human Nature 1:179–206.

McKenna, J. J., and N. J. Bernshaw

1995 Breastfeeding and Infant-Parent Co-sleeping as Adaptive Strategies: Are They Protective against SIDS? *In* Breastfeeding: Biocultural Perspectives, edited by P. Stuart-Macadam and K. A. Dettwyler, pp. 265–303. Foundations of Human Behavior. New York: Aldine de Gruyter.

McKeown, T.

1976 The Modern Rise of Population. New York: Academic Press.

McKern, T. W., and T. D. Stewart

1957 Skeletal Age Changes in Young American Males, Analyzed from the

Standpoint of Identification. Technical Report EP-45. Natick, MA: Headquarters, Quartermaster Research and Development Command.

McKinney, M. L., and K. J. McNamara
1991   Heterochrony: The Evolution of Ontogeny. New York: Plenum Press.

McMahon, T. A., and J. T. Bonner
1983   On Size and Life. New York: Scientific American Books.

McNab, B. K.
1963   Bioenergetics and the Determination of Home Range Size. American Naturalist 97:133–140.

1980   Food Habits, Energetics, and the Population Biology of Mammals. American Naturalist 116:106–124.

McNeil, W. H.
1977   Plagues and Peoples. New York: Doubleday.

Meindl, R. S., C. O. Lovejoy, R. P. Mensforth, and R. A. Walker
1985   A Revised Method of Aging Using the *os pubis*, with a Review of Tests of Accuracy of Other Current Methods of Pubic Symphyseal Aging. American Journal of Physical Anthropology 68:29–45.

Melton, L. J., S. C. Bryant, H. W. Wahner, W. M. O'Fallon, G. D. Malkasian, H. L. Judd, and B. L. J. Riggs
1993   Influence of Breastfeeding and Other Reproductive Factors on Bone Mass in Later Life. Osteoporosis International 3:76–83.

Mennella, J. A., and G. K. Beauchamp
1998   Early Flavor Experience: Research Update. Nutrition Reviews 56:205–211.

Mensforth, R. P., and C. O. Lovejoy
1985   Anatomical, Physiological, and Epidemiological Correlates of the Aging Process: A Confirmation of Multifactorial Age Determination in the Libben Skeletal Population. American Journal of Physical Anthropology 68:87–106.

Merchant, K., and R. Martorell
1988   Frequent Reproductive Cycling: Does It Lead to Nutritional Depletion of Mothers? Progress in Food and Nutrition Science 12:339–369.

Merchant, K., R. Martorell, and J. Haas
1990a   Maternal and Fetal Responses to the Stresses of Lactation Concurrent with Pregnancy and of Short Recuperative Intervals. American Journal of Clinical Nutrition 52:280–288.

1990b   Consequences for Maternal Nutrition of Reproductive Stress across Consecutive Pregnancies. American Journal of Clinical Nutrition 52:616–620.

Meredith, H. V.
1970   Body Weight at Birth of Viable Human Infants: A Worldwide Comparative Treatise. Human Biology 42:217–264.

Miles, A. E. W.

1963   The Dentition in Assessment of Individual Age in Skeletal Material. *In* Dental Anthropology, edited by D. R. Brothwell, pp. 191–209. Oxford: Pergamon Press.

2001   The Miles Method of Assessing Age from Toothwear Revisited. Journal of Archaeological Science 28:973–982.

Milla, P. J.

1991   Feeding, Tasting, Sucking. *In* Pediatric Gastrointestinal Disease: Pathophysiology, Diagnosis and Management, vol. 1, edited by W. Walker, pp. 217–223. Philadelphia: B.C. Decker.

Millar, J. S.

1977   Adaptive Features of Mammalian Reproduction. Evolution 31:370–386.

Milner, G. R., J. L. Boldsen, and B. M. Usher

1997   Age at Death Determination Using Revised Scoring Procedures for Age-Progressive Skeletal Traits. Abstract. American Journal of Physical Anthropology. Suppl. no. 24:170.

Minugh-Purvis, N., and K. J. McNamara, eds.

2002   Human Evolution through Developmental Change. Baltimore, MD: Johns Hopkins University Press.

Moggi-Cecchi, J., P. V. Tobias, and A. D. Beynon

1998   The Mixed Dentition and Associated Skull Fragments of a Juvenile Fossil Hominid from Sterkfontein, South Africa. American Journal of Physical Anthropology 106:425–465.

Molleson, T., M. Cox, H. A. Waldron, and D. K. Whittaker

1993   The Spitalfields Project. Vol. 2 of The Anthropology. York: Council for British Archaeology.

Montgomery, R. K., H. A. Buller, E. H. H. M. Rings, and R. J. Grand

1991   Lactose Intolerance and the Genetic Regulation of Intestinal Lactase-Phlorizin Hydrolase. The FASEB Journal 5:2824–2832.

Mooney, V.

1997   Sacroiliac Joint Dysfunction. *In* Movement, Stability and Low Back Pain, edited by A. Vleeming, V. Mooney, T. Dorman, C. Snijders, and R. Stoeckart, pp. 37–52. London: Churchill Livingston.

Moore, J.

1996   Savanna Chimpanzees, Referential Models and the Last Common Ancestor. *In* Great Ape Societies, edited by W. McGrew, T. Nishida, and L. Marchant, pp. 275–292. Cambridge: Cambridge University Press.

Moore J. A., A. C. Swedlund, and G. J. Armelagos

1975   The Use of Life Tables in Paleodemography. *In* Population Studies in Archaeology and Biological Anthropology: A Symposium, edited by A. C. Swedlund, pp. 57–70. Memoirs of the Society for American

Archaeology, no. 30. Washington, DC: Society for American Archaeology.

Moorrees, C. F. A., E. A. Fanning, and E. E. Hunt
1963   Age Variation of Formation Stages for Ten Permanent Teeth. Journal of Dental Research 42:1490–1502.

Morey, D. F., G. M. Crothers, J. K. Stein, J. P. Fenton, and N. P. Herrmann
2002   The Fluvial and Geomorphic Context of Indian Knoll, an Archaic Shell Midden in West-Central Kentucky. Geoarchaeology 17:521–553.

Morin, P. A., J. Wallis, J. J. Moore, and D. A. Woodruff
1994   Paternity Exclusion in a Community of Wild Chimpanzees Using Hypervariable Simple Sequence Repeats. Molecular Ecology 3:469–478.

Morse, J. M., C. Jehle, and D. Gamble
1990   Initiating Breastfeeding: A World Survey of the Timing of Postpartum Breastfeeding. International Journal of Nursing Studies 27:303–313.

Morwood, M. J., P. Brown, Sutikna T. Jatmiko, E. W. Saptomo, K. E. Westaway, R. A. Due, R. G. Roberts, T. Maeda, S. Wasisto, T. Djubiantono
2005   Further evidence for small-bodied hominins from the Late Pleistocene of Flores, Indonesia. Nature 437:1012-17.

Morwood, M. J., R. P. Soejono, R. G. Roberts, T. Sutikna, C. S. Turney, K. E. Westaway, W. J. Rink, J. X. Zhao, G. D. van den Bergh, R. A. Due, D. R. Hobbs, M. W. Moore, M. I. Bird, and L. K. Fifield
2004   Archaeology and Age of a New Hominin from Flores in Eastern Indonesia. Nature 431:1087–1091.

Mowbray, K., S. Marquez, S. Antón, C. C. Swisher III, T. Jacob, G. J. Sawyer, D. C. Broadfield, J. T. Laitman, R. Holloway, E. Delson, and I. Tattersall
2000   The Newly Recovered Poloyo Hominin (PL-1) from Java. American Journal of Physical Anthropology. Suppl. no. 30:233.

Mueller, K., and V. Loemberg
1992   Development of Speed of Repetitive Movements in Children Is Determined by Structural Changes in Corticospinal Efferents. Neuroscience Letters 144:57–60.

Müller, G. B., and S. A. Newman
2003   Origination of Organismal Form: Beyond the Gene in Developmental and Evolutionary Biology. London: A Bradford Book, MIT Press.

Muller, H.-G., J.-M. Chiou, J. R. Carey, and J.-J. Wang
2002   Fertility and Lifespan: Late Children Enhance Female Longevity. Journal of Gerontology: Biological Sciences 57A:B202–B206.

Murdock, G. P.
1949   Social Structure. New York: The Free Press.

Murray, K. A., and T. M. Murray
1991   A Test of the Auricular Surface Aging Technique. Journal of Forensic Sciences 36:1162–1169.

Myowa-Yamakoshi, M., and T. Matsuzawa

2000 Imitation of Intentional Manipulatory Actions in Chimpanzees (*Pan troglodytes*). Journal of Comparative Psychology 114:381–391.

Nakano, Y., and T. Kimura

1992 Development of Bipedal Walking in *Macaca fuscata* and *Pan troglodytes. In* Topics in Primatology, vol. 3, edited by S. Matano, R. H. Tuttle, H. Ishida, and M. Goodman, pp. 177–190. Tokyo: University of Tokyo.

National Academy of Sciences

1989 Nutrition and Diarrheal Diseases Control in Developing Countries. Washington, DC: National Academy Press.

Nee, S., N. Colegrave, S. A. West, and A. Grafen

2005 The Illusion of Invariant Quantities in Life Histories. Science 309:1236–1239.

Neel, J. V., and K. M. Weiss

1975 The Genetic Structure of a Tribal Population, the Yanomama Indians. American Journal of Physical Anthropology 42:25–52.

Nelson, A. J., J. L. Thompson, and G. E. Krovitz

2003 Putting It All Together. *In* Patterns of Growth and Development in the Genus *Homo*, edited by J. L. Thompson, G. E. Krovitz, and A. J. Nelson, pp. 436–445. Cambridge Studies in Biological and Evolutionary Anthropology, vol. 37. Cambridge: Cambridge University Press.

Nerlove, S. B.

1974 Women's Workload and Infant Feeding Practices: A Relationship with Demographic Implications. Ethnology 13:207–214.

Neville, M. C., J. C. Allen, P. C. Archer, C. E. Casey, J. M. Seacat, R. P. Keller, V. Lutes, J. Rasbach, and M. R. Neifert

1991 Studies in Human Lactation: Milk Volume and Nutrient Composition during Weaning and Lactogenesis. American Journal of Clinical Nutrition 54:81–92.

Neville, M. C., R. Keller, J. Seacat, V. Lutes, M. Neifert, C. E. Casey, J. C. Allen, and P. C. Archer

1988 Studies in Human Lactation: Milk Volumes in Lactating Women during the Onset of Lactation and Full Lactation. American Journal of Clinical Nutrition 48:1375–1386.

Neville, M. C., and J. Morton

2001 Physiology and Endocrine Changes Underlying Human Lactogenesis II. The Journal of Nutrition 131:3005S–3008S.

Neville, M. C., J. Morton, and S. Umemura

2001 Lactogenesis: The Transition from Pregnancy to Lactation. Pediatric Clinics of North America 48:35–52.

Newcomb, P. A., B. E. Storer, M. P. Longnecker, R. Mittendorf, E. R. Greenberg, R. W. Clapp, K. P. Burke, W. C. Willett, and B. MacMahon

1994   Lactation and a Reduced Risk of Premenopausal Breast Cancer. New England Journal of Medicine 330:81–87.

Nicolosi, R. J., and R. D. Hunt

1979   Dietary Allowances for Nutrients in Nonhuman Primates. *In* Primates in Nutritional Research, edited by K. C. Hayes, pp. 11–37. New York: Academic Press.

Nicolson, N. A.

1987   Infants, Mothers and Other Females. *In* Primate Societies, edited by B. B. Smuts, D. L. Cheney, R. M. Seyfarth, R. W. Wrangham, and T. T. Struhsaker, pp. 330–342. Chicago and London: University of Chicago Press.

Nielsen, R., C. Bustamante, A. G. Clark, S. Glanowski, T. B. Sackton, M. J. Hubisz, A. Fledel-Alon, D. M. Tanenbaum, D. Civello, T. J. White, J. J. Sninsky, M. D. Adams, and M. Cargill

2005   A Scan for Positively Selected Genes in the Genomes of Humans and Chimpanzees. PLOS Biology 3:976–985.

Nishida, T., N. Corp, M. Hamai, T. Hasegawa, M. Hiraiwa-Hasegawa, K. Hosaka, K. D. Hunt, N. Itoh, K. Kawanaka, A. Matsumoto-Oda, J. C. Mitani, M. Nakamura, K. Norikoshi, T. Sakamaki, L. Turner, S. Uehara, and K. Zamma

2003   Demography, Female Life History, and Reproductive Profiles among Chimpanzees of Mahale. American Journal of Primatology 59:99–121.

Nishida, T., H. Takasaki, and Y. Takahata

1990   Demography and Reproductive Profiles. *In* The Chimpanzees of the Mahale Mountains: Sexual and Life History Strategies, edited by T. Nishida, pp. 63–97. Tokyo: University of Tokyo Press.

Nissen, H. W., and S. H. Riesen

1964   The Eruption of the Permanent Dentition of Chimpanzee. American Journal of Physical Anthropology 22:285–294.

Nowicki, S., W. Searcy, and S. Peters

2002   Brain Development, Song Learning and Mate Choice in Birds: A Review and Experimental Test of the "Nutritional Stress Hypothesis." Journal of Comparative Physiology A 188:1003–1014.

Nozaki, M., F. Mitsunaga, and K. Shimizu

1995   Reproductive Senescence in Female Japanese Monkeys (*Macaca fuscata*): Age- and Season-Related Changes in Hypothalamic-Pituitary-Ovarian Functions and Fecundity Rates. Biology of Reproduction 52:1250–1257.

Nunn, C. L., and R. A. Barton

2001   Comparative Methods for Studying Primate Adaptation and Allometry. Evolutionary Anthropology 10:81–98.

O'Connell, J. F., K. Hawkes, and N. G. Blurton Jones

1988   Hadza Hunting, Butchering and Bone Transport and Their Archaeological Implications. Journal of Anthropological Research 44:113–162.

1999   Grandmothering and the Evolution of *Homo erectus*. Journal of Human Evolution 36:461–485.

O'Connell, J. F., K. Hawkes, K. D. Lupo, and N. G. Blurton Jones

2002   Male Strategies and Plio-Pleistocene Archaeology. Journal of Human Evolution 43:831–872.

O'Connor, K. A.

1995   The Age Pattern of Mortality: A Micro-Analysis of Tipu and a Meta-Analysis of Twenty-Nine Paleodemographic Samples. Ph.D. diss., State University of New York, Albany.

O'Connor, K. A., D. L. Holman, and J. W. Wood

2001   Menstrual Cycle Variability and the Perimenopause. American Journal of Human Biology 13:465–478.

Oeppen, J., and J. W. Vaupel

2002   Broken Limits to Life Expectancy. Science 296:1029–1031.

Oftedal, O. T.

1984a   Body Size and Reproductive Strategy as Correlates of Milk Energy Output in Lactating Mammals. Acta Zoologica Fennica 171:183–186.

1984b   Milk Composition, Milk Yield and Energy Output at Peak Lactation: A Comparative Review. Symposia of the Zoological Society of London 51:33–85.

1985   Pregnancy and Lactation. *In* The Bioenergetics of Wild Herbivores, edited by R. J. Hudson and R. G. White, pp. 215–238. Boca Raton, FL: CRC Press.

1986   Milk Intake in Relation to Body Size. *In* The Breastfed Infant: A Model for Performance, pp. 44–47. Columbus, OH: Ross Laboratories.

1991   The Nutritional Consequences of Foraging in Primates: The Relationship of Nutrient Intakes to Nutrient Requirements. Philosophical Transactions of the Royal Society London, Series B 334:161–170.

Oftedal, O. T., and S. J. Iverson

1987   Hydrogen Isotope Methodology for Measurement of Milk Intake and Energetics of Growth in Suckling Young. *In* Marine Mammal Energetics, edited by A. C. Huntley, D. P. Costa, G. A. J. Worthy, and M. A. Castellini, pp. 67–96. Society for Marine Mammalogy Special Publications. Lawrence, KS: Allen Press.

Olshansky, S. J., B. A. Carnes, and C. Cassel

1998   The Future of Long Life. Science 281:1612–1613.

Olson, M. V., and A. Varki

2004   The Chimpanzee Genome—A Bittersweet Celebration. Science 305:191–192.

466

Ovchinnikov, I. V., A. Gotherstrom, G. P. Romanova, V. M. Khritonov, K. Liden, and W. Goodwin

2000   Molecular Analysis of Neanderthal DNA from the Northern Caucasus. Nature 404:490–493.

Overall, J. E., and J. A. Woodward

1977   Nonrandom Assignment and the Analysis of Covariance. Psychological Bulletin 84:588–594.

Packer, C., M. Tatar, and A. Collins

1998   Reproductive Cessation in Female Mammals. Nature 392:807–811.

Pagel, M. D., and P. H. Harvey

1988   How Mammals Produce Large-Brained Offspring. Evolution 42:948–957.

1989   Taxonomic Differences in the Scaling of Brain on Body Weight among Mammals. Science 244:1589–1593.

1993   Evolution of the Juvenile Period in Mammals. In Juvenile Primates: Life History, Development, and Behavior, edited by M. E. Pereira and L. A. Fairbanks, pp. 528–537. New York: Oxford University Press.

Paine, R. R.

1989   Model Life Table Fitting by Maximum Likelihood Estimation: A Procedure to Reconstruct Paleodemographic Characteristics from Skeletal Age Distributions. American Journal of Physical Anthropology 79:51–62.

1997   The Role of Uniformitarian Models in Osteological Paleodemography. In Integrating Archaeological Demography: Multidisciplinary Approaches to Prehistoric Population, edited by R. R. Paine, pp. 191–204. Center for Archaeological Investigations, Occasional Papers no. 24. Carbondale: Southern Illinois University Press.

2000   If a Population Crashes in Prehistory and There Is No Paleodemographer There to Hear It, Does It Make a Sound? American Journal of Physical Anthropology 112:181–190.

Paine, R. R., and J. L. Boldsen

1997   Long-Term Trends in Mortality Patterns in Preindustrial Europe. Abstract. American Journal of Physical Anthropology. Suppl. no. 24:183.

2002   Linking Mortality and Population Dynamics. In Paleodemography: Age Distributions from Skeletal Samples, edited by R. D. Hoppa and J. W. Vaupel, pp. 169–180. Cambridge Studies in Biological and Evolutionary Anthropology, vol. 31. Cambridge: Cambridge University Press.

Panter-Brick, C.

1991   Lactation, Birth Spacing and Maternal Work-Loads among Two Castes in Rural Nepal. Journal of Biosocial Science 23:137–154.

1995   Child-Care Strategies in Nepal: Responses to Ecology, Demography, and Society. In Human Populations, edited by A. J. Boyce and V. Reynolds, pp. 174–188. Oxford, New York, Tokyo: Oxford University Press.

Panter-Brick, C., D. S. Lotstein, and P. T. Ellison
1993   Seasonality of Reproductive Function and Weight Loss in Rural Nepal Women. Human Reproduction 8:684–690.

Panter-Brick, C., A. Todd, and R. Baker
1996   Growth Status of Homeless Nepali Boys: Do They Differ from Rural and Urban Controls? Social Science and Medicine 43:441–451.

Parker, S. T., J. Langer, and M. L. McKinney, eds.
2000   Biology, Brains, and Behavior: The Evolution of Human Development. School of American Research. Santa Fe, NM: SAR Press.

Parker, S. T., and M. McKinney
1999   Origins of Intelligence: The Evolution of Cognitive Development in Monkeys, Apes, and Humans. Baltimore, MD: Johns Hopkins University Press.

Parkin, T.
2003   Old Age in the Roman World. Baltimore, MD: Johns Hopkins Press.

Partridge, L., and P. H. Harvey
1988   The Ecological Context of Life History Evolution. Science 241:1449–1455.

Partridge, L., and M. Mangel
1999   Messages from Mortality: The Evolution of Death Rates in the Old. Trends in Ecology and Evolution 14:438–442.

Partridge, T. C., D. E. Granger, M. W. Caffee, and R. J. Clarke
2003   Lower Pliocene Hominid Remains from Sterkfontein. Science 300:607–612.

Patino, E. M., and J. T. Borda
1997   The Composition of Primates' Milks and Its Importance in Selecting Formulas for Hand Rearing. Laboratory Primate Newsletter 36:8–9.

Patterson, B., and W. W. Howells
1967   Hominid Humeral Fragment from Early Pleistocene of Northwest Kenya. Science 156:64–66.

Patterson, C., D. M. Williams, and C. J. Humphries
1993   Congruence between Molecular and Morphological Phylogenies. Annual Review of Ecology and Systematics 24:153–188.

Pavard, S., A. Gagnon, B. Desjardins, and E. Heyer
2005   Mother's Death and Child Survival: The Case of Early Quebec. Journal of Biosocial Science 37:209–227.

Pavelka, M. S. M., and L. M. Fedigan
1991   Menopause: A Comparative Life History Perspective. Yearbook of Physical Anthropology 34:13–38.

Peccei, J. S.
2001   Menopause: Adaptation or Epiphenomenon? Evolutionary Anthropology 10:43–57.

Pennington, R. L.

1996   Causes of Early Human Population Growth. American Journal of Physical Anthropology 99:259–274.

Pereira, M. E., and J. Altmann

1985   Development of Social Behavior in Free-Living Nonhuman Primates. *In* Nonhuman Primate Models for Human Growth and Development, edited by E. S. Watts, pp. 217–309. Monographs in Primatology, 6. New York: Alan R. Liss, Inc.

Pereira, M. E., and L. A. Fairbanks.

1993   Juvenile Primates: Life History, Development, and Behavior. New York: Oxford University Press.

Pérez-Escamilla R., S. Segura-Millán, J. Canahuati, and H. Allen

1996   Prelacteal Feedings Are Negatively Associated with Breast-Feeding Outcomes in Honduras. Journal of Nutrition 126:2765–2773.

Persson, L. A.

2001   Breaking the Cycles of Malnutrition: Are Pregnancy Nutrition Interventions Effective? Journal of Health of Population Nutrition 19:158–159.

Peters, R. H.

1983   The Ecological Implications of Body Size. Cambridge: Cambridge University Press.

Pettay, J. E., L. E. B. Kruuk, J. Jokela, and V. Lummaa

2005   Heritability and Genetic Constraints of Life-History Trait Evolution in Preindustrial Humans. Proceedings of the National Academy of Sciences USA 102:2838–2843.

Pianka, E. R.

1970   On "r" and "K" selection. American Naturalist 104:592–597.

Picciano, M. F.

2001   Nutrient Composition of Human Milk. Pediatric Clinics of North America 48:53–67.

Pickford, M.

1975   Late Miocene Sediments and Fossils from the Northern Kenya Rift Valley. Nature 256:279–284.

Pickford, M., B. Senut, D. Gommery, and J. Treil

2002   Bipedalism in *Orrorin tugenensis* Revealed by Its Femora. C. R. Palevol 1:1–13.

Pisev, V.

1985   Age-Sex Changes in the Speed of the Movement in Students Aged 7–17. Khigiena-I-Zdraveopazvane 27:462–465.

Pollitt, E.
1984   Methods for the Behavioral Assessment of the Consequences of Malnutrition. *In* Methods for the Evaluation of the Impact of Food and Nutrition Programs, edited by E. Sahn, R. Lockwood, and N. Scrimshaw, pp. 179–203. Tokyo: United Nations University.

Pond, C. M.
1997   The Biological Origins of Adipose Tissue in Humans. *In* The Evolving Female, edited by M. E. Morbeck, A. Galloway, and A. L. Zihlman, pp. 47–162. Princeton, NJ: Princeton University Press.

Poppitt, S. D., A. M. Prentice, G. R. Goldberg, and R. G. Whitehead
1994   Energy-Sparing Strategies to Protect Human Fetal Growth. American Journal of Obstetrics and Gynecology 171:118–125.

Portmann, A.
1941   Die Tragzeiten der Primaten und die Dauer der Schwangerschaft Beim Menschen: Ein Problem der Vergleichenden Biologie. Revue Suisse Zoologie 48:511–518.

Power, M. L., O. T. Oftedal, and S. D. Tardif
2002   Does the Milk of Callitrichid Monkeys Differ from That of Larger Anthropoids? American Journal of Primatology 56:117–127.

Powers, D. A., and Y. Xie
2000   Statistical Methods for Categorical Data Analysis. San Diego: Academic Press.

Prentice, A.
1986   The Effect of Maternal Parity on Lactational Performance in a Rural African Community. *In* Human Lactation 2: Maternal and Environmental Factors, edited by M. Hamosh and A. S. Goldman, pp. 165–173. New York: Plenum Press.

Prentice, A., A. Paul, A. Prentice, A. Black, T. Cole, and R. Whitehead
1986   Cross-cultural Differences in Lactational Performance. *In* Human Lactation 2: Maternal and Environmental Factors, edited by M. Hamosh and A. S. Goldman, pp. 13–43. New York: Plenum Press.

Prentice, A., C. Spaaij, G. Goldberg, S. Poppitt, J. van Raaij, M. Totton, D. Swann, and A. Black
1996   Energy Requirements of Pregnant and Lactating Women. European Journal of Clinical Nutrition. Suppl. no. 1:S82–S111.

Prentice, A., R. Whitehead, S. Roberts, and A. Paul
1981   Long-Term Energy Balance in Child-Bearing Gambian Women. American Journal of Clinical Nutrition 34:2790–2799.

Prentice, A. M., and G. R. Goldberg
2000   Energy Adaptations in Human Pregnancy: Limits and Long-Term Consequences. American Journal of Clinical Nutrition. Suppl. no. 5:1226S–1232S.

Prentice, A. M., and A. Prentice
1988   Energy Costs of Lactation. Annual Reviews of Nutrition 8:63–79.

Prentice, A. M., and R. G. Whitehead
1987   The Energetics of Human Reproduction. Symposia of the Zoological Society of London 57:275–304.

Promislow, D.
1991   Senescence in Natural Populations of Mammals: A Comparative Study. Evolution 45:1869–1887.

Promislow, D. E. L., and P. H. Harvey
1990   Living Fast and Dying Young: A Comparative Analysis of Life History Variation among Mammals. Journal of Zoology London 220:417–437.

1991   Mortality Rates and the Evolution of Mammal Life Histories. Acta Oecologica 12:119–137.

Prothero, J. W., and K. D. Jürgens
1987   Scaling of Maximum Lifespan in Mammals: A Review. *In* Evolution of Longevity in Animals: A Comparative Approach, edited by A. D. Woodhead and K. H. Thompson, pp. 49–74. New York: Plenum Press.

Purvis, A., and P. H. Harvey
1995   Mammal Life-History Evolution: A Comparative Test of Charnov's Model. Journal of Zoology London 237:259–283.

Pusey, A. E.
1983   Mother-Offspring Relationships in Chimpanzees after Weaning. Animal Behaviour 31:363– 377.

1990   Behavioural Changes at Adolescence in Chimpanzees. Behaviour 115:203–246.

2001   Of Genes and Apes: Chimpanzee Social Organization and Reproduction. *In* Tree of Origin, edited by F. B. M. de Waal, pp. 10–37. Cambridge, MA: Harvard University Press.

Pusey, A. E., J. Williams, and J. Goodall
1997   The Influence of Dominance Rank on the Reproductive Success of Female Chimpanzees. Science 227:828–831.

Quandt, S.
1985   Biological and Behavioral Predictors of Exclusive Breastfeeding Duration. Medical Anthropology 9:139–51.

Quartz, S., and T. Sejnowski
1997   The Neural Basis of Cognitive Development. Behavioral and Brain Sciences 20:537–596.

Rabb, J. E., B. H. Passey, J. B. Coltrain, and T. E. Cerling
2004   Detecting Weaning through Incremental Stable Isotope Analysis of Human Tooth Enamel Using Conventional and Laser Sampling Techniques. Poster, Paleoanthropological Society Meetings, Montreal.

Ragsdale, G.
2004   Grandmothering in Cambridgeshire, 1770–1861. Human Nature 15:301–317.

Ramírez Rozzi, F. V., and J. M. Bermúdez de Castro
2004   Surprisingly Rapid Growth in Neanderthals. Nature 428:936–939.

Rasmussen, K. M.
1992   The Influence of Maternal Nutrition on Lactation. Annual Review of Nutrition 12:103–117.

Read, A. F., and P. H. Harvey
1989   Life History Differences among the Eutherian Radiations. Journal of Zoology London 219:329–353.

Reid, D. J., G. T. Schwartz, C. Dean, and M. S. Chandrasekera
1998   A Histological Reconstruction of Dental Development in the Common Chimpanzee, *Pan troglodytes.* Journal of Human Evolution 35:427–448.

Remer, T., and F. Manz
2001   The Midgrowth Spurt in Healthy Children Is Not Caused by Adrenarche. Journal of Clinical Endocrinology and Metabolism 86:4183–4186.

Reno, P. L., R. S. Meindl, M. A. McCollum, and C. O. Lovejoy
2003   Sexual Dimorphism in *Australopithecus afarensis* Was Similar to That of Modern Humans. Proceedings of the National Academy of Sciences 100:9404–9409.

Richardson, S. J., V. Senikas, and J. F. Nelson
1987   Follicular Depletion during the Menopausal Transition: Evidence for Accelerated Loss and Ultimate Exhaustion. Journal of Clinical Endochrinology and Metabolism 65:1231–1237.

Ricklefs, R. E.
1998   Evolutionary Theories of Aging: Confirmation of a Fundamental Prediction, with Implications for the Genetic Basis and Evolution of Life Span. American Naturalist 152:24–44.

Ricklefs, R. E., and A. Scheuerlein
2001   Comparison of Aging-Related Mortality among Birds and Mammals. Experimental Gerontology 36:845–857.

Righard, L., and O. Alade
1992   Sucking Technique and Its Effect on Duration of Breast Feeding. Birth 4:185–189.

Rightmire, G. P.
1985   The Tempo of Change in the Evolution of Mid-Pleistocene *Homo. In* Ancestors: The Hard Evidence, edited by E. Delson, pp. 255–264. New York: Alan R. Liss.

Rizvi, N.
1993   Issues Surrounding the Promotion of Colostrum Feeding in Rural Bangladesh. Ecology of Food and Nutrition 30:27–38.

Roberts, S. B., T. J. Cole, and W. A. Coward
1985   Lactational Performance in Relation to Energy Intake in the Baboon. American Journal of Clinical Nutrition 41:1270–1276.

Robine, J.-M., and M. Allard
1998   The Oldest Human. Science 279:1834–1835.

Robinson, J. T.
1960   The Affinities of the New Olduvai Australopithecine. Nature 186:456–458.

Robson, A. J., and H. S. Kaplan
2003   The Evolution of Human Life Expectancy and Intelligence in Hunter-Gatherer Economics. American Economic Review 93:150–169.

Robson, S. L.
2004   Breast Milk, Diet, and Large Human Brains. Current Anthropology 45:419–424.

Roche, A. F., W. C. Chumlea, and D. Thissen
1988   Assessing the Skeletal Maturity of the Hand-Wrist: Fels Method. Springfield, IL: Charles C. Thomas.

Rodriguez, G., P. Ventura, M. P. Samper, L. Moreno, A. Sarria, and J. M. Perez-Gonzalez
2000   Changes in Body Composition during the Initial Hours of Life in Breast-Fed Healthy Term Newborns. Biology of the Neonate 77:12–16.

Roff, D. A.
1992   The Evolution of Life Histories: Theory and Analysis. New York: Chapman and Hall.

Rogers, A. R.
1993   Why Menopause? Evolutionary Ecology 7:406–420.

Rogoff, B.
1996   Developmental Transitions in Children's Participation in Sociocultural Activities. *In* The Five to Seven Year Shift: The Age of Reason and Responsibility, edited by A. J. Sameroff and M. M. Haith, pp. 273–294. Chicago: University of Chicago Press.

Rosenberg, K. R., Z. Lu, and C. B. Ruff
1999   Body Size, Body Proportions and Encephalization in the Jinniushan Specimen. American Journal of Physical Anthropology. Suppl. no. 28:235.

Rosenblatt, K. A., and D. B. Thomas
1993   WHO Collaborative Study of Neoplasia and Steroid Contraceptives. International Journal of Epidemiology 22:192–197.

Ross, C.
1998   Primate Life Histories. Evolutionary Anthropology 6:54–63.
2003   Life History, Infant Care Strategies, and Brain Size in Primates. *In* Primate Life Histories and Socioecology, edited by P. M. Kappeler and M. E. Pereira, pp. 266–284. Chicago: University of Chicago Press.

2004   Life Histories and the Evolution of Large Brain Size Great Apes. *In* The Evolution of Thought: Evolutionary Origins of Great Ape Intelligence, edited by A. E. Russon and D. R. Begun, pp. 122–139. Cambridge: Cambridge University Press.

Ross, C., and K. E. Jones
1999   Socioecology and the Evolution of Primate Reproductive Rates. *In* Comparative Primate Socioecology, edited by P. C. Lee, pp. 73–110. Cambridge Studies in Biological and Evolutionary Anthropology, vol. 22. Cambridge: Cambridge University Press.

Rowland, M. G. M., R. A. E. Barrell, and R. G. Whitehead
1978   The Weanling's Dilemma: Bacterial Contamination in Traditional Gambian Weaning Foods. The Lancet 1:136–138.

Ruff, C. B., E. Trinkhaus, and T. W. Holliday
1997   Body Mass and Encephalization in Pleistocene *Homo*. Nature 387:173–176.

Russell, J. C.
1948   British Medieval Population. Albuquerque: University of New Mexico Press.

Sacher, G. A.
1959   Relation of Lifespan to Brain Weight and Body Weight in Mammals. *In* Ciba Foundation Colloquia on Ageing, vol. 5, The Lifespan of Animals, edited by G. E. W. Wolstenholme and M. O'Connor, pp. 115–133. London: Churchill.
1975   Maturation and Longevity in Relation to Cranial Capacity in Hominid Evolution. Primate Functional Morphology and Evolution, edited by R. H. Tuttle, pp. 417–441. The Hague: Mouton.

Sacher, G. A., and E. F. Staffeldt
1974   Relation of Gestation Time to Brain Weight for Placental Mammals: Implications for the Theory of Vertebrate Growth. American Naturalist 108:593–615.

Sadleir, R. M. F.
1967   The Role of Nutrition in the Reproduction of Wild Mammals. Journal of Reproduction and Fertility. Suppl. no. 6:39–48.

Saether, B.-E.
1988   Pattern of Co-variation between Life-History Traits of European Birds. Nature 331:616–617.

Safi, K., M. A. Seid, and D. K. N. Dechmann
2005   Bigger Is Not Always Better: When Brains Get Smaller. Biology Letters 1:283–286.

Sahi, T.
1974   The Inheritance of Selective Adult-Type Lactose Malabsorption. Helsinki: Vammala.

Sahi, T., M. Isokoski, J. Jussila, and K. Launiala
1972   Lactose Malabsorption in Finnish Children of School Age. Acta Paediatrica Scandinavica 61:11–16.

Sahlins, M. D.
1972   Stone Age Economics. Chicago: Aldine.

Sameroff, A. J., and M. M. Haith, eds.
1996   The Five to Seven Year Shift: The Age of Reason and Responsibility. Chicago: University of Chicago Press.

Sanderson, M. J., and M. J. Donoghue
1989   Patterns of Variation in Levels of Homoplasy. Evolution 43:1781–1795.

Santos, A. L.
1995   How Old Is This Pelvis? A Comparison of Age at Death Estimation Using the Auricular Surface of the Ilium and Os Pubis. *In* Aspects of African Archaeology: Papers from the 10th Congress of the Pan African Association, edited by G. Pwiti and R. Soper, pp. 29–36. Harare: University of Zimbabwe Publications.

Satake, T., F. Kirutka, and T. Ozaki
1993   Ages at Peak Velocity and Peak Velocities for Seven Body Dimensions in Japanese Children. Annals of Human Biology 20:67–70.

Sattenspiel, L. R., and H. C. Harpending
1983   Stable Populations and Skeletal Age. American Antiquity 48:489–498.

Sauther, M. L.
1994   Changes in the Use of Wild Plant Foods in Free-Ranging Ring-Tailed Lemurs during Pregnancy and Lactation: Some Implications for Human Foraging Strategies. *In* Eating on the Wild Side: The Pharmacologic, Ecologic and Social Implications of Using Non-cultigens, edited by N. L. Etkin, pp. 240–246. Tucson: University of Arizona Press.

Schew, W., and R. Ricklefs
1998   Developmental Plasticity. *In* Avian Growth and Development: Evolution within the Altricial-Precocial Spectrum, edited by J. Starck and R. Ricklefs, pp. 288–304. New York: Oxford University Press.

Schmitt, A., P. Murail, E. Cunha, and D. Rougé
2002   Variability of the Pattern of Aging on the Human Skeleton: Evidence from Bone Indicators and Implications on Age at Death Estimation. Journal of Forensic Sciences 47:1203–1209.

Schmitt, D.
2003   Insights into the Evolution of Human Bipedalism from Experimental Studies of Humans and Other Primates. Journal of Experimental Biology 206:1437–1448.

Schneiberg, S., H. Sveistrup, B. McFadyen, P. McKinley, and M. F. Levin
2002   The Development of Coordination for Reach-to-Grasp Movements in Children. Experimental Brain Research 146:142–154.

Schoeninger, M. J., H. T. Bunn, S. Murray, T. Pickering, and J. Moore
2001   Meat-Eating by the Fourth African Ape. *In* Meat-Eating and Human
        Evolution, edited by C. B. Stanford and H. T. Bunn, pp. 179–195. New
        York: Oxford University Press.

Schoetensack, O.
1908   Der Unterkiefer des *Homo heidelbergensis* aus den Sanden von Mauer bei
        Heidelberg. Leipzig: W. Engelmann.

Schrire, C.
1980   An Inquiry into the Evolutionary Status and Apparent Identity of San
        Hunter-Gatherers. Human Ecology 8:9–32.

Schultz, A. H.
1924   Growth Studies on Primates Bearing upon Man's Evolution. American
        Journal of Physical Anthropology 7:149–164.

1941   The Relative Size of the Cranial Capacity in Primates. American Journal of
        Physical Anthropology 28:273–287.

1949   Ontogenetic Specializations in Man. Archive Julius Klaus-Stiftung
        24:197–216.

1950   The Physical Distinctions of Man. Proceedings of the American
        Philosophical Society 94:428–449.

1956   Postembryonic Age Changes. Primatologica 1:887–964.

1960   Age Changes in Primates and Their Modification in Man. *In* Human
        Growth, edited by J. M. Tanner, pp. 1–20. Oxford: Pergamon Press.

1969   The Life of Primates. New York: Universe Books.

Schwartz, G. T., and C. Dean
2000   Interpreting the Hominid Dentition: Ontogenetic and Phylogenetic
        Aspects. *In* Development, Growth and Evolution, edited by P. O'Higgins
        and M. Cohn, pp. 207–233. London: Academic Press.

Schwartz, J., and I. Tattersall
2002   The Human Fossil Record, vol. 1, Terminology and Craniodental
        Morphology of Genus *Homo* (Europe). New York: Wiley-Liss

Sear, R., R. Mace, and I. A. McGregor
2000   Maternal Grandmothers Improve Nutritional Status and Survival of
        Children in Rural Gambia. Proceedings of the Royal Society London,
        Series B 267:1641–1647.

2003   The Effects of Kin on Female Fertility in Rural Gambia. Evolution and
        Human Behavior 24:25–42.

Sear, R., F. Steele, I. A. McGregor, and R. Mace
2002   The Effects of Kin on Child Mortality in Rural Gambia. Demography
        39:43–63.

Seger, J., and J. W. Stubblefield
1996   Optimization and Adaptation. *In* Adaptation, edited by G. Lauder and
        M. R. Rose, pp. 93–123. New York: Academic Press.

Sellen, D. W.

1998   Infant and Young Child Feeding Practices among African Pastoralists: The Datoga of Tanzania. Journal of Biosocial Science 30:481–499.

1999   Growth Patterns among Semi-nomadic Pastoralists (Datoga) of Tanzania. American Journal of Physical Anthropology 109:187–209.

2000   Seasonal Ecology and Nutritional Status of Women and Children in a Tanzanian Pastoral Community. American Journal of Human Biology 12:758–781.

2001a   Comparison of Infant Feeding Patterns Reported for Nonindustrial Populations with Current Recommendations. Journal of Nutrition 3:2707–2715.

2001b   Of What Use Is an Evolutionary Anthropology of Weaning? Human Nature: An Interdisciplinary Journal 12:1–7.

2001c   Weaning, Complementary Feeding, and Maternal Decision Making in a Rural East African Pastoral Population. Journal of Human Lactation 17:233–244.

2002   Sub-optimal Breast Feeding Practices: Ethnographic Approaches to Building "Baby Friendly" Communities. Advances in Experimental Medicine & Biology 503:223–232.

Sellen, D. W., and R. Mace

1999   A Phylogenetic Analysis of the Relationship between Sub-adult Mortality and Mode of Subsistence. Journal of Biosocial Science 31:1–16.

Sellen, D. W., A. E. Tedstone, and J. Frize

2002   Food Insecurity among Refugee Families in East London: Results of a Pilot Assessment. Public Health Nutrition 5:637–644.

Senut, B., M. Pickford, D. Gommery, P. Mein, K. Cheboi, and Y. Coppens

2001   First Hominid from the Miocene (Lukeino Formation, Kenya). Comptes Rendus de l'Academie des Sciences Paris 332:137–144.

Setty-Venugopal, V., and U. D. Upadhyay

2002   Birth Spacing: Three to Five Saves Lives. Population Reports, series L, no. 13. Baltimore, MD: Johns Hopkins University, Bloomberg School of Public Health, Population Information Program.

Shanley, D. P., and T. B. L. Kirkwood

2001   Evolution of the Human Menopause. BioEssays 23:282–287.

Shea, B. T.

1981   Relative Growth of the Limbs and Trunk in the African Apes. American Journal of Physical Anthropology 56:179–201.

1983a   Allometry and Heterochrony in African Apes. American Journal of Physical Anthropology 62:275–289.

1983b   Paedomorphosis and Neotony in the Pygmy Chimpanzee. Science 222:521–522.

1989   Heterochrony in Human Evolution: The Case for Neotony Reconsidered. Yearbook of Physical Anthropology 32:69–101.

2002 Are Some Heterochronic Transformations Likelier Than Others? *In* Human Evolution through Developmental Change, edited by N. Minugh-Purvis and K. J. McNamara, pp. 79–101. Baltimore, MD: Johns Hopkins University Press.

Shea, B. T., and R. C. Bailey
1996 Allometry and Adaptation of Body Proportions and Stature in African Pygmies. American Journal of Physical Anthropology 100:311–340.

Sheppard, J. J., and E. D. Mysak
1984 Ontogeny of Infantile Oral Reflexes and Emerging Chewing. Child Development 55:831–843.

Shi, J., H. Xi, Y. Wang, C. Zhang, Z. Jiang, K. Zhang, Y. Shen, L. Jin, K. Zhang, W. Yuan, Y. Wang, J. Lin, Q. Hua, F. Wang, S. Xu, S. Ren, S. Xu, G. Zhao, Z. Chen, L. Jin, and W. Huang
2003 Divergence of the Genes on Human Chromosome 21 between Human and Other Hominoids and Variation of Substitution Rates among Transcription Units. Proceedings of the National Academy of Sciences 100:8331–8336.

Shibaguchi, T., J. Kato, M. Abe, Y. Tamamura, M. J. Tabata, J. G. Liu, M. Iwamoto, S. Wakisaka, A. Wanaka, and K. Kurisu
2003 Expression and Role of Lhx8 in Murine Tooth Development. Archives of Histology and Cytology 66:95–108.

Shibata, Y., Y. Shirai, and M. Miyamoto
2002 The Aging Process in the Sacroiliac Joint: Helical Computed Tomography Analysis. Journal of Orthopaedic Science 7:12–18.

Short, R. V.
1976 The Evolution of Human Reproduction. Proceedings of the Royal Society London, Series B 195:3–24.

1987 The Biological Basis for the Contraceptive Effects of Breastfeeding. International Journal of Gynaecology & Obstetrics. Suppl. no. 25:207–218.

Short, R. V., N. England, N. E. Bridson, and D. M. Bowden
1989 Ovarian Cyclicity, Hormones, and Behavior as Markers of Aging in Female Pigtailed Macaques (*Macaca nemestrina*). Journal of Gerontology 44:B131–B138.

Shoshani, J., C. P. Groves, E. L. Simons, and G. F. Gunnell
1996 Primate Phylogeny: Morphological vs. Molecular Results. Molecular Phylogenetics and Evolution 5:101–153.

Silverman, N., B. Richmond, and B. Wood
2001 Testing the Taxonomic Integrity of *Paranthropus boisei sensu stricto*. American Journal of Physical Anthropology 115:167–178.

Skelton, R. R., and H. M. McHenry
1992 Evolutionary Relationships among Early Hominids. Journal of Human Evolution 23:309–349.

Skinner, M. F.
1997   Dental Wear in Immature Late Pleistocene Hominines. Journal of Archeological Science 24:677–700.

Skytthe, A., and J. L. Boldsen
1993   A Method for Computer Aided Estimation of Age at Death from Skeletons. Abstract. American Journal of Physical Anthropology. Suppl. no. 16:182.

Smith, B. H.
1986   Dental Development in *Australopithecus* and Early *Homo*. Nature 323:327–330.

1989a   Dental Development as a Measure of Life History in Primates. Evolution 43:683–688.

1989b   Growth and Development and Its Significance for Early Hominid Behavior. Ossa 14:63–96.

1991a   Dental Development and the Evolution of Life History in Hominidae. American Journal of Physical Anthropology 86:157–174.

1991b   Age at Weaning Approximates Age of Emergence of the First Permanent Molar in Non-human Primates. American Journal of Physical Anthropology. Suppl. no. 12:163–164 (abstract).

1992   Life History and the Evolution of Human Maturation. Evolutionary Anthropology 1:134–142.

1993   The Physiological Age of KNM-15000. *In* The Nariokotome *Homo erectus* Skeleton, edited by A. Walker and R. Leakey, pp. 195–220. Cambridge, MA: Harvard University Press.

1994   The Sequence of Eruption of Teeth in *Macaca, Pan, Australopithecus,* and *Homo*: Its Evolutionary Significance. American Journal of Human Biology 6:61–76.

2000   "Schultz's Rule" and the Evolution of Tooth Emergence and Replacement Patterns in Primates and Ungulates. *In* Development, Function, and Evolution of Teeth, edited by M. F. Teaford, M. M. Small, and M. W. J. Ferguson, pp. 212–227. Cambridge: Cambridge University Press.

Smith, B. H., T. L. Crummett, and K. L. Brandt
1994   Ages of Eruption of Primate Teeth: A Compendium for Aging Individuals and Comparing Life Histories. Yearbook of Physical Anthropology 37:177–231.

Smith, B. H., and R. L. Tompkins
1995   Toward a Life History of the Hominidae. Annual Review of Anthropology 24:257–279.

Smith, C. C., and S. D. Fretwell
1974   The Optimal Balance between Size and Number of Offspring. American Naturalist 108:499–504.

Smith, D. W. E.
1993   Human Longevity. New York: Oxford University Press.

Smith, K. R., G. P. Mineau, and L. L. Bean
2003   Fertility and Post-reproductive Longevity. Social Biology 49:185–205.

Smith, R. J.
1996   Biology and Body Size in Human Evolution. Current Anthropology 37:451–481.

Smith, R. J., P. J. Gannon, and B. H. Smith
1995   Ontogeny of Australopithecines and Early *Homo:* Evidence from Cranial Capacity and Dental Eruption. Journal of Human Evolution 29:155–168.

Smith, R. J., and W. L. Jungers
1997   Body Mass in Comparative Primatology. Journal of Human Evolution 32:523–559.

Smith, R. J., and S. R. Leigh
1998   Sex Dimorphism in Primate Neonatal Body Mass. Journal of Human Evolution 34:173–201.

Smith, S. L.
2004   Skeletal Age, Dental Age, and the Maturation of KNM-WT 15000. American Journal of Physical Anthropology 125:105–120.

Smuts, B. B., and D. J. Gubernick
1992   Male-Infant Relationships in Nonhuman Primates: Paternal Investment or Mating Effort? *In* Father-Child Relations: Cultural and Biosocial Contexts, edited by B. S. Hewlett, pp. 1–30. New York: Aldine de Gruyter.

Smuts, B. B., and R. Smuts
1993   Male Aggression and Sexual Coercion of Females in Nonhuman Primates and Other Mammals: Evidence and Theoretical Implications. Advances in the Study of Behavior 22:1–63.

Southgate, D. A. T., and E. N. Hey
1976   Chemical and Biochemical Development of the Human Fetus. *In* The Biology of Human Growth, edited by D. F. Roberts and A. M. Thompson, pp. 195–209. London: Halsted Press.

Spencer, H.
1886   *The Principles of Biology.* Vols. I and II. New York: D. Appleton.

Sprott, D. A.
1970   Note on Evans and Anastasio on the Analysis of Covariance. Psychological Bulletin 73:303–306.

Stacey, P. B.
1986   Group Size and Foraging Efficiency in Yellow Baboons. Behavioral Ecology and Sociobiology 18:175–187.

Stanford, C. B.
1999   The Hunting Apes: Meat Eating and the Origins of Human Behavior. Princeton, NJ: Princeton University Press.

Stearns, S. C.

1977   The Evolution of Life History Traits: A Critique of the Theory and a Review of the Data. Annual Review of Ecology and Systematics 8:145–171.

1992   The Evolution of Life Histories. Oxford: Oxford University Press.

Steenbeek, R.

2000   Infanticide by Males and Female Choice in Thomas's Langurs. *In* Infanticide by Males and Its Implications, edited by C. P. van Schaik and C. H. Janson, pp. 153–177. Cambridge: Cambridge University Press.

Stevenson, R. D., and J. H. Allaire

1991   The Development of Normal Feeding and Swallowing. Pediatric Clinics of North America 38:1439–1453.

Stiner, M. C.

2000   Carnivory, Coevolution and the Geographic Spread of Genus *Homo*. Journal of Archaeological Research 10:1–63.

2002   Thirty Years on the "Broad Spectrum Revolution" and Paleolithic Demography. Proceedings of the National Academy of Sciences 98:6993–6996.

Strait, D. S., and F. E. Grine

2001   The Systematics of *Australopithecus garhi*. Ludus Vitalis 9:17–82.

2004   Inferring Hominoid and Early Hominid Phylogeny Using Craniodental Characters: The Role of Fossil Taxa. Journal of Human Evolution 47:399–452.

Strait, D. S., F. E. Grine, and M. A. Moniz

1997   A Reappraisal of Early Hominid Phylogeny. Journal of Human Evolution 32:17–82.

Stringer, C. B.

1979   A Re-evaluation of the Fossil Human Calvaria from Singa, Sudan. Bulletin of the British Museum of Natural History: Geology 32:77–83.

Sturesson, B., A. Udén, and A. Vleeming

2000   A Radiostereometric Analysis of Movements of the Sacroiliac Joints during the Standing Hip Flexion Test. Spine 25:364–368.

Sugiyama, Y.

2004   Demographic Parameters and Life History of Chimpanzees at Bossou, Guinea. American Journal of Physical Anthropology 124:154–165.

Sullivan, P. G.

1986   Skull, Jaw, and Teeth Growth Patterns. *In* Human Growth, vol. 2, Postnatal Growth, edited by F. Falkner and J. M. Tanner, pp. 243–268. New York: Plenum.

Sutherland, W. J., A. Grafen, and P. H. Harvey

1986   Life History Correlations and Demography. Nature 320:88.

Suwa, G.

1988   Evolution of the "Robust" Australopithecines in the Omo Succession: Evidence from Mandibular Premolar Morphology. *In* Evolutionary History of the "Robust" Australopithecines, edited by F. E. Grine, pp. 199–222. New York: Aldine de Gruyter.

Suwa, G., B. Asfaw, Y. Beyene, T. White, S. Katoh, S. Nagaoka, H. Nakaya, K. Uzawa, P. Renne, and G. WoldeGabriel

1997   The First Skull of *Australopithecus boisei.* Nature 389:489–492.

Swisher, C., G. Curtis, T. Jacob, A. Getty, A. Supurijo, and Widiasmoro

1994   Age of the Earliest Known Hominids in Java. Science 263:118–1121.

Takahata, Y., H. Ihobe, and G. Idani

1996   Comparing Copulations of Chimpanzees and Bonobos: Do Females Exhibit Proreceptivity or Receptivity? *In* Great Ape Societies, edited by W. McGrew, T. Nishida, and L. Marchant, pp. 146–155. Cambridge: Cambridge University Press.

Tanner, J.

1986   Growth as a Target-Seeking Function: Catch-Up and Catch-Down Growth in Man. *In* Human Growth: A Comprehensive Treatise, vol. 1, Developmental Biology, Prenatal Growth, edited by F. Falkner and J. Tanner, pp. 167–179. 2d ed. New York: Plenum Press.

Tardieu, C.

1998   Short Adolescence in Early Hominids: Infantile and Adolescent Growth of the Human Femur. American Journal of Physical Anthropology 107:163–178.

Tardif, S. D., M. L. Harrison, and M. A. Simek

1993   Communal Infant Care in Marmosets and Tamarins: Relation to Energetics, Ecology, and Social Organization. *In* Marmosets and Tamarins: Systematics, Behaviour, and Ecology, edited by A. B. Rylands, pp. 200–219. Oxford: Oxford University Press.

Teleki, G. E., E. Hunt, and J. H. Pfifferling

1976   Demographic Observations (1963–1973) on the Chimpanzees of the Gombe National Park, Tanzania. Journal of Human Evolution 5:559–598.

Thompson, J. L., G. E. Krovitz, and A. J. Nelson, eds.

2003   Patterns of Growth and Development in the Genus *Homo.* Cambridge Studies in Biological and Evolutionary Anthropology, vol. 37. Cambridge: Cambridge University Press.

Thompson-Handler, N.

1990   The Pygmy Chimpanzee: Sociosexual Behavior, Reproductive Biology, and Life History. Ph.D. diss., Yale University, New Haven, CT.

Tilden, C. D., and O. T. Oftedal

1997   Milk Composition Reflects Pattern of Maternal Care in Prosimian Primates. American Journal of Primatology 41:195–211.

Tinbergen, N.

1963   On Aims and Methods of Ethology. Zeitschrift für Tierpsychology
         20:410–433.

Tinkle, D. W.

1969   The Concept of Reproductive Effort and Its Relation to the Evolution of
         Life Histories of Lizards. American Naturalist 103:501–516.

Tobias, P. V.

1971   The Brain in Hominid Evolution. New York: Columbia University Press.

1995   Thoughts on *Homo erectus* and Its Place in Human Evolution. Acta
         Anthropologica Sinica 14: 297–312.

Tomasello, M., and J. Call

1997   Primate Cognition. Oxford: Oxford University Press.

Tonz, O.

2000   Breastfeeding in Modern and Ancient Times: Facts, Ideas, and Beliefs. *In*
         Short and Long Term Effects of Breast Feeding on Child Health, edited by
         B. Koletzko, K. F. Michaelsen, and O. Hernell, pp. 1–21. New York: Kluwer
         Academic Plenum Publishers.

Tooby, J., and I. DeVore

1987   The Reconstruction of Hominid Behavioral Evolution through Strategic
         Modeling. *In* The Evolution of Human Behavior: Primate Models, edited
         by W. Kinzey, pp. 183–237. Albany, NY: SUNY Press.

Top, F. H., and P. F. Wehrle

1976   Communicable and Infectious Diseases. St. Louis, MO: C. V. Mosby.

Towne, B., E. W. Demerath, and S. A. Czerwinski

2002   The Genetic Epidemiology of Growth and Development. *In* Human
         Growth and Development, edited by N. Cameron, pp. 103–137.
         Amsterdam: Academic Press.

Tracer, D.

1991   Fertility-Related Changes in Maternal Body Composition among the Au of
         Papua New Guinea. American Journal of Physical Anthropology
         85:393–405.

Trevathan, W. R., and J. J. McKenna

1994   Evolutionary Environments of Human Birth and Infancy: Insights to Apply
         to Contemporary Life. Children's Environments 11:88–104.

Trinkaus, E.

1995   Neanderthal Mortality Patterns. Journal of Archaeological Science
         22:121–142.

Trinkaus, E., and R. L. Tompkins

1987   Femoral Diaphyseal Histomorphometric Age Determinations for the
         Shanidar 3, 4, 5 and 6 Neanderthals and Neanderthal Longevity.
         American Journal of Physical Anthropology 72:123–129.

1990   The Neanderthal Life Cycle: The Possibility, Probability, and Perceptibility of Contrasts with Recent Humans. *In* Primate Life History Evolution, edited by C. J. De Rousseau, pp. 153–180. New York: Wiley-Liss.

Trivers, R. L.
1972   Parental Investment and Sexual Selection. *In* Sexual Selection and the Descent of Man, edited by B. Campbell, pp. 136–179. Chicago: Aldine de Gruyter.
1974   Parent-Offspring Conflict. American Zoologist 14:249–264.

Tronick, E. Z., G. A. Morelli, and P. K. Ivey
1992   The Efe Forager Infant and Toddler's Pattern of Social Relationships: Multiple and Simultaneous. Developmental Psychology 28:568–577.

Tronick, E. Z., and S. A. Winn
1992   The Neurobehavioral Organization of Efe (Pygmy) Infants. Developmental and Behavioral Pediatrics 13:421–424.

Tucker, B., and A. G. Young
2005   Growing Up Mikea: Children's Time Allocation and Tuber Foraging in Southwestern Madagascar. *In* Hunter-Gatherer Childhoods, edited by B. S. Hewlett and M. E. Lamb, pp. 147–171. New Brunswick, NJ, and London: Aldine Transaction.

Turnbull, C. M.
1983a   The Human Cycle. New York: Simon and Schuster.
1983b   The Mbuti Pygmies. New York: Holt, Rinehart, and Winston.

Tutin, C. E. G., and P. R. McGinnis
1981   Chimpanzee Reproduction in the Wild. *In* Reproductive Biology of Great Apes: Comparative and Biomedical Perspectives, edited by C. E. Graham, pp. 239–264. New York: Academic Press.

Tymicki, K.
2004   Kin Influence on Female Reproductive Behavior: The Evidence from Reconstitution of the Bejsce Parish Registers, Eighteenth and Twentieth Centuries, Poland. American Journal of Human Biology 16:508–522.

Ulijaszek, S. J., and S. S. Strickland
1993   Nutritional Anthropology: Prospects and Perspectives. London: Smith Gordon.

Underwood, B. A., and Y. Hofvander
1982   Appropriate Timing for Complementary Feeding of the Breast-Fed Infant. Acta Paediatrica Scandinavica S294:5–32.

Vallois, H. V., and B. Vandermeersch
1972   Le Crâne Moustérian de Qafzeh (*Homo* VI). l'Anthropologie 76:71–96.

van Noordwijk, M. A., and C. P. van Schaik
2005   Development of Ecological Competence in Sumatran Orangutans. American Journal of Physical Anthropology 127:79–94.

van Schaik, C. P.

1983   Why Are Diurnal Primates Living in Groups? Behaviour 87:120–144.

1989   The Ecology of Social Relationships among Female Primates. *In* Comparative Socioecology: The Behavioural Ecology of Humans and Other Mammals, edited by V. Standen and R. Foley, pp. 195–218. Oxford: Blackwell.

1996   Social Evolution in Primates: The Role of Ecological Factors and Male Behaviour. Proceedings of the British Academy 88:9–31.

2000   Vulnerability to Infanticide by Males: Patterns among Mammals. *In* Infanticide by Males and Its Implications, edited by C. P. van Schaik and C. H. Janson, pp. 61–71. Cambridge: Cambridge University Press.

2004   Among Orangutans: Red Apes and the Rise of Human Culture. Cambridge, MA: Harvard University Press.

van Schaik, C. P., and R. O. Deaner

2003   Life History and Cognitive Evolution in Primates. *In* Animal Social Complexity: Intelligence, Culture, and Individualized Societies, edited by F. B. M. de Waal and P. L. Tyack, pp. 5–25. Cambridge, MA: Harvard University Press.

van Schaik, C. P., and P. Kappeler

1997   Infanticide Risk and the Evolution of Male-Female Association in Primates. Proceedings of the Royal Society London, Series B 264:1687–1694.

van Schaik, C. P., G. R. Pradhan, and M. A. van Noordwijk

2004   Mating Conflict in Primates: Infanticide, Sexual Harassment and Female Sexuality. *In* Sexual Selection in Primates: New and Comparative Perspectives, edited by P. M. Kappeler and C. P. van Schaik, pp. 131–150. Cambridge: Cambridge University Press.

van Schaik, C. P., M. A. van Noordwijk, and C. L. Nunn

1999   Sex and Social Evolution in Primates. *In* Comparative Primate Socioecology, edited by P. Lee, pp. 204–231. Cambridge Studies in Biological and Evolutionary Anthropology, vol. 22. Cambridge: Cambridge University Press.

Vaupel, J. W.

1997   Trajectories of Mortality at Advanced Ages. *In* Between Zeus and the Salmon, edited by K. W. Wachter and C. E. Finch, pp. 17–37. Washington, DC: National Academy Press.

Vaupel, J. W., K. G. Manton, and E. Stallard

1979   The Impact of Heterogeneity in Individual Frailty on the Dynamics of Mortality. Demography 16:439–454.

Vekua, A., D. Lordkipanidze, G. P. Rightmire, J. Augusti, R. Ferring, G. Maisuradze, A. Mouskhelishvili, M. Nioradze, M. Ponce De Leon, M. Tappen, M. Tvalchrelidze, and C. Zollikofer

2002   A New Skull of Early *Homo* from Dmanisi, Georgia. Science 297:85–89.

Venables, W. N., and B. D. Ripley
1999 Modern Applied Statistics with S-PLUS. 3d ed. New York: Springer-Verlag.

Vernon, R. G., and D. J. Flint
1984 Adipose Tissue: Metabolic Adaptation during Lactation. Symposia of the Zoological Society of London 51:119–145.

Victora, C. G.
1996 Infection and Disease: The Impact of Early Weaning. Food and Nutrition Bulletin 17:390–396.

Vignaud, P., P. Duringer, H. T. Mackaye, A. Likius, C. Blondel, J.-R. Boisserie, L. de Bonis, V. Eisenmann, M.-E. Etienne, D. Geraads, F. Guy, T. Lehmann, F. Lihoreau, N. Lopez-Martinez, C. Mourer-Chauviré, O. Otero, J.-C. Rage, M. Schuster, L. Viriot, A. Zazzo, and M. Brunet
2002 Geology and Paleontology of the Upper Miocene Toros-Menalla Hominid Locality, Chad. Nature 418:152–155.

Voland, E., and J. Beise
2002 Opposite Effects of Maternal and Paternal Grandmothers on Infant Survival in Historical Krummhorn. Behavioral Ecology and Sociobiology 52:435–443.

vom Saal, F. S., C. E. Finch, and J. F. Nelson
1994 Natural History and Mechanisms of Reproductive Aging in Humans, Laboratory Rodents, and Other Selected Vertebrates. *In* The Physiology of Reproduction, edited by E. Knobil and J. D. Neill, pp. 1213–1314. 2d ed. New York: Raven Press.

Vrba, E. S.
1998 Multiphasic Growth Models and the Evolution of Prolonged Growth Exemplified by Human Brain Evolution. Journal of Theoretical Biology 190:227–239.

Wake, D. B.
1999 Homoplasy, Homology and the Problem of "Sameness" in Biology. Homology, Novartis Foundation Symposium 22:24–46. Chichester: John Wiley and Sons.

Walker, A., and R. Leakey
1993 The Nariokotome *Homo erectus* Skeleton. Cambridge, MA: Harvard University Press.

Walker, A., R. E. Leakey, J. M. Harris, and F. H. Brown
1986 2.5 Myr *Australopithecus boisei* from West of Lake Turkana, Kenya. Nature 322:517–522.

Walker, M. L.
1995 Menopause in Female Rhesus Monkeys. American Journal of Primatology 35:59–71.

Walker, P. L.
1995   Problems of Preservation and Sexism in Sexing: Some Lessons from Historical Collections for Palaeodemographers. *In* Grave Reflections, Portraying the Past through Cemetery Studies, edited by S. R. Saunders and A. Herring, pp. 31–47. Toronto: Canadian Scholars Press.

Walker, P. L., J. R. Johnson, and P. M. Lambert
1988   Age and Sex Bias in the Preservation of Human Skeletal Remains. American Journal of Physical Anthropology 76:183–188.

Walker, R., and K. Hill
2003   Modeling Growth and Senescence in Physical Performance among the Ache of Eastern Paraguay. American Journal of Human Biology 15:196–208.

Walker, R., K. Hill, H. Kaplan, and G. McMillan
2002   Age-Dependency in Hunting Ability among the Ache of Eastern Paraguay. Journal of Human Evolution 42:639–657.

Wallis, J.
1997   A Survey of Reproductive Parameters in the Free-Ranging Chimpanzees of Gombe National Park. Journal of Reproduction and Fertility 109:297–307.

Wardle, J., M.-L. Herrera, L. Cooke, and E. Gibson
2003   Modifying Children's Food Preferences: The Effects of Exposure and Reward on Acceptance of an Unfamiliar Vegetable. European Journal of Clinical Nutrition 57:341–348.

Washburn, S. L.
1960   Tools and Human Evolution. Scientific American 203:62–87.
1981   Longevity in Primates. *In* Aging: Biology and Behavior, edited by J. L. McGaugh and S. B. Kiesler, pp. 11–29. New York: Academic Press.

Washburn, S. L., and I. DeVore
1961   Social Behavior of Baboons and Early Man. *In* Social Life of Early Man, edited by S. L. Washburn, pp. 91–105. Chicago: Aldine.

Washburn, S. L., and D. Hamburg
1965   Implications of Primate Research. *In* Primate Behavior: Field Studies of Monkeys and Apes, edited by I. DeVore, pp. 607–622. New York: Holt, Rinehart, and Winston.

Washburn, S. L., and C. S. Lancaster
1968   The Evolution of Hunting. *In* Man the Hunter, edited by R. B. Lee and I. DeVore, pp. 293–303. Chicago: Aldine.

Washburn, S. L., and R. Moore
1974   Ape into Man: A Study of Human Evolution. Boston: Little, Brown and Co.

Waterlow, J. C.
1981   Observations on the Suckling's Dilemma—A Personal View. Journal of Human Nutrition 35:85–98.

REFERENCES

Watts, D. P.

1991   Mountain Gorilla Reproduction and Sexual Behavior. American Journal of Primatology 24:211–226.

2000   Causes and Consequences of Variation in Male Mountain Gorillas: Life Histories and Group Membership. *In* Primate Males: Causes and Consequences of Variation in Group Composition, edited by P. M. Kappeler, pp. 169–179. Cambridge: Cambridge University Press.

Watts, D. P., and A. E. Pusey

1993   Behavior of Juvenile and Adolescent Great Apes. *In* Juvenile Primates: Life History, Development, and Behavior, edited by M. E. Pereira and L. A. Fairbanks, pp. 148–167. New York: Oxford University Press.

Watts, E. S., and J. A. Gavan

1982   Postnatal Growth of Nonhuman Primates: The Problem of Adolescent Spurt. Human Biology 54:53–70.

Weidenreich, F.

1940   Some Problems Dealing with Ancient Man. American Anthropologist 42:375–383.

1943   The Skull of *Sinanthropus pekinensis*: A Comparative Study of a Primitive Hominid Skull. Palaeontologia Sinica (n.s.) D10:1–291.

Weisner, T. S.

1987   Socialization for Parenthood in Sibling Caretaking Societies. *In* Parenting across the Life Span: Biosocial Dimensions, edited by J. B. Lancaster, J. Altmann, A. S. Rossi, and L. R. Sherrod, pp. 237–270. New York: Aldine de Gruyter.

1996   The 5–7 Transition as an Ecocultural Project. *In* Reason and Responsibility: The Passage through Childhood, edited by A. Samaroff and M. Haith, pp. 295–326. Chicago: University of Chicago Press.

Weiss, K. M.

1973   Demographic Models for Anthropology. Society for American Archaeology, Memoir 27. Published as American Antiquity 38(2):part 2.

1981   Evolutionary Perspectives on Human Aging. *In* Other Ways of Growing Old, edited by P. Amoss and S. Harrall, pp. 25–52. Stanford, CA: Stanford University Press.

Westendorp, R. G. J., and T. B. L. Kirkwood

1998   Human Longevity at the Cost of Reproductive Success. Nature 396:743–746.

Western, D.

1979   Size, Life History and Ecology in Mammals. African Journal of Ecology 17:185–202.

Western, D., and J. Ssemakula

1982   Life History Parameters in Birds and Mammals and Their Evolutionary Interpretations. Oecologia 54:281–290.

Westrheim, S. J., and W. E. Ricker
1978   Bias in Using an Age-Length Key to Estimate Age-Frequency Distributions. Journal of the Fisheries Research Board of Canada 35:184–189.

White, T. D., B. Asfaw, D. DeGusta, H. Gilbert, G. D. Richards, G. Suwa, and F. C. Howell
2003   Pleistocene *Homo sapiens* from Middle Awash, Ethiopia. Nature 423:742–747.

White, T. D., G. Suwa, and B. Asfaw
1994   *Australopithecus ramidus*, a New Species of Early Hominid from Aramis, Ethiopia. Nature 371:306–312.

1995   *Australopithecus ramidus*, a New Species of Early Hominid from Aramis, Ethiopia—a Corrigendum. Nature 375:88.

Whiten, A., and R. A. Byrne
1988   Taking (Machiavellian) Intelligence Apart: Editorial. *In* Machiavellian Intelligence: Social Expertise and the Evolution of Intellect in Monkeys, Apes, and Humans, edited by R. A. Byrne and A. Whiten, pp. 50–55. Oxford: Oxford University Press.

Whiten, A., J. Goodall, W. C. McGrew, T. Nishida, V. Reynolds, Y. Sugiyama, C. E. G. Tutin, R. W. Wrangham, and C. Boesch
1999   Culture in Chimpanzees. Nature 399:682–685.

WHO (World Health Organization)
1979   Joint WHO/UNICEF Meeting on Infant and Young Child Feeding: Statement and Recommendations. Geneva: World Health Organization.

1985   The Quality and Quantity of Breast Milk. Report on the WHO Collaborative Study on Breast-Feeding. Geneva: World Health Organization.

1996   Global Data Bank on Breastfeeding. Geneva: Nutrition Unit.

1998   Complementary Feeding of Young Children in Developing Countries: A Review of Current Scientific Knowledge. Geneva: World Health Organization.

2001   Global Strategy for Infant and Young Child Feeding: The Optimal Duration of Exclusive Breastfeeding. Rep. A54/INF.DOC./4. Geneva: World Health Organization.

WHO Collaborative Study Team on the Role of Breastfeeding on the Prevention of Infant Mortality
2000   Effect of Breastfeeding on Infant and Child Mortality due to Infectious Diseases in Less Developed Countries: A Pooled Analysis. The Lancet 355:451–455.

Wich, S. A., S. S. Utami-Atmoko, T. M. Setia, H. D. Rijksen, C. Schurmann, J. van Hooff, and C. P. van Schaik
2004   Life History of Wild Sumatran Orangutans (*Pongo abelii*). Journal of Human Evolution 47:385–398.

Wickes, I. G.

1953a   A History of Infant Feeding, part II, Seventeenth and Eighteenth Centuries. Archives of Disease in Childhood 28:232–240.

1953b   A History of Infant Feeding, part III, Eighteenth and Nineteenth Centuries. Archives of Disease in Childhood 28:332–340.

1953c   A History of Infant Feeding, part V, Nineteenth Century Concluded and Twentieth Century. Archives of Disease in Childhood 28:495–502.

Widdowson, E.

1950   Chemical Composition of Newly Born Mammals. Nature 166:626–629.

Widström, A.-M., A. B. Ransjo-Arvidson, K. Christensson, A. S. Matthiesen, J. Winberg, and K. Uvnas-Moberg

1996   Gastric Suction in Healthy Newborn Infants: Effects on Circulation and Developing Feeding Behaviour. Acta Paediatrica Scandinavica 76:566–572.

Wildman, D. E., L. I. Grossman, and M. Goodman

2002   Functional DNA in Humans and Chimpanzees Shows They Are More Similar to Each Other Than Either Is to Other Apes. *In* Probing Human Origins, edited by M. Goodman and A. S. Moffat, pp. 1–10. Cambridge, MA: American Academy of Arts and Sciences.

Wildman, D. E., M. Uddin, G. Liu, L. I. Grossman, and M. Goodman

2003   Implications of Natural Selection in Shaping 99.4% Nonsynonymous DNA Identity between Humans and Chimpanzees: Enlarging Genus *Homo*. Proceedings of the National Academy of Science USA 100:7181–7188.

Williams, G. C.

1957   Pleiotropy, Natural Selection, and the Evolution of Senescence. Evolution 11:398–411.

1966a   Adaptation and Natural Selection: A Critique of Some Current Biological Thought. Princeton, NJ: Princeton University Press.

1966b   Natural Selection, the Cost of Reproduction, and a Refinement of Lack's Principle. American Naturalist 199:687–690.

1992   Natural Selection: Domains, Levels, and Challenges. Oxford: Oxford University Press.

1999   The Tithonus Error in Modern Gerontology. 1999 Crafood Prize Lecture. Quarterly Review of Biology 74:405–415.

Wilmsen, E.

1989   Land Filled with Flies: A Political Economy of the Kalahari. Chicago: University of Chicago Press.

Wilson, A. C., and V. M. Sarich

1969   A Molecular Time Scale for Human Evolution. Proceedings of the National Academy of Sciences USA 63:1088–1093.

Winckler, W., S. R. Myers, D. J. Richter, R. C. Onofrio, G. J. McDonald,
R. E. Bontrop, G. A. T. McVean, S. B. Gabriel, D. Reich, P. Donnelly,
and D. Altshuler
2005   Comparison of Fine-Scale Recombination Rates in Humans and
        Chimpanzees. Science 308:107–111.

Winkvist, A., F. Jalil, J.-P. Habicht, and K. M. Rasmussen
1994   Maternal Energy Depletion Is Buffered among Malnourished Women in
        Punjab, Pakistan. Journal of Nutrition 124:2376–2385.

Winkvist, A., K. M. Rasmussen, and J.-P. Habicht
1992   A New Definition of Maternal Depletion Syndrome. American Journal of
        Public Health 82:691–694.

Wittwer-Backofen, U., and H. Buba
2002   Age Estimation by Tooth Cementum Annulation: Perspectives of a New
        Validation Study. In Paleodemography: Age Distributions from Skeletal
        Samples, edited by R. D. Hoppa and J. W. Vaupel, pp. 107–128. New York:
        Cambridge University Press.

Wittwer-Backofen, U., J. Gampe, and J. W. Vaupel
2004   Tooth Cementum Annulation for Age Estimation: Results from a Large
        Known-Age Validation Study. American Journal of Physical Anthropology
        123:119–129.

Wolpoff, M. H.
1999   Paleoanthropology. New York: McGraw-Hill.

Wolpoff, M. H., A. G. Thorne, J. Jelinek, and Z. Yinyun
1994   The Case for Sinking Homo erectus: 100 Years of Pithecanthropus is Enough!
        Courier Forschungs-Institut Senckenberg 171:341–361.

Woo, J.-K.
1966   The Skull of Lantian Man. Current Anthropology 7:83–86.

Wood, B. A.
1974   Olduvai Bed I Post-cranial Fossils: A Reassessment. Journal of Human
        Evolution 3:373–378.

1988   Are "Robust" Australopithecines a Monophyletic Group? In Evolutionary
        History of the "Robust" Australopithecines, edited by F. E. Grine,
        pp. 269–284. New York: Aldine de Gruyter.

1992   Origin and Evolution of the Genus Homo. Nature 355:783–790.

2000   Investigating Human Evolutionary History. Journal of Anatomy 197:1–17.

Wood, B. A., and M. C. Collard
1999a   The Changing Face of the Genus Homo. Evolutionary Anthropology
        8:195–207.

1999b   The Human Genus. Science 284:65–71.

2001   The Meaning of Homo. Ludus Vitalis 9:63–74.

Wood, B. A., and P. Constantino

2004   Human Origins: Life at the Top of the Tree. *In* Assembling The Tree of Life, edited by J. Cracraft and M. J. Donoghue, pp. 517–535. New York: Oxford University Press.

Wood, B. A., and B. G. Richmond

2000   Human Evolution: Taxonomy and Paleobiology. Journal of Anatomy 196:19–60.

Wood, B. A., C. W. Wood, and L. W. Konigsberg

1994   *Paranthropus boisei*—An Example of Evolutionary Stasis? American Journal of Physical Anthropology 95:117–136.

Wood, J. W.

1994   Dynamics of Human Reproduction: Biology, Biometry, Demography. New York: Aldine de Gruyter.

Wood, J. W., D. L. Holman, K. A. O'Connor, and R. J. Ferrell

2002   Mortality Models for Paleodemography. *In* Paleodemography: Age Distributions from Skeletal Samples, edited by R. D. Hoppa and J. W. Vaupel, pp. 129–168. New York: Cambridge University Press.

Wood, J. W., D. J. Holman, K. M. Weiss, A. V. Buchanan, and B. LeFor

1992   Hazards Models for Human Population Biology. Yearbook of Physical Anthropology 35:43–87.

Wood, J. W., G. R. Milner, H. C. Harpending, and K. M. Weiss

1992   The Osteological Paradox: Problems of Inferring Prehistoric Health from Skeletal Samples. Current Anthropology 33:343–358.

Woodburn, J.

1968   An Introduction to Hadza Ecology. *In* Man the Hunter, edited by R. B. Lee and I. DeVore, pp. 49–55. Chicago: Aldine.

Wrangham, R.

1979   On the Evolution of Ape Social Systems. Social Science Information 18:335–368.

1980   An Ecological Model of Female-Bonded Primate Groups. Behavior 75:262–292.

Wrangham, R., and D. Peterson

1996   Demonic Males: Apes and the Origin of Human Violence. New York: Houghton Mifflin.

Wright, A., F. E. Marino, D. Kay, P. Micalos, C. Fanning, J. Cannon, and T. D. Noakes

2002   Influence of Lean Body Mass on Performance Differences of Male and Female Distance Runners in Warm, Humid Environments. American Journal of Physical Anthropology 118:285–291.

Wright, L. E., and H. P. Schwarcz

1998   Stable Carbon and Oxygen Isotopes in Human Tooth Enamel: Identifying

Breastfeeding and Weaning in Prehistory. American Journal of Physical Anthropology 106:1–18.

Wrigley, E. A., R. S. Davies, J. E. Oeppen, and R. S. Schofield

1997 English Population History from Family Reconstitution 1580–1837. Cambridge: Cambridge University Press.

Wrigley, E. A., and R. S. Schofield

1989 The Population History of England 1541–1871: A Reconstruction. Cambridge: Cambridge University Press.

Wu, R., and X. Dong

1982 Preliminary Study of *Homo erectus* Remains from Hexian, Anhui. Acta Anthropologica Sinica 1:2–13.

Wu, X.

1981 A Well-Preserved Cranium of an Archaic Type of Early *Homo sapiens* from Dali, China. Scienta Sinica 24:530–539.

Wunderle, J. M.

1991 Age-Specific Foraging Proficiency in Birds. Current Ornithology 8:273–324.

Yoerg, S.

1994 Development of Foraging Behaviour in the Eurasian Dipper, *Cinclus cinclus*, from Fledging until Dispersal. Animal Behaviour 47:577–588.

Zhang, Y., O. A. Ryder, and Y. Zhang

2001 Genetic Divergence of Orangutan Subspecies (*Pongo pygmaeus*). Journal of Molecular Evolution 52:516–526.

Zhao, Z.

1997 Long-Term Mortality Patterns in Chinese History: Evidence from a Recorded Clan Population. Population Studies 51:117–127.

Zhu, R. K., K. A. Hoffman, R. Potts, C. L. Deng, Y. X. Pan, B. Guo, C. D. Shi, Z. T. Guo, B. Y. Yuan, Y. M. Hou, and W. W. Wang

2001 Earliest Presence of Humans in Northeast Asia. Nature 413:413–417.

Zihlman, A.

1997a Natural History of Apes: Life-History Features in Females and Males. *In* The Evolving Female: A Life-History Perspective, edited by M. E. Morbeck, A. Galloway, and A. Zihlman, pp. 86–103. Princeton, NJ: Princeton University Press.

1997b The Paleolithic Glass Ceiling: Women in Human Evolution. *In* Women in Human Evolution, edited by L. D. Hager, pp. 91–113. New York: Routledge.

Zihlman, A., D. Bolter, and C. Boesch

2004 Wild Chimpanzee Dentition and Its Implications for Assessing Life History in Immature Hominin Fossils. Proceedings of the National Academy of Science USA 101:10541–10543.

REFERENCES

Zihlmann, A., and N. Tanner
1978   Gathering and the Hominid Adaptation. *In* Female Hierarchies, edited by
         L. Tiger and H. T. Fowler, pp. 163–194. Chicago: Beresford Book Service.

Zohary, D., E. Tchernov, and L. K. Horwitz
1998   The Role of Unconscious Selection in the Domestication of Sheep and
         Goats. Journal of Zoology London 245:129–135.

Zollikofer, C. P., M. S. Ponce de Leon, D. E. Lieberman, F. Guy, D. Pilbeam,
A. Likius, H. T. Mackaye, P. Vignaud, and M. Brunet
2005   Virtual Cranial Reconstruction of *Sahelanthropus tchadensis.* Nature
         434:755–759.

Index

gender: and division of labor, 92; and subsistence contributions in hunter-gather societies, 42, 254–55

genetics: genomics and explanations of life history evolution, 83–90; genotype and definition of living taxa, 331–32; and hormonal regulation of human life history traits, 225–27

Gerber, L. M., 71

gestation, length of and size at birth, 27–28

Godfrey, L. R., 83

Gombe Stream National Park (Tanzania), 198, 213–14

Gompertz model, of mortality, 66, 285–87, 289, 290, 291, 302

Goodall, Jane, 24, 198, 221

gorilla (*Gorilla gorilla*): and age at first birth, 25; and avoidance of risk, 131; and dental development, *36–37t*; gestation length and size at birth, 27; primary life history parameters for, 20–21, *22–23f*; and skills learning, 144; stacking and cooperative breeding in, 42. *See also* primates

Gould, Steven Jay, 7, 31, 55–57, 59, 61–66, 79, 81, 86–87, 90, 92

Grandmother hypothesis: and Charnov's symmetry approach, 54, 234; defined, 6; hunting hypothesis compared to, 122–25; and Pleistocene foraging, 309–11; and residence patterns of hunter-gatherers, 258–65; and slow human maturation, 117–20, 126; and slow life history, 152–53

growth hormone, 226

growth rates: and hunter-gatherers, 242–53; and paradox of human evolution, 201;

of primates compared to human, 209; stages in human life cycle and velocity of, 205, 207–208. *See also* body size; slow maturation

Hadza (Tanzania): and adult mortality, 235, 236, 237, 238–39; extended family and childcare in, 215; Grandmother hypothesis and residence patterns of, 258–65; and growth rates, 242; and juvenile foraging, 41; learning and length of juvenile period in, 254–58; as model for evolution of human life history, 232–33; and slow maturation, 117–18. *See also* hunter-gatherers

Haile-Selassie, Y., 368

Hakeem, A., 136

Hamada, Y., 226

Hamburg, David, 96

Hamilton, W. D., 49, 67

Harpending, H. C., 269

Hartono, D. B., 247–48

Hartwig, W. C., 340

Harvey, Paul H., 29, 49, 51, 52, 98–101, 110, 112, 232

Hawkes, Kristen, 6–7, 7–8, 41, 83, 119, 120, 129, 234, 236, 242, 244, 253, 260, 309

hazard model, of age-at-death structure, 284–85, 290, 301

Headland, T. N., 290–91

health benefits, of lactation, 173–74

height, and adolescent growth spurt, 248–50

Hens, Samantha, 289

Herndon, J. G., 33

Herrmann, Nicholas P., 12–13, 78, 237, 261, 318

heterochrony, 59–60, 61–62, 90

Hiernaux, J., 247–48

Hill, K. R., 105, 240, 241, 243, 244, 258, 260, 262, 269, 291

historical demography: and life expectancy in

European populations, 311–17. *See also* demography

Historical Perspectives on Human Demography Database (HPHD), 318–24

Holliday, R., 67–68

Holliday, T. W., 28, 72–73

Hollingsworth, T. H., 313, *316t*

Holloway, R. L., 350

Holocene: and epidemics, 324; and farming, 308; and Grandmother hypothesis, 310–11; paleodemography and reconstruction of selective pressures in, 329

Holt, S. J., 66

homelessness, and street children, 211

homeobox domains, 227

hominins: classification of fossil record, 335–43; paleoanthropology and hypotheses about evolution of modern human life history, 361–63; paleoanthropology and life history of extinct taxa, 343–60; reconstruction of common ancestor with great apes, 19–21; taxonomy of, 365–93. *See also* archaic *Homo*; australopiths; Neanderthals; primitive *Homo*

Homo antecessor: and cranial capacity estimates, 399; and dental development, 356, 358, 359; and hypotheses about evolution of modern human life history, 363; and taxonomy, 381–82

Homo erectus: and body mass estimates, 396; and cranial capacity estimates, 398–99, 400; and dental development, 80, 81, 82, 358, 359; and hypotheses about evolution of modern human life history, 362, 363; and sexual dimorphism, 350; and slow maturation, 118;

School of American Research Advanced Seminar Series

PUBLISHED BY SAR PRESS

PUBLISHED BY UNIVERSITY OF CALIFORNIA PRESS

WRITING CULTURE: THE POETICS
AND POLITICS OF ETHNOGRAPHY
James Clifford &
George E. Marcus, eds.

PUBLISHED BY UNIVERSITY OF ARIZONA PRESS

THE COLLAPSE OF ANCIENT STATES AND
CIVILIZATIONS
Norman Yoffee &
George L. Cowgill, eds.

PUBLISHED BY UNIVERSITY OF NEW MEXICO PRESS

NEW PERSPECTIVES ON THE PUEBLOS
Alfonso Ortiz, ed.

STRUCTURE AND PROCESS IN LATIN
AMERICA
Arnold Strickon &
Sidney M. Greenfield, eds.

THE CLASSIC MAYA COLLAPSE
T. Patrick Culbert, ed.

METHODS AND THEORIES OF
ANTHROPOLOGICAL GENETICS
M. H. Crawford & P. L. Workman, eds.

SIXTEENTH-CENTURY MEXICO:
THE WORK OF SAHAGUN
Munro S. Edmonson, ed.

ANCIENT CIVILIZATION AND TRADE
Jeremy A. Sabloff &
C. C. Lamberg-Karlovsky, eds.

PHOTOGRAPHY IN ARCHAEOLOGICAL
RESEARCH
Elmer Harp, Jr., ed.

MEANING IN ANTHROPOLOGY
Keith H. Basso & Henry A. Selby, eds.

THE VALLEY OF MEXICO: STUDIES IN
PRE-HISPANIC ECOLOGY AND SOCIETY
Eric R. Wolf, ed.

DEMOGRAPHIC ANTHROPOLOGY:
QUANTITATIVE APPROACHES
Ezra B. W. Zubrow, ed.

THE ORIGINS OF MAYA CIVILIZATION
Richard E. W. Adams, ed.

EXPLANATION OF PREHISTORIC CHANGE
James N. Hill, ed.

EXPLORATIONS IN ETHNOARCHAEOLOGY
Richard A. Gould, ed.

ENTREPRENEURS IN CULTURAL CONTEXT
Sidney M. Greenfield, Arnold Strickon,
& Robert T. Aubey, eds.

THE DYING COMMUNITY
Art Gallaher, Jr. &
Harlan Padfield, eds.

SOUTHWESTERN INDIAN RITUAL DRAMA
Charlotte J. Frisbie, ed.

LOWLAND MAYA SETTLEMENT PATTERNS
Wendy Ashmore, ed.

SIMULATIONS IN ARCHAEOLOGY
Jeremy A. Sabloff, ed.

CHAN CHAN: ANDEAN DESERT CITY
Michael E. Moseley & Kent C. Day, eds.

SHIPWRECK ANTHROPOLOGY
Richard A. Gould, ed.

ELITES: ETHNOGRAPHIC ISSUES
George E. Marcus, ed.

THE ARCHAEOLOGY OF LOWER CENTRAL
AMERICA
Frederick W. Lange &
Doris Z. Stone, eds.

LATE LOWLAND MAYA CIVILIZATION:
CLASSIC TO POSTCLASSIC
Jeremy A. Sabloff &
E. Wyllys Andrews V, eds.

Participants in the School of American Research advanced seminar "The Evolution of Human Life History," Santa Fe, New Mexico, November 2–8, 2002.
Back row, from left: Kristen Hawkes, Barry Bogin, Daniel Sellen, Lyle Konigsberg. Front row, from left: Richard Paine, Carel van Shaik, Nicholas Blurton Jones, Bernard Wood, Leslie Aiello, Caleb Finch